DOUBLE AGENT VICTOIRE

DOUBLE
AGENT
VICTOIRE

MATHILDE CARRÉ AND
THE INTERALLIÉ NETWORK

DAVID TREMAIN

Dedicated to my mother,
Barbara

First published 2018

The History Press
The Mill, Brimscombe Port
Stroud, Gloucestershire, GL5 2QG
www.thehistorypress.co.uk

British Library Cataloguing in Publication Data.
A catalogue record for this book is available from the British Library.

ISBN 978 0 7509 8804 9

Typesetting and origination by The History Press
Printed and bound in Great Britain by TJ International Ltd

Contents

	Abbreviations	7
	Author's Note	15
	Acknowledgements	16
	Dramatis Personae	17
	Introduction	19
1	'An Exceedingly Dangerous Woman'	25
2	'A Man of Great Daring and Initiative'	37
3	*Interallié* is born	46
4	'A Squalid Tale'	62
5	An American in France	78
6	'The Kraus Affair'	85
7	The *Interallié* Network	99
8	Betrayal	109
9	MAURICE's Escape	120
10	Colonel Henri's Story	129
11	Turning the Tables	140
12	Penetration of the LUCAS Network	160
13	Gloria in Excelsis	173
14	LUCAS's Story	185
15	BENOIT's Story	194
16	'An Important Affair'	197
17	'A Nasty Taste in One's Mouth'	224
18	WALENTY and the 'Great Game'	237
19	Pointing Fingers	256
20	Winding Up a Troublesome Affair	271
21	Accounts Payable: The Cost of Doing Business	297
22	What Are we Going to Do about Mathilde?	302

23   Disposing of the Body   323
24   Strong Evidence from Many Sources   339
25   The Final Reckoning   360
      Epilogue   386

Appendix 1   Members and Contact of the WALENTY Organisation
              Carded in VICTOIRE   401
Appendix 2   Particulars of Members and Associates of the WALENTY
              Organisation   407
Appendix 3   Chronology of the Betrayal and Arrests of *Interallié*   415
Appendix 4   The Case Against VICTOIRE: The Allegations of her
              Betrayals   419
Appendix 5   Members of the *Interallié* Organisation who Escaped to
              England   425
Appendix 6   Regulations for Special Internees at Aylesbury   427
Appendix 7   Major Ische's Personnel in 1942   429
Appendix 8   Proposed Messages Relating to the Return of LUCAS
              and VICTOIRE to France   431

      Notes   433
      Select Bibliography   471
      Index   477

Abbreviations

27 Land	SIS term for France
48 Land	SIS term for USA
A4	Country section dealing with Free French and Polish government-in-exile (MI6/SIS)
A5	Overseas Services, Organization and Administration; later (1943) Special Services (MI5)
ACSS	Assistant Chief, Secret Intelligence Service (MI6/SIS)
ADB1	Assistant Director, B Branch (MI5)
ADC	Aide de Camp
ADE	Assistant Director, E Branch (MI5)
AFS	Auxiliary Fire Service
ARC	Aliens Registration Card
ARO	Aliens Registration Office
ARP	Air Raid Precaution
B1a	Espionage, Special Agents (MI5)
B1b	Espionage, Special Sources section (MI5)
B1d	Special Examiners (MI5)
B2	Counter-espionage (MI5)
B3a	Censorship (MI5)
B3d	Communications: liaison with censorship (MI5)
B4a	Counter subversion section involved with suspected cases of espionage by individuals living in the UK (MI5)
B4b	Enemy espionage, industry and commerce (MI5)
B5b	Counter subversion (MI5)
B5d	Political subversion section (MI5)
B6	Watchers (MI5)
BAOR	British Army of the Rhine (post-war)
BEF	British Expeditionary Force

BLA	British Liberation Army
BRCS	British Red Cross Society
BSS	Bayswater Special Security Section (SOE)
CCU	Canadian Concentration Unit
CIA	Central Intelligence Agency (US)
CIC	Counter-intelligence Corps (US Army)
CID	Criminal Investigation Department
C-in-C	Commander-in-Chief
COBRA	Cabinet Office Briefing Room A
CSDIC(WEA)	Combined Services Detailed Interrogation Centre (Western European Area), also known as the 'London Cage' (*q.v.* **MI19**)
CX	Reports prepared by MI6 (SIS)
D4b	Port intelligence (MI5)
DC & D	War Office – unknown
DDMI O&S	Deputy Director Military Intelligence, Operations & Security
DFC	Distinguished Flying Cross
DMI	Director (or Directorate) of Military Intelligence
DSO	Defence Security Officer (MI5); also Distinguished Service Order
DZ	Drop zone
F Section	Section of SOE dealing with France
F2c	Russian intelligence (MI5)
F3C2	Nazi sympathisers and fifth columnists (MI5)
FANY	First Aid Nursing Yeomanry
FIC	Fellow of the Royal Institute of Chemistry (now Royal Society of Chemistry)
FSP	Field Security Police
FSS	Field Security Section, Intelligence Corps
G2	Home Office (N.B. It can also mean the Security and Intelligence Branch of the British or US Army)
G3	Responsible for operations, staff duties, exercise planning, training, operational requirements, combat development and tactical doctrine (British Army)
GPO	General Post Office
GSI	General Staff Intelligence
HO	Home Office

HOW	Home Office Warrant
IB	Intelligence Branch
IOM	Isle of Man
IP2 (a)	Ministry of Information (MOI) and Propaganda; liaison between War Office, Ministry of Information (MOI), the Press and BBC
IRA	Irish Republican Army
IRB	Inter-Services Research Bureau; cover name for SOE
IRC	International Red Cross
ISOS	Intelligence Service Oliver Strachey/Illicit Services Oliver Strachey
JIC	Joint Intelligence Committee
KOSB	King's Own Scottish Borderers
LCI	Landing Craft Infantry
LCS	London Controlling Section
LNU	Last name unknown
LRC	London Reception Centre (*q.v.* **RVPS**)
LRCP	Licentiate Member of the Royal College of Practitioners
LZ	Landing zone
MA	Military Attaché
MAP	Ministry of Aircraft Production
MC5	Ministry of Information branch
MEW	Ministry of Economic Warfare
MGB	Motor gun boat
MI1a	Part of the Directorate of Military Intelligence in WW1 responsible for distribution of reports and intelligence records; remobilised in 1939 to interrogate enemy prisoners
MI5	British Security Service
MI6	British Secret Intelligence Service (*q.v.* **SIS**)
MI9	Escape and Evasion organisation of British Intelligence
MI14	A branch of Military Intelligence specialising in intelligence about Germany
MI19	Directorate of Military Intelligence (War Office): branch responsible for obtaining information from prisoners of war (*q.v.* **CSDIC**)
MM	Military Medal
MOI	Ministry of Information
MPD	Metropolitan Police District

MRCS	Member of the Royal College of Surgeons
NASA	National Aeronautics and Space Administration
NCO	Non-commissioned officer
NID	Naval Intelligence Division (Royal Navy)
NKVD	Narodni Kommissariat Vnutrennikh del – People's Commissariat for Internal Affairs (Soviet Union, 1934–46)
NLT	No living trace
OBE	Officer of the Order of the British Empire
OC	Officer commanding
OSA	Official Secrets Act
OSS	Office of Strategic Services (wartime US equivalent of **SOE**)
OTU	Operational Training Unit (RAF)
PAIR	OSS code name for deciphered German intelligence messages (*q.v.* **ISOS**)
P&PO	Pass & Permit Office
POW or **PW**	Prisoner of war
POWN	Polska Organizacja Walki o Niepodległości – Polish resistance movement based in Lyons
PRU	Photographic Reconnaissance Unit (RAF)
PUSD	Permanent Under-Secretary's Department (Foreign Office)
PW1	War Office directorate of Prisoners of War dealing with enemy prisoners
RAF	Royal Air Force
RAFVR	Royal Air Force Volunteer Reserve
RAMC	Royal Army Medical Corps
RANR	Royal Australian Naval Reserve
RASC	Royal Army Service Corps
RLL	Refused leave to land (Immigration)
RN	Royal Navy
RNAS	Royal Naval Air Service
RNVR	Royal Navy Volunteer Reserve
RPS	Royal Patriotic School (*q.v.* **LRC**, **RVPS**)
RSLO	Regional Security Liaison Officer (MI5)
RVPS	Royal Victoria Patriotic School (*q.v.* **LRC** and **RPS**)
SAAF	South African Air Force
SAS	Special Air Service
SCI	Special Counter-Intelligence (**OSS**) (104 SCI was a British unit)

SCO	Security Control Officer (MI5)
Section V	SIS counter-espionage section
SHAEF	Supreme Headquarters Allied Expeditionary Force
SIME	Security Intelligence Middle East
SIS	British Secret Intelligence Service (*q.v.* **MI6**)
SLA1	MI5 legal section
SLB	MI5 legal section
SLD	Services Liaison Department
SOE	Special Operations Executive
UNRRA	United Nations Relief and Rehabilitation Administration
VB3	Counter-espionage sub-section which dealt with France, Corsica, Andorra and the Benelux countries (Belgium, the Netherlands, Luxembourg) (MI6)
VB5	Counter-espionage sub-section (MI6)
VBZ	Counter-espionage sub-section (MI6)
VCIGS	Vice Chief of Imperial General Staff
WO	War Office
WR-A	War Room Registry A (MI5) – supplies and internal information
WRAF	Women's Royal Air Force
WRC1	War Room Registry (MI5). **WRC** was the Assessments Section; **WRC1** dealt with officers and agents of the old Abwehr I and III
WSWoj	Wyźsza Szkola Wojenna or Higher War College, Warsaw (Poland)
W/T	Wireless telegraphy
X-2	Counter-espionage branch of OSS
XX	Double-Cross Committee
ZB	SIS symbol for MI5

French Organisations

BCRA	Bureau Central de Renseignements et d'Action (French WW2 forerunner of **SDECE** and **DGSE**)
BCRAL	Bureau Central de Renseignements et d'Action Londres (London branch of **BCRA**)
BMA	Bureau des Menées Anti-Nationales (organisation created by Vichy government to counter anti-nationalism)
CCI	Centre de Coordination Interarmées
CST	Contrôle de la Surveillance du Territoire (predecessor to the **DST** (France))
DCRI	Direction Centrale du Renseignement Intérieur (French security service, 2008–12, superseded **DST**)
DGSE	Direction Générale de la Sécurité Extérieure (French overseas intelligence service, superseded **SDECE**, 1982)
DGSI	Direction Générale de la Sécurité Intérieure (French security service, 2012 to present, superseded **DST**)
DIA	Division d'Infanterie Algérienne
DSDOC	Direction des Services de Documentation (or **DSDoc**)
DST	Direction de la Surveillance du Territoire (French security service, 1944–2008)
FFI	Forces Françaises de l'Intérieur (Gaullist Resistance fighters)
FTPF	Francs-Tireurs et Partisans Français
LN	Libération-Nord (left-leaning Resistance organisation)
PSF	Parti Social Française
PTT	Postes, Télégraphes et Téléphones (French Post Office)
SDECE	Service de Documentation Extérieur et de Contre-Espionnage (French intelligence service, 1947–82)
SFIO	Section Française de l'Internationale Ouvrière (French section of the Communist Internationale)
SMH	French Resistance network
SNCF	Société National des Chemins de Fer (French national railway system)
SNM	Service National Maquis
SR Guerre	Services des Renseignements Guerre
SSM	Service de la Sécurité Militaire (France)

German Organisations

Amt IV	Gestapo (part of **RSHA**)
Amt IVE	Gestapo Counter-intelligence (part of **RSHA**)
FAK 313	Frontaufklärungskommando (front reconnaissance [spy] command 313)
FAT 350	Frontaufklärungstrupp (front reconnaissance [spy] troop 350)
GAF	German Air Force (Luftwaffe)
GFP (Luft)	Geheim Feldpolizei (German field security police) Luftwaffe
GIS	German Intelligence Service
MBF	Militärbefelshaber Frankreich (military commander in France)
MK	Meldekopf (advanced message centre)
NSDAP	Nationalsozialistische Deutsche Arbeiterpartie (National Socialist German Workers' Party – Nazi Party)
OKH	Oberkommando des Heeres (Supreme Command of the Army, Germany)
OKW	Oberkommando der Wehrmacht (Supreme Command of the Armed Forces, Germany)
RSHA	Reich Main Security Office
SD	Sicherheitsdienst (SS intelligence service)
Sipo	Sicherheitspolitzei (department which controlled the Gestapo and the Kripo (Kriminalpolizei)
SS	Schutzstaffel (security service of the Nazi Party); also German Secret Service
V-Mann	*Vertrauensmänn* or confidential person
WAKO	Waffenstillstandkommission (German Armistice Commission)

Abwehr Abbreviations

Abt.	Abteilung (Abwehr branch)
Branch I	Espionage
H	Heer (Army)
L	Luft (Air)
M	Marine (Navy)
Wi	Wirtschaft (Economics)
I	Communications
G	False documents, secret inks
Branch II	Sabotage
Branch III	Counter-espionage
Abt. IIIF	(Feind) Abteilung III F (penetration of enemy intelligence services; the largest and most important section)
Alst	Abwehrleitstelle (head Abwehr station)
AO	Auslandorganization; also Abwehrofficizier (Abwehr)
Ast.	Abwehrstelle (Abwehr station)
Ic	Third general staff officer (Abwehr) c.f. AO
KO	Kriegsorganization (War Organisation), Abwehr in Allied and neutral countries
1T/LW	Technik/Luftwaffe

Author's Note

Unless otherwise specified in the Notes, all quotes and extracts have been taken from files in the National Archives at Kew (TNA). When quoting from these files some minor formatting changes have occasionally been made to ensure the text flows better, and accents added to French and German words where they were missed out in the original text because the typewriters of the time lacked those keys; otherwise, no changes have been made to the original punctuation or spelling. In these files many MI5 documents use the term 'German S.S.'; in this context it is generally meant as a generic name for the German Secret Service rather than Schutzstaffel, the Nazi Party's intelligence service. Likewise, the terms 'MI6' and 'SIS' are used interchangeably to mean the overseas branch of the British Intelligence Service.

The accounts of the *Interallié* and LUCAS networks are peppered with numerous code names or aliases indicated in official documents by the symbol @ meaning alias, with some people having more than two, their code names sometimes being used interchangeably, depending on which document is being cited, causing some confusion. Therefore, those code names have been compiled into Appendix 1. Where possible, only one code name will be used in the text unless another appears in a quote, in which case the alternate code name(s) will also be given in parentheses. The identities of some individuals still remain vague or unknown, but where possible, attempts have been made to identify them.

Acknowledgements

All files in the National Archives are © Crown Copyright and are reproduced with permission under the terms of the Open Government Licence.

Quotes from Hansard contain parliamentary information licensed under the Open Parliament Licence v3.0.

Every attempt has been made to seek and obtain permission for copyright material used in this book. In certain cases this has not been possible. However, if we have inadvertently used copyright material without permission/ acknowledgements we apologise and we will make the necessary correction at the first opportunity.

The author and publisher would like to thank the following for permission to use copyright material in this book:

Amberley Publishing (*The Women Who Spied for Britain*)
Bloomsbury Publishing (*Agent Zigzag*; *John le Carré: The Biography*)
Crécy Publishing (*We Landed by Moonlight*)
Gerry Czerniawski (*The Big Network*)
Frontline/Pen & Sword (*No Cloak, No Dagger*)
Lauran Paine Jr (*Mathilde Carré: Double Agent*)
Nigel West (*The Secret War*)

Every effort has been made to verify the information in this book. Any mistakes are of my own doing and will be rectified in any subsequent editions that are produced.

I would like to thank my editor, Mark Beynon, and all those involved at The History Press, as well as Monica Aguiar; Cécile Carret, *Secrétariat de la Société Chimique de France*; Gerry Czerniawski, son of Roman Garby-Czerniawski; Katherine Doyle, Centre for Buckinghamshire Studies; Laura Sapwell, Governor of HM Prison, Aylesbury; Evelyn Tremain, and Nigel West.

Dramatis Personae

Maj. Hugh Waldorf Astor (1920–99): MI5 officer, B1a

Roger Bardet (ROGER): Member of *Interallié* network

S/Ldr Terence Elliot Beddard: MI5 officer

Hugo Bleicher (1899–1982): Abwehr Feldwebel, III F, *Ast* Paris

Renée Borni (VIOLETTE): Member of *Interallié* network; mistress of WALENTY

Michel Brault (MIKLOS) (b.1895–?): Paris lawyer

Princess Jacqueline de Broglie (1912–60 or 1918–65): Wife of Alfred Kraus

Col Maurice Buckmaster (1902–92): Head of F Section, SOE

Mathilde Carré (VICTOIRE) (1908–70): Member of *Interallié* network

Lieutenant Michel Coulomb (EVE): SOE agent.

Maj. Benjamin Cowburn (BENOIT) (1909–94): SOE agent

Comtesse Colette Dampierre (1911–69): Alleged Abwehr spy

Monique Deschamps (MONO): Member of *Interallié* network; first wife of Garby-Czerniawski

Cmdr Wilfred 'Biffy' Dunderdale (1899–1990): SIS officer, Section V; pre-war SIS Head of Station, Paris

Det. Sgt Louis V. Gale: Scotland Yard Special Branch; minder of Mathilde Carré

Roman Garby-Czerniawski (ARMAND; WALENTY; BRUTUS) (1910–75): Founder of *Interallié* network

Robert Goubeau (BOB): Member of *Interallié* network

Maj. Tom Greene: SIS Section V

Maj. Christopher Harmer (1910–96): MI5 officer, B1a; case officer of Mathilde Carré

Herbert Lionel Adolphus Hart (1907–92): MI5 officer, B1b

Col William Edward Hinchley-Cooke (1894–1955): MI5 interrogator and legal advisor, SLA1

Claude Jouffret (MICHEL): Member of *Interallié* network

Robert/Jean Lucien Kieffer (KIKI): Member of *Interallié* network

Maj. Maxwell Knight (1900–68): MI5 officer, B5b

Alfred Ignatz Maria Kraus (b.1908–?): Abwehr agent; husband of Jacqueline de Broglie

Suzanne Laurent (b.1914–?): Bleicher's girlfriend

Capt. Guy Maynard Liddell (1892–1958): Director, MI5 B Branch; later Deputy Director General, 1945–53

Richard Dafydd Vivian Llewellyn Lloyd (1906–83): Welsh Guards officer; lover of Mathilde Carré; author

William 'Billy' Luke: MI5 officer, B1a

William Mackenzie: Friend of Mathilde Carré

John Marriott: MI5 officer, secretary of Double-Cross Committee

Maj. John Cecil Masterman (1891–1977): MI5 officer; chairman of Double-Cross Committee

Helenus Padraic Seosamh 'Buster' Milmo (1908–88): Assistant Director, B1 (ADB1)

Lt Roger Mitchell (ADAM): SOE agent

Lt Col Thomas Argyll 'Tar' Robertson (1909–94): MI5 officer, B1a; in charge of double agents

F/Lt Alfred Philip Frank Schneidau (1903–84): Also known as S/Ldr Philipson (FELIX); RAF liaison with SIS

Cmdr John Senter (1905–66): SOE Director of Security, 1942

Lt Col Robin William George 'Tin Eye' Stephens (1900–?): Commandant, Camp 020

Jona 'Klop' Ustinov (1892–1962): Part-time agent for MI5, SIS

Pierre de Vomécourt (LUCAS) (1906–86): SOE agent

Dick Goldsmith White (1906–93): Head of MI5's B1b and assistant to Guy Liddell

Introduction

A cat is mercurial: she plays to her own rules, no one else's. She is independent and does what she pleases, when she wants to, not when others think she should. She owes her loyalty to no one but herself. Then, when the fancy takes her, she is off, returning at her convenience. Female cats also like to be the boss; put two of them together and they will fight for dominance. The spy known as 'La Chatte' (the female cat) was much the same. In her lifetime she served three masters, but ultimately was serving herself. A report (undated) written by Patricia McCallum of MI5's Registry about the woman later known as VICTOIRE begins:

> On 28.2.42 there arrived in the U.K. a remarkable woman agent: Mathilde Lucie (or Lily) CARRÉ ... Her case was later to receive the maximum publicity, although her arrival is not mentioned in the Curry History[1] or in the record of Camp 020.[2] Nor is there a reference to her in the Masterman Report[3] though for several months she worked as a B1A double agent. Yet Mathilde CARRÉ (referred to hereinafter as VICTOIRE) was a highly successful agent, firstly on behalf of the Allies, secondly on behalf of the Germans, and thirdly – apparently – once more on the British side. The reason for the official silence about her arrival is that she came to England, not by parachute or as a refugee like other spies, but was brought over by the Royal Navy in company with one of SOE's most important Resistance organisers: Pierre de VOMÉCORE @ LUCAS [sic]. Moreover their escape from occupied France was aided and facilitated in every way by Abt. III/F of the Abwehr.[4]

Remarkable she may have been, but for all the wrong reasons. Like most spies she was temperamental, untrustworthy, scheming, manipulative, jealous, and above all, treacherous.

Given that several MI5 officers were directly involved in her case, in particular Christopher Harmer, it is strange that John Curry's official history of MI5 does not mention her, even in passing, particularly as Guy Liddell's war diaries do from time to time, as do agents involved in other spy cases. She was never interned in Camp 020, which is why Robin Stephens never mentioned her in his account, even though he and his staff were occasionally involved in the case.

The Masterman Report, which only came to light in 1972 amidst controversy when the British government tried to suppress its publication, was a secret report by Oxford don Sir John Masterman, chairman of the Twenty Committee, about the Double-Cross System employed by MI5 to use spies who had been captured and then deemed suitable to be 'turned' against their original employer (mostly the German Abwehr) to work as double agents. Even though Masterman was to some extent involved in MI5's dealings with 'La Chatte' by attending meetings where she was discussed, she was only 'turned' in the sense that once in England she continued to transmit to the Germans under the control of British Intelligence, which is perhaps why he does not mention her in his report as a *bona fide* double agent. Indeed, he states that 'this was never my case beyond serving this woman with a Detention Order'.

The silence on behalf of the British Intelligence community may also have been because she had become an embarrassment to them, and once the war was over they were happy to be rid of her when they handed her back to the French to face trial.

VICTOIRE, the woman who would become notorious as 'La Chatte', was employed by the *Interallié* network, an organisation working on behalf of the Polish Secret Service in Occupied France. On 18 November 1941, she was arrested by the Abwehr, along with some of the more important members of the organisation. Shortly thereafter, she became one of their most trusted agents and worked for them as a double agent while still operating the *Interallié* network's radio. Allegedly, she briefly became the mistress of Feldwebel (Sergeant) Hugo Bleicher, the senior Abwehr NCO who worked against the French Resistance in breaking up *Interallié* and other networks. While working for the Germans, Mathilde Carré provided them with the names and locations of organisation members still at large, as well as acting as a decoy or as an *agente provocatrice,* so they could be arrested by the Gestapo. Her motivations for betraying them are complex and will be examined during the course of this book and summed up in the final chapter.

VICTOIRE's story, and those of the other two main protagonists – Roman Garby-Czerniawski @ ARMAND @ WALENTY (later also known as BRUTUS), and Hugo Bleicher of the German Abwehr – are inextricably linked. In the 1950s and '60s they all wrote accounts of their involvement in the *Interallié* affair, but at that time did not have the benefit of access to official MI5, Special Operations Executive (SOE) or other files, some of which are now publicly available from the National Archives at Kew. Therefore, their versions of events have become blurred, glossed over, even romanticised; facts have been omitted, or simply merged together. As Garby-Czerniawski wrote in *The Big Network*:

> Still, after publication of as many as four books in English which deal directly or indirectly with the story of the *Interallié* Network, I felt I could not, and should not, remain silent any more; not only from my own personal point of view but also in fairness to everyone engaged in the work of this Big Network.
>
> I could no longer bear the inadequate or wrong pictures of the organization and the many people in it, nor the very inaccurate remarks about myself.[5]

Apart from their books mentioned in the Bibliography, the fourth was *The Cat. A True Story of Espionage*, written in 1957 by wartime Abwehr officer Michael Alexander Graf (Count) Soltikow. Soltikow was born Walter Richard Max Bennecke in Potsdam on 17 November 1902 but was adopted by Leo Graf von Soltikow and Alexandra Tzvatkoff in 1926. During the war he served with the Oberkommando der Wehrmacht (OKW) and claimed to have worked for Admiral Canaris and Hans Oster. He died in 1984. Both Garby-Czerniawski and Benjamin Cowburn (BENOIT) would later claim over £12,000 damages against Soltikow and Nannen Publishing Company, the publisher of the German edition of Bleicher's book, alleging that their characters had been damaged by revelations in the book.

Until recently, the many authors who have subsequently written accounts of SOE – the Special Operations Executive established by Winston Churchill 'to set Europe ablaze' – in most cases also did not have complete access to the official files. Indeed, as one of Mathilde Carré's biographers, Gordon Young, acknowledged in 1957, 'the Home Office politely but firmly refused me any information on this subject'. Even after the release of those MI5 and SOE files to the National Archives, the many recent accounts of SOE and its agents have barely scratched the surface, only mentioning VICTOIRE and *Interallié* in passing, which seems strange, given the importance of what was then the largest network operating in France. Instead, they have tended to focus on the men and women agents who have now become household names, without necessarily adding anything new to their stories.

The story has also been portrayed in other media: On Tuesday 2 January 1962 *The Big Network*, based on Garby-Czerniawski's book, was aired on the radio on the BBC Home Service, with James McKechnie as Garby-Czerniawski and Mary Wimbush as Mathilde Carré. A German TV film directed by Wolfgang Glück was made in 1972, entitled *Doppelspiel in Paris*, starring Luitgard Im as Mathilde Carré, Hartmut Reck as Roman Garby-Czerniawski, Barbara Lass as Renée Borni, and Ferdy Mayne as Maître Brault.[6] Given the current interest in wartime exploits, perhaps the time is now right for a full-length feature film to be made on the subject.

Roman Garby-Czerniawski (as BRUTUS), together with Juan Pujol García (GARBO), would later go on to play an integral part in the D-Day deception plan, Operation *Fortitude*. However, this part of Garby-Czerniawski's career is outside the scope of this book and will not be dealt with here; nor will the many other operations in which Bleicher was later involved. The sole purpose of this book is to examine the '*Interallié* affair' and how it came to be broken up, as well as Mathilde Carré's subsequent involvement in the LUCAS network.

How the betrayals came about, who may have 'cast the first stone' of betrayal, and the motivations behind them will be explored in detail in these chapters, as well as how this affected the lives and careers of those involved and, to some extent, other networks with which they came into contact – the main ones being the LUCAS and SMH/GLORIA networks. Initially, Roman Garby-Czerniawski and Pierre de Vomécourt (LUCAS) were considered in part to blame and came under suspicion from British Intelligence and the Polish government-in-exile, but they were later exonerated. Those accusations will also be examined. *Interallié* was not alone; other networks were also betrayed from time to time, perhaps the most controversial being the *Prosper* network, which has already been the subject of a number of books and studies, but never fully resolved to some historians' satisfaction.

During the four-year occupation of France by Germany from May 1940 to August 1944, many disparate groups emerged, with different political affiliations, some Communist, some Gaullist (centre right), all seeking to disrupt their occupiers' operations, if not to rid them altogether of this 'plague', as Camus called it. But in reality, as has been revealed in recent years, the number of French men and women claiming to have been members of the Resistance is greater than the actual size of the networks. Many citizens preferred to sit out the war quietly, while a comparatively small percentage actively collaborated with the enemy, in some way or the other. That these French networks could be betrayed was largely the result of a climate of evolving mistrust of their fellow countrymen, and not necessarily the result of the competence of the German intelligence services, which was often questionable.

The overall picture that emerges from the '*Interallié* affair' reveals a tragic set of circumstances caused by a morass of lies, scheming and treachery. This was symptomatic of the many factions struggling to assert themselves against the Nazi occupation of war-torn France, as well as, to some extent, the response by the various British Intelligence agencies and their refusal, in some cases, to acknowledge that a problem existed. This account is my attempt to set the record straight.

David Tremain
Ottawa, 2018

CHAPTER 1

'An Exceedingly Dangerous Woman'

The woman known as 'La Chatte' was born Mathilde-Lucie Belard at 13, rue de la Barre in Le Creusot, Saône-et-Loire on 30 June 1908. Some of the correspondence about her refers to her as Ly Carré-Belard, Ly Carré de Roche, or Lily. In the summary of her case in one of her MI5 files she was also known by a variety of other names – Maintena Barrel, Micheline Donnadieu, Madame Berger and Marguerite de Roche – as well as by her code names LA CHATTE, BAGHERRA and VICTOIRE.[1] Her father, Arsène Narcisse Joseph Belard, a draughtsman, and her mother, Jeanne (*née* Gros), both born in 1886, had little time for her as a child. Her parents had a very active social life, so she was forced to live a sheltered life under the care of her maternal grandfather and two 35-year-old maiden aunts, known to her as Aunty 'Tine', later known as Isoline, and Lucie, or Aunty 'Cie', whom she called 'the Sad One' because she 'never laughed …only preached morality, modesty, virtue, duty, devotion and self-sacrifice',[2] all traits that Mathilde would later eschew. Her maternal grandfather was 'very tall and very old. He had to be treated with great respect. He spoke very little and frightened me, yet he was tender and indulgent to his little granddaughter.'[3] She described her father as 'small, thin and looked mild and good', her mother as 'a large lady who always looked to me on the point of flying into a passion or getting angry'. During the war her father, who had served as an engineer at Verdun in the First World War, was taken prisoner, but was released because of his age and honoured with the Légion d'Honneur and the Croix de Guerre.

At the age of 12 she went to the Lycée Jeanne d'Arc, a private school at 2, rue Dupanloup, Orléans, where she discovered boys for the first time. This served as a distraction from her schoolwork, which she regarded as intruding on this new-found interest. Her MI5 file gives her age as 14, depending on which account is read, but her autobiography says that in 1920 she was in her first of four years as a boarder, which would indeed make her aged 12. When she was 16 she transferred to the Lycée Victor Hugo in Paris at 27, rue de Sévigné in the 3rd arrondissement. This was, according to her, on 1 October 1924. One particular date – 30 June 1924 – she speaks about as being one she would never forget. A guest at dinner that evening, whom she described as 'gentle and loving' was a 19-year-old boy, the son of an old friend of her aunts, who they hoped would one day make her an excellent husband. His name, and what became of this encounter are not recorded, except to add that on that night, her sixteenth birthday, she 'shed my tainted innocence', which could be taken to mean that she lost her virginity, although this appears to be contradicted later on when she got married.

In her autobiography she speaks of other men who drifted in and out of her life: a tall, attractive man whom she had met in the church of Saint-Julien-le-Pauvre on the Left Bank, whom she refers to as 'Philippe', who brought her books – *Les Nourritures terrestres* (*Fruits of the Earth*) by André Gide, and *À la recherche du temps perdu* by Marcel Proust – but who went out of her life just as quickly as he had come into it. There was also 'Robert' whom she had met at the Sorbonne when they were both studying philosophy. He gave her flowers, talked of love and death, took her to the Louvre and drove her on outings to the Bois de Boulogne and the forest of Fontainebleau – 'the epitome of youth, dreams and love'. She had wanted to follow him to study medicine, but her mother declared that it was an unseemly profession for a girl, so she entered the Faculty of Law instead.

Then there were 'Adolphe' and 'Louis' (not their real names), thirty years older than her, who competed for her affections and 'wooed this girl who was irresistibly drawn towards evil'. While Adolphe's attraction to her was purely physical, Louis was mainly attracted to her intelligence and culture. Adolphe tried to get her to read Flaubert instead of Gide and Proust, while Louis wanted her to read about Saint Teresa of Avila. A clue to how she came to be attracted to evil may be explained in her autobiography when she spoke of her classmates at the school in Orléans who taught her the facts of life, something her aunts had failed to do. Exactly what she interpreted as this 'evil' is inferred to be carnal relations as a means of manipulating men by using her body to obtain what she wanted.

As well as literature, she showed an interest in music, listening to Johann Sebastian Bach and plainchant. She also took singing lessons, liking French composers Henri Duparc, Maurice Ravel, Ernest Chausson and Gabriel Fauré. After struggling to play Edvard Grieg, she gave up the piano, claiming to be a mediocre pianist. She once told a close friend named Marc, whom she had met in the Faculty of Law at the Sorbonne, that she wanted Mozart's *Requiem* played at her funeral – a comment that would later come back to haunt her – but she also told herself that she wanted *Pavane pour une infante défunte* by Fauré.

According to some sources, she never graduated, although she claimed to have passed two baccalaureates. Yet in spite of a not-so-stellar performance at school, she still managed in the 1930s to enrol in the Faculty of Law at the Sorbonne in Paris. As Gordon Young writes, she obtained her diploma and became a schoolteacher.[4] The account in her MI5 file states that she 'took degrees in science, mathematics, philosophy and law'.[5]

While at the Sorbonne, working as what would now be referred to as a 'supply teacher' at a small school in Montmartre in May 1932, she met a handsome, well-dressed man of about 30, a schoolteacher named Maurice Henri-Claude Carré. His mother was Corsican, and he had a brother, Roger, who would later be killed in an air crash in March 1939. The problem was that Maurice had no money and came from a lower class than her, but he wanted to marry her anyway, declaring:

> 'Nothing more, Lily, a man does not marry his mistress. You must respect the woman you have chosen to be your wife.'
> I was completely unmoved. I had never envisaged marriage and particularly marriage in these conditions. A teacher for a husband![6]

However, her choice of partner did not meet with her parents' approval, who thought that being a school teacher was beneath her and wished she would find someone better suited to their class. In contrast, another biographer, Lauran Paine, claims that Mathilde's parents did not openly oppose the marriage to Maurice, even though it was really Marc she yearned for. He was someone who was 'intelligent, cultured and delicate and had exquisite manners. We appealed very much to each other,' she wrote.[7]

When Marc returned from his military service in North Africa they continued to see each other but his attitude towards her was very possessive. He declared that he still loved her and wanted to take her back to North Africa with him. She was concerned that, while she wanted to marry him, he would not be able to provide for her in the way that she had become accustomed as a member of the middle class; nor did she want to become a pauper. On top of all that, her parents would not provide her with a dowry. She had to make a choice: who would it be? Sitting on the steps of the grand staircase to the Palais de Justice

(Law Courts) she flipped a coin: heads Marc, tails Maurice; it came up tails, so sadly Marc left Paris without her. Part One of a summary of her life and career compiled for her MI5 file comments on the story of how she came to choose her husband, saying that it was by 'cutting cards' and not the flip of a coin:

> This story is probably told in order to enable her to emphasise how many different people wished to marry her, but it does demonstrate at the outset the irrational way in which she conducted her life and the absence of any deep-rooted loyalty.[8]

Mathilde and Maurice were married on 18 May 1933 and honeymooned in Italy.[9] Their marriage, however, was not a particularly satisfactory or happy one and she took no pleasure in being Maurice's wife. She recalled that on their wedding night Maurice, obviously aware of her previous boyfriends, had remarked:

> With your free and easy life as a student I should never have believed that you were a virgin … I did not reply. I merely closed my eyes to keep back the tears that welled up in them. The whole affair seemed to be false, comic and a complete illusion.[10]

They would live apart – he with his mother, and she with her parents – until they moved to North Africa.

Maurice had hoped to get a posting to the military zone south of Oran, Algeria. Instead, he obtained a teaching post as director of European and Arab Schools in Ain Sefra, Southern Algeria, where Mathilde would work as his assistant. By 18 September 1939 they were in Oran, 'the noisiest of the North African ports'. Being the restless soul she was, it is not surprising that she became disillusioned with Maurice, yet as Patricia McCallum reported, 'VICTOIRE maintains that she was faithful to her husband in spite of the very many defects in his character, the worst of which appears to have been that he did not pay her sufficient attention.'[11] Her claim of fidelity was not strictly true as she did have many affairs, one in Ain Sefra with a Muslim friend of Maurice, possibly Mustapha Ben Aliona to whom she later wrote on 12 March 1944 while she was in Holloway and he was living in Oran.[12] (The typed envelope says Aliona, which, judging from her handwriting on the original envelope, is correct. In her autobiography she refers to him as 'Mus'.) In that letter, apart from general news about her situation, she told 'Mus', 'I very much regret not to have followed your advice and those of Khellardy in 1939 and stayed in Africa!'[13] MI5 regarded her conduct towards Maurice as an example of 'all the same defects of character that appeared later on when she became involved in Intelligence matters'.

Maurice became tired of teaching and reverted to his old military career, going to an École de Guerre (Reserve). When war broke out he had had the opportunity to go to the Western Front or to Syria. Not wanting to actively participate in the war, much to Mathilde's annoyance, he chose Syria, later becoming a Staff officer in Beirut. The revelation by her mother-in-law that a bout of childhood mumps had left Maurice impotent (her autobiography says it was peritonitis and a mastoid), and the fact that his father had died in a lunatic asylum, not during the First World War as he had originally told her, gave Mathilde the excuse she needed to leave him. On 18 September 1939, her marriage had come to an end as far as she was concerned, and Maurice was to all intents and purposes dead. Now 'full of fire and want[ing] to get at the enemy',[14] she decided to become a nurse. As a result of these mitigating factors the couple would divorce in 1940, and her Paris lawyer, as we shall discover, 'later became of considerable importance' and would feature prominently in her Resistance activities.

A recent short biography of Mathilde in a chapter of *The Women who Spied for Britain* describes her as 'not a pretty girl but she possessed a certain physical attractiveness that made her appealing to both boys and men. She had numerous admirers and had an active dating life while attending the Sorbonne.'[15] Yet, in spite of having an active libido, she claimed that she had remained a virgin until she was 23. (She was 25 when she married Maurice, which tends to contradict his claim that she was a virgin on their wedding night.) A photograph of her taken in 1933 from a Le Creusot website shows a not unattractive young woman with a haircut similar to a young Mireille Mathieu, the French singer popular in the mid-1960s.[16]

Her MI5 file describes her as being 5ft 4in with dark brown hair, an oval face and slightly turned-up nose, as well as being extremely shortsighted, 'but never wears glasses, except for reading, when she puts the paper practically up to her eyes'.[17] (A prescription for glasses in one of her files indicates that it was -15 diopters, or high myopia.) Elsewhere she is variously described as:

A small, chic figure, with abundant dark hair, strikingly intelligent green eyes, a lively sense of fun, and even at that age, a certain taste in dress. To all outward appearances she was the ideal type of the French *jeune fille bien elevée* [young, well brought-up girl].[18]

She is also described as having a wide and sensuous mouth and a voluptuous body that 'attracted men young and old'.[19] Her biographer Gordon Young described her at 23 as:

A woman if not of beauty at least of a striking appearance which people noticed. Her figure was the characteristically stocky one of many French women of her class. Her nose was a little too large and prominent, her jaw a shade too square and determined, her wide, sensuous mouth would part sometimes to reveal teeth which were widely-spaced and somewhat fang-like. Yet there was always a provocative look of intelligence in her staring green eyes – she suffered from shortsightedness all her life.[20]

Less charitably, she was later described as a 'whore, traitor, a liar, a killer and, most of all, an ingenious spy'.[21] At her trial she was even called a 'dangerous nymphomaniac' by an unnamed witness. By her own admission she was 'deceitful, untruthful and vicious'.[22] Lauran Paine, on the dust jacket of his biography, notes, 'She was not vicious nor spiteful, but she was a woman possessed of a tremendous sexual motivation, and from this ... came her unreasoning periods of violent jealousy.' He also refers to her as a 'green-eyed nymphomaniac' in his book on the Abwehr.[23] The MI5 report on her also says:

She is undoubtedly intelligent and certainly selfish and self-centred. With no extraordinary powers of attraction, she has managed throughout her life to attract a great deal of attention and limelight by a combination of vanity, cunning, ruthlessness and complete absence of deep-rooted loyalty and emotions. One searches for signs of genuine feeling and the only stable thing in her life appears to be her love for her mother ... The outstanding point about her is her complete lack of ordinary human understanding and sympathy, and her inability to judge any person or problem except in relation to herself ... She is fundamentally vicious, spiteful and amoral. Her redeeming features are her intelligence, her culture (she has a very wide range of knowledge), her industry (if, and only if, it serves her immediate ends) and her charm and conversational abilities, best expressed by the French word 'spirituelle' [lively, witty, humorous].[24]

Another report in one of Mathilde's MI5 files, dated 4 May 1942, to John Marriott of the Double-Cross Committee from Mrs S. (Susan) Barton of MI5, refers to her as having:

A very thin veneer of charm, kindness … consideration; utterly egotistical … who cares for nothing and nobody but herself and her own well [being?] and pleasures … very lazy and will only do what amuses her. When happy she can be very amusi[ng] and although she goes in a lot for dirty stories her sense of hum[our] at times is almost infantile.

She is clever but not as clever as she thinks she is, and has an enormous vanity and with flattery it is possible to guide her to a certain extent and for a limited period. On the other hand, she has an enormous arrogance, completely unfounded and a sense of her own infallibility which results in the most offensive remarks and behaviour, particularly against unfortunate Free French officers whom she may come across in restaurants and whom she has a habit of lecturing by simply butting into their conversation.

As long as she gets what she wants she is perfectly charming and merely asks for more, but at the slightest sign of opposition she will either burst into fury, ending up in a pathetic scene or, if that is not successful, act the injured party and become difficult and obstinate and refuse to eat … as she is very vindictive, she would quietly try to get her own back on the person or persons opposing her, and if she did not get what she wanted for herself she would try and find somebody else who would give it to her. In fact, given a chance she would sell any information she has to the other side …

Added to all this there is, of course, her interest in men. She feels she is irresistible to men anyhow and to sleep with a man seems a necessity to her. But once she gets hold of a man it is up to her to drop him or be unfaithful to him, and God help the man or for that matter the Service he is in, if he dares to drop her. From all her talk and the hints she has given me there does not seem to be a [limi]t to her vindictiveness.

Summing up, I think she is an exceedingly dangerous woman when [cross]ed.[25]

With such damning character assassinations it is easy to understand how later events came to unfold.

Susan Barton was the cover name for Austrian-born Gisela Ashley, who worked in B1a as the case officer for Double-Cross agents GELATINE (Friedl Gartner) and TREASURE (Nathalie 'Lily' Serguiew) and had initially served as Thomas Argyll Robertson's secretary. Robertson, better known as 'Tar' from his initials, was in charge of running double agents for MI5's B1a. According to Christopher Andrew's magisterial official history of MI5, Barton had worked as a 'casual agent' for MI5 before the war, 'providing information on the German colony in Britain before moving to the Netherlands in 1939'. There she had also worked with Jona 'Klop' Ustinov.[26] In The Hague she had renewed contact with Serguiew, almost penetrated the German legation, and was offered a job by Kapitän Kurt Besthorn, the German naval attaché.[27] After the 'Venlo Incident' on 9 November 1939, when the German Sicherheitsdienst (SD), the intelligence arm of the Schutzstaffel (SS), set a trap for Captain Sigismund Payne Best of the British Secret Intelligence Service (SIS) and Major Richard Stevens working for SIS under cover as a passport control officer, and the two were arrested, she was pulled out. Ben Macintyre describes Barton as 'vivacious' and the only woman in B1a, who was:

> … a most formidable intelligence operative … and vigorously anti-Nazi, Gisela had left Germany [sic] in the 1920s appalled by the rise of German fascism. She married a British man and then divorced him when he turned out to be homosexual, retained her British citizenship, joined MI5, and established a lifelong partnership with another intelligence officer, Major Gilbert Lennox.[28]

When war was declared in September 1939, Mathilde left Oran and took a boat to Marseilles. From there she headed to Paris, where she joined 'L'Union des Femmes de France', one of three companies that formed the French Red Cross before 1940, and volunteered with them as a nurse, training at a surgical hospital outside of Paris. In her autobiography she mentions her studies began on 1 November 1939 and finished on 1 May 1940. Her MI5 file incorrectly notes that when she studied nursing in Paris at the age of 20 (which would have made the year 1928) she took a particular interest in psychological cases and psychiatry.

In April 1940 she was posted to a hospital near the Maginot Line where she proved to be a capable and conscientious nurse. As the German Army advanced into Belgium and France the field hospitals were evacuated, with Mathilde as one of only eighty of the original nursing candidates ending up at a hospital in Beauvais on 10 May. There she made friends with Dr Raymond Legros, who had lived in Scotland for two years before the war, Dr Pierre Vernette, a surgeon living at 45, rue St Honoré, Paris and a 'woman of doubtful morals called Jane Smiro'. Jane later joined her at a first aid post in Beauvais where Mathilde was matron. Mathilde described how the dying men were brought to her in wheelbarrows or whatever was available to transport them. They worked round the clock, fortified with sandwiches from the village and whisky provided by a kindly major, which helped to raise their spirits. Completely unfazed by the attacks by the Luftwaffe, she remarked to Dr Guy, a doctor attached to the hospital,

'There's almost a sensual pleasure in real danger, don't you think? Your whole body seems suddenly to come alive.'[29] This vicarious thrill of living dangerously, knowing that at any moment she could be killed, was to become a recurring theme throughout Mathilde's life.

In June 1940, when the Germans had captured Paris and France had capitulated, she met a young lieutenant named Jean, referred to in her autobiography as 'Jean M'. This was probably Jean Mercieaux, a lieutenant in the 1st Regiment of Engineers who is referred to in the MI5 report; however, Mathilde says he had been in the Foreign Legion and the Tank Corps.[30] According to her, it soon became common knowledge that the other soldiers in his unit regarded them as a married couple. At a seminary outside Cazère-sur-Garonne they slept in a bed in the bishop's cell above which was a large crucifix, made love under the watchful eye of the Virgin Mary, and ultimately she became pregnant.[31] But Fate would take its hand; early in the pregnancy in September 1940 she suffered a miscarriage. Mathilde was heartbroken, and their relationship fell apart because she somehow blamed Jean for her loss.

Mathilde, it seems, was always prone to melodrama and at first contemplated suicide by flinging herself into the Garonne, but instead decided to put her heart and soul into the war to 'commit a useful suicide'. This was not the first time she had shown suicidal tendencies, nor attempted to draw attention to herself. She described in her autobiography how, while she was at school in Orléans, she had drunk a bottle of blue Waterman ink, largely it seems, because she did not feel at home there.

She met another engineer, named Camille Riy, and a couple of old friends who would go on to work for the WALENTY organisation. One was René Aubertin (RENÉ), a French officer who at one time was Mathilde's lover,[32] the other ONCLE MARCO @ MARCHAL or Kawovic, a distinguished French scientist of Russian extraction and president of the Association of French Chemists, who became head of the sabotage section. (Unfortunately, the Société Chimique de France has no record of any such person holding this office.) At some point during this time, probably after 12 June 1940 when the 51st Highland Division had surrendered at Saint Valéry-en-Caux, Normandy, according to 'Michael' (Stella Lonsdale), Mathilde had a 'mild flirtation' for a day in Rouen with a certain 'Dr Garrow'. This was Lieutenant Ian Grant Garrow of the 9th Battalion, Highland Light Infantry, who by that time was on the run from the Germans and would later join up with Nancy Wake and Albert Guérisse ('Pat O' Leary') to help British and Allied internees escape using the 'Pat' Line.

On 22 June 1940 the Armistice was declared in France and signed in the same railway carriage near Compiègne where the Germans had surrendered in 1918. On 17 September 1940 Mathilde found herself in Toulouse, having unsuccessfully tried to reach Bordeaux. This date and place are significant since it was there that she met a young fighter pilot on the General Staff of the Polish Air Force named Captain Garby-Czerniawski who was sitting next to her at dinner at La Frégate restaurant on the corner of the rue d'Austerlitz and the Place Wilson.[33] How the two of them actually met depends on who is telling the story.

On 21 October 1942, Garby-Czerniawski (who would become code-named WALENTY, but known to her as ARMAND) described in a report given to MI5 in the presence of Major Witold Langenfeld of Polish Intelligence, his version of how he had met Mathilde.[34] At La Frégate he had been unable to find a table so the head waiter had sat him at one where two women, one of whom was Mathilde, were seated. Neither objected to this interloper joining them. He described her as:

> … small, and in her thirties. Her pale thin face, with thin lips, was animated by very vivid eyes. She wore a black, tailored costume of good cut and elegant taste. With my lowered eyes I could see her lovely hands with slim, long fingers carefully kept. I could hear her voice as she talked to her companion, a slightly older, plumper woman.[35]

Mathilde's own account quite naturally suggests it was she who invited him to sit with her, which may well have been the case, given her flirtatious nature. The draft manuscript of her autobiography in her MI5 file states that because the restaurant was always full she and her friend Mimi Muet (mentioned in her autobiography simply as 'Mimi M') were forced to share a table with two men – 'un capitaine sans gloire certainement et un juif sans guerre' (literally, 'certainly an undistinguished captain and a Jew without war' – but perhaps this is a metaphor for something else). However, she changed this in her published autobiography to, 'A man was sitting near us alone at a small table and he had smiled at me from time to time.' She described how Mimi, a beautiful 35-year-old woman, hair wonderfully coiffed, well-dressed in a much-sought-after black ensemble and the latest style of hat – 'a charming, gay creature but quite feather-brained' – and she, her hair dishevelled and dressed as she usually was in a classic 'tailleur' (coat and skirt), sat opposite him. She remarked that it was one of those evenings she hated, as it made no sense and she wondered what she was doing there. It was only after dinner, when the two women had stopped at Fregaton for a drink, that Mimi had said, 'Don't look to your right, but he's there again.' The officer, who, she observed, was a fighter pilot, had followed them.[36]

Christopher Harmer's MI5 report on Mathilde (hereinafter referred to as 'the Harmer report', unless other reports are specifically quoted from) states that 'WALENTY and VICTOIRE made eyes at one another and he followed her out into the street and spoke to her.' According to her account in the draft manuscript, this was after she and Mimi had gone their separate ways. During the course of their conversation he asked her if she could give him some lessons so that he could brush up on his French. He also asked if he could see her home. Reportedly, Mathilde taunted him by asking:

> 'Why do you come to me when there are plenty of other girls around here who are prettier?'
> And in broken French, with a serious look in his dark eyes, the Major replied 'Because you look so intelligent and gay. You know what I shall call you? My little Spitfire.'[37]

Translated from the French in Mathilde's autobiography, it actually reads, 'You're like a Spitfire.' When they met at the Café Tortoni (now a McDonald's) in the Place du Capitole at eleven o'clock the next morning they both discovered that they were restless and fed up with nothing to do. Clearly she was intrigued by his appearance:

> As soon as he saw me coming he rushed up, kissed my hand and thanked me for coming. He was a man of about the same height and age as myself, thin, muscular, with a long narrow face, rather large nose and green eyes which must have originally been clear and attractive but were now flecked with contusions as the result of a flying accident. All his teeth were false or crowned. With his dark, sleek hair he could have been mistaken for a tough, excitable Corsican. He was not handsome but he radiated a kind of confidence and the enthusiasm of youth, an intelligence and a will-power which would alternately give place to a typical Slav nonchalance, or the airs of a spoilt, affectionate child.[38]

As Garby-Czerniawski later told MI5:

> From that time onwards I met her more and more frequently. Apart from the
> lessons I entered in no closer relations with her. She told me her real name and
> many details of her life. After about a fortnight, during our long conversations,
> she told me of her outlook. At the same time I hinted that I was working in
> some organisation. 'La Chatte' grew very interested and she, in turn, hinted that
> she would like to work in this organisation. As I was not yet certain of her, I
> explained that to her that I was engaged in helping Poles to get from France
> to England.[39]

According to Part Two of Mathilde's memoirs covering the period
17 September 1940 to 18 November 1941, written when she was in prison
in England, after their meeting they continued to see a lot of one another,
purportedly so that Garby-Czerniawski could receive French lessons. He told
MI5 that because he needed a cover to be in Occupied France, he had been
looking for someone of French origin to take care of matters concerning
finding a flat and facilitating his registration card with the French authorities,
but he thought his Polish accent would attract too much attention. 'They found
they had much in common and their friendship became intimate.'[40] This is
contrary to the Harmer report, where Mathilde (VICTOIRE) claimed that
they became lovers 'but that there was no serious affair between them', which
MI5 doubted.

CHAPTER 2

'A Man of Great Daring and Initiative'

Roman Garby-Czerniawski was born on 6 February 1910 to Stefan, a financier who died in 1941, and Zusanna, or Susanna (*née* Dziunikowska), in the village of Tłuste in the county of Skałeckiego, later Ternopil (now part of the Ukraine). His brother, Stefan, was an artillery lieutenant who later became a prisoner of war in Germany. The young Roman was educated at the Lycée in Pomerania before joining the Aviation Cadet School in Deblin, from which he graduated on 15 August 1931. Upon graduation he was assigned to 11 Squadron, No. 1 Aviation Regiment. There he received high marks as a pilot and was transferred to 11 Fighter Squadron with the rank of lieutenant. From 1936 to 1938 he spent two years of advanced training at the Wyższa Szkola Wojenna (WSWoj) or Higher War College, in Warsaw. In 1938 he was promoted to captain and organised the Aviation Command of the Polish Air Force HQ in Warsaw.

At the outbreak of war, on 9 September 1939 he was assigned to organise the Defence Command in Lviv (Lvov) to liaise with the Supreme Commander. After the surrender of Lviv he flew to Romania, but to avoid being interned by the Romanian authorities he escaped with forged documents by car via Yugoslavia to Italy and then into France, travelling with fellow pilot Zbigniew Czaykowski (1911–85). Czaykowski would go on to serve in the famous 303 Fighter Squadron, and 315 (City of Deblin) Polish Fighter Squadron, RAF, as a Spitfire pilot, claiming at least two 'kills' and two other 'probables'. From November 1942 to May 1943 he commanded 317 Polish Fighter Squadron. He was awarded the Distinguished Flying Cross (DFC) and ended up as a squadron leader. After the war he settled in the USA.

In Paris Garby-Czerniawski took over a flat owned by 'my old friends the Jankowskis' and attended a course at the École Supérieur de Guerre (now l'École de Guerre) in the Champ de Mars. In March 1940 he became head of Division II in the 1st Grenadier Division.[1] (According to MI5 this was actually the 1st Polish Armoured Division.) During this time he wrote a treatise entitled *The Duties of a Deuxième Bureau of a Large Unit*, which was circulated throughout the Polish Army. He had already been awarded the Polish Croix de Guerre and two Bars in 1939, and the French Croix de Guerre in 1940, but would later be awarded the Virtuti Militari in 1941 by General Władisław Sikorski, who personally presented it to him in London in October of that year. The Virtuti Militari was Poland's highest decoration for heroism and courage in the face of war, instituted by King Stanisław II in 1792, the equivalent to the Victoria Cross.

In his memoir Garby-Czerniawski describes how, on his first morning in Paris while walking down the Champs-Élysées, he came across two of his old colleagues – Lieutenant Krótki, aide de camp (ADC) to General Duch, and Lieutenant Stefan Czyż, his coding officer – seated at Le Colisée Café, 44, Avenue des Champs-Élysées. While they chatted, they showed him how easy it was to produce false identity cards using a stolen rubber stamp and blank cards bought at Au Printemps, the department store on the Boulevard Haussmann. Duch was Brigadier General (later Major General) Bolesław Bronisław Duch (1885–1980), who would become commander of the Polish 1st Grenadier Division in France in 1940 and hold other appointments throughout the war.

When France collapsed in May 1940, Garby-Czerniawski was stationed in the Strasbourg area. From there he managed to escape to Toulouse, where he met Mathilde Carré and founded a Resistance organisation that would become known as *Interallié* and whose membership ran well into three figures. The idea was born during his return to Paris from St Dieu where he had been visiting a wounded comrade, Jerzy Kossowski.

Colonel Wincenty Zarembski, part of General Sikorski's headquarters, informed him that he was in regular touch with London from a radio in Toulouse. With the approval of General Duch, they would start an intelligence network in France; all it needed was London's approval. Garby-Czerniawski described how, 'Two unusual men and one even more unusual woman played important rôles in the preparation of the network.'[2] The first of these men was Józef Radzimiński (b.8 June 1910), a Pole nicknamed Buster Keaton because of his sad face, who had worked as a correspondent for the Polish Foreign Ministry and the Polish Telegraphic Agency before the war. His file in the National Archives at Kew indicates that he had worked for SOE. Radzimiński would later be an assistant to Krystyna Skarbek (Christine Granville) (1915–52) and would fall madly in love with her, although his love was unrequited. Christine trusted him, regarding him as 'energetic and courageous', and put him in touch with Section D, the precursor of SOE. However, the War Office did not have the same faith in him, stating in his file, '[I] cannot conceive of him being the slightest use. On general grounds I consider him useless and untrustworthy and suggest that he should be got rid of at once, or at least interned.' Clare Mulley's book on Christine, *The Spy who Loved*, records how he made several failed attempts at suicide when Christine rejected his affections. He later disappeared after jumping from a train en route from Spain to Poland.[3] The other man was Philippe Autier – 'More than middle-sized, slim, blond, with a nice open face and exquisite, quiet manners'.[4] The woman was Mathilde Carré.

Initially Garby-Czerniawski was known as ARMAND, but was then code-named WALENTY. When he was later involved with the D-Day deception plans, British Intelligence gave him the code name BRUTUS, all of which are used in the MI5 files relating to him and to Mathilde Carré. The *Interallié* organisation was, according to an MI5 draft report written in 1945 by Hugh Astor, his case officer in B1a, 'extremely successful and was the first large organisation to be established in France; it was, indeed, our sole source of information from France at that time'.[5] The organisation also had four wireless telegraphy (W/T) transmitters that were used to send intelligence from all over France and enabled British Intelligence to learn the entire German order of battle for France. Astor described him as 'a man of great daring and initiative and had contacts among both Vichy and Gestapo authorities'.

Shortly after their meeting in Toulouse on 15 October 1940, ARMAND suggested to Mathilde that they travel to Marseilles, Lyons, Limoges and Vichy in the Unoccupied Zone, which she was more than willing to do to help take her mind off Jean, her former lover. He also suggested that she join him in building up an Allied network. The idea of becoming part of this network greatly appealed to her sense of adventure 'and she soon came to picture herself as the "Mata Hari of the Second World War"'.[6] Indeed, Mathilde's autobiography is subtitled 'The Truth about the Most Remarkable Woman Spy since Mata Hari – by Herself'. Exactly how true remains to be seen, but it was an indication of her own feeling of self-importance.

In Limoges they met an old friend, Philippe Autier, the son of a colonel, who had lived in Poland before the war and who would accompany them to Vichy. The other was Jacques G., a French NCO airman (the full name is not given). In Vichy Mathilde reacquainted herself with Captain (later Commandant) André Achat, an old friend whom she had known when she had lived in Morocco before the war with her husband. Achat was secretary to De Bergeray [*sic*], actually General Jean Marie Joseph Bergeret (1895–1956), Air Minister to the

Vichy government and later Vichy ambassador to Turkey. Both Authier and Achat had influence in the Deuxième Bureau, which she knew would prove useful one day. At the beginning of November Mathilde and ARMAND travelled to Marseilles to contact the Polish organisation, TUDOR, which, according to MI5, was 'already in contact with London (SIS)'.[7] There they learned that French troops had returned from Syria.

The identity of TUDOR is far from certain. Some sources and documents suggest it was an organisation, rather than an actual person. Garby-Czerniawski and others, give Wicenty (or Siegfried) Zarembski (1896–1996), who was RYGOR's deputy, as TUDOR. RYGOR was the code name of Major Mieczysław Zygfryd Słowikowski (1896–1989), who was responsible for setting up Allied spy networks in Occupied France and later in North Africa. RYGOR had been made the chief of the Polish Deuxième Bureau in France.[8] Another possibility is General Juliusz Edward Kleeberg (1890–1970), born at Trembowla, Galicia, Austria-Hungary (Poland). During the First World War (1915–17) he was a Staff officer in the Polish Legion. By 1937 he was promoted to brigadier general and awarded the Cross of Valour with two Bars, and the Gold Cross of Merit with Swords. At around that time he was also appointed to the Order of Polonia Restituta (Fourth Class). After Poland had been overrun by the Germans in 1939, he escaped to Paris, where he headed the Polish government-in-exile's military mission to the Allies. In November 1939 he went to Belgrade to organise the transfer of 40,000 Polish soldiers to France. When France capitulated in June 1940 he served briefly as Polish military attaché in Vichy. There he led a Resistance cell that smuggled downed airmen to Britain over the Pyrenees, for which he was awarded the Légion d'Honneur in 1941 and Croix de Guerre in 1947.[9] He went on to act as a liaison officer with the Allies in the Mediterranean theatre. In fact, as indicated later in this chapter, it appears that Kleeberg @ TUDOR/Zarembski are one and the same.

Bleicher's account in his book refers to TUDOR as Kadomtsev, whom he described as 'a dangerous man before the war. A fanatical Communist, he had been involved in various acts against the French State.'[10] He talks about 'a man in Paul's Paris group called "Tudor", who lived in Compiègne and was a specialist in the most dangerous acts of sabotage. [He] was extremely dangerous and had to be rendered harmless as soon as possible.' 'Paul' was Henri Jacques Paul Frager (1897–1944), who was executed at Buchenwald on 5 October 1944.

In Bleicher's account, sometime in August 1943 he set off with KIKI to arrest TUDOR, which he did at the République Métro station. From there he was taken to Fresnes by Military Police truck under escort. However, when

Bleicher arrived at the Place de la République two hours later TUDOR was dead. 'Ten minutes ago the prisoner threw himself out of a window on the second floor. He is dead,' someone reported to him.[11] Clearly, whoever Bleicher's 'Tudor' was, he was not the same one to whom WALENTY reported. Nor for obvious reasons was he the revolutionary, Mikhail Samuilovich Kadomtsev (1886–1918), Ivan Samuilovich Kadomtsev (1884–1918) or Boris Kadomtsev who was involved with Im Thurn of the London Steamship & Trading Company, mentioned in the report on the Zinoviev Letter.[12]

Mathilde's husband, Maurice, had shown up to visit her while she was in Toulouse but she had refused to accompany him when he went to Vichy. She viewed him as a Germanophile, a defeatist and a collaborator when, at her suggestion, he refused to join Brigadier General Charles de Gaulle's forces: 'Maurice, who had always been more or less pro-German and a partisan of a Franco-German Alliance, had returned from Syria completely pro-Nazi and hating the British.'[13] To her he was a coward. She was so disgusted with his apathy that she told him to stay with her parents, where she would later join him; however, she went off to Vichy instead.

A coward he was not. Captain Maurice Henri-Claude Carré was later killed around 29/30 January 1944 during the Allied invasion of Italy when he was first attached to the 4e Tirailleurs Tunisiens (4th Tunisian Sharpshooters), then to the 3e D.I.A. (3rd Algerian Infantry Division). The citation read that, while temporarily commanding the 1st Company of the 1st/4th Tunisians, he was killed heroically by a grenade during an enemy counter-attack while two assaults were being launched on Hill 771 at the First Battle of Monte Cassino.[14] He was recommended for the Chevalier de la Légion d'Honneur for his bravery.

Written sometime after her arrival in England, the undated MI5 report on VICTOIRE by Patricia McCallum states that while ARMAND returned to Marseilles, VICTOIRE 'for some reason never fully explained, went to Vichy'.[15] Although it is not recorded in ARMAND's statement to MI5, it has been suggested that this trip was so that Mathilde could learn espionage techniques, such as the recruitment of agents, methods of coding, and the delivery and dissemination of information from former members of the Deuxième Bureau. In Vichy she was introduced by Captain André Achat to two men. One was a certain Capitaine Simonaux [sic], also known as 'Dr S' or 'Mons. S', 'Dr Sorg', 'M. Sejournet' and 'M. St Simon'; her preferred name for him was 'SARDANAPALE' (Sardanapalus): 'He had a self-satisfied air, wore a monocle, had beautiful hands and fine features.' Capitaine Léon Simonau, as he is more correctly referred to in Raymond Ruffin's *Résistance P.T.T.*, about the French Post Office's contribution to the Resistance effort, was responsible for collecting information from 'Source K', a listening station at Noisy-le-Grand, and passing it on to London.[16] Simonau was later promoted to colonel and worked for the Service de Renseignements de l'Armée de Terre[17] and the Centre de Coordination Interarmées (CCI).[18]

The other man to whom Achat introduced Mathilde, whose name she could not remember, was known as 'Dr Bernard' or 'Sir Raoul'. In fact, this was Raoul Georges Bernard Beaumaine (1890–1971), according to her file. Before the war Beaumaine had been the general agent for Heidsieck & Co. Champagne, in America. He worked for Colonel Louis Baril of the Deuxième Bureau and liaised with the US embassy in Vichy and the British embassy in Bern. The file adds that he was expelled from Vichy on 10 October 1941. On 25 November he sent a telegram to Lisbon saying that he was returning to Montreal where his wife lived. He left Lisbon on 26 December.

Other agents with whom she became acquainted were Jacques Labourot @ JACKIE, or JACKY, as Mathilde writes in her memoirs, who was a 24-year-old sergeant pilot sent by Simonau; Richard d'Harcourt [sic]; and a French-Russian born in Cairo known as Duvernoy @ WIRTZ, whose first name was unknown. (Paine's biography of Mathilde refers to him as Inspector Duverney of the Vichy Deuxième Bureau). Pierre d'Harcourt (1913–81), as he was correctly known, and his brother Charles (1921–92) were the sons of Robert d'Harcourt (1881–1965), all of whom were involved with the Resistance.

An account in Freddy Kraus's MI5 file of Lieutenant Colonel Richard Lowther Broad (in 1940 a lieutenant) of the Seaforth Highlanders mentions Comte Pierre d'Harcourt in connection with Jacqueline de Broglie, who had hidden the colonel and seven of his men when they had become trapped in France after the Armistice. Kraus described d'Harcourt as young, aged about 22, hot-headed and very indiscreet, 'whose imprudence would one day land himself and his friends in trouble'. Indeed, Pierre was arrested on 20 July 1943, first sent to Neue-Bremme in Saarbrücken on 29 November, then to Buchenwald in December. Charles was sent to Buchenwald on 22 January 1944. Both survived the war. Pierre would later write of his experiences in *The Real Enemy*.[19]

In what is perhaps the earliest example of her duplicity, during the course of her conversation with the Deuxième Bureau, Mathilde told them that she was to accompany a Pole to Paris who was going to set up an espionage organisation on behalf of the Poles, and also offered to work for the Deuxième Bureau. They agreed and gave her instruction in secret writing with ink made from alum and water, as well as how to identify the markings of the German Army. These markings were those normally found on vehicles, helmets etc., a comprehensive list of which, complete with coloured illustrations, can be found in her MI5 file.[20] The bureau made her promise not to tell ARMAND that she 'also had a Vichy mission'. Predictably, she could not keep a secret and told him, but there is no record of his reaction to this disclosure. The Deuxième Bureau also said they would provide her with information to send to London via the Polish link.

While in Vichy, she stayed at the Hôtel des Ambassadeurs, where she developed the habit of scratching the hotel's leather chairs. This was how she reportedly obtained the name 'La Chatte', coined by some American reporters staying there, although other accounts say it was because of her predatory nature. Pierre de Vomécourt, whom we shall meet later, said it was because of 'her strange, wide-set eyes', and even said that she was 'undeniably attractive'.[21] ARMAND's own account, which may be more accurate, went like this:

> 'You know, Lily, you walk, especially in your soft shoes, like a cat; so quietly –'
>
> 'And I can scratch as well if I wish!' she said, raising her slim hands with the long fingers and long nails. 'Some other people have also compared me with a cat!'
>
> 'I would rather call you "She-cat" – *La Chatte*!'
>
> 'I like it!'
>
> 'So "*La Chatte*" in our organization you shall be!'[22]

This, he said, was the name used in reports and instructions, but between the two of them he always called her 'Lily' and she called him 'Toto'. Whether this was an allusion to Dorothy's dog in *The Wizard of Oz*, which appeared in 1939, is unknown. But the very mention of her being able to scratch if she wished was perhaps a veiled threat that she should not be crossed.

While they were in Vichy ARMAND still did not explain to her exactly what he was doing. It was only when they had returned to Toulouse on 18 October 1940, according to Mathilde, that he told her that he was engaged in intelligence work for the Poles in the Unoccupied Zone and had been authorised to set up an espionage organisation for them. This contradicts her earlier claim of also working for Vichy. The tendency to contradict herself and others is a common running element in many of her statements.

ARMAND suggested to her that they should go to Paris and collaborate on intelligence work, having determined during their conversations that she was 'intelligent, eager for adventure and might render me great services'. He disclosed that he was going to start up a similar network in the Occupied

Zone and would leave for Paris on 15 November (the Harmer report says it was the 14th). 'He would be the general and he asked VICTOIRE, the code name by which she became known, to be his chief of staff and Colonel of this organisation.'[23] Mathilde readily accepted his offer and arranged to live with ARMAND in Paris, 'giving out that he was her cousin and sp[oke] bad french because his parents had al[ways lived] abroad and because he had been, before the war, an ... the Rou[manian] oil fields'.[24]

In Marseilles they were offered an apartment at 2, rue du Porto Riche by Jean Ziromski [*sic*], a Pole who was a militant Socialist, which Mathilde rented under the name of Madame Berger, although she never used the flat. It would later be used by RAPIDE and JAG. Jean Zyromski (1890–1975) was leader of the SFIO (Section Française de l'Internationale Ouvrière) between the wars and had supported the Republican side in the Spanish Civil War, later becoming active in the Lot-et-Garonne Resistance. After the war, he joined the Communist Party.

Together, Mathilde and ARMAND made their journey to Paris, she travelling officially as a member of the Red Cross, ostensibly to re-join her unit, but ARMAND had to cross the border illegally into Occupied France. On 16 November 1940 they met in Paris at her mother's house at 14, Avenue des Gobelins, in the 5th arrondissment. For the first three days ARMAND lived in a hotel, while VICTOIRE rented an apartment at 26, Faubourg St Jacques, Montparnasse, in the 14th arrondissement, close to the Observatory and opposite the Cochin Prison. Her memoirs state that it was a studio near the La Santé prison and that it was on 17 November. La Santé prison stands close by between the 13th and 14th arrondissements on the rue de La Santé; the Cochin is the Hôpital Cochin at 27, Faubourg St Jacques, founded in 1780, referred to as a prison by Mathilde, but now the central burn treatment centre for Paris.

They subsequently lived together – 'We mutually agreed, "La Chatte" and I, soon after our arrival in Paris, that we should cease to exist for each other as man and woman and would become merely pals in Intelligence work.' This implies that the relationship was purely platonic, which seems unlikely both from Mathilde's and Garby-Czerniawski's points of view, given their proclivity for forming sexual relationships easily. That was certainly the feeling of her mother, who was convinced that she was 'living with the Pole' and refused to visit them. Indeed, as the 'Summary of VICTOIRE's Memoirs' noted, 'She is at pains to point out ... that while they lived together it was not as lovers and that each had their own love affairs on the side with which the other was familiar.' Whichever apartment, it was:

In this studio they sat down to work out the establishment of an organisation which would cover the whole of occupied France … and obtain detailed and comprehensive/information [*sic*] about the German […] forces. The country was to be divided into sectors, with a chief in each sector responsible for the work of the agents under him, and separate agents who would specialize in press matters, politics, industry and propaganda. All would report to ARMAND and VICTOIRE, would c[ode …] reports and dispatch them weekly to … [Remainder of page missing or severely damaged][25]

CHAPTER 3

Interallié is Born

The *Interallié* network was born on 18 November 1940 and derived its name from the international aviation news bulletin *Interavia* that ARMAND had read before the war. As it was to be an interallied organisation he called it by its French translation, *Interallié*. At the beginning it consisted of a few maps of France, some coloured pictures bearing information about the German Army, and *Le Guide d'Interpretre Militaire*. As McCallum's undated report notes, the various early recruits to the fledgling organisation were mainly Poles living in Paris whose names ARMAND had been given while he was in Marseilles, or friends of VICTOIRE:

> It was inevitable that the larger share of the 'recruiting campaign' which they now launched should fall to VICTOIRE as BRUTUS still spoke poor French. However, a number of his Polish friends joined him in the enterprise, notably Lieut. Bernard KRUTKI @ CHRISTIAN, at one time on the Polish Staff with BRUTUS; a commercial artist named Wladimir LIPSKY @ OBSERVATEUR, and his 17 year-old daughter Cipinka;[1] Stanislas LACH @ RAPIDE, who acted as courier for the group; Lucien ROCQUIGNY @ PAUL, an ex-lecturer at the University of Warsaw and journalist [a Pole who had been in Germany and who handled press work]; and (much later) Janusz WLODARCYK @ MAURICE, who became the principal W/T operator; and a great many others. Among the principal French men and women recruited presumably recruited by, and through, VICTOIRE, were René AUBERTIN @ RENÉ, a childhood friend of the BELARD family and an ex-Tank officer; who, in turn, brought in the distinguished scientist Marco MARSCHALL (born KAWOVIC) @ ONCLE MARCO; Charles LEJEUNE @ BOBY-ROLAND, a Police inspector who was chief organiser of the Paris (R) Sector and his wife, MIREILLE, a concierge who ran one of the original post boxes, and was a great friend of VICTOIRE's; Claude JOUFFRET @ MICHEL, another dear friend who

proved to be less than satisfactory; the HUGENTOBLE couple who came from Alsace-Lorraine: he under the cover-name RICHARD (NOEUD) obtained information from the Germans, while his wife, another concierge, ran a post-box, both were devoted to VICTOIRE. Two other prominent Frenchmen in the network were René LEGRAND @ YOLÉ, who supplied information on sea-transport under the cover of collaborating with the Germans; and Maitre Michel BRAULY [sic] @ MIKLOS, a lawyer of Polish extraction, who was in touch with a number of other underground organisations, and who gave BRUTUS and VICTOIRE their first start in Paris. Other important members of INTERALLIE were Fernand GANE @ MONO and his mistress Simone DESCHAMPS [sic] @ MOUSTIQUE, head and second-in-command of Sector A; Robert GORBINOT or GORRIOT @ BOB-EDGAR, head of Sector E; Robert KIFFER @ KIKI, head of Sector D, and his mistress Mme. BUFFET @ DENISE; Henri GORCE @ LOUIS, a friend of MONO and MOUSTIQUE's and an agent of Sector L; Francis TABAT @ MARCEL, a friend of VICTOIRE's who acted as W/T operator; George or Gaston LURTON @ JEAN [also written as LIORTON, who lived on the demarcation line], head of Sector J; Théophil[e] BURLOT @ CHARLES, a sub-agent in Sector C, whose head was COCO (name unknown); there were many, many others – the network and its ramifications ran well into three figures – but those names play principal parts in its tragic break-up.[2]

Théophile Burlot was a friend of Guy Chaumet (1913–80), who was already in touch with London and the *Copernicus* network, and a member of the Resistance (Réseau F2) in Caen in the Calvados region. In 1941 Chaumet had been a member of the *Ali-Tir* network as agent P2. He was arrested in December of that year and spent a year in Fresnes. After his release he was picked up by Lysander and flown to London, where he joined the Bureau Central de Renseignements et d'Action (BCRA, the French intelligence service until 1947), and later parachuted back into France. Jean Lapeyre-Mensignac (1922–2015), an old schoolfriend of Chaumet, was Agent P2 in the *Sol* network. MOUSTIQUE ('Mosquito'), was actually Monique Deschamps, not Simone, described as a 'tiny, chain-smoking firebrand of a woman'.[3]

Janusz Włodarczyk (MAURICE), referred to in Carré's MI5 file as Eugeniusz Włodarczyk, was born in Kraków (Cracow), Poland, on 5 October 1909. Before the war he had trained as a wireless-telegraphist with the Polish Navy, in which he served until his compulsory service had been completed in January 1933. Between that time and July 1939 his career was spent in the Polish Merchant

Marine on various ships and as a radio-telegraphist at various establishments. At the end of July 1939, when he was called up for service in the Polish Army, he spent three weeks training at Bydgoszcz. On 20 August 1939 he was called up by the Polish Ministry of Foreign Affairs and worked for them in Warsaw in 'special service' while all his family remained in Kraków during the war.

Just after Germany invaded Poland on 1 September, Włodarczyk and the ministry staff were evacuated on 7 September 1939 and managed to cross into Romania. He remained in Bucharest until 25 October, when he was issued with the necessary travel documents to go to France. He arrived in Paris on 1 November 1939, where he worked at the Polish embassy. On 13 June 1940, the day before the Germans marched into Paris, the ministry staff escaped to Libourne, arriving there on the 17th. A week later, on 21 June, he and the staff went to Langon, and from there, having lost all their equipment to General Marian Włodzimierz Kukiel (1885–1972), General Officer Commanding the 1st Polish Corps in Coatbridge, Scotland, they went to Lourdes, and finally Salies de Salat.

On 16 May 1941 Włodarczyk received orders from a radio-telegraphist named Zygmunt Masłowski to proceed to Paris. These orders had originally come from TUDOR. He crossed the demarcation line in the Rouvres region on the night of 17/18 May 1941 and travelled to Paris. There, with Masłowski, he set up a wireless station under the orders of 'Mr ARMAND (Pole)', who was obviously WALENTY. ARMAND sent Włodarczyk to Marseilles to try to find someone capable of establishing wireless communications with Poland, but he was unsuccessful. On his return, he was arrested around Loches, having just crossed the demarcation line, and kept in prison for fourteen days, after which he was released, arriving back in Paris around 13 September. He went to live at 8, Villa Léandre in Montmartre.

Lipsky was Prince Wladimir de Korczak Lipski, a direct descendant of Prince de Korczak, King of Hungary in 1120, who had fought with the British Army during the First World War. At the end of the war until 1922 he served under Lieutenant General Sir Adrian Carton de Wiart, VC, in the British Secret Service as a lieutenant with the British Poland Military Mission (1919–21). His role as a Secret Service agent is unclear.[4] Colin Gubbins, later of SOE, also served under de Wiart in that Mission.

Lipski's daughter was named Lydia Lova de Korczak Lipski, born in Warsaw on 8 January 1925; the *Interallié* network code-named her CIPINKA. When the network was broken up, Lydia was imprisoned in La Santé and Fresnes prisons, before being deported to Ravensbrück in July 1943; Wladimir was sent to Mauthausen. Both survived, but Lydia had been experimented on by SS doctors who gave her a mysterious injection that they told her would have a delayed reaction over a number of years. One website states that it was 'Dr Hans Gerhart'. If this was actually meant to be Dr Gerhardt August Heinrich Rose (1896–1992), he carried out typhus experiments on prisoners at Buchenwald. There is no mention of his ever being at Ravensbrück. He may have been confused with Dr Karl Franz Gebhardt (1897–1948), who carried out surgical experiments at Auschwitz and Ravensbrück. He was one of the doctors who treated Heydrich after the botched assassination attempt in 1942, and almost killed Albert Speer when he treated him for a swollen knee in 1944. He was hanged after being convicted at the Nuremburg Trials. More likely it was Herta Oberheuser (1911–78), who carried out experiments on women at Ravensbrück, infecting their wounds with sulfonamide, and was later convicted at the Nuremburg 'Doctors' Trial'.[5]

After the war Lydia was decorated with the Croix de Guerre avec Palme and the Légion d'Honneur. She went on to become a successful dancer at the Folies-Bergère in Paris and in London under the name Lydia Lova, but died suddenly on 3 February 1966 at the age of 41.[6] Whether her sudden death had anything to do with the mysterious injection was never proved.

A couple of others added to the network were Lieutenant André Laporte @ MARIUS, a French airman who specialised in air force information in the Paris district, and GEORGES I, a Pole who was to be the wireless operator, who came from Toulouse.[7] Unfortunately, no name was given for him. When ARMAND was not satisfied and wanted more members, he turned to VICTOIRE to approach her friends. One of those was Maître Michel Brault (MIKLOS), whose name she had been given by Captain Achat while she was in Vichy.[8] According to her memoir, Brault chose the name MIKLOS himself. He would also become the lawyer who would handle her divorce. A chat had also given them Pierre de Froment's name, described as 'a peasant of about forty whom we baptized JEAN. A stout, honest fellow, we realized he was ready for anything,' and 'an excellent recruit'.

Lieutenant Georges-Pierre de Froment (1913–2006), who lived near the demarcation line at Loches, helped them cross the line secretly, but later faded out of the picture. Using the code name DEBLÉ, de Froment had met Captain Henri Frenay Sandoval (1905–88) in Marseilles after the French capitulated. Sandoval went on to form the *Combat* resistance movement in the Zone Libre in 1940, some of which was later subsumed by SOE's *Carte* network in 1942. When Jean Moulin was captured on 21 June 1943, Sandoval fled to Algiers and worked for de Gaulle. On 14 January 1943, de Froment was betrayed by a comrade and arrested by the Abwehr. He was first imprisoned in Fresnes and would end up in Mauthausen, from which he was liberated in May 1945.

Another who became part of the network was René Aubertin, whom VICTOIRE had met during the retreat from northern France. He put her in touch with other friends, such as MARCO M., also known as ONCLE MARCO (Uncle Marco), MARSHALL or MARCHAL. Two others provided by the Deuxième Bureau, whom Mathilde had met in Vichy, were JACKIE (Jacques Labourot),[9] and Richard d'Harcourt @ Pierre RICHARD. In her memoirs VICTOIRE described the latter as tall, shortsighted and very intelligent; he acted as a liaison between her and the Deuxième Bureau in Vichy. In turn, JACKIE provided NOEUD (Richard Noeud) and BOBY-ROLAND (Charles Lejeune), whose wives were both concierges. NOEUD was a Swiss-German living at 1, Avenue Lemarck [sic], and BOBY-ROLAND, a policeman, lived at No. 6. The latter was able to provide ARMAND with information from the Gestapo via the French police and duplicates of all the police stamps for Paris. In this way, ARMAND was able to issue all his agents with false identity cards. (The address is actually more likely to be rue Lamarck in the 18th arrondissement as there does not appear to be an Avenue Lamarck in Paris, so rue Lamarck will be used instead of what erroneously appears in the report and other documents, unless it is a direct quote.) These addresses were used as post boxes for the agents.

By the end of 1940 the network had many members but little money, and ARMAND was forced to sell his camera for 1,500 francs at a pawnshop. According to the 'Summary of Victoire's Memoirs' in her file, the day after the camera was sold, MARIUS (André Laporte) returned from Marseilles with money, news and handbooks identifying the various units, ranks and branches of the Wehrmacht and Luftwaffe. Information was sent to Marseilles via RAPIDE (also known as LACH) by unscrewing a notice on a train and inserting the message behind it. Someone would board the train at the first stop after the demarcation line and retrieve the message. RAPIDE's name had been given to ARMAND by TUDOR. The organisation was now divided into a number of sectors:

Sector A (from the Spanish frontier to Bordeaux): This was covered by ALBERT, a friend of JACKIE.

Sector B (from Bordeaux to Brittany): NOEUD used to go here occasionally, but otherwise there were no permanent agents.

Sector C (Brittany): a young pilot called COCO had been found to deal with this sector.

Sector D (Normany and Cherbourg peninsula): A commercial traveler aged 50 named DANIEL was the agent for this sector.

Sector E (The country between the Seine and the Somme): A young pilot called BOB-EDGAR was the agent for this sector, and in view of its great importance at that time they also used the mistress of the agent of sector J. JEANINE-ERNESTINE, who was a waitress in a café at Rouen.

Sector F, G and H (comprising the 'zone interdite'): They were uncovered because of the difficulty of getting agents in and out, but a friend of MIKLOS went there occasionally.

Sector I (the country to the south-east of Paris, with Dijon as its centre): An Air Force N.C.O. known as GUY was in charge of this sector [Guy VEDERO].

Sector J (the area due south of Paris): This sector was looked after by JEAN [Georges or Gaston LURTON].

Sector K and L (the country to the west and south-west of Paris, excluding the coastal regions): These were empty.

Sector R (the Paris region): The official chief of the Paris region was RICHARD-NOEUD, who had under him sub-agents, known only to him, called RAOUL, ROBERT, RAYMOND and ROGER. RENÉ was to a great extent VICTOIRE's personal assistant, and quite evidently her lover, he also dealt with the industry of the Paris region, and so could be classed in a sense as an agent of Sector R, though he took a considerable part, too, in the direction of the organisation so far as preparing reports was concerned.

Industry: This was looked after by RENÉ for the Paris region, and OBSERVATEUR [@ De LIPSKI].

Press and Propaganda: As stated earlier, the agent PAUL looked after this.

Liaison with TUDOR, Marseilles: This was in the hands of RAPIDE.

Liaison with the Deuxième Bureau: VICTOIRE looked after this through RICHARD D'HARCOURT.

Liaison with PATRIE organisation: This was an organisation working in the chemical and engineering factories. The liaison was in the hands of VICTOIRE and ONCLE MARCO of PATRIE.

Liaison with L.N. organisation: This was a resistance organisation with whom INTERALLIEE were in touch through VICTOIRE and MIKLOS, a member of L.N.

Radio: This was nominally in charge of GEORGES, who was later injured in a train accident, and in any event the radio did not work.

Miscellaneous: There were also miscellaneous agents acting as casual and general
sources of information, such as JACKIE, CHON and a new friend of
WALENTY known as PAULETTE PORCHER. ONCLE MARCO also
introduced a man called Oscar STEININGER, who was a rich German with
properties on the Riviera, and who had been appointed by the Germans to
deal with the administration of property belonging to British subjects in Paris.
Another Deuxième Bureau contact known as PAOLI [Lieutenant ROBERT]
was introduced by RICHARD D'HARCOURT, but VICTOIRE did not
approve of him and complained, as a result of which she was interviewed by a
Deuxième Bureau chief called Captain DANIELLE.[10]

Based on the list in Mathilde's file (see Appendix 1), it is assumed that the
ALBERT referred to here is Roger Cottin. ARMAND's Polish family friends,
the Janowskis living at 64, Avenue de la Grand Armée, situated between the
16th and 17th arrondissements, were also recruited. Their daughter, Madeleine,
whom he had previously known as CHON, would later become one of his
girlfriends. But, that being said, ARMAND became tired of living alone and
celibacy and brought from Rouen the wife of a dentist, Madeleine de Quellec
[sic] (also referred to as Maude and ORION) to become his mistress. In her
memoirs VICTOIRE says that she was a 'charming girl friend, with whom
he had lived at Mégève [sic]', a ski resort in the Alps of south-eastern France.
A Madeleine le Quellec (née Hamel), born 5 April 1904 in Auxerre, is listed
as having her place of residence as Saint-Étienne-du-Rouvray in Normandy,
which is just outside Rouen, so this is likely the same person. She was deported
first to Sarrebrück on 27 July 1943, then Ravensbrück on 1 August 1943, and
finally to Mauthausen on 7 March 1945 under the ('Nacht und Nebel' ('Night
and Fog') decree. She was liberated from Mauthausen on 22 April 1945 and
repatriated to Annecy four days later.[11]

  The Harmer report supposed that 'by this time he [ARMAND] had got
tired of VICTOIRE'. Whether this was so, in March 1941 (the Harmer report
says 12 January), he and VICTOIRE switched to another apartment at 14, rue
Colonel Moll (written as 'Mole' in the MI5 file) near the Porte Champerret in
the 17th arrondissement, where they stayed for only two months before moving
again, this time to Square du Trocadéro in the 16th arrondissement, not far from
the Trocadéro and the Palais de Chaillot. It is probably this flat that is referred
to in 'Summary of Victoire's Memoirs', which it says it was near the Étoile, and
VICTOIRE engaged a maid named Marie. The next flat was occupied by a
Gestapo officer 'who became VICTOIRE's "flirt in the lift" and to whom she

gave the impression that the flat was inhabited by some gay young things who played dance mus[ic] on the radio all day'. Again, they only stayed there for two months, with ARMAND returning to his old apartment at 14, rue Colonel Moll and VICTOIRE renting a room in the rue Grenelle in the 6th arrondissement.

It was arranged that when agents visited Paris on a weekly basis, all their reports were to be deposited at the post box at 1, rue Lamarck, with the concierge, Mireille Lejeune, BOBY-ROLAND's wife. VICTOIRE would then collect them and hand them to ARMAND to review and critique. Together, they would then compile a report which would be sent to Marseilles via the train notice system mentioned earlier. Harmer's report notes, 'Confirmation has been received from the appropriate Intelligence section of the War Office that the WALENTY reports were of the utmost value and the best source of military information in France at that time.' The military information appears to be mostly troop movements based on markings they had observed on vehicles, helmets, uniforms, etc. which are illustrated in VICTOIRE's MI5 files.

In early 1941 JACKIE introduced two new recruits, MONO and LOUIS. MONO was Fernand Gane or Ganne (d.1978) @ GAUTHIER @ GRENIER @ GARNIER, a Frenchman aged between 35 and 40 who was recruited to organise the W/T activities, but later became chief agent of Sector A. He is listed in the 'Members and Contact of the WALENTY Organisation Carded in VICTOIRE' as KENT (see Appendix 1). He would also be code-named ICARE (ICARUS) in *Libération-Nord*, part of the *Phalanx* network founded by 'Colonel Passy' of the BCRA and Christian Pineau in 1942, who would become head of the network in 1943 following Pineau's arrest. Passy was actually André Dewavrin (1911–98), who had been selected by Charles de Gaulle to run the BCRA and help organise the French Resistance. Gane is also listed as being an unconfirmed member of the *Phidias* network.[12] He was also a member of *Phalanx*, where he was known as 'Jacquot'.

McCallum's report mentions that LOUIS was Henri Gorce (1906–2000), a Frenchman also aged between 35 and 40, a friend of MONO and MOUSTIQUE and the agent for Sector L. As noted earlier, MOUSTIQUE was Monique Deschamps, the mistress of MONO and an agent in Sector A; she would later marry ARMAND in 1944.

Prior to being in Toulouse, ARMAND had been billeted during the early part of the war with a young blonde widow, Renée Borni (*née* Petitjean) in Lunéville, a commune in the Meurthe-et-Moselle département, with whom he had fallen in love. According to a US Army Counter-Intelligence Corps (CIC) interrogation report dated 7 October 1944 prepared by agent Otto

Wirth,[13] Renée was born on 6 May 1919 at Epinal and her last permanent address was 6, rue Boffrand, Lunéville. Her husband, Ernest Borni, had died on 18 or 19 January 1939 in Metz. At the time of the report, her daughter was living with her grandfather, Joseph Borni, at 43, rue Drogon, Metz, having moved there in 1940. Renée was educated at the Collège des Jeunes Filles, Place de la Cathédral in Strasbourg, from which she graduated in 1934. She lived with her parents at 19, rue St Barbe, Strasbourg, until she married Ernest c.1937. They then moved to Thionville for six months until he died, whereupon she moved in with her parents-in-law in Metz. That being the case, their marriage must have taken place later in 1938. In Metz she worked as a cashier in a department store until she moved to Lunéville in 1939 at the outbreak of war. The report also includes some of the aliases that she recalled of 'VALENTIN INTERALLIE' [sic]:

THEO, agent in the Brittany sector.
COCO, agent.
MANNOT, agent.
MOUSTIQUE, agent.
ADAM, English agent.
PAMELA, an English woman who decoded in London.
MARCO, agent.
POUSSIN, alias for Subject, who also had the alias VIOLETTE.
VICTOR, agent.
MAURICE, W/T operator, a Polish officer.
POUSSIN, alias CARRÉ, alias BORNI, alias Bene VERNON for
    CZERNIAWSKI.
GEORGES, W/T operator, a young French aviator who also drew maps, etc.
ROSTOV, who acted as courier between London and Paris.
GUY, agent, and LA CHATTE, chiffreuse [encoder] whose real first name
    was LILLI.[14]

It has not been possible to establish exactly who agents ROSTOV and PAMELA were, although it must be assumed that the latter worked for either MI5 or MI6. There is a reference to a Pamela being the fiancée of ADAM in Garby-Czerniawski's memoirs, but whether she is the same woman referred to in the CIC report is unknown. It is also somewhat confusing that VIOLETTE claimed to have the code name POUSSIN as well as the alias CARRÉ, which was Mathilde's (VICTOIRE's) real name.

Renée had given ARMAND her late husband's papers in April 1940 (some accounts say he had persuaded her to give them to him), and so he adopted the name of Armand Borni. When he moved back to his old digs, he made the 'fatal mistake' of sending for her, and she moved in with him as his resident mistress. The idea of bringing Renée to Paris came to him when he was talking to Paul Martin (HONORÉ), the head of H Sector. ARMAND was concerned that VICTOIRE was spending most of her time typing reports, and he was having to work late to encode them: 'I did not wish to give our precious code to anybody I could not trust one hundred percent.' That statement alone is interesting as it indicates that already he had realised that VICTOIRE was perhaps not entirely trustworthy. He gave Renée the code name VIOLETTE and employed her as a trainee cipher clerk in the intelligence office. This arrangement was initially acceptable to VICTOIRE, who by this time had given up on the idea of ARMAND being her lover. Indeed, her mother had even asked her if they were lovers. VICTOIRE's reply to her was that she simply loved working with ARMAND. As he records their conversation about his idea:

'Thank you, Lily, and you *are* an excellent work companion!'

'She would be perfect for this work. She is accustomed to figures, adding and subtracting, being an accountant, and she is a very nice girl too!'...

'But you need a different sort of companion too! I spoke with René Aubertin a few days ago and we agreed we must find some girl friend for you!' ...

'Oh, my dear Lily, I don't complain about the lack of company! The Jankowskis have invited me several times. Chon-Chon and Simone are awfully nice girls and their friend Paulette a charming person. I have spent some enjoyable evenings with them and their families and indeed I know I can always count on their hospitality, but really that is not the problem; the problem is a question of time!'

'And you cannot invade them just at the time you are free and feel lonely! Yes, your Renée of Lunéville could be a good idea if she agrees to come!'

'Thanks, Lily. I was half afraid you might be – discontent –'

'You mean – jealous. No! No fear! You know how much time I spend in the company of men and you have never shown any sign of jealousy!'[15]

An understatement if ever there was one! However, this situation was not to last for very long, and, according to Patricia McCallum, 'the two women became violently jealous of one another, which led to a number of repercussions'. As Harmer's report attests:

There is now [*sic*] doubt, however, that VIOLETTE, since she eventually lived with the chief, was bound to exercise a decisive influence in the administration of the organisation, and this gave rise to the most shocking form of petty jealousy between them. VICTOIRE's descriptions of VIOLETTE are completely contaminated with this jealousy. For instance, she describes her as being a girl with no education, whereas in fact she came from a good family. She is biting about her personal appearance, whereas both ADAM [Lt Roger Mitchell @ BRICK] and MAURICE [Janusz Włodarczyk] have confirmed that she was a very nice looking and attractive girl. VICTOIRE says she had a foul character, and ADAM and MAURICE say she was very nice.[16]

Wirth's CIC report explains how VIOLETTE was recruited. It seems that after ARMAND had stayed with her for a week in Lunéville he left for Paris. In May 1941 he sent GUY (Guy Vedero) to persuade her to come to Paris and work for him. At first, VIOLETTE was reluctant to do so, but finally relented a month later and left with GUY on 24 June 1941. Sometime between meeting ARMAND and his being arrested by the Germans in June 1940, the two became engaged, but he managed to escape in July. In Paris, she lived with ARMAND, first at 5, rue Colonel Moll and later at 8, Villa Léandre. All messages sent from 8, Villa Léandre were to begin, 'LA CHATTE COMMUNIQUÉ', unless there was an emergency in which case they were to begin, 'VICTOIRE COMMUNIQUÉ'. When they were both arrested on 18 November 1941, Renée was sent to La Santé, where she said she was ill-treated, stripped naked and beaten by a German matron before being interrogated by Borchers (more about him later).

Initially the main Paris organisation consisted of VIOLETTE, VICTOIRE, ARMAND, CHRISTIAN, RENÉ and ONCLE MARCO. McCallum's report recounts that PAUL studied press reports and handled propaganda; RAPIDE remained both a courier and a news-gathering agent; OBSERVATEUR collected information on French industry; MAURICE ran the W/T side, operating the main set himself, and supervised the running of two others. VICTOIRE also made contact with other réseaux, including one of an SIS agent who had arrived, whose name is redacted from McCallum's report but was in fact Michel Courtois, code-named EVE, who had been given ARMAND's name as a contact. VICTOIRE was instructed to go and see EVE at the house of the Comtesse Colette 'Coco' de Dampierre (*née* Colette Cahen d'Anvers, 1911–69), in Neuilly. The Comtesse had married Comte Armand de Dampierre (1902–44) on 5 July 1933. Harmer thought that as VICTOIRE and EVE had got along well she must have become EVE's mistress. On the other hand, ARMAND didn't like him. When EVE was later captured during the summer of 1941 he never spoke or revealed anything to the Gestapo.

During a partial reorganisation of the network JEAN left the direction of Sector J to his mistress, who became JEANNINE, and MOUSTIQUE was nominated to assist with the running of Sector E. Communicating with London was a prime concern because at first the wireless set did not work. ARMAND therefore came up with the idea of having a sea link between England and Brittany. One of the network's minor agents had a sister living in Saint-Pol-de-Léon, in the Finistère département of Brittany, and he thought she might be able to arrange a sea link. He sent VICTOIRE off to Brest to investigate, but her mission was unsuccessful, and she only succeeded in attracting the Gestapo's attention by inspecting air raid damage. The Gestapo official, whom she knew as Max, had an Irish mother. By using her charm and having lunch with him, she told him that she had gone off to Brittany as a joke and spoke with an English accent in order to find out how they reacted to the bombardment. The problems with the wireless were only sorted out when Zygmunt Masłowski @ MASSENET arrived from Marseilles in May.

RENÉ was responsible for coming up with a method of shading using India ink to illustrate the various German markings on their vehicles in France. These drawings were then sent to Marseilles in small medicine packets. In March or April Mathilde rented an apartment at 14, rue Raffet in the 16th arrondissement, not far from the Jasmin Métro station under the name Madame Donnadieu. The apartment consisted of two large studios at the top of the house that proved good for communications, so ARMAND turned them over to MONO for his wireless transmissions. Other changes took place, with MOUSTIQUE being given responsibility for Sector A; a pilot named Robert Gorriot (BERTRAND) was introduced by BOB-EDGAR and took over Sector B (confusingly, Kieffer's MI5 file states that BOB-EDGAR was Robert Gorriot @ CORBINOT); and Sector F was given over to FRANCK, a Jew who changed the group's money on the black market.

Jean Lucien Kieffer (sometimes spelled Kiffer) was known by a number of aliases: Raoul @ Michel @ André Berger @ Edmond Clisse @ Edouard Valentin @ Robert Heuzy @ Lieutenant John Sharp. Not to be confused with SS-Sturmbannführer (Major) Hans Josef Kieffer, head of *Abt.* IV E of the Sicherheitsdienst (SD, the SS intelligence service) at 84, Avenue Foch in Paris, he was an engineer born at Moncel-sur-Seille (Meurthe-et-Moselle) on 30 August 1913. His father Lucien died in December 1938; his mother was Lucie (*née* Gribeling). He was educated at the École de l'Est and the École

Supérieure de l'Industrie in Nancy. In 1933 he trained at the École de Pilotage as an '*élève pilote*' (student pilot) at Ambérieux. A year later he was posted as a 'sergeant pilote' (sergeant pilot) to the 33me Escadre Aerienne at Nancy, a reconnaissance squadron. In 1937 he returned to civilian life to become an engineer at the Tuileries Mécaniques at Champignolles (Côte d'Or), where the director was DENISE (Madame Buffet).

In March 1938 Kieffer was recalled to the air force to the Groupe Aérienne d'Observateurs 2/520, which fought in the Ardennes during the war. Repatriated via Perpignan to La Senia, the airbase at Oran in Algeria, in June 1940, it was not until September 1940 that he returned to Moncel-sur-Seille as a 'sergeant chef' (flight sergeant). His first encounter with the intelligence services was meeting a man named Holvecq, an '*ingenieur en chef en construction navale*' (chief naval engineer) in Marseilles after he had crossed into the Unoccupied Zone. There he also met a man whom he knew as 'Jean' (Gaston Lurton), an artillery officer working for the Deuxième Bureau, for whom he worked under the name RAOUL. This lasted until May 1941, when he made an unsuccessful escape to Spain. He and his fellow escapees were arrested at Figueres in Catalonia, Spain, and imprisoned for a month. This seems to have been a common practice with the Spanish authorities throughout the war; even though they were supposedly neutral, they were not always friendly towards escapees from Occupied France.[17] At the end of 1941 Kieffer went to Paris. In 1944 he was still living at Moncel-sur-Seille. What is interesting about Captain O.H. Salmon's report of 29 August 1944 is that there is no mention of Kieffer's involvement in the *Interallié* network, only mention of his links with that of Roger Bardet in 1942 and the *Donkeyman* circuit. It is only a later report that mentions his recruitment by VICTOIRE, and later as an agent of Gruppe III F of Abwehr station *Ast* St Germain.

Alsace-Lorraine was considered the 'forbidden zone' and was run by IRENEE I (Guy Vedero), using his first name, Guy, who had previously been in charge of Sector I, and was assisted by MONO; Sector I became the responsibility of IRENEE II; Sector J was run by JEAN and JEANINE. MIKLOS lent his secretary Ginette Letonturier to assist VICTOIRE with her duties, which helped to increase her liaison with Richard d'Harcourt. MIKLOS was also responsible for introducing the network to the second-in-command of another organisation that was arranging escapes, run by a Russian (no name is given anywhere). PAOLI interviewed the young Frenchman, named Jean Pierre, in the hope that they could set up a liaison with Richard d'Harcourt; however, the Russian disappeared before VICTOIRE could arrange anything.

In the spring of 1941, DANIEL (Jean Carbonnier), who ran Sector D, was arrested by the Gestapo.[18] This caused the network to abandon 1, rue Lamarck as a post box in favour of MONO taking another apartment in the Maison Berlitz in the rue de la Michodière in the 2nd arrondissement, where he would now work, leaving RAPIDE (LACH) and JAG (Jagielowicz @ JACQUES) at the rue Lamarck. This was the Agence Inter-France, Palais Berlitz, 29, rue de la Michodière. They also decided that agents should only deliver their reports every ten days, on the 4th, 14th and 24th of each month.

The other most important agent to arrive in the summer of 1941, together with MAURICE (Janusz Włodarczyk), was ADAM (Lieutenant Roger Mitchell), 'the young [redacted] agent of S.I.S. who came into contact with the organisation through TUDOR in Marseilles', described as a 'Franco-Scottish gunnery officer'.[19] With the help of MONO and MAX, MAURICE set up three secret radio stations in Paris. This enabled them for the first time to operate effectively until the organisation was broken up. Garby-Czerniawski's book lists the radio stations as:

1st: Rue du Faubourg St. Jacques, used for first trials only. Jan–Apr. 1941
2nd: Near the Trocadéro. First contact with London was made here, then a daily link four times a day. May 10th 1941 and after.
3rd: Place Peréir; became our main station. June to August 1941.
4th: Boulevard St. Honoré. June to August 1941.
5th: Villa Léandre, our main station. Oct–Nov. 1941.[20]

Their first successful message was sent from the second radio station near the Trocadéro on 10 May 1941: 'FROM INTERALLIÉ STOP VERY HAPPY TO ESTABLISH THE DIRECT LINK STOP VALENTIN'.[21] A reply came back: 'TO INTERALLIÉ STOP CONGRATULATIONS …' VALENTIN would be the name ARMAND used when communicating with London.

There are many records of Mitchell passing in and out of France during 1941 and 1942. One source, Henri Noguères, states that Mitchell (BRICK) had parachuted into France on 19 June 1941,[22] although the date is also given as 18 June and no drop zone (DZ) mentioned.[23] The discrepancy in the date could simply mean the night of 18/19 June. As Hugh Verity notes, Mitchell must have been known as ADAM at that time. Another reference mentions him as part of Operation *Fitzroy B* on 4 July 1941 sent in to assist Polish intelligence networks operating in the south of France and to arrange landing zones (LZ) for pick-up operations and drop zones.[24] When he was in Marseilles he met with TUDOR, who gave him the address and password for the post box at 1, rue Lamarck. Harmer's report, however, states that ADAM had been sent out by SIS in August.

On the night of 1/2 October 1941, Mitchell (mentioned as BRICK) was flown in by a Lysander piloted by Squadron Leader John 'Whippy' Nesbitt-Dufort of 138 Special Duties Squadron, so called because he had once had to make a forced landing at Whipsnade Zoo in Bedfordshire among the wild animals while trying to land at RAF Tempsford. The aircraft landed at a field west-north-west of Compiègne, 2 kilometres north-east of Estrées St. Denis, where Garby-Czerniawski, then referred to as ARMAND, was picked up along with Claude Lamirault (FITZROY) and flown to England on 6/7 November 1941 by the same pilot.[25]

As part of Operation *Beryl II* Mitchell was flown in by Lysander on 28/29 January 1942, again by Nesbitt-Dufort, together with Maurice Duclos @ SAINT-JACQUES to a landing ground at Le Coudray in the département of Cher. However, the aircraft had to make a forced landing 2 kilometres south-west of Saint-Florent-sur-Cher on account of low fuel and ice build-up on the windscreen and leading edge of the wings. As the record notes, 'Aircraft damaged beyond repair and written off.' Attempts by Nesbitt-Dufort to sabotage the aircraft and destroy it failed. The three were later hidden by the stationmaster at Issoudon, on account of Duclos giving everyone at the station a Masonic handshake and finding that the stationmaster was a fellow Mason.[26]

Another report on the incident tells that the aircraft had dropped off André Simon, and that Mitchell was responsible for bringing Duclos back to England. On the night of 1/2 March 1942, Mitchell, Maurice Duclos @ SAINT-JACQUES were recovered, as well as General Juliusz Kleeberg @ TUDOR/Zarembski, in Operation *Beryl III*. The operation was carried out from a site located 1.5 kilometres north-east of the town of Ségry in the Indre département, in a twin-engined Avro Anson piloted by Squadron Leader Alan 'Sticky' Murphy. This was the only time such an aircraft was used.[27]

In Paris Mitchell stayed at a hotel in the rue Duplex [*sic*], possibly Le Marquis Eiffel at 15, rue Dupleix, in the 15th arrondissement. There he was visited by KIKI (Jean Lucien or Robert Kieffer @ DESIRE @ POVIC), then ARMAND, now known as WALENTY, whose visit Mitchell (ADAM) did not welcome, presumably because it drew the attention of the Gestapo, who may have been watching him, to his location. Confirmation that Jean Lucien Kieffer and Robert Kieffer are one and the same can be found in a note from D. Ian Wilson in B1b to Colonel H.J. Baxter of B1d on 10 January 1945.[28] KIKI is described in one of Mathilde Carré's MI5 files as a flight sergeant and an agent of Sonderführer

(Specialist Leader) Verbeck (Bleicher), with the number E-7010, working in the Lisieux and Caen areas. He was also a friend of ROGER, agent E-8010, a former flight lieutenant who was arrested in 1943.[29]

WALENTY set up a system of communications and engaged a fisherman from Roscoff in Brittany. He brought in two agents, CHARLES (Theophil Burlot) and CLAUDE (Claude Jouffret), to reinforce Sector C (Brittany). CHARLES in turn found another fisherman in Roscoff, code-named CÉSAR, who would take out documents to British ships in the English Channel. By November this amounted to a large heavy suitcase.

In addition to VIOLETTE, Harmer's report mentions a number of other agents considered important to the *Interallié* organisation, including CHRISTIAN (Bernard Krutki), a Pole who was a personal friend of WALENTY and worked out of their headquarters and helped him keep in touch with agents; and Claude Jouffret @ MICHEL, a young Frenchman who the report says 'occupied a place of no particular importance, and who had been brought into the organisation by VICTOIRE and assisted her in preparing reports, drawings, etc'. This is also confirmed in Kieffer's MI5 file. There are two agents called CLAUDE listed in the 'Members and Contact of the WALENTY Organisation Carded in VICTOIRE' in Harmer's report, so the CLAUDE brought into Sector C is obviously a separate person.

CHAPTER 4

'A Squalid Tale'

In the summer of 1941 EVE (Michel Courtois) and Richard d'Harcourt were arrested. In VICTOIRE's file there is a letter dated 28 December 1942 from Harmer to Susan Barton in which he mistakenly claimed the arrests of d'Harcourt, Alfred Kraus, and the Comte and Comtesse de Dampierre as having taken place in December 1941.[1] However, d'Harcourt's arrest was on 8 July, betrayed by Kraus, according to Captain Danielle of the Deuxième Bureau. D'Harcourt and EVE had been in touch with the Comte and Comtesse de Dampierre, as well as Freddy Kraus, an Austrian married to the daughter of the former Mrs Daisy Fellowes. The Comtesse told VICTOIRE that Kraus had seen EVE on 1 July, leading her to believe that it had been he who had given EVE away. Months later, VICTOIRE would learn from the Germans that the only photograph d'Harcourt had in his possession was one of her with her name and telephone number on it, which caused her to wonder why the Germans hadn't arrested her sooner. VICTOIRE, who knew Kraus, claimed that he was generally pro-Allies and had helped prisoners of war escape, although 'during the second half of the year 1941 he was employed in Paris by Abteilung IIIF of Abwehr (the C.E. [Counter-Espionage] section of the German Intelligence Service).'

Kraus claimed during his later interrogation at Camp 020 on 30 December 1944 that in April or early May 1941 he had been summoned to appear before officers of *Abt.* III F, who told him that they knew all about Jacqueline de Broglie and her work for the Allies. This contradicts his earlier statement: he had told MI5 on 24 November 1944 that he had been a German agent who was first recruited in November 1940 by Giskes. In exchange for Jacqueline de Broglie not being arrested and to save her life, the Abwehr told him that he must work for *Abt.* III F to penetrate Allied organisations. Part of this work would entail planting information about the Tiger tank, Condor aircraft, and oil production and oil stores (see below) on a British agent. That agent was Lieutenant Michel Coulomb @ Michael Cartwright @ Courtois of the SIS, who was dropped at Chateauroux on 16 January 1941 from a Whitley bomber. However, Verity gives the date as a 11/12 April landing by Lysander, referring to Coulomb as 'Lt. Cartwright'.[2] Coulomb/Cartwright would go on to be the founder of the *Cartwright* network and become known to Major Hermann Giskes and others as EVE. The Germans also agreed to arrange that Kraus be exempted from military service. Following this episode he said he did nothing more for the Abwehr but remained a contact through Hauptmann Theo Schade of the Luftwaffe, his former friend and colleague from Siemens & Halske, a V-Mann (*Vertrauensmänn* or confidential person) for 1T/LW (Technik/Luftwaffe).

This concurs with Giskes' claim that he first got to know Kraus in April or May 1941 in Paris and gave him the name KURT. As Giskes describes in his book *London Calling North Pole*, they had a chance encounter in the vestibule at Berlin's Potsdamer station prior to Operation *Nordpol* in 1942. By this time Kraus was already working for him, as Giskes refers to having got to know him in Paris the previous winter. He described Kraus as the '"Ace" of my Paris contacts, charming and elegant as ever … this intelligent, splendid-looking scion of an old Austrian family'. When they had met in Paris the previous year, Kraus had been seeking Giskes' protection:

> … for a beautiful young Frenchwoman, the bearer of one of the best-known ducal names in France. He had discovered by accident that she had helped a friend of the family, a French General Staff captain serving in the English Secret Service, in his dangerous work, and he knew that the captain's espionage group had already come to the attention of the Abwehr.
>
> What should one do in the circumstances? I made up my mind that a twenty-year-old girl who had become the accidental accomplice of a skillful secret agent would be warned off once and for all by the arrest of her friend and his group. I thought I could probably 'square' my immediate superiors if I let her off after taking this action, but it could prove fatal if my helpful attitude became known in unfriendly quarters. Fortunately the incident had passed off without attracting undue attention, and a few months previously my now sworn friend Freddy had married his blonde, blue-eyed 'Daisy', having already himself become a German national through the annexation of Austria. They were the happiest, handsomest and most elegant couple in Paris.[3]

During their conversation Giskes learned that Kraus was regularly visiting his fiancée Daisy de Broglie in Neuilly, that a certain Sonderführer Bernberg-Gossler had asked her at a party: 'Are you now prepared to work for the German Abwehr or not?' Bernberg-Gossler, whom she had got to know at the Hôtel Bristol, had begun to question her about the route taken by escapees over the demarcation line. When she denied any knowledge, he had telephoned the Hôtel Lutetia, the headquarters of the Abwehr. Afterwards, Kraus arranged to meet Bernberg-Gossler and Fraulein Abshagen of the Abwehr to try to smooth things over. On another occasion Bernberg-Gossler had tried to interrogate Jacqueline and had twisted her arm and pushed her against a map of France hanging on the wall and insisted that she point out the crossing points on the demarcation line. When Kraus complained, Giskes intervened and Bernberg-Gossler was removed from the case. This statement is strange since the account in Giskes' file states that he denied that Bernberg-Gossler worked for the German Intelligence Service. Giskes said that he had got the impression that Kraus wanted to be put in touch with someone in *Abt*. III F.

A note in Kraus's file refers to the possibility that Bernberg-Gossler might be Heinrich (Cornelius Johann von) Berenberg-Gossler (1907–97), whose father was Freiherr (Baron) Cornelius von Berenberg-Gossler of Hamburg (1874–1953):

> A well known banker who is known to be a very honest and decent minded individual and who is said to have been the only Aryan in Hamburg who dared to help a Jewish refugee after his release from a concentration camp.[4]

In another note, Kraus said that Bernberg-Gossler spoke perfect English and was probably connected with the Abwehr. The French General Staff captain to whom he was referring was most likely Lieutenant Michel Coulomb (EVE).

Alfred Ignatz Maria Kraus, sometimes referred to as 'Freddy' or 'Freddie', was born in Sarajevo on 28 November 1908, of German, originally Austrian, nationality, and undoubtedly the same man whom Eddie Chapman (Agent ZIGZAG) met at the Paris *Dienststelle* and described as 'slightly built and effeminate so Eddie surmised that he was homosexual', as well as 'sinister'.[5] This is confirmed in Ben Macintyre's book *Agent Zigzag*:

> Chapman had been allocated a new 'shadow', in the shape of a young, slightly built man from the Lutétia known as Kraus, or Krausner. Von Grönig warned Chapman that Kraus, a homosexual who frequented the Paris underworld, had a reputation as a spycatcher and had trapped more enemy agents than anyone else in German counter-espionage.[6]

Homosexual or not, for reasons that will become apparent later, in Paris in October 1941 Kraus married Princess Jacqueline Marguerite (*née* de Broglie, 1918–65), the daughter of Prince Jean de Broglie and novelist, poet, and magazine editor, the Honourable Daisy Fellowes (*née* Marguerite Séverine Philippine Decazes de Glücksbierg, 1890–1962), who was also involved in espionage with the Comtesse. Daisy Fellowes was variously described as 'rich, ugly, dissolute and the destroyer of many a happy home'; 'the very embodiment of Thirties chic'; 'a man-eater' and 'the very picture of fashionable depravity', who lived on morphine, opium or cocaine.[7]

Some correspondence exchanged between Ann Gregory in B1d's Information Section and Harmer sheds some light on the arrest of the Comte and Comtesse de Dampierre. Gregory wrote on 24 April 1943:

> I see from our report on the interrogation of Viscount Richard Roger Etienne de DAMPIERRE[8] [*sic*] that this man stated that in December 1941 – after working in a secret organisation in the Occupied zone – he left Paris with his wife for Switzerland.
>
> In view of the possibility that the two de DAMPIERRES may be identical I think that this file should be brought to your notice.[9]

Harmer replied on 29 April:

> I agree that at first sight it looks rather alarming and it is possible that he is identical with the agent mentioned by VICTOIRE as having been captured. I have, however, been able to make an independent check on this through the leader of VICTOIRE's organisation [WALENTY], who is now in this country. He met the Comte de DAMPIERRE referred to by VICTOIRE on two occasions, and describes him as being a man of about 45, with a wife of about 35, who had lived for a long time in England. I produced the photograph of your de DAMPIERRE and it was pronounced as being nothing like the man who was in the same organisation as WALENTY.
>
> I think we can, therefore, assume that they are not identical. On the other hand it appears to be possible that the de DAMPIERRE who worked in the VICTOIRE Organisation was the father of Richard de DAMPIERRE who passed through the L.R.C. [London Reception Centre] I say this because VICTOIRE mentions him as having a partly Jewish wife and I see he is reported to have married a Mlle DREYFUS. The age might also fit in. I therefore return your file herewith.[10]

Comtesse Colette 'Coco' de Dampierre had been first introduced to Freddy
Kraus through Michel Coulomb (EVE), the founder of the *Cartwright* réseau
in France, and her friend, Jacqueline de Broglie, Freddy Kraus's wife. However,
her nickname should not be confused with that of COCO, the unnamed head
of Sector C, who was employed by Coulomb as his codist. COCO's real name,
according to the organisational chart of *Interallié* in *The Big Network*, also
reproduced in Nigel West's book *MI6*, was J. (Jacques) Collardey.[11] There is also
a Polish Jew named Abraham Zemsz who worked in the Resistance under the
code name COCO, mentioned in the file of Gabrielle Cecile Martinez Picabia
(GLORIA), as having come to England in April/May 1943, where he joined the
Polish Air Force as a parachutist.[12]

In April 1941 Coulomb brought Kraus to meet the Comtesse at her home
at 9 bis, Avenue Richard Wallace in Neuilly, adjacent to the Parc de Bagatelle.
(Actually, it is the Boulevard Richard Wallace.) At first, she disliked him because
he was Austrian, but shortly thereafter they met regularly for dinner about
twice a week. Any information that Kraus thought might be useful he passed to
Coulomb, who would then have COCO send it to London. When Coulomb
went to England in May COCO passed that information to VICTOIRE to
send to London via Spain. Coulomb was arrested on 7 July 1941 two hours
after seeing COCO deliver an envelope that was passed on to Kraus. Kraus told
VICTOIRE that he had given the envelope to Jacqueline de Broglie so that the
contents could be reproduced in a smaller format. The following day, Kraus told
Jacqueline de Broglie that the papers were too hot to handle and gave them to
her to pass on to VICTOIRE, which she did a couple of days later. In a report
on Kraus by D.I. Wilson to Dunderdale of SIS on 2 January 1945, he refers to:

> ... plant material [which] we should be extremely interested to see it, both for
> comparison with the corresponding efforts sent out from this side and also to
> see if there is any evidence of material being included for deceptive purposes
> as distinct from merely censored material being allowed to go through for
> C.E. [counter-espionage] purposes. In particular, his reports sent at this period
> (Summer 1941) the Germans may well have attempted to mislead about their
> intentions toward Russia.[13]

A report on Kraus in Giskes' file[14] states that Coulomb, calling himself Courtois,
had told Kraus at a meeting at 19, rue St James, Neuilly, sometime after May 1941
that he was a British intelligence officer and solicited his help in providing
information on military matters. At first Kraus demurred, saying that he was too

scared to become involved in espionage, but later changed his mind and offered to help. Information requested by Courtois consisted of the following:

(i)   Constructional work being carried out at Brest, Lorient and the French coast in general;
(ii)   Troops, their locations and movements;
(iii) The quantity of petrol coming into France monthly; and above all,
(iv)   Details about troop concentrations on the Russian border.[15]

Kraus reported this to Giskes, who told him in no uncertain terms not to provide this information unless he (Giskes) was consulted on it. What Kraus actually 'planted' on Courtois was:

(i)   Details of bomb damage, which KRAUS was supposed to have seen or heard about during his visit to Berlin. KRAUS had to learn these reports by heart and was required to pay particular attention to the definite order in which they were drawn up.
(ii)   There was one report giving details of the performance of an aeroplane, possibly the 'Condor'.
(iii) At least one report concerning the number of U-Boats in Lorient or the number that could be harboured there.
(iv)   Finally, a blue-print [sic] of a tank chassis, possibly the 'Tiger', which was being turned out by the SAMOA (?) works in France.[16]

This is most likely SOMUA, an acronym for *Société d'outillage mécanique et d'usinage d'artillerie* based at Saint-Ouen, a suburb of Paris, which had built the French 20-ton S35 cavalry tank and the Char B1 tank.

Plans for the tanks were made available to Courtois so that they could be photographed. Since Siemens was working on the electrical layout for them they had been easy for Kraus to obtain. When he met Courtois at the Ritz Hôtel, Kraus had arranged for Sonderführer Graf Kreuz and Herbert to shadow them. Sonderführer Alex Graf Kreutz was with *Ast* Paris, IIIc2, later with *Ast* Hamburg IIIc. He was aged about 35, of medium build and around 6ft tall, with dark hair, dark eyes, of Slavic appearance, and spoke German, French and possibly Russian, and always dressed in civilian clothes. Herbert was likely Obergefreiter Berthold @ Bertrand. They then went to the Palais Luxembourg, and while Courtois and Kraus went to a nearby café, the two men who had joined them north of the rue Lafayette photostatted the plans. Kraus reported all of this to Giskes at his office at 2, rue du Cirque near the Champs-Élysées. He later learned from Schade that the two men who had copied the plans were known as Invernell and Eglise, the latter a well-known French technician or inventor. Eglise and his wife were also later arrested and made to work at a laboratory in Berlin. All the information supplied to Courtois, purportedly from a 'German engineer', was sent to the RAF Intelligence Centre in Berkeley Square, London.

A letter to D. Ian Wilson at MI5 from C.H.S. Garton of SIS dated 16 January 1945 states, 'EGLISE is unknown to us. INVERNELL was one of EVE's [Michel Courtois] agents.'[17] Garton quoted from a report on him in French that had been made during one of EVE's visits to England. He said that it had been impossible to identify the 'plant' material (referred to above) as most of the reports from EVE had since been destroyed. It seemed likely, he said, that none of the information obtained from Kraus had ever been received in England as EVE had been experiencing trouble making contact with England.

Robert Invernell, of 60, rue Chardon Lageche, Paris in the 16th arrondissment, left for Gibraltar in July (the year is not given, but may have been 1944). Before returning to England he was ordered by someone referred to as Fitzgeorge 'des services de Gibraltar' (of the services in Gibraltar), to go and help certain French aviators to leave North Africa. This was most likely Commander George William Frederick Fitz-George (1891–1960), who was involved in Operation Dragoon, the Allied invasion of southern France on 15 August–14 September 1944. He was also on the staff of the Allied Naval Liaison Officer (Captain E.L. Wharton) at HMS Hannibal, the Royal Navy base in Algiers, which would fit with the North African connection. When the authorities in Oran discovered what Invernell was up to he was forced to return to France, where he re-established contact with England. In about February (possibly 1945) he was put in charge of organising an 'aviation' network for Vichy, as he was an excellent pilot and moved in all the right aviation circles. The service in Vichy that had instructed him to undertake this mission pretended that all the information he obtained was destined for England.

Invernell's aim was to work exclusively for the British, building up his network for SOE. As a cover story he officially worked for the Ministry of Youth. His reports were only sent to Vichy after they had first been communicated to Courtois. He would be expected to know the functions of all the networks in both the 'Zone Libre' (Unoccupied Zone) and the 'Zone Occupée' (Occupied Zone), in case he was needed to replace Courtois, who was frequently required to be in Paris.

A report of an interview with Invernell dated 15 June 1945 found in Kraus's file states that he had first seen Kraus outside COLLOMB's [sic] office on 15 June 1941 but did not actually meet him until sometime between 20–25 June when they went to photograph the documents. He had picked up Coulomb and Eglise in his Peugeot 202 car and driven them to the Ritz, which he said was on the rue Scribe, to pick up Kraus. He must have meant the InterContinental, which is at 2, rue Scribe, because the Ritz is in the Place Vendôme. From there they went to a café at the corner of the rue Médicis and the Boulevard St Germain. However, it must have been on the corner of the Boulevard St Michel, *not* the Boulevard St Germain. The photographer lived in a small street near the Odéon Théâtre, which is on the corner of those two streets, and close to the gardens of the Luxembourg Palace. This would make the street possibly the rue Rotrou or rue de Vaugirard.

Wilson replied to Garton the following day saying that, unbeknown to Bleicher, who was exploiting the break-up of *Interallié* when he set a trap for Kraus and Comtesse Dampierre, Kraus was actually working for III F; because Bleicher was only a junior rank, he would not have known Kraus's real function.

By about the middle of June 1941 Courtois had so much information that Jacqueline de Broglie was typing it for him — all approved by Giskes, to whom Kraus reported. However, Kraus stated that Jacqueline did not disclose any of the contents to him, which were written in French. As can be expected, all the information received from Kraus came at a price. Giskes ordered Kraus to ask for a cash payment from Courtois to cover the costs of obtaining the information. As part of their deception, Giskes arranged for Kraus to meet with German Army and Luftwaffe staff from time to time, although Kraus said that nothing ever came of these meetings. Of course, this was not what he told Courtois, who paid him 3,000 francs for the cost of entertaining these men.

When in July 1941 Courtois was having trouble getting his information to England, Kraus offered to act as a courier for him. It will be recalled that there had been problems when the *Interallié* network was trying to establish a sea link, and documents were being placed behind notices on the train to Marseilles. Kraus told Courtois that he was going to Marseilles 'to look into some petrol business', which also happened to be information Courtois was asking for. Courtois immediately asked him to take a letter there for him. To facilitate matters, Kraus obtained a courier's pass so that he would not be searched. With all the correct documentation, Kraus was ready to set off for Marseilles. His orders were to hand over the letter to Major Schneefuss at the offices of the Waffenstillstandkommission (WAKO), the German Armistice Commission in Marseilles. Courtois had asked him to deliver the envelope to a Mr Spoldini, chief accountant of the Gibbs soap factory in Marseilles.

Courtois and Kraus met at a café near the Champs-Élysées where Courtois handed over the envelope. Kraus had not expected to actually receive the package until he was on the train, but since he already had it, he went straight to the Hôtel Majestic and handed it over to Giskes. He was instructed to wait in a bar on the Boulevard St Germain while Giskes went to the Hôtel Lutetia to examine the package. Herbert showed up half an hour later to say that Kraus could not proceed to Marseilles that day. Meanwhile, the package was being inspected by personnel at the Luteitia, who became very excited about its contents. The reports would first be scanned by Luftwaffe staff at the Palais du Luxembourg. Giskes had once let out a report without altering it first, which had caused losses to the Luftwaffe at a certain aerodrome, and they were determined not to make the same mistake again.

The next day Kraus went to Giskes' office at 2, rue du Cirque to pick up a similar-looking package to be handed over to Spoldini. He was also to report to Major Schneefuss to let him know that the documents had already been vetted. Kraus duly handed over the package to Spoldini and spent some time at WAKO. Spoldini took Kraus to his flat, where he locked the package in a suitcase. They then went to the Hôtel Noailles for a drink. Kraus reported that Spoldini was very discreet and only asked about his nationality. Having spent an hour or so with him, Kraus left for Paris again that evening. Judging from the interview with Invernell, it seems that he had been sent by Courtois to prepare the way for Kraus's visit, as he travelled to Marseilles on 1 July to warn Spoldini. On 9 July, the day after he returned from Marseilles, Invernell was arrested by German military police and taken to the Hôtel Matignon, then Fresnes. The Hôtel Matignon at 57, rue de Varenne is the official residence of the prime minister of France, but during the war it was occupied by the Gestapo. Later, Invernell was sent to Buchenwald and returned to Paris in May 1945.

When he reported back to Giskes, Kraus was told that Courtois was going to be arrested the following day. Jacqueline de Broglie continued to type Courtois's reports and he left at about seven o'clock in the evening. At nine o'clock, Kraus was summoned to Giskes' office and informed that Courtois had been arrested in the rue St James. He had no incriminating papers on him, which Kraus told Giskes were at 19, rue St James. Giskes then insisted that they get access to these documents. They met at midnight on the corner of the Avenue de Madrid and the Avenue des Grandes Armées (this is now part of the Avenue Charles de Gaulle). They took the documents and made copies at the Hôtel Lutetia, with Kraus insisting that they be put back exactly where they had been found so that Jacqueline de Broglie would not become suspicious. Kraus had to promise with his life that he would not let the documents out of his reach, and that he would be in a position to destroy them or hand them over to Giskes if necessary.

Jacqueline de Broglie was surprised by Courtois's non-appearance the next day; two days later 'Coco' Dampierre told Kraus that Courtois had disappeared. She assumed that he had been arrested and would have to inform London right away. Kraus pretended to be very upset and suggested that all papers relating to Courtois be destroyed; however, both Jacqueline and 'Coco' Dampierre felt that they should be sent to London in the normal way. Giskes and Kraus then contrived to obtain the documents by sending a policeman round to the house to say that the Germans were looking for Jacqueline de Broglie. She was out at the time, but when she returned Kraus intimidated her into handing over all the papers. When Giskes had finished altering them they were returned. The two women still wanted to send them to England, with 'Coco' telling Kraus that she had a secure way of doing so. To that end, she arranged a rendezvous for him to meet a 'Polish girl' at three o'clock at Au Rendez-Vous restaurant, 14 Avenue de Wagram, close to the Étoile. That so-called 'Polish girl' was VICTOIRE.

This meeting in the restaurant was VICTOIRE's first encounter with Kraus. She entered with another woman, whose name is not recorded, who sat at a nearby table. She then went over to join Kraus and 'Coco' Dampierre, who carried out a conversation in French that he did not understand. Kreutz was also there, but left to give a description of VICTOIRE to Herbert, who was waiting outside. Kraus finally handed over the letter to VICTOIRE. He later learned that Kreutz had got her description wrong and had therefore failed to arrest her. He only learned on 27 August 1944 that VICTOIRE's name was Micheline Carin [sic].

Three days later, while Kraus and Jacqueline de Broglie were in the Pam-Pam bar on the Avenue Royale, d'Harcourt came over and invited them to have dinner with him at the Pavillon d'Armenonville restaurant in the Bois de Boulogne, which they accepted. After dinner they all left at around eleven o'clock at night, with d'Harcourt heading to his home in Vincennes. In the interrogation report on Kraus by MI5 he insisted that there had never been any friction between the two of them, nor that d'Harcourt had any interest in Jacqueline. In fact, the dinner party had been quite amicable. D'Harcourt was arrested at the Métro station by Herbert shortly after the party had broken up. When he tried to escape he was shot in the leg. In his possession was an envelope containing 'espionage material'. Kraus pleaded with Giskes to spare his life, which Giskes said depended on how much information he was prepared to reveal.

Herbert told Kraus that he had tracked down d'Harcourt because he had made the dinner reservation in his own name. He thought it might look better if Kraus claimed responsibility for the arrest when dealing with Giskes, which Kraus did and Herbert backed him up. Herbert also told him that the Courtois case was even bigger than first thought, and the best thing Kraus could do was marry Jacqueline de Broglie to avoid having her arrested. Thus Kraus's marriage to Jacqueline de Broglie on 6 October 1941 was a 'marriage of convenience'.

VICTOIRE told COCO that she had to meet Kraus, and even though it proved difficult, she made an appointment to see him. This, she was sure, was on 18 December 1941. COCO had gone to meet them at a bar in the rue de Tilsitt in the 8th and 17th arrondissements. VICTOIRE arrived accompanied by a tall man aged about of about 33 to 40 who spoke with an Alsatian accent. She told COCO that ARMAND (WALENTY) and a Frenchman had been arrested.

While their meeting took place a tall, good-looking man, aged about 30, was eavesdropping on their conversation. VICTOIRE produced an envelope containing a note, which she gave to Kraus. It read, 'Please ask FREDDY and COCO to help me to escape. I am in a camp at Fougère. Sgd MICHEL.' VICTOIRE said it had been brought to her by one of their agents in Brittany. In fact, the note had been faked by Karl Gustave Propst, who worked for *Abt.* III F. Kraus said he would go and try to help. According to Bleicher, once Kraus had committed himself to saving EVE, he was arrested and later sent to Germany and shot. Of course, Kraus was not shot but became involved in another affair before coming to England (of more later).

Ironically, the Comtess Dampierre and her husband had been planning to go to the Unoccupied Zone but had put it off in favour of helping Coulomb. In the meantime VICTOIRE consulted Maître Michel Brault at his home at 22, rue Raynouard in the 16th arrondissement. In a report dated 21 October 1942 and entitled 'Additional questions connected with the liquidation of the "PROGRESS" I.O.' (intelligence organisation), WALENTY supplied answers to questions about Brault posed by Major Witołd Langenfeld:

BRAULT, p.s. 'Miclos', worked for a short time in our office by supplying occasional information. He was a Paris lawyer and I made his acquaintance through Mr. AUTIER who was his nephew. 'La Chatte' met him through me. My opinion about him is as follows: He wished to work for Intelligence rather for sentimental reasons and in order to be able to boast of it later on. He had no genuine channels for obtaining information. He always told stories which were valueless from the point of view of Intelligence. He wished to make money from contacts with me, his idea being to supply the French 2nd Bureau with excerpts from or whole, reports, which I was to give him.

In principle I regard him as an honest and conscientious man. I believe that he would have gladly helped us if we should have asked him for help. His idée fixe was to combine the efforts of our Organisation with those of the French I.S. against the Germans. He therefore tried to put me in direct touch with Colonel MICHEL. 'Miclos' frequently visited VICHY where he had many important contacts. I avoided him as a rule because I was afraid of his indiscretions. 'Miclos' had some contacts with a British officer and with some secret organisations.[18]

At three o'clock in the morning of 19 December 1941 the Comte and Comtesse Dampierre were arrested and taken to the Hôtel Edouard VII. Seated at a desk on the other side of the room was Kraus, who was also under arrest. The 'Interim Interrogation Report' on Bleicher cites VICTOIRE (whom the report refers to as MICHELINE) as saying that Kraus belonged to another organisation headed by an Englishman, YVES @ COURTOIS (Michel Courtois). Under the pretext of getting news of YVES, VICTOIRE had arranged a meeting with Kraus (referred to as FRED) and the Comtesse at a small bar. She was accompanied by Bleicher posing as a Polish officer. After an hour, Bleicher was satisfied that he had enough evidence on them, and they were arrested the following day.

Bleicher's statement in Appendix J of the report sheds more light on the circumstances of the arrest and, while long, is worth repeating verbatim:

It was VICTOIRE who first mentioned to me the Comtesse de DAMPIERRE and a certain FRED. While belonging to another organisation, the Comtesse de DAMPIERRE knew also TCHERNIAVSKI [sic] @ ARMAND. If my memory does not fail me, there was a courier of the Polish organisation TUDOR at Marseilles, named LACH [cover name RAPIDE], of Polish nationality, who arrived in Paris furnished only with the Comtesse de DAMPIERRE's address. The Comtesse de DAMPIERRE arranged a meeting between the courier and TCHERNIAVSKI which took place in the Comtesse's flat at Neuilly, and I believe that VICTOIRE was there also.

To the best of my recollection, TCHERNIAVSKI would know nothing about the Comtesse de DAMPIERRE, having met her only on this occasion, but VICTOIRE must have seen her more frequently. She told me that Madame DAMPIERRE and one FRED (I do not know whether she knew FRED or not) were members of an organisation the chief of which named YVES, an English subject, had been arrested by the Germans some weeks previously.

On referring to the dossier of the service concerned, I saw that it was a question of a big espionage affair carried out by one Yves COURTOIS, who had numerous agents and contact points well scattered, and in the list of personnel appeared the Comtesse de DAMPIERRE and this FRED, alleged Austrian subject, who also lived at Neuilly.

According to VICTOIRE, FRED was an intimate friend of YVES, and under the pretext of having received news from YVES asking for his liberation from the prison camp in which he had been placed, VICTOIRE asked the Comtesse de DAMPIERRE for the meeting. VICTOIRE had her telephone number and thus the meeting was arranged in a small tea room [Au Rendez-Vous, 14 Avenue de Wagram] near the Étoile (going up the Champs Élysées, the last street on the right, opposite the block where the 'Meldekopf d'Angers' had its offices).

When I entered the café, the Comtesse de DAMPIERRE was already there with FRED. I was introduced by VICTOIRE as one of her friends in the organisation, a Polish officer. VICTOIRE and the Comtesse de DAMPIERRE made most of the conversation. FRED was agreeable to try to get YVES freed, being egged on by DAMPIERRE, who hotly declared the utmost must be attempted to get YVES out of prison. The discussion lasted at least an hour, being concerned exclusively with the plan of escape.

After my report had been made to Major ESCHIG, we gave instructions to the GFP [Geheim Feldpolizei, the German Field Security Police] to arrest this couple, FRED and DAMPIERRE, on the following day at 06.00 hours. On arriving at the GFP at 9.00 hours we learned the whole set-up. FRED was there in the company of several officers of the Lutetia [headquarters of the Abwehr, 43 Boulevard Raspail], making violent protests. An hour later, there was a conference with Oberstl. REILE.[19] Major ESCHIG was heavily jumped on. What did he mean by making an arrest before consulting the registry, etc, etc. In any case, the blunder was made.

Major ESCHIG later gave me the 'low-down' saying that FRED was a celebrated agent of the OKH [Oberkommando des Heeres, the German Supreme Command of the Army] Berlin, who had married a French or English Countess (de BROGGLIE?) [sic] with the Government's approval, so that he could move more easily and infiltrate suspected circles. And that … far from being a friend of YVES, it was he who had played this COURTOIS game and had YVES arrested. Moreover, he had handled the Comtesse de DAMPIERRE, so that he could, through her, infiltrate into other organisations. Warning of his meeting the evening before with VICTOIRE and we had already been given to the service (he had even been given a pistol) and having already handed in his report, he had then asked for the arrest of VICTOIRE and her Polish officer.

I also learnt that following the unfortunate incident and realising that he had been 'blown' in Paris, FRED had left the city a few days later to go to Berlin to see his wife and celebrate Christmas. The incident took place a few days before Christmas 1941, round about 20th December, 1941.

I saw FRED again in the autumn of 1943 in the Hôtel Lutetia, Paris, when he was visiting Count KREUZ [sic].[20] He did not recognize me. I think he told KREUZE he was coming from or going to Hamburg (I am not sure). They seemed to be on very friendly terms.

When he had gone I asked Count KREUZE who he was. He replied, 'One of my friends from Berlin.' Not being sure whether I had recognized him, I asked Kreuze if he was called FRED. 'Do you know him?' he asked me. So I told him the incident of his arrest. Count KREUZE was well informed about the Yves COURTOIS affair and without knowing anything for certain, I would not be surprised if the two of them, FRED and Count KREUZE, had played that game together. This visit lasted no more than about half an hour.

That is all I know about FRED, and I never saw him again nor heard speak of him again.[21]

At the Hôtel Edouard VII an officer had thrust a briefcase at Kraus and shouted at him in German for several minutes before a soldier grabbed him by the scruff of the neck and took him out of the room. Kraus, as noted earlier, was actually working for another branch of *Abt.* III F, and Bleicher was reprimanded for being over-zealous. The Comtesse de Dampierre was later taken to La Santé prison, while her husband was taken to Fresnes. In all, she was kept there in solitary confinement for ten months and three months at Fresnes, remaining in Fresnes until July 1943.

At some point during her incarceration the Comtesse was condemned to death. A note sent to Harmer on 15 March 1942 informed him that both Armand Dampierre and his wife had been shot; however she was reprieved, and sent to work in the Lévitan factory, named after its Jewish owner Wolff Lévitan, whose shop was at 85–87, rue Faubourg Saint Martin in the 10th arrondissement. Following its liquidation in 1941 the shop was repurposed by the Germans in 1943 to sell goods stolen from the Jews. On 11 August 1944 the Comtesse and the other prisoners were told they would be sent to Drancy internment camp and thence to Germany, but she and some friends managed to escape. Armand, the

Comtesse's husband and a member of the Resistance, died in Buchenwald Dora concentration camp on 8 January 1944.[22] Following her escape:

> She made her way to Madame Le HIDEAUX's house. She eventually saw her own mother who later saw Alec de CASTEJA. The latter rang up COCO and to her amazement passed over the telephone to KRAUS who expressed the desire to see her. COCO immediately went to 19 rue St. James [in Neuilly], Lady FELLOWS' [sic] house, where she saw KRAUS and Alec de CASTEJA. She challenged KRAUS about his activities. Alec was present during the interview and therefore knew everything at that time about KRAUS' activities.

<u>The CASTEJAS</u>
They were living in the Zone Libre when COCO worked for KRAUS. Alec was a fool. He was arrested as being a De Gaullist and released through intervention by KRAUS. COCO does not know about the activities of EMMA [Emeline de Casteja *née* Broglie], but believes that husband and wife were not on good terms.

COCO believes that there was much jealousy between Miss ROCHESTER and Emma de CASTEJA [sic]. The rumour went that they both had an affair but that eventually Emma transferred her affections to De la CHAUME.[23]

Madame Le Hideaux is possibly Françoise Lehideux *(née* Renault, 1904–86) of the Groupe Renault based at Boulogne-Billancourt, the wife of François Lehideux (1904–98), the French industrialist and politician in the government of Admiral Darlan, whom she had married on 6 May 1929. As noted in his file, Comte Alexandre de Casteja @ Alec, Marquis de Casteja (1907–83), and his wife Emeline *(née* Broglie, 1911–86) were living at 19, rue St. James, Neuilly, a suburb of Paris. The file also states that he was Kraus's brother-in-law and was imprisoned by the Gestapo at Toulouse in 1944:

> ... on account of alleged correspondence with the UK – subsequently released. Supplied KRAUS with cover address in Lisbon. This was used by the German Intelligence Service. November 1944. Through the intervention of M.I.5 relieved of the post he held as French Liaison Officer with 21 Army Group attached to the Czech Forces.[24]

Emmeline de Casteja was also suspected of working for German Intelligence. However, another document in de Casteja's file referring to Kraus (also in the Kraus file) mentions that she, along with Maximilienne (Baby) Boréa and Madame Thion de la Chaume, were involved in organising the Resistance in the Lille area. The cover address in Lisbon was c/o Maxime Vaultier, Calcada Marques de Abrante 43, Cintra, Lisbon, and also the Marquesa de Cadaval. Vaultier (1898–1969), a renowned archaeologist, was known to be pro-German and pro-Vichy. His address is mentioned in a note from someone, most likely in MI6, to R.E. Bird of MI5's B3a, Liaison with Censorship, dated 8 December 1944.

Madame Thion de la Chaume is possibly Marie Madeleine Louise LeBlanc (also written in Kraus's file as Manette Thion de la Chaume, and elsewhere as Le Blan), born in Lille in 1906, who married Robert Thion de la Chaume (1906–70) in 1938. Given her later Resistance activities in Lille, there is a good possibility that they are one and the same. She was twice raided by the Gestapo for helping British prisoners, once in the winter of 1940–41, and again later. According to Hugh Verity, a Thion de la Chaume was brought out of France by a Lysander flown by Flying Officer Bathgate on 6/7 November 1943 from a field near Jouy-le-Châtel, along with cellist Maurice Maréchal and Yvonne Rudellat @ Jacqueline Gauthier, as part of Operation *Amoureuse*, except another entry gives the name as MacMahon @ Marechal.[25] Strangely, there is no mention of this operation in Stella King's biography of Rudellat, *Jacqueline*.[26] Verity must have been wrong with his dates as by that time Yvonne Rudellat had been shot and captured and transferred first to Fresnes, then Ravensbrück, and finally Bergen-Belsen, where she died of typhus on 23 April 1945. Given that Manette Thion de la Chaume was still in France at the end of the war it seems likely that the person brought out by Lysander was Simone Thion de la Chaume.

CHAPTER 5

An American in France

Kraus alleged that Thion de la Chaume, Maximilienne (Baby) Boréa, born 30 July 1920,[1] and Deverell Denise Rochester, a young American woman who was living with a young Swiss woman, Mademoiselle d'Andiran, at 118, rue de la Faisanderie in the 16th arrondissement, were all lesbians. (This property is now the residence of the former president of Peru, Alan Garcia.) Thion de la Chaume complained to Kraus that Rochester had seriously compromised the security of her Resistance group by talking too freely.

Maximilienne Boréa was the daughter of Vera Boréa – Contessa Boréa de Buzzaccarini Regoli – founder with Princess Dilkusha de Rohan (*née* Alis Wrench, born in 1899) of a French fashion house in 1931 at 29, rue d'Artois, one of the first to offer luxury women's sportswear. The Princess, who had been educated at Roedean, had married in London on 14 December 1922 Prince Joseph Carlos de Rohan (1895–1931), a German aristocrat, and went to live with him at Herkules Haus in Charlottenburg, Berlin. The marriage was barely consummated because of de Rohan's homosexuality, and she met and fell in love with Catherine Devilliers, known as Katusha, a ballet dancer who had been associated with the Bolshoi Ballet. After the Prince was killed in a car accident in 1931 Dilkusha moved to Paris, where she collaborated with Vera Boréa. The fashion house remained open at 376, rue Faubourg St Honoré until 2007. When Dilkusha later moved to London she established a fashion house with Nancy Mitford at 4 Savile Row. During the war Princess Dilkusha de Rohan was head of the Swiss desk at the British Ministry of Information.[2] There she got to know Guy Burgess and would later attend the farewell party for him given by Moura Budberg in July 1950 before he left for Washington in August.

Some correspondence in Kraus's MI5 file between Major R. Ansell Wells of SIS and D. Ian Wilson of MI5 offers more information on Miss Rochester, who apparently worked for an unnamed section of SIS, and later in Paris for

George Darling of MI9. It may in fact have confused the name of Donald Darling, code-named 'Sunday' who worked for MI9 as head of the Gibraltar office (1940–44), and George William Darling (1899–1943), who had organised the *Physician* circuit in eastern Normandy and was later fatally injured in a gunfight with the Gestapo on 26 June 1943 (he died the following day). Miss Rochester told Lieutenant Colonel Warden that Madame Thion de la Chaume and Madame de Casteja were both 'pretty bad hats', although this does not appear to have affected her work unduly. Her section head described her as 'indiscreet … slightly eccentric but is nevertheless perfectly honest'.

References in Kraus's files and elsewhere have created some confusion as to whether there were actually two Miss Rochesters. This is largely because his file refers to a Deverell Denise Rochester @ Denise Renaud for whom very little biographical information is given. It seems that this was a pseudonym for Elizabeth Devereux Rochester (1917–83), whose activities are far better recorded. To begin with, there are some obvious similarities in name (Deverell and Devereux sound similar; both have the surname Rochester), which could easily have been misheard or mistyped in reports. Another similarity is that they were both American. But the report of an interview with Miss Deverell Rochester on 23 February 1945 found in Kraus's MI5 file – a copy of which is also in the de Casteja file – tends to muddy the waters.[3] In the National Archives at Kew there are SOE files available for Margaret Elizabeth Churchill Reynolds, born 15 December 1924,[4] and for Elizabeth Devereux Reynolds @ Elizabeth Devereux Rochester @ Elizabeth @ TYPIST @ D.B. Rochester @ Denise Berthe Roquette, born 20 December 1917.[5] Margaret Reynolds can probably be eliminated, because her birth date and age do not fit the profile of Elizabeth Devereux Rochester or the so-called Deverell Rochester.

Elizabeth Devereux Rochester's mother was Aimee Lathrop (Babe) Gunning and her father was Richmond Rochester, both of whom were American, although one reference says her father was English; however, Gordon Thomas's book claims that it was her mother who was English, as does Beryl Escott.[6] Elizabeth was born in Nyack, New York, on 20 November 1917. Her mother later divorced and married Myron Reynolds, from whom she later took the name Reynolds. Thomas describes Elizabeth as 26, tall, long-legged and athletic, with grey eyes 'that she knew men found attractive', dark hair, 'très joli' [*sic*] (very pretty) and 'sympathique' ('likeable'). Her family was wealthy, so she was educated by a governess; at Roedean, a leading girls' public school near Brighton, England, and at Swiss finishing schools. During the 1930s she was living in Paris with her mother. When war was declared she was on holiday in Greece and instead of returning to the US, she left her ship in Marseilles, pretending that she needed to go shopping for sanitary pads, and caught the train to Paris. In France she worked as a driver for the French Red Cross, although one reference says it was the American Hospital Ambulance Corps, the same organisation that Deverell Rochester allegedly worked for.[7] In fact, it *was* the American Hospital Ambulance Corps, as Elizabeth states in her autobiography, *Full Moon to France*. In 1940, Elizabeth's mother was interned in Vittel internment camp in the Vosges département, a camp reserved for US and British citizens. According to Escott, her stepfather had left by then.

Sometime in late January 1943 she came to the attention of Allen Dulles in Bern while she was helping Allied airmen to escape across the border into Switzerland from Chalon-sur-Saône, but for reasons unspecified he found her unsuitable for recruitment to OSS (the Office of Strategic Services, wartime US equivalent of SOE).[8] Contrary to this, Gordon Thomas records that Dulles decided to use her as a courier.

At some point after that in 1943 she made her way to England via Spain, where she was then recruited by SOE as a member of FANY (First Aid Nursing Yeomanry). As Elizabeth Reynolds, using her stepfather's name (Myron Reynolds), she was sent to France by Hudson aircraft flown by Wing Commander Lewis Hodges on the night of 18/19 October 1943, together with Jean Rosenthal (CANTINIER) of the BCRA, Major Richard Harry Heslop (1907–73) (XAVIER) and American Captain Owen Denis Johnson (PAUL). They landed west-north-west of Lons-le-Saunier in the Jura département, 4 kilometres west-south-west of Bletterans.[9] Working as a courier with Heslop in the *Marksman* circuit in the Jura region, her code name was TYPIST or DACTYLO in French. She would later record her experiences in *Full Moon to France*:

> I returned to France by the moon of October. There was a nip in the air and the sky was studded with stars. It was not a winter sky nor yet a summer one. A farewell and hello one, disputing the mellowness of summer, heralding the sharpness of winter.[10]

Information in Major Robert Bourne-Patterson's account *SOE in France 1941–1945* tells us that the officers sent out to the *Marksman* circuit were:

> Xavier (Lieut-Colonel R. Heslop), D.S.O., Legion d'Honneur, Croix de Guerre.

Gaël (Captain D. Johnson) of the American Army, his extremely competent
    original radio operator.
Parsifal (Major Parker), R.A.M.C., D.S.O.
Bayard (Lieutenant Nornable), M.C.
Yvello (Lieutenant Veilleux) a French Canadian and a very competent radio
    operator and Elizabeth (Miss Rochester), courier.[11]

The use here of the name Elizabeth suggests that this was indeed Elizabeth
Devereux Rochester, which she also confirms in her book. This also concurs
with Peter Jacobs's account *Setting France Ablaze*, which refers to her as
25 years old (which would be correct) and using the name Elizabeth Reynolds.[12]
This contradicts some of the names and code names used in Verity's account,
but since Bourne-Patterson's was an official account, it is probably correct.
Another account says that a landing with Heslop @ XAVIER of SOE's
F Section, Jean Rosenthal of SOE's RF Section @ CANTINIER, François
Michel @ JACQUES of BCRA and Longpierre @ COSTE took place on
21 September 1943 as Operation *Peashooter*.[13] This is confirmed by Verity, who
mentions R. Heslop, J. Rosenthal and F. Michel. On that mission the pilot was
Verity, flying a Hudson, and took place on the night of 21/22 September 1943.
The field was north-north-west of Pont-de-Vaux, 3 kilometres west-north-west
of Arbigny in the Ain département of the Auvergne-Rhône-Alpes region.[14]

   While visiting her mother in Paris, Elizabeth was arrested by two men from
the Gestapo and a *milicien* – 'a French militia punk aged about twenty' – on
20 March 1944 and taken to their headquarters at 11, rue des Saussaies, before
being imprisoned in Fresnes. Escott says it was actually a safe house owned
by one of her friends in the Ambulance Service. Rochester confirms in her
book that a Swiss friend (presumably Mademoiselle d'Andiran) was sheltering
her. The same day, Mademoiselle d'Andiran was also arrested, but later released
because she was Swiss.

   In a note to Milmo in Kraus's file from the French BCRA headquarters at
10 Duke Street dated 17 April 1945 (the signature cannot be discerned), a 'Mlle
Reynolds' is mentioned, suggesting that this was in fact Elizabeth Devereux
Rochester who, as stated before, was also known by that name. The note also
says that Mademoiselle d'Andiran had formally accused Evelyne de Casteja [*sic*]
of being responsible for the arrests, as did Mademoiselle Reynolds. However,
Mademoiselle d'Andiran later retracted her accusation. This caused the author
of the note to conclude that Kraus had not been the source of EVE's arrest.
When questioned by the Gestapo about where she had obtained her identity

card, Elizabeth in her book refers to Madame de C as the person who had
given it to her – obviously Madame de Casteja. The 'Austrian' present at her
interrogation must have been Kraus, as she refers to Madame de Casteja as
being his sister-in-law, which is correct. When in June 1944 Elizabeth was
tried for possession of a false identity card, the judge confirmed to her that
Madame de Casteja had indeed been responsible for her arrest. She believed
that Madame de Casteja had also been responsible for the arrest of the Marquis
de Vogüé – Pierre de Vogüé (1921–2011), who had worked with the Forces
Françaises de l'Intérieur (FFI, Gaullist resistance fighters) in Vercors, and then
in Cher-Nord as 'Lieutenant François'.[15]

As noted earlier, there is very little biographical information available
on 'Deverell Rochester' in any of the MI5 files accessed. What is known
is that she was fluent in French, having grown up in France since the age
of 5. According to her interview with MI5 on 23 February 1945 she had
been working for 'an Allied organisation', although exactly which one is not
mentioned, but most likely SOE. In 1940 she joined the American Ambulance
Corps. In September 1942 her mother was arrested in Paris and interned at
Vittel internment camp. In June 1940 Deverell Rochester's unit left Paris for
Angoulême under the direction of Madame Thion de la Chaume, but the
women were informed in August by Thion de la Chaume that they were
leaving to escape the Germans. Miss Rochester returned to Paris in December.
When America finally declared war on Germany on 11 December 1941,
she decided to escape from France. She and her roommate, Mademoiselle
d'Andiran, approached Madame de Casteja to see if she could help them escape.
This did not work out and Miss Rochester went to unoccupied France to live
with a French cousin. When France was totally occupied by the Germans she
returned to Paris and Mademoiselle d'Andiran.

When she contacted Madame de la Chaume again to ask for help getting
to the UK she was advised again to contact Madame de Casteja. Madame de
Casteja suggested she should join the Normandy unit of the Red Cross under
Maximilienne Boréa, but when she did so, she discovered that Miss Boréa had
no means of sending her to the UK. The account recalls that she finally managed
to leave with a woman named Bridget who worked for Major 'Jimmy' Langley
of MI9. What is interesting is that the woman known as Bridget is also recorded
as being a friend of Elizabeth Devereux Rochester and is mentioned a number
of times in her book, although there is no mention of MI9.

The report on Deverell Rochester states that it was at this point she began
working for Maurice Buckmaster of SOE in the Haute-Savoie region.

She apparently operated in the same region of France as with Elizabeth Devereux Rochester, although it seems unlikely that there would have been two women of similar names working for SOE in the same region at more or less the same time. When Deverell Rochester found herself in Paris in March 1944, she discovered that Miss Boréa was in prison. She therefore got in touch with Madame Thion de la Chaume to try to get her released, giving her a cigarette case to ease her anxiety. At that time Miss Rochester was hiding in Mademoiselle d'Andiran's house. Miss Boréa asked Deverell Rochester to return her bicycle, which had been left with Madame Thion de la Chaume. She said she would fix it up and asked her to be at the house at 41, rue Vital at 10.30 a.m. (or eleven o'clock as one document states) on 20 March. When Rochester kept the appointment, the Gestapo showed up and arrested her. She was taken to the rue des Saussaies and interrogated by a man she described as aged between 35 and 40, about 5ft 9in tall, grey eyes, square head, light brown hair which was receding, and with high cheek bones. He said he was from southern Germany. He spoke very little French, wore a ring on his left hand and had very nice hands. There was also a secretary in her early thirties present. When she was interviewed a second time Kraus was present for a few minutes. She had been told some time ago by Madame de Casteja that he wanted to help her. Deverell Rochester got the impression that:

> Madame de la CHAUME had spoken to Madame de CASTEJA about her work for Buckmaster and that this had been reported by KRAUS. She bases this on the following facts. The interrogator told her that she must have money as she was able to give away cigarette cases. The secretary said, 'These women (referring to de la CHAUME and CASTEJA) worked for us.' In addition Miss ROCHESTER saw in front of the interrogator a type written paper signed in a manner that reminded her of CASTEJA's signature.
>
> Miss ROCHESTER was kept in Vittel until September 1944.[16]

'Coco' Dampierre was a friend of de la Chaume, and when she was arrested Deverell Rochester recalled that de la Chaume had said that 'the rumour is that KRAUS [organ]ized her arrest'. After the liberation, Deverell Rochester went to see 'Coco' Dampierre and told her what Kraus had told her: that he had worked for the British but after being beaten by the Germans he was made to promise them to only work for the Gestapo. She also went to see Kraus at Madame de Casteja's house and challenged him about it. He denied being responsible for her arrest and told her that he was about to leave for

England. This would have made it late August (see below). The response she received when she challenged Madame de la Chaume, Madame de Casteja and Maximilienne Boréa was, 'Well, you can never prove it.' This would suggest that they were indeed guilty, or at least culpable.

In the summer of 1944 Elizabeth Devereux Rochester was transferred to Vittel until the liberation. After the war she lived in France, working in advertising, and died in Pontchaillou Hospital in Rennes, Brittany (now the Centre Hospitalier Universitaire), on 19 March 1983, suffering from multiple sclerosis (MS). Other references say it was either Dinan or St Mâlo; they also say she died unmarried, although one suggests that she had married a Mr Reynolds, which is not true as she is quoted as saying in her memoir that she was glad she had been unmarried, as having MS would have put an unbelievable burden on whoever had to take care of her.

Deverell Rochester also alleged that Boréa had been responsible for the arrest of a Captain Michaels, having been tipped off by a nurse at the Vittel camp. She was told that this was a well-known rumour and that Boréa, while in prison near Lille, had been a stool pigeon. Since then Miss Boréa had become engaged to an English major (whose name is not mentioned).

In summary, both women were fluent in French from an early age; both were living in Paris before the war; both worked for the American Hospital Ambulance Corps; both their mothers were arrested and imprisoned in Vittel, although the dates do not concur (one was in 1940, the other in 1942); both Elizabeth Devereux Rochester and Deverell Rochester were arrested on 20 March 1944 in Paris and also imprisoned in Vittel; both women apparently operated in the Jura at more or less the same time. There are too many coincidences for there to be two separate women, which leads one to conclude therefore that Deverell Rochester must have been Elizabeth Devereux Rochester.

CHAPTER 6

'The Kraus Affair'

A statement in Kraus's MI5 file written by Colonel Hinchley-Cooke on 27 October 1944 observes:

> The exact nature of KRAUS' [*sic*] activities since the outbreak of war has not yet been fully ascertained but it is known both from his own statements and other sources that at least during the second half of the year 1941 he was employed in Paris by Abteilung III F of Abwehr (the C.E. [Counter-Espionage] section of the German Intelligence Service) and that he played an important part in the penetration and breakup of an extremely valuable Allied Intelligence organization in France.[1]

This 'Allied Intelligence organization' was the *Interallié* network. The statement was written in the context of Kraus having recently arrived in Britain and at that time confined at Camp 020. A memo in his file by D.H. Sinclair of SLB1 states:

> On the information available it seemed clear that KRAUS was responsible for breaking up the effective VICTOIRE organisation. Previously Madame CARRÉ had been suspected of this, and whilst there was no reason to alter the conclusions reached in her case, there seemed no doubt that KRAUS was also responsible for this effective organisation being betrayed.[2]

A further report written by Milmo dated 20 October 1944 on the interrogation of Kraus conducted at the Oratory Schools says:

> I think there are strong grounds for suspecting that KRAUS's pre-war visits to this country were made partially, if not wholly, on behalf of the Abwehr … In view of our interest in VICTOIRE and WALENTY it will be important to to get to the bottom of KRAUS's activities of behalf of Abteilung IIIF, and to

obtain full information as to how and to what extent he was successful in his penetration of this particular Allied organisation. It may be that VICTOIRE has been held responsible for some of, though I am sure not all, the sins which were properly attributable to KRAUS ... The story which he has told of severing his connection with the Abwehr after his very successful coup in penetrating the WALENTY set up is wholly unconvincing, and one is left with strong suspicions that it may have been the intention of the enemy that he should operate as a stay behind agent after their evacuation of Paris and once more exploit the qualifications and connections that on a previous occasion had enabled him to achieve such successes amongst the English speaking community in that city.[3]

Kraus's pre-war visits to the UK referred to: (a) his visit when he arrived at Harwich on 26 March 1938 and stayed until 23 September 1938, posing as a commercial traveller representing Siemens & Halske; and (b) on 18 March 1939 when he attempted to re-enter the UK at Folkestone but was refused entry by F.J. Ralfe, H.M. Chief Inspector Immigration Branch. He brought this refusal to the attention of the German ambassador to Britain, Herbert von Dirksen, who intervened on his behalf by contacting Lord Halifax, the foreign secretary, but his approaches cut no ice with the British authorities and Kraus was sent back to Boulogne.

It seems that once Paris had been liberated in 1944, Kraus became involved with a certain Captain Lee of the Special Air Service (SAS), whom he approached to join the British forces. The 'Special Appendix to the Interim Report on Alfred Kraus' states that he had been arrested on suspicion of being a German officer by the French police on 28 August 1944, while at 19, rue St James in Neuilly, the residence of the Marquis de Casteja. However, when he produced his Wehrpass proving that he was a German civilian he was released but instructed to remain at that address. The following day two SAS officers, Captain Lee and Lieutenant Lord John Manners, the second son of the Marquis of Granby, came to the address. Lee asked Kraus and de Casteja what their intentions were. Both said they would like to join the British Army, with de Casteja saying that he would like to join the SAS if he could be brought to England. Given that de Casteja had been commissioned into the French Army as an officer, he was told that he could be a lieutenant, but in Kraus's case, because he was an Austrian he would only be able to enlist as a private. It was not until 4 September that Lee gave Kraus a full British Army paratrooper's uniform and equipment.

Captain Lee was Jack William Raymond (also called Ramon) Lee, also known as Raymond Couraud, born on 12 January 1920 at Surgères, Charente-Maritime, who died in 1977.[4] Described as a former Legionnaire and a gangster, he was second-in-command of the 2nd SAS Regiment under Major Roy Farran, who led a seven-man team to Orléans in an unsuccessful attempt to kill or capture Field Marshal Rommel at Rambouillet between 25 July and 15 August 1944 (Operation *Gaff*).[5] Lee was 'gazetted' on 29 June 1944 and awarded a Military Cross for his service in Italy.[6] In an extract from his statement, given on 5 May 1944 to London District, he elaborated on how he became involved in the whole affair with Kraus:

Three days after (c.middle August 1944) we arrived in Paris.

The next morning, after my arrival, I went with Lt. Lord John MANNERS to 19, rue St. James Neuilly. My reason for going there was that I knew it to be the house of the Comte de CASTEJA [*sic*] whom I had previously known in France. Furthermore, I had been asked by his family, whom I knew in England, to look him up in Paris and bring them news of him. When we arrived at the house, the concierge told us there was no one at home … The next day I went again to the house, and this time I found the Comte de CASTEJA and his brother-in-law Alfred KRAUS. I knew the latter, having met him before the war on the Riviera. I also contacted him in 1942 when I went to France on a mission for the British Government, and I contacted him again on one of my previous missions at the end of July 1944.[7]

As Wilson noted, Kraus's claims were 'inconsistent with Captain LEE's statements – first Kraus claimed not to have met Captain Broad before 29 August 1944, yet he had also claimed to have met Lee in 1941. Lee also claimed to have met Kraus before the war on the Riviera. He explained that it was during the third week in August when he was travelling through Bayeux that he had had the following conversation with de Casteja:

CASTEJA explained that Alfred KRAUS was in trouble with the F.F.I. and he suggested to me that I should take KRAUS back to England. This I agreed to do, after some discussion. CASTEJA then asked me if he could come as well with us. To this I also agreed. At this time, I was faced with the prospect of taking three Frenchmen [the other two are not named here] and one German

(KRAUS) back to England. I never anticipated any trouble about taking three Frenchmen but I did realise there might be trouble taking a German ... On arrival at Bayeux I contacted the Movement Control Authorities and asked if I could take four Frenchmen back to England. I was told it was impossible. I then decided to send them back to Paris. KRAUS was substituted for the driver and eventually arrived in England but the Frenchmen were not heard of again.[8]

Statements made by Lieutenants Edmund Frederick Astley 'Frog' Birtwistle (1924–86) and Lord John Manners (1922–2001), which do not appear in Lee's account, tend to contradict him: Birtwistle said that Lee did not know de Casteja until 22 August, and Manners said that when they called at de Casteja's house in Neuilly the family was away in Lyons.

Milmo noted in his report that Lee's wife worked for the Home Office. Furthermore, Lee had told Kraus, who was becoming suspicious of the way in which he was being brought to England, that his wife would probably be able to 'arrange matters'. This was apparently not the first time that Lee had done this, having once brought out a Portuguese girl with the help of his wife at the Home Office. D.I. Wilson doubted this story, which he thought was 'pure invention on LEE's part ... in order to relieve any doubts that might have been in KRAUS' mind on their proposed joint conduct'.[9] He requested that Mrs Lee be invited to explain her side of the story and to have her solicitor present. That interview took place on 11 January 1945 at the offices of solicitors Messrs Gordon, Dadds & Co., with J.M. Davis of B5, the Investigating Staff under Superintendent Leonard Burt, at which Lee was also present. Annoyingly, his wife's first name is not mentioned. Both Lee and his wife denied the story about the Portuguese girl. He suggested that he had once known a Portuguese girl, one Maria Jose Viana, daughter of Rachel Rodriguez of 109 Avenida Barbosa du Bocage, Lisbon, who told him she wanted to come to England after the war. He thought that this story had been taken out of context and spread around by Betty Palson [sic], a friend of Lady Swinfen.

It has not been possible to determine the exact identity of Mrs Lee, and it may be just a coincidence that there happens to be a Mrs K.G. Lee in the Home Office Aliens Department who features in a number of MI5 documents. Nor has it been possible to establish any connection between them. Raymond Lee was also known to have had a number of lovers – one was the American socialite and heiress Mary Jayne Gold (1909–97) whom he met in Marseilles and became her lover, although they never married. Gold, with American art student

Miriam Davenport and American journalist Varian Fry, helped many Jewish refugees to escape, including artists Marc Chagall (1887–1985) and sculptor Jacques Lipchitz (1891–1973). Another of his lovers was Mary Aline Mynors Wesley (*née* Farmar, 1912–2002), later to become well-known author Mary Wesley, whose first husband was Charles 'Carol' Swinfen Eady, 2nd Baron Swinfen. Her second husband was Eric Siepmann (1903–70). Another reference states that on 27 May 1952 Lee first married Hélène Louise Nancy de Bono (1918–95), and later Katherine Davis.[10]

On the night of 6/7 September 1944 Lee and Kraus set sail for Southampton. At Lee's suggestion, Kraus had taken on the identity of Private Gosselin, Lee's driver/batman, to avoid immigration problems. Whilst on board Kraus was allowed to take a turn at guarding some of the German prisoners. By travelling in this way, he managed to pass through Britain without being examined at the London Reception Centre, which would have been standard operating procedure for an alien or refugee arriving in Britain. Kraus's MI5 file states that Lee hid Kraus at his flat at 61 Christchurch Street, Chelsea. The account in Mary Wesley's official biography offers a different explanation, stating that Lee, referred to in the biography as Raymond, concealed Kraus in an army camp in the Cotswolds for six weeks, which did not sit well with him because of the poor quality of the food.

Wesley had first met Kraus, referred to as 'the Czech', in late September at a restaurant in London where she had arranged to meet Lee, but he failed to turn up. Instead, 'she was greeted by a tall man with a mid-European accent wearing a good suit, who told her he was a fellow guest [and] said he was Czech.'[11] Her lunch partner turned out to be Kraus. Lee arrived at the end of the meal and ordered more wine. They spent a drunken afternoon at a club to which Mary belonged, resulting in Mary and Kraus pouring Raymond (Lee) into a taxi and setting off for Richmond Stopford's [*sic*] house in Chelsea. The biography refers to Stopford as a senior member of MI6. In fact, at that time he was head of MI5's B1l (seamen and airline personnel) but had served in MI6 before the war. Mary had hoped that the encounter with Kraus would not jeopardise her chances of resuming a career in MI5. An article in the *Spectator* refers to her being recruited by an unnamed friend (possibly Stopford) to MI5 to decode German military signals, although her biographer does not elaborate on this either.[12] Nor does this seem likely, as the German codes would have been broken first at Bletchley Park, then passed on to MI5 and MI6, the end-users, as 'Most Secret Sources'. Another review of Mary's biography claims that when she had been asked to move to Bletchley she declined because it wasn't close to the Ritz![13]

Other reviewers of her biography have suggested that her role may have been to keep an eye on Czech exiles in London, which might fit in with her encounter with the so-called 'Czech', alias Kraus. Later that evening at Stopford's flat 'the "Czech" was arrested, held on remand and deported to Nuremberg, where he was eventually tried for war crimes and convicted of several murders.'[14] That was the official party line at that time. Many years later Mary learned the truth about the so-called 'Czech' and his real identity from Richman Stopford.

Owing to their collaboration, Daisy Fellowes' daughters, Jacqueline and Emmeline de Casteja, had their heads shaved by a Paris mob in the 16th arrondissment and were imprisoned with prostitutes in Fresnes for five months. There, she said, they would 'jiggle their bare breasts at the men in the block opposite'.[15] Emmeline, who was apparently a lesbian, was also accused of betraying an unnamed girlfriend in the Resistance, thought to be Elizabeth Devereux Rochester.

Daisy Fellowes asked Duff Cooper, the newly arrived British ambassador (1944–47), to intervene on her behalf. Cooper responded that it would have to go through official channels, but shortly thereafter, Raymond Lee arrived in Paris. Wesley's biographer posed the question: Was Lee sent to Paris to rescue Kraus, or had it been a chance encounter? If there is anything in Kraus's MI5 files that sheds more light on the matter it is now sadly illegible.

On the night of 8 September Lee introduced Kraus to his sister-in-law, Mrs Rosamond Daisy Gladstone (1921–98), daughter of the Honourable Reginald Ailwyn Fellowes and Marguerite Séverine Philippine Decazes de Glücksbierg, who was married to Captain James Gustavus Gladstone (1917–72) of the King's Own Scottish Borderers (KOSB). (They divorced in 1945.) Kraus had apparently told MI5 that while he had promised to work for the Germans, he had in fact been working for the Allies. While doing so:

> He was put in touch with a girl, who he thought was Polish but subsequently proved to be French. He evidently confided in this girl and he says as a result he, and a number of other people working for him were arrested [sic] because the girl was, in fact, working for the enemy. Incidentally he says he knows that she is in this country.[16]

Clearly, this was VICTOIRE, as Hinchley-Cooke avers in a Minute to Wilson of B1b dated 30 October 1944. In the same document it refers to a statement that had been taken from Lieutenant Lord John Manners of the 2nd SAS Regiment by G2 I (b) London District in which Hinchley-Cooke drew attention to the following:

MANNERS states that at a din[ner] party prior to it being decided that KRAUS should be brought to England by L[EE] the former gave it out that he wished to go to England:-

(a) to get hold of the girl who had caused him and his friends in France a great deal of trouble
(b) to do his bit.

The girl at (a) I think you will agree is unquestionably VICTOIRE.[17]

During his interview at Headquarters G2 I (b) London District in Kensington Palace Gardens Manners told them that the Marquis de Casteja, with whom Lee and Kraus were connected, was currently serving with the 21st Army Group in the Netherlands as a liaison officer. Further enquiries revealed that de Casteja was actually serving as a French liaison officer with the Independent Czech Armoured Brigade in Dunkirk. A report to B1b on 27 October 1944 by Hinchley-Cooke states:

We have no evidence that Captain LEE was aware that KRAUS had been connected with the German Intelligence Service nor have we any evidence on the motives which led Captain LEE or KRAUS to cooperate in bringing KRAUS irregularly to this country.[18]

Milmo reiterated this in his report to Stephens of Camp 020, when he said:

It is felt that there is no evidence, and it is highly improbable that Captain LEE had any real idea of KRAUS's true character when he sent the man over here. It is also felt highly improbable that KRAUS has in fact any espionage mission in this country, or that he was intended by the Germans to come here; however, this is not to suggest that these matters should not be explored.[19]

It appears that this was not Lee's only misdemeanour. His so-called 'mission for the British Government' in 1942 must have been the operation for SOE in August 1942, a beach raid near Cannes, or the mission in November near Narbonne, where he had had to kill three Vichy policemen. He had then escaped over the Pyrenees to Barcelona and Lisbon. In Gibraltar he had been interviewed by a Mr Morul who worked for SOE about the misappropriation of 4 million francs. The letter from SLB3 of MI5 to British Army Group MI5 Liaison in Paris, dated 19 February 1946, states that in the interests of security,

Lee was not prosecuted. It was only after various indiscretions during 1942 that he was dismissed from SOE and joined 62 Commando under Bill Stirling, David Stirling's brother, which later became 2SAS.

The story of Kraus and Lee's association was first told to J.R. (Richman) Stopford of MI5's B11 by Lady Swinfen, an old friend who brought Kraus and Lee over to Stopford's house to introduce them. Lady Swinfen was Averil, Lady Swinfen (née Averil Kathleen Suzanne Humphreys, d.2007). MI5 arranged that Kraus should be taken to the Immigration Office at Ibex House in the Minories, near the Tower of London, where he would be officially refused leave to land (RLL) and handed over to the Oratory Schools for interrogation. Lee would then be arrested by London District and disciplinary action taken against him. In fact, he was court-martialled and pleaded guilty. According to Wesley's biography, he was cashiered (dismissed in disgrace) and deported. At his court martial he was represented by the firm of Gordon, Dadds, solictors, who requested that KRAUS attend as a witness, although as it turned out, he did not.

B.H. Townshend of SIS's Section VB5 reported in September 1944 to Lieutenant Colonel Baxter of MI5's B1d that a reliable resource in Paris had reported that Kraus had been arrested by the Gestapo in 1941 and forced to work for them, and should therefore be treated as suspect. As already noted, in 1944 he had tried to leave Paris and join the Parachute Regiment. Proof that Kraus was indeed working for the Abwehr in 1941 can be seen in an ULTRA intercept dated 1 July 1941:

1.7.41.
7226 Wiesbaden – Toulon. No.137. From PAUL for K.O. MARSEILLES. On 3/7 ALFRED KRAUS is arriving in MARSEILLES. Identity card (Austria?) in this name. It is urgently necessary that he should be received by someone at the Armistice Commission Building. In immediate W/T is requested stating in which building and to whom KRAUS can report. Agent (VM) [?] is to present proof to R.N.D. [?] that he was concerned with the installation of technical Apparatus at the Armistice Commission.
RUDOLPH.[20]

K.O. were the Kriegsorganisationen, which were operated by the Abwehr in neutral countries; V.M. could simply mean V-Mann. 'JACQUELINE [de Broglie] told Kraus that Bernberg-Gossler [sic] had passed [illegible] information he had to his girlfriend Inge ABSHAGEN at the Hôtel Lutetia.'

Ingeborg Helen Haag (*née* Abshagen), a secretary at the German Foreign Ministry and at one time secretary to Colonel Helmut Groscurth (1898–1943) and Admiral Canaris, was born into an upper-middle-class Prussian family in Berlin on 13 August 1918 and died in London on 10 December 2009. After the rise of Hitler, on 10 April 1937 she had travelled on the *Bremen* from Bremen to Southampton to study at Exeter University and the London School of Economics under Harold Laski, but her family recalled her to Berlin before the Second World War broke out. Canaris dubbed her 'The Painted Doll' because of her good looks; later she acquired the nickname 'the Mata Hari of Marylebone' as she had a flat in Upper Wimpole Street, London, after the war. Canaris sent her to work in Paris in 1940, where one of her missions was to supply false passports to Jews. Throughout the war she was fervently anti-Nazi. In 1942 she married Werner Haag (1909–85), a senior German officer (later Generalleutnant), and was later implicated in the plot to kill Hitler in July 1944, although she was having lunch with two Gestapo officers at the time. However, an interview she gave to the *Guardian* in 2004 claims that she and Werner were in Romania at that time.[21]

Giskes asked Kraus to find out what was going on in the de Broglie circle. As Giskes described it in his file:

> The results were serious. It was absolutely clear that a certain circle of well-known personalities in Paris had organized a spy net, which collected and analysed particular material. In the de BROGLIE house in Neuilly, meetings and the collecting and sifting of material was taking place. To what extent Mlle. de BROGLIE overlooked the great danger she was running in so doing was not clear. Nevertheless it was obvious what action would have to be taken rightaway if I was to get her out of the business, as I had already promised KRAUS I would do. In June or July 1941, amongst others, COURTOIS and Pierre d'HARCOURT were arrested in connection with the affair. In this connection there were later a few further arrests.[22]

Shortly afterwards Giskes was transferred to The Hague, so does not remember the names of the others. He added that later on he met Kraus socially in Paris when he needed to visit there but said that 'there was no more talk of espionage or the Abwehr'. Furthermore, he believed that Kraus's wife, Daisy, had no idea that he (Giskes) was involved with the Abwehr or that he had been involved with her case.

With the collaboration of his brother-in-law, de Casteja, Kraus set up a cover address in Lisbon belonging to a Gräfin (Countess) in Lisbon that the Germans could use. He also told de Casteja to write to his mother-in-law, the Honourable Mrs Reginald Fellowes, to let her know that de Casteja could receive letters at that address. The address, as far as he could remember, was Comtesse Galvani, Villa Maria, Estoril, Portugal. (There is a Villa Maria in Sintra that is now a hotel, also the Casa Santa Maria in Cascais, which could both be candidates.)

A letter to Lieutenant Colonel N. MacDermot at Headquarters G2 I (b) London District from Lieutenant Colonel P.R. Barry of Room 055 at MI5 explained that although Kraus was a German agent, there was no evidence to suggest that either his wife or de Casteja knew of his secret service activities, and she may actually have assisted the resistance movement. He emphasised that:

> … the Security Service are quite satisfied that up to date KRAUS has not told the truth or anything like it and it may conceivably happen that, if and when the ture [sic] story comes to light, KRAUS's wife and possibly others, including the de CASTEJA's, may stand in a more unfavourable light than they do now.[23]

It was further stated by D.I. Wilson in a letter to Bernard Townshend of SIS on 21 November 1944:

> You refer to the penetration of the INTERALLIEE organisation by KRAUS but I imagine this is a slip. There is no evidence that KRAUS was responsible for the break-up of this organisation. What he was responsible for was certainly the 'planting' of information on the organisation run by EVE, and probably he was at least in part responsible for the arrest of EVE and of Richard d'HARCOURT. The INTERALLIEE organisation appears to have broken down when the IIIF officer, BLEICHER, got on to the agent DESIRE in Cherbourg, through him got on to CHRISTIAN, and through CHRISTIAN got onto WALENTY, VIOLETTE and VICTOIRE. With the help of VICTOIRE and papers captured at WALENTY's flat the almost complete round-up of the organisation followed. KRAUS was not responsible for this.[24]

Unfortunately, most of the documents in Kraus's files are of such poor-quality photocopies that they are almost illegible, including's Townshend's original letter to Wilson. However, a copy exists in one of Mathilde Carré's files.

When Jacqueline de Broglie was interrogated in 1945 a report prepared by VBZ (the SIS counter-espionage sub-section that dealt with France, Corsica, Andorra, Belgium, the Netherlands and Luxembourg) stated that she confirmed what Kraus had told MI5 during his interrogation at Camp 020, that she did not know that he was working for the Abwehr, and that he did everything he could to prevent her from being arrested. He also attempted to get de Casteja released. This was also confirmed by Lieutenant Colonel Richard Broad, who had been hidden by de Broglie at her house in Paris.

In his inimitable way, Lieutenant Colonel Robin Stephens at Camp 020 concluded, 'It is a squalid tale which in a novel would fail for improbability.' He recommended that de Casteja be removed from his present position for three reasons: (1) he had allowed himself to be used to set up a cover address in Lisbon; (2) he knew that Kraus worked for the Abwehr and did nothing about it, something which Stephens, uncharacteristically charitable, felt he might be excused for because Kraus was his brother-in-law; and (3) de Casteja was fully aware that Kraus had been sent to England to join the armed forces. In a report dated 31 December 1944, Stephens noted that, 'No evidence, however, has been forthcoming that KRAUS came to this country under orders of the Secret Service or that they were even aware of his intention in this respect.'[25] Nevertheless, he was interned under the Royal Prerogative as of 21 November 1944.

The matter didn't end there. Ladislas Farago, in his book *The Game of Foxes* writes how in the House of Commons on 8 April 1945 (it was actually the 17th, published on the 26th) questions were asked by Edgar Granville (later Baron Granville of Eye), Independent MP for Eye in Suffolk, about the presence of Kraus in the UK. All quotes are taken from Hansard as reported in the Kraus file. Granville stated that he had been tipped off by a war correspondent of the News Chronicle, most likely Norman Maynard Clark, that 'a "handsome German officer" identified as a "Captain Klause" [*sic*] had flown to Britain from the Continent, probably from Sweden, and landed by parachute "in a country area about a month ago".' The so-called 'Klause' had then headed to London under the guise of a refugee. Granville asked the Secretary of State, Herbert Morrison, about representations he had allegedly made regarding Kraus being treated as a refugee. Home Secretary Morrison replied that no such representations had been made. He further added that Kraus was interned as a civilian alien and that 'there are no grounds for suspecting that this alien engaged in any harmful activities in this country', nor was he prepared to allow him to remain at liberty, based on information he had received:

> **Mr Granville:** ... may I ask has he any information whether this man was a Nazi and a member of the Reichswehr; and, if so, can he say how it came that he was running loose in this country for a whole month before he was apprehended?
>
> **Mr Morrison:** It was admitted when the War Secretary was questioned about it, that there were irregularities in his arrival. We got track of him as quickly as we could and I put him "inside". Therefore my hon. Friend may take it that he is being safely taken care of and need not have any undue loss of sleep at night owing to his apprehensions about the security of the State.
>
> **Mr Granville:** But is my right. Hon. Friend quite sure that he has the fullest information about this man, and did this man make a full statement to the Home Office when he was arrested?
>
> **Mr Morrison:** I think we know all about him; in fact, the Hon. Member would be surprised how much we know about all sorts of things. [26]

Farago quotes Granville as saying that the plan was, according to the war correspondent, for Kraus 'to use information he gained in Paris during the German occupation as his bargaining point to enable him to change sides at this late stage of the war'. [27]

It appears from Farago's account that Daisy Fellowes had invited her daughter and son-in-law Kraus to London after the Liberation of Paris and intervened with Churchill to allow this to happen. This may have been an allusion to Duff Cooper's alleged, but unproven, intervention. However, Jacqueline was ill and Freddy Kraus had to go on his own. With the help of Churchill, 'all red tape was cut'. The account also says that Churchill invited him to Chartwell as his guest for several weekends. Kraus apparently told Churchill that he could act as a liaison between German anti-Nazi dissidents and Britain to try to bring an end to the war. 'The Prime Minister put him in touch with the people who handled such delicate matters.'

In the House of Commons, some of Granville's questions were also answered by Ellen Wilkinson, the Labour MP for Jarrow and a junior minister in the Ministry of Home Security under Herbert Morrison. She informed the House of Kraus's real name, that he was not all he first appeared to be, that it had been decided he was someone 'who should not be at liberty' and that 'he was accordingly interned'. She reassured the House, 'Herr Kraus was not receiving any preferential treatment.' It was also admitted that Kraus had been brought to London 'without explicit permission to leave France'.

The Kraus affair also generated some correspondence between MI5 and Sir Frank Newsam at the Home Office. Draft responses were prepared by Milmo in which it was made clear that Kraus was known to them. Copies were also sent to Mr Drew at the Army Council and Mr M.F. (later Sir Michael) Cullis, then head of the Austrian section of the Central Department of the Foreign Office. Lieutenant Colonel P.R. Barry of MI5 wrote to Drew saying that 'Captain Klause' was in fact an Austrian civilian named Kraus and:

> … we have been again reassured by P.W.1 [the War Office Directorate of Prisoners of War dealing with enemy prisoners] that they do not know of any Prisoner of War to whom the question could possibly refer.
>
> On this assurance, S of S might properly answer the question in an entirely negative sense, but we do not think that this course would be advisable as we are informed that the Press are very anxious to follow this story and a mere denial of any knowledge of 'Captain Klause' might tend to stimulate curiosity and give the impression that there was something to hide.[28]

A note to file written by Milmo on 12 April 1945 elaborates on this:

> I was asked by G.3./D.C. & D., in the absence of Colonel Barry, to attend upon the D.D.M.I. (O.S.) at the War Office who was seeing the V.C.I.G.S. on the KRAUS case and wished a representative of M.I.5. to be present.
>
> I saw the V.C.I.G.S. in company with the D.M.I. and, at his request, told him generally about the facts of the KRAUS case and answered a number of factual questions which he raised. I explained that the Security Service did not wish to express any view as to the desirability or otherwise of mitigating LEE's punishment, and the V.C.I.G.S. accepted this attitude.[29]

The Vice Chief of Imperial General Staff (VCIGS) at that time was Lieutenant General Sir Archibald Nye; the Director of Military Intelligence (DMI) was Major General John Sinclair, who would later become the Chief of the Secret Intelligence Service from 1953 to 1956, taking over from Sir Stewart Menzies. As Barry predicted, the exchange in the House of Commons was widely reported in the national newspapers – the *Sunday Pictorial*, *Daily Express*, *Daily Mail* and *News Chronicle*.

As we have seen, Kraus was *not* parachuted into Britain from Sweden, but arrived by boat from France, courtesy of Captain Lee. Nor was his arrival in a 'country area'; he arrived at Southampton, whereupon he was taken to London. Of course, the matter of Lee's involvement would need to be kept secret from the general public, and presumably, much of the government. Morrison may have been correct when he informed the House that there were no grounds for suspecting Kraus of being 'engaged in any harmful activities in this country', as members of MI5 had already noted, and had informed Morrison of that fact, but because he was an alien who had entered the country illegally he was interned anyway. Whether Churchill had indeed taken him to his home at Chartwell remains to be seen. In Giskes' MI5 file there are mentions of Kraus's early career working for him, but certainly not in the context of being an 'agent of influence' with Churchill. It would certainly have been an embarrassment had that emerged at the time. With the benefit of hindsight, it must be borne in mind that not everything Farago wrote, or which he believed to be true, was in fact true, as he did not have access to official government (i.e. MI5) files detailing the case. Even with this access now, the information is at times sparse and far from conclusive, in part because of the aforementioned poor quality of some documents, and the selective 'weeding' of others. On 4 May 1945 Kraus was sued for divorce by Jacqueline de Broglie – 'French wife of mystery Austrian'. The divorce became absolute on 3 February 1958 in Münster. Kraus was deported to Germany on 3 July 1945 and was held by the British 21st Army Group. On 16 January 1952 Kraus left for Canada to work as a director of production at Webb & Co. Ltd, import merchants of Montreal. Unfortunately, Access to Information requests to Canadian Border Services have drawn a blank, and no other information is currently available.

CHAPTER 7

The Interallié Network

During the winter of 41 and 42 Abwehrstelle St GERMAIN discovered an espionage organisation known as *Interallié*. The organisation covered the whole of Occupied France and carried out excellent work for the Allies. The leader of the organisation was a Captain in the General Staff of the Polish Air Force. He was known under a variety of extraordinary names, some of which were double-barrelled. PW [prisoner of war] can only remember one of them, which was BIELAWSKI. This man was subsequently given the cover name HUBERT by the Germans. Abwehrstelle St GERMAIN was in due course able, with the help of the GFP, to arrest about sixty members of this organisation and to capture its transmitter in PARIS and a considerable amount of documentary evidence. The documents showed that the organisation had carried out extremely successful espionage and had obtained very good information about the German Air Force, Navy and Army. The organisation contained several main agents who worked under the Polish Captain. They were known as Section Leaders and were also Poles. Most of the agents were French nationals.[1]

As noted earlier, WALENTY and VICTOIRE had moved out of their flat in the rue du Colonel Molle and into one at 3, Square du Trocadéro under the name Donnadieu. The proprietress suspected them of being Fifth Columnists, so they moved again, he to the rue Picot in the 16th and she to 146, Boulevard Pereire in the 17th arrondissement, now the Hôtel Étoile Pereire. However, at the end of July they moved back to the rue du Colonel Molle address they had occupied before. When he went to England in October 1941 WALENTY was seriously concerned about the amount of time spent at the rue du Colonel Molle, so he found VICTOIRE another flat at 3, rue Cortot in Montmartre, run by two women who VICTOIRE referred to as '*Les deux sorcières*' (the two witches), one of whom was called Alice.

The organisation's wireless station was by this time in the Villa Léandre, a two-storeyed house in the rue Junot in the 18th arrondissement where MAURICE lived. It had started out in an apartment at 26, Faubourg St Jacques where WALENTY and VICTOIRE had first lived, and had then been moved by MAURICE to the Boulevard Berthier, then to the Villa Flora in Montmartre, before finally transferring to the Villa Léandre. Subsidiary stations were set up at 217, rue du Faubourg St Honoré at the home of ARTOS, the painter, and a third at 13, rue Miguel Hidalgo in the 19th arrondissment, known only to MAURICE and MAX. The radios had all been constructed by MONO and MAX, with the cipher invented by WALENTY.

Information in the report compiled by the Combined Services Detailed Interrogation Centre (CSDIC) dated 6 July 1945, obtained during the interrogation of Oberstleutnant Reile, HUBERT/BIELAWSKI, refers to WALENTY (Garby-Czerniawski) as BRUTUS. This is also mentioned in the note to Major Luke from WRC4A (it is signed DW – D.I. Wilson (War Room)). A further report goes on to say that at the beginning of November 1941 the Gestapo office in Cherbourg had tracked one of the sub-agents, Raoul Kieffer (KIKI/DESIRE), of the network and arrested him.[2] Exactly who had betrayed him is unclear, but a report prepared on 28 February 1942 on the interrogation of VICTOIRE states that it had been Madame Denise Buffet (*née* Marie-Thérèse Fillon), described as a former German intelligence service agent[3] within the Cherbourg network, who had betrayed KIKI to the Gestapo on 3 or 4 November.[4]

A report to Stephens at Camp 020 on the interrogation of Hugo Bleicher compiled by Squadron Leader Beddard, dated 9 July 1945, posed the following questions:

> Was it LEMEUR? Had KIEFFERS's mistress BUFFET no part in this denunciation? Was KIEFFER arrested before or after the other agents of the group? What were the conditions of release of these agents? Was it because KIEFFER had agreed to work for the Germans?[5]

Bleicher told Beddard that he thought it was in October 1941 that Kieffer had been denounced by Émile Lemeur, a municipal worker in Cherbourg, described as one of Mme Buffet's former agents, at the office of the GFP (Luft) – Geheime Feldpolizei Luftwaffe – in the Place Napoléon in Cherbourg. Lemeur is also referred to as Le Meur in a recent book on the French who collaborated with the Third Reich.[6] Lemeur had been recruited either by Kieffer or by his mistress Denise Buffet, but Bleicher did not know why Lemeur had denounced Kieffer.

GFP (Luft) then sent a report on Lemeur's denunciation to Paris, whereupon Hauptmann (Captain) Erich Borchers of III F, *Ast* St Germain came to Cherbourg to investigate further.

Borchers, aged 47, had been a journalist before the war and was subordinate to Major Eschig @ Salzberg, the chief of III F.[7] Bleicher described Borchers as completely useless in III F, and as a rake and a drunkard, which is perhaps why there was no one competent enough in GFP (Luft) to deal with Kieffer; the case was therefore handed over to Bleicher to carry out the arrest. Kieffer was arrested when he arrived from Paris. Bleicher later told his MI5 interrogator that when Kieffer was first arrested he was uncooperative, saying, 'It's a pity you've caught me. I should have caused you a lot of trouble in Normandy.' Finally, Kieffer agreed to give away the other agents of the Normandy organisation providing their lives were spared. The less important ones were later released.

Denise Buffet was also arrested a few days later but was unwilling to give away any information. However, according to the book on French collaborators with the Third Reich, Bleicher and Borchers discovered a list of twenty-one names, including Raoul Kieffer [*sic*], who was about to go to Cherbourg on 3 November.[8] Described as an artist-painter, Denise Buffet was later deported to Sarrebrücken (27 July 1943), to Ravensbrück (1 August 1943) and finally Mauthausen (7 March 1945), all under the 'Night and Fog' decree; she was liberated on 22 April 1945.

In an attempt to spare his organisation, Kieffer invented a rendezvous with an imaginary agent at the Place de l'Opéra and led Bleicher on a wild-goose chase, walking around and waiting for the 'agent' to appear. On the 15th Bleicher forced him to write a letter to the La Palette post box inviting WALENTY to an interview, and to reveal WALENTY's address. Neither WALENTY nor VICTOIRE came to the rendezvous as they had had other matters with which to attend. Kieffer was then forced to write another letter to CHRISTIAN (Lieutenant Bernard Krotki) inviting him to a rendezvous at the Café Monte Carlo at 9, Avenue Wagram (the file says Boulevard), where he was arrested on Sunday 16 November. Ironically, further down the avenue at number 128 was the headquarters of the GFP. CHRISTIAN was beaten up and as a result gave up WALENTY's address. This led VICTOIRE to believe that the Gestapo must have obtained WALENTY's address from someone else first, otherwise GEORGE and MAURICE would not have been allowed to escape so easily.

Harmer's report notes that there was a discrepancy in the date of CHRISTIAN's arrest. VICTOIRE was adamant that it was on Sunday 16 November, whereas in MAURICE's statement he could not have been arrested before midday on Monday 17th. It meant that whoever had given up the address hadn't known that the two were living in the apartment above, which VICTOIRE certainly did. Alternatively, they had received information on Monday night. However, Harmer also cautioned that information in VICTOIRE's statement was liable to be inaccurate as she had obtained it second-hand from Bleicher. Both MAURICE and ADAM believed that CHRISTIAN was not someone who would have betrayed his boss. Harmer considered this as a point against VICTOIRE's account, particularly given that CHRISTIAN had been arrested once before and had not told the Gestapo anything. It was only after Bleicher visited him in his cell that he was persuaded to give up WALENTY's address. Harmer notes:

> In either event it appears to provide evidence that it was not VICTOIRE who gave away WALENTY's address. She maintains that she knew perfectly well that the wireless set was operated from the top floor of the Villa Leandre. MAURICE was doubtful about this, but thought she probably knew. It is inconceivable that VICTOIRE did not have this bit of information, and I have always held the view that whatever the cause of the break-up it was not as a result of a voluntary betrayal on her part.[9]

Garby-Czerniawski's (WALENTY) book *The Big Network* says that CHRISTIAN and VICTOIRE were put in the same cell and their conversation bugged, which was how Bleicher found out where he lived. What it does not say is which one of them actually gave up the address, but perhaps that is a moot point. According to VICTOIRE, when CHRISTIAN had first been arrested, he was caught red-handed. Through KIKI the Gestapo would have obtained a great deal of information about the network. As Harmer noted, the behaviour of anyone caught in such a position would be unpredictable 'and I certainly would not regard VICTOIRE's account as untrue merely because of a supposition of this sort. As before stated, the circumstances of the arrest are consistent with a betrayal such as she has recorded.'

WALENTY has recorded in his book *The Big Network* that he had been anxious about CHRISTIAN. He had briefed him about the meeting with KIKI at the Villa Léandre at 6 p.m. but he had not shown up for the party. It would be the last time that he saw him. On the morning of the 17th he was still worried; by the evening CHRISTIAN had still not appeared, so WALENTY went out for dinner with VIOLETTE. At the restaurant in Montmartre they were accosted by a man in a raincoat and beret who WALENTY said seemed a bit drunk. He had seen the same man earlier in the street, and he appeared to be following them. That man would again show up on the morning of his arrest – 'Medium build, slightly taller than myself, rather slim, about forty, with an intelligent face and sharp, but not violent eyes'. He also wore glasses. 'I did not know then that by this very act, the man standing in front of me, Hugo Bleicher, German Agent, had started his unusual, famous career!'[10] Bleicher appearing drunk must have been an act as, according to his file, he didn't drink.

How had this all come about and why had VICTOIRE betrayed them – or had she? It appears that the green-eyed spectre of jealousy had reared its ugly head. VICTOIRE was jealous of VIOLETTE and competed for WALENTY's attention. During the five weeks that he was away in England a dispute had arisen between the two women, when VICTOIRE quite naturally assumed that she was in charge as far as messages and the workings of the organisation were concerned. The problem was the interpersonal relationships between the main members of the network: ADAM got along with MAURICE, but not with VICTOIRE; VIOLETTE was also on good terms with MAURICE and ADAM, but not VICTOIRE. Since VIOLETTE was a great friend of WALENTY, she 'had rather been left by him holding a watching brief over the organisation, was well in with the powers-that-be to dictate her wishes and override VICTOIRE'. ADAM and MAURICE would later confirm that while WALENTY was away, 'if anybody was in charge of the organisation … it was in fact VIOLETTE.' As Harmer noted, 'For a person with a nature as jealous as that of VICTOIRE, this was obviously a cause of friction.' ADAM explained that VIOLETTE was a rich girl whose first language was German, the daughter of a wealthy landowner in Nancy, and 'a high class girl of adequate intelligence'. Because she was extremely attractive, VICTOIRE 'conceived a violent hate for her and never lost an opportunity of being unpleasant to her and making her cry'.[11]

However, this was not the only source of trouble. VICTOIRE had also told Harmer that while WALENTY was away there had been a conspiracy between MONO and MOUSTIQUE, who had wanted to depose him and take over the network. MOUSTIQUE partly confirmed this to MI5, saying that there had been problems between her and WALENTY. MONO had originally been brought in to control wireless communications but proved to be incompetent, so was replaced by a Polish operator, Janusz Włodarcyk (MAURICE). MONO was then assigned to Sector K, which covered the Le Mans area, which MOUSTIQUE was unhappy about and this caused friction between her and WALENTY.

Monique Deschamps (MOUSTIQUE) told Harmer that she didn't think there was any animosity between them, although it appears that she had made a threat to kill VICTOIRE. It was apparently said in jest but served to create a rift between the two women, with VICTOIRE saying that she never wanted to see MONO again. MOUSTIQUE, who had slept with WALENTY too, was also jealous of VIOLETTE. BOBY-ROLAND approached ADAM and told him that he had uncovered a plot to poison WALENTY when he returned, having first thought that ADAM may have something to do with it. WALENTY's womanising was such that while he was in England British Intelligence warned him that his chief danger was the jealousy of his girlfriends, and that he should decide who he wanted to live with and keep her under control. VICTOIRE also claimed that she had heard from M. Victon @ Paul PRIVAT that MONO and MOUSTIQUE wanted to poison her as well.

On the night of 1/2 October WALENTY set out, together with ADAM (Lieutenant Mitchell), who had been trained to lay out the flare path, and VOLTA (Auguste Brun), one of his agents who was a French Air Force officer, to fly to London with a portable gramophone laden with intelligence. He was picked up by an SIS Lysander flown by Squadron Leader John 'Whippy' Nesbitt-Dufort of 138 Special Duties Squadron from a disused aerodrome landing ground west-north-west of Compiègne, 2 kilometres north-east of Estrées St Denis, and landed at RAF Tangmere in Sussex.[12] The airfield had been chosen, apparently by KIKI, because he thought it would attract less attention than landing a Lysander in an empty field. Hugh Verity gives a fine account of the pick-up in his book *We Landed by Moonlight*:

> The 1st October was a lovely day. His local agent [VOLTA] told him that all was quiet on the airfield, but that soldiers from the infantry regiment in barracks one mile away passed the road alongside it. Armand did not worry as the soldiers would not walk along the road at midnight. The three of them travelled from Paris to Compiègne by train … From the station they moved separately towards the aerodrome, followed the road on the south side and turned along an unused path which was covered on both sides by overgrown bushes. Armand said: 'Let's sit here quietly in the bushes and wait until darkness comes, then we will move to the hangars. They are nearer to our proposed "flarepath". They are obviously abandoned. How nice of the Germans to leave them open for us, and unguarded!'[13]
>
> Five minutes to midnight; then out of the quietness of the night a distant sound. No … yes … now louder, louder, but still very distant. Now – there

was no mistake now! It was a low-flying 'plane approaching ... The Lysander made a short landing, bumping strongly, stopped, braking briskly, turned sharp left and taxied quickly back to the take-off position near Adam. Running beside it, caught in the wind produced by the propeller, hearing the roar of the engine, Armand felt himself suddenly back in the Air Force – a pleasant feeling, temporarily suppressing any other sensation. Adam took the gramophone box and helped Armand to scramble upwards. Then he thrust the gramophone up into his outstretched hand and shouted: 'Good luck!'[14]

As WALENTY described it, after they landed at RAF Tangmere they were met by two officers, one of whom was Flight Lieutenant Philipson, the other a group captain who was the station commander. They were invited for drinks and dinner, then the next morning driven to London to meet with the liaison officer with Polish Intelligence, who Garby-Czerniawski referred to as 'Commander' and that he spoke seven languages, including Polish. This would have been Commander Wilfred 'Biffy' Dunderdale of SIS – 'a tall, slim, elegant man, with an extremely interesting and vivid face'. Later he was taken to the Rubens Hotel in Buckingham Palace Road, the headquarters of the Polish General Staff. There he met Colonel (later General) Stanisław Gano (1895–1968), the deputy head of Polish Intelligence, the Deuxième Bureau. Colonel Gano is regarded as the hero of Polish military intelligence who, in November 1941, became head of the Polish Deuxième Bureau. Gano then took him to see his deputy, Major Żychón – Jan Henryk Żychón (1902–44), who was later killed at the Battle of Monte Cassino on 17 May 1944 – and General Tadeusz Klimecki (1895–1943), the chief of the General Staff. Klimecki then took him to see General Sikorski, the Polish prime minister. Both Klimecki and Sikorski were killed in an air crash on 4 July 1943 at Gibraltar.

After only six days of being away, WALENTY received a message from VICTOIRE handed to him by Żychón:

'IMPORTANT STOP LA CHATTE TO VALENTIN STOP HAVE SERIOUS TROUBLE WITH KENT AND HIS FRIENDS STOP THEY REFUSE TO COOPERATE AND THREATEN SECESSION STOP WHAT SHOULD I DO STOP LA CHATTE.'[15]

On the strength of this message, he decided to cut his trip short and return to France, rightly believing that serious trouble could develop if he didn't nip it in the bud. He quickly sent a message back, saying: 'TO LA CHATTE STOP COMING BACK IN TWO DAYS STOP NO RECEIVING PARTY REQUIRED STOP GREETINGS TO ALL STOP VALENTIN.'[16] The message arrived on the day he was scheduled to jump, but the jump had to be cancelled because of the bad weather. That same day he was awarded the Virtuti Militari Cross.

The truth about why WALENTY was allowed to leave France with ADAM when KIKI had already been arrested and knew of the landing zone will become clearer as the story unfolds. Were the Germans complicit in facilitating his departure and turning a blind eye, and if so, for what reason? When he was arrested, had they hoped to 'turn' him and use him against the Allies?

When WALENTY returned to France on 7 November 1941, having parachuted from a Whitley bomber, he first went to live in the same house as VICTOIRE at 3, rue Cortot, but 'Les deux sorcières' accused him of being a Fifth Columnist, which scared him, so he went to live with VIOLETTE on the first floor of the Villa Léandre in which MAURICE was operating the transmitter. At that time VIOLETTE lived under her maiden name, Borni, while WALENTY called himself first Armand Borni, then Bornier. In the meantime, VICTOIRE moved into 6, rue Lamarck under the name BARREL but left all her papers at 3, rue Cortot, which she still used as an office. WALENTY then took a flat for himself and VIOLETTE in Asnières, a commune in the suburbs of north-western Paris, which he did not tell VICTOIRE about. His first task on being back was to deal with MARCEL, MAURICE's second-in-command. He also tackled VIOLETTE about the spat that had brought him back to Paris prematurely.

VIOLETTE told him that it was some friction that had occurred between VICTOIRE and Fernand Gane (MONO/KENT) over the fact that he resented having VICTOIRE in charge while WALENTY was away. Gane had suggested to VIOLETTE that he help her with the coding, but she had told him that the only person allowed to do that was herself, not even VICTOIRE. When VICTOIRE arrived that evening, he asked her about it. She told him that Gane (referred to as KENT) had started it all by quarrelling with her 'about some trifling things':

> There was no doubt that there was a dissentient tendency in Kent's mind, but knowing him I could feel that it was produced mostly because of friction

with *La Chatte*. The other motive could be a desire for far more freedom, independent action and initiative among the circle of friends he had introduced to our service.[17]

WALENTY managed to straighten things out with Gane, saying that he needed him, LOUIS and Aouta (MOUSTIQUE), whom he recognised as being experienced, to help him reorganise and make things more efficient and safe.

Patricia McCallum's report on the rift between the two women said that 'VIOLETTE was not only closer to BRUTUS but she seems also to have been a younger and prettier girl and very popular with other members of the group – notably with MAURICE, the W/T Chief, and with ADAM himself.' Certainly, from her photograph in the MI5 files, she is a young, attractive-looking woman, and nothing like the way VICTOIRE portrayed her, as aged 23, 5ft 2in tall, plump, with brown hair dyed platinum blonde, and a 'Jewish nose', which, in Harmer's opinion, was probably inaccurate. WALENTY described her as:

> Pretty, young with dark eyes. She was quiet but vivacious, had no high-school education, and no high-society background. She had no interest in literature, liked going occasionally to cafés and restaurants, seeing people and being among them, but she did not mix easily with them. She relaxed in cinemas but the theatre did not attract her. She was a perfect gay and pleasant companion with people whom she knew.

Whereas VICTOIRE was:

> Not exactly pretty, but interesting to men, a sophisticated type of woman, *une femme de lettres*, with Sorbonne background, society interests, ambitious, very often nervous and highly strung. She was interested in meeting people, being in the company of men – though never too long with any of them – and she tired of people who did not share her interests.[18]

MARCEL (François Tabet, also referred to as Henri Tabet)[19] was a radio operator brought in by VICTOIRE who she thought could help MAURICE; however, WALENTY considered him unstable and unreliable, always wanting money, and lazy. Because of this MAURICE was unable to get along with him and had given WALENTY unfavourable reports about him. What unnerved WALENTY even more was when MARCEL said that all it would take was one phone call to get them all arrested. He was so unpopular that WALENTY had paid him two weeks' leave and told him to get lost. Someone suggested killing him by putting him in the central heating furnace of a block of flats, or at the demarcation line. ADAM had even approached someone through CLAUDE who would have been willing to do the job for 20,000 francs. As it transpired, WALENTY approached MAURICE with a view to having MARCEL establish a radio station in Brittany in connection with a courier service as a quick means of communication, saying that VICTOIRE had vouched for him. He also set up a new post box at a café in the rue de la Palette in the Saint-Germain-des-Prés area of Montparnasse in the 6th arrondissement. This is possibly La Palette, which is on the corner of the rue de Seine and rue Jacques-Callot. Agents were instructed to bring their reports there instead of to the address in the rue de la Michodière in the 2nd arrondissement where they had an office.

When ADAM left for England on the night of 8/9 November from the same landing ground at Estrées St Denis he informed KIKI about the new post box. This did not sit well with KIKI, who did not like having to communicate with WALENTY through a post box that was only cleared three times a month (on the 4th, 14th and 24th of each month). ADAM (code-named BRICK) was also picked up by Nesbitt-Dufort along with 22-year-old Claude Lamirault (FITZROY), born 12 June 1918 and a founder member of the SIS *Jade-Fitzroy* network with Pierre Hentic.[20] Lamirault would later be arrested in 1943 at the Richelieu-Drouot Métro station at the intersection of the Boulevard Haussmann and the Boulevard des Italiens. He was deported to Dachau on 2 July 1944, where he would spend the rest of the war. He was killed in a car crash on 27 May 1945.

On 16 November, to celebrate the first anniversary of the *Interallié* network, WALENTY held a party to which VICTOIRE, VIOLETTE, RENÉ, MICHEL (Claude Jouffret), MAURICE, GEORGES and numerous other agents were all invited. WALENTY had announced at their celebration that it would be the last day of *Interallié*. 'What did this mean?' they asked. While he was in London he had been told that the name was to be changed to *Progress*, but he'd managed to delay the change until the day of the party. He could not possibly have known on that day that his announcement presaged the real end of the network. Two days later, on 18 November 1941, the principal members of the organisation, including himself, VICTOIRE and VIOLETTE, were arrested. By Christmas the entire network had been rolled up and was under German control, and *Interallié* was no more. One factor that had made it easy for the Germans was that WALENTY did not practise good operational security – he kept a card index of all his agents and the German order of battle in his flat, which, when the network was betrayed, made it easy for the Germans to round up so many members.

CHAPTER 8

Betrayal

The first raid came at the Villa Léandre on the morning of Tuesday 18 November. MAURICE (Włodarczyk) awoke at 5.30 a.m. to the sound of what he thought were gunshots, footsteps on the stairs and shouting. It was the Gestapo. Since WALENTY had not heard the bell ring, the Gestapo must have rung Madame Blavette, the concierge, to let them in. Ironically, he had planned to move yet again and had packed up all his things. In the flat above, MAURICE and GEORGE, who were staying with him, managed to escape over the rooftops. As MAURICE described in a report compiled by M.B. Stokes at the Royal Victoria Patriotic School (RVPS) on 28 May 1942:

GEORGE ran into his room saying that the Germans had broken into ARMAND's flat and then they could clearly hear commands being given in German. As neither WLODARCZYK nor GEORGE was armed and it was obvious that ARMAND had been trapped, they decided to escape, if possible …

WLODARCZYK and GEORGE dressed themselves hurriedly and by knotting together the sheets off the bed, they lowered themselves down to the small roof above the terrace at the back of the house. There they hesitated for a moment, not knowing, in the complete darkness, which way to turn; there was still no light from their windows. Then GEORGE decided to climb over the parapet to the next house. He jumped over, forgetting that the other was a glass roof and he crashed through the kitchen of the adjoining house. This, of course, caused a tremendous noise, but nothing happened.

With WLODARCZYK's assistance he climbed back on to the parapet, in spite of the bad cuts on his arms. They then began to climb the roof of the house opposite and moved along from roof to roof until they came to the point where two rows of houses joined, in the triangular block; they could, of course, proceed no further. They they found a fanlight through which they lowered themselves on to a staircase. They proceeded downstairs and, as the door was unlocked, they walked out into the street.

They went to GEORGE's parents' house where they washed and then left to warn the other members of the Organization. It was arranged that GEORGE should go to another of the wireless transmitters in order to inform London that the Organization had been discovered and the codes and secret papers etc. had fallen into German hands and they decided to meet again at the flat at 3 o'clock in the afternoon and, later on in the evening at the Station Montmartre where they were expecting to meet KIK [*sic* – obviously KIKI] – another member of the organization. As GEORGE did not appear at 3 p.m. WLODARCZYK was certain that he had been caught, so alone he went to the station in the evening and there he met GEORGE who told him that when he arrived at the house in which the wireless transmitter was installed, he went up to the third floor and knocked on the door. It was opened by a German soldier whom GEORGE pushed violently and ran back down the stairs. Some shots had been fired, he said, but nothing had happened to him.[1]

They escaped to Dax in the Landes sub-prefecture of Nouvelle-Aquitaine and crossed the demarcation line at Tartas, eventually making it to the safety of the Unoccupied Zone by way of Montpellier and Marseilles. MAURICE crossed into Spain on the night of 13/14 December and reported to the British consulate in Barcelona on the 15th. From there on 7 January 1942 he was sent to the British embassy in Madrid, where he stayed until 20 February. Accompanied by Lieutenant Jósef Rzepka ('Krzysztof' and 'Znicz') and two Belgians, he was sent back to Barcelona via Badajoz. At Gibraltar he embarked on the RMS *Llanstephan Castle* belonging to Union-Castle Mail Steamship Company on 4 May 1942 and arrived in Gourock on the Clyde, Scotland, on 11 May. He was taken on 14 May to the Camberwell Institute, an outstation of the London Reception Centre.[2] MAURICE's account of his escape is detailed in Chapter 9.

WALENTY and VIOLETTE were not so lucky and were arrested. Later MAURICE estimated that there had been up to six Gestapo members making the arrest. This set off a cascade in which almost every member of the network was rounded up. VICTOIRE's account offers the most details on a day-to-day basis of how this happened, which Harmer included in his extensive report, and will be referred to here.[3] However, she was not the only one involved, as it was noted in Kraus's MI5 file that:

On the information available it seemed clear that KRAUS was responsible for breaking up the effective VICTOIRE organisation. Previously Madame CARRÉ had been suspected of this, and whilst there was no reason to alter the conclusion reached in her case, there seemed no doubt that KRAUS was also responsible for this effective organisation being betrayed.[4]

VICTOIRE described that fateful Tuesday morning as 'cold and foggy. Montmartre seemed colder than elsewhere and Paris lay below shrouded in mist.' Not suspecting anything was amiss, she kept her meeting with MICHEL (Jean Lucien Kieffer) at 10.30 a.m. at the Café Lamarck. When no one turned up she went back to her rooms, where Mireille Lejeune told her that the rue Junot, where the Villa Léandre was located, was being searched. Realising that there was a problem, she went to the old apartment in the rue Cortot to retrieve some incriminating papers, and left instructions with Mireille that she was to destroy all her papers if VICTOIRE failed to return. Always the 'drama queen', she claimed that as she passed by the Sacré Coeur she felt as if people were watching and following her: 'I continued up the street when I suddenly sensed that the men who had been gossiping by the lamp post had started to follow me.' As Harmer noted, 'in any event we know she is so short-sighted that she could not have seen who was following her' – if indeed anyone was, at this stage. Her final undoing was when she stopped to speak to Alice, one of the 'deux sorcières', who was standing outside her home in the rue Cortot, and was arrested by a Gestapo official named Tritche.[5] 'You have made us wait a long time, Mme BARREL,' he said, to which she replied, 'I have played a good game and lost, but I have always been a good player.' While there is no proof, it is possible that Alice may have been acting as a look-out to warn Tritche when VICTOIRE approached and help identify her.

WALENTY described Tritche as being aged about 35 to 37, 6ft 2in tall, athletic and clean-shaven, looking like an intelligent boxer, well-dressed, very conceited and self-important.[6] He had previously been employed in a POW camp. Bleicher described him as stupid, conceited and completely 'Nazi-fied'. A message from TUDOR in Toulouse, which appeared in 'Report on Traffic of Walenty Station in Paris' dated 15 March 1942, stated:

Five agents of Walenty escaped into the free zone; they report that Walenty, his secretary and 14 other agents as well as the Post Box have been arrested by the Germans on the 18th November; all three W/T stations of Walenty as well as the codes are in German hands.

Tudor requests, therefore, for cessation of W/T work in PARIS, because the Germans are working on this station with HQ in London. Walenty was caught in bed with papers. Walenty was in the habit of writing down addresses. I never had any contacts with Walenty. Gloria contacted Walenty a few months ago but they did not know each other's addresses. I suppose that Walenty's arrest does not threaten our Officers' Post.[7]

The identity of Gloria has already been revealed; her involvement will be expanded upon in Chapter 13. A further report from Marseilles followed up on the arrests:

I wish to report that Walenty and approximately 14 of his agents were arrested by the Gestapo on the 18th November. To-day, five agents fled to me from there. Papers, 3 W/T sets, the codes of the whole network and the like have been caught. The station is in German hands. Please cease liaison at once. Listen in to me always at 15.30 hours.[8]

The reports in VICTOIRE's files of her arrest differ somewhat from this. According to the account compiled on 28 February 1942 the Gestapo took her first to the Hôtel Edouard VII at 39, Avenue de l'Opéra, described as one of the offices of the Gestapo in Paris; another document states it was on the rue Edouard VII, north of the Boulevard des Capucines.[9] Either way, the locations are close as the Boulevard des Capucines bisects the north of the Avenue de l'Opéra. Then at one o'clock she was taken to La Santé prison, where she was searched and all her possessions confiscated. The following morning at eight o'clock she was questioned by a captain of the Deuxième Bureau in the presence of two female interpreters. In this case, 'Deuxième Bureau' is taken to mean either the Abwehr or the GFP, not the French intelligence service. Harmer's report states that upon being arrested she was first taken back to the Place du Sacré Coeur, then to the Villa Léandre, where she was identified by VIOLETTE. When she was taken back to the Hôtel Edouard VII she was interrogated again by Captain Erich Borchers and the commissioner of the Gestapo at Cherbourg, with Hugo Bleicher and three or four other people present. The Gestapo also had an office behind the Bon Marché alongside the rue du Cherche-Midi, but in fact it was a few blocks away on the other side of the Boulevard Raspail.[10]

Harmer states: 'It is difficult to assess the exact moment that VICTOIRE's collaboration with the Germans began.' From what VICTOIRE related, it was on 19 November at eleven o'clock in the morning. What seemed strange to Harmer was a couple of the accounts she gave him: how first Tritche had complained of having no cigarettes and she had given him a packet of hers; the second was how she had complained about how damp and dirty the bed was where she was incarcerated, whereupon it was changed immediately, which, Harmer observed, 'appears to be most peculiar that an arrested spy should be treated so well before any interrogation or examination of her story'. He concluded that she had embellished her story to satisfy her own vanity. She was left alone for the rest of the day, but given dinner, consisting of four slices of meat, vegetables, bread, cheese and ersatz coffee. It seems overly generous for a spy to be given so much food, and not just bread and water.

As with any arrest of Resistance members, a certain amount of damage control immediately followed. After his escape, at around 8 a.m. MAURICE went to warn CHRISTIAN, but found he was not there so he left a message in Polish instructing him to get to Marseilles as quickly as possible. Then he telephoned his girlfriend, who was supposed to call at the Villa Léandre at 9 a.m., to warn her not to go there or she would be arrested, even though she had nothing to do with their organisation. MAURICE met her at a restaurant at the appointed time and summoned MAX. It was not until MAX arrived that they told him that WALENTY had been arrested, and said he had to warn MONO and MOUSTIQUE. Fortunately for the latter, they were able to escape to Marseilles and then proceed to England. GEORGES had managed to warn JAG about WALENTY's arrest. Later, when JAG met MAURICE he told him that when he went to VICTOIRE's flat, Alice had informed him that VICTOIRE had been arrested and shot herself that afternoon. This, of course, was incorrect.

The following day, the 20th, VICTOIRE awoke to be given a cup of coffee and was taken to La Santé prison, where she met an officer who gave her more coffee and a cigarette. From there she was taken back to the Hôtel Edouard VII and given a continental breakfast, of which she said, '*rien ne manquait*' ('nothing was left out'). They handed back the packet of cigarettes she had given Tritche, who was present together with Bleicher. As she recounted later, Bleicher told her:

Mme. BARREL, we have decided that you are too intelligent and too interesting to stay in prison. You know everything and you are going to be a valuable help to us in clearing up the whole INTERALLIEE affair. Having arrested WALENTY, we are in possession of all the documents, but we need you, because you are known by everybody, for the remaining arrests. I see in

your diary: 'Wednesday, 19th November, 9 o'clock Pam-Pam.' This means
that in a short time you are going to meet an agent; I will accompany you.
I will be in your organisation; you will introduce me as so-and-so, and when
this agent has spoken sufficiently I will arrest him. We will work thus, you
and I, and if you do not try to double-cross me you can be sure that you will
be free from to-night. If you betray me you will be immediately executed
without trial. Save your skin and regain your liberty. You have done quite
enough to be shot several times, having hidden this escaped Polish officer
and passed him off as your cousin, more than a year's espionage, and certainly
crossing the demarcation line clandestinely, and saving English people; all
things punishable by death and you know it. You had better save your skin
and start to understand that England is beaten. You can do similar sort of work
for 6,000 francs a month. England always makes other people do her work for
her and doesn't even know how to pay them.[11]

Whereupon they took her in a military car to the Pam-Pam restaurant.
Conveniently, she omitted to say in her statement that she had already agreed to
collaborate with the Abwehr.

Pam-Pam was a restaurant originally created by an American named Parker
to serve American-style steaks and hamburgers. It was purchased in the 1930s by
the Café de la Paix. One branch was at 73, Champs-Élysées, another at 5, Place
de l'Opéra. It attracted the likes of jazz musicians such as Stéphane Grapelli,
Michel Warlop, Jacques Hélian, Count Basie, Duke Ellington, Erroll Garner,
Ella Fitzgerald and Charles Aznavour. Harmer's report does not specify which
location they went to, although VICTOIRE's memoirs, in both the manuscript
and published form, describe them as arriving in the Champs-Élysées:

En arrivant aux Champs-Élysées la voiture s'arrêta et en descendant je lui fis
remarquer dans quell état j'étais : pas coiffée, sans chapeau, sans gants, sans sac, le
visage rincé à l'eau de la prison.

'When we arrived on the Champs-Elysée the car stopped, and when we got
out I remarked to him [Bleicher] about the state I was in: my hair wasn't
brushed, I had no hat, no gloves, no handbag, my face only washed with water
from the prison'.[12]

While they were at the restaurant Duvernoy (real name Wirtz) arrived. He
was one of VICTOIRE's contacts with Vichy. He sat down at her table and

talked openly about various matters of interest to the Deuxième Bureau after being reassured by her that Bleicher was 'a trusted friend'. Their conversation centred on the Vichy order of battle which he had promised to give her. As they were leaving the café Bleicher offered him a lift to his next appointment and then promptly arrested him, saying, '*Eh bien Monsieur, vous êtes maintenant dans une voiture de la Police Allemande et je vous arrête*' ('Well Monsieur, you're now in a car belonging to the German police and I'm arresting you'). VICTOIRE recorded that 'Duvernois [*sic*] turned green, literally green, for he was normally pasty-faced. He turned to me. "What a slut you are!"'[13] Bleicher later told him that he could save himself by betraying his comrades. Under questioning he readily gave away the entire Vichy set-up, and a man named Binet who was an inspector of finances at the Ministry of Finance. VICTOIRE's account goes on to say that he told Bleicher everything he needed to know about Vichy and 'wept like a woman'.

Bleicher knew from VIOLETTE that VICTOIRE called her mother every day and he ordered her to call her immediately. Her mother informed her that ONCLE MARCO and RENÉ had heard about the arrests and were worried about her. Bleicher told her to make a date with them to meet at the Café Graff. This was probably Chez Graff at 62, rue de Bellechasse in the 7th arrondissement, close to the rue Grenelle. Harmer thought that this was:

> … an example of what is probably a twist given by VICTOIRE to her story. Having justified the first arrest by saying it was written in her diary, she seeks justification of her next betrayal by the complicated story of VIOLETTE having given away that she telephoned her mother every day. VICTOIRE probably did telephone her mother every day, who gave away the message recounted above, but she embroiders the story and seeks to put the whole responsibility for the arrests of ONCLE MARCO and RENE on to VIOLETTE.[14]

Further arrests were to follow. At La Palette café, where VICTOIRE would go every day to pick up agents' reports, the proprietress, Madame Gaby, had been arrested but was then released. A Polish website claims that she was actually a lavatory attendant there.[15] While there, Bleicher was approached by a woman who he claimed to be his mistress, but he spoke to her harshly, and told VICTOIRE that since their meeting he was no longer interested in this woman. This was, as Harmer records, how Bleicher had started to play on her vanity, even though he believed it to be 'an inconceivable story', but VICTOIRE had fallen for it. Bleicher also told her that he wanted to arrest

Mireille, BOBY-ROLAND's wife, but VICTOIRE had tried to stop him. Contrary to VICTOIRE's instructions, Mireille had not burnt all the papers and had allowed the apartment to be ransacked, with most of VICTOIRE's possessions going missing. Bleicher blamed it on the French, who he said had taken advantage of the arrests, to which VICTOIRE declared, 'Oh, stupid sentimental Boche!'

When they went to the rue Lamarck Bleicher told her that VIOLETTE had given away the cipher and they had read all their latest messages, claiming that there should be half a million francs lying around. VICTOIRE retorted that if that were true about being able to read the cipher then he would have known that they only had 137,000 francs, which Mireille kept in a small box. She asked Mireille for the money and it is assumed that she handed it over to Bleicher. BOBY-ROLAND was hunted down and arrested at the Petit Palais and taken to Fresnes. There he sold out the entire Paris sector, Sector R. In an attempt to mitigate his act he claimed he had written to the Germans and denounced the organisation. Mireille was taken to La Santé but never said a word.

At dinner that evening at the Café Madeleine, 1, rue Tronchet, near the Place de la Madeleine in the 8th arrondissment, Bleicher introduced VICTOIRE to Erich Borchers and two other Germans. It was there, she claimed, that Bleicher had first started to make advances to her. As she described it in her memoirs, 'Bleicher spoke German, boasting of his successes and slapping me on the thigh, which only made him appear more repulsive in my eyes. I could not hide my disgust.' Ever the cynic, Harmer observes, 'Knowing VICTOIRE, one may be certain that the truth was the exact reverse.'

The trap had been set. At the Café Graff later that evening VICTOIRE sat alone at the bar at the end of the room waiting for the others to arrive. ONCLE MARCO arrived first, greeting her affectionately, and began to prepare a message for London; he also asked her for 12,000 francs. When RENÉ arrived he greeted her in much the same way, kissing her on the cheeks and calling her 'ma petite princesse' ('my little princess'). Bleicher then arrested them both. As VICTOIRE described in her memoirs:

> I trembled more violently. What thoughts could be going through the heads of my two friends at the moment? I had assured them that nothing had happened to me and now they had been arrested. They must have thought that I had betrayed them. It was true. But I could not have done otherwise. I could never have saved them. The wheels of fate ground inexorably and no miracle occurred.[16]

Following their arrest it was the turn of RICHARD NOEUD and his wife in the rue Lamarck. Their real name was Hugentobler, and they came from Alsace. When Bleicher and VICTOIRE entered their flat, Madame Hugentobler was preparing dinner. Also present were her husband, a 14-year-old daughter and a baby less than a year old: 'She was a large, emotional, very strong family person, happiest at this moment of the day surrounded by her family … His wife, a good soul, a domestic woman without guile, reacted with an outcry.'[17]

The daughter was hysterical as Madame Hugentobler was separated from her baby and the couple led off under arrest. She looked at VICTOIRE, whom she knew as Micheline, for some sort of explanation and begged her to intercede, but VICTOIRE reacted only by uttering 'Pardon', as the couple were dragged away. Bleicher was reported as saying, 'France will look after your children.' As Gordon Young was to add, it was 'The Cat's cruelest stroke of all', because while NOEUD never spoke, his wife hanged herself in her cell that night. What became of the children is unknown. Garby-Czerniawski would later dedicate his book to Lucien de Rocquigny and Madame Hugentobler, 'who died in its service'. Ironically, while expressing an element of remorse for what she had done to ONCLE MARCO and RENÉ, VICTOIRE wrote nothing about her feelings on the arrest of the Hugentoblers.

VICTOIRE's account of MARCO's arrest was contradicted in an account written by Major William E. (Billy) Luke of B1a to Christopher Harmer on 24 July 1945. Two questions had been put to ONCLE MARCO in Paris: (1) Was VICTOIRE entirely responsible for his arrest? (2) Had she any opportunity of warning him? To the first question was an emphatic 'Yes, entirely.' Further qualification was to come:

(a) Because she called him on the phone though it was by no means necessary (her argument about her Mother asking her to call MARCO as soon as possible is undoubtedly false). Oncle MARCO was not at all trying to get in touch with her by that time.

(b) She said to MARCO that there was a long time since she had the pleasure of seeing him and initiated an urgent appointment so that she could 'recevoir des fleurs de son jardin' (receive flowers from his garden).

(c) When MARCO keeps the appointment at 'Café GRAFF,' VICTOIRE openly produced two false identity cards 'in blank' in such a funny way that MARCO did not touch them and asked her what was the idea. As VICTOIRE insisted on MARCO taking the cards, he thought it so extraordinary that he asked her to put them herself in a book that was lying on the table. VICTOIRE took a long time to do so.

(d) VICTOIRE is lying when she says that MARCO asked her for twelve thousand francs. [*sic*] In fact, it is she who asked MARCO for some money (and it was not the first time) and MARCO, owing to the insistence of VICTOIRE, gave her a thousand francs.[18]

The answer to the second question, Luke reported, was also 'undoubtedly yes'. He concluded that she could have easily warned MARCO either on the telephone, or through her mother. She could have even done so at the Café Graff, if only to prevent RENÉ's arrest. She had insisted that he also come to the café, thereby ensuring that he would be arrested.

VICTOIRE and Bleicher slept together that night at Maisons-Lafitte, where the famous French film actor Harry Baur (1880–1943) lived in the guard house at 39, rue des Côtes. Baur was later arrested and tortured by the Gestapo for allegedly being a Communist and a Jew. Reflecting on the events of her first day of betrayal, Harmer itemised several points 'worthy of mention':

The first is that whatever the responsibility of, for example, VIOLETTE, whom VICTOIRE blamed for having betrayed people wantonly, it was VICTOIRE who accompanied BLEICHER from the start and acted as the decoy for arresting the agents. There can be no better proof than this being that, of the people arrested, the Germans regarded VICTOIRE as being their most valuable ally. Secondly, it will be observed that on the evening of the first day's collaboration VICTOIRE was allowed to go into the bar of the café alone and talk to two people she was supposed to meet, without BLEICHER being in her company. Thirdly, of course, her relations with BLEICHER had developed in a phenomenal way since 11 o'clock when he had first proposed collaboration. Knowing VICTOIRE, it is absolutely certain that this was largely a result of her wishes, and the fact that a responsible German officer was prepared to fall in with them demonstrates the importance they attached, even at that stage, to obtaining her collaboration.[19]

The day after the arrests VICTOIRE reflected on what she had done:

Now I was fully cognisant of the greatest act of cowardice in my life committed on 19th November with Bleicher. It was a purely animal cowardice, the reaction of a body which had survived its first night in prison, had suffered cold, felt the icy breath of death and suddenly found warmth once more in a pair of arms … even if they were the arms of the enemy. I hated myself for my weakness and as a result of my abasement I hated the Germans even more. That morning under my cold shower I swore that one day I would make the German pay.[20]

In the days that followed, TUDOR sent messages from Toulouse and from Marseilles (already cited) informing British Intelligence of the arrests.

Report from Marseilles: I wish to report that Walenty and approximately 14 of his agents were arrested by the Gestapo on the 18th November. To-day, five agents fled to me from there. Papers, 3 W/T sets, the codes of the whole network and the like have been caught. The station is in German hands. Please cease liaison at once. Listen in to me always at 15.30 hours.

One of the five agents who fled was MAURICE. His report on his escape is the subject of the next chapter.

CHAPTER 9

MAURICE's Escape

The following report sent from Madrid on 29 January 1942 addressed to 'William' offers up a clearer, more detailed account of the arrests and break-up of *Interallié*. 'William' refers to Wilfred Dunderdale of SIS; Harmer explained that MAURICE's report was set out in a letter from the Poles to Dunderdale. It is worth repeating in full:

Dear William,

I am sending you herewith details concerning the arrest of the Chief of our Intelligence Office 'Progress', WALENTY, and his collaborators, on 18.11.41 by the Gestapo. The developments are described in a partial report may by MAURICE, the W/T operator of the Intelligence Office 'Progress', who was able to escape from France to Spain. On 13.1.42, MAURICE submitted his report, dated 9.1.42, to our Chief Agent 'M' MADRID. MAURICE sent the following information:

MADRID – 9.1.42

'MAURICE'

Report for the Period 18.1.11 to 15.12.41

I wish to add the following details to my report sent via MARSEILLE concerning 'VALENTIN's and 'VIOLETTE's arrest and my escape.

The arrest took place on 18.11.41 at 0530 hours in a small two-storeyed villa, 8 rue Villa Léandre/Montmartre/, where the W/T station No.1 and my apartment were situated and where VALENTIN [WALENTY] and VIOLETTE temporarily took up their abode. The ground floor was occupied by the owner, Mme BLAVETTE, the first floor by Valentin and Violette, and the second floor by the W/T station and myself. 'GEORGE', who was awaiting his departure for England at the time, spent the night in the room in which the W/T station was placed.

On 18.11.41, at 0530 hours, I was awakened by the noise of the door on the first floor being broken down, one revolver shot, the noise of

6 or 7 persons talking German, heavy footsteps on the stairs – then I heard VALENTIN's voice, several German orders, and then I understood what had happened. As I had neither arms nor dynamite, / these things were in VALENTIN's flat / I could offer no help whatever, and so, after brief consideration, I destroyed the code and the plan of work which I had with me. Wishing to warn the remaining members of the organisation of the impending danger, I decided somehow to escape. At that moment, GEORGE, who was asleep in the next room and who had been awakened like myself, caught up some of his clothes and rushed into my room; having made an improvised rope of torn-up sheets and tied it to the window in my room which faced the back of the house, we crawled on to the roofs of the houses facing rue Caulincourt [sic – it should be Caulaincourt], which runs parallel to rue Villa Léandre, but the level of which is some seven storeys lower. While we were descending past the window of the room where the arrest was taking place, I managed to hear a German telephoning. We finished dressing on one of the roofs and while trying to find our way in the dark we fell on to a neighbouring roof which happened to be a whole storey lower and got bruised and wounded. GEORGE was bleeding and marked our track with blood. After a long time we succeeded in reaching the attic of one of the houses by breaking a skylight. We descended the staircase and got through the yard and the gate and got to the Avenue Coulincourt [sic]. Thanks to the darkness we got safely to GEORGE's cousin who lives near the Place Clichy. After dressing our wounds and supplementing our wardrobe, we separated at 7.a.m. in order to go and warn as many as possible of the people concerned. I tried to telephone from this quarter, but two call-boxes and the telephone in one bistro were out of order, so I suppose that as soon as our escape was noticed all telephones in Montmartre were put out of order. Fearing that I might be caught on the Métro stations, because I had an identity card issued in the name in which the flat was leased, and unfortunately I had left my other identity cards in the flat, I proceeded on foot, carefully avoiding police agents, to the flat of the third Pole, CHRYSTIAN [sic], in order to warn him. Unfortunately, he was already out and I suppose that he had gone to see VALENTIN. I telephoned therefore to one of our helpers, a young Frenchwoman, asking her to watch CHRYSTIAN's flat. I myself warned the second W/T operator, MAX, and agents MONO and MOUSTIQUE. GEORGE warned JACK and EDGAR. At 1200 hours I met JACK and GEORGE and I sent the former to warn LILI/CHATTE/

and the latter to EDWARD. In the afternoon I proceeded with MAX to the W/T station No.2/13, rue Miguel Hidalgo/ in order to establish liaison with LONDON. Unfortunately, I had to answer London calling us with crystals belonging to W/T set No.2. / Those of No.1 were caught in rue Léandre / and London did not hear us. After very many unsuccessful attempts I had to wait till the following day. I left the crystals with MAX and instructed him to proceed on the morrow to W/T station No.3/86, Faubourg St. Honoré / during the hours set for liaison as the transmitting set there was stronger.

At 1900 hours I met GEORGE and JACK. It appeared that LILI was arrested during the afternoon in her flat together with EDWARD. She fired, seriously wounding two or three Germans and it may be assumed that she poisoned herself by taking one of our pills which she always carried on her. Somewhat later the Frenchwoman detailed to watch CHRYSTIAN's flat returned with appalling news. CHRYSTIAN did not return home and by about 1700 hours the Gestapo was already on the spot. I began to suspect that under 'pressure' VIOLETTE must have betrayed the address of LILI and CHRYSTIAN. I spent the night with GEORGE at W/T station No.2, the address of which was known only to MAX and myself.

On 19.11 at 10.00 hours I sent GEORGE to Station No.3 where he was to meet MAX and from whence, after notifying LONDON, they were both to proceed to Station No.2 at 14.00 hours for a general conference. I myself met the Frenchwoman mentioned above, from whom I borrowed some money and received suggestions concerning the route by which one might despatch [sic] someone to MARSEILLE in order to organize work. Neither MAX nor GEORGE returned until 15.00 hours, which again convinced me that VIOLETTE must have betrayed us, as the address of station No.3 was again known only to WALENTY, VIOLETTE, MAX and myself. So I lost my last crystals, the W/T set, again two workers, the 'archives' and the tiny stock of arms which were placed there. At 19.00 hours I met JACK, EDGAR, and, thank God, GEORGE. The latter gave the following explanation: 'In the rue St. Honoré he had encountered Germans in the doorway, but in spite of pursuit and shots he succeeded in making his escape. He did not come to HIDALGO, because he feared that there too there might be people caught and he was sure that I too had got caught.' He drew up a balance sheet of the general position and considered what to do next. He had no money, no means of establishing liaison with LONDON and GEORGE and myself were pursued by the police and Gestapo.

As the Gestapo got hold of all our things, the whole material and even some of our means of liaison, there was danger that they might try and work 'under cover of our firm' and I hardly need explain what results that would have brought about. It is true that my escape and GEORGE's checked them slightly, but it became the more urgent to notify LONDON and MARSEILLE; because among the archives which had fallen into German hands was included the whole numbering of the stations/ NICE, MARSEILLE, TOULOUSE, etc. / We decided that JACK and EDGAR should wait for COCO, who was due to arrive from BORDEAUX, and that together they would undertake everything in their power to prevent the catching of a larger number of victim[s]. GEORGE and myself were to warn MARSEILLE. At 21.50 hours, after luckily slipping through the German control, we left from the Gare d'Austerlitz.

On 20.12 at 09.00, we were at DAX, from whence we walked to TARTAS, about 30km away. Here we obtained the necessary directions and some food. That evening we proceeded, partly on foot and partly by bus to HAGEDMONDE, situated on the frontier.

On 21.11.41 at 00.30 hours we successfully crossed the demarcation line, by walking from early morning we reached AIR SUR ONDE, and thence proceeded by train to MARSEILLE.

On 22.11.41, at 01.40, dropping with exhaustion, we had to stop at MONTPELLIER. Here after a short rest, I obtained, thanks to GEORGE's contacts, 'new' identity cards and sent out a short report to our H.Q. through the local representative of I.S. [Intelligence Service] / I do not know if it arrived, it was signed 'VOLTA' /

On 23.11. at 01.00 hours we left MONTPELLIER, at 00.00 hours we reached MARSEILLE. We succeeded in avoiding police control and at 09.00 hours I was already seeing Mr.Z. [This implies that TUDOR was indeed Wincenty Zarembski referred to earlier]. I reported to him the whole course of events, and of the winding up of NICE, as the Post most easily caught. As we continued to be uncertain whether matters in MARSEILLE had not come to a head / we thought VIOLETTE might have known the address /, we agreed that I only would enter the building, and if I should not get out after 5 minutes, it would mean that I had been caught and GEORGE would make his escape. Unfortunately, after about 4 minutes an automobile full of police drove into this street and the waiting GEORGE, expecting the worst, left immediately for MONTPELLIER, whence he sent a second message to H.Q. / signed VOLTA /.

Mr.Z. instructed me to wait for a few days in order that he might organize my escape to Spain. After leaving him after 5 minutes, I did not find GEORGE and in the evening I left in the direction of TOULOUSE. By a miraculous coincidence, when changing trains at TOULOUSE, I met GEORGE on his way to MONTPELLIER. / I must mention that the 'new' identity cards were issued by the Mairie [Town Hall] at MONTPELLIER. / Overjoyed, we made plans for further escape. I gave the address of the friends I was going to, and he was to notify me should he have any news via the I.S.

On 29.11. I received instructions from agent JACK, /sec[tor]. TOULOUSE /, to proceed to PERPIGNAN.

On 2.12 I was in PERPIGNAN and after waiting until 13.12.41 I left for Spain via the PYRENEES.

On 15.12 I reported to the British Consulate in BARCELONA.

On 7.1.42 I reported to the British Embassy in MADRID.

Since my departure from France, GEORGE has not given a sign of life, and I have no idea what has become of him.

To sum up: the following were arrested; VIOLETTE, VALENTIN, LILLI, EDWARD, CHRISTIAN, MAX and probably two or three more agents, who were to report on that day to VALENTIN.

The Gestapo got hold of the whole '*etat major*' [general staff] codes /old and new /, originals of reports already sent or prepared for despatch [*sic*], copies of telegrams, money, identity cards, seals, stamps, etc, 2 W/T sets, complete with crystals, which were in archives, als[o] the codes which were on MAX when he was caught, as well as the plans of work, numbering of stations and list of crystals and the photographic laboratory. I do not know in detail what else was in WALENTY's possession, but I suppose that there were no names or localities where agents were at work in the original papers.

This dreadful breakdown and the terrible loss in men must be ascribed to fatal coincidence, and under no circumstances to the watchfulness of the Gestapo.

Two facts go to prove this contention irrefutably:

1. If our organization had been watched, trailed and discovered, the arrests would have taken place on our 'feast day', i.e. 16.11, when all important agents and chiefs of sectors gathered at WALENTY's flat.

2. On 18.11, when breaking in on WALENTY, they would have immediately broken into my flat above, thus preventing my escape.

On the day when he was arrested WALENTY was to have changed his habitation. The fact that he was taken by surprise, prevented him from using arms and destroying all the material by means of a small charge of dynamite. He was simply taken by surprise in bed, his way cut off from everything, ~~prepared for the~~ the cupboard standing at the other end of the room, where everything, prepared for the move, had been accumulated. The disposition of the flat did not allow me to take with me, before making my escape, the crystals and to destroy the W/T set and photographic laboratory. I had the choice either of destroying them and being caught or leaving them and escaping. I chose the latter alternative for reasons previously stated. Even the destruction of that station would not have amounted to much in view of the fact that VIOLETTE knew MAX's address.

I do not know what happened afterwards, but I am sure that the remaining chiefs of sectors and single agents/ as MONO, JACK, EDGAR and MOUSTIQUE kept assuring me/ would be willing to continue working. I myself would gladly return to this work if it were only possible.

If it is possible please arrange that during the evening broadcast of news in French at 20.15 hours, the following message should be given for our agents and people who are left in PARIS and who helped me to escape, both materially and morally: 'Pour YOYO and MARGUERITE: JANEK boit whisky.' ['For YOYO (YOLÉ?) and MARGUERITE: JANEK drinks whisky.'] This will be a signal for them that we were not caught and that we will not let anyone down and for JACK and EDGAR it will be a signal that the reorganization of work will take place in the future/if it has not already taken place /.

MAURICE

MADRID – 9.1.42

In sending you the above I wish to inform you that we are trying to establish through our own channels further details concerning the factors which might have contributed to the liquidation of WALENTY, and we shall not fail to let you know anything we find out.

In order to give you an idea of the position, I am giving you a list of the persons mentioned in the report:

1. 'VALENTIN' – WALENTY, chief agent of 'PROGRESS' – Capt. CZERNIEWSKI [sic].
2. 'VIOLETTE' – young Frenchwoman, assisted WALENTY – codes.

3. 'LILLI' – LA CHATTE, Frenchwoman, WALENTY's secretary.
4. 'MAURICE' – W/T operator from PROGRESS. Pole, name: WLODARCZYK.
5. 'MAX' – W/T operator, French officer.
6. 'GEORGE' – agent 1620, French, air force N.C.O. Head of sector 'G'.
7. 'AOUTA-MOUSTIQUE' – agent 296, French. Head of sector 'A'.
8. 'EDGAR' – agent 1550, French. Air Force N.C.O. Head of sector 'E'.
9. 'COCO' – agent 294, French. Air Force N.C.O. Head of sector 'C'.
10. 'VOLTA' – Head of photographic laboratory.
11. 'MONO' – agent 1580, present pseudonym 'KENT'. French air force N.C.O. Head of sector 'K'.
12. 'JACK' – probably agent 279 'YAG'. Formerly registered as 'JACK'. Pole, N.C.O. micro photographer worked in sector 'Y'.
13. 'EDWARD' – unknown, not registered with 'PROGRESS'.
14. 'CHRYSTIAN' – "   " "   '   '
15. Z. – Major ZAREBSKI [sic], Chief of Intelligence Office 'F' – MARSEILLE.

I am firmly convinced that VALENTIN, VIOLETTE, LA CHATTE, MAX and several others are in the hands of the Gestapo. I think that all three W/T stations together with codes, ciphers, and the whole archives fell into German hands. The mere fact that telegrams from PARIS are now signed VICTOIRE, gives one furiously to think. It seems to signify the Gestapo's victory over us. We have had no information of an intelligence character from PARIS since WALENTY's arrest, and yet if LA CHATTE, now allegedly VICTOIRE, wished to inform us simply of the things she sees, we would be having some intelligence information from time to time.

She knew the methods of work, knew the agents, was in touch with them so she would not have found it too difficult to establish contact with them. I think therefore that VICTOIRE is the Gestapo and that we are in contact with the Gestapo – although the future may prove that I am mistaken.[1]

Clearly, MAURICE was wrong when he claimed that VICTOIRE 'fired, seriously wounding two or three Germans and it may be assumed that she poisoned herself by taking one of our pills' as there is no evidence to suggest that she had a firearm or used it; nor does she claim to have done so. Had she fired, being so shortsighted, she would have probably missed anyway! A bit of dramatic licence to embellish his account, which tends to make it somewhat suspect. As Harmer noted when he wrote to Ronnie Haylor of B1d (Camp 020) on 21 May 1942 on behalf of Tar, MAURICE's evidence on the break-up of the network would be invaluable to them because he had stayed behind in Paris for a few days after the arrests, but:

> His report made in Marseilles quite obviously needs clarification in certain points and he ought to be questioned thoroughly on this ... It will ~~would~~ aid us considerably in investigating her case [VICTOIRE] when ~~if~~ we ~~could~~ have the unbiased testimony of MAURICE.[2]

Harmer added that Janusz Włodarcyzk was someone known to MI5 and SIS as MAURICE. This was followed up by a visit to MAURICE at the RVPS on 23 May 1942, together with Captain Scott, whom he described as the examiner there, Major Langenfeld and Lieutenant Ehrenburg of the Polish Deuxième Bureau.[3] According to a report by the NKVD (Narodni Kommissariat Vnutrennikh del, the Soviet People's Commissariat for Internal Affairs) in Nigel West's *Triplex*, Captain Scott (cover name 'Stokes') was head of the Polish section at the RVPS.[4] As Harmer reported:

> MAURICE does not seem to have any definite idea as to how the WALENTY organisation came to be broken up beyond a vague reference to a friend of one of the agents, who was a Pole and might have betrayed them. He thinks, however, that immediately on her arrest VIOLETTE gave everything away. He obviously does not suspect VICTOIRE, nor did we inform him that VICTOIRE was in this country. I did tell him that ADAM was in this country and suggested a joint meeting which he thought would be a good idea.
>
> It will be remembered that VICTOIRE's account of the break-up of the organisation disclosed a ~~change~~ chain starting with KIKI who betrayed CHRISTIAN, who in turn gave away WALENTY's address. She has always said that CHRISTIAN was not at the big meeting on November 16th. MAURICE was convinced that CHRISTIAN was present in spite of the fact that I pressed him on this point. Here, therefore, there is a clear inconsistency. MAURICE had never heard of Mme. BUFFET so that I do not think we will get any vital information out of him.[5]

Copies of Harmer's report were also sent to Major Foley and Tom Greene at SIS.

It is perhaps appropriate that at this point we should turn away briefly from VICTOIRE, and examine Bleicher's early career.

CHAPTER 10

Colonel Henri's Story

The title of this chapter is also the title of Hugo Bleicher's memoirs, first published in 1954.[1] His book states, 'These war memoirs of Hugo Bleicher were related to Captain Erich Borchers, formerly of the German Intelligence Service,' yet the editor's Preface claims, 'the German edition of this book was published under the authorship of Erich Borchers.' As Borchers was his superior officer, the editor suggested that it may have been ghost-written by him. What is surprising is that Bleicher should have confided his story to Borchers at all for, as we saw earlier, Bleicher had spoken disparagingly about him. Perhaps by the time the war was over he had few friends left to tell it to. Equally remarkable is that Bleicher is decidely reticent about what he describes in his book as being a 'landmark in my career in Intelligence', the 'Allied Circle', as he calls it, or *Interallié*. Instead of capitalising on it and getting as much mileage out of it as possible, as one might expect, the dearth of information about it is in direct contrast to his boastful nature, as noted by the various spies with whom he came into contact. As a consequence, he is also coy about his relationship with VICTOIRE, to the point where he doesn't even mention her!

Bleicher was not, in fact, a colonel at all; he was a Feldwebel, or sergeant in the Abwehr, German Military Intelligence, seconded from the GFP. 'Colonel HENRI' was one of many aliases he adopted; others being 'Monsieur JEAN', 'VERBECK' and 'Jean CASTEL'. When Squadron Leader Terence Elliot Beddard[2] debriefed him at Camp 020 on 2 July 1945, Bleicher said that he was called Monsieur JEAN:

> … vis-à-vis all my agents and throughout the whole of my stay in France, i.e. from November 1941 until July 1944; Colonel HENRI alone that I am known to Captain FRAGER @ PAUL and by his connections Colonel BUCKMASTER, London, Major BODINGTON and finally Captain Pieter [*sic*] CHURCHILL.[3]

When he was in Cherbourg during the summer of 1941 his identity was Jean CASTEL, which was also the name of one of Suzanne's friends. Suzanne, who came to feature in his life at that time, will be discussed later. Jean VERBECK was the name he went by to the porter and owners of the various apartments where he and Suzanne lived in Paris.[4]

Hugo Ernst Bleicher was born in Tettnang, Germany, a town in the Bodensee district in south Baden-Württenberg, known as Swabia, 7 kilometres from Lake Constance, on 9 August 1899. His father was Karl Bleicher, the owner of a large bicycle store, and his mother was Emma (*née* Vogel). He had two brothers, Karl and Oscar. Before the Second World War Bleicher was an agent for a chemical firm in Hamburg. His file notes that he was taken prisoner during the First World War as a spy in British uniform, although he also does not mention this in his book either.

The various people with whom he came into contact remember him as being between 5ft 10in and 6ft tall, of strong build, but growing fat, and round-shouldered; with either greying or brown hair; a puffy red face, hooked nose, dark eyes, and wearing glasses. The MI5 report gives his weight as 12 stone 5lb, height 5ft 10in, well built, oval face with a longish nose, brown eyes, and brown hair receding at the forehead. WALENTY's description of him bears a passing resemblance to these. VICTOIRE described him as having a clumsy gait, saying he 'walks like an elephant'. He never drank, was intelligent, quick-witted and always boasting. WALENTY also said he was invariably slovenly dressed in civilian clothes. He spoke German, French (with a Belgian accent), English and Spanish. The photograph in his file shows a high forehead, with greasy hair combed back away from his face, and a down-turned mouth.

Between 1906 and 1910 he was educated at the local Volkschule in Tettnang, then in 1910 transferred to the Realschule, where he stayed until 1912. After completing his education at the Oberrealschule in Ravensburg (1912–13) and passing the 'Einjäerhrig-Freiwillinger' (one-year volunteer) examination, he wanted to either join the navy or become a concert pianist, but neither was to be. His eyesight was considered too poor for the navy, and he lacked the talent to be a professional musician (although his file says that he was an excellent pianist). He therefore went to work from 1914 to 1916 in the Gewerbebank, Ulm, Filiale Ravensburg in Kirchstrasse 7, thanks to his father, who knew the manager. From 1916 to 1917 he stayed on with the bank until in June 1917 he was called up and served first as a private in the Infantry, then in the Pioneer Gas Corps. He was captured on the Somme and taken to British POW camp 165 near Abbeville. An attempted escape failed and he was finally repatriated to Germany in 1919.

At the end of 1919 he went to Wiesbaden with a Frau Favre and her daughter Lilly, with whom he had fallen in love, and worked for a year for M. Glasser with the railways of the Occupied Rhineland. In 1921 he worked in Mainz as an interpreter in an office for compulsory taxation, where he succeeded in becoming its head. At the end of 1922 he returned home to Tettnang, then went to Hamburg where his aunt Marie worked as a lady's maid to the wife of General Levinski [sic]. This may have been Fritz Erich George Edouard von Lewinski, who was also known as General Erich von Manstein (1887–1970). If so, von Manstein's wife was Jutta Sybill Viktoria Elisabeth von Loesch (1900–66), 'a slightly built, dark-haired girl of 19 years, delicate physically but of strong character'[5] whom he had married in 1920. Lewinski helped him to get a job with an export firm in Hamburg, Afrikanische Händelskompagnie, run by M. Gleichman von Oven, which mainly dealt with North Africa. This company amalgamated in 1924 with several other companies and became known as E.L.K.A. Irish novelist Edward Jerrard Tickell, an early biographer of Odette Churchill (née Hallowes), writing about Bleicher in 1949 states:

> It was galling indeed for the suave and cultured Bleicher to have to own to an aunt in domestic service and even more galling to be forced to accept the General's good offices in getting a job. He would have preferred the approach to have been through the drawing-room rather than the servants' hall but he took the post offered him and immediately severed all connection with his aunt.[6]

This revealing description shows that Bleicher was not only a snob and pretentious, but even at this early stage he was prepared to use people, including his own family, to his own ends.

It is curious how much access Tickell must have had to at least some of Bleicher's file at such an early time. The frontispiece to the chapter 'Portrait of Henri' in his book on Odette Churchill[7] depicts the front page of the MI5 'Interim Interrogation Report' on Bleicher, complete with photograph and personal details. Given that the files on Bleicher and Odette were not released to the Public Record Office until at least fifty years later in 1999, and Tickell had been dead since 1966, how had he obtained access to what would then have been considered secret records?

Matthew Sweet's book *The West End Front* sheds some light on Tickell's wartime career that may help to explain this, at least partially. Tickell had joined the British Censorship Department from the advertising agency for which he was working and was transferred in 1940 to MC5, the Ministry of Information's Postal Censorship Service, at that time located in the Littlewoods Pools building in Liverpool. But as Sweet notes, 'Until his MI5 file is declassified, it will be impossible to say for certain why this happened, but police records insist that his political views had made him obnoxious to his colleagues.'[8]

There is more to this than meets the eye, linked to a scandal that was covered up. In 1940 Tickell joined the Royal Army Service Corps (RASC), first as a driver and then commissioned in 1941, serving in the Quartermaster General's Department of the War Office on unspecified 'special duties'.[9] Could this have meant MI5? Between 1943 and 1945 he was in Africa and the Middle East, which could have meant being assigned to SIME (Security Intelligence Middle East) or even SOE. This may explain why his name does not appear in the *Army List* for 1943. His postings to Washington DC, Canada, and the West Indies may have had something to do with British Security Coordination, although there is no mention of him in the official record of the organisation. He was also in Europe, and in 1945 appointed to the General Staff. As noted in Sweet's book, Tickell became embroiled in a murder charge in 1941, involving an illegal abortion for Margaret Pickwoad who, according to Sweet, was Tickell's girlfriend – referred to as 'Helen Mary Pickword' in her Metropolitan Police file – who had become pregnant by him, but he succeeded in getting off lightly.[10]

The company sent Bleicher to Tetuan, Morocco, to manage the Bazaar Aleman and he maintained contact with the German Colony there. As Tickell wrote, he 'looked forward keenly to the sunshine, the palms and the golden-skinned girls of the Mediterranean'. When the company went bankrupt in October 1927 he returned to Hamburg. In 1928 he found a job as a foreign correspondent with the Jewish firm of Bodenheimer, Schuster & Co. (founded by Hermann Bodenheimer and Joseph Elias Schuster), exporter of chemicals, through Max Friedrich, whom he had met in Morocco. The firm is listed in the Hamburg telephone directory as being a manufacturer of surgical products in bulk and for export at Kaiser Wilhelm Strasse

89.91 Mercurhof in Hamburg. Later, in 1936, with the rise of Hitler and anti-Semitism in Germany, the company's name would be changed to Wilhelm Friedrich & Co.

In 1928 he married Luzie, or Lucie, (*née* Mueller); their son Gerhard was born in 1936. That same year, 1936, Bleicher joined the Nazi Party for appearances' sake for the firm. 'How much he actually believed in Hitler is hard to say. Some of his subsequent actions indicated that his was merely lip-service and that he was ready to hitch himself ... to any star that happened to be in the ascendant.'[11]

When war was declared in September 1939 Bleicher was put on the reserve list and in October he applied to work in Postal Censorship as they needed people with foreign languages. As noted earlier, he spoke four in total. He waited, but heard nothing until November when he was called up for military service and told to report to Hindenberg Barracks, still thinking it was to do with Postal Censorship. As he recounted in his memoirs:

> We did not have to do much reading of letters. We were fitted out in uniform from head to foot, received our packs, side-arms, steel helmets and gasmasks [*sic*]. Was that all for the censorship of letters? Something seemed to be wrong. ... At last at the beginning of December we were mustered and a captain explained to us that we were to become a new formation and were to be trained in Duisberg. He did not say anything about postal censorship, but he hinted that our call-up had been camouflaged.[12]

This unit became the Geheime Feldpolizei (GFP) Gruppe 312, formed on 26 August 1939 at Küstrin. In May 1940 the entire Gruppe was sent to The Hague. In June he was posted to Rugles, near Verneuil in the Eure département of Haute-Normandie. He wrote that the entire Gruppe was posted to Paris at the end of July to handle the security for the route that Hitler would take during his triumphal arrival in France. When this did not take place, after two weeks the Gruppe was posted back to Rugles. In fact, Hitler had visited Paris on 23 June 1940, so Bleicher was mistaken, unless a second visit had been planned.

In August 1940 he was posted to Caen in Normandy, where he met Suzanne Laurent (*née* Renouf), the beautiful *patronne* of the Bar Pelican in the rue d'Auge[13] with whom he became entranced, and who became his mistress. That Bleicher was a womaniser does not really become apparent in his book, but in somewhat of a swoon he talks about her:

A fine face, under deep brunette hair. It was a face of such unusual beauty than on an impulse I was through the door and into the bar … I was quite out of this world … That was my Suzanne. Twenty-five years old, a striking beauty.[14]

The woman he had spoken to so harshly in front of VICTOIRE at the La Palette café could not have been Suzanne, unless this was all a charade, as he continually refers to her being with him in 1942 and later, long after the thrill of VICTOIRE had subsided. There are also references to her in 1945, as we shall see later. Where his wife was all this time is unclear, but most likely in Germany. Bleicher's file supplied details of many Abwehr agents, some of whom were recruited by him. One of these was Suzanne, a portrait of whom appears in Bleicher's book.[15]

—*m*—

Marie-Suzanne Laurent was born on 2 February 1914 in Laize-la-Ville, in the Calvados département of Normandy, and had a sister, Renée. When her husband died, Suzanne bought the Bar Pelican in Cherbourg. In September, while Gruppe 312 was posted to St Lô in the Manche département of Normandy, she visited Bleicher regularly. When, in March 1941, he was posted to Cherbourg, she sold the bar and lived with him, moving with him to Paris in November 1941 and setting up their apartment at 31 bis, Boulevard Suchet, near the Bois de Boulogne and the Musée Marmottan. According to a document in the National Archives & Records Administration in Washington DC, artworks from the apartment belonging to a Monsieur A. Touche, which had been requisitioned by the Germans, disappeared during their occupancy, given as 1 December 1941 to 20 August 1944. These included two cases of Sèvres porcelain, a Persian carpet, 690 volumes of books, 18 drypoint prints, etc.[16] Later, in June 1942, she would accompany him to the Unoccupied Zone; in July 1944 to Auxerre, and on the retreat into the Netherlands.

In 1944 Hauptmann (Captain) Wiegand @ WALTER @ Dr Bergmann, aged about 45, a member of the *Leitstelle* and head of Frontaufklärungstrupp (FAT – Front Reconnaissance [spy] Troop) 350 in Zwolle, had ordered that she be sent to Wiesbaden and into forced labour, but Bleicher, with the help of Oberst. Reile's intervention, had her sent back to Rorup in November 1944. A fortnight later she joined Reile in Bad Ems, who then sent her to Oberstleutnant Dernbach at Bad Kreuznach. There she completed a W/T course. When Bleicher was posted to the Netherlands in 1945 they lost contact with each other but had agreed to write after the war to a *poste-restante* at Avenue Victor Hugo or to M. Fol at Chaussée de la Muette, Paris, not far from where they had lived on the Boulevard Suchet. More information on Suzanne appeared at the end of the war in an extract from an interrogation report on SCI penetration agent BABY after returning from a mission:

ANNEX III – French Personalities
8. SUZANNE (first name: LNU)[17] [last name unknown]
Status: French W/T Trainee with FAK 313. Description: B.2.2.14 in a village 12 km. from Caen, 70 km. from Lisieux, and where there were two iron mines worked by the Germans, and a marble quarry. 1 m. 63; round face, brown hair; full-bosomed, large-hipped, small white rectangular scar, about 6mm. largest dimension, about 1½ cm. from the left eye toward the middle of her forehead – scar said to have come from an illness. Career: W/T Training; was to be parachuted into France.

Further Notes on SUZANNE:
Has a daughter born 13 February 1934, living with her spinster sister, 47 years old [Renée]. Claimed to own with her sister houses in Normandy. After her husband's death was mistress of a pharmacist, probably at Cain [sic] or Rouen; kept a bar opposite the pharmacy, made much money, first from English customers, then, in the occupation, from Germans. She kept away French customers, who did not bring in enough. At her bar she got acquainted with Feldwebel Hugo BLEICHER, who became her lover, and whom she followed to Paris, after selling her property. Intended to go to France, either parachuted in as W/T operator when her course was over, or (in case the Americans arrived) with a false card as a French labourer in Germany. Intended to see her daughter in Normandy and also go to Paris to get her trunks which she had left in a flat near the Etoile. This flat, its rent unpaid since October 1944, is owned by a woman who runs a private hotel and rents flats or rooms to rich customers etc.

At Kuhberglager, SUZANNE, while waiting for her 'Jean' (Hugo BLEICHER), granted her favours to a Frenchman GASTON, b.c.1917, who came to Germany with his wife in August 1944. Before going to Bad Kreuznach area, SUZANNE was at Bad Ems, about October 1944, with a group of collaborators of both sexes. Ex-prisoners and French workmen there watched them, with bad grace, go through the shops and stuff themselves with cakes. SUZANNE's group, hearing the workmen planned to duck them in the river, armed themselves. SUZANNE and another Frenchman (going under an alias, is or rather claims to be the son of a French noble, and speaks German perfectly) went ahead of the group to provoke the workmen, but in vain. Extracted B.1.A./HL on 2.7.45[18]

Kuhberglager was most likely Fort Oberer Kuhberg prison in Ulm, which from 1942 was used for French prisoners. The reference to BABY is is possibly the same Maximilienne (Baby) Boréa referred to earlier; alternatively, it could have been an agent controlled by Kapitänleutnant Behrend Schuchman, as this comment in his file states: '"BABY" was to have operated in Amsterdam. He was trained by WURST for this purpose, under WEISHEIT's directions, but SCHUCHMAN said that since no W/T had been installed for 'BABY' no reports were received from him.'[19]

Exactly what happened to Suzanne later Bleicher describes in his book. On 31 May 1945 he was captured in Amsterdam, where he was head of the Abwehr (FAT 365), by the 1st Canadian Corps which had liberated the Netherlands (Milmo gives the date as 11 June). On 16 June he was flown to Croydon airport, England under the false Canadian identity of Charles Lorne Davidson born 10 April 1921 in Penticton, British Columbia. Interestingly, the real Charles Lorne Davidson, also born in Penticton, British Columbia, had served as a sergeant in Canadian Army Intelligence during the Second World War and died on 24 March 2005, aged 83.[20]

From Croydon Bleicher was taken to Camp 020, but later brought back to France. He described how a superintendent of the Sûreté had enquired about what had happened to Suzanne and their reunion. After the training course in Bad Kreuznach she had made her way to Tettnang to visit his mother. From there she fled to Lindau in Austria as the Allies advanced, finally ending up in Salzburg, where she got a job with UNRRA, the United Nations Relief and Rehabilitation Administration. There an unnamed American colonel who had employed her at UNRRA offered to marry her in order to make life easier for her and protect her from the French authorities. Her undoing came when she wrote to her sister to obtain a copy of her birth certificate and other papers in order to register her marriage. It was then that she discovered she was on a list in France as being 'an important German spy'. The French military police arrested her and took her to Feldberg, where she was tried before a court martial and sentenced to death for collaboration. However, the authorities received instructions from Paris that she was being sent to Strasbourg. Later she was imprisoned in a cellar at 11, rue des Saussaies, the former headquarters of the Gestapo, and later the headquarters of the Direction de la Surveillance du Territoire (DST), the French security service.[21]

Suzanne was released in November 1945, but rearrested in December and sent to Fresnes. The Ministry of Justice intended to try her, but Bleicher was able to secure a temporary release so that she could go and live with her sister in Caen until her trial. In December 1949 she was tried along with Roger Bardet, Claude Jouffret, Robert Goubeau and Robert Kiffer (KIKI). On 3 January 1950 she wrote a final letter to Bleicher:

My dear Hugo,

So you did not come then! I sent you a telegram and it was returned to me. I had to face the court alone.

During this trial I have lived through the past ten years again. I have lived through them quite alone.

But I sensed that your shadow was hovering over this busy courtroom. Roger Bardet [more about him later] and Kiki were sentenced to death. Their records in the Resistance made as little impression on the Public Prosecutor as the favourable evidence of the witnesses, who were convinced of the sincerity of Roger and Kiki. I was sentenced to three years' imprisonment, confiscation of my possessions and a fine of 100,000 francs. The Public Prosecutor made his case with extraordinary intelligence and talent. He had studied all four thousand pages of the documents.

The case for the prosecution took eight hours, and the examination of witnesses and the hearing of the case lasted fourteen days after that.

There was not one witness for me among the 120 called. Even La Chatte was brought from Rennes prison. Poor cat, she is nearly blind, has heart trouble and has lost her old vitality. She told the Court that she had nothing to say. She said no more than that.

Two essential things emerged from this trial. That there were apart from the genuine and decent men of the Resistance, a horde of traitors and cowards too, hiding their base instincts behind the mantle of the Resistance. Their secret rivalries were a disgrace to the movement. They had long been a sore to the genuine patriots.

Secondly the trial made it plain that the German soldier was not just a rogue and looter, such as many would gladly brand him today. Of course there were cowards, traitors and criminals among them too, but they were in a small minority.

The Public Prosecutor spoke for a quarter of an hour in his indictment about Hugo Bleicher. It was almost a eulogy – Bleicher's gifts as a psychologist, his keen intelligence and his decency. The handsome and persuasive Bleicher, the intrepid Bleicher with his amazing luck. The man of courage who led the troops against the Maquis of Auxerre. The man who was active till the last minute, although he knew the war was lost. An upright German patriot, and a sincere friend of France too, who was magnanimous and left many men of the Resistance at liberty.

The verdict was a shock to me. I shall never forget those moments. I thought Roger and Kiki would have saved their lives.

And where are you? Are you happy? Go to America or the Argentine. I would like to go to the Argentine too later on. I have a good friend there. Well, I have crossed the Rubicon now and believe that in my life there has only been one great love. Farewell, Jean! The curtain has fallen.

Suzanne.[22]

There is no indication what happened to her after she was released from prison, or the American colonel who had suggested that they marry.

—◁◁◁—

Bleicher told his MI5 interrogator that between March and October 1941 he was confined to police work, which was not intelligence-related. During this time he applied for a transfer to the Abwehr. In October, his luck was about to change and he would receive his first big case. The account of the start of the *Interallié* case, referred to by III F as NOBEL I, is described in Bleicher's MI5 'Interim Interrogation Report':

1941 Oct.
KIEFFER @ KIKI, an agent of the INTERALLIÉ organisation and the first of this group to be arrested, had been denounced by one of his associates, LEMEUR [Émile Lemeur], to the G.F.P. (Luft) Cherbourg. A report was sent to Paris and Htm. BORCHERS of IIIF St. Germain was sent down to Cherbourg to investigate. As there was no suitable person attached to G.F.P. (Luft) to deal with KIEFFER's arrest it was decided to pass the matter to G.F.P. (Heer), to which BLEICHER was attached, and BLEICHER himself was selected as the most suitable man for the job.

Nov.

BLEICHER, accompanied by LEMEUR and a contingent of G.F.P. consequently arrested KIEFFER while he was walking from Cherbourg station to the house of his mistress, Madame BUFFET. A few days after the departure of Htm. BORCHERS, who had taken KIEFFER to Paris, a telegram arrived from the Feldpolizeidirektor [Philip Greiner] summoning BLEICHER to St. Germain.[23]

With the help of VICTOIRE, whom Bleicher knew as MICHELINE, the following agents were released:

KIEFFER @ PAUL @ RAOUL @ KIKI
CARREE @ LA CHATTE @ MICHELINE @ VICTOIRE
BORNI @ VIOLETTE
X [François Tabet] @ MARCEL, W/T operator
JOUFFRET, Claude
X [Robert Gorriot] @ BOB [@ BOB-EDGAR]
X [Marcel Kléber] @ KLÉBER
LAVALLEE, KLÉBER's fiancée[24]

Bleicher told his MI5 interrogators that at first he had not heard of MICHELINE (VICTOIRE) until VIOLETTE had denounced her, but that the *Leitstelle* (Defence Headquarters) in Paris had been looking for the heads of *Interallié*, without success. When she was arrested, VICTOIRE had immediately demanded to see 'Le Chef' (Bleicher) and had been willing to give up the names of everyone in the organisation even before they had discussed any terms. She was released the same day and went to live with him until March 1942, when she was sent to London (of more later). He said that this arrangement gave him no personal satisfaction; that it was just part of his job, but it was entirely due to her that the Abwehr was able to 'liquidate almost the entire organisation'. This seems a trifle ironic, given Bleicher's habit of womanising. He also said that VICTOIRE was 'insatiable in her treachery and was prepared to denounce her nearest and dearest. In all BLEICHER's experience he has never seen anyone who betrayed her friends with such cynicism and zest.'[25]

CHAPTER 11

Turning the Tables

On 20 November VICTOIRE, accompanied by Bleicher and Borchers, who was dropped off at the Gestapo headquarters behind Le Bon Marché, went to La Palette, but no one turned up. Then they visited her mother, Madame Jeanne Belard, with Bleicher posing as the commissaire de la Gestapo. He informed Madame Belard that he understood from VICTOIRE that she had always helped her daughter, but this cut no ice with her. He then went off to the rue des Deux-Ponts on the Ile St Louis, where he arrested the Pole, Stanislas Lach, code-named RAPIDE, who was a courier for the network.

VICTOIRE had briefed Bleicher that Lach would not be someone who would come quietly, so armed guards were positioned ready to intercept him if he were to make a run for it. Lach and his wife were having lunch at the time. VICTOIRE stood in the open doorway and told him that she had to alert London and Marseilles because something had happened to ARMAND. However, she did not know how to reach TUDOR, which astonished Lach as he thought that if anyone would have known how to contact TUDOR it would have been her. When he queried the fact, saying that he thought she had visited TUDOR in Marseilles, she denied it. Their conversation was awkward: he becoming more and more suspicious, and she more and more agitated. Finally, as she made to leave, Bleicher, in Paine's words, lunged forward, 'a weapon in each hand, in the best Wild West tradition', and ordered Lach, his wife and VICTOIRE against the wall with their hands up. This move was deliberate as he did not want Lach to suspect that VICTOIRE was a double agent. VICTOIRE described it somewhat differently:

> Rapide and his wife ... received me with their usual cordiality. I don't remember what I mumbled. I wanted to leave as quickly as possible but the two Germans [Bleicher and Kleiber], who were at the door, pushed me inside and Bleicher cried: 'German police!' The room started to swim before my

eyes. It was on the face of this couple that I saw the greatest distress and the most bitter hatred. They looked as though they could have killed me. I was in despair. Bleicher held me close to him for he must have thought I was going to faint. 'I can't do it … I can't do it,' I kept repeating and this made him even more tender. In the car Rapide did not deign to glance at me but his wife continued to stare at me with implacable hatred.[1]

Lach was born in Lwówek (La Fondation pour la Mémoire de la Déportation via Trêves says Lvov), Poland, on 3 May 1908. Before the war he had worked in the Citroën factory as a metallurgist, and would end up being sent first on 27 March 1943 to Trêves (Trier), a concentration camp run by the SS, known as KZ Hindert, used as a transit camp for deportees under the 'Night and Fog' decree, then Mauthausen two days later. He was liberated on 5 May 1945 and repatriated on 21 May. It has not been possible to discover what happened to his wife other than that she survived the war, according to Mathilde's memoirs. There was also a Władysław (or Ladislas) Lach, born 20 June 1900 in Wrociery, Poland who was a member of the Polska Organizacja Walki o Niepodległości (POWN) resistance movement in the southern zone of France based in Lyons, but there appears to be no connection between the two men.

That evening VICTOIRE dined with Propst. When she returned to Maisons-Lafitte, she drank champagne with Kayser (Kaiser) and Commandant von Eiffel [sic], who was actually von Ehfeld @ von Eiffel, on the staff of Major Ische in III F.[2] In Bleicher's file von Ehfeld is described as aged 55, white-haired, wearing a monocle, quite important and aristocratic;[3] VICTOIRE's description was less charitable: 'an old monocled major who resembled a Parisian tramp'; and she described Kayser as looking like a 'Levantine trader'. Propst, aged 32, was fat and heavy, efficient and subservient, but lacking in imagination. He had worked in England before the war as a representative for a typewriter company, but hated the British intensely. Bleicher too was no fan of them either: 'He loathed England but loved France and his little "Lily" who was so adorably French.' This dislike was most likely directly related to his being a prisoner of war of the British in 1917 and, according to VICTOIRE, being treated inhumanely in the camp at Abbeville.

MAX, the radio operator, was brought to the Café La Palette on 21 November but VICTOIRE failed to recognise him. This is hardly surprising since she was so myopic. Harmer's report speculates as to how he was caught, given that MAURICE had warned him. He thought that probably when ARTOS was caught on the 20th, MAX may have been caught at the radio station at the rue

Faubourg St Honoré. Alternatively, since the Germans were watching the house, they may have arrested him when he returned to try and warn CHRISTIAN, who by that time had already been arrested. Whatever the reason, MAX gave away MONO's address and offered to work for the Germans.

At a meeting at the Hôtel Edouard VII later that day VICTOIRE was confronted by Bleicher, Borchers, Kayser and another officer, who told her:

> We have decided to continue the INTERALLIÉE affair. We wish to play a little game with the British. We will tell them that WALENTY and VIOLETTE have been arrested, since we can't do otherwise, having regard to the fact that MAURICE and GEORGES have escaped. We will tell them for the moment that you have been able to save yourself with the radio post at the painter's house, that you have with you all the papers, telegrams and codes, and that you are continuing the affair with the provincial agents. Whether you like it or not all telegrams will be signed LA CHATTE by us. You are the only one who can continue, and in whom London, Marseilles and Vichy all have confidence, and nobody still at liberty will know that you are in our hands. You are going to telephone to MARCEL, the radio operator, and give him a rendezvous; he is a weak boy who likes money, whom MONO wished to bump off. He will be excellent.[4]

When questioned about the third radio post she denied any knowledge of it, but Harmer assumed that it would have been given away by MAX anyway. VICTOIRE would later explain to MI5 that she had seen a chance to warn London, so agreed to Bleicher's proposal. However, he found it interesting that MARCEL should have been mentioned, since he was apparently on holiday at the time and:

> There was no reason why he should have come to the notice of the Germans. It is perfectly obvious that VICTOIRE herself suggested that he come as a suitable person to work the radio. He was a friend of hers, and the fact that she could, three days after the initial arrests, nominate people who were to be used by the Germans is in itself significant.[5]

Mathilde suggested that instead of LA CHATTE she use the name VICTOIRE, which the Germans accepted but said that they would always know her as 'Kätze' (she-cat) or 'Kätzchen' (kitten). The Germans wasted no time; the first radio message sent out that day was as follows:

Following German search have moved. WALENTY probably arrested. I am continuing work in tranquility with the radio in a new place. I await your instructions and money urgently.[6]

The text of the message, according to MI5 actually read:

1018 – Following German round-up have moved. WALENTY probably arrested. I am continuing work undisturbed, with the radio in a new place I await your instructions and money urgently. LA CHATTE.

This was followed up with a second message the following day:

In our previous message we told you that we are being looked for by the Germans and have been obliged to move. We await your instructions. Money urgent. We are forced to move.[7]

Again, the exact wording of her second message was:

1019 – In our No.1018 we told you that we are being looked for by the Germans and had been obliged to move. We await your instructions. Money urgent. We are again forced to move. CHATTE.

Harmer noted that both messages appeared to have been written by VICTOIRE, although in the original French the word 'Allemands' to mean Germans was used instead of 'Boche'. This may have been her way of letting them know she was being controlled.

When VICTOIRE visited ARTOS's house she found nothing, so she went off to the rue Lamarck, but no one showed up. Later she was taken to the Villa Léandre, only to find VIOLETTE sitting between Borchers and Kayser. Oberleutnant Kayser, aged 42, had been a lawyer in Mannheim before the war. Known as 'Le Juif' (the Jew) and disliked by his friends, he was thin, with an olive complexion and a hooked nose, black hair and eyes, of medium height (5ft 6in). They cross-examined VICTOIRE about a friend of hers, a bacteriologist named Dr Collins, who was nothing to do with her organisation, as well as Jean Bailly @ OSCAR, the son of her godfather, the novelist Auguste Bailly (1878–1967), who was also not a member. She would claim to MI5 that VIOLETTE had told the Germans that they were agents of *Interallié*, saying that she 'lied with every breath and everybody knew it'. Again, Harmer states that this demonstrates her vanity and how, even at this early stage, the Germans believed her completely. VICTOIRE spent the evening having dinner at the Weber restaurant, although it does not specify with whom, but one can assume it was Bleicher. This may have been the Restaurant Weber, 1, Parc des Buttes-Chaumont in the 19th arrondissement. She was then taken to the cinema, before returning to Maisons-Lafitte.

On 22 November PAUL (Lucien Rocquigny), an ex-Polish journalist who was responsible for monitoring press and propaganda, and OBSERVATEUR (de Lipsky), another Pole responsible for information on small French industry, were arrested; again, VICTOIRE acted as a decoy. To disguise the fact that she had betrayed them, she claimed that the Germans had found in her bag a letter from PAUL requesting a meeting. However, when they went to his address in the Boulevard St Michel in the 7th arrondissement he was not there. She remained in the car and did not attempt to escape while Bleicher and an NCO went into a hairdresser's. PAUL was arrested later when they returned to his address, where he also gave up OBSERVATEUR's address. In the meantime, they had gone to the Hôtel de Ville in the 1st arrondissement in the Place du Louvre to arrest colleagues of BOBY-ROLAND, although all but one had managed to escape. OBSERVATEUR was arrested after VICTOIRE and Bleicher had had lunch at La Palette, but he pretended that he knew nothing about what was going on.

The next domino to fall was FRANCK at their old office in the rue de la Michodière, having left a message for VICTOIRE saying he would be there at 5 o'clock. He went on to betray FERNAND, a young French Air Force NCO who lived at Boulogne and a sub-agent of Sector F. Bleicher and VICTOIRE had dinner again at the Madeleine restaurant. When they returned to Maisons-Lafitte she learned that STEPHEN (Lieutenant Stefan Czyż) had also been arrested. Czyż, according to one source, operated a safe route to Bordeaux.[8] This may have been the Stefan Czyż born in Lublin in 1906, who married Franciszka Konarska on 3 September 1932.

VICTOIRE's betrayals did not stop there, and at every opportunity she made sure that blame was clearly laid on VIOLETTE for them. On 23 November it was the turn of YOLÉ (René Legrand), MIKLOS (Maître Michel Brault) and Robert Poulain.[9] VIOLETTE, however, claimed that only VICTOIRE had known about them. Poulain was not one of their agents but was in touch with semi-active underground movements led by Général Benoît de Fornel de la Laurencie (1879–1958) – who had led the French Third Corps at Dunkirk and was later appointed by Maréchal Pétain as délégate general of the French government to the occupying German forces – and Michel Clémenceau (1873–1964), a staff officer in the Deuxième Bureau and the son of Georges Clémenceau, prime minister of France during the First World War.

Monday 24 November was the day that all the agents representing the various sectors were supposed to deliver their reports. VICTOIRE had therefore arranged that she would await them at La Palette and send them to the basement to collect a message. The Gestapo was waiting in the restaurant and basement to arrest them. The only one to show up was COCO, who had offered to go in disguise, the others having heard about the previous arrests and considering it too dangerous to go to the meeting. It was thought afterwards that, had VICTOIRE not been there, no one would have recognised COCO, but she, of course, sent him down to the basement for the message, where he was arrested. At the Hôtel Edouard VII she had to identify him. Harmer's report on VICTOIRE refers to COCO's subsequent shooting after his arrest, but no other evidence has emerged to confirm this, other than to say that he was 'probably now shot'.[10] VICTOIRE described in her memoirs how Bleicher arrested 'Poor little Coco' at La Palette after he had arrived and spoken to her. When he tried to deny being a spy he was rewarded with a slap in the face from Bleicher.She then set the wheels in motion to entrap YOLÉ, MIKLOS and Robert Poulain.

On 25 November Bleicher set up 'La Chattière' ('the Cattery') at the Petite Prieuré Villa, rue du Prieuré in Saint-Germain-en-Laye where VICTOIRE was now established with a radio set and all her papers. The house was shared with Borchers, Kayser, who was in charge of interrogation, and three NCOs – Tritche, Propst and Todt. It was arranged so that the living area was on the ground floor, she and Bleicher were in a double room on the first floor, with Borchers next door. The top floor housed the office and radio station where Propst had his living quarters and, much to VICTOIRE's disgust, VIOLETTE, sharing a room with Propst. In an attempt to flatter her and appeal to her vanity, Bleicher told VICTOIRE that his mistress, who he had yelled at when he had first met her, had committed suicide. Harmer offered an opinion on the reason why VICTOIRE and VIOLETTE shared the same premises:

VICTOIRE has always maintained that VIOLETTE was necessary to the Germans for enciphering, at which she was very good. It was rightly pointed out at the outset that the Germans had no need of anyone but themselves to do the ciphering as the cipher was easy to operate. This is another example of how VICTOIRE's intelligence, which is pretty good, can be affected by her vanity. Undoubtedly [h]ad it been anybody but VIOLETTE she would have realised that the [p]roposition that a person was essential to do the ciphering was [f]allacious, and her intelligence would have prevented her from putting it on record. Therefore I believe this explanation to have been given to her in fact by the Germans. They were by this time running both VICTOIRE and VIOLETTE, and assigned one of their immeasurably better dividends that was VIOLETTE, but they did not want to have VIOLETTE in prison altogether; she might have come in useful for catching some of the smaller fry. They therefore told VICTOIRE that she was necessary for the ciphering in order to try and sugar the pill. They were prepared to lay on rules which apparently relegated VIOLETTE to the position rather of a servant, in that she was never allowed to come out of her room when VICTOIRE was in the house. However, VIOLETTE, who appears to have been an amiable, if weak, creature, was anxious to get on, if she could, with VICTOIRE, and applied to see her. VICTOIRE agreed, and VIOLETTE told her that she had become engaged to WALENTY in prison and had been to see him, and had promised not to work for the Germans. WALENTY had also asked her to extract the same promise from VICTOIRE. VICTOIRE says she could have strangled VIOLETTE for having been false to WALENTY. One is tempted to ask what punishment she would have reserved for herself on this basis. Yet another unimportant but interesting incident recorded by VICTOIRE is that when she went into her bedroom at La Chattière and found that the Germans had provided no flowers for her she made such a tremendous row that they never committed the error again. It was certainly worth their while to try and humour her.[11]

That same day she went to La Palette again to see if anyone had shown up, but only found a letter from YVES making a rendezvous for the next day at Café Ruc, 159, rue St Honoré, across from the Comédie Française. It is unclear which YVES is referred to here – there is an YVES also known as '*Le Petit Turc*' because he was half Turkish, and Michel Courtois, also known as YVES – but this must have been '*Le Petit Turc*' for reasons explained in Chapter 12. She also collected her things from the rue Cortot and rue Lamarck, but when she saw BOB-EDGAR there she simply ignored him.

On the morning of 26 November Bleicher, accompanied by VICTOIRE, visited La Santé and Fresnes prisons. He left her to have lunch at her parents' house and met her later at the Café Madeleine. VICTOIRE records in her memoirs that the atmosphere was decidedly frosty between her and her mother, who thought (rightly) that she was collaborating with the Germans. As Harmer notes, 'It is quite clear at this stage that VICTOIRE really was working whole-heartedly for them.' Bleicher returned to Fresnes with her after lunch and confronted her with Marcel Kléber, who denied knowing her, but VICTOIRE recognised him. Coincidentally, their driver's name was Kleiber. That day she had had two occasions in which to escape: the first when Bleicher left her to walk from her parents' house to the Café Madeleine; the second, when she left the driver and went to sit in a nearby café to keep warm. Possibly she considered it futile to try, but more likely it was because she was by this time fully cooperating with the Germans.

YVES was arrested that evening at six o'clock just as he was coming out of the Café Ruc and VICTOIRE and Bleicher were going in. He was carrying his report, which he tried to drop, but Kleiber the driver picked it up. But who was the Englishwoman whose address in Asnières YVES gave up? Her identity is not revealed in the files.

The events that followed on subsequent days are not as clearly recorded by VICTOIRE, but 27 November marks the date when the plan to deceive YOLÉ, MIKLOS and Robert Poulain by getting them to write incriminating letters was put into effect. With her arm in a sling, she went to YOLÉ's office at eleven o'clock and asked him to write down a list of convoys of French ships passing between French African possessions and Occupied France. (This is taken to mean the Straits of Gibraltar.) MIKLOS also remembered her coming to his office and having him write a note. Again, she was left alone, unsupervised, and apparently honoured the trust bestowed upon her by the Germans. In spite of the warmth shown to her by YOLÉ and his generosity in giving her some of his black-market products, he was arrested later that day. When she visited MIKLOS he wrote out a message to London, but for some reason was not arrested later and remained at liberty. VICTOIRE claimed that she had persuaded the Germans that he was unimportant. As Harmer astutely notes, 'It is more probable, however, that she had told them that he was in touch with other underground movements, and they thought it better perhaps to let him run and keep him under observation,' which is probably more to the point. In her memoirs VICTOIRE records:

I found this train of arrests nauseating. They followed in quick succession and Bleicher was insistent that I should be present as often as possible ... I understood Bleicher's game. He wanted to compromise me, to bind me morally, and thus prevent me trying to escape.[12]

It was not until the following day, the 28th, that VICTOIRE unsuccessfully attempted to obtain any incriminating evidence from Robert Poulain when they met at the Café Graff. She dined with VIOLETTE but 'found the experience so degrading that she stipulated that she should never see VIOLETTE again'. To avoid this, VIOLETTE was moved to another villa. Harmer records in his report that the 29th was the day when British Intelligence received the first message signed 'VICTOIRE', a name she had chosen, but which the Germans did not accept right away. As Harmer observes:

> One wonders whether they did not suspect, as we did, that she might slip in a code word meaning that she was controlled, and possibly they were unhappy about signing a message with a name chosen by herself. As their confidence in her grew, however, they started later on.[13]

The message read:

> 1023 – I am regaining courage. Have traced several agents … We are installed in peace because of the theft of certain documents I am taking from now on the name VICTOIRE and dropping Inter-alliee [sic]. You can send someone to me. The need of money is urgent.

Further arrests were to follow due to Kléber's mistress, Jacqueline Lavallee, and took place sometime between 30 November and 6 December. In La Santé, Lavallee gave the Gestapo the addresses of MONO and MOUSTIQUE, as well as offering to take them to the address of IRINEE (Guy Vedero) near Rambouillet, and also betraying KENT (Fernand Gane). However, when Bleicher and VICTOIRE went to see MONO and MOUSTIQUE they found that both had flown the coop. Nor was IRINEE at home so they left a note arranging a rendezvous at a post box in the rue d'Amsterdam. 'On our return to Paris in the car Jacqueline was terribly nervous, crouching in the back seat like an animal,' VICTOIRE observed.

During their return to La Santé Lavallee suggested that one of the other agents might be at the Café du Sport near the Porte Maillot.[14] When they stopped there, as Harmer's report recounts, 'this rather miserable and frightened woman about whom VICTOIRE writes with the utmost contempt, managed to outwit the Germans by making for the ladies' cloakroom and escaping by the back entrance'. Apparently, Bleicher didn't care and let her go, considering her to be unimportant. IRINEE was later arrested, with VICTOIRE once again acting as a decoy when they went to his house. There was an emotional scene when he and his wife kissed goodbye, and then he was bundled out in handcuffs. In the car, he revealed the address of ISIDORE, who told her that there was going to be a meeting of the free agents at the Café Louis XIII on 6 December. This may now be Le Relais Louis XIII, a two-star Michelin restaurant at 8, rue des Grands Augustins, in the 6th arrondissement.

At an unspecified date, which must have been before the end of the year, VICTOIRE went to the Unoccupied Zone. As she insisted to Kayser, going to Vichy would prove to the Deuxième Bureau that she had never been arrested. In her memoir she said that the plan never amounted to anything, but other reports in her files state that she did. Before doing so, she went to visit her parents; her mother gave her 30,000 francs. Bleicher, in the meantime, went to arrest ÉMILE, but he had already disappeared. He was finally arrested when Bleicher and VICTOIRE went to ÉMILE's address in Courbevoie or Asnières (the account does not specify which). They found him locked in a second-floor room, in spite of the occupants trying to tell Bleicher that he was not there. The place was surrounded by soldiers, so he came out. Later, Bleicher told VICTOIRE that he had kicked ÉMILE in the stomach, an uncharacteristic act.

Harmer records that 6 December was 'the most tragic day of all since the 18th November' because BERTRAND and BOB-EDGAR were arrested. '[T]hat once again they had both been warned, and only VICTOIRE's willing collaboration with the Germans caught them.' A trap was set, with VICTOIRE again acting as a decoy at the Café Louis XIII. BERTRAND was the first to arrive, followed by BOB-EDGAR. They were both pleased to see her, thinking that she had been arrested, as they had been told by Alice. Under interrogation after their arrest BOB-EDGAR revealed that CHARLES (Theophil Burlot) was with CLAUDE (Claude Jouffret), and both men gave away the addresses of other agents: BOB-EDGAR revealed CLAUDE's address, and BERTRAND revealed those of the fisherman BERTHE, and BERNARD. BOB-EDGAR also had on him the plan of the SOE organisation code-named OVERCLOUD, referred to by VICTOIRE as the 'Rue Gît-le-Coeur affair'.

Rue Gît-le-Coeur is in the Latin Quarter of Paris in the 6th arrondissement. OVERCLOUD was a network set up in north-west Brittany by Jöel Letac ('Joe') and his brother Yves.[15] The network was later penetrated and broken up by using BOB-EDGAR, who was allowed his freedom so that the Germans could penetrate it. Members of the network, who also included André Peulevey (André Joseph Scheinmann), were arrested and he and Jöel Letac spent the rest of the war in a variety of prison camps: Natzweiler-Struthof, Dachau, Neuengamme, Gross-Rosen, Dora and Bergen-Belsen, before being liberated by the British on 15 April 1945.

After the arrests Bleicher and VICTOIRE still expected to see MONO and MOUSTIQUE at La Palette, as well as members of the Jankowski (Madeleine Jankowska @ CHON) and Bradkowski (Madame Bradkowska @ METCHKA) families. They also visited the home of Guy Chaumet @ CHARAL,[16] the former minister of industry, whose wife told them that CLAUDE had been associated with CHARLES and the black market. Tritche and Propst were left behind to arrest CHARLES when he arrived the following day. When he was arrested, he gave away everything, including the address of the fisherman CÉSAR, and even offered to set up a Gestapo office at Rennes. Bleicher was eager to accept the offer but VICTOIRE warned him that CHARLES was untrustworthy.

During the month of November the sea route normally used to send over suitcases of documents each month was not used, perhaps because the Channel was too rough. The suitcase that should have been sent over was left by CHARLES with a friend, Mimi Debray. ADAM pointed out that before he left France he had given WALENTY some documents for that suitcase, but it had never been found. The documents contained compromising information about his friends living in the Unoccupied Zone. Since these friends were still free, he argued that it was proof that CHARLES could not have given everything away. But since VICTOIRE was unaware of this, and because she claimed that the suitcase had never been found, it tended to negate ADAM's evidence against her.

While Bleicher was away on leave from 19 December for three days, Borchers saw his chance to make a move on VICTOIRE by taking her to dinner at the Grande Restaurant at the Gare St Germain. True to form, he got hopelessly drunk. 'Aperitif, dinner, wine and a great deal of brandy ... Borchers opened his heart. He was sick of the surroundings in which he lived; no one understood him, etc., etc.' In his inebriated state, he complained to her about his job and said he was trying to go to Istanbul. If he did, he said, he would take her with him as his secretary and called her 'Le plus grand espionne international de cette guerre' (the greatest international female spy of this war). VICTOIRE had avoided drinking the vast quantities of champagne that Borchers and the NCOs had consumed – 'I never drink champagne' – and quietly sipped an orange juice. 'Now let's visit Madame's "Cat's nest,"', he declared. It was then, she claimed, that she would outwit the Germans by playing what she called 'the long game'. She also contrived to get Borchers into trouble the next morning with his colonel by claiming that the colonel wanted to see him at eleven o'clock. Borchers did not believe her and ignored it, going back to bed to sleep off his hangover; however, the colonel had wanted to see him and telephoned to give him a severe dressing-down. A slightly different account of 'l'affaire Eric Borscher' [*sic*] can be found in one of VICTOIRE's files:

> Borscher one evening to celebrate the Interalliée affair had been in a cafe in St. Germain with Victoire where, after having had a lot to drink, he invited the proprietors of the cafe as well as three N.C.O.s to drink with him. He boasted of being employed by the German deuxieme bureau and that the woman who was with him was a spy. Then Borscher invited the three N.C.O.s to La Chattiere as well as Victoire. Borscher, more and more drunk, let drop all the papers about the Armand and Victoire affair. Victoire hesitated, wondering whether she should make them disappear, however she decided to do nothing. In addition she got rid of the three N.C.O.s before Borscher awoke to avoid a row. When Borscher woke up: 'I told him of all that had happened during the night, I told him how the papers were scattered about (those of the Armand affair) I told him that I had done nothing though I could have done something easily. He begged me to say nothing of what had happened and I got him to promise to do nothing against me.'[17]

Whatever situation arose, VICTOIRE managed to cause trouble. When Borchers' secretary was brought in to the house, probably to try to keep VICTOIRE in line, VICTOIRE had her dismissed. The woman had come up from Bordeaux and was introduced to her by Major Ische, alias Malloy, whom she always called 'Freddie' and described as a very handsome Austrian. Harmer adds more on both Ische and the secretary:

> The position of ISCHE is rather peculiar. VICTOIRE describes him as being the chief at the Maison Lafitte [*sic*]. I suspect that he was specially brought along to deal with VICTOIRE, as the coincidence of BLEICHER's leave, the arrival of the woman secretary and the particularly handsome Austrian, all seem to suggest a desire on the part of the Germans to create a set-up to keep VICTOIRE, who by this time must have been an agent of inestimable value, happy. From our own experience of looking after her [this would come later] we know how difficult it was to keep her quiet, and also it can

be deduced that BLEICHER had probably had enough. I would not be surprised if the handsome ISCHE was not a man holding an entirely bogus position, who was laid on to impress VICTOIRE. The description of his visit to La Chattière would bear this out. He came at 11 o'clock in the evening, and frantic steps were taken by all the German officials to be busy when he arrived. VICTOIRE records this as an example of the Germans' stupidity. It might rather be a well staged plan to convince VICTOIRE of ISCHE's importance. VICTOIRE describes him as being a large, strong, handsome Colonel, typically Viennese in his beauty, charm and gallantry!

The secretary from Bordeaux, called SONIA, was obviously intended to look after the house, and a maid was also laid on known as LUCIE. We may suppose that this was what the Germans hoped would be a working arrangement. However, VICTOIRE set out to sink SONIA. In the first place she insisted that the maid LUCIE should be directly under her orders, which was of course granted. Then she caught out SONIA slinking off to Paris without tidying her room in the morning and took BLEICHER and showed him her room. Finally she set about making the poor woman ridiculous and eventually got her dismissed from the house around Christmas.[18]

Bleicher's file offers a brief description of Sonia as being aged 53, 5ft 5in tall, plump, with a red face, black hair and eyes, and looking like a Spaniard. She had, in fact, been in Spain before the war and was stationed in Bordeaux. Ische was described as aged 40, 6ft 5in tall, with a strong build, but developing a large stomach, a fat face with a fresh complexion, thick black hair brushed back, very handsome, and with good manners. Although hailing from Vienna, he had lived in France for twelve years. Consequently, he spoke excellent French and was very much a Francophile. He was married with two children aged 13 and 5, who remained in Vienna with his wife. He was also described as being very intelligent and sincere, and mistrusting of others.

Bleicher's return from Cherbourg heralded more arrests: those of the Jankowski family, including their daughter CHON (Madeleine); Paulette Porchers and the family of Capitaine Philippe, whose address Bleicher had been given by VIOLETTE. The latter's address was amongst documents intented be sent over to Britain in the November suitcase previously mentioned. Bleicher was also interested in finding ADAM. One clue he had was that VIOLETTE had asked him to bring back from London some crocodile skin. A parachute and this type of material had been found in the Occupied Zone; however, ADAM never came back to Paris when he returned to France.

VICTOIRE was used once again as an *agente provocatrice* to force Madame Bradkowska to write a letter to WALENTY, thus incriminating her. She was also used to find out about a certain TADY @ BERNARDSKI @ CAROLA who may also have been working for the Germans. The Philippe family were luckier: they had gone away to relatives for Christmas and Bleicher simply forgot about arresting them. When JEANNINE (ERNESTINE) was arrested it was as a result of VICTOIRE making her write a letter, which was left with the concierge during one of her visits to La Palette. VICTOIRE later claimed that she had tried to warn JEANNINE by pretending not to recognise her, but JEANNINE blurted out her name and was arrested.

At Christmas, Borchers, who was going on leave, threw a party at the Café Madeleine. Once again he managed to disgrace himself by getting 'crazed' (drunk) and having to be carried to the train by a soldier. Also present at the party were Bleicher, Sonia and VICTOIRE, Kayser having disappeared. Another party was held at Maisons-Lafitte, but Bleicher and VICTOIRE both stayed away – she wanted to have a quiet time and he wanted to be with her. He was furious to find out later that all the items confiscated from the round-up of agents had been distributed amongst the guests, but no one had thought to save him anything. It also made him furious when he was offered a sum of money for his part in the break-up of *Interallié*. As of Christmas Day, all the agents from *Interallié* had been arrested, except MIKLOS. The exact number of those arrested has been redacted from VICTOIRE's file, but it has been estimated that it was at least 100, which would include sub-agents and probably their families. Of those who were arrested, not all cooperated: WALENTY, ONCLE MARCO, RICHARD NOEUD, COCO and KLÉBER never talked; but VICTOIRE of course did, as did KIKI, BOB-EDGAR and MARCEL, although KIKI kept having attacks of conscience.

Up to this point the Germans had not shown much interest in the radio traffic and were more preoccupied with receiving money. Nonetheless a message sent by the British on 1 December reads:

> **485** – In reply to your 1023. Please propose by what means we can send you the money.

A message was received saying:

1024 – Have found agents for sectors D, E, F, K, R. Am worried about MOUSTIQUE and liaison with MARSCHAL and CHARLES. Send to CESAR for maintenance of organisation. I have courage but no more money. VICTOIRE.

1025 – Propose you send money by plane. The place used for the departure of WALENTY. Fix date, password and signal. DESIRE, ex KIKI and VICTOIRE will be on the ground.

Other messages sent and received during this time were as follows:

Message sent 2.1.2.41
484 – Send DESIRE immediately to KIKI, where he was the beginning of August and who awaits him.

Message received 3.12.41.
1025 – Reply immediately if you agree to air operation. Have also found agent for Sector J and YOLÉ. Because of dangerous situation we will remain quiet until about 1st January. If you have urgent news to ask us we can always send it for you. We are completely out of money for paying the agents. VICTOIRE.

Message sent 5.12.41.
485 – In reply to your telegram of 3.12.41. Your proposal for sending money is slightly risky under present conditions. Give us another suggestion. You are right to stop work until 1st January. What is happening to WALENTY and his comrades. JANIO. [There is no record of who JANIO was]

Message received 9.12.41.
1026 – I agree to your proposal. Tell us if it is to wait at Bujaleuf or to go to Marseilles. We do not understand your fear of coming by plane. If impossible to land drop money in a package by parachute in well settled place. We cannot make you any other proposal since the fisherman CESAR has not been found. Can you send us money by another organisation here. Have also traced agents EDGAR and BERTRAND. Absolutely impossible to continue holding together organisation without immediate dispatch of money. VICTOIRE.

Message sent 12.12.41
486 – For VICTOIRE. We do not understand the word Bujaleuf. DESIRE should know the rendez-vous well. How many copies of the code existed before the German round-up. JANIO.

Message received 14.12.41.
1027 – VIOLETTE was arrested together with WALENTY. The Germans searched the place. Cypher department was transferred by me; so it was not searched. They had only a dictionary and Polish notes as well as all the telegrams. As WALENTY had only one W/T set I do not think that the Germans know the code. Bujaleuf is a locality in the free zone where DESIRE will await the parachutist. Do you want to send money to Bujaleuf or to the place of WALENTY's departure?

Bujaleuf is a village located in the Haute-Vienne département of the Limousin region.

On 14 December the Germans sent a message that indirectly threatened to close down the network if they did not receive any money. They also indicated that they had located a number of agents who would reveal everything they knew about the Pétain–Goering negotiations:

Message received 14.12.41
1028 – We are surprised by your silence. Yes or no, do you want to help us in our future work? We are not at all disturbed at present and have found a sufficient number of agents, especially on the whole of the coast sectors B, C, D, E, and F. In connection with Petain-Goering negotiations work promises to be most interesting. Sabotage and subversive activities are increasing in strength, this is not the right time to abandon our aims.[19]

The negotiations had taken place on 1 December 1941 in Saint-Florentin-Vergigny (in the Yonne département of Bourgogne-Franche-Comté) between Reichsmarshall Hermann Goering, Admiral Jean Louis Xavier François Darlan and Marshal Henri Philippe Pétain, where Pétain and Goering reaffirmed Franco-German collaboration. After his meeting on 11 May 1941 at Berchtesgaden, Hitler's mountain retreat in Bavaria, Darlan declared:

My choice is made: it is collaboration ... France's interest is to live and to remain a great power ... In the present state of the world, and taking into account of our terrible defeat, I see no other solution to protect our interests.

On 27 December the Germans sent an ultimatum that if they did not receive any money by 10 January they would abandon the organisation and move on to another one:

1031 – I have moved completely and changed my identity. Impossible for you to trace me if you and I do not fix a rendez-vous at a fixed time with a password, in Paris or the occupied zone.

1032 – If on 10th January I am still without money I will abandon you and will pass with my agents to the other organisation for the liberation of my country.

The Germans had also said they would send KIKI to the Unoccupied Zone to await a parachutist who would bring money. As Harmer noted, 'Either this is a complete bluff, or they had complete confidence in KIKI at this stage. If the latter, it would bear out VICTOIRE's statement that he was working for them.' As reported by McCallum:

It seems that at first, at any rate, London was completely spoofed by the 'new' INTERALLIE and messages were exchanged almost daily. Although the Abwehr, advised by VICTOIRE, kept to routine traffic (raising in particular the agents' perennial cry of 'send me money'), they did claim two successes.[22]

The first of these successes was that when the German battleships *Scharnhorst* and *Gneisenau* were getting ready to put to sea in February 1942, the famous French Resistance leader 'Colonel Rémy' (Lieutenant Colonel Gilbert Renault-Roulier, 1904–84) sent out urgent warnings from Brest. Contradicting this, messages sent from La Chattière stated that the two ships were too badly damaged to be moved. The Admiralty, in its infinite wisdom, preferred to accept these messages as true, since previous messages they had received from *Interallié* about shipping had always been accurate, rather than trust 'Colonel Remy's agent'. The result was that the two ships, accompanied by the cruiser *Prinz Eugen*, slipped through the English Channel and through the Straits of Dover back to Kiel under the noses of the Royal Navy on 11–13 February 1942. The operation had been code-named by the Kriegsmarine as *Unternehemen Zerberus*

(Operation *Cerberus*). The second success was prior to the St Nazaire raid (Operation *Chariot*) that took place on 28 March 1942. London had asked for details of port installations, thereby alerting the Germans. As McCallum points out, both these claims – made in Carré's biography, *The Cat with Two Faces*, and in an interview with Erich Borchers for the *Daily Mail* in January 1951 – are considered 'dubious'.

At some point VICTOIRE and the Germans came up with a plan for the notional new 'Victoire Organisation', which appeared in her second interrogation report:

Sector A	ANDRÉ (ex. EDGAR) to recruit new personnel on the spot to re-open liaison between IRUN and Spain.
Sector B	BARBE (ex. BERTRAND), BEBERT (ex. BERNARD) To go on as before.
Sector C	COCO will resume the direction of his old sector with his old personnel. CÉSAR the fisherman is ready to resume activity (I never knew what happened to Charles yet I was informed at Vichy at the end of November that he had crossed over).
Sector D	KIKI (ex. DESIRE) to go on as before.
Sector E	EDOUARD (ex. ÉMILE) and his brother EUGÈNE are going on.
Sector F	FRÉDÉRIC (ex. FRANCK), FELIX (ex. FERNAND) to go on as before.
Sector G	
Sector H	I have not yet been able to re-establish the liaison.
Sector I	IRENE continues.
Sector J	JEAN (ex. ISIDORE) takes back this section again.
Sector K	KING
Sector L	I am looking for a chief agent for this sector.
Paris Region	ROBERT (CLAUDE in report No.1) will be in charge of this region.
INDUSTRY	RENÉ will continue.
PRESS	PIERRE, French journalist, will begin from 1st February (I don't know where PAUL and OBSERVATEUR are).

RADIO	MARCEL, operator; MARIKA, coding. I need a second operator to help MARCEL and a second post will have to be set up in case of an accident to the first.
Political information	PAUL
General information	YVES as before.
TYPING	YVONNE

The O de B [*Ordre de bataille* – Order of Battle] will be kept up to date by me and will be sent to you regularly.
I will re-establish the liaison with L.N.
PATRIE network remains ours.
If necessary we could re-establish the microphotography system?[23]

Harmer's report of 15 March 1942 appears to confirm that VIOLETTE had been responsible for many of the arrests, saying:

> At the end of the month [January 1942] S.I.S. received MAURICE's report in which it stated that VICTOIRE was arrested in the evening in her flat with EDOUARD. It will be remembered that S.I.S's agent ADAM had commented on the fact that MAURICE could not have known anything about the arrest of VICTOIRE as he left before that happened. MAURICE, however, in his report states definitely that he was several days in Paris before he fled to the non-occupied zone and that he therefore would have had the opportunity of finding out about VICTOIRE's arrest. This point will, however, be clarified when he reaches this country. Another most interesting fact about MAURICE's report is that it provides confirming evidence that VIOLETTE did betray a lot of secrets of the WALENTY organisation; in particular the address of one of the W/T sets was known to only three people, including VIOLETTE. One of these people is MAURICE, who has escaped, and as the other two were WALENTY and VIOLETTE the assumption is that it was VIOLETTE who betrayed it.[24]

On 27 April 1942 Harmer, writing on behalf of Tar, responded to Buckmaster to explain some of the names that had appeared in the plan for the new 'Victoire Organisation', such as KING, EDOUARD and FREDERIC. These, he said, were the agents for Sector K (KING), Sector E (EDOUARD), and Sector F (FREDERIC), but without identifying their actual names; ALBERT, he said, was the name of a town (in the Somme region).[25] Here he must have been mistaken, as ALBERT is also Jean Lejeune who had been covering Sector A, as shown in the 'Members and Contact of the WALENTY Organisation Carded in VICTOIRE' in VICTOIRE's file, and also in 'The *Interallié* Network, Autumn 1941', in Nigel West's *MI6* and Garby-Czerniawski's *The Big Network.*[26] A Jean Lejeune, born on 12 October 1913 in Toul in the Meurthe-et-Moselle, a printer, shows up in a charred fragment of a document 'Tatbestandziege. Personalien des Beschuldigten', meaning 'Personal details of the accused', dated 21 April 1944, but there is no other information available from the fragment to confirm whether or not he is the person referred to above.[27]

CHAPTER 12

Penetration of the LUCAS Network

Just after Christmas, the LUCAS network appeared on the scene and served to distract the Germans from *Interallié*. It seems that Bleicher's idea was 'to organize a fictitious resistance network and infiltrate narks into all the clandestine organizations'. VICTOIRE's task, according to her memoirs, would be 'to see LUCAS, listen to all he had to say, give nothing away, ask a maximum of questions, play up my past in *Interallié*, give him advice and of course repeat everything faithfully to Bleicher'. She was to offer him everything he needed. If LUCAS had been paying attention, this should have been suspicious and a little too good to be true. Asking too many questions and offering too much in return should have rung alarm bells.

Exactly how VICTOIRE came into contact with LUCAS is at first not at all clear, and was initially thought to have occurred on 26 December 1941 when she met MIKLOS, who was her lawyer, to discuss her divorce from Maurice Carré.[1] As we shall see, though, LUCAS contradicted this when he was interviewed later by Tar Robertson. His side of the story will be explained in Chapter 14. MIKLOS is reported to have said at some point: 'I was present yesterday at a very important meeting where there was a young chief who, having returned from England, is going to co-ordinate all the organisations.' That meeting was the one with LUCAS and VICTOIRE.

LUCAS was Edouard Pierre Fourrier De Crevoisier de Vomécourt, referred to as Pierre to distinguish him from his brothers Philippe @ GAUTHIER (1902–64) and Jean (1899–1945), who died at Orianenberg concentration camp on 12 February 1945. Pierre was born on 1 January 1906 at Chassy-lès-Montbozon, in the Haute-Saône département of Bourgogne-Franche-Comté. His father, Jean François Maxime Constantin De Crevoisier de Vomécourt, had been killed during the First World War; his mother (*née* Louise Adrienne Marie De Carrey d'Asnières) took the entire family to England on 11 April 1919.

There he was educated at St John's School, Old Windsor, and Beaumont College, a Jesuit public school also in Old Windsor. (It closed in 1967.) After going into business, when the family returned to France he did his national service in 1926. At the beginning of the Second World War he was attached as a liaison officer to the 7th Battalion, the Cameronians (Scottish Rifles), a Territorial Army unit and part of the British Expeditionary Force (BEF). The battalion would serve during the latter part of the Dunkirk campaign, from where it was evacuated in June 1940. After becoming a naturalised Briton on 14 October 1940, he refused to return to France, but was recruited by F Section SOE, which sent him back as one of their agents.

Pierre de Vomécourt founded and led SOE's *Autogiro* network, and it was agreed by them that VICTOIRE should act as the conduit for the network's messages. As Nigel West points out:

> Once London's acknowledgement had been received, via the Canadian Legation in Vichy, de Vomécourt was fully satisfied that Carré was trustworthy. Accordingly, he channeled all his communications through her, which meant that her Abwehr lover, Hugo Bleicher, was reading every word.[2]

On 13 May 1941 he parachuted into Chateauroux, France, according to West's account, which is also confirmed by Marcel Ruby.[3] However, Mackenzie's official account of the history of SOE contradicts this date, which he says was 11 May.[4] LUCAS's own statement made to MI5 on 14 May 1945 also states that it was the 11th. According to Mackenzie, LUCAS's contacts were all through Major Georges Bégué (1911–93) @ GEORGE NOBLE, who had been dropped the week before, on 6 May, to set up wireless communication (some accounts say the 5th, but this could be the night of 5/6 May to account for such discrepancies). The dates in Freddie Clark's book *Agents by Moonlight* muddle things by getting the dates reversed:

> On the 10/11th May in reply to Bégué's wireless report to London on the 9th May, Knowles [Squadron Leader E.V. 'Teddy' Knowles] flew another operation to France AUTOGYRO D&E/JOULY and parachuted two more agents: Pierre de Vomécourt (Lucas) and Baron Emanuel d'Astier de la Vigerie (Bernard) into the same area as Bégué was dropped.[5]

On 24 October 1941 Bégué was arrested by the Germans in a Marseilles safe house and imprisoned in a camp at Mauzac but would later escape.

Michel Brault, known as MIKLOS, gave a statement to William Skardon of MI5 on 4 and 11 April 1944 in the presence of Christopher Harmer in which he elaborated on Mathilde Carré (VICTOIRE) and the events leading up to the break-up of *Interallié*. Before the war he had been a member of the Paris Bar with an office at 22, rue Raynouard in the 16th arrondissement. Since August 1940 his office had been at 21, Avenue Georges V, which he had taken over from the American Max Shoop, the managing partner in the law firm of Sullivan & Cromwell's Paris branch.[6] The law firm was described by Douglas Waller as 'one of the most powerful law firms in the world'.[7] Shoop was covertly working for the head of the American Coordinator of Information (the forerunner of the OSS), Allen Dulles, who was a partner in Sullivan & Cromwell. Shoop would funnel money to Resistance groups and handle military intelligence that the groups sent back. When he gave his statement, Brault was an officer with the Forces Françaises Libres, which were based at the headquarters of the BCRA at 10 Duke Street, London. Born in 1893, he was variously known as Jérome Levy, Colonel Jérome, Marcel Robert Barrault and Maizeray.[8]

Brault described how he had first met VICTOIRE, known to him then as Micheline Carré, when she came to him accompanied by Armand Borni (WALENTY). They left him in no doubt that they had come from Philippe Autier, the son of his first cousin, Theresa Autier. He said that the meeting was either at the end of September or the beginning of October 1940. It will be recalled that the pair had met Autier in Limoges sometime after the 15 October 1940 but before the 18th, when they had returned to Toulouse. In fact, they had not arrived in Paris until 16 November, when they met up again, so Brault must have been wrong about the timeframe. They told him their instructions were to set up an intelligence network and asked his assistance. They especially needed introductions to people working for the railway companies (SNCF) and young boys who were unemployed. When they asked whether he could find them work as a cover to their activities, Brault told them this would be difficult, given that everyone had to register for employment. Nor was he sure how trustworthy his staff were. That being said, his secretary, Ginette Letonturier, also worked for them but he thought that Philippe Autier had been responsible for that introduction. Also known as GENEVIÈVE or CLAIRE, she later became the secretary, then on the staff of the Maquis of the Auvergne under Georges Louis Rebattet (CHEVAL). After the liberation she worked with Henri Ingrand, the regional commissioner of the Republic at the prefecture in Clermont-Ferrand.[9]

Brault continued to meet with them on a semi-regular basis, two or three times a week, first together, then just with VICTOIRE. He refused to be part of the organisation as an agent, but agreed to the code name MIKLOS to be used in their reports. Henceforth, he will be referred to as such here. Among the others MIKLOS introduced them to were Captain Davout, Gerard Dampierre and Teddy Rason. Captain Davout was Jacques Davout d'Auerstaedt (1913–2003), who was a civil mining engineer. Brault also introduced them to one of his friends, Henri Boussel, who became known as LE PETIT HENRI and worked for the Northern Railway Company in their traffic office:

> He was, I think, their best informant … He created I think a network of information in connection with railway matters and supplied them with information relating to troop movements and requests by the German Staff for train allocations. In my belief Henri Boussel was a most important agent for them and supplied quite invaluable information.[10]

Louis-Henri Boussel was born in Smyrna, Turkey, on 2 January 1916. He was arrested on 26 November 1941 (he says 22 November), due to VICTOIRE informing on him, and spent from then until 18 February 1943 in Fresnes. When he was interrogated, the Abwehr officer – who was in possession of all the wireless messages he had sent – who was undoubtedly Bleicher, said: '*Capitaine vous ne pouvez pas vous imaginer le mal que votre réseau a fait à l'Armée allemande*' ('Captain you can't imagine the harm your network has done to the German Army').

From Fresnes he was first sent to the fort at Romainville just to the north of Paris, then on 25 March to Mauthausen-Gusen concentration camp (prisoner number 48261). He died in Paris on 19 January 2014 aged 98, having made his career with the SNCF after the war. Interestingly, he refers to Brault as 'Colonel Michel' and founder of the *Étoile* and *Interallié* networks.[11] Boussel confirms in his article that he had been recruited by Brault and also that he was known as YVES @ LE PETIT TURC (the little Turk). Interestingly, the official biographer of Samuel Beckett refers to a Pierre Turc and Gaston Passagez as being railway engineers.[12]

In November 1941 VICTOIRE came to see MIKLOS about her divorce and informed him that Armand Borni (WALENTY) had been arrested, so this would make it around 17 November or just after. His arrest, she told him, was because he had fired his Polish secretary who was also his mistress

(VIOLETTE), who she suspected was a Gestapo agent. MIKLOS advised her to go immediately to Vichy since he knew from what she'd told him that she was apparently an agent of the French Deuxième Bureau assigned to keep an eye on ARMAND. He added:

> At the meeting when she, Micheline, informed me that Borni had been arrested and at several other meetings in the next few weeks before I went to Vichy, Micheline had frequent and ample opportunity of warning me that I was in danger of being arrested by the Gestapo. Had she warned me or told me that she had been arrested, I would have recognized the danger in which the Dampierres stood and I could possibly have saved Henri Boussel.[13]

At their first meeting MIKLOS had apparently explained to VICTOIRE that LUCAS and his network had no quick means of communicating with London and had offered him the use of the radio set operated by her. But this was not quite how LUCAS explained it. He said that their first meeting had only been of a general nature and had lasted about a quarter of an hour, during which he had simply promised to keep in touch with VICTOIRE; there had been no mention of VICTOIRE's offer of communication. VICTOIRE described her first impressions of him:

> I immediately took a liking to Lucas. He was a clean, robust idealist with a number of good ideas, but without the necessary drive to run an organization, little physical stamina and no knowledge of military information. Later I ascertained that he had great will-power, icy courage, and the gestures of overkeen men.[14]

Colonel Gano of the Polish Intelligence Service observed that LUCAS had made a major mistake on first meeting her: even though he knew nothing about her at that point, he gave away too much information.

They met on at least a couple more occasions, including at eleven o'clock the following morning, when LUCAS told her that he was going to Chartres to wait at a landing ground. It seems that it was only after this that he finally decided she should send a message for him. Harmer was also sceptical of VICTOIRE's account:

> There are so many inconsistencies in this story that there seems to be something seriously wrong somewhere. It appears however absolutely inconceivable that

MIKLOS in his state of nerves would have told VICTOIRE on the telephone what he wanted to talk about. It also seems inconceivable that VICTOIRE should have been so very certain when she first arrived in this country [of more later] that she went to see MIKLOS to discuss her divorce, whereas in her written memoirs she does not mention this. And it also seems inconceivable that LUCAS should have forgotten that he mentioned the quick means of communication at his first meeting. I regard the account given by VICTOIRE in her memoirs as a fabrication designed to cover up the real story, which was that by this time she was being allowed to circulate pretty freely (KIKI, BOB and MARCEL were all allowed complete liberty by this time), that she had gone to MIKLOS to discuss her divorce and other matters, that when with MIKLOS she had met LUCAS and heard about him from MIKLOS, and that she had then betrayed him to curry favour with her German masters. If she therefore deserves any credit for having rescued LUCAS from the Germans' clutches this is cancelled out by her initial crime of having betrayed him.[15]

The message LUCAS gave her, which was received on 31 December, read:

Please give the following message to Room 055 War Office urgently [cover name for MI5]. I confirm my message of 10th December by a different route. Send LYSANDER to fetch me the 3rd, 4th or 5th January on the ground used for the departure of WALENTY to see the Polish Secret Service. Send one wireless operator, two W/T sets and important funds. If LYSANDER impossible, send by man on the landing ground at Vaas near Le Mans with one wireless operator, funds, a container … (illegible). If operation is impossible send me money by the U.S. Military Attache at Vichy and tell me when to go and fetch it and what password, necessary before 10th January. I am fusing all healthy organisations in both zones, counting on you. Reply urgently by the Polish channel if you are sending LYSANDER or by man or money to Vichy. LUCAS. VICTOIRE.

A reply was sent the following day:

For LUCAS. Very pleased to have had your news. We are hoping to send you money and wireless operator. A message will follow shortly.

For VICTOIRE. We are waiting impatiently for the address to which we can send you money. Reply urgently.

At LUCAS's office the next day, Bleicher had also shown up but waited and watched outside in the car, apparently intending to kill him if VICTOIRE did not appear. LUCAS told VICTOIRE that he would return to Paris if he did not succeed in escaping. Again, Harmer reports an inconsistency in this account:

> It does appear peculiar that the Germans were prepared, on VICTOIRE's showing, to allow LUCAS to go back to England without knowing to any degree who he was or what he represented. Therefore, again it appears to be probable that LUCAS' account is correct, and that he did not tell VICTOIRE anything about his organisation until after his return from Chartres, and the failure of the operation.[16]

MIKLOS said that the Gestapo came for him at 6.30 on the morning of 16 January 1942 at his residence at 22, rue Raynouard, but he managed to escape. As VICTOIRE recounted in her memoirs, MIKLOS was able to escape via the backstairs reserved for servants while the soldiers sent to arrest him 'clumped up the main stairs'. A week later he left for Vichy and met Sejourne (Capitaine Simonaux), whose name he had been given by VICTOIRE, as well as two of his colleagues who were in French Counter-Espionage, one of whom was chief of the division. This was likely Major (later Colonel) Paul Paillole (1905–2002), who was head of the Counter-Espionage division at that time. Sometime after that LUCAS received a note from MIKLOS saying he had escaped to Vichy and wanted to meet with him. LUCAS had to go there to collect some money anyway so the two arranged to meet. MIKLOS told him that he was certain he had been set up and given away by VICTOIRE, but eventually they both concluded that this had not been the case, although it is not recorded who else they thought it might have been.

LUCAS sent a message to London, which was received on 23 January 1942, reporting that MIKLOS was currently in Cannes. He also told Tar Robertson that he thought MIKLOS was all right because he had met him in company with Roosevelt's personal representative to Vichy, whose name he thought was Schuler but it was, in fact, Robert Daniel Murphy (1894–1978) who, in February 1941 had successfully negotiated the Murphy–Weygand Agreement allowing the US to export to French North Africa in spite of a British blockade and trade restrictions on Vichy France, as well as plans for Operation *Torch*. When MIKLOS met him, Murphy was the American *chargé d'affaires* in Vichy.

Once back in Paris that same day, LUCAS challenged VICTOIRE about her suspected involvement in the attempted arrest of MIKLOS. She was horrified, stating categorically that she had had nothing to do with it. Then she changed her story and confided in him how she had been caught by the Gestapo and was working for them; she had also been put in charge of finding out everything she could about the LUCAS organisation. As Tar recounted in his report:

> I asked LUCAS why it was that VICTOIRE had never previously at any of their meetings told LUCAS the correct position. LUCAS said that VICTOIRE had said that she had been trying to but had not been able to bring herself to do it. I also asked LUCAS, in connection with this matter, whether at any time VICTOIRE had aroused his suspicions at all and he said that he had been suspicious on one or two occasions when VICTOIRE had asked him for the real names of certain people who were doing subversive work in France. LUCAS explained that this was one of the things which is never done by people who are doing this type of work.

Tar noted:

> This point is exceedingly curious and interesting, especially in view of the fact that at the interview which Mr. Harmer had with VICTOIRE on 3.3.42, VICTOIRE made an attempt to find out WALENTY's real name. I regard this fact as most suspicious.[17]

These occurrences should have made LUCAS much more wary of VICTOIRE and raised a red flag or two, so why didn't they? Had LUCAS even at this early stage decided to find a way of 'turning' her yet again? It seems that this was indeed the case, as we shall see.

Patricia McCallum's report outlines the many reasons why MIKLOS and LUCAS had reason to suspect VICTOIRE of betraying *Interallié*. One was that she was quickly able to produce papers that the organisation needed, papers that were considered too good to be forgeries, meaning that they had to have come directly from the Germans. When VICTOIRE asked MIKLOS to identify a friend from a photograph, it also could only have come from the Germans. She also claimed to LUCAS that she had been 'forced' to do things because Bleicher had followed her, listened to her phone calls, read her diary, while also blaming VIOLETTE for many of the betrayals. As McCallum sums up:

The facts remained: she was BLEICHER's mistress; she had collaborated with the Germans to the fullest extent; she had betrayed (or at least failed to warn) a number of old friends; and she had 'blown' AUTOGIRO. The orthodox course for LUCAS to take was to liquidate VICTOIRE then and there and himself disappear.[18]

LUCAS later admitted that he had considered doing so but realised that there was no time to warn agents before she met with Bleicher.

Once the *Interallié* affair was wound up VICTOIRE was only useful as a conduit to obtain money from the British. Had it not been for the LUCAS organisation, which was now considered more important, the Germans would most likely have used her to infiltrate the Rue Gîte-le-Coeur organisation run by BOB-EDGAR. They held a meeting with VICTOIRE, BOB and KIKI to decide what to do. Their decision was to assign Ische to deal with the Rue Gîte-le-Coeur organisation, while Bleicher and VICTOIRE would handle LUCAS; the operation was code-named NOBEL II. VICTOIRE, in turn, was given the code name BAGHERRA, exclusively for this operation. True to form, VICTOIRE made a number of demands of the Germans: that she be given carte blanche to deal with everything in Paris; that she should be completely free; and that one of the captured agents, RENÉ (René Aubertin), be released to help her. The Germans would not agree to the latter demand, but allowed MICHEL (Claude Jouffret), renamed CLAUDE, to be released instead.

René Camille Aubertin, who was born on 18 August 1911 in Montmorency, in the Val-d'Oise, département, was first deported to Trêves on 25 March 1943, then to Mauthausen on the 27th under the 'Night and Fog' decree; he was released on 5 May 1945.[19] (Another online entry gives his birth date as 27 July 1912 and his birthplace as Saint-Dizier in the Haute-Marne département;[20] in both cases, the release date from Mauthausen is the same.) VICTOIRE used him to assist her with making contacts with LUCAS and his agents, and he would later keep in touch with ROGER (Roger Cottin) when VICTOIRE was in England. A 'Preliminary Interrogation of SYLVAIN @ LUCAS' dated 21 April 1945 noted that ROGER met with CLAUDE regularly while VICTOIRE was away. When ROGER disappeared, after weighing all the odds and going to his rooms, LUCAS assumed that he had been arrested. He then sent DAISY to Lyons with a telegram saying that ROGER had been arrested and to bring back a W/T operator. An interview with Philippe de Vomécourt @ GAUTHIER dated 18 March 1944 states that DAISY was a *girl* working in 'the other zone' (presumably the Unoccupied Zone) who had first informed him of his brother's arrest, and was herself presumed to have been arrested: 'She told GAUTHIER that LUCAS had gone to the appointment at a café with three persons and then went to another café to pick up someone else (GAUTHIER did not know who) when he was arrested.'[21] This means it could not have been Daisy Fellowes, who was married to Kraus, as she was much older and still around.

In Bleicher's file in the list of 'Principal Personalities' of NOBEL II, DAISY is listed as 'MARTEGOUTTE @ DAISY, mistress of LUCAS and agent';[22] she is also described as '*Secretaire et Maitress*' (secretary and mistress) in another of Bleicher's files[23] and referred to as Madame MARTE-GOUTTE in 'Comte Rendu de Pierre de Vomecourt' of 14 May 1945 in the same file. As Squadron Leader Beddard observed in his report on 9 July 1945, 'By January 1942 MICHELINE [VICTOIRE] had LUCAS completely under her thumb, and they joined forces, taking an office at the Lido, where they worked together.'

Shortly thereafter, VICTOIRE moved into a flat at 26, rue de la Faisanderie, in the 16th arrondissement near the Porte Dauphine and the Université Paris-Dauphine, one of many that had been requisitioned by the German High Command, and that had been previously owned by an Italian Jew, later occupied by a German captain who had been sent to the Russian Front. In her published memoirs she said it was formerly the François de Curel Hôtel. By this time she was also on more intimate terms with Ische, whom she called 'Freddie'. As Harmer recounted in his report:

> The flat was magnificent; although it was mid-winter, flowers were brought round several times a day. She was not subject to the restrictions of rationing of fuel and light, but on the contrary had special fires fitted, and a maid called MARGUERITE was put entirely at her disposal. BLEICHER, she says, moved his things to the new flat and they lived as Monsieur and Madame Jean CASTEL. She explains that as her confidence grew she was able to withstand the advances of BLEICHER, whom, of course, she really detested, by pretending that she was ill. Here again one wonders whether, even if this was true, it was due to her dislike of BLEICHER or perhaps to the fact that she had now received the attentions of ISCHE.[24]

Instead of deciding to eliminate her, LUCAS opted to 'turn' her yet again. VICTOIRE had told him that she 'wished to redeem herself' and work for the Allies again; exactly why is unclear, but perhaps this was part of her 'long game'. But why should LUCAS believe it? As BENOIT described it:

> Because a few seemingly minor details such as the delay in the transmissions of a message or an inconsistency had aroused Lucas' curiosity: also, a couple of more serious matters (the arrest of a friend, the procurement by Victoire of over-perfect false papers bearing genuine German stamps) had strengthened his doubts ... He decided that her repentance was sincere and that her obvious megalomania and shame at having given way to the Germans could be put to good use with skillful handling. She was a great subversive worker. Why should she not become the greatest of all 'treble' agents by working for us? He had struck the right chord. She jumped at it and I really believe she began to hate Bleicher from then on.
>
> Her peculiar nature must have experienced a queer kind of elation at the idea of playing an even more complicated version of the game to which she had devoted herself. And perhaps the idea of personal revenge spurred her on.[25]

To that end, LUCAS invented a story for her to tell Bleicher: that 'he (LUCAS) had suddenly become confidential and revealed his plans to her'. He said he wanted to return to London but that when he returned he would meet with all the heads of the Resistance and might even bring back a British general to meet them. VICTOIRE, of course, duly reported this to Bleicher, who was delighted. It was agreed that LUCAS should be allowed to return to London, with the proviso that it would have to be cleared at a higher level, and also with the Gestapo. According to BENOIT, the Gestapo found the whole plan 'too clever to be feasible and were pressing for our immediate arrest. A big noise had arrived from Berlin to decide between the two proposals!' Clearly the envoy from Berlin agreed to allow them to escape as the plan went ahead. This enabled LUCAS to contact his brother, Philippe, who would send a message to SOE. As noted in the report, 'Although for the rest of the war she was regarded with considerable suspicion nothing has come to light to show that after her "re-conversion" she ever went back on her Allied allegence [sic].' In the meantime, LUCAS held a meeting with BENOIT (sometimes written as BENOIS), Ben Cowburn, whom we shall meet later, and ROGER (Roger Cottin), who both agreed to the plan.

Complications occurred around how to pay VICTOIRE's notional network through an SIS source and also through LUCAS; how to get money for LUCAS and his organisation; how to arrange for a pick-up, first by air, then by sea, and finally by air again, but nothing worked out. LUCAS eventually decided that VICTOIRE should accompany him to London. As VICTOIRE records it, on the day that had been arranged for LUCAS's departure, 30 January, the aircraft had not appeared. A message sent by VICTOIRE the following day to London reported, 'LUCAS has been at the landing place since yesterday evening. I am in touch with him each day to send him his instructions.' The following Sunday they went for a walk in the snow. It was then that he suggested that she accompany him. When she protested, saying that the Germans restricted her movements, he insisted that she should try, saying that she would be in a better position to tell the British what had happened to her, rather than him recounting it second-hand. In his next message to the British, he told her, he would say that he would be bringing 'another important, small sized, lightweight passenger, but without saying who it is'.[26] If he sent such a message it is not recorded in any of their files. Had he done so, SOE would almost certainly have recommended against it. However, the 'Conte Rendu de Pierre de VOMECOURT' (Account of Pierre de VOMECOURT) dated 14 May 1945, copies of which are contained in the files of VICTOIRE, BRUTUS and Bleicher, somewhat contradicts this when LUCAS said:

> *Entre temps, j'avais dit à* <u>*Victoire*</u> *de dire aux Allemands que je lui avais proposé de l'emmener avec moi en Angleterre et qu'elle déplois toute son habileté pour faire accepter cette solution à la Gestapo.*

> Meanwhile I told <u>Victoire</u> to tell the Germans that I had suggested that she accompany me to England and to use all her skill to persuade the Gestapo to accept this idea.[27]

In VICTOIRE's mind, going to London would have several benefits: it would prove to LUCAS that she was being straight with him, as well as saving her from the Germans once they had discovered she was double-crossing them. On the negative side, if she was still working for the Germans, she could be 'kept where she could do no more harm'. Her cover story to the Germans would be that she was going as an Abwehr agent to collect information on British Intelligence, to whom LUCAS would introduce her. She was to get a list of 'agents working in France for the Allies, obtain a documentation from the Secret Service and return with Lucas. After that the great "round up" would take place.' It would also enable the Germans to monitor the pick-up and learn about methods and techniques. As McCallum's report notes: 'It is perhaps noteworthy that LUCAS did not warn SOE, either through the Polish link or Vichy, of the treat that was in store for them.' Most of the ensuing messages concerned the receipt/non-receipt of 200,000 francs to be passed on to VICTOIRE.

There followed a heavy exchange of messages between Paris and London regarding the pick-up. It was decided that BENOIT should accompany them, leaving ROGER to hold the fort. LUCAS suggested Lannion Bay at Moulin-de-la-Rive in Brittany for a sea pick-up, to which London agreed on 7 February. These sea pick-ups were part of Operation *Overcloud*; this particular operation was given the code name *Waterworks* (which was an unfortunate choice in light of what prevailed).[28] On 11 February they all left by train, shadowed by the Abwehr, who were anxious to arrest BENOIT. VICTOIRE had told them that he was only going to assist with the pick-up, not that he would leave with them.

Ische obtained an order signed by General Carl-Heinrich von Stülpnagel (1886–1944), which was sent to the Commander-in-Chief Naval Forces Brest, Generaladmiral Otto Schultze, to ensure that 'no night patrols by the German navy were to be carried out along the coast of Brittany between Perros Guirec and Loquirec'. This order was also sent to the Luftwaffe's Jagdgeschwader 2 (JG2) 'Richthofen', the Second Fighter Wing at Ploujean-Morlaix airfield. Eckert (of whom more below) was also sent to ensure that no patrols questioned a woman in a black fur coat and red hat. The black sheepskin coat she had bought for 10,000 francs with money her mother had given her.

In spite of the Germans making plans to withdraw their shore patrols in the area, the whole exercise was doomed. The sea was too rough, the boats dispatched by the destroyer were too small and capsized when VICTOIRE and BENOIT tried to embark, and London had ignored or not acted upon warnings from Vichy by sending over two W/T operators as requested by LUCAS – George William Abbott (PAUL) and Gustave Claude Brooks Redding (GEORGES 30) – but when they came ashore with a naval officer, an Australian named Lieutenant Commander Ivan Black, they were 'left wet and furious on the beach'.

CHAPTER 13

Gloria in Excelsis

In addition to the *Interallié* network, another network, the SMH/GLORIA organisation, began operating in both Occupied and Unoccupied France, first for the Polish Deuxième Bureau then the British Intelligence Services during most of 1941 and the first half of 1942. SMH was, according to James Knowlson, Samuel Beckett's official biographer, a reversal of the letters HMS – 'His Majesty's Service'.[1] A leading role in this organisation was played by Gabrielle Cecile Martinez Picabia (1913–77) @ GLORIA @ CLAUDE @ JEANNINE (to her sub-agents) @ Marie MONNET @ MARTINEZ @ Jean PICKARD, who some sources say actually founded it. She was the daughter of the French/Spanish-Cuban Cubist artist Francis Martinez Picabia (1879–1953), who counted among his artist friends Marcel Duchamp (1887–1968) and poet and writer Guillaume Apollinaire (1880–1918), and her mother was Gabrielle (*née* Buffet), born 1881 (no apparent relation to Denise Buffet). GLORIA first became an agent in 1940 when driving an ambulance for the French Red Cross. This brought her into contact with several prison camps in Brittany and Bordeaux, and she reported what she saw to a certain Marie Thérèse Briel (1909–52), another ambulance driver, who in turn was in touch with the British representative at the American consulate in Marseilles. Someone else with whom she was in contact was the American agent Virginia Hall @ MARIE, who had also been an ambulance driver, in spite of having a wooden leg.

While in Marseilles GLORIA met several people who would be instrumental in recruiting her to the Resistance: one was an ambulance mechanic named Gambier who was known to Briel; another was Armand Lowengard, a Jew who was a friend of her mother, Gabrièlle Buffet. He put her in touch with René Gimpel (1881–1945), who was a prominent French art dealer of Alsatian-Jewish descent. He would later be arrested in Monte Carlo, interned by the Vichy authorities, released in 1942, then rearrested, dying in Neuengamme concentration camp in 1945. His sons, Charles and Peter, founded an art gallery, Gimpel Fils, in London in 1946.

In February 1941 she was recruited by a Pole named Leblon, who gave her the name GLORIA and said she would be working for the 'English Intelligence Service' as Agent 253. He sent her to Paris to contact a Frenchman, Jacques Legrand, a chemist at the Institut Curie. Her job was to travel around and try to organise an information service in Brest. In case of emergency, she was to contact ARMAND (WALENTY) at 14, rue Raffet. Her first contact with him was in June 1941 when she went to see him to ask if he would send some communications for her, but he refused. He insisted that SMH subordinate themselves to *Interallié*, claiming his organisation to be the only Polish information service in France. She, in turn, rejected his demands. He told Harmer on 20 March 1943 that:

> He was satisfied that not only had they no proper organisation working but they were far too inexperienced and incompetent to run one ... In short, he regarded the whole SMH/GLORIA outfit as not being a serious effort at all and he wanted to have as little do with it as possible ... [but] he was prepared to use them as sub-agents, if they were prepared to join him on his terms, but they refused to do this.[2]

He also set her straight about who she was working for, which was the Poles and not British Intelligence. When he asked her for a list of her agents and their photographs, she refused. It seems that he did not trust the accuracy of the reports she had given him about U-boats at Brest, so refused to send them. As Buckmaster noted in 1943, 'The history of Gloria, Lucas, Walenty, Miklos and others is inevitably frightfully interwoven.'

Henri Boussel (LE PETIT TURC), a member of *Interallié* who had been arrested when the network was broken up, had been put in touch with GLORIA by Michel Brault (MIKLOS) and was supplying her with information without WALENTY's knowledge. She narrowly escaped arrest when she visited MIKLOS the day the Gestapo came to arrest him, but bluffed her way out of it by saying she had come to see him as a client about a piece of land.

According to a report in her file, it was between 15 and 20 January 1942 that she first met LUCAS, erroneously referred to as 'Jean de Vomecourt'. The report states that she was 'in fairly close touch with him from this time until his arrest at the end of April or beginning of May 1942'.[3] She first thought it was on 24 April or 1 May. She told him of her dissatisfaction with WALENTY and the Poles, and he promised that when he next went to England he would try to arrange that she could work for the French–English service. He also told her about the break-up of *Interallié*, caused by VICTOIRE's treachery.

When she returned from a holiday in Nice she arranged to meet him on 15 April at the Café du Dome, 108, Boulevard Montparnasse, a favourite meeting place for artists and writers. The others who accompanied her to the café were Hélène Roussel, who was actually Suzanne Roussel @ HÉLÈNE, GLORIA's deputy, aged 30, and Gilbert Thomasson. LUCAS gave GLORIA 100,000 francs and told her he had arranged that SMH could maintain its independence. In exchange she promised to supply him with men for his para-military organisation, a promise she lived up to. Roussel was later arrested in August 1942. Interestingly, Knowlson describes Roussel as sometimes being called 'La Chatte', 'on account of her large eyes', but of course she should not be confused with Mathilde Carré, who also had that soubriquet.

Thomasson @ GIL was a reserve officer aged 40. He was arrested on 12 August 1942, the same day as Jacques Legrand. (Beckett's biographer says that Thomasson was an engineer with the Public Works department at the Porte d'Orléans responsible for the Paris catacombs.) In Bleicher's file SOE gives GIL as being Lieutenant T.C. Coppin, part of the *Carte* network sent to Marseilles in June 1942 to link up with OLIVE (Captain F. Basin).[4]

Edward 'Ted' Cyril Coppin (1915–43) was born at Brightlingsea in Essex on 20 May 1915 and recruited by F Section SOE as an instructor for the *Donkeyman* circuit.[5] Code-named OLIVIER, he was infiltrated into France on 11 June 1942. He was arrested by the Gestapo on 23 April 1943 and executed on 27 September 1943, thought possibly to have been at Ravensbrück, although never proven.

GLORIA and LUCAS continued to see each other on a regular basis. One of LUCAS's post boxes was on the Boulevard des Italiens, where she arranged to meet him, but only a sub-agent, Guy Walter @ LEON, was there. A note in GLORIA's file in the MI5 Registry states that Walter, born circa 1897, had claimed to have parachuted into France as a British agent, which the note says is untrue and suggests that he was probably a Belgian working for the Germans. It was only after having waited for him to show up, and then meeting Jean CLAUDE, another of LUCAS's agents, that GLORIA found LUCAS in the café opposite with a woman named Betty, and another man. Betty, according to GLORIA, was the liaison agent between the two zones of JOSEF (real name Jean Maxime Aron, born 1 November 1901)[6] in the Unoccupied Zone. Aron was a Jewish engineer for Citroën and also an SOE agent who had been responsible for recruiting Denise Bloch (1916–45), another SOE agent, who became his secretary. Bloch would later die at Ravensbrück on 5 February 1945 along with Lilian Rolfe and Violette Szabo. LUCAS informed GLORIA of ROGER's arrest and that the post box was probably under surveillance; he gave her an alternative address at 1, rue de l'Université.

It was on Tuesday 5 May that she learned of LUCAS's arrest when she met Hélène Roussel and Jacques Legrand @ SMH at the Vikings restaurant. Most likely this was Le Viking at 55, rue du Faubourg in Montmartre. Of all those arrested, LEON was the only agent to be released. Information from an SIS report, originally dated 23 November 1943 and extracted on 29 May 1944, described Guy Walters [*sic*] @ LEON as:

> Aged 45, well built, grey hair receding at temples, gross features, scar on right cheek in form of a cross. Spoke with a Belgian accent. Said to have a brother working in the Belgian Intelligence Service. Claimed that he had been parachuted from England. In Paris an associate of LUCAS, S.O.E. agent, 1942.[7]

A note in the same document states:

> S.O.E. inform us that Guy WALTERS @ LEON was never parachuted from England and has never, in fact, visited this country in connection with his S.O.E. activity. The second LEON may very well be a confusion for an agent called NOEL, whose name has been spelt the wrong way round on several occasions and thereby got confused. It seems pretty clear that the one who is suspected of being a German agent is LEON, and not NOEL.[8]

This appears to be contradicted by a question in the 'Proces-Verbal' prepared by the Direction du Comité Français de la Libération Nationale, Direction Générale des Services Spéciaux of the BCRAL dated 10 March 1944 in their investigation of '*le sieur* MIKLAUS [*sic*]'. The report posed the question: '*Quels on été les pseudonyms de* PIERRAT?' ('What were the pseudonyms of PIERRAT?'), to which the answer was 'LEON et NOEL'.

PIERRAT was Paul Leon Pierrat, also referred to as Leon Henri Pierrat, who came under suspicion of working for the Germans as an *agent provocateur*. He was born in Calvi, Corsica, on 3 April 1908. His file states that in 1933 he went to Germany at the behest of M. de Margery, first secretary of the French embassy in Berlin, to study the Nazis. Margery was the cousin of Baron Robert Fabre-Luce (1897–19??), who was a writer and far-right activist known to be a National Socialist. In Berlin he gained access to some high-ranking Nazis, including Dr Alfred Rosenberg and Otto Meissner, Hindenburg's closest advisor, and attended a couple of receptions given by Joseph Goebbels. A report in his file notes that 'PIERRAT makes it clear that throughout his stay in Germany he never showed sympathetic interest to the Nazi movement, and while he never expressed his dislike of it to them he also never claimed to be a convert to their ideas.'[9]

A lengthy report by A. Newman in Pierrat's file dated 13 January 1944 avers that 'Leon WELTER is certainly identical with Guy WALTER @ LEON'. Interestingly, there are SOE files in the National Archives at Kew on a Guy Walter @ CHARRUE[10] and Jean Étienne Sriber (1918–2012),[11] who were both involved in the *Faucheuse* mission in 1944 to collect arms and sabotage high-tension cables. An interview with Philippe de Vomécourt @ GAUTHIER on 18 March 1944 states:

> GAUTHIER definitely believes that 'LEON' refers to WALTER and that WALTER was responsible for LUCAS' arrest. He was told on the 7th January by his wife who had seen her sister in law that LUCAS had told her that WALTER had denounced him.[12]

It appears that WALTER had given LUCAS the impression that he knew that VICTOIRE was working for the Germans. When Michel Brault (MIKLOS) was interrogated by MI5 on 23 March 1944 two questions were posed to him that are significant in this regard:

LUCAS Organisation
1. Which of LUCAS's [*sic*] agents was known as LEON?
Two were known as LEON – PIERRAT and WALTERS. PIERRAT was also known as NOEL. I never met WALTERS and do not know which of the two was arrested with LUCAS. I was told by PIERRAT that it was WALTERS. He put up a strong defence for WALTERS. The arrested man was released 24 hours later. Therefore either both PIERRAT and WALTERS are traitors or else PIERRAT believed WALTERS. I do not know which of the two was more generally known as LEON.

Arrest of LUCAS
How did you hear of LUCAS' arrest?
I heard from GAUTHIER that LUCAS was arrested in a café. I also received this message from Philippe AUTIER:- 'LUCAS, LEON and two others arrested on Monday in a café; LEON released 24 hours later; it looks very

suspicious; believe LEON is the man who denounced the party.' I thought that LEON was PIERRAT and very nearly had him killed.[13]

Pierrat said that he first met LUCAS in November 1941, introduced by an old journalist friend, Daniel Bernstein @ JULIEN @ ANDRÉ @ VICTOR (born 27 January 1904), whom he had met around September 1941 at the Brasserie Lorraine, 2, Place des Ternes in the 7th arrondissement. He was later introduced to Roger Cottin and Leon Welter, who was of Russian origin and had been wounded in the right leg. Also at that time he introduced LUCAS to Michel Brault. In January 1942 LUCAS introduced him to VICTOIRE, who he described as having beautiful black eyes, very elegant, and of 'extremely easy virtue'. However, his account of his activities since the Armistice in 1940, according to John Day of MI5 in March 1944, 'seems profoundly unsatisfactory'. Major Richard Warden of SOE wrote to Geoffrey Wethered at MI5 in February 1944, saying:

> I cannot for one moment believe that there is any truth in PIERRAT's story that LUCAS had instructed him to establish relations with [Pierre] LAVAL with the aim of building up an information service for his organisation … it was certainly not in either LUCAS' mind, or – as far as we know – anyone else's, that any contact with LAVAL or the Gestapo should be permitted … It looks as if PIERRAT … has given free rein to his imagination in order to account for any dealings he may have had with the enemy.[14]

On 1 February 1942 in a report possibly by Harmer (the name is not given), it states, 'LUCAS desires to see General Sikorski, as he saw LEON NOEL before leaving Paris and that he had given him messages for General Sikorski.'[15] Harmer suggested to Major Wethered on 4 February 1944 that VICTOIRE be asked whether Pierrat was the man referred to as 'LEON' in the organisation and 'whether the messages received from the Germans at the end of April referring to LEON in fact referred to PIERRAT'. Two of these messages found in Pierrat's file[16] were a telegram from Paris dated 1 May 1942 transmitted over a channel controlled by the Germans. The first said:

> *Pour* VICTOIRE. CLAUDE *a appris déperdition* ROGER *par* LEON *qui averti par concierge de plutôt perquisition a pu se sauver. D'après* LEON, ROGER … (? Parassait) *être très inquiet les derniers jours au sujet retard agent expedie en zone libre.* LEON *suppose que cet agent est arreté en route et a trahi. Aucune autre*

explication possible. Suivant enquête LEON quelques autres agents on été arretés. Qui être SYLVAIN [this sentence not clear]. LEON *a parlé de lui comme étant un des dirigements de l'organisation. Il … son arrestation … pas venir au rendezvous fixe 27 avril.* LEON *est parti en zone libre pour quelque temps. Prière informer* LUCAS *immédiatement pour prendre decision concernant votre retour.* KIKI.

[For VICTOIRE. CLAUDE learned of the loss of ROGER from LEON who was warned by the concierge in plenty of time to save himself. According to LEON, ROGER … (? appeared) to be very anxious these last few days about the delay of the agent sent to the Unoccupied Zone. LEON assumes that this agent has been arrested en route and was betrayed. There is no other possible explanation. After making enquiries LEON learned that several other agents had been arrested. What has become of SYLVAIN [this sentence not clear]. LEON spoke of him as being one of the leaders of the organisation. He … his arrest … not coming to the fixed meeting of 27 April. LEON has left for the Unoccupied Zone for a while. Please inform LUCAS immediately so that we can plan for your return. KIKI.]

The other was a telegram received from the Polish chief agent 'F' in France on 15 April 1942 in which LEON is mentioned: 'LEON *relache le 1er mai a disparu trois jours après*' ('LEON was freed on 1 May then disappeared three days later').

On 26 April 1942 Harmer reported on the message received regarding ROGER's arrest and discussed it with VICTOIRE. She was of the opinion that, had he actually been arrested, the Germans would have been unlikely to have broadcast it in such a way. Her rationale was that if they knew she was double-crossing them they would not have revealed such information to her. That would have told her that there was a danger of ROGER betraying her under interrogation, and this would have prevented her from returning to France. Harmer argued that:

> If on the other hand they did not know that she was double-crossing them but thought it wise as a precaution to put ROGER under restraint, they would not have arrested him because of the complications that would ensue on this side in the preparation of her plans over here for going back with LUCAS and helping them to break up the LUCAS organisation.[17]

VICTOIRE thought that there were two possible explanations: either he had been arrested on a misdemeanour, as had happened once before, or he had never returned from Vichy and had arranged for someone else to hand over the 100,000 francs and deliver a message to the effect that he had collected it there.

When LUCAS left Paris it had been arranged that he would give ROGER 'a certain sum of money' and on 15 April and 1 May he would be instructed by MI5 to go to Vichy to collect it, then return after a suitable period of time. It occurred to Harmer that since there had been a change of government in Unoccupied France, these arrangements 'might give rise to difficulties and might compromise even further the relations between the U.S.A. and the Vichy authorities'. Bodington proposed that on 19 April a message be sent to Paris saying, 'Go to Vichy immediately to collect money. The old method has been abolished therefore you must utilize the the alternative method we discussed before I left France. LUCAS.' The reasoning being that the Germans wouldn't ask what the new method was, and it would ensure that ROGER went there instead of the Germans sending one of their own. 'We were, however, forestalled in this plan by the arrival of the message on the 18th saying that ROGER had left in any event.'

Harmer was inclined to agree with VICTOIRE's explanations and thought that it was likely that LUCAS had ordered ROGER to go underground. The Germans feared that he had escaped because he had discovered the real position:

> In that event they know that he will try to get a message through to England, and this is their way of warning VICTOIRE that he has fled, so that she can take steps to arrange her return for the earliest possible moment.

However, he remained unconvinced that the Germans wouldn't have announced ROGER's arrest, saying that if they had actually arrested him, they might still have made the announcement in order to lure British Intelligence into sending them the money some other way:

> Assuming that they have realized that we are playing with them and that in point of fact they will never see VICTOIRE and LUCAS again, they might very well decide to give us as much trouble as possible with regard to paying the money.

He believed that ROGER had indeed gone underground and that when a direct communication was received through LUCAS, this would be confirmed.

He approved two messages drafted by VICTOIRE to be sent to Claude Jouffret, knowing full well that Bleicher would see them, explaining that if Bleicher had been responsible for ROGER's arrest then VICTOIRE was annoyed with him for messing up her plans. If ROGER had been arrested for a serious offence she was afraid that LUCAS would abandon his organisation, and if he had been arrested for something trivial, or as a precaution, 'this will tell them that they must release him if they hope to have the remainder of the LUCAS organisation'.

A copy of Warden's document and a report on the interrogation of Pierrat by Wethered and Harmer, but signed on Harmer's behalf by H. Leggatt, appears in one of VICTOIRE's files.[18] The interrogation report focused on Pierrat's involvement with, and knowledge of, the *Interallié* and LUCAS organisations. Pierrat told them that he thought VICTOIRE was a member of a group of Polish saboteurs. He also seemed to know about several members of LUCAS's organisation, such as Roger Cottin, Leon Walter, Lucien Ambrosini (born 1 April 1910, employed by the Service de l'Air at Calvi) and Grimaldi (a Corsican police inspector), but said he knew nothing of the members of the GLORIA network or Picabia herself. There is no indication whether VICTOIRE was able to confirm or deny the allegation that Pierrat was in fact LEON or the messages sent by the Germans. What is interesting is that the SIS report dated 6 September 1943 concluded that there were two unsatisfactory points that emerged:

(a) Pierrat's story that he worked for the Gestapo in the interests of LUCAS suggests that he, as well as VICTOIRE, may in reality have been working for LUCAS in the interests of the Gestapo.

(b) There is a hitherto act of treachery in that someone betrayed to the Germans that LUCAS had returned to Paris after his visit to London from 28.2.42 to 4.4.42. It is considered that this responsibility can hardly be laid at the door of VICTOIRE who had, of course, not returned to France with Lucas. In view of (a), it is felt possible that the traitor may have been PIERRAT.[19]

What tends to confuse the issue even more is that another member of the LUCAS organisation was code-named LEON. As Harmer noted on 31 August 1943:

One of the LEONS was definitely released three days after his arrest, and GLORIA's original statement made it clear that this man was Leon WALTERS, referred to as WETTERS in PIERRAT's statement. It was the fact that somebody called LEON was released so soon afterwards and started to make enquiries about contacts in the LUCAS organisation that made us suspect that this LEON was working for the Germans. As PIERRAT also reports that the other LEON was released shortly after his arrest, it seems to point to WALTERS @ WETTERS being the person on whom suspicion fell at this time.[20]

Pierrat's file also notes that while LUCAS was in London he spoke of him but not that he had instructed him to work on behalf of the Gestapo. Furthermore, LUCAS's brother Philippe, as told by LUCAS to SOE, had 'absolutely no confidence in him'. MI5 decided to discount the allegation by GLORIA that LEON was an agent for the Gestapo as it was only third-hand information.

—ᴍ—

Amongst the other members of the SMH/GLORIA network were the writer and playright Samuel Beckett and his wife Suzanne (née Dumesnil). According to GLORIA's (Picabia) file, both dealt with photography. The file also mentions that he acted as a secretary and micro-photographed their reports. But a report on Beckett by Hugh Astor to John Marriott and Guy Liddell dated 16 April 1945 describes his job as being to collect reports from the various agents and type them up; the photography would be done by a Greek named Nazarov in the Avenue de Parc Mont Souris [sic]. Knowlson clarified the matter in his biography of Beckett:

Beckett was very insistent that he was not responsible for the photography as has been claimed [by Deirdre Bair, another of Beckett's biographers]. Instead … he delivered his typed sheets to a man known to him only as Jimmy the Greek. The photographer of Gloria was André (in reality Hadji) Lazaro, who indeed had a Greek father and was also known within the group as Tante Léo (Aunt Léo). Lazaro lived, as Beckett said he did, in the avenue du Parc de Montsouris, now known as the avenue René Coty. It was he, Beckett said, who produced the miniaturized film for dispatch to London.[21]

Neither Nazarov nor Lazaro appear in the list of the GLORIA/SMH network in either of her files. André Hadji Lazaro was born in Athens, Greece, on 31 October 1914, and, having been interned in Fresnes and Romainville on 24 February 1943, was deported first to Sarrebruck Neue Bremm on 28 September 1943, followed by Mauthausen on 16 October 1943 under the 'Night and Fog' decree. He was liberated on 22 April 1945 and repatriated to Annecy on the 29th.

Beckett was described as 'an Irishman known to GLORIA before the war' and as 'Age 38, 6ft. Well built but stoops. Dark hair. Fresh complexion. Very silent.' His whereabouts at that time were given as near Avignon. His wife was described as 'Age 35. 5ft 6in. Dark hair. Smart appearance.'[22] Beckett also had an assistant, Yvonne Boneval. As he told his biographer James Knowlson, he joined the Resistance because, 'You simply couldn't stand by with your arms folded.'[23] Beckett is reported to have joined the Resistance on 1 September 1941.[24] A key factor, according to Knowlson, was the arrest of James Joyce's unpaid secretary and helper, Paul Léopoldovitch Léon (1893–1942), who was arrested in August 1941 and imprisoned at Drancy internment camp; he died in Auschwitz on 27 March 1942. Astor reported that:

> Although BECKETT appears fairly intelligent and well educated, he knew very little about the organisation of S.M.H./GLORIA. He received his orders direct from S.M.H., and the other members who were known to him personally included GLORIA, THOMASSON, PERON and Hélène ROUSSEL. He had heard speak of LUCAS and of LEON, but had not met either of them. He did not appear to have heard of MIKLOS or of MARIE [Virginia Hall].[25]

Beckett told MI5 that he knew nothing about LUCAS's arrest except that LEON came under suspicion from GLORIA and SMH. In the days following the arrests of the SMH/GLORIA network Beckett and his wife were forced to keep moving constantly until a man named Delau provided them with safe lodgings. Unlike many in the organisation, he did not escape to the Chalet de Ski hide-out in Megève, but was helped by an American, Mary Reynolds,[26] a bookbinder and art patron active in the Resistance, who put him in touch with a Dr Roux living at Foix who helped Madame Picabia to escape. Mary Louise Hubachek Reynolds was born in Minneapolis in 1891 (d.1950) and was in an intimate relationship with Marcel Duchamp, although they never married; she was also friends with the American artist Man Ray. An essay by author Page Dougherty Delano observes:

Most puzzling, in my view, is Reynolds' absence in the list of members of the Gloria network accounted for in the SOE debriefing of Jeanine Picabia in London, 1943, shortly after Picabia had escaped from France, when the Germans had arrested so many of this network. Yet, among Reynolds' papers in the Chicago Institute of Art's Library is a membership card in the Fédération des Amicales de Réseaux de la France Combattante, stamped 28 November 1945, of the network Gloria SMH.[27]

Nor is she mentioned in the list of members of the GLORIA/SMH network in Picabia's MI5 files. Dr Roux was most likely the French artist Gaston-Louis Roux (1904–88). Beckett managed to escape to Lyons, then went to Vichy to get his papers put in order before moving to Roussillon, where he stayed until October 1944. During this time he was part of the Maquis and also worked on the land. In October 1944 he returned to Paris. Harmer added, 'So far as BECKETT himself is concerned, he appeared helpful and created a favourable impression. I can see no reason to regard him with suspicion from a security point of view.'

—ᴍ—

It may be just a coincidence that a woman connected with the network named BLANCHET @ PETITJEAN, who was thought to be a former SIS agent suspected of working for the Germans, shared the same name as Renée Petitjean (Borni) @ VIOLETTE, but there does not appear to be any connection. The GLORIA/SMH network was betrayed by 32-year-old Abbé Robert Alesch (1906–49) @ Jean ACKOUIN or ACQUIN. As the report on the network by Captain John Mair (previously the deputy to the RSLO in Edinburgh and now with B1a) dated 11 April 1943 concludes, he was 'very likely an agent provocateur working for the Germans' and was responsible for the arrest of sixty-five agents and the break-up of the network. He was shot by firing squad at the Fort de Montrouge, Arceuil, France, on 25 January 1949.

During interviews in London in 1943 after she had escaped from France to England via Spain, GLORIA confirmed that, from what LUCAS had told her, VICTOIRE had betrayed 'Armand, his Organisation, Les Dampierre, Maitre Broult [sic], who escaped, Henri Boussel and some others'.[28]

CHAPTER 14

LUCAS's Story

In May 1945 LUCAS gave an account of his arrest and other events to MI5. When he parachuted into Chateauroux, France, on the night of 12/13 May 1941 his mission had been to organise propaganda and sabotage, and to see what the possibilities were for a general uprising, based on the activities, known and unknown, of the Resistance at that time. The first agent to be sent into France and given carte blanche to organise the Resistance, he had the advantage of being able to revert to his old identity and have many of his old contacts rally around him. Other agents were parachuted into the Occupied Zone sometime afterwards.

On 7 March 1942 he was interviewed by Tar Robertson at 6 Orchard Court, Portman Square, one of SOE's F Section offices. It was here that agents were normally briefed before going out on their missions, or new agents vetted. A four-roomed flat on the second floor had the famous black-tiled bathroom, an onyx bidet, subdued pink lighting, and peach-pink mirrors engraved with scantily clad maidens, now all since disappeared. LUCAS told him that it was on 28 December 1941 that MIKLOS, the lawyer Maître Michel Brault, had suggested that if he was interested he should meet the head of the Franco-Polish information service operating in the Unoccupied Zone. Tar reported that LUCAS, 'In the main … answered his questions with much more conviction and without any hesitation.' He divided his report into four subject headings:

1. The two attempts made by boat to get him away from France with particular emphasis on the first attempt.
2. LUCAS' reasons for not reporting that VICTOIRE would be with him.
3. The story of LUCAS' first meeting with MIKLOS.
4. The story of the first meeting with VICTOIRE.[1]

In the first – their two attempts to get away – LUCAS explained that he and VICTOIRE had waited on the shore for the boat to arrive. When it did, the occupants (Abbott and Redding) reported that their boat had sunk and the suitcases and containers had been lost; however, a second boat was being sent. It was pointed out to them that Sonderführer Joseph von Eckert or Ekkerth @ EVANS of III F at *Ast* St Germain had arranged for them to be allowed through the checkpoints and had been keeping a watch on them from a safe distance. LUCAS was surprised that the two occupants of the first boat were destined for Paris, as London had not informed him about them. SOE had sent him a message but it had not reached him. With nothing but the clothes they were wearing, LUCAS instructed them to go to Paris, but if for any reason they were unable to make it, they were to return the following night. He subsequently learned that they had been caught the following night when they tried to return. The second boat also capsized twice when they tried to right it and he and VICTOIRE got very wet. They managed to get dry by the fire in a small café nearby and returned to the site the next night.

In the second – LUCAS's reason for not reporting that VICTOIRE would be with him – he said it was because he knew the wireless was being controlled by the Germans, so he avoided sending a message as he wasn't sure how London would receive it. He was also completely unaware of what they knew about VICTOIRE and how she was viewed by SOE.

Thirdly – concerning his first meeting with MIKLOS – he said he knew about him through some unnamed mutual American friends and thought he was running a 'resistance group' somewhere, but he wasn't sure where. His contact with MIKLOS was through NOEL, the head of the PSF group (Parti Social Français). NOEL was probably Nöel Ottavi (1892–1945), and actually one of the vice-presidents of the party's central committee, who was arrested on 9 March 1943 and died at Stalag XB, Sandbostel, west of Hamburg on 21 April 1945. NOEL had apparently mentioned MIKLOS's situation to him at the beginning of December, but LUCAS had told him that at that time he was not ready to make any further commitments. However, he met with MIKLOS on Christmas Day; NOEL was present for the first part of the meeting, which which was 'chiefly concerned with the work which MIKLOS' people were doing'. Their second meeting was on Boxing Day and not the 28th as he had already told MI5 on another occasion.

MIKLOS had told him that the first chief, known as ARMAND or VALENTIN (WALENTY), had been arrested on 17 November, but his assistant, known as MICHELINE or VICTOIRE, who had formed the Polish service with him, had some very important information to send to England and had managed to regroup the organisation and carry on their work. According to Tar, MIKLOS said that he had known both of them for a long time even though he was not actually part of their organisation. LUCAS understood that MIKLOS had supplied a number of agents to them and 'was very much taken with the idea of getting a direct contact by wireless'.

On the final point – LUCAS's first meeting with VICTOIRE – he said that a few days after his meeting with MIKLOS he met with VICTOIRE for the first time at the Café George V on the Champs-Élysées; he thought that it was on either 29 or 30 December. He emphasised that at that meeting there was no mention of wireless communications and the conversation was only about general matters.

At the beginning of January LUCAS began organising a return trip to England. However, the aircraft that was supposed to pick him up and take him back to England was grounded because of bad weather. He said it was on 7 January that a landing was scheduled at the site at Vaas, but with such little notice, it was already six o'clock in the evening, and the aircraft was supposed to leave sometime in the early morning. VICTOIRE had offered to get hold of a car so that they could drive there, accompanied by a Polish agent: 'I was to introduce him as Jean, a good Belgian friend who had a car and a little petrol.' It was only after this and an attempt to contact London through a Belgian network that VICTOIRE sent a telegram to London that he was sure that the Polish service had established a working wireless link with London.

Harmer's report of VICTOIRE's account gives it as the night of 6 January that LUCAS had sent ROGER to prepare the site. This apparent minor discrepancy is correct as it took place during the night of 6/7 January. It appears that the so-called Belgian 'friend' was Bleicher, but since Bleicher could not drive, he provided a German soldier disguised as a Frenchman to be their chauffeur. Harmer's report details the timeframe of the rendezvous. First, they met at a café near the Église St Germain at 5 p.m., then drove to the site, arriving at 9 p.m. There they were met by ROGER and the local schoolmaster who ROGER had designated to bury the containers that were to be dropped:

As the night wore on and they still waited hopefully with one person keeping guard in case the plane should arrive, BLEICHER and the chauffeur both went to sleep; as VICTOIRE herself admits, at that moment she had BLEICHER entirely in her power.[2]

As VICTOIRE admitted in her memoirs (according to Harmer's report), when she first met LUCAS she realised that this was her chance to get her own back on the Germans – 'I was delighted. Lucas would be my revenge.' That she did nothing on the night of the 6/7 January was, according to her, because the cunning plan she had hatched required that she first build up the Germans' confidence in her. This she had done to a large extent, which resulted in their giving her more freedom and the chance to go and see the son of her godfather, Jean Bailly, from time to time and whom she introduced to LUCAS.

LUCAS, in the report of 14 May 1945, states that shortly afterwards he became wary of VICTOIRE, largely because of the attempted arrest of Michel Brault (MIKLOS): 'The Gestapo came at four o'clock in the morning but the Feldgendarmerie (the operation wasn't run by the SD) handled the arrest very badly.'[3] Here there is a discrepancy with the time of the arrest, with MIKLOS saying 6.30 a.m. A message was received in London on 10 February 1942 from Geneva, which, given the CXG designation, came from SIS:

GENEVA 9.2.42 2122
10.2.42 1025
CXG 110

A. FOLLOWING MESSAGE SENT BY 48 LAND W.M. VICHY. NO EXPLANATION AS TO HOS [sic] HE OBTAINED IT.

B. BEGINS: MIKLOS ESCAPED ARREST TWO WEEKS AND NOW ARRIVED IN UNOCCUPIED ZONE. WILL NEED MONEY SHORTLY ALSO INSTRUCTIONS. CAN BE REACHED AT FOLLOWING ADDRESS. CLOS ST. JACQUES CHEMIN DE BENEFIAT, CANNES.

C. MIKLOS REPORTS ORGANISATION GOING WELL IN PARIS AND LUCAS HAS EVERYTHING WELL IN HAND.

D. EVERY EFFORT SHOULD BE MADE TO SEND INSTRUCTIONS BY SOME OTHER MEANS OTHER THAN LILI REPEAT LILI [VICTOIRE]. RELIEVED SHE WAS ARRESTED END NOVEMBER AND RELEASED AGAIN AFTER PROMISING TO ACT AS INFORMER. SHE WAS PROBABLY RESPONSIBLE FOR ARREST ABOUT DECEMBER 15TH OF ARMAND DAMPIERRE WHO WAS LIAISON OFFICER IN VICHY, AND WIFE ALSO OF MARCHAL AND OBERTIN, HEADS OF THE SABOTAGE SECTION.[4]

It is worth noting that '48 Land' was SIS code for the US, so the message would have been sent from Vichy via the SIS station in Geneva, Switzerland.[5]

LUCAS sent a telegram at 2316 (11.16 p.m.) on 20 February 1942 and received at 0430 (4.30 a.m.) on 21 February from Lisbon via the US Military Attaché in Vichy. A pencilled note at the top says, 'Received about 12 Feb by Vichy US MA'; underneath another note states, 'Should be about 4th or 5th'. The two messages state:

LOCAL 837.
LISBON. Despatched   2316 20.2.42
 Received 0430 21.2.42
[Redacted]
MY IMMEDIATELY PRECEDING TELEGRAM.

1. FIRST MESSAGE BEGINS,
    FOR GOD'S SAKE RESUME AT ONCE MESSAGES VIA
    VICTOIRE. AM FULLY AWARE OF REAL SITUATION.
    ARRANGE MY TRIP TO ENGLAND VIA VICTOIRE EARLIEST
    POSSIBLE. NO DANGER FOR ANYONE TRIP ITSELF AND
    RETURN. DANGER IF TRIP DELAYED. REAL DANGER WILL
    BEGIN ABOUT THREE WEEKS AFTER MY RETURN BUT
    BY THEN MY COUNTERMINE WILL HAVE EXPLODED. AM
    PREPARING FINEST COUP YET REALIZED BUT MUST COME
    TO ENGLAND AT ONCE FOR DETAIL. MUST BRING BACK
    NECESSARY SUPPLIES. AUTOMATICS WITH SILENCERS
    ABSOLUTELY NECESSARY. THE BOATS FETCHING ME MUST
    ABSOLUTELY BRING A GEORGE BUT MAKE NO MENTION
    OF HIM IN MESSAGES VICTOIRE. BENOIT WILL RECEIVE AND
    GUIDE HIM AS I MUST HAVE MEANS OF COMMUNICATING
    WITH TEAM HERE WHEN IN ENGLAND FOR SECRET
    INSTRUCTIONS USING VICTOIRE FOR HARMLESS ONES.
    DEADLY DANGER MY INFORMER AND MYSELF IF YOU DO
    NOT IMMEDIATELY RESUME VICTOIRE MESSAGES FOR
    REAL INSTRUCTIONS MY TRIP AND HARMLESS GENERAL
    TOPICS. SEND BOAT VIA (GP MUT) AS BEEN DONE BEFORE.
    FIX DATES AND SIGNALS. NO DANGER UNTIL MY RETURN.
    FOR GOD'S SAKE DO NOT TAKE ANY ACTION AGAINST
    VICTOIRE UNTIL I SAY SO ENDS.

2. SECOND MESSAGE BEGINS
    INFORM ONE OF YOUR PARIS AGENTS CALLED JEAN
    PROBABLY ENGLISH AND PROBABLY M.I. WHO IS IN TOUCH
    WITH BELGIAN BAT 33 REAL NAME STOCKMANS THAT
    LATTER LIABLE TO ARREST ANY DAY. TELL BAT 33 TO
    DISAPPEAR. JEAN TO MY KNOWLEDGE NOT YET LOCATED
    BY THEM. YESTERDAY MAXINE BELLEVILLE ARRESTED.
    APPARENTLY HIS REAL NAME. WAS APPARENTLY IN
    TOUCH WITH BRITISH COLONEL IN FRANCE. MEANS
    TO INDUCE SAID COLONEL TO COME TO PARIS AND
    THUS ARREST HIM ARE BEING EXAMINED. CHARLES IN
    CHARGE OF BRITTANY FOR ARMAND NOW IN PRISON
    HAS OFFERED TO HELP LAY TRAP SAYING HE KNOWS THE
    COLONEL   LUCAS ENDS.

3. MESSAGES WRITTEN IN INK EXCEPT FOR LAST PARAGRAPH
    OF EACH WRITTEN IN PENCIL. APPARENTLY IN SAME
    HANDWRITING.

4. IN FIRST MESSAGE WORD VICTOIRE IS IN + INSTANCE
    CROSSED OUT IN PENCIL.[6]

The message on 25 February read:

LOCAL 38
TELEGRAM FROM GENEVA   CXG.187 25.2.42

MOST IMMEDIATE
A. FOLLOWING MESSAGE RECEIVED FROM GOOD SOURCE.
B. FROM LUCAS REPEAT LUCAS TO ROOM 055A, WAR OFFICE.
C. MESSAGE BEGINS. OPERATION 13TH. BOTH BOATS
    CAPSIZED ALL EQUIPMENT LOST. OFFICER CAPTURED
    ON ACCOUNT OF UNIFORM. GEORGE PAUL EN ROUTE
    PARIS. BE CAUTIOUS ALL MESSAGES VIA VICTOIRE
    AND ALL FOREIGNERS WISHING HAVE HAND IN
    BUSINESS ESPECIALLY POLES, MARSEILLES. SEND ALL
    INSTRUCTIONS RE DEPARTURE VIA VICTOIRE BUT FOR

REST KEEP TO GENERALITIES AND QUESTIONS ON WHICH
YOU WISH TO APPEAR TO REQUIRE INFORMATION.
VITAL FOR INFORMER AND SELF BE IN LONDON BY
MARCH 1ST. IF NOT I MAY BE A FATAL CASUALTY. DO
YOUR UTMOST. SENDING BENOIT VIA SPAIN WITH ALL
INFORMATION IN CASE OF ACCIDENT TO SELF. IF I CAN
BE IN LONDON BY MARCH 1ST. GREATEST COUP MAY BE
SCORED AND MANY LIVES SAVED. MESSAGE ENDS.

TP 1025 27.2.42   MFB[7]

It would appear that the first two messages were taken by LUCAS's brother
Philippe to Vichy and given to Colonel Robert A. Schow (pronounced Scow),
the US Military Attaché there.[8]

On 16 March C. Brooke of B1a had met with LUCAS to ask him about the
telegrams sent on 9, 20 and 25 February, referred to above:

I asked LUCAS whether he thought that there was any chance of his
channel through Colonel SCHOW being compromised. His reply was 'I
hope not'. He then added that the Germans could not possibly be aware of
the contents of his messages dated 20.2.42 and 25.2.42 for had they been
they would most certainly have arrested him instead of allowing him to
come to England.

LUCAS was not sure of the dates on which he passed the messages but he
thinks those dated 20.2.42 left him about Feb.12th or 13th and that Colonel
SCHOW may have been away from Vichy at the time they arrived there.
Someone had told him that these messages had not arrived in London until
Feb.23rd he thought.[9]

A letter sent by Dansey to Tar Robertson, but readdressed to Harmer
and marked 'Secret and Personal' on 22 March 1942, appears to confirm
VICTOIRE's involvement in the Germans' attempt to arrest MIKLOS.
A copy of the letter was sent to SOE's F Section (probably Maurice
Buckmaster) and 'Biffy' Dunderdale at SIS. The second paragraph is of
interest here:

(ii) 'It is learned from MIKLOS, who recently had to flee from Occupied
Zone, that there is positive proof that LILI, otherwise Micheline CARRE
also believed to be VICTOIRE, has been working for the Germans and
is responsible for many arrests. Man I know as LUCAS and who may
be individual now in London, was introduced to me by mutual
friend. Later he called at my office and fulfilled formalities required
for obtaining package which had been forwarded to me from Lisbon'.
Message ends.[10]

The message sent from Geneva designated CXG 293 and dated 19.3.42 to SOE
(F) and SIS A4 from Dansey on 22 March, which included the paragraph above,
reads as follows:

A telegram has been received from Switzerland which accounts for the
reception of a message from LUCAS which was passed from Vichy to Geneva
on or about 25th February, the contents of which message were, I believe, at
any rate known to the Germans if not initiated by them.

I draw attention to the following points – in that message it was stated
that a man named BENOIT was being sent out via SPAIN in case anything
happened to the sender, i.e. LUCAS.[11]

A4 was the SIS Country Section that dealt with the Free French and the Polish
government-in-exile under Dunderdale, with a junior officer, possibly Tom
Greene, who had been his pre-war deputy head of station in Paris, or Captain
Heath, acting as liaison with the Polish Deuxième Bureau.[12]

When LUCAS returned from England on 10 April 1942 he told Pierrat that
he was 'brulé' (burnt – in other words, betrayed) and that he was convinced it
had been by VICTOIRE. It was for this reason, he said, that he had taken her
with him to England and left her:

… where she would be powerless to do further harm to the organisation.
He added that he was convinced that when VICTOIRE returned to France
she would renew her old loyalty, on account of her passionate love for him,
LUCAS. This accusation against VICTOIRE was repeated to PIERRAT
shortly afterwards by other members of the organisation whom he met at
Cannes in the course of a journey to the unoccupied zone.[13]

It was shortly after this, when he returned on 28 April, that he learned that LUCAS and other members of his organisation had been arrested. Harmer's report on Pierrat dated 26 March 1944 concluded:

> That in all probability WALTER was responsible for the arrest of LUCAS. A suggestion by MIKLOS that VICTOIRE had passed over a message to the Germans in some way while she was in England appears to be based on no evidence. LUCAS himself accuses WALTER of having denounced him.[14]

CHAPTER 15

BENOIT's Story

Benjamin Hodkinson Cowburn was an oil engineer, born in Lancashire in 1904. As a young boy aged 8 he had been educated at an English school in Boulogne sur Seine, also known as Boulogne-Billancourt, in the western suburbs of Paris, then at a lycée. He had been recruited by F Section, SOE in 1941 and trained at Wanborough Manor near Guildford, along with Pierre de Vomécourt (LUCAS) and Georges Bégué. On the night of 6/7 September 1941 Cowburn had parachuted from a Whitley bomber into Chateauroux, France with LUCAS. In his book, he described how they came to arrange for a seaborne landing for the W/T operators, and his departure with LUCAS:

> A few days later Lucas declared that parachuting was obviously unreliable in winter and asked whether I could organize an M.T.B. [motor torpedo boat] landing on the north coast. I approached Nel Marcorelles for a contact and again he had the very thing. A cousin of his, Monsieur Bousquet, hastened to Brittany and returned with an ideal set-up: a patriotic friend of his owned a villa near Moulin-de-la-Rive – a small beach between Lannion and Morlaix. He also had a motor-lorry which we could use for transporting our supplies … Whereas air drops needed a bright moon, beach landings required total darkness and the operation was fixed for February 12th at midnight.[1]

Emmanuel Bousquet @ Jean de Boissière was identified in 1944 as working for the Gestapo and had betrayed Charles Skepper, Arthur Steele and Eliane Plewman. He was executed by the French on 15 November 1946.

Over dinner in January LUCAS confided in BENOIT and ROGER that VICTOIRE's story about how she had escaped arrest was untrue. BENOIT observed that LUCAS was obviously unsettled by her confession. Bleicher had also decided that once LUCAS and VICTOIRE had escaped, BENOIT would be arrested. This begs the question that when LUCAS had decided to involve BENOIT in his departure with VICTOIRE from France did he not realise that he would be putting him in danger by exposing him in this way, given that unbeknown to him, Bleicher had accompanied them on their first attempt, and von Eckert had been keeping an eye on them? Or, had he intended to betray him?

On the day in question they had taken the Paris–Brest train as far as Plouigneau and begun their walk to the landing site. It took them two hours to reach Lanmeur, where they stopped for lunch. Cowburn (BENOIT) later described what happened:

> London's instructions (which had been faithfully relayed to us by the enemy) were that from midnight onwards we were to point a torch-lamp straight out to sea and flash a certain signal at regular intervals. When we saw the first arrival land on the beach, we were to exchange passwords and make ourselves known to each other.[2]

In the subsequent pages of Cowburn's book he described what happened next. As part of Operation *Waterworks* the two agents, George Abbott and G.C.B. Redding, were landed separately by dinghy from MGB (motor gun boat) 314, as well as a Royal Australian Naval Reserve (RANR) officer who said he was second-in-command of the MGB. The sea had become rougher and the agents' luggage was lost in the sea, tossed overboard from the 'pram-dinghies' (small rowing boats with a transom – flat – bow rather than a pointed one):

> A short while ago the beach had been deserted and the silence of the moonless night broken only by the gentle lapping of the water's edge and now the darkness was agitated by eight people struggling in the foam and the roaring and pounding of the breakers. It was like battling against the powers of darkness.[3]

The sea was too rough and it was impossible to pick them up. The lifeboat had been sent out to assist, but then had to return to the MGB. The operation had failed, and the six of them – LUCAS, VICTOIRE, BENOIT, the two agents and the RANR officer – were left on the beach. One of the agents, Lieutenant George William Abbott @ Georges Marie MARC,[4] described how he was told, '"Nobody lands, you have to re-embark immediately." Nobody was able to re-embark; the sea was very rough; the dinghies collapsed and lost their oars. It was a complete catastrophe.' He went on:

We hid in this little hut and we were in pretty poor shape. Three of us had been in the sea. We were soaked, were shivering, we were feverish, and it must have been eight o'clock in the morning when the naval officer and I said, 'I can't stick it any more. I'm in uniform, I'm going to give myself up.'[5]

As Cowburn described it, LUCAS decided that the two new arrivals, plus the RANR officer, should hide, while the three others should stay in the neighbourhood until the following morning when VICTOIRE would contact the Germans. Still wet, they were forced to stay in Loquirec until the morning, when they returned to Moulin-de-la-Rive. VICTOIRE went to the local barracks to tell them what had happened. Needless to say, the Germans were thrilled. They had arrested Ivan Black, the RANR officer, because he was in uniform, but the other two had not been found, although their luggage, containing two W/T sets, had. Black was later imprisoned in Marlag O (Milag und Marlag Nord) in Lower Saxony, a camp for Merchant Navy and Royal Navy POWs. George Abbott was later taken to Fresnes, and finally Colditz (Oflag IVC). Together with Lieutenant Ben Waters, RNVR, Black helped Lieutenant David James, RNVR to escape – a story that was made into the film *Albert RN*, whereby a dummy was used to deceive the German guards into believing that everyone was 'present and correct' at *Appel*.

LUCAS decided that he and VICTOIRE should return to Paris and get a message back to London about another pick-up, while he instructed BENOIT to leave. This he did and headed to Tours. Plans were made for another pick-up for the night of 20/21, but the two of them went to the wrong beach. It was not until the 26/27 that they were finally picked up and taken to London. Shortly afterwards, on 28 March 1942, *MGB 314* was scuttled during Operation *Chariot*, the Saint Nazaire Raid, after being heavily damaged by shore batteries.

CHAPTER 16

'An Important Affair'

In London VICTOIRE and LUCAS were put up in a flat together at 39 Porchester Terrace, Bayswater, as lovers. In her memoirs she says that the first night was spent at the flat of 'Major B', who was Buckmaster's adjutant, so that must have been Bodington. From the moment they arrived, they were subjected to a number of interrogations, mainly by SIS and MI5. Much of the information from the transcripts of these interrogations has already been recorded in various parts of this book, in particular Tar Robertson's report on LUCAS, as well as Harmer's on VICTOIRE. She had obviously made a good impression for, as McCallum's report notes:

> SIS 'supplied certain facts which are all to the credit of VICTOIRE. The first of these is that she had been working as an SIS agent since the late summer of 1940 and had done remarkably good work. Secondly the facts regarding the arrest of MIKLOS are as stated by her, namely that he managed to escape into unoccupied France …' Her MI5 interrogator, later her case officer [Christopher Harmer], noted 'VICTOIRE herself created a favourable impression. She is without any doubt very intelligent and gives every appearance of being sincere and speaking the truth.' He concluded his report 'I was very much struck by her personality and on this afternoon's interview would certainly accept her as genuine.' LA CHATTE had done it again![1]

McCallum added, 'Above all, VICTOIRE was, and remained, a superb liar.' And while SOE 'did not care what she might or might not have done so long as they could keep their greatest agent, LUCAS, happy', SIS 'had certainly a good deal to do with INTERALLIÉ, although it was not "their" organisation'. They did not want to believe that one of 'their' agents was guilty of betraying the network, but 'The MI5 officer [Harmer], who should perhaps have had a cooler judgement, was the more deceived.'

An SIS report dated 28 February 1942[2] by an unnamed member of A4, but possibly Tom Greene, mentions that he had visited Bodington's flat at 20 Charles Street, W1, the previous evening at eight o'clock. There, 'Cadet. [sic] Humphreys, and two officers of their organisation, shortly afterwards Buckmaster, De Cellis, Boddington [sic] arrived with LUCAS and VICTOIRE, having arrived there from the Coast.' L.A.L. (Leslie) Humphreys, formerly head of SIS's Section D in Paris, was now SOE's head of DF, their escape section, according to M.R.D. Foot.[3] He had also been responsible for recruiting Vera Atkins. Cadet was Thomas Cadett, who had been Henry Marriott's deputy; Marriott (not to be confused with John Marriott of MI5) was with F Section and had been replaced as head by Buckmaster. De Cellis may actually have been Charles de Salis of MI6's Section V. While they were all having dinner, Lewis Gielgud, brother of actor John Gielgud, and Squadron Leader Philipson also arrived. Gielgud worked as a recruiter for SOE. The author of the report said that when VICTOIRE was talking about current conditions in France, he asked her 'avez vous des nouvelles de vos collègues?' ('Have you any news of your colleagues?'), to which she simply shrugged and didn't answer. It appears that she had been instructed by Bodington only to answer questions of a general nature 'until she had been told to whom she might speak on such matters'. While Philipson spoke with her, all the SOE officers crowded around LUCAS.

What the author of the report learned was that both VICTOIRE and LUCAS had come to England with the connivance and cooperation of the Germans, engineered by Eckert, and that she had a mission from the Germans. He related:

VICTOIRE, I formed the impression that this woman was a sensual sensitive and highly intelligent woman who would be capable of great loyalty, in proper hands, likes flattery and would be capable of extreme jealousy.

LUCAS. A very intelligent clear minded man with very definite opinions. I should say that he is very attracted by VICTOIRE and on most intimate terms with her, during dinner they were always exchanging glances and he paid her every possible attention.

He also described LUCAS as 'physically small and unattractive' and believed that he knew his brother in Paris (taken to mean Philippe). It was recommended that the following information be obtained:

1. All details connected with the arrest of Walenty and his present position. Who were arrested with Walenty and also since that date.
2. How did VICTOIRE meet LUCAS.
3. Details of VICTOIRE's arrest and doings since that date.
4. Proposals made by the Germans to VICTOIRE.
5. Particulars of Mission given by Germans.
6. Her proposals to the Germans.
7. Proposals for return.
8. Future plans, etc.[4]

A note from Tar Robertson in VICTOIRE's file, dated 4 March 1942, reported:

One of the subjects of this file [LUCAS] may shortly be returning to France to do very important work on behalf of S.O.E. His present mistress VICTOIRE, the other subject of the file, admits to having been in contact with the Gestapo and German espionage organisation in France and will probably accompany him back. In view of this contact, the importance of the work he is to do makes it essential to keep watch on all their movements during their stay in this country and also learn as much as possible about ~~probable~~ contacts here. Since, however, the name under which he may be known cannot be indicated with any certainty, it will be necessary to make this check as wide as possible.

H.O.W. on 'any name' at the address at which he and his mistress are living is accordingly submitted for signature if approved, also telephone check on Bayswater 1343 & 6015.[5]

Dick White appended a handwritten note to the top acknowledging that 'D.G. knows about this case & has seen initiating papers. It is an important affair.' Telephone checks on the pair of them were quite revealing, as we shall see.

On 16 March C.B. Mills had been instructed to see LUCAS to try to establish whether certain telegrams, dated 9, 20 and 25 February, had in any way compromised the American military attaché in Vichy. This was Cyril Bertram Mills (1902–91), working in MI5's B1a section responsible for running double agents, whose father had created Bertram Mills's Circus. Later, he became the Defence Security Officer (DSO) in Ottawa. Following up on his note written to Harmer on 17 March 1942, he went on to say that he had tried to get in touch with Claude Dansey as well as a captain whose name he had forgotten (which has been redacted from the report) who apparently controlled the Geneva–Vichy channel, 'but I soon learnt that he knew so little of the VICTOIRE-LUCAS case that it was little good discussing it with him.' This was probably Count Frederick 'Fanny' Vanden Heuvel, the SIS head of station in Geneva.[6]

Mills thought that it would be a good idea to meet with Tom Greene, who then asked him to meet with Dunderdale. At that meeting Dunderdale agreed that the link between the American military attaché and Vichy had been known to the Germans and therefore compromised:

> Dunderdale says that he agrees also that it is established beyond all doubt that the channel through the M.A. [military attaché] at Vichy is known to the Germans and I said that we must therefore consider it most probable that the Germans have planted an agent on the M.A. otherwise they might have caused trouble with the French and asked for his removal.
>
> Within a few minutes [redacted] came into the room and said that at the interrogation this morning VICTOIRE had told them that there was not the slightest shadow of a doubt but that the Germans knew that LUCAS had communication with us through the M.A. in Vichy and that she added moreover that she believed that two Gestapo agents were working in his office.
>
> If anything that VICTOIRE has said is to be believed, this surely confirms my theory that the Germans know the channel and that they are not closing it because they have a means of tapping it and it therefore pays them better to keep it open.[7]

Mills thought they should consider the possibility that, since the Germans had not stirred up trouble with the French and asked for the removal of the military attaché, they must have planted an agent on him. An unnamed person – possibly the same person referred to earlier – entered the room and told them that at VICTOIRE's interrogation that morning she had confirmed that the Germans knew that LUCAS had communicated with them through the military attaché in Vichy. Mills confirmed that when he went to see LUCAS on the previous day Schow 'was not blown as a result of anything LUCAS had done'. That being said:

> Your statement that the M.A. is compromised is indisputably correct and I am quite at a loss to know why A.C.S.S. [Claude Dansey, assistant chief of SIS] should have asked us to try to check the matter through LUCAS unless, as I assume to be the case, he is not informed of the existence of the message sent on 31.12.41.[8]

The message to which he was referring has already been mentioned in Chapter 11. Mills followed this up with a note to Dunderdale on 17 March where he admitted, 'I was drawn into the case so hurriedly, and with so little knowledge of it, I may possibly have misunderstood A.C.S.S.'s question,' adding:

> If A.C.S.S. is aware of the contents of the LUCAS message sent over the VICTOIRE transmitter on 31.12.42 [sic], then there can be no doubt in his mind that the Germans know what the M.A. is doing.
>
> What I think that A.C.S.S. may be anxious to know is how much LUCAS knows of the channel between the M.A. and ourselves. As you know, the copy messages which I showed to LUCAS did not contain any references to the source (Geneva) from which we received them and I am satisfied from my talks with LUCAS that he does not know how the M.A. got the messages through to us and that it may be assumed therefore that LUCAS has not divulged to the Germans, either willingly or unwillingly, what channel the M.A. at Vichy uses for communication with us.[9]

Major Bodington met with LUCAS at St James's on 18 March. Present at that meeting were:

Commander Dunderdale, SIS
Mr Greene, SIS
Major Keswick, SIS
Major Buckmaster, SOE
Major Bodington, SOE
Mr D.G. White, MI5
Mr J.H. Marriott, MI5
Mr C.B. Mills, MI5
Mr C.H. Harmer, MI5

Major Nicholas Redner Bodington (1904-74) was second-in-command of F Section SOE under Buckmaster and had participated in the landing in Brittany to pick up VICTOIRE and LUCAS. In the 1930s he had worked for the *Daily Express*. He would later come under suspicion for his involvement in the Dericourt affair. A further unnamed member of SIS had been unable to attend owing to illness. Keswick was Major (later Colonel) David Johnston Keswick (1902–76), a former merchant banker and part of the Jardine, Matheson family. At that time as D/R, Regional Director for France and the Low Countries, he

supervised SOE's operations in France, Belgium and the Netherlands, having
taken over that responsibility from Robin Brook.[10] In 1942 he was moved to
Algiers and, as of 19 October 1944, would serve on SOE's Council as A/DH,
Director of the Mediterranean Group.[11]

The first item on the agenda was a plan for operating the transmitter.
Bodington agreed that SOE should take this on but thought it would be more
effective if VICTOIRE cooperated, warning that she might try to slip a code
word into one of the messages. Dunderdale, who also agreed with this plan,
suggested that they should keep two sets of traffic and paraphrase her suggested
messages. He was also in favour of informing the Poles, who he thought
would support the plan. Dick White, speaking on behalf of MI5, welcomed
her cooperation.

How then should they break this to VICTOIRE? Those representing SOE
told the meeting that LUCAS had been informed about it the day before and
had accepted it in principle. After 'a considerable amount of discussion' it was
decided that LUCAS should be given the unenviable task of breaking the news
to VICTOIRE, as well as Tom Greene from SIS, who would invite her to
lunch. They also agreed to perpetrate a long-term deception on her, of which
more will be outlined later. The next issue to be dealt with was her 'disposal' – a
term frequently used in MI5 and other documents, but not necessarily with the
sinister connotation it implies. It fell to Dick White to nominate someone with
whom she should stay for a few days in the country. Keswick announced that
LUCAS would be going away for a few days the following week.

Following the meeting on 18 March, Harmer had enquired as to how the
meeting with LUCAS had gone. Bodington told him that LUCAS had 'refused
point blank' to communicate the information to VICTOIRE, saying that British
Intelligence should do it themselves. However, he would accept VICTOIRE's
decision, whatever that might be. Harmer then had a long discussion with
Greene and Dunderdale, when it was agreed that Greene should:

> make known the decision in the matter as a decision of the chiefs of the British
> Intelligence Service and if she refused to accept it and there was considerable
> difficulty as a result, he would be prepared for Brigadier Gubbins, if the
> latter agreed, to see her and tell her quite firmly that the decision had to
> be accepted.[12]

Brigadier (later Major General) Colin McVean Gubbins (1896–1976) was
director of operations, Western and Central Europe, at SOE at that time.

Just prior to the lunch with VICTOIRE on 19 March a meeting was held, attended by Harmer, Philipson and Tom Greene, as well as Agent U.35 ('Klop' Ustinov); his name has been redacted from the report but handwritten in later. It was decided that Klop should invite VICTOIRE to spend a weekend at his country home in Gloucestershire, and that MI6's A4 representative (most likely Greene) should inform her that she would not be returning to France the following morning 'so that she might not get the impression that the lunch was only a blind to get her into good humour before bringing the bad news'.

When Tom Greene picked her up in a taxi to take her to lunch, in typical fashion VICTOIRE complained about how Bodington had interfered in sending her to a doctor, as well as the arrangements for the lunch. Harmer had reported on the 15th that at a meeting he had had with Flight Lieutenant Philipson on 13 March, VICTOIRE disliked Bodington intensely – largely, it seems, because he had been trying to get her to see a doctor. She had refused, but agreed to see Tom Greene's doctor instead, Dr Machugh of Trafalgar Road, Clerkenwell. What caused MI5 concern was that in 1940 Machugh's assistant had been Dr Yolande Friedl, the daughter of Mrs Henry de la Pasture (*née* Elizabeth Lydia Rosabelle Bonham), who was a left-wing pacifist. Bettine Marie Yolande Friedl (1892–1976), also known by her family as Yoé, was married to an Austrian and followed a 'rather sporadic medical career'. She featured as a character in her sister's books (Edmee Elizabeth Monica Dashwood *née* de la Pasture, otherwise known as E.M. Delafield).[13]

Philipson was actually Flight Lieutenant Alfred Philip Frank Schneidau, DSO, a member of SIS, also referred to as an RAF liaison officer. Over lunch VICTOIRE agreed to produce a joint paper with Klop on Gestapo activities. However, she would not agree to go and stay in the country with him until she knew about her situation regarding her return to France. She told the meeting how LUCAS had informed her of the previous day's meeting and the decision on his planned return to France, but that she would not be accompanying him at that time. Instead, she would remain in London and control the W/T VICTOIRE set until he returned in two months' time. Everyone pleaded ignorance of any such decisions and feigned surprise at not being informed, promising her to find out from their various chiefs and let her know the following morning.

Klop decided to broach the idea of her country stay again, asking that perhaps now she might reconsider. Still recalcitrant, she replied that she would have much to discuss with LUCAS. Besides, she replied petulantly, she had made arrangements for a dinner party and a concert at Queen's Hall on Sunday

22nd, but would be available the following week. She appeared satisfied that she would remain in England and be 'fooling the Gestapo over the wireless'. To say that those present had had their noses put out of joint by VICTOIRE's declaration that LUCAS had already informed her of their decision, is best summed up here:

> The fact that LUCAS had spoken to VICTOIRE of the new plans on the night of 18.3.42, after his previous refusal to do so that afternoon, came as a very great surprise to us and we are at a loss to understand how M.I.5 or S.O.E. were not aware of his action.[14]

Prior to the series of meetings on the 20th, Greene had been agonising all night about breaking the news to VICTOIRE and found the position completely untenable. He thought that he needed to meet with LUCAS first and find out what his attitude was about it. When this was communicated by Harmer to Major Keswick, he replied that the only reaction from LUCAS would be a very stern rebuke about the way VICTOIRE had been treated so far. Harmer discussed it further with Greene, telling him that it was not SOE's fault that they had had to deal with such a 'perpetually embarrassing subject' and that there was nothing to be gained by blaming each other. As Harmer put it, 'we were all responsible at one time or another, since when one is dealing with agents it is often the only way of heading off their grievances.' He also disagreed with Greene's views, feeling that the matter needed putting to VICTOIRE 'firmly as a joint decision of all the departments concerned of the Intelligence Service'.

They met at Greene's club to hash out the strategy for the afternoon's meeting. Harmer expressed the belief that it should be couched in the following terms:

- that the LUCAS/VICTOIRE case had been considered in the most minute detail by the heads of the various departments of the British Intelligence Service, who had given the matter their personal consideration;
- that there had been a great many meetings and discussions about it and that ultimately it had been jointly and unanimously decided that LUCAS should go back to France under a different identity during which time we would cover the position by the radio;
- that LUCAS would be coming back within a definite period of, say, two months and that therefore according to the success which our plans had achieved to date, we would set about getting her back to France or to Tangiers;

- that she probably would not like this decision and that LUCAS had not liked it either, but that he had accepted it and that we hoped that she would accept it and give us her cooperation.[15]

Greene and Philipson accepted Harmer's approach, but took great exception to telling her after lunch, reiterating what they had said at the 19 March meeting – that she would interpret the lunch as a means of breaking bad news. They preferred to tell her the following day, which Harmer agreed to, but that whatever the outcome, she ought to be told within the next twenty-four hours.

Later on, Philipson was still put out by being told by VICTOIRE how LUCAS had already been told of their plans. She seemed to derive great pleasure at the fact that they were all at sixes and sevens about it. Greene also communicated his distaste to Cyril Mills and Dick White, although the complaint was actually directed at SOE, not MI5. 'His attitude was that even if S.O.E. did not know, if they trained their agent properly he would have informed Bodington and the latter could have warned Greene.' This seems a reflection of the generally low opinion SIS had for SOE, frequently saying that SOE were amateurs.

On 20 March there was a series of meetings between MI5, SIS and SOE to discuss what should be done with VICTOIRE. Harmer first met her in the morning with Tom Greene of SIS and another, whose name has been redacted, 'to outline the plan of future operations in detail'. Both members of SIS expressed doubts and were unwilling to press her for a reply about staying in the country with agent U.35 ('Klop' Ustinov). VICTOIRE, Harmer records, was fully cooperative and willing to go along with their plan. She even suggested to them the contents of the first message to be sent, which was articulated by the unnamed SIS member (most likely Philipson).

That afternoon Tom Greene interviewed LUCAS and VICTOIRE, in the presence of Harmer and Greene's unnamed colleague. This meeting centred on the deception plan to be put in place to fool the Germans while LUCAS was in France for two months. The question of LUCAS's report on VICTOIRE's handling was raised again, and he was informed that it had not been received. As he pointed out:

Since her arrival in England at least three different departments, if not more, had interested themselves in VICTOIRE's case and that the net result had been that no single department had assumed the responsibility for giving her the treatment she deserved. He said he felt very strongly that VICTOIRE should be handled by one service alone and that this service [SIS] should be Mr. Greene's. VICTOIRE said that she had wished this all along and that everybody knew it. LUCAS also said that she ought to be seen out in uniform with Polish officers in case the Germans have anyone watching her in this country, because they would think it extremely odd that she was treated in the way she had been.[16]

LUCAS added that circumstances had changed since he had returned to England; therefore, because the 'General Staff appeared to have woken up to various things which they did not seem to have considered before', plans such as blowing up the Gestapo would have to take a back seat and other matters would have to take precedence. Indeed, at a meeting held on 11 March at which Dunderdale, Buckmaster, White, Robertson and Harmer were present, Gubbins had deemed the blowing up of Fresnes prison and the Gestapo buildings too risky. His prescience in making this decision was in direct contrast to Operation *Jericho*, the precision raid by RAF Mosquitos and Typhoons on Amiens prison on 18 February 1944 to release members of the French Resistance held by the Gestapo. That would prove to be somewhat of a pyrrhic victory since during the raid 100 resisters were killed and many who escaped were recaptured forty-eight hours later. It was because of these changed circumstances that LUCAS said he would not take VICTOIRE back with him when he returned to France. He told the meeting that he had only agreed to go back to France for two months if VICTOIRE was well treated in England, and also if he could be allowed to take her back on a second mission, which would be to set up an information bureau. VICTOIRE added that the organisation would not be anything like the size of the WALENTY organisation, but limited to four or five people with whom she was more comfortable.

None of the organisations present made any commitment to LUCAS's proposition, given that they had been unaware of any such conditions being imposed on his return mission, nor were any questions asked by LUCAS or VICTOIRE about the organisations' acceptance of them. It was only a matter of time, LUCAS said, before the Germans figured out what was going on, but if they could arrange the money issue properly it could avoid ALBERT being arrested. (It is not clear here whether he was referring to Roger Cottin or Jean Lejeune, both of whom had the code name ALBERT, but probably Cottin.) He thought the money should be paid in small, regular instalments, rather than large lump sums, thereby forcing them to keep the transmitter operational. He foresaw that after two months the Germans would have seen through their subterfuge and that neither he nor VICTOIRE had contemplated running the transmitter beyond the time needed to cover his return to France.

That evening, Tom Greene invited VICTOIRE and LUCAS to dinner. Also present were Harmer, and another whose name has been redacted, so it must have been another person from SIS, as the account relates how there had been 'fairly free criticism of Major Bodington and his Service by not only VICTOIRE but the representatives of S.I.S. as well'. Greene and his unnamed colleague were critical of Bodington and the fact that SOE had not kept them informed. Nor had they received the statement that LUCAS had prepared criticising their handling of VICTOIRE. She, in turn, complained about having to live under police protection and desired unrestricted access to a flat of her own. LUCAS defended Bodington, saying he had known him for some time and had no complaints about him, even though he admitted that he could occasionally be difficult.

Harmer thought that LUCAS looked tired but was impressed by him, particularly when he also stood up for the British:

... by which I assume him to mean the British Service for whom he is working. He said that although the British suffered from a lack of imagination, yet on the whole he would rather work for them than for any other people.[17]

But he was disturbed by LUCAS's association with VICTOIRE: 'They seemed such very different types and I cannot see what there is in her which would attract a man of this nature.' That being said, as noted earlier, she had already created a favourable impression with Harmer. What he had to say about her is worth repeating:

She spoke enthusiastically, and in my view completely genuinely about the old days when she had been working with WALENTY and she told stories about him in a way which seemed to me to be absolutely natural and unassumed. She did not over drink on this occasion, but on the other hand she did in telling stories reveal a streak of coarseness which certainly in an English woman would be very unusual indeed.[18]

When Harmer told her that he would be working with her on the radio messages she warned him that she 'had every fault and was an impossible woman'. Both she and LUCAS had a much more favourable impression of SIS than of SOE, the former had given her a much better exchange rate for some money they had changed for her.

At the 18 March meeting another topic up for discussion had been a telegram received on 12 March about a certain Jeannine Pradier that deserved looking into. Dunderdale wanted her interrogated. The telegram read:

POUR LUCAS VISITEZ JEANNINE PRADIER 25 WIGMORE STREET RAPPORTEZ PHOTO ET MESSAGE STOP HIMMEL ACCEPTE EMBRASSEZ M.PEGGY
ROGER[19]
[For LUCAS. Visit Jeannine Pradier 25 Wigmore Street Bring back photograph and message. Himmel accepts. Greet PEGGY. ROGER]

Bodington explained the meaning of the telegram and that 'Peggy' was in fact Rosina Bourn, a friend of LUCAS's in England (of whom more later). As he noted to Keswick on the 24th, 'Lucas presumes the name "Himmel" was put in by Roger [Cottin] in order not to give away too much to the Germans.' On the back of this telegram, initialled by Bodington, was a note saying:

This foreman however would not give 100% of his time and energy to our work unless he had some definite proof of LUCAS' authentic mission from the British, and it is to this purpose that that the photograph and message are required. The word HIMMEL is probably explained, according to LUCAS, by the fact that the foreman is Alsacien and it is very probably his name. PEGGY is a woman friend of ROGER's whom we know as Mrs. Bourne [sic].

LUCAS found it difficult to believe that this message was passed by ROGER over the Victoire line, and asked whether it had come through S.M.H. I have now verified that it did come through the Victoire line.[20]

ROGER, mentioned earlier, was born Roger Albert Cotton-Burnett on 31 May 1903 at Boulogne-Billancourt, the same place as LUCAS. Having been recruited by SOE F Section he had been parachuted into France on the night of 12/13 May 1941, together with LUCAS. On the 23 (or 25) April 1942 he was arrested by the Gestapo and imprisoned first in Fresnes, before being sent to Stalag 5A and Oflag 10C (one reference states it was Colditz, which is confirmed by M.R.D. Foot). He was repatriated on 18 June 1945 and died on 27 December 1972 in El Centro, California.

Further information in a note dated 24 March from Bodington to Keswick revealed that Pradier, born on 7 January 1891 in Clermont-Ferrand, in central France, was the sister-in-law of a foreman of the Citroën works in Paris named Thomas who was working for FRANCOIS, a sub-agent of LUCAS.[21] Bodington sent a note on 19 March informing Harmer that:

LUCAS is writing a note on her to the effect that he has recently arrived from France, failed to contact a relative of hers (at their request) and however has a message. He is asking Janine Pradier [sic] to come round and see him on Monday morning, and I will drop in sometime during the interview. I will let you know more about this when I have the details.[22]

To which Harmer has appended a note:

Mr Greene spoke to me about this 19/3. He said he thought we (MI5) ought to 'drop in' to see Pradier. I am however disposed to leave it to Boddington. Boddington's presence is only an excuse for holding the meeting in the flat, where we can observe it. Moreover we can always see Pradier officially later if necessary.[23]

It was also stressed that they should keep a close watch on her, 'having regard always to the necessity of not antagonizing LUCAS'.

Tar Robertson sent a note to Harry Hunter, head of B6, the Shadowing Staff also known as the 'Watchers', saying, 'Her name has cropped up in rather unusual circumstances and we wish very discreetly to obtain information about her.' He also wrote to Major Kenneth Younger, assistant director E Branch (ADE), responsible for Alien Control, on the same issue and requested Special Branch's assistance. Younger followed this up by writing to the deputy assistant commissioner, Special Branch and stressed, 'We do not wish her to be interviewed, nor her movements to be watched, at the present moment, nor do we wish her to be aware that an enquiry has been made.'[24]

Special Branch reported that Pradier had arrived in the UK on 20 April 1917. Based on information on her registration card issued on 29 July 1918, she had been living at Flat 4,120 Wigmore Street, London W1 since 22 September 1941 and at a variety of addresses in London since 1921. The registration card also listed a passport issued in Paris on 13 July 1919, but the entry had been scratched out. (It should be noted that the number of the Wigmore Street address in the telegram was incorrect.) Prior to this address she had been staying on holiday at a guest house at Kingsley Greene, Fernhurst, Sussex, in what had been designated as Aliens (Protected Areas) (No. 5) of West Sussex, meaning that aliens were not permitted to travel more than 5 miles outside that zone.

Discreet enquiries revealed that she was also known as Céline Pradier, who had traded from the Wigmore Street flat under the name of Janine and Sarita, court dressmakers. Sarita was a Miss Lewis who, when the partnership had been dissolved a few months earlier, had established a separate business but Pradier had continued to work out of the Wigmore Street address. It was believed that she may once have had a husband in France. A young girl, thought to be her niece (earlier claimed to be her daughter), occasionally stayed with her. A report of 23 March 1942, which appears to have been initialled by Cyril Mills, described Pradier as:

> Age 48-50, height 5'5", hair dark brown, slim figure, large nose, almond eyes, lines from nose to mouth, fall full – Mongolian type of face. Gesticulates when speaking and is of excitable nature. Walks with quick, short steps with a slight stoop.[25]

Bodington also noted to Harmer on 26 March that:

> You will find reference to Mrs. Bourn in your own records under Roger Cottin, whose particulars were submitted to M.I.5. for vetting on 10.2.41. Roger gave us her address in May 1941 as: Mrs. R.E. Bourn, B.R.C.S. Mobile Unit, Middlesex Hospital Annexe, London, W.1.[26]

At the meeting on the 20th Bodington had suggested that LUCAS invite Jeannine Pradier to his flat at 39 Porchester Terrace and MI5 would listen in to their conversation. This LUCAS did on Tuesday the 24th. Bodington reported to Keswick and Harmer that same day that LUCAS had confirmed Pradier's bona fides and that she had a 14-year-old daughter at school in the UK. She would provide a copy of a photograph of her daughter and a message giving news of her health to be sent to Thomas, the foreman of the Citroën works in Paris.

Harmer met with Brigadier Gubbins and Majors Keswick and Bodington on 21 March at Baker Street to communicate LUCAS's views expressed the previous evening. They were informed that LUCAS had accepted to return to France on the following conditions:

1. VICTOIRE being looked after properly by one Service, which in his view should be Mr. Greene's [SIS] and,

2. ~~that~~ if he returned in two months time VICTOIRE ~~should be~~ being allowed to go back to France and build up an information service there.[27]

He explained to them that LUCAS had not asked whether they agreed or disagreed with these terms, nor had anyone committed themselves one way or the other. SOE should be aware, however, that LUCAS was likely to ask for acceptance, or assume that there was already a tacit one. He thought that SIS had never intended to send VICTOIRE back, nor would MI5 support her return to France if the transmitter was still working after two months. Furthermore, MI5 would take no responsibility for LUCAS operating under any kind of misapprehension.

Gubbins was in favour of making conditions to LUCAS before he left and breaking them afterwards, rather than letting him be disillusioned. He also thought that LUCAS would probably not insist on VICTOIRE going back. It was, Bodington added, LUCAS's prime concern that she be looked after. MI5 would assume responsibility for her well-being and that she should remain in the flat at Porchester Terrace until she went to the country with Klop on 30 March. Keswick informed those present that VICTOIRE was costing them a lot of money and was unsure who should bear the cost. Dunderdale had suggested at a meeting at Gubbins's office on 11 March that the cost should be split between SOE and SIS. At Harmer's suggestion, they agreed:

a) That S.O.E. should continue to make payments until 30th March.
b) That we should thereafter assume responsibility for making all payments to VICTOIRE.
c) That since all three Services had an interest in looking after VICTOIRE well, the cost of her upkeep should be divided between the three Services in various proportions.[28]

When asked by Gubbins what those proportions should be, Harmer said he thought that each should bear a one-third share of the cost.

A note from ADB1 (Dick White) to DB (Guy Liddell) dated 22 March 1942 referred to the handling of the case as being 'triangular' with SOE and SIS:

The former are the guardians of Lucas, the latter of Victoire. M.I.5 have been the co-ordinators of the examination of this case and we have advised S.O.E. and S.I.S. that it would be unwise to allow Victoire to return with Lucas to France. I have myself seen both the principal characters, and feel that whereas

Lucas may have a future career with S.O.E. in France, Victoire cannot in the long run be trusted. She is a highly intelligent woman but one who can be turned round in her allegiance remarkable [*sic*] easily. [I] cannot believe that the Germans will have failed to consider after the departure of Lucas and Victoire from France the possibility that while in London we should discover that Victoire was under control. This seems to be inevitable since they made the mistake of sending messages over Victoire's wireless station in Paris of which both she and Lucas were unaware. Once we got down to the questioning of these two persons we must have discovered this fact and thereby have discovered the part Victoire was supposed to be playing for the Germans. These considerations seem to me to be over-riding, but in addition we can find no real basis for Victoire's loyalty to our cause.[29]

White agreed with Harmer's suggestion that MI5 bear one-third of the cost 'in connection with running Victoire as an agent in this country. I am further also of the opinion that we should control her ourselves.' However, her messages would still have to be passed through SIS.

On 23 March Harmer met with VICTOIRE at 39 Porchester Gate. There she had handed him drafts of messages to send to the agents that week and also suggested questions of a military nature to be sent to them. She cautioned that the questions should be of a nature that was of no importance to Britain since they might be misinterpreted by the Germans as relating to some impending operation. The omnipresent question of funds was raised, particularly to replenish LUCAS's coffers, and to make arrangements for payment to be made via a new route. She suggested that the amount they should be paid was 200,000 francs a month, in two biweekly instalments of 100,000 on the 1st and 15th of the month. The café in Paris to which the money could be left for CLAUDE was the Polo Alsacien at 172, Avenue de la Grande Armée in the 16th and 17th arrondissments near the Porte Maillot (close to where the Palais de Congrès is now located).

At their meeting Harmer asked her who had ultimately given her permission to come to England. She told him that after Bleicher had passed it to his commanding officer in Paris, the request had been sent to Berlin, who had given permission. She told him that her first meeting with LUCAS had been on 26 December – which, of course, was incorrect. Harmer informed her that they would be looking for a suitable flat for her and issuing her with all the necessary identity papers. At that time she had an emergency ration card under the name Denise Martin, which she said she didn't like as it was the sort of name a French servant girl would have. MI5 proposed to accommodate her in Flat 603, Stratford Court, Oxford Street, as Susan Barton mentioned in her note to Harmer on 28 April 1942:

> I have taken a 2-room flat No.603, Stratford Court, Oxford Street at Gns.8.p.week [8 guineas = £8.8s] incl.service plus 2/- p.week [2 shillings] for linen plus electricity used, for a period of 4 weeks, payable in advance, from Friday May 1st onwards. I have made it clear to the people there that although the rent is paid for 4 weeks in advance, the flat will nevertheless be on the basis of weekly notice. The flat is taken in the name of Madame de Roche. So far no references have been given, but should any be required I will give your name and private address.
>
> The flat will be vacant after midday Friday and she can move in on Friday afternoon.[30]

The day after the meeting, 24 March, VICTOIRE received two messages from CLAUDE, the second reporting that WALENTY had been relocated to Fresnes, but a Polish lawyer was negotiating his release 'for a very large sum'. When she had sent a message to him she was still expecting to return, as she spoke of arranging a suitable landing ground 'for the moon period end of April beginning May'. LUCAS also sent a message to ROGER (Bardet) requesting that he confirm VICTOIRE's message about their return and to send an agent to Lyons 'to find out the present position of the chief of LIBERTÉ organisation'.

MI5 also proposed getting a Home Office warrant to apply a telephone check on all incoming and outgoing calls. The problem was that each flat already had a telephone line connected to the main switchboard, so the request would have to be taken up with the General Post Office (GPO). Mrs Barton also wondered whether a wireless set should be hired, and whether VICTOIRE's address could be changed on her ration book because the building's restaurant had wanted her to surrender it up so she could get her meals. Harmer wrote a note at the bottom, 'I consider a wireless set essential, in spite of its effect on Mrs Grist's activities,' and, 'I will deal with the question of ration cards as Mrs B suggests.'

When John le Carré worked for MI5 at Leconfield House after the war, 'Mrs Grist ran the listeners' room, a stuffed parrot on the wall above her. Her typists sat in cubicles muttering and occasionally giggling at the conversations they were monitoring through their headphones.'[31] This was A5, listed in Curry's history of MI5 in 1941 as 'Overseas Services, Organisation and Administration', and in 1943 as 'Special Services' run by Mrs (Redacted, but was Mrs Evelyn Grist), and known in MI5 as 'the Gristery'. Evelyn Grist would later inform William Skardon that Klaus Fuchs had been lying during some of his interrogations.

The three principal agencies involved in this case, SOE, SIS and MI5, held a meeting to discuss how things should proceed: SOE wanted to keep the London end of the VICTOIRE link running, while SIS said that neither they nor the Poles wanted to make use of a 'tainted' source and were prepared to hand her over to MI5. This decision was largely influenced by ADAM (Roger Mitchell), who disbelieved VICTOIRE's story from her interrogation reports. However, his opinion was regarded as biased since he had been a friend of VIOLETTE and disliked VICTOIRE. In the meantime, MAURICE had shown up in Lisbon and was awaiting a passage to England. SIS also re-examined the circumstances of the arrest of EVE (Michel Courtois), who had been one of VICTOIRE's contacts and had been betrayed.

Harmer had written a note to ADB1 (Dick White) on 22 March 1942 regarding the meeting he had had on 20 March with SOE about the non-return of VICTOIRE with LUCAS to France, and a new plan, saying:

> The purpose of that interview was to make it quite clear to S.O.E. that if LUCAS goes back to France, having been deceived as to the acceptance of certain conditions, that is entirely the responsibility of S.O.E. [*sic*] This position is clearly appreciated by Brigadier Gubbins. LUCAS will be returning in little over a week.
>
> VICTOIRE has accepted the invitation to go to the country on March 30th. From that date I think we ought to assume entire responsibility for her and arrange for her accommodation when she returns to London.
>
> May I have your views on this and also on the suggestion made that the ultimate cost of looking after VICTOIRE should be borne in shares by the three Services concerned. If this is approved I will communicate the proposal to Commander Dunderdale through Section V.[32]

Harmer's report on that meeting, dated 21 March 1942, indicates that VICTOIRE, LUCAS, Christopher Harmer, Flight Lieutenant Philipson and Tom Greene were present. It is worth repeating in full:

> I wish to put on record the following points:-

1. Very shortly after the arrival of these people in London, 27.2.42., I formed the conclusion that their interests were so linked together in every point of view that it would be practically impossible to separate them if any benefit was to be obtained from their efforts, and I am still very much of this opinion.

2. Since the date of their arrival, many meetings and discussion[s] have taken place between the principals of M.I.5, S.O.E., S.S. and the Polish I.S.; at a conference held on 5.3.42, Col. GANO said the projects of LUCAS and VICTOIRE would have to be clarified as they appear to him to resemble too much a film story.[33] Commander DUNDERDALE was very much of the same opinion. They were both of the opinion that VICTOIRE was of no further potential value from the information point of view, even if her genuineness could be proved, due to the fact that she was well known to the German[s] in Occupied France and equally well known to the 2eme Bureau in Unoccupied France. Col.G. and Commander D. however said they were prepared to help S.O.E. as far as it was in their power.

3. S.O.E. sets great store on LUCAS, his organisation and work. They also regard VICTOIRE as an adjunct to the LUCAS affair.

4. Section V and M.I.5 are only interested in the handling of the W/T link between London and the German controlled Paris Station (VICTOIRE) and count on VICTOIRE's collaboration for this purpose.

5. As a result of several conferences attended by the interested Sections, it was finally decided that:

    (a) S.O.E. should send LUCAS back to France to carry on certain work.
    (b) VICTOIRE should remain in the U.K. and not return to France with LUCAS.
    (c) Section V and M.I.5 should run the W/T line with the Germans.
    (d) The Poles should be asked to grant [facilities] for transmitting messages through the[ir] [words missing] [W]/T.
    (e) That S.S. whilst having no [words missing] should assist as far as p[ossible] [words missing] carrying out their plans [words missing]

6. At the Meeting mentioned at the beginning of this paper, LUCAS commenced by saying that his one unchangeable condition fo[r] returning to France without VICTOIRE on this occasion, was: This mission was

anticipated to involve his absence from the U.K. for a period of two months. He would then return to England for a short period of about 14 days when he would insist that VICTOIRE should then return with him to France, having in the meantim[e] [been?] instructed and given a definite mission on our part for obtaining information, a type of work in which she is particularly interested.

7. LUCAS' ultimatum placed us in a very difficult position as a refusal on our part would have caused an immediate scene and also the risk of S.O.E. broadcasting to all their backers that we were sabotaging their scheme. Therefore, under the circumstances I thought it best to appear to accept LUCAS' proposal as if it was a matter already settled by S.O.E. My action was in accord with the decision taken at the meeting at M.I.5 on 18.3.42 when it was agreed in principle that it would be wise to perpetrate a long term deception on VICTOIRE, namely leading her to suppose that after a successful out come of the LUCAS affair, we would endeavor to send her back to France or to Tangiers.

8. There is no getting away from the fact that LUCAS is definitely an S.O.E. agent and that S.O.E. look on VICTOIRE as an accessory to the LUCAS scheme, therefore that organisation is fully responsible for his actions and work, and it is for them [to] decide whether they will or will not accept his conditions.

9. It should be definitely laid down by Section V and accepted [by] S.O.E. and M.I.5 that we are in no way involved in any arrangements they may make at present or in the future with LUCAS or VICTOIRE and that we refuse all responsibility.[34]

In his note of the 24th to John Marriott in B1a Harmer referred to the above report:

Please see the attached note and particularly paragraph 9. So far as we are concerned, we have no reason to hold S.I.S. Section A.4, responsible for any arrangements which may be made about LUCAS or VICTOIRE. Their sole function now is in connection with the messages and also any financial interest that may be agreed upon, therefore I can see no harm, if it sets Mr. Greene's mind at rest, in confirming that they undertake no responsibility for the future of LUCAS and VICTOIRE other than such financial responsibility as may be agreed.[35]

At the bottom of the note, Marriott has scrawled:

There's a catch in this somewhere but I can't see what it is. In any event however there's a war on and [illegible] major decision having been taken it doesn't matter if SIS want to head [?] at their [illegible] 'without prejudice.' As I understand it ADB1 is fully alive [?] to this ultimate possibility of Victoire becoming a security case and accept it.[36]

Sir David Petrie, the director general, wrote back on the 25th:

I have no objection to this as a temporary arrangement, but after she has been overhauled, and we are in a better position to judge what use we can be, I feel it would be better to pay from a single source – which ever may be shown to be the more appropriate.[37]

The following day Harmer informed John Marriott that:

We have decided to make VICTOIRE live under the name of Mlle. Marguerite ~~DE TREVISE~~ DE ROCHE. Do you think you could make arrangements to have her landed on 27.3.42 at London. Her particulars are as follows:-

Nationality: French
Born: 20.6.1908 at Creusot
She is not in possession of a passport. If you take the landing to Chief Inspector Robinson and obtain from him the Aliens Registration Certificate (I have the necessary photographs), after having her Registration Card signed she could go and draw her Identity Card and Ration Book in the normal way.
    I am very anxious to get this through by Monday so that she can go off to the country with her papers signed.[38]

On 25 March Tar wrote to Bodington regarding the telephone conversation LUCAS had had with Peggy Bourn and enclosed a transcript of the conversation. Unfortunately, that transcript is not in VICTOIRE's file; however, it appears that LUCAS had informed Peggy Bourn that he would be leaving that coming week and would shortly be seeing ROGER. As Tar pointed out:

In view of the fact that LUCAS has given her information over an open trunk line, which if it came into enemy hands would completely jeopardise the plans agreed upon, I think it essential that we make all enquiries possible to satisfy ourselves that this indiscretion will not have harmful effect.[39]

He suggested making further enquiries about her, that LUCAS be informed that his telephone conversation had been overheard, and that 'the security authorities in this country … are making enquiries'. Bodington replied the following day, saying, 'it is perhaps regrettable that the conversation held by Lucas with Mrs. Bourn should have referred to departures and to seeing Roger,' but he was not anxious about it nor inclined to take it up with him as 'it is not a moment, from our point of view to upset him by the suggestion that he is being too closely watched.' He added:

I may add that Lucas lived here for some time and was educated here. He has a very large circle of friends here and it is not surprising that he should communicate with one or two of the more trustworthy ones during his stay in this country.[40]

The MI5 file states that Mrs R.E. Bourn was Rosina Bourn formerly Fryer (*née* Holland), married to Harold John Bourn.[41] At least two conversations LUCAS had had with Peggy Bourn were in regard to her coming down from Manchester, where she had been temporarily assigned by the British Red Cross Service, to London to pick up a small package of perfume that had been given to him by ROGER (Cottin, referred to as Albert in the file, KV2/927) to pass on to her. This would make sense, since, according to M.R.D. Foot, Cottin had been a director of Roger et Gallet, the French perfume company before the war. Those conversations took place on 8 and 13 March. It seems that they arranged for her to come to his flat on Sunday 15 March. She already knew his first name as Pierre and referred to him as 'Mr Lucas'. In the end, the package was left at the Cumberland Hotel for a Mr Niebenhaus who was staying there to pick up on the 24th. He was, according to Peggy Bourn, 'a little Dutchman, a friend of mine from Switzerland actually', whose name turns out to be Hendrick Nieuwenhuis, born Amsterdam 27 June 1888, about whom nothing else is known.

Further messages were sent by VICTOIRE and LUCAS to CLAUDE over the next week. KIKI had been sent to find out the present position in the Estrées St Denis region. There were also questions about what crystals MARCEL needed. On 31 March a request was made for COCO to be sent to St Nazaire to report on the damage done by the raid on 28 March (Operation *Chariot*), the length of time necessary for repair and whether coastal anti-aircraft defences had been reinforced and more troops brought in. That same day, information from CLAUDE came back saying that, based on KIKI's recommendation, the Estrées St Denis landing ground was still good, and informing them that there were no German troops in the area. He also sent a list of crystals needed, and two condensers. On 2 April CLAUDE sent the following message regarding WALENTY:

For the evasion of WALENTY I am in touch with a Polish lawyer Dr. − de Cossecki of − 10,00 [*sic*] of money to be paid before April 8th. He is prepared to report in which prison WALENTY is held so as to organise escape through the intermediary of one of his German friends who is very devoted to him. Sum demanded for escape 250,000 in French money, payable in advance. Will not undertake anything without your instructions − with necessary money.[42]

The following day VICTOIRE informed him that the money would be deposited in his true Christian and surnames. Other questions related to the St Nazaire raid. A message from CLAUDE was received, stating:

COCO has returned from St. Nazaire and has found out in spite of great difficulty and strict control that the outside gate of the large lock is badly damaged. According to experts, repair will last for a pretty long time. The small lock is damaged also as well as the lock pumps. Submarine base undamaged. 2 tugs sunk. At St. Nazaire and round about reinforcements of troops, partly marines and partly infantry. A force of heavy artillery has also arrived in the region.[43]

CLAUDE repeated his message about the Polish lawyer, now spelling it de Kosseki, and the sum being 10,000 francs (partly missing from the original message) on 15 April. Clearly COCO was alive and well and still active!

LUCAS returned to France on the night of 1/2 April 1942, dropped onto his brother Philippe's estate south of Limoges from a Whitley bomber flown

by Squadron Leader William Twiston Davies, DFC.[44] McCallum's report
says that 'VICTOIRE's parting with him was described as not particularly
friendly.' Her case officer, Christopher Harmer, was shocked by her subsequent
behaviour and observed, 'She has behaved in a way towards him which even
if there was no other reason would convince me that she is completely out
for her own advancement and accordingly unworthy of any real long-term
trust.' However, she continued to be involved in the 'VICTOIRE transmitter',
reviewing incoming messages and paying agents, real and notional. McCallum
sheds more light on what was about to happen:

> After LUCAS left it was arranged that VICTOIRE should spent [sic] a few
> days in the country with U.35 ['Klop' Ustinov]. She much enjoyed the trip
> though it is doubtful if she would have done so had she been privileged to
> read the report he afterwards put in about her. He didn't, he wrote, believe
> a single word she said and, believed wrongly that she alone was responsible
> for the break-up of INTERALLIÉ. As for her motives these did not resemble
> patriotism, idealism or decency but were purely venal. Money appeared to
> be the dominating factor in her life ... These views undoubtedly carried
> a good deal of weight when the question of VICTOIRE's future came to
> be discussed.[45]

Guy Liddell commented in his diary for 1 April 1942 on his meeting with
Keswick of SOE that:

> One point in the whole [LUCAS] case which puzzled Keswick was the fact
> that LUCAS having discovered that VICTOIRE had betrayed him should
> have been at her throat but in actual fact within a very short time he seemed
> to be her slave. This could not be explained by the evidence of the mike which
> seemed to show that although VICTOIRE was very much in love with him,
> he was not nearly so enamoured with her.[46]

On 25 April CLAUDE reported that ROGER had been arrested. VICTOIRE
followed this up with questions regarding the circumstances of his arrest as
well as who had given CLAUDE money, and if it was ROGER. 'If ROGER
has been arrested for a serious reason I fear that LUCAS will abandon his
organisation.' The date of LUCAS's return in April is confirmed in 'Preliminary
Interrogation of SYLVAIN @ LUCAS' found in one of VICTOIRE's files.[47]

This was followed by a message from KIKI informing her that CLAUDE had been arrested, that he was taking over the organisation until she and LUCAS returned, and advising that their return be delayed.

At the beginning of May KIKI informed VICTOIRE that CLAUDE learned of ROGER's arrest from LEON, who had been warned by the concierge. He advised her that if they were not going to delay their return they should go to the Unoccupied Zone 'for the situation is too critical here'. She replied on 4 May that their return scheduled for 1 May had been cancelled. It seems that no money had been forthcoming for WALENTY's release/escape as RENÉ was still asking for 250,000 francs. When VICTOIRE replied, she referred him to her telegram of 19 April in which she had said:

> Subject WALENTY. We do not know KOSSEKI but will make enquiries. 250,000 francs appears to be an insufficient sum, therefore is this serious or a trap. If all precautions are taken, you can advance 10,000 francs to obtain present news of WALENTY. But approach the Pole and the Alsatian with great care. Send all details as soon as possible.[48]

Unfortunately, whatever information MI5 obtained about Kosseki from SIS (the Minute Sheet gives the date as 24 April 1942) is missing from VICTOIRE's file.[49] There is a mention in *Vichy Law and Holocaust France* of a Kossecki who was a former lawyer in Russia, who may be the same person, but no first name is given.[50] Her reply of 9 May stated:

> Nothing has changed. If this lawyer is serious he should give all news before receiving the sum required for freeing him and we await impatiently his news. All liaison is becoming very difficult and we are looking for a means of sending you money as soon as possible. We are doing all we can. You must have patience and courage.[51]

RENÉ's message to VICTOIRE on 13 May was clear that he and the others in France were miffed that her replies were not what they had hoped for:

> We start to have the impression that you are neglecting us for the profit of LUCAS. In previous telegram you tell us that instructions for money are coming by next message. You add you will keep us informed about your return with LUCAS. Another message mentions an important order for

KIKI. In spite of this you keep us in uncertainty. No reply to our telegrams concerning WALENTY. We understand the concern of LUCAS for his organisation which is also ours, but you must not forget your own organisation which needs all your support to continue work. The arrest of CLAUDE has demoralised agents greatly who ask every day for news of you.[52]

VICTOIRE replied on 17 May informing him:

Since situation is so bad and we have no precise news, LUCAS and I are going to leave England immediately … We are coming back to France by a longer but safer route and should be in Paris at the end of May.

On 1 June MICHEL (Claude Jouffret) told RENÉ that they had not heard from VICTOIRE or LUCAS for ten days and feared that their voyage had been held up.

All these messages exchanged between VICTOIRE and CLAUDE appear to contradict the date when LUCAS actually returned to France, as she informed CLAUDE: 'I await LUCAS return here this evening. I have not yet told him of the arrest of ROGER as I am awaiting further details on this arrest. Act quickly because we must decide about our return this week.'[53] However, they were all a bluff, obviously to confuse Bleicher, who was probably listening in.

Other proposed messages drafted by Harmer included in one of her MI5 files were designed to continue to proliferate this disinformation. Harmer wanted to exploit the new situation in Vichy, when Pierre Laval became prime minister on 18 April 1942, whereby:

3. The Germans should be told at the end of this month that, on account of the changed situation in the unoccupied zone, it is necessary for LUCAS to go there for a fortnight or three weeks to make a report on conditions there before moving into the occupied zone to build up his organisation. They can then be informed of the date of his arrival in the unoccupied zone and ROGER can be instructed to go and meet him at a certain place in Vichy when he goes to collect the instalment money for May 15th. The Germans could, however, be told that on his arrival in the occupied zone, about the 20th May, he will proceed to the coast to choose a suitable landing place for the rest of the organisation and the remainder of the plan will be as before, except that nothing will be heard, so far as the germans are concerned, of LUCAS or ROGER after the latter goes to fetch the 100,000 francs on May 15th.

4. As a further part of the plan it occurred to me that it would put the Germans in considerable difficulties if they were told that LUCAS, on arrival in the occupied zone, was to contact COCO and go with him to reconnoiter the various portions of the coast chosen for the landing operation. COCO we know is in prison and it would put the Germans in a difficult position to decide whether they would say that COCO would meet LUCAS or whether they would try and make us reconsider the idea. If they reply that COCO would be able to meet LUCAS they would be under the great difficulty of not being certain whether LUCAS had a description of COCO from VICTOIRE, and therefore whether they could risk sending somebody to take his place.[54]

Harmer proposed sending telegrams about this plan 'referring to message No. 1125 from Paris, in which CLAUDE raises questions about the return of VICTOIRE to France'. These telegrams are included as Appendix 8.

CHAPTER 17

'A Nasty Taste in One's Mouth'

VICTOIRE was installed in Flat 603 at Stratford Court, managed by Susan Barton, but as Tar Robertson noted to Dick White on 29 April, 'She is in a position at any moment to betray him [LUCAS] and his schemes and also to give information which, if it came into the enemy's hands, would enable them to track him down under his new identity in France.'[1] Susan Barton's report on her of 4 May has already been quoted at the beginning of Chapter 1. At the bottom of the report is a note written by John Marriott:

> I agree with the above almost in toto. I think it will be almost impossible to detect if she decides (or perhaps has decided) to work against us. We ought always to be on our guard and bear in mind that at one time she worked with the Germans and subsequently turned against them without their knowing it. Sooner or later, in this woman if she is not interned first, she will turn against us, because we will simply not be in a position to carry out her wishes.
>
> At the present we are trying to strike a happy mean between giving her everything she wants and giving her cause for going back. I think we have more or less succeeded up to date. I only hope we will detect the change if and when it comes.
>
> I think ADB1 would be interested to see this.[2]

Dick White (ADB1) added: 'I feel sure that proper treatment for this woman will ultimately be internment for the duration.'

As noted in the previous chapter, MI5 had made the decision to send VICTOIRE down to the country in Gloucestershire to stay with Jona 'Klop' Ustinov (Agent U.35) at Barrow Elm House, a Victorian farmhouse north of Fairford. Klop duly submitted his report on 10 June, referred to as the 'touched up copy'. The delay, he explained, was based on the weakness of his conclusions that were, in turn, based simply on his reactions to VICTOIRE's statements. He arrived at his final conclusions after comparing notes with MAURICE

(Janusz Włodarczyk) and ADAM (Lieutenant Roger Mitchell), adding that he did not 'believe a single word VICTOIRE says', and that it was 'pure eyewash from beginning to end'. When he tried to find further confirmation for his doubts, he was forced to admit that it was 'a hopeless task with a person so tricky and so alive to the dangers of contradiction … her confidence in her immunity from being unmasked grew in proportion to the comfort which surrounded her'. His original *J'accuse* of 23 April, as he referred to it, 'will, I hope, gain in weight and conviction'. The fact that he was 'more or less ignorant of the facts' of VICTOIRE's past gave him the opportunity to approach his confrontation with her with an open mind.

Klop's report is an extremely insightful document into how he, as the interrogator, was able to unravel VICTOIRE's twisted mind, to prise out of her how and why events developed and what motivated her to do the things she did. It is worth quoting in full to better understand how he arrived at these conclusions. Ever the contrarian, VICTOIRE remarked in her memoirs that she 'much preferred his landscape-painter wife [Nadia Benois]. She had something which delighted me: a love of nature coupled with a sweet innocence and an open, frank simplicity. She was the complete antithesis of a spy.'[3]

REPORT of 23.4.42 on VICTOIRE

VICTOIRE stayed with me from Friday, April 3 to Tuesday April 7. During these four days I adhered to my instructions to maintain her belief in her return to France and her willingness to collaborate. I refrained, therefore, from continuing the elaborate cross-examination which she seems to have undergone at the hands of ourselves [MI5], S.O.E. and the Polish 2me Bureau.

My approach was the following: 'I am more or less ignorant of the facts of your past. My particular hobby is the psychological aspect of the German counter-espionage organisation and its procedure.' My contact with VICTOIRE was therefore, so I said to her, mainly concerned with the elucidation of a number of points still nebulous to me. The only clear and unassailable fact was, from my point of view, her journey with Pierre [deVomécourt @ LUCAS] to England with the sanction and even blessing of the Germans. VICTOIRE agreed that the journey to England was undertaken with the full knowledge and concurrence of the German authorities. I then proceeded to point out to her that a major enterprise such as the despatch to England of two valuable individuals – VICTOIRE in possession of important clues concerning the German Intelligence Service in Paris, and Pierre, the prospective head of an anti-German sabotage organisation in France – could never have rested in the hands of the Gestapo, as VICTOIRE had originally alleged, but would have belonged to the sphere of the German Counter-Espionage Service. VICTOIRE agreed that she had been acting under the orders of the German Counter-Espionage Service in Paris.

I further pointed out to VICTOIRE that the essential condition for allowing her to proceed to England in the circumstances known to you – i.e. in charge of Pierre – was complete confidence in her on the part of the German Counter-Espionage Service. VICTOIRE replied:- 'The German confidence in me is 100 percent.'

I then dealt at length with the grounds for such confidence. It is here, where VICTOIRE showed signs of being on less firm ground, that her answers tended to be vague and that irritation manifested itself in her replies. Whilst not visibly resenting questions connected with the German confidence in her, VICTOIRE treated them, according to the amount of embarrassment they caused her, as naïve, ill-informed, tactless or stupid. As a last resort, instead of a concrete answer there always remained the monotonous retort: 'I do not understand the whole thing myself – *que voulez vous – c'est une histoire de fous*'. ['What do you expect – it's a crazy story'] VICTOIRE, in fact, found it difficult to explain this 100 percent German confidence in her. Having discovered this weak point in her armour, I made the question of German confidence in VICTOIRE the pivot of all future research. I laid particular stress on:

1. VICTOIRE's active and passive role in the 'cascade' (attached in her own handwriting) i.e. the breaking up of the ARMAND organisation.
2. VICTOIRE's relations with BLEICHER and his colleagues.
3. The mission to England.
4. VICTOIRE's plans for the future.
5. VICTOIRE's motives.
6. A study of VICTOIRE's character and technique.

ADDENDUM I

It soon became apparent to me that VICTOIRE's whole case is built up on the 'cascade'. In other words, VICTOIRE came to England fully prepared to meet the inquisition of the organisation that had originally employed her and to answer any and all questions connected with her 'conversion' from an important member of the ARMAND organisation to an instrument of the

BLEICHER show. In her story a wise balance is maintained between guilt and fate, initiative and coercion, loyalty to our cause and 'collaboration' in the French sense of the word. The speed with which VICTOIRE was able to record the sequence of events in November down to the actual time of many of the arrests confirmed my suspicion that her power of minute reconstruction is less due to memories, however vivid, than to a carefully prepared and well-rehearsed foolproof vindication of her actions. This consideration and other evidence which I shall presently enlarge upon strengthens my belief that VICTOIRE is more responsible than she is prepared to admit for the breaking up of the ARMAND organisation.

Before proceeding further, let us look at ARMAND through the eyes of VICTOIRE. One could reasonably have expected that the secretary and close collaborator of a man who, as the head of a vast anti-German organisation in France, has done most valuable work for the Allied cause and who then fell into the clutches of the Germans and is now facing certain death, should in the safe atmosphere of the British Isles pay tribute to her gallant ex-chief and give a favourable account of the man. Far from it! ARMAND, according to VICTOIRE, was indiscreet, both in his work and in his love affairs. He was dirty – hardly ever taking a bath – and altogether, from a womanly point of view, repulsive. ARMAND had many women. Amongst his five mistresses VICTOIRE cites Paulette PORCHER, Maud Le QUELLEC, Madame BRADKOWSKA, and, of course, VIOLETTE. VICTOIRE herself slept only once with ARMAND at Toulouse – 'by mistake'. She did not repeat the experience. To all those women ARMAND talked carelessly and recklessly about his work and the 'family'. Now everything VICTOIRE says has a meaning. Why should she paint ARMAND, this man, as rather disgusting, and ARMAND the chief, as indiscreet? In my view the reason is obvious; VICTOIRE tried to eliminate any suspicion that she was jealous of VIOLETTE, ARMAND's official mistress, and other women, and at the same time widen the scope of possible leakages. This attempt to prove that had not Madame BUFFET of Cherbourg set the ball rolling and started the 'cascade' of denunciations and arrests, the show would have been wrecked all the same sooner or later owing to ARMAND's own carelessness, reveals a thoroughly bad conscience on the part of VICTOIRE and the desire to remove betrayal of ARMAND's organisation as far as possible from her own name. VICTOIRE goes further: she introduces spare parts into the system of possible leakages. According to her, an officer called de MARIGNY belonged to the organisation of the Polish major 'TUDOR' at Marseilles. De MARIGNY was a Vichy agent, and through Vichy the Germans might therefore also have been kept informed. (The possible MARIGNY leakage plays a role too in the forthcoming despatch of Pierre to France. I shall deal with it later.) In order to make quite sure that the Germans were in possession of the 'TUDOR' facts, VICTOIRE sees to it that 'Rapide' gave TUDOR's address in Marseilles to the Germans.

VIOLETTE does not fare better with VICTOIRE than does ARMAND. VIOLETTE was 'ugly', of Jewish appearance and endowed with a prominent back [this should probably be 'beak', i.e. nose]. VICTOIRE had 'no reason to be jealous of VIOLETTE'. VICTOIRE's excessive zeal in attempting to eliminate every trace of personal animosity or affection from her relationship with VIOLETTE and ARMAND reveals, in my opinion, the defensive character of her position in the question: 'Who killed the WALENTY organisation?' This fact is all the more convincing as VICTOIRE's attitude in the matter was not only unprovoked, but spontaneous and persistent.

Looking at the 'cascade' proper, one is struck by two facts; VICTOIRE's insight into the circumstances that preceded her own arrest and her detailed knowledge of the developments that followed her arrest. If one excludes the arrests which she, according to her own statements, helped to bring about and at which she was present, one is driven to the conclusion that all the information must come down from the Germans themselves or must be pure guesswork. I cannot imagine that the Germans would care to provide VICTOIRE, however much they took her to their hearts, with all the dates concerning the break-up of ARMAND's organisation except with the intention of providing her with an alibi and helping her to whitewash herself in the eyes of the British. It will be noticed that VICTOIRE attributes her own arrest to the fact that 'VIOLETTE parle' [VIOLETTE talked, or 'squealed']. It would have astonished us if VICTOIRE had made anybody else but VIOLETTE responsible for being caught by the Germans. VIOLETTE to VICTOIRE is like red rag to a bull. It may not be out of place to state here that in the course of discussions quite unconnected with the 'affaire' and only concerned with her private life and character, VICTOIRE never hesitated to paint herself as a woman prone to extreme fits of jealousy and capable during such fits of resorting to almost any form of vengeance. I cannot help feeling, therefore, that it was VIOLETTE who owed her arrest to VICTOIRE, and not vice versa. In expressing this opinion I am, of course, fully conscious of my inability to provide any proofs of my indictment of VICTOIRE. I prefer, however, to base my judgement on my instinct in the matter instead of attaching importance to the statements of a person whom I consider to be wrong all through.

ADDENDUM II

VICTOIRE's conversion from ARMAND's creed to that of BLEICHER was effected in record time. This is what her moral speedometer records:

18.11.41   VICTOIRE is arrested.
19.11.41   '   is out of prison.
20.11.41   '   is BLEICHER's mistress.

VICTOIRE claims that German confidence in her was mainly based on a few acts of grace on her part – i.e., her intimacy with BLEICHER and her generosity towards PORCHER after the incident the night of December 20th, 1941. With all the respect for German primitiveness, I cannot believe that the confidence of the German Intelligence Service can be won by giving yourself to one member of this service and by not giving away another member. With all due respect, too, to VICTOIRE's seductive powers, I firmly believe that every German officer in Paris had the opportunity to 'write on better paper' (as they so delicately say in Germany) and was not dependent for his amorous exploits on the rather '*faisandé*' [gamey, as of meat] charm of VICTOIRE. This is all nonsense. In my opinion German confidence in VICTOIRE started earlier than one day after her arrest. It was based on a more solid foundation than a bed. The Germans needed VICTOIRE. They needed her for rounding up the rest of ARMAND's organisation; they needed her for maintaining W/T contact with England, and they needed her, as later events proved, as a bait for future fry, small and big. That is the meaning of VICTOIRE's ultimate installation in the rue Faisanderie.

The fact that the Germans needed VICTOIRE is not enough; they had confidence in her – '100 percent confidence', as she herself admits. Three days sufficed for the Germans to accept one of the three most important members of ARMAND's staff as a collaborator and three months sufficed to grant her all facilities to join, if only temporarily, her former employers in company with Pierre without any guarantee that either of them would choose to return to France. Nothing will ever make me believe that the Germans, however stupidly they may sometimes behave, would take such risks without good reason. It may be said with some justification that VICTOIRE from the moment of her arrest onwards proved such a willing tool and delivered so many of her former colleagues into the hands of the Germans, that even the most hardened amongst the German Intelligence Officers must have been impressed by her obvious will to collaborate and must have been moved to confidence. I still maintain, however, that even in German eyes the capacity for betraying friends is no guarantee of the incapacity for betraying enemies.

I see in this 100 percent confidence in VICTOIRE the most convincing proof for my belief that VICTOIRE had rendered services to the Germans prior to her arrest and that everything that happened afterwards is only the logical result of those services. In view of this firm belief of mine I attach no importance whatsoever to the sexual background provided by VICTOIRE for her relationship with BLEICHER. Apart from the fact that sex plays an important role in this woman of waning sexual powers and that she therefore never misses an opportunity depicting herself as being desired, it offers a most convenient and romantic explanation for the very thing VICTOIRE cannot and dare not otherwise explain – the amazing confidence displayed by BLEICHER & Co. in this fresh recruit to their cause. If there were nothing else, this German confidence in VICTOIRE alone would be sufficient for me to find VICTOIRE guilty.

It is not difficult, but impossible for me to go into all the details of VICTOIRE's account of her relations with BLEICHER and his colleagues, considering as I do this account to be pure eyewash from beginning to end and only intended to confuse the issue. These people, whose names VICTOIRE has given to you, may well exist and even their names may be correct, but all their words and actions have in my opinion been shaped to fit into the general plan devised by VICTOIRE for her own ends. BLEICHER, for instance, embezzles funds which VICTOIRE has to account for, and instead of denouncing him to his chiefs and thereby removing him painlessly, VICTOIRE suggests the more complicated method of poisoning him. This latter method has, however, the great advantage of making VICTOIRE's return to France imperative and denying BLEICHER the chance of proving that he did not appropriate the sum in question. If I were asked who was the more likely to embezzle money – BLEICHER or VICTOIRE – I should answer without a moment's hesitation, VICTOIRE. I am only giving this as an instance of how futile any approach to VICTOIRE's case seems to me as long as we depend on her word alone. It is sheer waste of time to weigh statements of purely fictitious value. This seems to me to be one of those cases where the accused ought to be considered guilty until convincing proofs of innocence are offered. It may not be lawful, but it would certainly be right.

ADDENDUM III

I am, as you know, not sufficiently acquainted with the character and scope of VICTOIRE's mission to England to enter into a detailed examination of this part of VICTOIRE's case. As all the questions concerning Pierre are at present sub judice I displayed no inclination to trespass on territory which is at the moment 'out of bounds'. I can therefore only give you my general impression of this part of VICTOIRE's programme.

I have mentioned in the first part of this report the 'wise balance' that is maintained in VICTOIRE's 'cascade'. This balance was to be tipped in our favour (from our point of view) by her journey to England as the shepherdess of Pierre. The journey was not only meant to be a convincing demonstration of her own good conscience vis-à-vis the British, but was to entail an even more striking proof of her loyalty by preparing the return journey to France of Pierre and herself – Pierre with full powers in the 'affaire Nobel' and VICTOIRE as an absolved and re-instated British agent. I believe VICTOIRE for once when she says that from the German point of view an important object of her journey to England was '*de tuer tout soupçon du côte de l'Angleterre*' [to kill all suspicions on the coast of England].

This is how I see the mission to England, leaving Pierre (about when I know nothing and about whom I have asked no questions) outside my more detailed calculations. Pierre is being used as a sort of Trojan horse which produces VICTOIRE who has, after all received instructions from ISCHE. These instructions, which you know, sound convincing to me. We do not know, however, if VICTOIRE is telling the whole truth. There may be instructions (and I am inclined to believe that there are) of which we know nothing. BLEICHER's instructions – 'bring back foreign exchange, cigarettes, etc. for me' – I do not take seriously and only regard as another conjuring trick to fill VICTOIRE's own pockets.

With the return journey to France once completed, I see VICTOIRE playing in the '*Affaire Nobel*' the same role which I suspect her of having played in the '*Affaire Interalliee*' – the role of informer. The other side of this typical 'agent double' [double agent] would be set working again after having been idle whilst under British jurisdiction. If Pierre is right (and I hope he is) then I consider him a doomed man in the company of VICTOIRE. The Greeks had a word for it – VICTOIRE is like the shirt of Nessus that inevitably kills the man who wears it.[4]

I have referred before to VICTOIRE's long-term policy on the question of leakages. It is significant that she is already making provision for the possibility that the Germans might learn about Pierre's return to France. Apart from the 'de MARIGNY' leakage mentioned before, she does not rule out the chance that the Czech friend with whom Pierre is staying, and to whom he tells everything concerning his activities, past, present and future, might be a channel by means of which a 'fuite' [escape] would be possible. About Pierre's discretion VICTOIRE seems as doubtful as about that of ARMAND. I must confess that all this is rather disturbing to me. The analogy with the case of ARMAND is too close (down to VICTOIRE's cold-blooded description of physical infirmities) not to make one reflect. But even if VICTOIRE for some reason or other did not bring Pierre himself back with her to France, one of ISCHE's instructions could easily be complied with by her; she could impart information about various Intelligence services in this country more complete, probably, than that imparted by any agent before her. This alone would have made her mission to England worth while.

ADDENDUM IV

VICTOIRE's plans for the future can be crystallised into a few words. They are: 'To get out of England as quickly as possible'. The absolute necessity for her speedy return to France is the recurring leitmotiv of her thoughts and words. She advances various reasons which demand her return. There is the question of her mother. VICTOIRE's mother is like Voltaire's God: She would have to invent her if she did not already exist. This mother has served, and continues to serve, many useful purposes. In this particular question of VICTOIRE's return to France the poor mother would be made to suffer at the hands of the Germans if VICTOIRE did not keep her appointment with them. When VICTOIRE sees that contrary to her expectations the sob stuff does not work with the sentimental British, the old mother is put in cold storage for a while and VICTOIRE decides to return to France in order to poison BLEICHER. When this plan does not prove sufficiently attractive, VICTOIRE suggests pro-British propaganda on her part amongst – the harem women of French Morocco. Why should VICTOIRE be so keen on departing from our hospitable shores?

There is no doubt in my mind that VICTOIRE has been greatly perturbed by expressions of distrust which she has met with in certain quarters, and she begins to wonder whether she will be able to weather any forthcoming storm. On the other hand, she envisages the resumption of life in Paris with calm confidence and seems to be sure that, thanks to some physical make-up mainly concerning a fringe on her brow, her life in Paris will pass undetected and undisturbed by the Germans. The only positive conclusion which I can draw from this attitude on the part of VICTOIRE is that at the moment she seems to fear the British more than she fears the Germans. That in itself is hardly a recommendation.

ADDENDUM V

VICTOIRE's motives are not related to anything resembling patriotism, idealism or decency, but are purely venal. Money is the dominating factor in this girl's life. As you know, she is very fond of dancing. The dance she likes best is the one round the golden calf.

VICTOIRE expressed great admiration for her mother, who was buying up in Paris as many dollars and as much jewellery as she could find. When asked why she herself did not do the same, VICTOIRE replied: 'Where should I have taken the money from?' VICTOIRE did not explain how her mother obtained the funds for these transactions. I am convinced that mother and daughter were close collaborators in these matters and that VICTOIRE provided the cash.

Money being the prime motive of her actions, with 'having a good time' as second in the field, truth in the case of VICTOIRE is served best if everything she has done or is doing is viewed from this angle. It is no use looking for other motives.

ADDENDUM VI

You will have gathered by now from my report that my opinion of VICTOIRE's character is not particularly favourable. In my view she possesses all the qualities, good and bad (and many others besides) that make for a perfect 'agent double'. She has a high intelligence, physical courage and sangfroid, and is a good actress. She has no scruples of any sort, no attachment to causes or persons and no affection for anything except her own interest. Her technique, like her acting, is rather crude and more suited for provincial audiences. VICTOIRE believes in reiteration. A source of preoccupation or worry would reveal itself by daily frequent references to it. Flattery and appeal to human vanity, showing prolonged intercourse with inferior minds form another important part of VICTOIRE's professional make-up. When embarrassed, VICTOIRE ignores her predicament, and after full reflection unfailingly provides an explanation later with an air of complete detachment. If the indifference with which such action is met should trick VICTOIRE into the belief that the point has not been driven home sufficiently, then the method of reiteration is resorted to again.

REPORT OF MY MEETING WITH ADAM AND MAURICE

The meetings which I have had with ADAM and MAURICE [Lieutenant Roger Mitchell and Janusz Włodarczyk respectively] have enabled me to go over some of the ground covered in my report on VICTOIRE of 23.4.42. As I expected, VICTOIRE's facts did not remain unchallenged. Though Adam and Maurice make their exit at a fairly early stage of the WALENTY play, their knowledge of some of the events and of the central figures provides a valuable help in the destruction of part of the fabric so skillfully woven by VICTOIRE. To begin with, there is ARMAND himself. The picture which the two men, one of whom, MAURICE, lived under one roof with him, drew of ARMAND, is diametrically opposed to that sketched by VICTOIRE. ARMAND lived for his work only; he had no time for women. He lived with VIOLETTE, who was devoted to him, and not one of the other women mentioned by VICTOIRE and known to ADAM was ever ARMAND's mistress. ARMAND was discretion personified. He took the greatest care with all the documents and spoke to nobody outside the 'famille' about the work, and to members of the 'famille' only about what concerned them directly. There was therefore, as far as ARMAND was concerned, very little chance of a leakage. ADAM and MAURICE agree that VIOLETTE might have been less discreet. She would talk but only within the 'famille', and would not dream of giving information to the enemy. Physically, VIOLETTE was attractive – young and fresh. MAURICE had tried hard to win her favour, but she remained faithful to ARMAND. Two other agents well known to ADAM and MAURICE, 'Kiki' and CHRISTIAN [Robert Kiffer or Kieffer and Lieutenant Bernard Krotki respectively], also seem to be very different from their description by VICTOIRE. Both ADAM and MAURICE think it impossible that either of these two would ever have given away any of their colleagues except perhaps, after passing through long stretches of third degree. Both were reserve officers and both were very brave men. This emphatic contradiction of VICTOIRE's account of two colleagues and friends of Kiki and Christian upsets the very source of VICTOIRE's 'cascade' and throws serious doubts upon the rest of her story. But this is not all. ADAM knows as a definite fact that the meetings at the letter box 'La Palette' took place on the 4th, 14th and 24th of every month. Nobody ever went there in between. When one bears this fact in mind, then the time-table of the 'cascade', at least up to the arrest of ARMAND and VICTOIRE becomes entirely unconvincing. Moreover, MAURICE himself met Christian and

ARMAND on the morning of November 17th. Christian's arrest and ill-treatment could therefore only have taken place in the afternoon or evening of that same day, and he would have to have given ARMAND's address at once for ARMAND to be arrested in the early hours of the 18th November. Christian had been arrested by the Germans before and ultimately released without a single secret passing his lips. The possibility that he should have broken down within a few hours after his arrest is therefore completely ruled out by ADAM and MAURICE.

Two further facts about VICTOIRE have emerged in the course of the talks with ADAM and MAURICE:

1. The worst man of the whole ARMAND organisation, a man who after having tried theft, resorted to blackmail and was even listed by ARMAND to be 'eliminated', MARCEL [Francis or François Tabet] was a special protégé of VICTOIRE's. It was she who brought him into the organisation, lived with him, and exerted her influence in his favour when he got into trouble with his colleagues and ARMAND. You will see from VICTOIRE's notes that MARCEL 'a toujours été libre 100 percent' ['has always been 100 per cent free'].

2. ADAM found out from ARMAND that the dollar exchange which VICTOIRE, the cashier of the organisation, received and entered in the books was 120, whilst the official quotation was 160. This remark of ADAM's interested me very much indeed in view of the suspicion expressed in my report of 23.4.42 that both VICTOIRE and her mother were engaged in some sort of dollar racket. If one takes into consideration the accusations of VICTOIRE against BLEICHER about the embezzlement of money sent to the organisation from England and the fact that she makes Moustique & Co. disappear from Paris with 40,500 frs. (whilst ADAM says that they arrived in Marseilles without a sou in their pockets) one begins to wonder if VICTOIRE has not been quietly building up a nest egg of her own which she hoped to enlarge by serving two masters at the same time. In this respect, in my view this woman has no scruples whatsoever and least of all when money comes into play. She would sell anybody, even her 'pauvre mère' [poor mother].

I am certain that more use could be made of the presence of ADAM and MAURICE in this country, and that a confrontation of these two men with VICTOIRE would yield further and even unexpected results.

In the meantime I hope to have produced a few proofs of VICTOIRE's mendacity. For me she remains from beginning to end a person who is not to be trusted and whose whole past predestines her for a safe place, where she can do no harm.[5]

A handwritten note at the top of the pages that follow Klop's report in the file (which relate to meetings held to discuss the break-up of the WALENTY organisation) by Tar to Harmer says, 'Excellent. This note leaves a nasty taste in one's mouth. It seems as if VICTOIRE has not quite told us the truth. Perhaps one day she may.'[6] An understatement if ever there was one!

CHAPTER 18

WALENTY and the 'Great Game'

If I have acted wrong in organizing the 'Great Game' the news that I have
perished in an air accident will save my family and my colleagues.

Roman Garby-Czerniawski

It is now worth considering WALENTY's situation after his arrest in Paris: the
events following the break-up of his organisation; the role VICTOIRE may
or may not have played in them; and his so-called 'escape' from France. Some
aspects of this case have been covered in other literature,[1] but in order to try to
understand what really happened, the focus of this chapter will be his interaction
with VICTOIRE, and that of a few key members of their circle, as well as what
arrangements he made with the Germans, and what his subsequent mission in
Britain was intended to be. Later, as BRUTUS, he would go on to play an
important role in the D-Day deception plan known as Operation *Fortitude*.
However, it is not the intention here to spend any time on an in-depth study of
this later phase of his career as it is outside the scope of this book.

The many reports that were produced on these events, mainly by MI5, found
in the BRUTUS and Mathilde Carré files, each tend to put a slightly different
perspective on things, according to whoever has written them, making it
sometimes hard to decide when to believe WALENTY and when not. There is
also the inevitable finger-pointing, allegations and counter-allegations.

A summary of a report dated 4 January 1943 prepared for the Wireless
Board (W Board) by B1a asserts that either WALENTY approached, or was
approached by, the Germans 'with a view to his collaborating with, and
working for, the Germans and returning to England to raise the Polish nation
on the side of the Axis in return for generous peace terms'.[2] The W Board began
life as the W Committee in October 1940, an interdepartmental committee that
monitored the use of double agents for 'the dissemination of false information'.[3]
Later that year it became known as the Wireless Board or W Board. One of
its sub-committees was the Twenty Committee or Double-Cross Committee

(from the Roman numerals XX), formed on 2 January 1941, and chaired by the Christ Church, Oxford don John Cecil Masterman (later Sir John) then working for MI5, with Tar Robertson of MI5's B1a in charge of running these double agents, and John Marriott as board secretary.

As the W Board report summary continues, 'These arrangements finally came to a head, and at the end of July the Germans facilitated his escape from prison and instructed him to come here and tell his story that he had escaped.' The details of these arrangements and his so-called 'escape' are far more involved than the summary makes out and are contained in the 'Walenty Report' prepared by Christopher Harmer, dated 3 December 1942 and circulated to only a handful of people: Tar Robertson in B1a; Frank Foley, the SIS representative on the Twenty Committee; 'Biffy' Dunderdale in Section A4 of SIS; Colonel (later General) Stanisław Gano of Polish Military Intelligence, and Beavers.[4] Tar was very complimentary of it and described it as 'such a masterly report and represents so much more detailed knowledge of the case than I possess that I hesitate to criticise it in any way'.

Harmer's 'Walenty Report'[5] (TNA KV2/72, hereinafter referred to as such, with WALENTY's original account in Appendix A of the report referred to as 'Appendix A') states that WALENTY had arrived in the UK from Gibraltar on 2 October 1942, having been imprisoned by the Germans since his capture on 18 November 1941 until 29 July 1942, when he apparently escaped. How he 'escaped' will now be explored by first looking back to what happened to him after his arrest. All quotes are from the 'Walenty Report' unless otherwise stated.

When WALENTY arrived back in the UK he was extensively debriefed by the Polish Intelligence Service (Deuxième Bureau) and subsequently court-martialled (more about this later). Harmer reported that through WALENTY's reports he was able to piece together and confirm what was already known about how the *Interallié* network came to be broken up. Harmer's report attempted to establish:

A. Whether WALENTY's new story is a true one and what is his position from a security point of view.
B. What his true motives were for holding it back.
C. Whether it is possible to play 'the great game' as suggested by WALENTY.

He took the approach of first looking at WALENTY as chief of the *Interallié* network, and second, as a German agent.

Following his arrest in Paris by Bleicher, WALENTY was taken to the 'Feld Gendarmerie' [sic] where Michel Brault (MIKLOS) had also been taken; however, this could also have been the GFP at the Hôtel Bradford, 10, rue Saint-Philippe du Roule in the 8th arrondissement (now called the Hôtel Bradford Élysées-Astotel). According to Otto Wirth's CIC report on VIOLETTE in 1944, WALENTY and VICTOIRE had been taken to the GFP 610 headquarters at the Avenue de l'Opéra, the Hôtel Edouard VII, then to Fresnes. There he experienced an unspecified act of brutality at the hands of the duty officer. When he reported this to Ische he was informed that the officer would have been punished had this been known by him at the time. He also said that for the first few days he was not interrogated, which does not seem entirely believable. When he was, it was by a naval commander who fitted the description VICTOIRE had given of someone known as the 'Colonel' who had also visited her. This person, mentioned in Appendix B of the report, is described as aged 50, height 6ft, thin, wearing spectacles, and almost completely bald; he gave WALENTY the first interrogation but did not reappear.

The officer who accompanied VIOLETTE when she came to visit him on 27 November appears to have been Borchers. WALENTY heard that he had been sacked for making improper advances to VIOLETTE, although another reason, that of being drunk and incompetent, had been given by VICTOIRE. When questioned about TUDOR he refused to disclose any information. He said it was on or about 29 November that Borchers and Bleicher first approached him about collaborating with them, which he refused to do. When asked for his opinion of VICTOIRE he was equally non-commital.

Between December and January he was left alone and not interrogated, with only a visit from Borchers to check on his well-being. In mid-January he was moved to a better cell on the fourth floor, but it was not until March that he was interrogated about the 'Interallié affair' by two 'Inspectors de Justice' [sic], who MI5 thought must have been Bleicher and Eckert. After that, the Germans lost interest in the whole thing. That there had apparently been so few interrogations of WALENTY beggars belief. It suggests that they already had all the information they needed from the other agents who had been arrested, and wanted him for another purpose.

That other purpose would come to light on 27 November during VIOLETTE's visit with Borchers – what has been described as the 'opening move' on him becoming a German agent. Borchers left them alone for half an hour, during which WALENTY quizzed her about what had happened to members of the network. It was then that she suggested that he collaborate on technical, as well as Army Intelligence matters, but he refused, saying that to do so would mean betraying his comrades, something he was not prepared to do.

In WALENTY's original story, he refers to *Interallié* as TER, VIOLETTE as RENÉE, and VICTOIRE as LA CHATTE. He stated that:

> The only untrue part of this affair is the story of my escape, which, however, has no bearing on the affair, and which <u>for the good of the cause must continue to be regarded as true.</u> It was absolutely necessary to introduce this 'story' (which, as a matter of fact, covers only the space of a fortnight) into the 'TER' affair, in order to satisfy all those persons who are investigating it, but have nothing and will have nothing to do with the plans I wish to submit.
>
> I fully realised that the 'TER' affair and my subsequent re-appearance was too sensational (especially among the Air Force which, after all, form the majority of the forces – and a very mobile majority at that) to make it possible to conceal any secrets whatever in their entirety. I know that it would prove impossible to avoid small 'sensations'.

He was concerned that nothing should be leaked out to anyone in the Air Force as to do so 'would cause the failure of the whole affair'. However, he hinted that there might actually be 'agents among the leading circles. My present report will supply proof such possibilities do actually exist (!)' This may have been an allusion to how the Germans had come to know about his previous trip to England. However, that proof is not included in any of the files. He then went on to explain what he called 'My new affair'.

This new 'affair' came about as a result of Renée Borni's (VIOLETTE's) visit when she had revealed that the Germans had no real information that could be used as a means of provocation against the WALENTY (*Interallié*) organisation. It seems that the Germans admired the way the organisation worked and the methods they used, and would do their utmost to persuade him to work for them '<u>if not in an active manner, then at least in their study department on methods and the organisation of Military Intelligence</u>'. While VIOLETTE knew that WALENTY would not work for the Germans in any way, she thought that he might want to exploit this to mislead them and save himself. Whatever he chose to do, she begged him not to kill himself, something he confessed he had considered doing, 'had it not been for RENÉE's visit, I should probably have done so on that very day, because I was afraid of interrogation "by force"'.

After due consideration, he realised that maybe she had a point and that the plan would work. His speculations were, he said, 'based exclusively on RENÉE's assurance that the Germans were very anxious to win me over'. He therefore came up with the following conclusions:

- I would continue to refuse to supply any data about mine or other organisations as well as any data whatever concerning my personnel; such an attitude might even strengthen my position; – With regard to Polish and British military secrets – I had nothing to betray, not even unconsciously, as I had no information on the subject – so that I would not be running any risks in that respect;
- By stressing the fact that I was working for the Polish and not for the British government, I might plant the suggestion that they might reckon on my collaboration if they offered me work for Poland (!) based on German collaboration (!) I thought that they might be impressed if I gave them to understand that in my opinion England was leading us, Poles, up the garden path …
- As I was fully aware that the Germans would not believe my too sudden ideological 'conversion' I decided to present a long resistance and to put forward great demands. I realised fully that I would only win the 'great game' if I could match my nerves against theirs

Two days after RENÉE's visit, the German captain came back with the same proposals as before, which he said came from Stülpnagel's office. WALENTY reiterated his views and said that unless an officer authorised by Berlin was prepared to speak with him then he would refuse to cooperate and give them any information about the network. The officer agreed that such conversations would take place, but requested that he show 'good will' and provide them with some information. His reply, which took the officer completely aback, was that 'if they thought me capable of treason, surely they could not reckon on any loyal collaboration on my part in the future.'

There followed what he referred to as a 'war of nerves'. During this time he suffered from hunger and cold; it was not until later that he was moved to a better cell. In January the same officer returned, saying that some interest had been shown and he should be given the chance to speak with staff officers; however, he should still provide them with answers to some of their questions. This was met with the usual 'no' from WALENTY.

Much of the rest of this Appendix has already been mentioned or discussed elsewhere. Suffice to say, he was visited by a member of Stülpnagel's staff who asked him to write down his ideas. He explained those ideas as being:

> ... one of the best propaganda articles I ever wrote in my life (and I used to write lots of them in Poland before the war). I used as my 'leitmotive' my <u>deep</u> conviction, allegedly contracted after my conversation with the Germans, that I really saw that Poland's future lay in her collaboration with the German nation, etc. I 'confessed' that 'actually' such thoughts had crossed my mind at an earlier time ... that many of my colleagues had seriously envisaged this possibility; that I was sure I would find many followers – naturally provided the Germans did show their good will ... I even hoped to win over for this idea some of my colleagues in France ... etc.

This 'manifesto' of WALENTY's must have done the trick, as the Germans' attitude towards him improved immensely and further discussions took place, leading to the escape plan.

Despite Renée's encouragement, he was firm in his decision not to work for the Germans. Nor did he bend to Borchers' propaganda about working for the Jews and Britain. Instead, he developed a strategy to accept any proposal over the long term, rather than immediately. To that end, he wrote a letter to General Carl-Heinrich von Stülpnagel in which:

> ... he set out his position as a Polish officer and many things also about the position of Poland, pointing out that the assurances given by Britain were insufficient and all Poland's sacrifices in vain, that only if Germany gave suitable assurances to Poland as to her position in the new Europe would any form of collaboration be possible.

Stülpnagel, who had succeeded his cousin Otto in February 1942 as commander of German-Occupied France, was later implicated in the July Plot to kill Hitler in 1944 and was hanged from a meat hook after a failed attempt at suicide (he shot himself in the head and was blinded as a result).

—ɯ—

Later, when he was in England, WALENTY reconstructed the two letters he wrote. The first was written after his interview on 27 November, and handed to Borchers on the 29th:

> I carried out my duty as a soldier during the war in Poland as a fighter for the rights of the Polish Nation. I continued this struggle during the war in France, now I am continuing the struggle in the ranks of the Polish Army allied with England.
>
> In all three cases I have done everything possible merely for the good of my Nation. No collaboration which might be proposed to me could come about unless I was convinced that I was working for the good of the Polish Nation.
>
> I consider that in the New Europe all the nationality problems ought to be solved. The Polish Nation represented by thirty million Poles cannot disappear and this will obviously be one of the questions to be solved by the Germans after the war. If the German nation has amongst its plans the reconstruction of the rights of the Polish Nation, in this case alone discussions about my collaboration could take place.
>
> Even in this case all conversations could only take place with an officer of the General Staff who knows these problems and who is authorized to discuss them with me.

The second letter was written in May 1942 after Ische had visited him:

> Having reflected for a long time in prison, I have arrived at certain conclusions which are the following:
>
> That Poland is in the German sphere of influence.
>
> That England, who knows that she is not capable of giving aid direct or indirect to Poland, has nevertheless given on two occasions false promises, once before the start of the war in 1939, the second after the war in France.
>
> Whatever collaboration Poland might have with Great Britain would be merely to help the selfish aims of Great Britain.
>
> That after the war, if the Allies win it, Russia would be in a position to decide the New Order in Eastern Europe and Poland would thus be under the heels of the barbarians and Communists in Russia. In these circumstances England would not be able to help us and Russia on the contrary would do us harm.
>
> That all things considered, the best solution would be to come under the cultural protection of Germany, since German culture is preferable to barbarian culture.

That Germany in constructing a New Europe would be forced to create the possibility of life for all the nations which form this Europe.

That the military collaboration of the Poles would be a great help to Germans in achieving and speeding up the realisation of their programme, and that this military collaboration would be much appreciated by the Germans.

That collaboration in the sphere of military information and in the sphere of the Fifth Column would also give good results.

That in the sphere of military information they would be in touch with a well organised service in England, since at this time they could have good information not only from England but also from America, Canada, North Africa and Russia.

That in the sphere of Fifth Column politics they could rely not only on the collaboration of certain persons in the army, but what is more important on the Fifth Column ready at the moment that Germany attacks England.

That a direct collaboration with the Germans and certain Polish organisations working in Europe would not necessarily be excluded.

That according to my considered opinion the result of all these conclusions would be the accelaration [sic] at the end of the war and the realisation of a New Order in Europe.

Two days after Borchers and Eckert had visited him they returned, but he declined to collaborate with them, and they left him alone.

But was this apparently subversive talk in the second letter an attempt by WALENTY to ingratiate himself with the Germans? Certainly he was not in a position to speak for the Polish nation, but only to express his own opinion as a Pole in a very precarious situation who was trying to save his own neck.

These letters represent his prescience that 'Russia [or rather, the Soviet Union] would be in a position to decide the New Order in Eastern Europe', which is, of course, what later happened at the end of the war. Poland did become 'under the heels of the barbarians and Communists in Russia' as part of the Warsaw Pact until its withdrawal at the end of the Cold War in 1989/90. Like many members of the British aristocracy prior to, and during, the Second World War, he seems to be saying that Nazism was preferable to Communism. As we now know, if Germany had won the war, it had no intention of reconstructing the rights of the Polish nation, nor any other nation that it had conquered, given its devastating and ruthless suppression of the Warsaw uprising in 1943, for example, and the extermination of Polish Jews at Auschwitz and elsewhere during the Holocaust. The New World Order that Nazi Germany had espoused, and was already carrying out, was nothing like the idealistic view that WALENTY seemed to hold.

The so-called 'second move' was made in March when he was interviewed by a colonel on the General Staff, and an infantry lieutenant. He stated that he had nothing to add to what he had already told Borchers and Eckert, but described the meeting thus:

> In the prison office I found a Colonel wearing the uniform of a Staff Officer attended by an A.D.C. in the rank of Lieutenant. Upon my entering the room, in reply to my bow they gave the military salute. Their behaviour during the interview was tactful.
>
> Personally I did not feel well during this interrogation. I was cold and unshaven, hungry, and on that particular day in an exceptionally bad temper.

That interview was, in the words of the colonel, to establish the 'state of mind in Polish Units'. A whole list of questions and answers are supplied in the WALENTY report under 'Course of Interrogation' but will not be addressed here; other questions related to General Sikorski and WALENTY's meeting with him. The colonel was aware of WALENTY's previous visit to England and his meeting with Sikorski, which would suggest that there had been a leak or 'mole' in the Polish Intelligence Service. At the end of March VIOLETTE came to see him in Fresnes and gave him a note, slipped to him while shaking hands, which explained what had happened with the break-up of *Interallié*, VICTOIRE's role in helping the Germans, and who had been arrested.

The 'third move' was made by Ische a couple of weeks later in which he spoke of a United States of Europe, but never mentioned *Interallié*. There was a great deal of anti-Communist talk but no anti-Semitism. WALENTY played along with it and was allowed to read German newspapers. Another two weeks passed before Ische returned to repeat his propaganda spiel. He then suggested that WALENTY become an agent for them and go to England. The colonel used WALENTY's family in Poland, his imprisoned comrades and VIOLETTE as bargaining chips to secure his agreement, saying that if he agreed, all his comrades would be released. Ische asked him to write down his suggestions for such a mission, which WALENTY did. Sometime around the end of May he was again interviewed by the colonel. WALENTY would only agree to work for them 'for ideological reasons and there will be no need of reprisals', to which the colonel replied, 'You will be required to sign a declaration that these people are held as guarantee for you.' WALENTY repeated that it would be for ideological reasons and not money, nor simply to get out of prison.

The Germans set out his mission with two objectives: first, he was to find out about aircraft production, tank production, troop movements and the British order of battle. Secondly, he was to investigate the possibility of creating a Fifth Column against the Poles in Britain, which would include subversive propaganda and sabotage. This latter did not sit well with the Poles when they later interviewed him in London, but as we shall shortly see, all of this appears to have been part of WALENTY's end-game to lure the Germans into trusting him to become a double agent.

It is worth noting that the Germans already had other spies who were supplying them with this kind of information. One was the counter-intelligence and trade attaché in Stockholm, Dr Karl-Heinz Krämer, code-named HEKTOR by the Germans, who worked for Abwehr 1L (1 Luft) under Nikolaus Ritter. Krämer was supplying them with monthly production summaries from the Society of British Aircraft Constructors and from other contacts in Sweden, such as JOSEFINE (a code name for a number of sources in the Swedish government, but also thought to be Count Johann Gabriel Oxenstierna, the Swedish naval attaché in London). One of Ritter's agents, Walter Dicketts (CELERY), SNOW's accomplice, known to the Germans as 'Der Kleine', was also furnishing information on the state of the British aircraft industry and the RAF, as well as TATE (Wulf Schmidt), and SNOW (Arthur Owens) himself.

It was not until July that a plan was put in train for his 'escape' to take place. The chronology can be summarised as follows: on or about 26 July Ische informed him that an escape from hospital would not work. On 29 July WALENTY was taken into Paris, to 5/7, rue Dufrenoy, close to the rue de la Faisanderie, where he was met by Ische and the colonel. He asked after VIOLETTE and what had happened to her. They told him that she had been allowed to return to her family in Lunéville and was now living under house arrest at 10, rue Boffrand. On 31 July he again met with the Germans at the rue Dufrenoy in the early afternoon between twelve noon and one o'clock. He sent a postcard to VIOLETTE, and later went to see her sometime after 2 or 3 August (she said it was the 6th), with the assistance of two German NCOs who drove him there. WALENTY and VIOLETTE spent the night together, during which she told him that after April the Germans had decided that they had no further use for her, which was why she had been allowed to return to Lunéville.

VIOLETTE seemed to want to talk about *Interallié*, although he tried to change the subject several times. What she did tell him was that the trouble had started with KIKI, although he had tried to save WALENTY. She confirmed that CHRISTIAN had been arrested on 18 November and had given the Germans details about him and VICTOIRE. Had VICTOIRE not gone to her home that day she could have avoided arrest as she had apparently known that the Germans were searching the area:

> VIOLETTE spoke at great length about the discreditable role which VICTOIRE had played and was particularly incensed because on one occasion she had asked VICTOIRE what 'TOTO' (i.e. WALENTY) would have said and VICTOIRE shrugged her shoulders. VIOLETTE told him that VICTOIRE had given all the necessary information to enable the Germans to restart the radio link and had arranged that MARCEL be appointed operator.

She also complained that she had lost her life savings of 75,000 francs during the raid on the *Interallié* office. WALENTY gave her 5,000 francs, with the reassurance that he would send her 3,000 francs on a regular basis until the end of May 1944. This he did, with the money always being wrapped in white paper inside a plain envelope. On two occasions, a typewritten note was also included and signed 'Edgar'. He left instructions that should she experience any difficulties she should write to GABY at 43, rue des Écoles.

WALENTY enquired how the British had been deceived after MAURICE's escape. She told him that everyone had been suspicious but their suspicions had been allayed; the British had sent money and he was able to restart the radio network. VICTOIRE had also begun to work with the LUCAS network through MIKLOS. She initially said that she thought VICTOIRE had gone to England with LUCAS, but then when he asked how sure she was, she said she'd heard that VICTOIRE had gone to Marseilles and may now be back in Paris. Then she told him that the British had gone to great lengths to save him, even paying a Polish or Alsatian lawyer named Kossecki half a million francs, and had also sent ADAM back to England. She confirmed to him that those who ran Sectors G and H in the forbidden zone had been arrested. What she told him next he found amazing: she had requested permission to see Stülpnagel to plead for leniency. Stülpnagel obviously held WALENTY in high esteem as he had a photograph of him in his office and held him up as an example of how a soldier should carry out his duty. WALENTY and VIOLETTE had sat up half the night drinking coffee and talking.

On 15 August WALENTY met one final time with the colonel, Ische, the two NCOs and Todt. Much of what was initially discussed was the same ground that had been covered before. The arrangements for his escape were that he was to proceed to Vichy, accompanied, at his suggestion, by a German who could smooth out any problems which might arise. That task fell to Bleicher, but WALENTY dictated many of the logistics. He said he would first go to Vichy, then to Lyons, where he would stay at the Hôtel de Bordeaux and meet up with Bleicher at the Restaurant Brasserie Georges each day. Bleicher informed him that Suzanne Laurent would be accompanying them, and that she could be used as a contact if he needed to get in touch. Throughout all of this, WALENTY only knew Bleicher as JEAN, never his real name.

The Germans instructed WALENTY to make contact with the chief of the Polish organisation in the Unoccupied Zone so that they might know what sabotage organisations existed there. This he played along with but later made excuses to Bleicher. They handed him a document that was an acknowledgement by him that he was:

> Acting on the dictates of his conscience, he was starting to work for the National Socialist State and in a military capacity. The document also stated that he was undertaking the mission voluntarily, and that if he failed in his duty the Germans would be entitled to take reprisals.

After he had signed it, the Germans saluted him and they all parted amicably.

WALENTY's journey began on the morning of 15 August at the Gare de Lyon, travelling alone and crossing the border at Paray-le-Monial. When he met up with Bleicher in Lyons two or three days later at the Restaurant Brasserie Georges as arranged, Suzanne Laurent was with him. She was staying at the Hôtel Terminus in Aix-les-Bains, which they arranged should be his contact address. The notes in Bleicher's file[6] however, give this date as 9 September, by which time he and Suzanne were in Toulouse and staying at the Grand Hotel d'Orléans, 57, rue Bayard. Bleicher then went off to Chamonix – the report says that he seemed to be much more interested in the scenery and very pleased he was having a holiday at the expense of his organisation.

Before Bleicher returned, WALENTY received orders to move, so he left a note at the Hôtel Terminus arranging to meet Bleicher at the Brasserie Belossi in Toulouse, which they did on 8 September. On his way to the railway station WALENTY sent a note via the porter, to be given to Bleicher, which read, 'long live Hitler, the great creator of New Europe'. Postcards were also sent via Suzanne Laurent from Madrid and finally Gibraltar. In Madrid his escape was assisted by Michael Justin Creswell (1909–86), code-named 'Monday', who was actually working for MI9, the escape and evasion organisation of British Intelligence and connected with Andrée 'Dédée' de Jongh (1916–2007) and the 'Comet Line'. The late Conservative MP Airey Neave (1916–79), who also worked for MI9 during the war, described Creswell as 'a big genial member of the British Embassy staff'.[7]

When it came time to cross into Unoccupied France, WALENTY contacted a Mademoiselle Noël, an assistant teacher at the École Arts et Métiers, who he thought would be able to help. She in turn put him in touch with Pierre Morreau [sic], who owned a W/T shop at 5, rue Roger in the 14th arrondissement. WALENTY made the mistake of telling the Germans who this man was when they asked him, and they suggested that he might be an *agent provocateur*. They also told him that they had had Morreau under surveillance for some time and warned him not to have anything to do with him, leading him to wonder whether Morreau really *was* an *agent provocateur*. What he didn't know was that Morreau was acting as liaison between a Belgian organisation in Belgium and an American one in Unoccupied France.

Morreau should not be confused with Pierre Léonce Demalvilan @ Jean Moreau (1926–2015), a member of F2, the British–French–Polish resistance network, as he was only 14 at the time. Instead, this was Pierre Moreau, listed in one of the BRUTUS files.[8] Confusingly, his code name was LUCAS, although this is not the same LUCAS (Pierre de Vomécourt) mentioned earlier. As WALENTY noted, it was interesting that the Germans had warned him that some of his former agents – DESIRE (Robert Kieffer), BOB (Robert Gorriot @ EDGAR) and MICHEL (Claude Jouffret) – were now working for them against the Communists and the Jews. The Germans had instructed them to look out for him in the hope that he would lead them to Polish organisations in France. While he never ran into any of these men, he wrote in his report that he hoped that DESIRE at least would have warned him.

The Germans told him that LA CHATTE had left for England with the leader of the LUCAS organisation. Not unreasonably, they also assumed that she had been arrested and betrayed everything. As WALENTY said, 'The supposition that she had betrayed everything appeared to be supported by the fact that there had been "some echoes in France" and in particular "an attempt" made on the flat of one of her former collaborators.'

In referring to avoiding making any slip-ups in Unoccupied France,
WALENTY mentions NESTOR, whose identity remains unknown – he even
admits to not knowing his real name – and has not been identified in any of
the MI5 files: 'NESTOR observed the necessary caution (even though I did
not acquaint him with the new affair) and he, too, did not notice anything
suspicious.' NESTOR is again mentioned when WALENTY was with Bleicher
in Toulouse, giving rise to the likelihood that he was probably someone working
for the TUDOR network in Unoccupied France:

> I reported that, in my opinion, the Polish organisation had more or less
> collapsed after the winter arrests. All chiefs had left as they felt in danger. Only
> NESTOR had remained and was now in charge of the work. I did not know
> his present name and address (NESTOR had given me this information). I
> knew that NESTOR was going to leave and then the work would come to
> a standstill.

Whoever it was, the two most likely contenders must be ruled out as the
chronology does not fit:

(1) It cannot have been Jean Loncle @ NESTOR @ PIKE as WALENTY
     had arrived back in England before Loncle had been landed by a Lysander
     of 161 Squadron on the night of 25/26 November 1942 4 kilometres east
     of Chateauneuf du Cher and 0.88 kilometres north of Chavannes, along
     with W/T operator Paimblanc @ CARP MINOR @ Eric W and twelve
     W/T sets;[9]
(2) Nor could it have been the man who Foot mentions: J.R.E. Poirier, DSO
     @ NESTOR, part of the *Author/Digger* network and assistant to Henri
     Peulevé, as he also came later.[10]

There are also a number of other SOE agents with Nestor as a Christian name, but
these cannot be verified sufficiently to qualify as contenders.[11] Mathilde Carré's
biographer, Gordon Young, refers to NESTOR as being an organisation rather
than an individual when he wrote: 'When all were rested, the trio proceeded
to Toulouse where Armand made contact with an underground organisation
named "Nestor" which undertook to smuggle him safely to Britain.'[12] Garby-
Czerniawski's book describes how Colonel Zarembski (TUDOR) was sending
a Major Szymanowski to take over from ARMAND in Toulouse and would
give the name 'Nestor'. This may have been Major Stefan Szymanowski who in

1943 would command the Polish Independent Grenadier Company, considered the Polish equivalent of the SAS. Someone mentioned by VICTOIRE who worked for NESTOR was Jacques Marie Christophe Grassal, who was born in Nantes on 28 October 1913, deported from Compiègne on 6 April 1944, and died in Mauthausen on 17 or 22 April 1945. He is described as being a lieutenant in the FFI but must also have trained with SOE as a file on him exists in the National Archives at Kew.[13]

A 'Brutus Supplementary Report' dated 31 December 1942 was prepared by MI5 on the WALENTY case.[14] As listed at the beginning, it deals with:

Part I   The acts and decisions taken on the discovery that BRUTUS was a German agent.

Part II   Evidence which has come to light during the past year bearing on BRUTUS' motives and intentions.

Part III   Conduct of BRUTUS in Polish internal politics, his arrest and court martial.

Part IV   Evidence disclosed by the various checks kept on BRUTUS.

Part V   Progress of the BRUTUS case.

Part VI   Present assessment of the position and prospects in regard to BRUTUS (a) as a Security Service case, (b) as a double agent.

Part I of the report states that initially doubts had been expressed about the credibility of his story of how he had been imprisoned but without revealing any secrets, and his subsequent escape, although it concluded with the unanimous decision that he had been telling the truth. 'The admission by him a month after his arrival that he had been given a mission by the Germans was a bombshell, particularly for the Polish Service.' This jarred with the two Polish officers in charge of his case – Major Jan Henryk Żychón, Colonel Gano's deputy, and Major Siegfried Zarembski, who had been a personal friend of WALENTY with whom he had teamed up in Toulouse at the beginning of the *Interallié* network.[15] Captain Plocek of the Deuxième Bureau acted as secretary to the Commission. This is probably Rudolf Jósef Plocek, who would later go on to translate documents used in the investigation of the Katyn massacre.

WALENTY's court martial began on 26 November 1943 and ended on 9 December 1943, resulting in his being condemned to two months' imprisonment first in London, then at an unnamed fortress in Scotland, from which the six weeks he had already spent in prison in Scotland were to be deducted, with the remaining two weeks deferred until after the war. Part VI of the report concluded that he had only received a nominal punishment, with Harmer noting, 'He has probably come out of it a little tinpot hero in the eyes of his fellow Polish airmen.'

In spite of Colonel Gano's insistence that there be a Military Court of Inquiry to look into his escape – a rule of Polish military law that any escaped prisoner had to go before a Court of Inquiry – the Commission, which was held in secret at Dunderdale's house on 17 and 22 December, suggested that WALENTY's story be accepted, but it recommended that he be 'severely reprimanded for jeopardising several persons, including an officer from a neighbouring post, by his behaviour because he did not report the whole matter to his superiors on his arrival'.

The Twenty Committee, represented by Guy Liddell and Tar Robertson on behalf of MI5, discussed his case on 31 December 1942 to consider whether as BRUTUS he should be run as a double agent. Once the W Board had approved it, they informed Gano and Dunderdale of the committee's decision. As J.C. Masterman explained to Guy Liddell that same day:

> At the Twenty Committee to-day the case of BRUTUS was explained by Major Robertson. The Committee took the view that we ought not to proceed with the case without the approval of the W. Board, on the ground that it was necessary to give the Poles full information about the case and that some of the members of the Board were always sensitive about the passing of information to officers of Allied countries. In these circumstances I hope that you will be able to ask D.M.I. to summon the Board in order to clear the matter up.
>
> I think that you and Robertson will have little difficulty in persuading the Board to carry on with the case if you so wish. Perhaps it would be best for you to have a word with Robertson about the whole matter before the Board is summoned.[16]

A summary of the case for the W Board was duly drawn up by B1a, dated 4 January 1943, in which Tar noted that, 'Apart from himself [Gano] and his chief officers the Poles who know are General Klimecki, the Polish Chief of Staff, and Colonel Orlovsky, head of the Polish C.E. [counter-espionage].' As mentioned at the beginning of this chapter, WALENTY's later role as double agent BRUTUS will not be dealt with here, but henceforth, the British referred to him by his new code name. However, we will continue to use the code name WALENTY unless he is being quoted as BRUTUS.

When WALENTY arrived in England MOUSTIQUE (Monique Deschamps) had already preceded him by escaping from the Occupied Zone (although an MI6 CX report from Townshend states she arrived on 12 October; see Appendix 4) and was now living with him as his mistress at 41 Redcliffe Square, Kensington, London, SW10. Part II of the 'Brutus Supplementary Report' noted that in the messages sent to BRUTUS by the Germans about VIOLETTE, 'they have shown that they are still in contact with her, and it seems to indicate that she is in [on] the secret as well'. On 21 October 1943 he received the message, 'VIOLETTE is very well. Because of our dealings with her she seems to have deduced that you are fighting on our side. Her friends also are well.'[17] He wrote back on 26 October:

Many thanks for news but I am very much displeased that VIOLETTE should have guessed the real situation because I fear any involuntary indiscretion which might destroy all my efforts. I should therefore like to send her a personal letter in French via Antonio. He should change the envelope in Lisbon. Do you agree?[18]

Hugh Astor suggested that BRUTUS reply and try to establish exactly how VIOLETTE had been arrested, and to what extent she had collaborated with the Germans. He proposed that BRUTUS recruit her as a sub-agent, provided the Germans could assure him that she was agreeable to it. She would then send back chicken feed to the Germans via BRUTUS, or be run independently of him and direct to the Germans. 'If the latter course is adopted it should be possible to devise a means whereby even if VIOLETTE subsequently becomes blown it would not react against BRUTUS.'

On 14 December Harmer reported that BRUTUS, as he was now referred to, had asked him whether MOUSTIQUE could be used:

I told him that any request of this sort would be dealt with refused categorically and outlined to him our reasons, namely that it was not essential for the running of the case that MOUSTIQUE be taken into our confidence and that, although I felt certain that her personal loyalty to him was sufficient to make her keep her mouth shut for the time being, her attitude might change in the future and we would not take the risk.[19]

Harmer commented that while BRUTUS did not openly show he was annoyed, he was probably hurt. A lengthy report on Bleicher prepared by D.I. Wilson of B1w to Colonel Robin 'Tin Eye' Stephens of Camp 020 on 5 July 1945 sheds some light on WALENTY's escape:

10.   There is no special secrecy about the arrest of the head of the INTERALLIÉE Service, WALENTY @ ARMAND @ TCHERNIAVSKY, etc, nor of the fact that he susbsequently escaped. What is Top Secret is that his escape was arranged by the Germans and that he came over here with a mission which he subsequently proceeded to carry out under British control. All references to his escape having been arranged or his subsequent history should, therefore, be excluded from the Interim report, but I would like to have a separate report on the extent to which WALENTY in the course of his assisted escape gave away to BLEICHER the patriots who helped him to escape without knowing that the escape was taking place at the instigation of the Germans. WALENTY admitted that some patriots might have suffered through this act and I would like to ascertain from BLEICHER whether WALENTY told us the whole truth about this matter.

11.   There is no reason why BLEICHER should not realise that we are now aware that WALENTY came over here with a mission. We have, in fact, been told it by Oberst. REILE. BLEICHER should, therefore, be left with the impression that we only recently learnt of this fact of which we had not been aware at the time and he should be made to think that we are now trying to find WALENTY who has disappeared.

The report goes on to add:

14.   As you know, the Germans arranged that after the breakdown of the INTERALLIÉE Organisation VICTOIRE should come over to this country with LUCAS, an important agent of S.O.E., who, in German eyes, was not to know that VICTOIRE was working for the Germans. LUCAS in fact returned to France secretly while wireless traffic from this country was trying to make the Germans believe that both LUCAS and

VICTOIRE were staying in this country longer than at first anticipated in order to undergo further training and courses etc. In fact LUCAS was arrested not long after his return. We would like to know exactly how this arrest took place, that is to say how the Germans discovered he was in France. He was probably betrayed by one WOLTERS but we do not know how BLEICHER got on to WOLTERS.

15. After the breakdown of the INTERALLIÉE BLEICHER was understood to have employed KIKI as a penetration agent in the neighbourhood of Lisieux. The report should contain details of this activity.[20]

Wolters was the Belgian Leon Wolters @ GUY, born 14 October 1903 with whom LUCAS was living in Paris.[21]

CHAPTER 19

Pointing Fingers

While all this was happening, on 20 October 1942 WALENTY wrote another report looking at who could have been responsible for the break-up of the *Interallié* network in which he offered his 'personal conjectures respecting the following problems' and singling out a few obvious suspects for criticism:

- how did the Germans come upon the trail of the Organisation.
- in what way did they strive to liquidate it.
- how did this liquidation finally occur.[1]

First of all, he stressed that the investigations started by Schwerbel via Madame Bratkowska and Biernacki did not contribute to the liquidation of the network, due to the security measures he had put in place. However, in his interview with Major Langenfeld, he admitted that he thought it possible that Biernacki had stolen his and VIOLETTE's photograph from Mademoiselle Magdalena Jankowska (also known as Madeleine, or CHON), with whom VIOLETTE was friendly, and who used to visit Madame Bratkowska. He said that he regarded DESIRE's arrest on the 15 or 16 November as the direct cause of the break-up and also the arrest of Lieutenant Krotki. This assertion was borne out by how ADAM had been picked up on 2 November without any difficulty. Krotki had been in possession of notes and addresses linking him to a resistance organisation, but he felt that if Krotki had broken down and confessed, it was probably because he 'had not as yet been bound with it by ideological and spiritual ties'.

Schwerbel was 'an official delegate for Polish matters in the Paris aliens' office and at the same time in the service of the German Intelligence', according to WALENTY. He is mentioned in a report on 'Walenty/Victoire/Szumlicz' by J.P. de C. Day (John Day) of B1b, dated 13 January 1943 and may have been the Dr Scherbe or Dr Schwelbe referred to in Szumlicz's MI5 file. Aged 33/35, 5ft 5in tall, of broad build, fair hair, clean-shaven, given to wearing plus fours

PART I

PERSONAL PARTICULARS AND PREVIOUS HISTORY OF VICTOIRE

Full Name:	Mathilde Lucie CARRE (nee BELARD)
Aliases:	Maitena BARREL (nom-de-plume)
	Micheline DONNADIEU
	Mme. BERGER
	Marguerite DE ROCHE
Code Names:	LA CHATTE
	BAGHERA
	VICTOIRE

Nationality:	French
Born:	30.6.1908 at Creusot, Saone et Loire, France.
Father:	Arsene BELARD, born 1886.
Mother:	Nee Jean GROS, born 1886.
Married:	18.5.33, Maurice Henri Claude CARRE.

Description:
Height:	5' 4".
Build:	Slight.
Face:	Oval.
Hair:	Dark brown.
Eyes:	Green-brown.
Nose:	Slightly turned up.
Distinguishing Features:	Two teeth missing at side. Extremely short-sighted but never wears glasses, except for reading, when she puts the paper practically up to her eyes.

Mathilde Carré, from her MI5 file (© Crown Copyright, The National Archives, KV2/931)

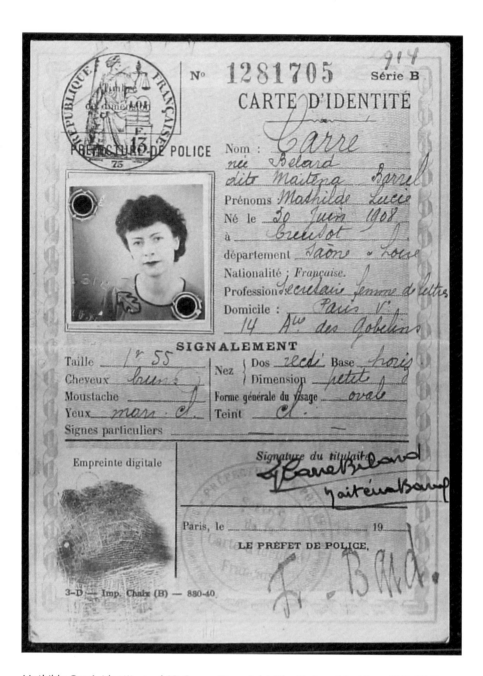

Mathilde Carré, identity card (© Crown Copyright, The National Archives, KV2/933)

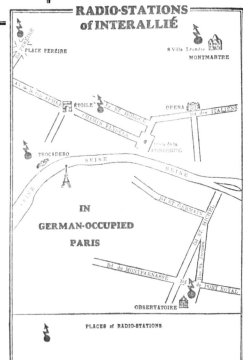

INTELLIGENCE SECTORS
as designed in November 1940
for the
INTERALLIÉ NETWORK

The plan was carried out and this " field organisation " gradually uncovered the entire dispositions of the German Army in occupied France

Intelligence Sectors for
the November 1940
Interallié network
(© Gerry Czerniawski;
photo: Author's collection)

RADIO-STATIONS
of INTERALLIÉ

IN
GERMAN-OCCUPIED
PARIS

PLACES of RADIO-STATIONS

Radio stations of *Interallié*
(© Gerry Czerniawski;
photo: Author's collection)

Courier service from
German-occupied Paris
(© Gerry Czerniawski;
photo: Author's collection)

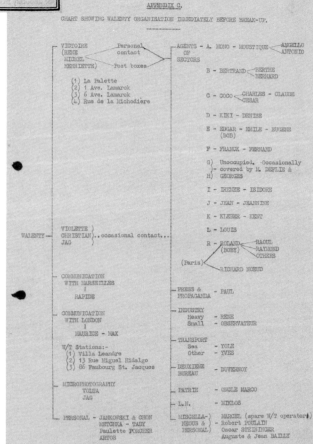

WALENTY organisation
before the break-up
in 1941 (© Crown
Copyright, The National
Archives, KV2/931)

Statement of expenses for Mathilde Carré, March–April 1942 (© Crown Copyright, The National Archives, KV2/935)

VICTOIRE.

Statement of Expenses.

MARCH, 1942.   £   s   d

        C. B. Mills,   5   -
        St. J. Horsfall,   1   7   -
        C. H. Harmer,   4 13   -
                                                 £6   5   0

One third of the cost = £2 1 8d.

APRIL, 1942.   £   s   d

April 10. Salary 1st - 14.4.42.   25   -   -
  "   13. W. G. Cole, Exes. w/e 12.4.42.   3 12   1
  "   14. Mrs. Barton, Housekeeping &
           other exes. to 13.4.42.   8 13   6
  "   17. Sgt. Gale, Exes. to 9.4.42.   4 16   3
  "   18. W. G. Cole, Exes. w/e 19.4.42.   6   3   -
           Mrs. Barton, housekeeping etc.   4 14   -
  "   22. W. G. Cole, Exes.to 21.4.42.   4   6   -
           Mrs. Barton, Exes to 21.4.42.   9 15   -
  "   27. W. G. Cole, Exes. to 27.4.42.   2 19   3
           Mrs. Barton, Exes. to 27.4.42.   9 18 10
  "   30. Salary 16th - 30.4.42.   25   -   -

           C. H. Harmer, Exes. for month   34   3   6
           L. C. Marshall,   do.   16 10
           St. J. Horsfall,   do.   10   6
           J. H. Marriott,   do.   6   6
                                               £ 140 15   3

One third of the cost = £46 18 5d.

SUMMARY.
           March, one third of cost,   2   1   8
           April, one third of cost,   46 18   5
                                                £49   -   1

No charge has been made of the rent of 19, Rugby Mansions,
nor for the services of Mrs. Barton.

B.1.A./4.5.42.

Statement of expenses for Mathilde Carré from B1a, March–July 1942 (© Crown Copyright, The National Archives, KV2/935)

Victoire
March – July

B1A
        Salary   125
        Rent   42:15:-
        Living Expenses   53:6:8
        Entertaining   122:17:5
        Trunk   6:-:-
        Dentist   4:14:6
        Contingencies   35:-:-
                          £359:13:7

        B1A   389:13:7
        SOE   300:17:10
        SIS   48:2:-
                      £708:13:5
              1/share £236:4:6

        B1A   Paid   359:13:7
                1/share   236:4:6   123:9:1
        SOE   Paid   300:17:10
                1/share   236:4:6   64:13:4
                                      £188:2:5
        SIS   1/share   236:4:5
                Paid   48:2   188:2:5

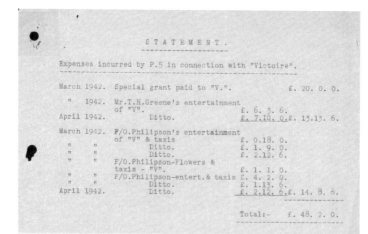

Statement of expenses for Mathilde Carré from P5 (SIS), March–April 1942 (© Crown Copyright, The National Archives, KV2/935)

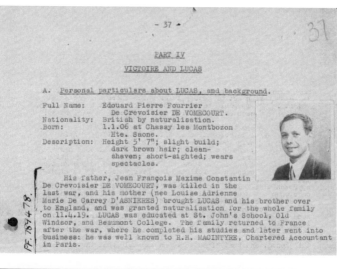

LUCAS, from Mathilde Carré's MI5 file (© Crown Copyright, The National Archives, KV2/931)

Mathilde Carré at her Paris trial (© Getty Images/Bettmann)

Mathilde Carré in a Paris court (Credit: Rue des Archives/Granger – All rights reserved)

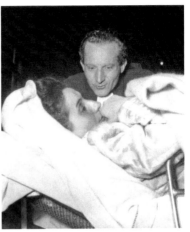

Renée Borni in a Paris court (Credit: Rue des Archives/Granger – All rights reserved)

Roman Garby-Czerniawski, portrait (© Gerry Czerniawski)

Roman Garby-Czerniawski and Hugo Bleicher in Paris after the war (© Gerry Czerniawski)

Left: Roman Garby-Czerniawski's award of Virtuti Militari (© Gerry Czerniawski)

Below left: Roman Garby-Czerniawski's wedding to Thelma, his second wife (© Gerry Czerniawski)

Below right: Hugo Bleicher (from *Colonel's Henri's Story*) (Credit: Author's collection)

Right: Suzanne Laurent, Bleicher's accomplice (from *Colonel's Henri's Story*) (Credit: Author's collection)

Far right: Hugo Bleicher after the war as a tobacconist in Tettnang (Credit: Keystone Pictures USA/Alamy Stock Photo)

and married to a Polish wife, he was the only official who spoke Polish. He also had a separate office in the Avenue Hoche in the 8th arrondissment, one of the streets radiating out from the Étoile. His main responsibility was for rounding up Poles and sending them to the Arbeitsdienst (Reich Labour Service) in Germany. His organisation also employed Tadeusz Biernacki, described as 'one of the most dangerous and active German agents',[2] and someone named Ołpiński. This was probably Stefan Eugeniusz Ołpiński (1898–1944), also known as von Ołpiński, described by Władsław Fejkiel (1911–95), a Polish physician and prisoner-physician at Auschwitz, in Hermann Langbein's book *People in Auschwitz* as a 'fine figure of a man with agreeable manners who mastered several languages'.[3]

Langbein's book states that Ołpiński 'became unfavourably known … [for] his connections with the Nazis and spoke on German radio stations before the war'. He also apparently had two sons who served in the Waffen-SS. He collaborated with the Gestapo as their chief informer in Paris, resulting in various members of the Polish Army being shot. When he was deported to Auschwitz (number 67214) on 9 October 1942 after the sabotage of a railway car he was also made an informer there. He died in Auschwitz in January 1944 of typhus, contracted from a typhus-infected lice-ridden pullover sent to him by some Polish compatriots seeking revenge for his treachery. Day observed that, based on other traces of Schwerbel and Ołpiński, the organisation concerned was the SD.[4] Day adds that Szumlicz was working for Neugebauer at the Paris SD, as well as Schwerbel and Bereznicki.

Tadeusz Wojciech Szumlicz was born on 2 June 1916 in Stanisławów, Poland. He attended the Officers' Training Centre in Tarnapol. When Germany invaded Poland in 1939 he was a 23-year-old officer cadet. After the Polish Army – in which he had served in Norway and France – had been dispersed, he was recruited by the Abwehr in Paris.[5] According to his MI5 file he worked for them for two and a half months and then, with German connivance, had escaped to Madrid via Marseilles. In Madrid sometime in late June he had reconnected with the Gestapo (Dr Ast) and revealed to them the Polish escape line from Marseilles to Lisbon. From Madrid he made his way to Lisbon and Gibraltar, from where he came to England, arriving in July 1941 aboard the HMT *Narkunda* [sic].[6] On 25 July he was taken to the RVPS, and later (around 2 August) to Camp 020, to discover whether he had been sent to England on a mission for the Abwehr. The fact that Szumlicz had used this route is interesting, given that MAURICE had used the same route to escape, yet the Germans – who by this time knew the arrangements – allowed MAURICE to escape unheeded. A document in Szumlicz's MI5 file initialled by 'F.C.D.' and dated 1 June 1942 posed *inter alia* the following question:

> Was the Polish secret escape route from Marseilles to Lisbon organised and in operation by the middle of January 1941?
>
> Presumably it was, but if not, if SZUMLICZ was sent on a mission by the Germans in Paris at the end of January, it could not have been to discover this route and report on it to Madrid.[7]

A reply from the Polish Ministry of War, Security Control Department at the Hotel Rubens on 29 July (the author is most likely E. Szarkeiwicz) informed MI5, 'we had several routes from Marseilles to Lisbon, which were used by us immediately after the collapse of France.'[8] Milmo concluded, 'On the present state of our information it seems to be a 95 per cent certainty that SZUMLICZ worked for the German Secret Service both in Paris and in Spain before he came here.'[9] In fact, at Camp 020 he admitted he had worked for the Germans.

Bereznicki was a Ukrainian using the name Muller @ Ostapczuk, who worked at a German office in the Hôtel Stella on the Avenue Carnot in Paris. Szumlicz had been instructed to denounce Bereznicki, a writer posing as a Ukrainian refugee, by Captain Majewski of the Polish Deuxième Bureau whom he had previously known in Lemberg and had run into in the Champs-Élysées on 1 July 1940. Szumlicz had been arrested by the Geheime Feldpolizei on 29 July and taken first to the Hôtel Crillon, then La Santé prison. It was there that he had been visited by Majewski, who informed him that Bereznicki had been responsible for his arrest.

A Dr Neugebauer is mentioned in a declassified CIA document as being a liaison of the Sicherheitspolitzei (Sipo – the department which controlled the Gestapo and the Kriminalpolizei) and SD with the Abwehr and Wehrmacht back in 1941, based at the Hôtel de Calais, 5, rue des Capucines, Paris; the same document lists Dr Schwerbel as being with the SS Sonderkommando, Polish Section, 72, Avenue Foch.[10] Although Neugebauer has been mentioned in the CIA document, there is also a First Lieutenant Neubauer named in a list of Abwehr personnel in Paris in one of VICTOIRE's files. Aged about 35 years old, 5ft 8in tall, a former athletics instructor from Central Germany, he had been in the Abwehr since 1940 and was used as a director of agents.[11] A description of Neugebauer in Szumlicz's MI5 file gives him as a head of a section at the Hôtel de Calais, aged 32, height 5ft 11in, strongly built, with straight fair hair and blue eyes, clean-shaven; long face; ruddy complexion, wearing dark clothes: a short overcoat and greeny-grey sporting-type soft felt hat with feathers on the side, much like one of those Tyrolean or Alpine hats much favoured in Bavaria. There is also the following description in one of VICTOIRE's files of a Neubauer: '1st Lt. (Res). About 35 years old, 5ft 8in tall, an athletics instructor from Central Germany, in the Abwehr since 1940, speaks good French, was used as a director of agents.'[12]

WALENTY did not question that VICTOIRE, or 'La Chatte' as he preferred to call her, had been guilty, or at least complicit, as he said she had been responsible for the increased number of those arrested:

> There is no doubt that even without her assistance the Organisation would have been entirely liquidated … Her guilt, therefore, consists chiefly in having facilitated to the Germans the quick arrest of other and numerous agents, who might have escaped in view of the notoriety, which the affair immediately won e.g. the escape of the group 'Moustique', 'Kent' and 'Louis', together with their agents as well as of all agents of the sectors 'G', 'H', 'S' warned by 'Hector'.
>
> 'La Chatte' is also guilty of contributing to the liquidation of the 'LN' and 'Patrie' organisations, which were connected with us. 'La Chatte' was the only person in possession of data necessary for this liquidation. It was she, too, who gave her assistance in catching W/T work and in continuing the work of the organisation for 'provocative' purposes.
>
> Her guilt is the greater since, in spite of the fact that she was immediately at one with the Organisation ideologically, and had organised it together with me, and in spite of the fact that she herself removed most of the agents and contacts, and although she must have fully realised the extent of the catastrophe, she helped the Germans in their work.[13]

LN was Libération-Nord, a left-leaning resistance organisation founded by Christian Pineau and Robert Lacoste on 1 December 1940.

At times, WALENTY's misguided loyalty to VICTOIRE comes across as extraordinary. In spite of the fact that he regarded what she had done to the Free French organisation as 'treason and betrayal', in an unwarranted gesture of magnanimity, he attempted to make excuses for her, saying that he could understand why she had had a grudge against the British, although at first he did not elaborate on what that grudge was or how she came to develop it. Later, he qualified that by saying that her grievance was related to the lack of appreciation that the British had shown her and the non-bestowal on her of any decoration, even though he had repeatedly asked them for one. That she was frustrated with the British response (or lack thereof) to her messages is clear from one sent on 14 December 1941 and received by SIS:

> We are surprised by your silence. Yes or No, do you want to help us in our future work. We are not at all disturbed at present and have found a sufficient number of agents especially on the whole of the coast, Sectors B, C, D, E and F.[14]

By this time, of course, British Intelligence was already aware of some of the arrests and this caused them to be suspicious and cautious, as witness their reply on 17 December:

> Subject your telegram 14/12. Your present position worries us a lot. Although we hope you are free of all enemy influence we cannot avoid the fear that your messages are being dictated by the Bosches. This for two reasons. 1) you have not replied to our question about the number of specimen codes existing before the arrest of WALENTY. 2) No details about him, for example, where he was arrested, what day and with which agents. Please prove to us that you work independently of all Bosche influence. Once we know this we will help you to the full as previously.[15]

Harmer's report of 11 March 1942 noted that at the end of his meeting with her, VICTOIRE had expressed her dissatisfaction at being in England and complained that so far she had only seen the Poles' and Tom Greene's organisations (SIS). She also felt that she should have been involved with all discussions relating to LUCAS's organisation since she considered herself to be inextricably linked with it; that she should be told of any progress being made with LUCAS's suggestion of Michel Clemenceau forming a provisional French government; and to be able to review previous reports sent by WALENTY to verify the facts. This sense of entitlement in which VICTOIRE believed is something that comes across time and time again in all MI5's confrontations with her.

In a back-handed compliment, WALENTY patronisingly described her work as 'not inferior to that of any British intelligence officer in France, although she was a "mere" woman, and she was intelligent enough to realise this'. These positive comments about her are in direct contrast to those published in his

memoirs. When asked later on when he was in England whether he wanted
see VICTOIRE in prison, he replied, 'I don't wish to see her. If by any chance
I do, I think I shall kill her. And I meant it.'[16] MOUSTIQUE also came in for
similar chauvinistic treatment when he said that, even as a 'mere' woman, she
was his best intelligent agent.

Harmer, writing on 4 March 1943 in 'Lessons to be Derived from the
VICTOIRE Case as to the German Methods of Penetrating Intelligence
Organisations', summed it up with the following:

> The case provides a valuable insight into the methods employed by the
> Germans, in showing the risks and chances they are prepared to take in order
> to win substantial prizes. It will be seen from the above that they put their
> trust in two agents who had shortly before been working whole-heartedly
> against them – in the first case they might well have missed their prize but
> in fact got it due to outside circumstances; in the second case they achieved
> what they wanted. The second lesson seems to be that, when using agents
> for penetration purposes, they allow them a very large amount of liberty and
> treat them very decently, to the extent even of making them personal friends.
> The third, and perhaps most singular lesson of the case is that in its broad
> outlines it was handled with great imagination by the Germans, whereas in
> detail they were very slovenly and failed to take a great deal of care. Some of
> their methods messages, for instance, were very bad and they did not prepare
> VICTOIRE's cover story in this country with any care at all. One's general
> feeling on investigating the case is that the Germans are playing for results
> rather than for safety, and either by successful handling or by good luck they
> achieved them in this case.[17]

When he was asked much later to write a critique of the memoirs VICTOIRE
had written while in prison, and to comment on the accuracy of the allegations
and assertions she had made therein, WALENTY commented that 'she
presents things as she saw them or rather as she wished to see them'. It would
be unnecessary and would take too long to wade through every single one, but
a few are worth mentioning as examples of whom she had betrayed.

At one point when VICTOIRE was angry, she had hinted that she might
leave the organisation but said she would be lost without it. WALENTY told
her that he would 'find an intelligent person, who knows how to type, I shall
take the trouble to train her from morning to night for a week and she will draw
up identical reports'. That statement could be interpreted in two different ways:

that VICTOIRE was neither intelligent nor able to type, or that he could easily replace her with someone with the same skills. Whatever he meant, he said he had exaggerated his statement, perhaps to put her in her place and remind her that no one was indispensable, adding that her intelligence was 'above the average'. Even so, it caused her to fear that perhaps one day this might happen. The power he had apparently given her had certainly gone to her head and was not something she wanted to relinquish. She saw herself running the organisation, and her admirers had added to the delusion by telling her that she might even become a second 'Jeanne d'Arc' (Joan of Arc); the French intelligence service 'flattered her out of all reason', and in the second part of her memoirs she portrayed herself as running the show while 'poor Toto' (WALENTY) languished in prison. Yet at other times in his critique he takes her to task over these delusions of grandeur, her sense of self-importance, and what he had initially allowed her to do. He goes to great pains to emphasise that her role in the organisation was limited, and not as inflated as her ego. She was not allowed to give instructions to agents – that was solely his prerogative – which he himself gave in detail. Nor did he allow her to draw up reports by herself; these he wrote himself and then she typed them up. He considered that she did not have the ability to work independently as she did not understand military matters and therefore could not follow the development of the German order of battle.

Her relations with the Deuxième Bureau also came in for criticism. WALENTY alleged that there had been several rows with them over requests for information, which were refused on the grounds that transporting them across the demarcation line into Occupied France was not safe. He also said that they were working 'very slowly and inefficiently'. As a result of this dispute, he stopped supplying the Deuxième Bureau with copies of *Interallié*'s reports, 'although I knew that La Chatte was very sorry about it. She did not show it because she was at one with me where the interests of our organisation were concerned.' He summed up by saying:

It is a great pity that La Chatte breaks off her Memoire and does not give a picture of subsequent periods, especially that before the catastrophe. La Chatte's picture gives only the 'sunny' period of our work. She did not include the most beautiful period when the Organisation had begun to work with the W/T set, when it had reached the apex of its possibilities and efficiency. The tempo of work would have slowed down afterwards. Neither did she give the 'shadowy' period containing the dangers and our fight with the C.E. [counter-espionage].[18]

He had further criticism to offer on Part III of her memoirs, both on how she presented the facts, and the inevitability of the outcome:

> In principle Part III of La Chatte's Memoires did not change my views on the catastrophe and the part played by La Chatte after the collapse of the Organisation.
>
> It provided me, however, with an answer to the question which I had been unable to solve as to the direct cause of 'Desire's' arrest. After all it was due to an ordinary denunciation lodged against him with the police dictated by personal spite.
>
> It follows that the collapse of the Organisation was due to chance and not to planned action worked out by the Germans. In this way we might have been caught a few months earlier or a few months later. They have no right to be proud of their C.E. methods. The Germans lost the game as soon as La Chatte got to England. Since my arrival in England the Germans are entering the final stage of losing the game. It has become my ambition to conclude this affair in grand style.
>
> I think that on the whole La Chatte's statements in her Memoires are true. Unfortunately, her style and her wish to lend her Memoire a litterary [sic] value, her desire to write up some scenes, her need to clear herself or at least to find justification for her actions – have affected the actual value of these Memoirs [sic] as statements.[19]

He went on to say that she was incapable of expressing herself objectively, ranging from 'extreme cynicism into outbursts of idealism'. It was incomprehensible how or why she accused certain people of treason, while ignoring or refusing to speak of her own act of betrayal. She had defied his instructions not to meet with VIOLETTE unless it was for operational reasons, and her hatred of VIOLETTE was based on her inability to confront her. Her attitude after the collapse of the organisation also changed: she made no attempt to contact him, unlike VIOLETTE who sent him several letters. As far as she was concerned, he no longer existed. As he put it, 'she was physically and mentally unable to do it'. In Part III she made little mention of him; when she did, it was with a kind of 'gêne' (discomfort), as he described it. He opined that possibly the Germans had deliberately not mentioned him to her, not wanting it to be perceived as a negative reaction, or that she had been blackmailed into believing the stories they told her, or what she chose to believe.

At no time, he said, did she reveal any psychological reasons for her mental breakdown, believing that there must have been some. Following her breakdown:

> La Chatte … began slowly but steadily to follow the downward path. She was given the chance to save her life at the cost of betraying the French organisation connected with us. Our agents must have played only a minor part in this after the collapse. La Chatte had to continue her policy in order to 'keep' her life, the moral foundations of which she had irretrievably lost. Her will ceased to function. Feeling her moral weakness, she must needs lean on the 'strong' Germans. She gradually loses her personality to such an extent that even when chances of escape arise, her will is atrophied.[20]

He drew the following conclusions about other members of the *Interallié* network:

> 'DESIRE' definitely accused owing to denunciation, and arrested, must have been carrying some documents supporting the charge. I think that he did his utmost to save the Organisation and his chief. In any case he said very little. He could not prevent the Germans from getting on the trail of KROTKI. I ascribe the fact that he did say something which led the Germans to us, to the poor moral resistance he was capable of putting up in moments of crisis. There was no baseness in his behaviour, a fact stressed even by the Germans. I am sure that had he wished, he might have compromised TUDOR's organisation.
>
> KROTKI, although arrested with compromising documents on him and although a whole set of reports on the land forces, testifying to the size of the Organisation, to which he belonged, were found in his flat, did not agree to collaborate – this is borne out by the fact that two days after his arrest the Germans had no details about me while arresting me and were not aware of the W/T station and the presence of a W/T operator in my house. I suppose that they found on KROTKI my telephone number and La Chatte's address.
>
> We have no illusions about La Chatte's role, and it is the factors which brought about her breakdown which are of interest to us.
>
> VIOLETTE did not play the part ascribed to her by La Chatte. It is possible that, lacking guile, she may have committed minor mistakes. It would appear that VIOLETTE did not betray anyone, because persons known to her and unknown to La Chatte were not arrested – I refer to the chiefs of the

forbidden zones, i.e. 'O' and 'H'. She knew them both personally and she knew their addresses. Neither did she betray coding details and did nothing to avoid mistakes in radio-correspondence. During her visit to me she told me with joy that 'so many mistakes have been made in the encoding that it is impossible that London should not twig something.'[21]

He wondered whether it would be possible to bring VIOLETTE to England to shed more light on what really happened, which ultimately the British did. Turning to other characters who committed 'the many major and minor betrayals', he singled out COCO, KLÉBER and OBSERVATEUR, who he said, 'proved their mettle'; however, the women, Mireille, RICHARD's wife, and KLÉBER's mistress Jacqueline 'showed a better spirit'. There then appears to be a few lines missing from his summary of the women.

MIKLOS's (Michel Brault) involvement in the whole affair also comes in for discussion, for as far as WALENTY was concerned, it was unclear. He suspected that MIKLOS might have been acting as a decoy. What has never been proved is the fact that a large Russian organisation connected with MIKLOS collapsed in the spring of 1941, and his subsequent connection with the collapse of *Interallié*, may not have been a simple coincidence. That being said, it has not been possible to establish exactly what this so-called Russian organisation was. What is also interesting is that many sources state that Michel Brault @ JÉRÔME was no mere Parisian lawyer, but a major figure in the French Resistance, later appointed head of the Service National Maquis (SNM) by Henri Frenay, and later credited with originating the term 'maquis', used as a synonym for the French Resistance.

In his more specific comments WALENTY pointed out that what LA CHATTE had failed to mention was what VIOLETTE had told him: that within ten minutes of VICTOIRE being arrested she agreed to collaborate with the Germans. He found it significant that VICTOIRE had the addresses of the two leaders of French organisations connected with *Interallié* and was convinced that this was her first betrayal, the details of their arrests being 'adjusted' by her to absolve herself of the blame. As to the allegation made by the Germans that MOUSTIQUE, MONO and ARMAND wanted to poison her, the real persons for whom the poison was intended were Tadeusz Biernacki, Stefan Ołpiński and possibly MARCEL.

He aired further comments about ROLAND-BOBY, whom he thought incapable of betraying his comrades, but he believed that MARCO and RENÉ's arrests had been the result of LA CHATTE. The arrest of RICHARD

NOEUD, and the subsequent suicide of his wife in prison was something that he found impossible to believe. How, he asked, had Bleicher found out about him, and had LA CHATTE told him, or somebody else? It could not have been VIOLETTE – she didn't have his address. This whole incident was treated by LA CHATTE with cynicism, which WALENTY found totally abhorrent, given that she was supposed to have been 'very intimate with them'.

The allegations against LA CHATTE, and refutations of statements that she claimed as fact, just kept pouring out of WALENTY's critique. There were many other accusations levelled against her and others, and inaccuracies that WALENTY set out to correct, such as her knowing TUDOR's exact address, which she did not. He pointed out:

> I think it highly probable that the direct cause of DESIRE's arrest was the betrayal on 6.11.41 by Mme BUFFET/La Denise of the 'D' sector. It appears from La Chatte's statements that DESIRE betrayed the names of his collaborators, but out of revenge he also caused the arrest of Denise![22]

KROTKI's betrayal of his and LA CHATTE's addresses was made under torture so WALENTY excused him, saying that he probably had her address in his notebook, having only recently arrived in Paris. But even though KROTKI knew his name and the existence of the W/T, he had not revealed this to the Germans. VIOLETTE's betrayal of LA CHATTE's address to the Germans was most likely the result of blackmail rather than a hatred for her, he thought. MAX was a coward and readily agreed to collaborate after his meeting with LA CHATTE on 20 November. However, he wondered why MAX was not working for the Germans and that they were asking for MARCEL. 'I suppose it was La Chatte's judgement that MARCEL was more suitable because he had no scruples and moreover he hated KENT and wished to revenge himself on him,' he wrote.

He commented that Alice, one of 'Les deux sorcières', had said that all the evil originated from VIOLETTE, and he pondered whether the Germans may have brought them together prior to LA CHATTE's arrest, just to create a confrontation or provoke a reaction. He also attributed the arrest of PAUL to LA CHATTE; in turn, PAUL betrayed OBSERVATEUR's address, even though ARTOT [sic – should be ARTOS] knew him better, but did not know his address. Most of LA CHATTE's assertions were either incorrect, or exaggerated to suit her own purpose and to cast herself in a better light. In reality, all they showed was that nothing she said could be taken at face value, nor could she be trusted.

That there was certainly no love lost between LA CHATTE and VIOLETTE is apparent time and time again, as WALENTY pointed out:

La Chatte writes that she would have gladly strangled Violette for swearing to me that she would not work for the Germans, and then working for them – but she makes no mention of the fact how often she swore to me before the catastrophe that should it come she would maintain her courage and dignity.[23]

He later elaborated on it in a document entitled 'Comments on the "Lucas – Violette" Statement':

With regard to relations between La Chatte and Violette, I wish to stress that there can be no question of any 'jealousy' but only of hatred. La Chatte could not be jealous of Violette's position in the organisation, because Violette did not occupy any, nor of her love for me, because La Chatte never was in love with me and had her own lovers. Previous to Violette's arrival La Chatte knew about my meetings with 'Orion' and she helped me to arrange them – a fact she mentions in her Memoirs.

La Chatte's hatred towards Violette was based on the following factors:

1. Violette refused to accompany La Chatte when going to town / this in accordance with my instructions as I did not wish them to attract attention. On the several occasions when she could not get out of it, Violette gave me a faithful account of 'the good time' she had enjoyed with La Chatte. La Chatte sensed this and regarded this as Violette's disloyalty to her.

2. On several occasions Violette pointed out to me La Chatte's mistakes in work and her private life, because she was of the opinion that these mistakes were unnecessarily jeopardizing the Organisation. La Chatte knew about it and being exaggeratedly ambitious, instead of admitting that I was right, she nurtured an unfounded grievance towards Violette, in spite of the fact that it was our principle for the members of our Organisation to watch each other's steps and to draw attention to mistakes committed.

Violette, on the other hand, for reasons unknown to me, was afraid of the smallest childish accusation against her made to me by La Chatte. Being deeply in love with me she was afraid of my smallest reproach. She was forever terrified lest La Chatte should by her intrigues cause her dismissal.

She was excessively touchy on this subject and I know that she confided this with tears to ADAM, MAURICE and MOUSTIQUE. I knew about it and I reassured her, because I was aware that this was exaggerated and she had no reasons to fear La Chatte's intrigues.

I initiated very few persons in the fundamental aspects of the Organisation, and I did not discuss under any circumstances my private affairs or relations between La Chatte and Violette with my agents. Hence all these tales must have originated from the exaggerated sensitiveness of Violette.

I am particularly anxious to address this point because many persons basing their judgement on mere guesses distorted the actual state of the La Chatte-Violette relationship.[24]

Harmer's report on VICTOIRE dated 11 March 1942 goes further into the intense hatred of VIOLETTE by VICTOIRE, who claimed that VIOLETTE had only been in prison for one night, whereas she had earlier said it was for longer, and also that she was 'working completely for the Germans'. VICTOIRE also claimed that VIOLETTE had now switched her allegiances as Propst's mistress, having formerly been Borchers', and that 'she had given away everything and that when the day of reckoning came [she] herself would be glad to be given the job of liquidating VIOLETTE'.[25] Clearly, the animosity and hatred between LA CHATTE and VIOLETTE was a classic case of 'Hell hath no fury like a woman scorned.'[26]

Others whose arrests VICTOIRE had brought about were KLÉBER (Marcel Kléber) and his mistress, and YOLÉ (René Legrand). LA CHATTE alleged that BOB (Robert Gorriot), when he collaborated with the Germans, had betrayed an organisation called 'rue Gît-le-Coeur', yet WALENTY claims not to know of any such organisation. This 'affair' has already been referred to in Chapter 11.

It may be worth mentioning that WALENTY regarded what LA CHATTE had said about the Comtesse Dampierre's acquaintance with Kraus as 'fishy'. They were all aware, he said, that Kraus had betrayed EVE, but as far as he knew, the Comtesse did not know Kraus personally. He added that the Germans had asked him for details of her handing over Renault plans to LA CHATTE, and that she must have told the Germans about it. He found it interesting that LA CHATTE, or 'Micheline' as he often refers to her, had admitted that VIOLETTE had no relations with the Germans, and 'noticeable that persons known only to Violette, persons who were directing the work in the "zone interdite" [forbidden zone], were not arrested'. Had VIOLETTE wished to betray the chiefs of sectors H (HECTOR @ Mr DEFLY) and G (Mr MARTIN), she could easily have done so. In summary, he had this to say:

> I have the impression that La Chatte's 'visions' about the part she would play in England, about diversion with regard to German C.E. posts and her desire to save the prisoners at FRESNES did [not] originate till she got here. I do not know the story of her f[irst?] days in England, which play a decisive role in this. In order [to] estimate La Chatte's activities in their entirety I would ha[ve to] study her first reports after her arrival in London.[27]

—⁂—

At the beginning of April 1942 Marriott sent a note to Felix Cowgill at SIS relating to information VICTOIRE had of the break-up of another network. He sought Cowgill's opinion as he thought the outcome would 'affect considerably the VICTOIRE affair'.

In 1940 Philip Schneidau (Flight Lieutenant Philipson) and his wife had formed an SIS circuit known as FELIX (some sources say that was his code name) financed by his father-in-law, prosperous cloth merchant Paul Shiffmacher. On 30 March 1942 VICTOIRE had apparently told Harmer that she wanted to do something for Philipson's wife, Simone, and his father-in-law who, along with other members of their network, had been arrested by the Gestapo in January 1942 and detained at Fresnes. If Hugh Verity's assertion is correct, that VICTOIRE had betrayed Shiffmacher, was she trying to do this to assuage her conscience?[28]

Simone was placed under house arrest and interrogated by the Gestapo, but she and her mother, Eveline, continued to shelter downed airmen in their Paris flat. The only one remaining in the network after the arrests was JULES who, Marriott's note says, ran it. JULES may have been Jules Villegas of Libre Résistance who worked with Francis Suthill and the PROSPER-PHYSICIAN network. Sometime after October 1942 her father, Paul, was shipped off to Buchenwald.[29] (Notes in the sale of Schneidau's medals state that this was in January 1944.)[30] There is no information in the files on the outcome of this affair, nor Cowgill's comments, but according to Hugh Verity, Paul Shiffmacher 'just survived the war in Buchenwald, but recovered enough to live until he was 93.'[31] In the auction catalogue notes it says that Shiffmacher was repatriated from Buchenwald on 23 April 1945. Philip Schneidau, born in 1903, died in January 1984.

CHAPTER 20

Winding Up a Troublesome Affair

It seems that at every available occasion VICTOIRE was capable of spinning a yarn to anyone who was prepared to listen. One of these was to Charles Mackintosh. His statement about a meeting he had had with her on 27 April 1942 is worth repeating in full as it provides an interesting insight into just how delusional she could be.

Charles Ernest Whistler Mackintosh (1903–74) was the son of Flight Lieutenant Charles Mackintosh and Lady Jean Norton-Bell (*née* Douglas-Hamilton, 1904–87), whom the Duke had married on 8 April 1927; they divorced in 1946. Mackintosh, who was living at 3 Chester Square Mews, London SW1, related:

> On Monday April 27th I met Mr Anthony Gillson at the '500 Club' where he introduced me to Madame de Roche.
>
> He suggested that I should take her out to dinner as he was unable to do so himself. I was unable to arrange this but agreed to take her to the '400 Club' at 11 pm on 27.4.42. I called for her at 11.10 pm at 19, Rugby Mansions, near Olympia. We proceeded to the '400 Club' [in Leicester Square] where I gained the following information from Madame de Roche:–
>
> She informed me that her father was Turkish & her mother Swiss. She had lived in Lausanne with her mother for some years.
>
> I asked her if she knew Mont Benon [*sic*]; she replied that she did not, so I concluded her statement was incorrect.
>
> I asked her how it was if she had been in England two years as she had stated, she could not speak English. She replied: '*Parce-que je suis bête.*' ['Because I'm stupid.']

I ultimately gleaned the following particulars from her:-

1. She has worked for a French sabotage organisation in collaboration with 'Pierre'.

2. She had then been arrested by the Germans & on the score of her intelligence, requested by them to act as their agent.

3. She kept in close touch with 'Pierre' at the same time as accepting liberal German treatment and financial support.

4. Ultimately they had decided to send her to this country 'en mission'. Pierre accompanied her.

5. Immediately upon arrival here she reported these facts to the authorities & offered to return to France as their agent.

6. She expected to return there at the end of May, and consequently wished to enjoy her short sojourn in this country.

7. Daily reports, compounded [?] in collaboration with the War Office, have been sent back to France by short wave transmission. This statement of hers immediately recorded by me put her integrity to the test. I therefore talked around the subject for some time. The following points of interest emerged:-

    (a) She had been in an 'Air France' machine witnessing the bombardment of Barcelona during the Spanish Civil War.

    (b) 'Victor' was a waiter in the restaurants of Toulouse, who had always been 'of assistance to her'.

    (c) She had to give the Germans some accurate information to justify her position.

I decided to make a further appointment to meet Madame de Roche, and arranged to give her lunch on Thursday April 30th.

Between Monday evening, April 27th & Tuesday morning, 8.30 & April 28th I discovered that my identification card & my M.A.P. (R.A.F.) car pass had disappeared. I ~~concluded~~ thought that they might possibly have been taken by her and decided to offer her 25 British passports.

At lunch on Thursday, on April 30th, I said that I was very keen to help her, and that the passports, which I had found by chance, in my Travel Bureau, might be of great interest if they were given to the German 'contact'. This, I agreed, would enable our Intelligence Dept. to check German agents coming to this country and would also serve her as bait to retain the confidence of the Germans.

I took great pains to explain that there might be serious trouble for me if I were caught giving her these documents. I suggested that the best course would be for me to hand them to Anthony Gillson. She asked me not to do this in any circumstances, saying that she would hand them to Uncle Tom. I said that she would have to explain from what source she acquired them & she suggested that she would inform Uncle Tom that she had bought them for £10 ('*Et alors nous allons bien dîner*' ['Now let's go and have a good meal'], she said.)

I thereupon arranged to go to my office to collect the passports and meet her at her flat, 19, Rugby Mansions, at 4.15 pm. This arrangement was made at 3.45 pm & she informed me that the person who shared her flat would return at 5 pm.

I immediately rang up Mr Gillson, and being unable to contact him asked to speak to his deputy.

I was put in touch with a Mr Bingham, whom I met at 4.5 pm at Dolphin Square. He suggested that the situation seemed to be an excellent one & that it would be better to delay handing over the documents on some pretext so that adequate arrangements could be made. I handed the bag containing the passports to him. I proceeded to 19, Rugby Mansions, & explained that the secretary of the company had been in the room & that it had been impossible to take the passports without arousing his notice.

I arranged to meet her for dinner on Monday ~~April~~ May 4th, and she promised to ring me up & let me know her telephone number as she was moving to a flat – '*où je serais seule et où on ne me surveillera plus.*' ['where I'll be on my own and where I won't be under surveillance any more.']

She gave me the following address:-
Margaret de Roche
Flat 603,
Stafford Court
Oxford St.
W.1.
The above statement has been read over to me and is true. [signed C.W.Mackintosh and witnessed by J.M. Bingham, dated May 1st 1942][1]

The business of obtaining passports was first brought to MI5's attention by Harmer on 7 May 1942 when he found out quite independently of VICTOIRE that she intended to do some work for British Intelligence which she thought would be valuable to them. These passports would be obtained from a person (redacted, but obviously Mackintosh) to whom she had been introduced by Gillson. Mackintosh had been a travel agent before the war and knew how to get hold of a quantity of old passports lying around the agency. This was before he knew much about her, but he did know that Gillson worked for MI5.

VICTOIRE had also spoken to Tom Greene about it and wondered whether they would be of use to him, which he said they would. Harmer was asked whether she should be allowed to proceed with the plan. Both he and Gillson agreed that it would be a test of her reliability to see if she actually handed them over to Greene, or whether she would keep some of them for herself. When she went out for dinner with Mackintosh on 3 May he handed them over to her; she in turn handed them to Greene the following day when he went round to her flat to collect them. Gillson finally handed them back to Mackintosh, with the matter being hushed up and with Harmer not supposed to know anything about it. But, as Harmer said:

> It all seems rather silly in retrospect, but having once told her that he would give her the passports, it seemed rather more advisable to let the thing continue than to stop it altogether. Had I stopped it she would have realized that [redacted, Mackintosh] is reporting to us and we might thereby have lost valuable information on a future occasion.[2]

Major Godfrey Anthony Gillson (1908–44) of the King's Own Scottish Borderers (KOSB), was the son of Major General Godfrey Gillson and Edith Christian Dugdale, and was married to Priscilla Gillson (*née* Dickerson). Nigel West described Tony Gillson as 'a nightclubbing playboy and racehorse owner who transferred to SOE, only to be killed in an air crash in 1943 en route for India'.[3] The Commonwealth War Graves Commission gives the date on the Rangoon Memorial as 3 March 1944.[4] He had been stationed in Cairo with SOE as the 'first Security officer to be sent abroad to another Mission by S.O.E'.[5] At MI5 he had worked in B5d for John Bingham in the Political Subversion Section[6] and was one of the few officers permitted access to Maxwell Knight's flat in Dolphin Square, most likely the flat mentioned in Mackintosh's statement – either 308 Hood House or 10 Collingwood House,[7] but there is also the suggestion that Knight used 709 Nelson House.[8] According to Christopher Murphy, Gillson underwent a training programme with SOE and was attached to the Security Section for a few months.[9] John Bingham, who later succeeded to the title of Viscount Clanmorris, worked in MI5 throughout the war and afterwards, and is now regarded as the most likely model for John le Carré's George Smiley.[10] He was also a writer of detective novels, but was largely eclipsed by le Carré and others, which caused him deep resentment.

Harmer reported to John Marriott of the Twenty Committee on 25 April 1942 that he had arranged to have dinner with VICTOIRE on the evening of the 23rd along with a captain from SIS (the name has been redacted). However, this captain had happened to mention it to Major Felix Cowgill, head of Section V at SIS, who had forbidden him or any of his officers to have anything more to do with VICTOIRE now that MI5 was running the case, given that 'the position of Section V is that they do not take any executive responsibility for the running of the case but reserve the right to oppose any course suggested by us which is contrary to their interest'. As a compromise, Harmer felt that all he could really do was to keep Cowgill apprised of any new developments.

The question first and foremost on MI5's mind was what to do with VICTOIRE over the long term, a difficult decision as it created a number of headaches for them. Her period of freedom prior to her internment, and her relationship with a 'well-known author' will now be explored.

Captain Richard Dafydd Vivian Llewellyn Lloyd (1906–83) of the Welsh Guards was that 'well-known author', better known as Richard Llewellyn, the best-selling author of *How Green is My Valley*, published in 1939. In June 1942 he was serving with IP2 (a) at the War Office, which was the Ministry of Information's liaison with the War Office, the BBC and the press. At a meeting at Room 055 on 1 July 1942 he explained to John Masterman how he had come to know VICTOIRE, which he said had been through Dr Herbert. Herbert urged him to be friendly to her as she had served Britain well and had recently escaped from France.

After she and LUCAS had arrived in England she had been taken to see Herbert by Detective Inspector Louis Gale, a Special Branch officer delegated to look after them.[11] Herbert had offered to introduce her to some artistic friends who he thought might take her mind off things. These included Lloyd, Mrs Mayerson and Lord Selborne. As Harmer noted, 'The latter appears to have been very much attracted to VICTOIRE and was about to entertain her when we intervened and stopped it as being undesirable in the circumstances.' Exactly when this intervention occurred is unclear but may have been at the event mentioned below, which also sheds further light on her encounter with

Roundell Cecil Palmer, the 3rd Earl of Selborne (1887–1971) and Minister of Economic Warfare, who was responsible for SOE from 1942 to 1945.

On 13 May Lloyd had invited VICTOIRE to his flat and said he was going to take her out to dinner afterwards. However, Mackintosh had rung her up to say that he was leaving London the following day and would she like to go out to dinner with him? At her instigation, Lloyd invited Mackintosh round to his flat for a drink and the three later went out for dinner to Hatchetts at 5 White Horse Street, in Shepherd's Market. There they also met Dr Herbert and Mrs Anna Mayerson, the artist (1906–84), who was Dr Herbert's fiancée.

Some sources say that Mayerson was German, others say British; in fact, Mayerson was Viennese and had studied at the Kunstgewerbemuseum in Zurich and at the Vienna Academy. She had emigrated from Vienna to London in 1938 to avoid persecution because she was Jewish. In London she studied at the Slade School of Fine Art, exhibiting with British artist Graham Sutherland (1903–80) and Polish artist Jankel Adler (1895–49) in 1946 at the Redfern Gallery. Truman Capote, writing to Robert 'Bob' Linscott, his editor at Random House, on 20 March 1951, told him that Mayerson had sent him drawings for the dust jacket and frontispiece of his novel *The Grass Harp*, which he described as 'superb – beyond anything'.[12]

Later, at a night club, Mackintosh and Lloyd both competed for VICTOIRE's attention, resulting in her going off with Mackintosh, much to Lloyd's annoyance and dismay. The following day Lloyd telephoned her and went round to pick her up at ten o'clock, returning her drunk later that evening. On the 15th he sent her flowers and intended to take her to the cinema in the evening, although he arrived too late, but they went out anyway. When they returned, he stayed the night. Exploiting the situation, as she seemed wont to do on every possible occasion, she told Lloyd that she felt uncomfortable in her flat, so he offered her the use of his since he was about to take a week's leave in North Wales. While she continued to stay there, he then booked into the Savoy, where he stayed from 27 May until 24 June. Masterman reported that 'He [Lloyd] had for some little time been anxious to get rid of her and had made up his mind that the arrangement could not go on much longer.'[13] Once he had returned to his flat that did not stop him from sleeping on the floor, as VICTOIRE had said she needed protection. Harmer concluded:

> His lending the flat to VICTOIRE was not prompted entirely by quixotic generosity. It is quite clear that he was VICTOIRE's lover, and also pretty clear that she was going to provide him with a copy. On 18.5.42 he rang

her up from North Wales and we have a complete copy of the conversation. On 23.5.42 he telegrammed her, saying 'Arriving about 8 o'clock. Love Chat Noir'. Telephone checks reveal that he spent the nights 23.5.42, 25.5.42 and 26.5.42 in the flat with her, or at least there is strong evidence to this effect.[14]

That evidence was Lloyd asking the telephone exchange to give his number a call at eight o'clock.

When VICTOIRE moved into his flat on the 16th Lloyd had apparently told her to keep it until the end of the war as he had no further use for it, being forced to live in barracks. This runs contrary to Harmer's report where he said that, while there was no way to prove Lloyd was trying to get her out of his flat, the evidence suggests that he was losing interest in her, and she was complaining on the phone to a friend, Henri, that he lacked emotion, as was revealed in a telephone check on 26 June. Harmer was also unable to shed more light on why Lloyd should have moved into the Savoy, except what VICTOIRE had said about his friends, in particular the doctor, who were jealous of her and tried to stir up trouble between them by making unpleasant remarks about Lloyd. To avoid further conflict, Lloyd had moved back into the flat. That Lloyd's circle of friends was creating trouble was, according to Harmer, apparent from the telephone checks. He also cleared up a point about Mackintosh not being connected with the intelligence services.

Susan Barton further reported on VICTOIRE on 17 May after having gone round to Stratford Court to take her out to lunch. At that lunch VICTOIRE had told her about 'Richard Ll.Ll.', as Barton referred to Lloyd. VICTOIRE's first impressions of him were not in his favour as he could not speak very much French. She told Barton that Mackintosh and Lloyd did not like each other very much and were very jealous of each other. Mercurial as ever, VICTOIRE, 'having seen Ll.Ll.'s pocket-book and also his flat ... decided that he was exceedingly charming after all and went out with him again'. In the typically patronising tone of the time, Barton reported that Lloyd's maid, Elizabeth, had a 'very strong accent ... and I should have said she was foreign, but perhaps she is Welsh'. When Barton asked her whether she was in love with Lloyd, VICTOIRE said she didn't think so:

... but he might be a little in love with her. She explained to me that it was a question of their souls having found each other, that she was Ll.Ll.'s inspiration, and that he told her there were only two women in his life, one his grandmother and the other she, Victoire. Apart from using his flat she is using a watch of his, his cigarette-holder and a gold cigarette case, all of which he lent her.

I think it is quite possible that Ll.Ll. has fallen for her but it also seems pretty certain that Victoire merely basks in his admiration, takes everything she can get, but not obviously, and enjoys herself.

I asked her whether she had told him her story and pointed out to her that it seemed to me a dangerous thing to do as he was a writer and would probably use it for one of his own books and she would not be able to publish her book. She assured me that she fully realised that danger and had told him nothing (which I doubt nevertheless).[15]

Lloyd had been made aware that she had been involved with the intelligence services when he had run into Mackintosh and someone older to whom VICTOIRE referred as '*mon oncle Tom*' ('my uncle Tom' – Tom Greene). In her book, VICTOIRE describes her first meeting with Greene, which took place on the first evening of her arrival in England. He seemed, she said:

… more hospitable than the others [unspecified] and very reassuring. He was a tall, fat man – what we should describe in France as 'a real wardrobe of a man' – who had given instructions to *Interallié* from London. He was known as Uncle Tom. His good humour and strength inspired great confidence.[16]

Lloyd also knew that someone called 'Christopher' (Harmer) had taken her out. Lloyd had offered to help her to get her memoirs published, even though he had neither the time to translate them, nor read them at that point. When he had met her there had been no reason to doubt her trustworthiness, nor did he question it. As Harmer put it:

At the time the policy in regard to VICTOIRE was to treat her as if we had complete trust in her and it is difficult to see how in these circumstances anybody would have had cause to suspect VICTOIRE of being a sinister person.[17]

It also appears that Lloyd was 'very much attracted by VICTOIRE', but Harmer's report concludes with the statement, 'There is no evidence … to show that at any time Captain LLOYD was guilty of indiscretion to VICTOIRE.' However, Mrs Barton asserted that even though 'she is exceedingly discrete [*sic*] as regards her love affairs and although I am convinced from all she has told me that she is sleeping with Ll.Ll. she would certainly never say so outright.' This sounds a bit out of character: given VICTOIRE's tendency to boast about anything and everything, is seems odd she would not have been more open to Barton about it. But perhaps because Barton was keeping an eye on her and she regarded her as 'staff' she did not feel disposed to treat her as a confidante and be more direct about it.

Mrs Barton also cautioned about allowing VICTOIRE to move into Lloyd's flat, 'as the complications which may arise from this will be very much greater than the few scenes we would have had to put up with if she had been forbidden to move'. She emphasised the amount of freedom she had been afforded and how well they had treated her, adding, 'After all, there was nothing to stop her spending the occasional night at Ll.Ll.'s flat if she wanted to.'

Harmer met with Brigadier Nevile and Masterman on 3 July 1942 to discuss Lloyd's conduct regarding VICTOIRE. The brigadier was not unduly worried about how Lloyd had met her, but said he was more concerned about whether any of Lloyd's friends had been indiscreet, which could make trouble for all concerned. 'He said it was only to be expected that a man of this sort [Lloyd] would have friends in artistic and film circles.' Harmer told the meeting that, from his record, Lloyd was 'a man who said exactly what he thought, often with rather unfortunate results'. Indeed, he had told VICTOIRE about shipping losses in a convoy to Malta; however, as Masterman had pointed out, since she was totally unreliable, she had probably boasted about being in possession of secret information. The brigadier resolved to give Lloyd a dressing-down about indiscretion, and a warning to avoid people 'who were not absolutely above suspicion'. Masterman appended a handwritten note to the bottom of the report on 5 July:

I think two points might be mentioned also:-

(1) That we told the Brigadier that we had evidence that Lloyd's relations with Victoire were more intimate in the early stages (i.e. before she went to Lloyd's flat) than Lloyd's own comments might suggest.

(2) That the circumstances of Lloyd's introduction to Victoire and the persons with whom she [was at] this meeting would actually and almost inevitably lead them to assume that she was a trusted person and above suspicion herself.[18]

Susan Barton reported to Harmer on a party that VICTOIRE had held at Claridges on 1 May 1942 in which Lord Selborne and Dr Herbert were present, as well as a woman painter whose name Barton did not know (most likely Anna Mayerson). According to MI5, Dr Herbert was 'connected in some way with Scotland Yard besides being the resident doctor at Claridges'. In addition to the intelligent conversation there were also some 'cochonneries' (smutty or dirty jokes). Selborne appeared impressed by the ideas VICTOIRE had expressed about propaganda and flattered her by saying that they had never been thought of before. VICTOIRE had also tried to impress him by mentioning a Frenchman who was a friend of her family, whom Selborne also probably knew. Since this was all obtained second-hand from VICTOIRE, who had woken up Barton at 11.30 p.m. to tell her about it, Barton was probably right in her assertion that VICTOIRE was 'giving herself airs'.

Lord Selborne told her he knew her entire story, much more than even 'Christopher' (Harmer) did. He had then offered to take her out for dinner the following Tuesday (5 May) to talk more about her background. He told her that 'a man who wanted to get on always needed the advice of a clever woman and that there were several women around Churchill'. Not only that, but he was going to talk to Churchill about her, and have the woman painter at the party paint her portrait. As Barton noted, 'As far as I can gather Victoire seems to be dreaming of becoming Lord S.'s mistress. According to her, he has all the attributes she admires in a man except that he cannot dance, but that for the moment has become a minor matter.' Selborne was at that time married to the Honourable Grace Ridley (1889–1959), daughter of 1st Viscount Ridley (Matthew White Ridley). Very much a 'ladies' man', Selborne was 'a small, stooping figure with protruding grey eyes, who would smile at any attractive woman who caught his attention'.[19] Barton went on:

> Lord S. may be merely playing up to her but even if only half of what she has told me is true it seems to me that he is behaving exceedingly foolishly and is not doing himself any good nor for that matter us as she will get more and more above herself. She seems to have told him that although she is treated very well she does not get everything she wants and he is supposed to have said that he would see to it that she should have everything.
>
> She made me promise that I would not to repeat anything she had told me as I was told these things as one friend to another. She would tell 'Christopher' a little about it and probably everything to 'Uncle Tom' [Tom Greene].

I would be interested to know what she has in fact told you, probably she will not be able to keep it to herself, but should she tell you something different I would be glad if you would let me know as it might help me to get things out of her in future if need be.[20]

Selborne's dalliance with VICTOIRE was brought up in Harmer's report to Marriott on 3 May in the context of VICTOIRE visiting a doctor recommended to her by Inspector Gale, Dr E.M. Herbert of 5 Devonshire Place, Upper Wimpole Street, W1:

He [Dr Herbert] also said that she was in need of company and distraction and promised to introduce her to a friend of his whom he described as a lawyer, a Lord, and who was one of the big chiefs of the British Intelligence. This subsequently turned out to be Lord Selborne of M.E.W. [Ministry of Economic Warfare] The doctor arranged for them to meet last Friday, 1st May.

What happened at the meeting has been recounted by VICTOIRE to Mrs. Barton, Mr. Greene and myself.[21]

According to VICTOIRE, Selborne had asked her if she knew 'somebody called VICTOIRE', to which she admitted she did. Selborne had said that he had always wanted to meet someone with such an interesting history as hers. It appeared that he knew everything about her, although they did not discuss the actual case. She had, however, told him that she had been kept under observation 'more or less as a prisoner'; Selborne told her that he thought it was 'outrageous for a person in her position'. As Harmer noted, with the promise of Selborne offering to take her dancing, it has 'left no doubt that she thinks it only a matter of time before she becomes his mistress'. What concerned him was how Selborne came to know so much about VICTOIRE, and he thought it should be taken up with a higher authority:

So far as I know there is a connection between M.E.W. and S.O.E. [SOE reported to the Ministry of Economic Warfare] but I should not have thought that it would have warranted a full disclosure to him of the relevant facts of VICTOIRE's case. The main point however is of course whether we are prepared to let the thing merely go on in a natural way or whether we want to have Selborne approached on our behalf. I am inclined to think the best thing we could do is to take it up with Keswick of S.O.E. and ask him to find out from Selborne exactly what is the position. From the point of view of running the case I don't much mind whether she goes on seeing Selborne or not, but whether we owe a duty to him to prevent him making a fool of himself is a matter which I must leave for someone else to decide.[22]

At the top of the report Marriott had written, 'I have spoken to ADB1 [Dick White] who agrees that Keswick should be told of this incident and asked how much Selborne knows and if the whole story, why.' Harmer duly met with Keswick and Buckmaster at SOE on 5 May:

We then discussed VICTOIRE's contact with a certain Cabinet Minister and I explained the position to Keswick, who thought it most undesirable that the association should continue and said that he would take steps to have the Minister warned. Later on in the day I was informed that Brigadier Gubbins had been to see him and had explained the true position and that the man in question had stated that he only knew a certain amount about the story and for that reason had assumed that he was perfectly alright [sic].[23]

An article that appeared in the *Independent* newspaper on 28 November 2002 also discusses this incident, but erroneously attributes the source of the information to a 'Mrs Barker', not Susan Barton, as well as saying that Harmer worked for SOE, which he did not. Several historians were quoted in the article, including Russell Miller, who said, 'The prospect of Selbourne [sic] having an affair with her would have caused substantial panic in high quarters in the security service'; and Oliver Hoare, historian at the Public Record Office (as it was then still called), who stated that there was no record of Selbourne [sic] being warned off by MI5, but that it was probably done orally, which is backed up by Harmer's report of his meeting with Keswick and Buckmaster, mentioned above. M.R.D. Foot, the leading expert on SOE, thought that while:

Carré might have dreamt of being Selbourne's mistress, there was very little chance she was successful.

The fact that she dreamt of capturing him from Lady Selbourne is one thing but I think the idea that she became his mistress can be ruled out straight away.

Selbourne knew how a gentleman should behave. He was also too busy running the SOE and the Ministry of Economic Warfare to have time to have a mistress.[24]

Another incident that caused MI5 to worry was when VICTOIRE reported that she had gone to a hairdresser called Paillard at 3 William Street, Knightsbridge sometime before 23 April and learned from him that LUCAS had been there to get his hair tinted before going to France and would be returning to England in two months' time. Fortunately, she feigned ignorance. Tar Robertson wrote to Keswick to see what should be done about it and whether it warranted a visit from the police. Marriott scrawled at the bottom, 'Spoke with Buckmaster 24/4. Decided no action desirable in circumstances.' It must be assumed that it was SOE's decision not to act, not MI5's.

At the time of Lloyd's interview with Masterman, VICTOIRE was on the point of being arrested, and he recommended that Lloyd be present when her possessions were removed from his flat. It would also be necessary for Lloyd to telephone his brigadier, Brigadier Nevile, and inform him of the situation. Harmer met with Charles Mackintosh to tell him of MI5's decision to intern her and thank him for his work. To cover his expenses, they paid him £15 in cash, even though Mackintosh had told them that he had not expected anything for his trouble and 'was only too pleased to do this for us'. What is interesting in Tar's report on 2 July is that Harmer had assured Mackintosh that 'all reference to him in our files will be deleted so he will not appear in our records as having been mixed up with somebody who was later interned as a person who was a menace to security'.[25] Little did he know what history, freedom of information and declassification would later reveal!

At a meeting with 'all the Intelligence departments concerned' in St James's in early June, a decision had been made to intern VICTOIRE, 'on the grounds that she was far too unreliable ever to be allowed out of the country and that in this country she would be, on her past record, a menace to security'. Those present were:

Commander Dunderdale, SIS
Major Foley, SIS
Mr Greene, SIS
Colonel Keswick, SOE
Major Buckmaster, SOE
Lt Commander Senter, SOE

Mr White, MI5
Major Robertson, MI5
Mr Robertson, MI5
Mr Harmer, MI5

As was pointed out in a report on her:

Had the plan gone as we hoped, all the LUCAS agents would have disappeared sometime about the middle of May, after which LUCAS would have made his way back to England for further instructions. We would then have been faced with a possible difficulty of persuading him that VICTOIRE could not accompany him back to France. We might also have had to intern VICTOIRE, and this might have disgruntled him to a dangerous extent. Once, however, he was arrested the problem was merely one of what to do with VICTOIRE herself. The only complications which would probably arise were those which might arise after the war, when she regained her liberty.

The most satisfactory way of dealing with her appeared to be to intern her. The objections to this were that she was a cunning and intelligent person and after she regained her liberty she would be in a position to make a great deal of trouble for us. There was also the objection that, having accepted her, entertained her and made use of her for drafting messages, we were under some sort of moral obligation not to turn against her. It was felt, however, that she was not only a very dangerous woman in herself but that she was in possession of valuable information about the activities of S.O.E. Even if she were left at liberty she was bound to be disgruntled because we had encouraged her in the belief (or rather not discouraged her in her belief) that one day she would be sent out by the British Intelligence en mission. A compromise was suggested that she might be told that any further work on our behalf was impossible, but that as she had worked for us she could have her liberty, coupled with threats of immediate internment if she did anything wrong. This was, however, objected to by S.O.E. and she was, therefore, interned under a 12(5a) order on July 1st. Since that date she has been at Aylesbury gaol.

In the latter stages of her liberty in this country she became acquainted with a well-known author in the army. He took her to live in his flat. Although the wisdom of the decision may be doubted, it was thought at the time that we could not prevent her from living there as we were creating the illusion that she was a free woman. Moreover it helped to rid us of a very embarrassing situation. She accordingly spent about six weeks in this man's flat, living in great comfort, but maintaining all the time that it was as nothing compared to the comfort of the surroundings as laid on by the Germans.[26]

Also on the agenda were: the future use of the WALENTY transmitter; the 'disposal' of VICTOIRE; finances for her, and whether to send a message via the BBC to let her parents know she was safe. The last two were the easiest to resolve. The matter of £324 4s 7d for the period 28 March to 9 June 1942 was submitted, with SOE agreeing to pay its one-third share, and subject to Stewart Menzies' approval, SIS also agreed to pay its one-third share. The meeting decided that it was not in their best interests to allow the BBC broadcast to go ahead, 'after discussion about the wisdom of sending this message'. The bottom line as far as VICTOIRE's future was concerned was that she had said she could never return to France for fear of being caught and shot. It is unclear here who would have pulled the trigger first – the Germans or members of the French Resistance. As Harmer recounted, there were three options which the group considered:

a) Sending her somewhere other than France:
   S.O.E. were opposed in principle because she might get back to France. Commander Dunderdale said though he would not accept her, she might be a counter espionage agent. Major Foley, however, said that this was not possible. It was therefore decided that she should not be sent away on any mission for any departments of the Service.

b) Sending her back to France to contact the Germans:
   I explained that as she had stated her objection to returning to France, this course could not arise.

c) Allowing her to live in this country in complete liberty:
   It was agreed that this would be no solution to the matter.[27]

There were two other ideas put forward: to pay her off with a generous sum of money (no actual figure was disclosed) and leave her to fend for herself, or to intern her. As Harmer pointed out, considering that she was writing a book about her experiences, the fourth part of which would be about the 'malfeasances of S.O.E.', she was a potential danger. Dunderdale, on the other hand, was not in favour of interning her:

Unless we were prepared to liquidate VICTOIRE altogether … because we would thereby be making an enemy of her for life and she might be able after the war to do immense damage to the British Intelligence Service, since she was an extremely clever woman.[28]

Whether Dunderdale's use of the words 'liquidate altogether' implied that he was willing to have her killed if necessary in order to ensure her silence, or if he meant something not quite so drastic, is unclear; nor whether this reflected an SIS 'licence to kill' policy or his own solution to the problem, but it strikes an ominous tone of how far British Intelligence might be prepared to go to eliminate a profound nuisance to them. Dunderdale therefore thought it might be better to pay her off. Colonel Keswick opposed this idea, saying that they were under no obligation to her for what she had done for Britain, and she was too dangerous to be allowed to stay free. Dick White thought that by interning her in an ordinary camp, such as the Isle of Man, she would come into contact with other internees, which would lead to as much leakage as if she were in London. A compromise solution would be to pay her off and let her go free, but if she were to leak any information about what she had been doing, she would immediately be interned. SOE again came out against this, saying that because of the valuable information she had about their organisation and plans, it would be safer to intern her. That being the case, White said that interning her must be done in 'the most thorough way possible'. Certainly, given her proclivity to 'spill the beans' whenever she could, paying her off was no guarantee that she would 'keep mum', to use a popular wartime expression.

Ultimately, it was decided that SOE should make a case for interning her, and that MI5 would make recommendations to the Home Office to intern her under a 12(5A) Detention Order. Dunderdale asked that it should be put on record that SIS had 'no primary reasons for wanting VICTOIRE interned'. The only information she had of any value was that there was still another working transmitter that they knew was controlled by the Germans. They agreed that the WALENTY transmitter should be shut down and a message was drafted to be sent regarding getting RENÉ out of the Occupied Zone, and the café where he was to go. That message was likely this one, sent on 15 June:

Because of silence from VICTOIRE we have made new arrangements. You alone must go next week to the Café Glacier near Toulouse well known to you and VICTOIRE, as we are arranging that somebody who knows you personally will meet you there. Friend who is going to meet you will give you new instructions and funds necessary and you must give him a report concerning the present position in Paris. Reply tomorrow if instructions understood and notify day on which you will be there.[29]

A message sent by ALEXANDRE on 17 June was received in response:

> For MICHEL. RENÉ left yesterday for Toulouse where he will wait on
> the 19th and 20th June at the Café Glacier from miday [sic] til 1 o'clock.
> We hope for a better result this time because failing a receipt of new
> funds we are going to stop all work in a month's time. Have you news
> of VICTOIRE? In what way did she leave? We are afraid that something
> may have happened to her on the line of demarcation since once in Paris
> it is easy to rejoin us [sic]. Agents refuse to continue work if VICTOIRE
> abandons organisation and we beg you to put situation right immediately.
> ALEXANDRE.[30]

RENÉ sent a message on 1 July reporting that he had returned from Toulouse,
where he had met no one at the rendezvous. He said that he would await an
explanation and a precise rendezvous in Paris, otherwise he would break off
contact. A reply was sent to ALEXANDRE the same day:

> Look out. Friend who ought to have met RENÉ has been arrested. We have
> news of VICTOIRE and LUCAS. To save those who remain and because of
> great difficulties, we have decided to close down the organisation. You must
> hide the set and disappear. In sending this message, the last, we repeat the motto
> of WALENTY in his last message No.1000: 'Every day and in every way against
> the Boches. Long live liberty.' Remember always the example of your chief
> WALENTY, respected even by the Boches for his courage and devotion.
> MICHEL.[31]

Dick White wrote to MI5's Legal Section, SLA, on 14 June informing them
that at the meeting that he had convened between MI5, SIS and SOE to
discuss the VICTOIRE case they had come to the conclusion, 'although not
without reluctance – that VICTOIRE ought to be interned in the interests of
National Security, and in particular, the security of our own secret services'.
A letter written to him on 11 June from SOE (the signature cannot be made
out, but is initialled HL at the top, which could be Hester Leggett, the head
of B1b's secretarial unit), pretty much sealed SOE's opinion of what needed
to be done: 'I regard it as most important, from the point of view of our
Security, that she should be under maximum control until the end of the
war.' The author pointed out that since most of the LUCAS organisation
who had been SOE-trained had now been arrested by the Germans, any

knowledge she still had of them could not do any harm; however, there was still one member of the group at large, as well as two local recruits who were known to her:

> We consider it most undesirable that VICTOIRE who has a first-hand knowledge of S.O.E. policy in France, acquired from Lucas himself, should be left in a position to divulge this knowledge to outside parties … we do not know how much Lucas, in his more intimate moments, may have revealed. We have evidence that, though he did not trust VICTOIRE implicitly, his security-mindedness was not on a very high level.
>
> We have proof that VICTOIRE is utterly unscrupulous, and we feel that she would not hesitate to use, in the most obnoxious manner, any information which she had acquired as to the methods of the Intelligence Services.[32]

Leggett was described by Ben Macintyre as 'a sharp-tongued dragon', who went on to oversee letters written for Operation *Mincemeat* and, in fact, may have written some of them.

Harmer reported on 12 June on a discussion he had had with Dick White, Helenus 'Buster' Milmo and A.H. Robertson, that a decision had been made to intern VICTOIRE on the Isle of Man; this decision was also included in the statement read out to her by Hinchley-Cooke, citing her various indiscretions and the mis-statements she had made to MI5:

> In these circumstances, having regard to your previous collaboration with the Germans, the mis-statements you have made to us, the uncertainty of your loyalty and your discretion, it is no longer possible for us to continue the generous treatment which you have been accorded hitherto. In normal circumstances we would have no doubt how to deal with you, but in this particular case as you have worked for us we intend to treat you leniently. You will therefore, instead of being imprisoned and tried, be sent to the Isle of Man as an internee where you will be provided with the means to live in comparative comfort.[33]

But instead of the Isle of Man she was sent to another prison where she would be unable to communicate with ordinary prisoners and thus pass on any information she might possess.

The paperwork – Deportation and Detention Orders – from Miss Nunn at the Home Office was duly forwarded to 'Toby' Pilcher in SLA on 27 June and arrangements made to pick up and arrest VICTOIRE at Lloyd's flat. This was scheduled for 17.00 hours on 1 July when the Detention Order would be served. Harmer pointed out to Hinchley-Cooke that VICTOIRE had in her possession some 'poison' that should be confiscated; also, that SIS had asked for any information on the Vichy agents she had supposedly betrayed, which should be included in the charges against her. The so-called 'poison', in the form of four pills, was sent to H.L. Smith of the Scientific Section of the GPO for analysis. Smith frequently carried out this kind of work for MI5's A6. He replied to Tar on 6 July that the pills were morphine weighing just over a grain each; other pills were barbiturates. Neither medication, he said, could be used for secret writing.

Toby Pilcher wrote to S. Hoare, an official at the Home Office, confirming what they had discussed earlier: that it was essential that VICTOIRE not be allowed to mix with other 12(5A) internees, preferring that she be accommodated in a prison with 'two or three other women of her kidney'. It should be stressed that this was not Sir Samuel Hoare, who had been home secretary under Stanley Baldwin and Neville Chamberlain, as at that time he had been posted as British ambassador to Spain (1940–44). Pilcher also said it was essential that she not be allowed to appeal to the Lindley Committee,[34] nor allowed to mix with anyone who might be released prior to the end of the war. The Lindley Committee was the Home Office, Aliens Department Advisory Committee, chaired by Sir Francis Oswald Lindley, a retired diplomat, A.V. Aveling (Foreign Office) and Sir Frank Newsam (under-secretary, Home Office), which met in London at 6 Burlington Gardens, W1 (now part of the Royal Academy). Pilcher and his colleagues suggested the following people with whom VICTOIRE could be allowed to mix:

Stella Lonsdale
My Eriksson
Mathilde Krafft
The Duchesse de Château-Thierry

Apart from Eriksson, who was being detained under Article 12(5A), the others were detained under Defence Regulation 18B. As Pilcher pointed out, Stella Lonsdale had not appealed, Mathilde Krafft's continued detention had been recommended by the Advisory Committee, and he thought the same criteria would apply to the Duchesse. He hoped that the Home Secretary 'will find little difficulty in making a detention order under Article 12(5A) against VICTOIRE'.

A complication arose a week prior to VICTOIRE's arrest and detention. A Mr Clayton of the Home Office Aliens Department had phoned E.A.S. Baxter in SLA1 on 25 June to say that the home secretary, Herbert Morrison, was out of the country and therefore would be unable to sign the Detention Order until Saturday 27th. If this was too long to wait, another minister could easily sign it instead, although this would not sit well with Morrison. There was also the issue of what would happen if the special accommodation being arranged for her 'and her future companions' at Aylesbury or Holloway Prison was not ready in time. Baxter explained to Clayton that Hoare was looking into it. Harmer said that he preferred to wait until the home secretary returned. Hoare then told MI5 that if the special accommodation was not ready in time, VICTOIRE would be placed in a room on her own and kept 'incommunicado'. The actual procedure for her arrest is worth repeating in full to illustrate how this was effected:

1. VICTOIRE will be collected at 16.45 at 32 Upper Brook Street [Lloyd's address, Flat A] by Mr. Robertson and Mr. Horsfall and will be driven to Scotland Yard, Embankment entrance. In the entrance hall they will be met by Colonel Hinchley-Cooke who will then take charge of VICTOIRE, and will interview her in the waiting room and inform her that she is to be interned for the duration of the war.

2. The Police are making arrangements for the immediate arrest thereafter of VICTOIRE and for taking her to Aylesbury Prison. She will leave Scotland Yard immediately after her arrest and will not return to her flat.

3. The Home Office have confirmed to Mr. Pilcher that they have made arrangements for her reception at Aylesbury Prison this evening. The other people to be imprisoned in the special wing there have already arrived.

4. At 16.45 an appointment has been fixed for Major Robertson to see Lt. LLOYD [sic] at Room 055 [referred to earlier]. After explaining the position, it is requested that Major Masterman ask Lt. LLOYD to ring up his flat and inform the maid there that VICTOIRE has got to leave London urgently and that someone will be coming round to pack her things. Lt. LLOYD should also ask the maid to give Mrs. Barton assistance in packing up VICTOIRE's clothes and so forth, and it is suggested that he himself should be advised not to return to the flat before about 7 o'clock in the evening.

5. After leaving VICTOIRE at Scotland Yard, Mr. Horsfall and Mr. Robertson should pick up Mrs. Barton and take her along to the flat, arriving there not before 17.15. All her things should be gone through and in particular the following should be confiscated for examination:

a) A copy she has of the instructions given to LUCAS before he left the country.

b) A copy of the various messages which have passed via the VICTOIRE transmitter.

c) A copy of the note on her first interrogation, which I believe she still has.

d) That part of the book of her life story which relates to her association with WALENTY.

e) Her diary in which the various events during last winter are recorded.

f) Various maps and documents which I know she possesses which have reference to her collaboration with the Germans.

g) Any letters she may have kept from Mr. Greene or me should be taken away from her. In this respect she may have in her possession two notes which I have written her.

In addition all her literary efforts and papers should be confiscated for a time with a view to examining them to see what they contain. The typewriter in the flat is my property and should be returned to me.

6. When VICTOIRE's things have been packed up Mr. Horsfall will take them and leave them at Aylesbury Prison later this evening. I will try and get a message for the Police to leave at this Prison when they hand over VICTOIRE to the effect that her luggage will be following by a separate car.[35]

In reference to 5(g) above, letters dated 2 July 1942 and written by VICTOIRE were addressed to both Greene and Harmer. Tar wrote to Buckmaster at SOE and Frank Foley at SIS informing them of her arrest and to tell them that MI5 had a suitcase containing some of LUCAS's effects, as well as copies of the last messages sent on the VICTOIRE transmitter. He also sent a note to Commander John Senter, then director of security at SOE, enclosing a document of LUCAS's programme on his return to France. Buckmaster sent back a Minute Sheet in which he thanked Tar for the winding-up 'of a troublesome affair which has only had the merit of causing us to exercise our brains in concert'.

On 6 July 1942, Cyril Mills visited Aylesbury Borstal Institution to meet with the governor, Miss Aliss Molly Mellanby[36] and discovered from her that this was the first occasion on which the prison had been sent any prisoners under DR.18B or 12(5A). As a result, he was of the opinion that neither the Home Office nor the Prison Commission had briefed Miss Mellanby as to how they were to be treated. Any misgivings Mills might have had were allayed by the presence of a former officer, Miss Baxter from Holloway, who knew the drill. They discussed the business of dealing with letters, other communications and visits. The only snag seemed to be that the wall at the back of the garden to the special wing overlooked a drive where 'other prisoners including those of the Anna Wolkoff category' were housed and that notes could be tossed over the wall.[37] Mills was not unduly worried about this, saying that the other prisoners were unable to see who these five special category prisoners were. Miss Mellanby added that even though the other prisoners, who were Borstal girls, knew about the presence of these five women they did not know their names and were unlikely to mix with them anyway, not wanting to 'mix themselves up in any of the affairs or troubles of people about whom they know nothing and who they may guess are spies or at least people who are not fit to mix with them'.

A further issue was seen in all prisoners being allowed access to the prison library and chapel. A simple solution was found by allowing these special prisoners access to the library when it was closed to other prisoners; in the chapel they would be placed on the opposite side of the aisle, and accompanied by prison warders. All these arrangements would have to be dealt with by the Home Office and Prison Commission, not MI5. Mills commented on how these prisoners were adapting to their new surroundings, beginning with VICTOIRE:

> VICTOIRE being new to the game began by adopting a high hat attitude towards the Governor but as soon as she saw that it would get her nowhere she was as pains [sic] to act the sweet little thing and has given no trouble at all.[38]

He also commented on the Duchesse de Château-Thierry and My Eriksson; his comments on Stella Lonsdale and Mathilde Krafft will not be quoted in full here as they are peripheral to this story, but the following is of note:

> Both LONSDALE and My ERIKSSON have now written letters to friends in which they exhibit nothing but the highest praise for their new quarters and from the descriptions they give it is quite clear that they are highly

delighted that they have been moved and I am not at all sure they do not think the move is in the nature of a priviledge bestowed upon them by a benevolent Government!

CHATEAU-THIERRY has written to one of the inmates at Holloway [Enid Riddell] in a way that indicates that she is almost as pleased as if we had given her a suite at Claridges.[39]

Mills noted that VICTOIRE had written to Christopher Harmer and Tom Greene, whom she spelled 'Grim', on 2 July 'more in sorrow than in anger and her chief concern seems to be to have something to do'. The letter to Enid Riddell from the Duchesse was to ask her to forward some of her things from Holloway that had been left behind. Eriksson had written a letter to a Christian Science 'practionner' [*sic*] which also mentioned a Mrs Gerald Stone, a copy of which was passed on to her case officer. She had written another letter to someone called Hohenburg who was in Holloway, which also mentioned Jessie Jordan. Hohenburg was Mrs Felicia Hohenburg (*née* Tyndel), born in Berlin in 1916, who was later transferred to the Isle of Man, Married Aliens Internment Camp at Port Erin in November 1942 with her chemist husband Dr Erich Hohenburg, both of whom were Jewish refugees. Dr Hohenburg was described by J.A. Cole as a 'quiet, well-mannered man', while his wife was 'rather odd-looking; she has a large, very pale face and a wide-eyed, frightened look'.[40] They were arrested and interned for 'a purely civil offence ... and ... are probably harmless from a Security point of view'. The offence was petty larceny, according to an internal memorandum from A.H. Robertson in B1a to Major Jock Whyte in B4a in one of Eriksson's files.[41] Mrs Gerald Stone, also known as 'Mollie', lived at 19 Barons Court Road, London.

The plan, as outlined by Mills, was for MI5 to request that the Home Office submit all mail, incoming and outgoing, as well as all visits, for B1a's approval. Harmer would read all VICTOIRE's mail and establish with the other case officers (for the Duchesse and Eriksson) whether they wished to do the same, and whether they needed to be consulted about permits being issued for visits to these two women. Mail would be sent to Harmer or Mills at Box 500, Parliament Street, 'as we know that the H.O. are particularly anxious that these internees should not be able to compare their treatment at Aylesbury unfavourably with that which they received at Holloway'; outgoing overseas mail was to be sent to Alan Grogan in B3a, liaison with Censorship (actually B3d). Telegrams 'which are not prima facie objectionable' would be allowed to proceed, but copied to MI5; telephone calls would not be allowed without permission from MI5, and only in special circumstances (complete details are provided in Appendix 6). Mills commented:

> I am not at all clear as to just what rights M.I.5. has to censor the mail of 18B internees (Mr. Pilcher is the expert I believe) but I did make it clear to the Governor that M.I.5. Censorship will be complementary to and not in substitution for the ordinary prison Censorship which should continue as usual.[42]

This is a little surprising, given that it was now 1942 and MI5 had been interning people of various stripes since 1939, some even earlier. That they were still fumbling around in the dark trying to establish what, if any, legal rights they had means that the entire process had not been clearly thought through. Since MI5 was not placed on a statutory basis until the Security Service Act of 1989, it could be assumed that during the Second World War they would have been able to do whatever they liked as far as mail opening and censorship were concerned. As J.L.S. Hale pointed out on 28 October 1943, 'I do not think that any question of law arises here. VICTOIRE is the Home Office's prisoner, and the Home Office can stop or send on her letters as they please.'[43]

A.H. Robertson in B1a recorded the following day (7 July) that VICTOIRE was safely installed in Aylesbury and 'behaving like a little angel'. He suggested that any of her personal property that was not intelligence-related should be returned to her, but that her memoirs, traffic on the VICTOIRE transmitter, documents relating to WALENTY and LUCAS, maps of Brittany, and her morphine be retained by MI5. Copies of LUCAS's summary of Part II of her memoirs could be made available to SIS and anyone else having an interest in the WALENTY organisation. Tar sent a note and a copy of the summary to Frank Foley at SIS on 9 July, and also to Tom Greene. This copy is in a poor shape in her file. He also thought there would be no harm in encouraging her to keep writing her memoirs as they might prove useful, but she would need to have access to what she had already written. However, if MI5 considered this undesirable, in case it was circulated to the other inmates, then they would have to retain Part III, but she would be unable to complete Part II without having access to the part of it that she had already written. He saw no problem in her retaining Part I since it only related to her work with the French Red Cross prior to the Occupation.

What Robertson also suggested was whether MI5 should 'do anything to make her detention there as agreeable as possible', and whether in light of the work she had done for the British prior to her capture and 'turning' by the Germans, she should be paid a small sum of money to cover any minor comforts. This he considered an inducement to have her complete her memoirs 'and, so far as possible, mitigate the bitterness which her enforced detention is bound to produce, having regard to such harm as she may be able to do to us at any future date'.

Once again, VICTOIRE continued to lead a charmed life. Whether instigated by her or not, it seems that MI5 felt they had some sort of obligation to pander to her every need and make life more tolerable for her. A search would continue for the diary MI5 knew she had kept on her time working for WALENTY but, strangely, was not looked for when she was arrested at Lloyd's flat, 'on which occasion no attempt was made to undertake an exhaustive search'. Leaping forward in time, this is strangely reminiscent of how Sir Anthony Blunt had first managed to remove potentially incriminating papers from Guy Burgess's three-bedroomed flat in 10 New Bond Street after he had disappeared with Donald Maclean in 1951, and the scanty search MI5 and Special Branch had carried out afterwards.[44]

Harmer wrote to VICTOIRE on 21 June referring to her as '*Ma Chère soeur*' ('My dear sister') and saying how he had promised to write to her but had been on holiday in the north of England. The tone was friendly and almost affectionate, signing off as '*Votre petit frère*' ('Your little brother'). On 27 June when he wrote to her he again referred to her as '*Ma Chère soeur*', thanking her for the third part of her memoirs and saying that he was going away for a few days and that he was handing her case over to Captain Robson. For that reason he was unable to have tea with her or help celebrate her birthday soirée. He also said that everything was up in the air for him at that moment and he was going to take some holidays.

On 10 July, he wrote again, referring to her as '*Chère Ly*', and he informed her that since it had been decided to intern her the matter was now out of his hands. Her case had been handed over to Captain Robson and that all her correspondence should be sent to him; also 'Uncle Tom' had been out of the country for a few weeks so he had been unable to pass on her letter to him. He advised her to try to make the best of her situation and adapt to it by focusing on her writing and to '*des choses d'esprit*' ('those things in mind'). He was sure that Robson could help her with her writing and obtain whatever books she needed. Robson was in fact, A.H. Robertson, as he admitted to Miss Mellanby, the governor of Aylesbury, in a letter to her on 17 July.

Never one to give up without a fight, VICTOIRE wrote to General Legentilhomme of the FFL, whose headquarters were at Grenville House, Dolphin Square, on 8 July asking him to use his influence to get her reinstated as a nurse with the 'fighting French Red Cross'. That information was conveyed by Tar to Claude Dansey at SIS in his letter of 17 July. Legentilhomme was Major General Paul Louis Victor Marie Legentilhomme (1884–1975), who had been condemned in absentia for treason by the Vichy government in 1941 but awarded the Compagnon de la Libération by General de Gaulle on 9 September 1942. The same day Tar also wrote to Keswick at SOE to ask his opinion on whether VICTOIRE's letter should be forwarded to the general or stopped by MI5. He hinted, based on a study Harmer was carrying out of her memoirs, that they might be able to bring a prosecution against her. Tar reported to Harmer on 20 July that he had spoken to Keswick, who was strongly opposed to MI5 passing on VICTOIRE's letter to General Legentilhomme, and that she should certainly not be allowed to join the French Red Cross. Not only that, but he was against lifting any of the current restrictions against her.

VICTOIRE had also written to Louis V. Gale, the Special Branch detective with whom she had developed a friendship while he was keeping an eye on her and LUCAS after they had come over to England. Tar wrote to the deputy assistant commissioner, Special Branch informing him of this, saying that 'no useful purpose could be served by allowing a correspondence to start which could not in any event achieve anything', and that 'she must appreciate that his position makes it impossible for him [Gale] to take a personal interest in her case.' Gale had responded to her letter of 16 July on 28 July in which she referred to him as '*Cher Ange Gardien*' ('Dear Guardian Angel'), saying that he was not familiar with her history or her '*famille*' (the note at the bottom of the translated letter states that '*famille*' refers to the department by which she was formerly employed, i.e. MI5) and that:

> The circumstances which exist at the present time and departmental discipline do not permit me to take any personal interest in a matter which, from the Police point of view, is ended. In the same way, in spite of our good friendship, I cannot continue any private correspondence with you. I can only offer my regrets.[45]

CHAPTER 21

Accounts Payable: The Cost of Doing Business

There were still financial issues to be resolved, one of which related to VICTOIRE's poor eyesight. Prior to her arrest, on 13 May she had been taken to see Eugene Wolff (1896–1954), the renowned opthalmologist,[1] at 46 Wimpole Street to have her eyes tested for new glasses. On 20 June the opticians Clement Clarke at 16 Wigmore Street sent MI5 an invoice for dispensing her glasses, described as 'brown rhodoid spectacles with flat lenses' costing £3 6s (rhodoid was an early form of celluloid made from cellulose acetate). While VICTOIRE was at Aylesbury A.H. Robertson (Captain Robson) had written to Miss Mellanby to say that her glasses were now ready and apologised for the fact that the original pair had been made incorrectly. Another issue was arranging for a dentist to make a plate for some missing teeth, and how much MI5 was prepared to pay; they opted for the cheapest version.

During 1943 she continued to experience problems with her eyesight. Wolff had examined her eyes again on 23 November, when he concluded that her current prescription should be sufficient to correct her high myopia, but in the opinion of Dr John Campbell McIntyre Matheson, the governor and chief medical officer of Holloway, where she was then kept, part of her problem was that she frequently did not wear her glasses. She complained to Matheson on 26 January 1944 that the examination performed by Dr Wolff in November had been a sham, as opposed to when he had examined her in 1942, and wished to have her eyes re-examined. Two days later she wrote a medical report in which she complained about the condition of her eyesight, stating that she was unable to read for more than fifteen minutes at a time and needed to wear her 'fifteen dioptrics spectacles' (for distance) in order to do so, 'which proves that my shortsightedness, which had not changed since my childhood, has got very much worse'. She was also experiencing violent headaches, 'black spots, veils and fogs', then white spots, which moved as her eyes moved. These were most likely what are commonly known as 'floaters'.

As to her teeth, there had been no further complaints since her examination and treatment at Aylesbury. Matheson noted that she liked being examined, particularly by male doctors, 'and this desire on her part is I think the explanation of her repeated complaints about her health'. She had also been examined by Dr Herbert on 10 November and Dr Saner on 26 January 1944 regarding a sub-acute inflammatory condition in the right lower pelvic region. Both doctors concluded that there was no need for surgical intervention. Saner had concluded that it might not be appendicitis but a Fallopian tube condition and had prescribed Stilboestral, also known as Diethylstilbestrol, a synthetic non-steroidal oestrogen, classified as an endochrine disruptor. It had started to be used in 1938 for women in their first trimester to prevent miscarriages, although it was found to be unsuccessful and banned in 1971. But this can hardly mean that VICTOIRE had become pregnant as she was in prison and had not received any male visitors, so it must have been another gynaecological condition.

There had been plenty of correspondence relating to the cost of keeping her in London before her internment, and also the cost of keeping her entertained. A note to Miss Constant in A4 from L.C. Marshall of B1a refers to the fact that 'Heavy expenses have been incurred in connection with the VICTOIRE case.' Another note to John Marriott is especially interesting:

> I am sorry that the VICTOIRE expenses are so high, but it is impossible nowadays to sustain anyone in the West End without spending a great deal of money. Entertainment of this particular character is extremely difficult without drink and that costs big money.[2]

A note at the bottom added: 'Drink is also necessary to keep up the morale of those doing the entertaining.' It had already been agreed that MI5 would pay VICTOIRE £50 per month, payable on the 15th and 30th of each month, but a third of that would be picked up by SOE and SIS, with SIS's share not to exceed £35. A Mr Gordon would also take her out and be paid £5 a week plus a further £10 for entertainment expenses.

Major Robert Bourne-Patterson of F Section SOE wrote to MI5 on 15 July that 'our expenses for the period during which we were in charge of the lady's up-keep, amounted to £300.17.10 and the third share, which it was agreed you should bear, is thus £100.5.11.' A handwritten note at the bottom, probably added by Bourne-Patterson, states, 'I spoke with Miss Atkins (SOE) who answers me that the above sum of £300.17.10 represents expenses solely to Victoire and not to Lucas.' Bourne-Patterson, designated as 'FP' in F Section, has been described as SOE's 'first historian' based on the account he wrote that has recently been declassified and published.[3] Vera Atkins (*née* Rosenburg, 1908–2000) was Buckmaster's assistant, and designated as 'FV'.

An example of the costs incurred by Greene and Philipson for VICTOIRE's upkeep, submitted by Frank Foley of SIS's VX section on 31 July, can be found in her file.[4]

P5 was the SIS Production Section that handled Poland and Polish networks in France during the Second World War.[5] An example of the expenses incurred by MI5 can be seen in the account covering March and April 1942.[6] MI5 had also calculated what it had cost them from March until July when VICTOIRE was interned. A handwritten note (no date) states:

> The total cost of the VICTOIRE case was £269 £738.13.5. In each of the three services [one word illegible] a third share. They will each pay £246.4.6. S.O.E. has already paid £300.17.10 leaving the sum of £54.13.4 owed to them. SIS' expenses paid amount to £48.2.0 and they thus owe £198.2.5.

The MI5 document from B1a is also handwritten.

E.M.I. had also loaned SOE a Model 347 radio receiver and had written to Masterman on 6 July to see whether he wanted to continue the loan. Masterman replied to the general manager offering to settle the account and on 11 August submitted a cheque for £2 to cover the cost of rental.

In December 1942 VICTOIRE wrote to Harmer to find out how she could obtain money to pay for clothes, linen and underclothes, as well as current expenses. Harmer replied:

> I have no doubt that the paying of any money to VICTOIRE would be an unpopular move but at the same time she must, I suppose, have something for day to day requirements. I do not exactly know what 18B Detainees of German nationality get as a right, but I think she should get at least as much as they do.[7]

J.L.S. Hale in MI5's Legal Section spoke to the Home Office Aliens Department and G2, the section dealing with detainees under DR.18B, to find out what funding might be available to 'sweeten the lot of the destitute detinu'. The Home Office in turn told him that there was no such fund available but that the Society of Friends (Quakers) and Red Cross might be able to help out. It was pointed out to Hale that prisoners were able to work while in prison and thus earn some money, although he was aware that this was usually a paltry amount. When Tar wrote to Ian Roy at the Home Office Aliens Department on 25 February 1944, the option of approaching the Red Cross for financial support was not on the table. SOE was strongly opposed to her communicating with any outside persons or organisations so MI5 had decided since January 1943 to subsidise her to the tune of 10 shillings to cover her day-to-day requirements. It had been in MI5's mind to give her an allowance of £1, commensurate with what My Eriksson was receiving from the Swedish consul, but it was eventually decided to award her 10 shillings to bring her in line with what the other detainees were receiving. But, as Tar noted in his letter to Ian Roy on 8 March 1944, 'Of course the remaining inmates of Aylesbury at that time were all receiving considerable sums from private sources.'

Hale wrote to Harmer on 4 January 1943 suggesting that next time he (Harmer) visited Aylesbury he meet with Miss Mellanby and sound her out. He added, 'I suppose that we could, as a matter of fact, readily justify, as a necessary security expense in order to keep Victoire as sweet as possible, an appropriate welfare payment from our own funds though this is, as you will appreciate, very far from being a matter for me.' Harmer appended a note requesting instructions from Marriott, who replied to Tar on the 7th saying that:

I personally consider that, having regard to the fact that presumably BRUTUS may one day be confronted with VICTOIRE and generally in the interests of the BRUTUS case, it would be proper for us to make some payment for the purpose of equipping VICTOIRE with clothes etc. This is, in my view, the only basis upon which a payment to VICTOIRE would be justified at all, since even supposing we were particularly sympathetic towards VICTOIRE, which as an office we are not, we should not be justified in making a payment on that score, more particularly since the Home Office, who are a more charitable department than we are, are not prepared to do so. I do think, however, that BRUTUS might, if he discovered the present situation, regard us as treating VICTOIRE rather shabbily if we refused to do anything at all.[8]

Miss Mellanby pointed out that under normal circumstances, in an ordinary civil case, prisoners did not need to be provided with cash since the prison authorities supplied them with food and clothing. VICTOIRE had been spending on average about 30 shillings (or £1 10s) a week on extra food, and consequently would need some extra cash unless she was prepared to wear prison clothes, which was highly unlikely in this author's view, given her predilection for being temperamental. Harmer seemed resigned to the fact that:

> Nothing we do or fail to do while VICTOIRE is in prison will prevent her from being disgruntled and, although I would like to agree with Mr. Marriott that a payment was necessary in the interests of running the BRUTUS case, I am afraid I cannot say so. It seems to me that the problem merely rests on the grounds of common sense – the question being whether we allow a woman, who worked as our agent and whom we feted and pampered to our own ends, to be on the same level as a common criminal. As I understand it, the internment was agreed upon as a precautionary measure to prevent her from doing more damage rather than as a punishment – the latter will obviously remain to be gone into and the end of the war by the French. I am sure that if the point had been specifically raised at the conference deciding to intern her, we would have all agreed to make some little payment towards her living expenses.[9]

L.C. Marshall followed this up by sending Miss Mellanby a cheque for £6 10s to cover VICTOIRE's weekly expenses up to 24 June 1943. After that date a further cheque for the same amount was sent to cover expenses up to 28 September 1943. By this time, Miss Mellanby had been succeeded by the Honourable Victoria A.K. Bruce.[10] These payments continued into 1944, by which time VICTOIRE had been transferred to Holloway prison.

CHAPTER 22

What Are we Going to Do about Mathilde?

As the war dragged on, VICTOIRE, desperate for human contact, continued to write to various people. However, steps were being taken to ensure that her letters did not reach their recipients. There were also concerns about where she was now interned. These measures served to cause a certain amount of friction between SOE and MI5, the former being quite adamant about how her case should be handled and the limits imposed on her freedom. In contrast, MI5 preferred to take a somewhat more relaxed approach, largely, one suspects, because the information VICTOIRE may or may not have possessed affected SOE's agents and operations more than their own. Throughout 1943 and well into 1944 much paper was expended with the two organisations exchanging letters and reports with each other and the Home Office in order to sort out the mess they had created. Noses were often put out of joint and egos bruised; it was time for all parties concerned to take a firmer stand.

Early in July 1943 VICTOIRE and her four companions – the Duchesse de Château-Thierry, Mathilde Krafft, Stella Lonsdale and My Eriksson – had been moved out of Aylesbury and into Holloway. VICTOIRE wrote to Hinchley-Cooke on 14 July 1943 saying that she had petitioned the Home Office to be transferred to the Isle of Man, only to be sent to Holloway instead, the order to move her to the Isle of Man being cancelled by Sir Frank Newsam at the Home Office. Tar informed Frank Foley at SIS on 15 July 1943 that the move to Holloway had taken place a few days before because 'the particular reason for which the Aylesbury special wing was instituted no longer applied'. It seems that MI5 no longer considered her a threat, as he added, 'there is no evidence to suggest that VICTOIRE made any effort to communicate vital information through the medium of any of her fellow internees … but my own view is that she could not now do any serious harm even if she did get into communication with the enemy.'

Christopher Harmer had written to Tar on 18 April 1943 expressing his view that 'since the total occupation of France, and in view of the lapse of time, there is absolutely no S.O.E. secret of importance which VICTOIRE could reveal, even if she wanted to'. Yet in spite of these prognostications about her not now being in a position to do any harm, it seems that MI5 and SOE were still concerned about the possibility of her being able to communicate outside the prison via other detainees. A case in point was expressed in a letter Harmer wrote to Tar, in which he also referred to a letter My Eriksson had written to MP Richard Stokes and the Home Office about conditions in Aylesbury, requesting to be moved back to Holloway or to the Isle of Man. Harmer wondered whether:

The Home Office or this office wish to keep on the special wing at Aylesbury for exceptional cases, but I suggest that all parties concerned, including the officers who concern themselves with keeping an eye on the special cases involved, be invited to express their views on the possibility of closing down the Aylesbury special wing and moving the five detainees there to Holloway or the Isle of Man.[1]

This, however, was not the view of SOE and clearly did not sit well with Air Commodore Archie Boyle (1887–1949), SOE's director of security, intelligence and personnel, who wrote to Guy Liddell, the head of B Division at MI5 expressing their dissatisfaction and disagreement with Tar's comments. Boyle said that 'the Home Office will not unnaturally have assumed that enquiries had been made before this advice was given', and reminded Tar that her internment had been agreed upon in June 1942. Furthermore, LUCAS's brother Philippe, who was well-known to VICTOIRE, was still at large. Boyle also pointed out that in Tar's letter of 27 June 1942 he had quoted from one of MI5's sources ('Klop' Ustinov) that, 'For me she remains from beginning to end a person who is not to be trusted and whose whole past predestines her for a safe place, where she can do no more harm.'[2] Boyle cited cases where prisoners who were about to be released had mixed with those having 'special information', including Admiral Muselier, listed by Dr Ingrao and recommended that it was time for the VICTOIRE case to be reviewed.

Vice-Admiral Émile Henry Muselier (1882–1965) was with the FFL, once accused of treason by the British, but later exonerated. Dr Andrew R. Ingrao, a psychologist and member of the Mazzini Society, had served in the Italian Army between 1915 and 1922, but afterwards resumed his medical studies.

The Mazzini Society was an anti-Fascist society created by Italian-Americans in Northampton, Massachusetts, on 24 September 1939 and named after Giuseppe Mazzini, who had been a leading figure in Italian reunification in the nineteenth century. Its headquarters were at 1775 Broadway, New York. Ingrao had been recruited by SOE in 1941 to persuade Italian prisoners of war to work for the Allies but was cited as being a 'chief source of discontent' within the society for being jealous of Alberto Tarchiani's role as their leader and attempting to undermine his authority. Tarchiani's group formed a para-military force that would be used to carry out covert operations in Italy. However, Ingrao proved to be extremely indiscreet and before his departure to the United States was arrested on 10 June 1941 at Euston Station and interned under DR.18B for twenty-three months in Swansea and on the Isle of Man. Roderick Bailey's book about SOE operations in Italy quotes an SOE report that stated, 'He is grumbler No.1 and the main factor in stirring up discontent among others,' and 'He is a 'know all' and will not be taught anything.'[3]

Interestingly, once released when it was thought he no longer knew any secrets of note, Ingrao returned to America in 1943 and lived with his sister Diana Ingrao Rizzo at 2145 Creston Avenue, New York City. There he threatened to spill the beans if SOE did not pay him off; their response was to tell him to 'go to hell'.[4] A report duly appeared in the *Chicago Sunday Tribune* on 12 September 1943 in which the headline read 'Held in British Prison 2 Years, says American. No Charge Filed. Tricked into Joining Army'. He claimed he had been locked in a cell for twenty-three hours a day and fed on bread and water. His detention, he said, was not because of what secrets he might know but 'for fear that I would tell how unfair Great Britain had been to me and my companions'.[5]

The transfer of the five women, in particular VICTOIRE, caused a whole flurry of meetings and correspondence between MI5 and SOE in order to try to clear up the bad feelings that had resulted. Referring to Harmer's comments that VICTOIRE posed no danger in passing on important information via other detainees due to be released, Tar wrote to Guy Liddell on 30 July 1943 to say that comments solicited by Harmer had been received from 'Buster' Milmo, Dick White and J.L.S. Hale, MI5's senior legal advisor, but unfortunately Hale had sent a letter to the Home Office before Harmer had been able to meet with SOE to discuss it. A suitably contrite Tar admitted that this was an oversight on his part, for which he felt responsible, but in mitigation, he said that Commander Senter at SOE had been told retrospectively about it and had not objected. Foley at SIS had also been informed, even though MI5 did not consider SIS to be particularly interested at that point. This, Tar also admitted, was his oversight. He suggested meeting Boyle, where 'I am afraid we shall have to grovel as it does not seem to me to get us anywhere if we start arguing the toss. We are at fault and we must therefore face up to it.' He further suggested that someone from MI5 should be present when Boyle went to the Home Office to sort things out.

Another point Tar thought worth mentioning was the possibility of My Eriksson being exchanged for SIS agent Andrée de Jongh, and the fact that she had been in close proximity to VICTOIRE. Milmo told Tar that the matter was in the hands of [redacted] at SIS. Milmo had also brought up the issue of what if any damage VICTOIRE could do to SIS. As Tar noted, 'The details she could give away about other people's causes are, to say the least of it, small.'

Andrée Eugenie Adrienne de Jongh, known as Dédée, was a member of the Belgian Resistance who had set up and run the 'Comet Line', an escape line for Allied prisoners, helping them escape over the Pyrenees to neutral Spain. De Jongh had been captured by French police on 15 January 1943, and after imprisonment in the Château Neuf prison, Bayonne and Fort du Hâ, Bordeaux, was taken to Fresnes prison in Paris, where she was brutally tortured by the Gestapo. Later she was sent to Ravensbrück and Mauthausen concentration camps.[6]

On 5 August 1943 Tar reported on the meeting he and Harmer had had with Air Commodore Boyle that morning in which he apologised to Boyle for having had VICTOIRE transferred without SOE's input. His manner seemed somewhat conciliatory, as he undertook to visit the governor of Holloway to ascertain whether conditions at Holloway were the same as at Aylesbury, namely, no contact with the other internees, etc. He agreed that any future transactions involving internees where SOE had an interest would be discussed with them first, reminding Boyle that Senter had expressed no objection at the meeting they had had some months before on the matter of Eriksson's possible exchange for Andrée de Jongh. Tar undertook to ensure that Eriksson was not told in advance of this in case VICTOIRE somehow got wind of it and reported it to the Germans through Eriksson.

The following day Tar discovered that in Holloway the special internees were not segregated from the others but housed in a special wing with 18B cases. He quickly passed this information on to Senter, again apologising for his mistake and asking him to accompany him when he met with the governor of Holloway the next day, Saturday. At that meeting Senter told the governor that he was anxious that VICTOIRE should not pass on any information about her involvement with SOE or any of the persons with whom she had come into contact. The deputy governor, Miss D. Wilson, informed them that although three internees under 18B had just been released it was unlikely that VICTOIRE would have used any of them to get messages out. It would be up to the Home Office to decide whether any re-opening of the special wing at Aylesbury was possible, but it was impossible with the limited resources she had available to segregate the five special cases from the others. Senter told Tar that it was not so much the ordinary 18B cases that he was concerned about but the three IRA cases, such as Mrs Kirsch. This was either Elisabeth Kirsch, born 8 July 1902 at Konstanz am Bodensee or Eva Kirsch, born in Berlin on 5 December 1901, both of whom were interned during 1939-42.[7] Tar commented:

> I can see no way out of the difficulty other than a joint discussion between M.I.5, S.O.E. and the appropriate individual at the Home Office in order to see whether any arrangements can be made, namely the re-opening of the Special Wing at Aylesbury or some other arrangement which might be suitable to S.O.E.[8]

He opined that SOE would probably want VICTOIRE treated as a special case throughout the war, adding 'that we shall find it impossible to fight against this view'.

Boyle wrote back to Tar on 11 August thanking him for the letter of 9 August in which Tar had referred to this case as being a 'chapter of accidents'. Ironically, this would also become the title of an autobiography by Goronwy Rees, who worked for MI6 during the war and who would later be implicated in the 'Cambridge Five' case.[9] Boyle said that he hoped VICTOIRE would soon be returned to Aylesbury. He took the view – 'If I may be rather pompous' – that everyone realised the importance of not taking action without consulting each other first.

Harmer wanted to put on record his latest meeting with VICTOIRE when he wrote to Tar on 20 August:

> In connection with the trouble we are having with S.O.E. about the internment of VICTOIRE, I have made a detailed note of my conversation with her yesterday. For the purposes of the advisability of moving her, I think it should be borne in mind by all parties interested that her present demeanour does not accord at all with the fears which S.O.E. have, and that so far from trying to get messages out, she appears to be trying to act as a stool-pigeon for us and give us information about the other detainees.

I put this on record because, if VICTOIRE is to stay at Holloway, it might set some of S.O.E.'s fears at rest to be told this, and also that there is another woman who is intimate with her whom we could use to check up on VICTOIRE's sentiments and activities.[10]

In another report, dated 20 August 1943, following an interview with her the previous day, Harmer states that 'she appears to have developed mentally in a way which is well-known to us, having now become institutionalized and having started to spy on the other inmates and take an interest in them. She wants, I think, to become a stool-pigeon.' On 4 October 1943 J.L.S. Hale had written to John Marriott saying:

It seems to me that in pressing the Home Office to reconstitute an isolated party for VICTOIRE, our and S.O.E.'s best point is that in my letter to the Home Office telling them they could disband the Aylesbury party if they wanted to, I expressly stated that we might want such a party again, and invited them to consider whether, in view of this possibility, it might be wiser to preserve the status quo.[11]

To which Marriott had appended a note:

We might bring this point forward if S.O.E. are not given satisfaction by the Home Office. I do not see that we are called on to fight S.O.E's battles at the present instance as they are acting independently of us.

The issue of VICTOIRE as a stool pigeon had been first raised by Mary Stanford, one of the other internees at Holloway, when she wrote to Sir Archibald Southby, the Conservative MP for Epsom, Surrey, on 7 January 1943, a copy of which had also been sent to Sir Ernest Graham-Little, the National Independent MP for London University. Mary 'Molly' Agnes Geraldine Stanford, described by P.M. Burke in F3C2 as looking on the war as 'a fight between the Powers of Light (the Nazis) and the Powers of Darkness (the Jew-controlled Bolshevik democracies)', was a supporter of the National Socialists, a member of the Right Club and friend of Anna Wolkoff at the Russian Tea Rooms, who was interned under DR.18B in 1940.

The letter Stanford had written to Southby made all sorts of allegations against VICTOIRE, such as how she had been supplied by the War Office with 'Enough poison to kill six people', which she allegedly carried in a ring; that she was getting money from the War Office to pay for lingerie and her dentist's bills; that she had been 'in close association' with Mrs Brett-Perring, who spoke French, and they were 'in each other's confidence over matters outside the ordinary detainee'. She added, 'The worst of people with special contacts with "Authority" is that they are often prone to invent or embroider in order to put feathers in their own caps or help themselves.' Another letter she had sent to Southby on 30 January 1943 repeated many of these allegations. At this point, according to Stanford, VICTOIRE was living in the married couples' wing in which Sir Oswald Mosley and his wife, the Honourable Diana Mitford, had stayed prior to their release, an option first proposed by Tar when he wrote to Senter on 26 November 1943, 'I suggest that the removal of Mosley and his wife presents an excellent opportunity for returning to the charge and trying to arrange for the Home Office and the Prison Authorities to take say four of the women, including VICTOIRE, and put them in these quarters.' Stanford pointed out that:

> She has also shown herself to be in possession of information about detainees here to whom she was a complete stranger before her internment ... [and] one is curious to know how she obtained the information. Such facts as all the above convey unavoidably the impression that she is not only an ex-employee of the W.O. but is still in receipt of salary and advantages in return for continuing, during internment, to act under their direction – in fact, put in to spy on us![12]

Evidence that VICTOIRE was telling tales on fellow inmates is mentioned in a report that Harmer sent to Tar Robertson on 20 August 1943. These inmates were: Mrs Brett-Perring, who she said was the only one who was pro-British; Mrs Christabel Sybil Caroline Nicholson,[13] the wife of Admiral (ret'd) Wilmot Nicholson; Magdalena Cecilia Colledge (1920–2008), the skating champion, who drove an ambulance with the Motor Transport Corps during the Blitz and was reported to be 'violently pro-German'; and Stella Lonsdale (1913–94). Christabel Nicholson had been arrested in possession of a document obtained illegally from the US embassy in 1940, in connection with the Anna Wolkoff-Tyler Kent Affair and charged under the Official Secrets Act. She was acquitted, but interned under DR.18B. It is ironic that VICTOIRE had reported the entire Colledge family to be 'violently pro-German' since Cecilia's brother Flight Lieutenant Maule William Colledge was killed returning from a mission in his Mosquito en route from Berlin on 14 September 1943. One theory is that he collided with David Maltby's (of Dambusters fame) Lancaster.[14]

Miss D. Wilson, deputy governor of Holloway, sent a letter to Captain Harman [*sic*] enclosing a copy of Stanford's letter, noting that 'there may be Parliamentary repercussions'. John Marriott sent a copy of the letter and a note to J.L.S. Hale, who wrote at the bottom:

> If I am right in thinking that it's not the fact of V's detention, but the story which she might tell which must be concealed. This is probably not as bad as it looks. Let me know if I can assist in any way.[15]

In the spirit of cooperation with SOE, Marriott also sent a copy to John Senter, reiterating Miss Wilson's supposition about possible Parliamentary repercussions. If there were any, *Hansard* does not record them.

Stanford's letter also contained complaints about Marie Anne Teresa de Styczinska Brett-Perring, a nurse during the First World War and the alleged mistress of a German officer in Bern, who had been interned from 1942 to 1944 under DR.18B for evading the censorship by sending messages through the Chinese and Soviet diplomatic pouches, as well as having Nazi sympathies.[16]

Harry Sporborg, deputy head of SOE under Colin Gubbins, had written to Sir John Moylan at the Home Office on 17 November 1943 about a letter VICTOIRE had sent to a friend of hers on 18 October 1943, a Madame Richard, at 4 Carlton Gardens, the headquarters of the FFL, in an attempt to get them interested in her case. He also sent a copy to Guy Liddell:

> My dear,
>   I am so glad to hear that you are in London since June. Could you come to see me now that I am a 'prisoner of war', it would give me a real pleasure to see you again. If you let me know you can come I shall send you a visiting order.
>   Affectionately yours,
>   'White mouse'[17]

Interestingly 'White Mouse' was also the nickname given to SOE agent Nancy Wake (1912–2011) by the Gestapo. Sporborg informed Moylan:

> We have taken the strongest possible objection to any risk being taken to complicate this case by allowing Allied French Headquarters to become interested in it. The political and operational consequences of such a development might be extremely grave as we have two Sections dealing with

France and the one which she injured by her activity for the Germans is the Independent one [F Section] and not the one which works in cooperation with the Allied French [RF Section].

I should like to make the strongest possible representations against any such visit being allowed and a fortiori[18] against the woman being allowed to leave the prison in any circumstances – I notice that Colonel Robertson of M.I.5 has also written to you about this.

I do hope you can give me an assurance that she will be restored to effective segregation with the least possible delay.[19]

Harmer noted to Hale on 26 October 1943, 'For all reasons, and particularly in view of S.O.E.'s interest in the case, this letter must not go forward. The question is whether we have authority to stop it.' He cited the similar case of when she had written to General Legentilhomme in July 1942 in which, after discussions with Toby Pilcher and SOE, the letter had not been forwarded. Therefore:

I should be very grateful if you would advise us on the legal position and authority for withholding the letter on this occasion also, especially having regard to the move from Aylesbury to Holloway. Perhaps I might refer you to the regulations for Aylesbury internees at 14a in S.F.85/2/20 sent herewith [see Appendix 5].[20]

Hale replied on 28 October 1943:

I do not think that any question of law arises here. VICTOIRE is the Home Office's prisoner, and the Home Office can stop or send on her letters as they please. To some extent we have acted in the past as the Home Office's agents in this matter and have stopped letters without reference to them, but I think that in view of what has occurred in this case it might be wiser for Mr. Milmo, who wrote to Sir John Moylan on the 17th October about VICTOIRE's doctor and dentist, to write to him about this letter, saying that we are stopping it, for reasons of which he will be aware. The letter might perhaps serve as a reminder to the Home Office that, so far as we are aware, no progress has been made with the matters discussed in S.O.E.'s letter of 28.8.43 (322k) and 1.10.43 (325k). My reading of these papers is that we have left S.O.E. to conduct their own negotiations with the Home Office, but I think that if difficulties are being experienced which do not look like being solved in the near future, Kinnaird House (see 47a in S.F.85/2/20) would be glad to lend a hand again.[21]

Edward Blanchard Stamp in B1b in a response dictated by Milmo wrote on 2 November that:

> I feel that if we stop this letter we are, in fact, evading the Home Office ruling … that the special internees at one time detained at Aylesbury should be allowed to have visits. I think for this reason that the letter should not be stopped without reference to the Home Office and I would suggest that the draft letter attached should accordingly be sent to Sir John Moylan with a copy to S.O.E.[22]

Guy Liddell, writing on 6 November to Moylan, referred to:

> [The] considerable amount of correspondence regarding her case passing lately between S.O.E., the Security Service and the Home Office, and a somewhat delicate situation now arises in connection with a letter which this lady has written addressed to a certain Madame RICHARD at the French Headquarters in Carlton Gardens.[23]

MI5 did not feel that it should stop the letter without referring to the Home Office and the regulations for the 100 per cent censorship of mail and visits for special internees and:

> Although permits for visits would only be issued with our written approval, we should bear in mind that it was not desirable that any restrictions imposed should compare unfavourably with those in force previously. The Home Office also stipulated that we should not refuse a permit to visit an internee without consulting them.
>
> If the letter addressed by Madame CARRE to her friend in Carlton Gardens is allowed to go forward, we feel that it will doubtless have the effect which the writer intends that it should have, namely to stimulate interest on the part of the French in her case; a result which in our view would be most undesirable. On the other hand if we stop this letter without reference to you we are, in fact, preventing Madame CARRE having visits and would thereby be disregarding the Home Office regulations referred to above.[24]

Tar also wrote to John Senter the same day as Liddell. A few days later, on 10 November 1943, VICTOIRE wrote to Tom Greene at his flat in Cranmer Court, Chelsea, inviting him to come and see her, enclosing a visiting order and signing the letter, 'Always affectionately, your poor little cat.'

The serials to which Hale referred were letters sent by Sir Charles Hambro of SOE to Sir Frank Newsam on 28 August 1943, and from Harry Sporborg to Sir John Moylan on 1 October 1943 respectively. In the former, SOE expressed their opinion on the cancellation of VICTOIRE's transfer to the Isle of Man, saying:

> As you know, we regard it of really vital importance from a security point of view that this lady should be held in effective detention of the nature originally agreed upon and, as I explained in my letter of the 24th August, the arrangements at Holloway are not of this character, in that the she has full facilities for the communication with persons who are likely to be released. I should be very relieved to receive your assurance that she will be moved as soon as possible either back to the Special Wing at Aylesbury or to some other place where suitable arrangements can be made for her to be kept separate from persons likely to be released before the end of the war.
>
> I think that the importance of the case from the security point of view is fairly outlined in my previous letter but if you thought a meeting would be helpful I should be very happy to come and see you upon this matter.[25]

In the latter, Sporborg reminded Moylan that VICTOIRE's case had been discussed at a meeting of the Security Executive at Kinaird House on 15 September that was chaired by Duff Cooper and attended by John Senter and himself. He reiterated his plea at that meeting for her transfer from Holloway into 'effective detention' whereby she would be prevented from associating with other detainees who might be released before the end of the war, saying:

> As you know, we are very anxious about this case for the reasons set out in Hambro's letter of the 24th August, and although we are aware of the difficult administrative problem caused by segregating 'VICTOIRE', we regard it as essential to press for this. I shall therefore be most grateful if you will let me know that steps for the effective segregation of this enemy agent will be taken.[26]

He felt that it was no longer necessary to have Guy Liddell present at the meeting Hambro had called because the discussion they had had on 15 September was sufficient and that the minutes of that meeting had clearly stated their position.

Mary Stanford had also written a letter to Hinchley-Cooke on 21 February 1944, saying that VICTOIRE had told her that she had been brought over to England to work for the 'British War Office, M.I.5. Deptartment [*sic*]', but referred to them as '*ces salauds de gens du War Office*' ('those bastards in the War Office') during a stamping and crying fit after they had stopped her allowance. It is interesting that although VICTOIRE claimed not to know any English, when excited 'it became so obvious that she knew English quite well that she finally gave up the pretence, and used, or openly understood it, whenever it suited her'. Stanford wanted to know why VICTOIRE was still receiving money from MI5 and, if she was supposed to be the same as the rest of the internees, why weren't they all getting such benefits? She drew the only obvious conclusion – that VICTOIRE was still working for MI5. That being the case, Stanford asked, 'could you please be so kind as to find someone more reliable and scrupulous, less irresponsible and therefore more suitable to fill the post in her place?' She thought it a 'low method of doing things', adding:

> She either (a) has a hair-raisingly colourful imagination or (b) has no common sense or discretion as to what kind of stories about herself it may be wise or unwise to relate in a community of already rather nerve-wracked women, or (c) she is non compos mentis, and therefore not accountable for what she says or does.[27]

The matter of VICTOIRE's general behaviour towards her fellow detainees obviously rankled so much with Stanford, who was speaking not just for herself but for others, that she delivered what appears to be an ultimatum to MI5:

> if it should prove impossible to get full satisfaction from Members of Parliament or yourself, I have decided to ask friends outside to send me the lawyer who is the most competent and experienced in dealing with such matters and with all the elements necessarily involved.[28]

Miss Mellanby had duly forwarded Stanford's letter to MI5. A note on the forwarding slip addressed to Harmer, initialled by John Marriott and signed by Hinchley-Cooke, states: 'Please see the attached letter from Margaret Stanford regarding 'Victoire'. If what this woman says about your pet is correct, we may find ourselves in some difficulty. We may even be faced with a question in the House.'[29] The note and letter had also been seen by Guy Liddell and Milmo, who added, 'I think this needs discussion.' Exactly what discussion took place or what action was taken is not included in VICTOIRE's files.

Sporborg wrote to Sir John Moylan, under-secretary of state at the Home Office, on 13 March 1944 to express his concern about 'certain facts ... which fill me with alarm' which he felt compelled to raise. He had just seen copies of the letters VICTOIRE had sent to Dr Herbert and Inspector Gale which Tar had passed to Ian Roy at the Home Office in which she hoped they would visit her in Holloway. Sporborg began his letter by saying that he thought the matter of her future custody for the remainder of the war had been settled once and for all. He also thought that any such visits were entirely at the discretion of the Home Office and said that it would be a 'most serious mistake to alter the position now and to allow her this privilege'. To allow her to have visitors, 'however respectable ... [they] might be ... it would be impossible to avoid giving her the chance of doing harm to this country, and in particular to certain people who are serving it overseas'. As to her being allowed to write letters:

> I cannot help feeling that she is lucky to be allowed to write letters at all, in view of the fact that, according to her own story she worked for the Gestapo and caused the arrests (and subsequent torture) of many persons at their hands. She can hardly be entitled to expect lenient treatment, or indeed, consideration of any kind at the hands of the British authorities.[30]

On the note sent to Tar by Major the Honourable Thomas Gabriel Roche, SOE's assistant director of security, Tar wrote, 'I am really appalled at this effort.'

On 22 February 1944 VICTOIRE wrote again to Detective Sergeant Louis V. Gale, now an inspector, again addressing him as '*Ange Gardien*' and saying that since she was back in London and that another prisoner had received visits from a 'police official' whom she had met at the airport when she had arrived in Britain, perhaps he would care to come and visit her. She went to great pains to impress upon him that her opinion of him had never changed – 'I always remember you with kindness to me'; nor was she annoyed with him – 'as I supposed that you were only following the rules laid down'. She closed by saying, 'in the twenty months I have been detained I have never had a single visit, I'm sure you'll understand how much pleasure a visit from you would give me'. She also wrote to her friend Dr Herbert in a similar vein, saying that she was fed up just seeing the other detainees and prison staff and was sure that 'neither you, nor, perhaps Anna, would mind coming to see me now and then'. The envelope in her file states that these were 'Original letters from VICTOIRE in respect of queries that are outstanding with the Home Office'.[31]

There is no indication in her files whether Inspector Gale visited her in Holloway or that MI5 or Scotland Yard tried to block him as they had earlier. However, Dr Matheson, the governor of Holloway, wrote to MI5 wondering whether it was all right for Dr Herbert to visit her not in a professional capacity but simply as a friend. Commander John Senter at SOE told Tar, 'You may certainly take it that we should hold the view that the correspondence of this woman is undesirable,' and asked that he should provide the Home Office with some guidance on this, which SOE would support.

Another person to whom VICTOIRE had written on 3 February 1944 and with whom MI5 was anxious that she should not start a correspondence was Mlle Simone Mousseigt – Simone Marie Antoinette Mousseigt (1921–2012), a member of Platoon I, B Company, of the Forces Françaises Libres based in Guildford, Surrey, who had recently been released from Holloway. She had escaped from France by crossing the Pyrenees on the night of 17/18 February 1943 and arrived in England in June of that year. Tar wrote to Ian Roy at the Home Office about it as well as John Senter at SOE but did not feel that they could hold up the letter. Mousseigt later married Claude Félix Saint-Genis, a French Marine Commando and graduate of St Cyr, the French military academy, who had arrived in Liverpool on 4 January 1944, having worked for the BCRA in Algeria.[32] She died at Salies-de-Béarn in the Pyrénées-Atlantique département on 26 September 2012. It is not known how VICTOIRE came to know her.

On 7 March VICTOIRE wrote the following letter to Hinchley-Cooke, a copy of which she intended to send to the Home Office:

I add here certain addition for you, connected with the seven requests I took the liberty of addressing to Mr. H. Morrison.

No.1. It is true no reason was ever given to justify my detention. During my arrestation [sic] you found one (Duvernay or Duvernais) a 'verbal' reason which you know better than I, is not a reason.

No.2. I only wish to explain anything which may seem strange to you, if there is something to explain. This I remember perfectly that only one person who did not make a reproach but a more objection one day in connection with the work of the Gestapo. It concerns Mr. UTZINOFF [Ustinov]. I beg of you urgently Colonel to allow Mr. UTZINOFF to come and see me for his objection may fall immediately in the face of certain details I can give him now, and if this objection is present in my mind somewhat too scrupulous and in vain search of what (or who) could accuse me, is any case these details can be of use to Mr. UTZINOFF for his study of the Gestapo.

No.3. Depends more on you than on the Home Office!

No.4. Why, Colonel, do you forbid me all correspondence and all visits?
You know very well whom I wish to see. They are all people more or less in
your entourage, or that little French girl who was with me here under detention
for a few months. Furthermore my internment in England since I have been at
Holloway cannot remain unknown to my family – as I was promised.

Nos.5,6,7. I can only still and always hope.

I wish that one day, Colonel, I may receive some satisfaction which ever it
may be ... and I remain,

Yours always devotedly,

Ly Carre.[33]

The numbered points, which were written in Roman numerals in the version
of the letter written to Herbert Morrison, referred to:

1. The reasons why she had been interned;
2. A request to face a Tribunal or a Committee (such as the Lindley Committee)
   to explain herself;
3. A desire to be allowed to take up a nursing position in England, since she was
   not going to be allowed to be repatriated to North Africa;
4. An agreement on correspondence and visits, and asking whether she
   was under the same regulations as the other detainees 'or under a special
   inhumane one which I wish to know of';
5. A request for a 'careful and serious examination' of her eyesight, which she
   claimed was getting worse;
6. A request to visit her dentist, Miss Waterson in Park Lane; and
7. A request to have a wireless set installed so that she could alleviate the strain
   on her eyesight.

Duvernoy (also spelled Duvernoit) mentioned in point 1, was one of
VICTOIRE's links with the French Deuxième Bureau in Vichy and had once
been engaged in espionage in Italy for the French. He had also been a member
of the WALENTY organisation[34] who had appeared when she had gone to
the Café Pam-Pam with Bleicher on 19 November 1941 (see Chapter 11).
WALENTY had commented in his review of Part III of VICTOIRE's memoirs,
'I am amazed that the secretary of LN was ready to betray his organisation after
5 minutes' (see comments in Chapter 19). VICTOIRE followed up her letter to
Hinchley-Cooke of 12 March with another letter to Tom Greene complaining

to him that she was the only detainee in Aylesbury not receiving any letters or visits – 'Oh! They do not really forbid it, but letters and "visiting orders" are stopped somewhere!' She continued:

It is now the 21st month that this situation prevails and I assure you that I am fed up, so fed up! … You do not know the pleasure it would be to see you again, for I'm perfectly certain you never wished me this present suffering … that you must know well that I have never done anything wrong.[35]

In keeping with all her other correspondence, MI5 forwarded copies to the Home Office and SOE. By April 1944, a 'Note on the Case of Madame Mathilde Lucie CARRE' dated 23 April by J.P.L. Redfern of SLB1 reported in the final point that:

S.O.E are continually pressing that VICTOIRE be kept incommunicado, due to the knowledge she has obtained about their activities. From LUCAS she certainly obtained a first hand knowledge of their policy in France and he may well have given her information about their headquarters organisation. There is no doubt she is a dangerous woman and it is clear that the longer she is kept in detention and prevented from receiving visitors the worse she will become. She has already stated that she intends to write her memoirs and expose the misdeeds of S.O.E.[36]

When the summer of 1944 rolled around, Captain Septimus Brooke-Booth, who had succeeded Kenneth Younger as assistant director, E Division (ADE), responsible for alien control and internment, received a letter from R.H. Rumbelow, under-secretary of state at the Home Office Aliens Department saying that 'Madame Carré is being informed that she cannot be allowed to send letters or receive visits and that her letters have been stopped.'[37] This was in response to letters Brooke-Booth had written on 28 July to Ian Roy at the Home Office Aliens Department regarding VICTOIRE's letters to the president of the International Red Cross.[38] In his letter of 8 July Brooke-Booth wrote:

As you will see, Mme CARRE is writing to the President of the International Red Cross and enclosing copies of her petition to the Home Secretary, dated 11th May, and of her letter addressed to the Governor dated 12th June. The writer appears to be complaining more of the physical conditions under which she is detained and or her state of health, than of the reasons for her detention, and I feel that the disposal of these documents should be left to the Home Office.

The point in which we are particularly interested is her suggestion to the I.R.C. that a delegate should visit her. As you know, the department who were employing Mme CARRE hold very strong views about her having any direct contact with the outside world. I have consulted them and they are adamant in their views that the I.R.C. delegate should not be allowed to visit her at Holloway.[39]

VICTOIRE's letter to the president of the International Red Cross contains mainly information about her physical condition – her eyes, teeth, general health – as well as the amount of money she receives, the fact that all her letters are being withheld – 'Somebody stops all my correspondence in England' – and that her detention is 'purely and simply solitary confinement'. She ends by saying, 'My last hope is in you and I ask you, I beseech you even, to do something for me. Whatever and however little it may be, it will be the only joy I have had for over two years.'

Her complaints continued well into 1945. A letter written to Hinchley-Cooke on 23 April 1945 (enclosing a copy of a letter to the Home Office forwarded by the deputy governor of Holloway) she bemoaned that:

The restrictions put into force by the Home Secretary since August 1944 go to such lengths that my life of complete isolation has become an existence without either sense or reason in the face of such stupidities as that which forbids the sending of a simple Christmas card to a detainee with whom I lived for two and a half years [Mathilde Krafft] or meeting with a saleswoman selling chiffon.[40]

According to the Home Office letter, this saleswoman was from 'the shop Jones (?) Bros' (possibly Dickins & Jones, then in Regent Street, or Jones & Higgins in Peckham, closed in 1980). She went on to claim that:

There has never been anything, either in my character or in my attitude, for rebuke ... My discretion has always been perfect ... You must realise that this can go on no longer and that it is absolutely essential that these [Home Office] regulations should be changed: it is really a scandal!

She also mentioned the 'K affair', a reference to Kraus and the reports she had read in the newspapers about his being in the UK, as well as asking that since Paris had been liberated whether she could receive news of her family. Whether she did is not known. Hinchley-Cooke scribbled a note at the bottom addressed to Masterman, 'I should be grateful if you would deal with the attached. As you are no doubt aware this was never my case beyond serving this woman with a Detention Order.'

On 30 April 1945 John Senter wrote to Masterman mentioning that LUCAS had returned to Britain, having been sent to Buchenwald.[41] According to Marcel Ruby, SYLVAIN, as LUCAS was now known, was captured on 25 April 1942, just three weeks after parachuting back into France on 1 April, and imprisoned first in Fresnes for eighteen months (ten in solitary confinement), then taken to Colditz Castle *not* Buchenwald, from which he was liberated by the Americans in 1945.[42] This is confirmed in Robert Bourne-Patterson's account of SOE circuits in France.[43] A letter on 2 November 1943 sent by LUCAS to Mrs Buxton of 156 Sloane Street from M-Stammlager VA, south of Ludwigsburg, Germany, explained to her that:

> After 18 months at Fresnes the Court has decided to consider us as prisoners of war and we are here temporarily until our final destination had been decided upon. Health of myself and my friends very good considering everything. I take the liberty of sending you the necessary label for a Red Cr. parcel. Letters and parcels will I expect be forwarded. I long to hear from you and do hope that you and your husband are in perfect health.[44]

He had been betrayed by the capture of documents carried by his courier, who was taking them to Virgina Hall (MARIE). Bleicher recognised the documents that had arrived on his desk as being in LUCAS/SYLVAIN's handwriting. This led to the arrests of other members of the *Autogiro* circuit: Roger Cottin; Leon Wolters, a Belgian sub-agent with whom SYLVAIN was living; Jack Fincken; Lieutenant Noël Fernand Raoul Burdeyron (GASTON), who had been a head waiter at the Dorchester before the war; Dr P. du Puy; SYLVAIN's brothers Philippe and Jean, and several others. Burdeyron, who had been dropped 'blind' on 9 July 1941 into Avranches with his radio operator XAVIER (Ernest Bernard, not to be confused with Major Richard Heslop, who was also code-named XAVIER), was arrested on 9 May 1942 and would end up in Colditz on 8 January 1944. As noted in Chapter 15, Abbott was sent to Fresnes and later to Colditz.[45]

John Marriott sent a note to Harmer on 5 January 1944 informing him that Buckmaster had received information 'from an unimpeachable source' that LUCAS, together with six or seven other members of his organisation, was in Stammlager VA, which Buckmaster thought was an overflow from Fresnes. A letter from Major Geoffrey Wethered to Major Richard Warden at SOE on 21 February 1944 referred to LUCAS's letter and mentioned that a Margaret Sample had been in touch with a Miss Waddeson about letters from the Stuttgart prisoner of war camp in which LUCAS was held. It is unclear just who Margaret Sample, Miss Waddeson or Mrs Buxton were.

Senter's letter added that LUCAS had somehow discovered that VICTOIRE was in prison although it was unknown who had told him. LUCAS was of the opinion that since her 'services to the British cause out-weighed her misdeeds' her continued incarceration was probably no longer warranted, and he wanted to see her. His aim was to find out more about Bleicher. It was pointed out to him that since she was known to be vindictive, setting her free would only cause harm to SOE and its officers. Senter proposed having a meeting with MI5 and SIS to discuss her case at their earliest convenience. He hoped that Bleicher would be taken alive, thus enabling them to learn more about his operations, in particular the truth about Roger Bardet and Jean Lucien Kieffer. He felt that it would be a good idea to find out from VICTOIRE exactly what she knew about Bleicher, but that LUCAS was not necessarily the one who should extract it. He also stressed that all those who had been imprisoned in concentration camps be treated gently 'until they have had some chance to recover'.

Harmer wrote to Masterman on 1 May from 104 SCI Unit, Rear HQ 21st Army Group, saying that Tom Greene was going to arrange a meeting between them and LUCAS, but he felt that interrogating LUCAS 'would serve no useful purpose' except to learn whether he had been told by the Germans whether BRUTUS was working for them. However, he thought it might be a good idea to ask casually whether he had heard anything about BRUTUS's escape. It would also be useful to find out the reason for LUCAS's arrest. He said that LUCAS should be questioned about it and shown the radio traffic that MI5 had passed through the VICTOIRE transmitter between March and July 1942, which was important in case VICTOIRE had slipped into the messages anything that might have revealed that she was now a prisoner of the Allies and working on their behalf. This would serve as a serious indictment against her and, while improbable:

If, for example, the Germans told LUCAS that VICTOIRE had secretly indicated that she was working for the Allies, he might be able, by reading the messages, to put his finger on the trap word or other method employed.[46]

It was important to debrief LUCAS about his movements 'from the moment he landed by parachute on 9th April 1942 until his arrest [sic]'. A preliminary report was provided on 21 April 1945. As far as VICTOIRE and her 'disposal' were concerned:

> The sooner she is handed to the French authorities the better. As time goes on, and particularly when the fighting ends, these cases will attract a great deal more public attention and if they go to trial, publicity. I think, therefore, that it is in the interests of all of us that VICTOIRE's case be disposed of by the French at the earliest possible moment. I think ~~we~~ you would be right to urge the Home Office to return her now.[47]

William 'Billy' Luke, writing to someone in VB5 at SIS (possibly Greene, R.C.S. Barclay or Bernard H. Townshend), felt that it would be inappropriate to ask VICTOIRE about a ring belonging to LUCAS that he had asked her to keep for him, and that they should not give her any indication that he was back in England. The ring bore an armorial crown with two bears rampant, according to Hinchley-Cooke's letter to the governor of Holloway on 11 May.

Hugh Astor attended a meeting at 58 St James's Street on 3 May with Dick White, Masterman, Major R.A. 'Tom' Wells of SOE's Bayswater Special Security Section (BSS), Bernard H. Townshend from SIS, and Luke, at which they decided that since the BRUTUS case was closed, and LUCAS had returned to Britain, 'we could raise no further objection to the Home Office deporting VICTOIRE to France'. Their main reasons for not deporting her had been: (1) to safeguard the interests of BRUTUS, and (2) to safeguard the interests of LUCAS, who was in German hands. Astor added:

> The representatives of both S.I.S. and S.O.E. pointed out that VICTOIRE could cause considerable mischief if she were at liberty, both in this country and in France, but they agreed that if she were deported to France one could safely assume that she would be kept in safe custody by the French.[48]

Astor further reported the following day that, nevertheless, the Home Office 'should at the same time be requested to inform us if and when they decided to make the deportation'. That being the case, he would inform Captain Vaudreuil that deportation was imminent. Captain François Thierry-Mieg alias Jacques Vaudreuil, head of France's BCRA counter-intelligence unit, was based at Wigmore House, 10 Duke Street, London.[49] Lieutenant Colonel the Honourable Thomas Gabriel Roche of SOE wrote to Astor on 10 May to express that:

> Now that hostilities have come to an end we cannot say such detention is essential on operational grounds. We are of course apprehensive that this lady may seek vengeance against various persons who have worked for us. This risk however would not be decreased by further detention and it is clearly impossible to ask for life long detention on such grounds.[50]

There would therefore be no objections on the part of SOE and they would leave it up to Home Secretary Herbert Morrison to decide when to deport her. The French Security Service would also be thoroughly investigating her case. Astor duly informed Vaudreuil, who asked for two days' notice of any deportation and informed him that Captain Ponsard would be taking over the case.

CHAPTER 23

Disposing of the Body

It was clear that once hostilities ceased VICTOIRE should be deported and handed over to the French but, as Squadron Leader Hugh E. Park, SOE's head of General Security pointed out, not 'until the French are ready to make suitable arrangements for her reception'. In 1944 decisions were already being made about what to do with her, with November and December 1944 seeing a flurry of correspondence between MI5, SOE and the French. D.I. Wilson, John Marriott and Captain Brooke-Booth of MI5 met with Sir Frank Newsam, under-secretary at the Home Office, on 14 November 1944 to discuss the VICTOIRE case. Wilson explained to Dick White and Hugh Astor that:

We considered it desirable that her deportation should not take place immediately because we had no control over what the French might do. They would certainly interrogate her, and might make her the subject of a trial to which publicity would attach, and in the course of the interrogation or trial facts might come to light which would prejudice the position of BRUTUS as a B.1.a agent used for operational purposes, or alternatively might further endanger the life of LUCAS who was believed to be a P/W in Germany.

Sir Frank agreed that in view of what we had told him VICTOIRE should remain in detention until our objections to her return to France had ceased to apply. It was also agreed that in view of the breaking up of the Bridge Party she would have to be associated with the other inmates of Holloway, but that M.I.5. would be afforded as many facilities for controlling her correspondence and visitors as was possible.

Sir Frank added that for the purposes of replying to the letter from the Home Office dealing with the question of the deportation it would be sufficient if we stated that, for reasons given verbally to him, this lady must continue to remain in detention for the time being, and we need not put the details in writing.[1]

Tar added a note at the top of Wilson's letter asking him, 'Will you please let S.I.S., S.O.E, the Polish and C.H.H. [Harmer] the decision in this matter.'

R.H. Rumbelow of the Home Office Aliens Department wrote to Brooke-Booth on 30 November to say that Holloway was able to accommodate all the women in 'E' Wing in the so-called 'flat'. At the time he wrote, Carré (VICTOIRE) was already there, along with the Duchesse de Château-Thierry and Stella Lonsdale. The others in 'E' Wing were: Manchello, a 12(5A) awaiting deportation; Pachitto, an 18(BA) case being sent to Cuba; Mitzi Smythe, 'an old 18B friend' who had been an active Fascist in the 1930s; Jessie Jordan, interned under the (Royal) Prerogative; and Brouwer, an Article 5A case.[2]

On 18 December 1944 John Marriott wrote to Christopher Harmer, now the Officer Commanding (OC) 104 SCI Unit, Main HQ 21st Army Group, British Liberation Army (BLA) to say that VICTOIRE's file had been handed over to Capitaine De Couëdic, head of the Service de la Sécurité Militaire (SSM) of the French provisional government in Britain – which had replaced the earlier Bureau des Menées Anti-Nationales (BMA) – based at Wigmore House, 10 Duke Street, 'who may by now have forwarded it to Paris. I observe that you find difficulty in seeing any reason for keeping VICTOIRE further in the U.K. but you will remember that the decision to keep her here was taken as a result of urgent representations by the Twenty Committee, who were anxious for the BRUTUS case to be kept in existence.'[3] De Couëdic had written to D. Ian Wilson in B1b regarding the VICTOIRE case.

In January John Marriott wrote again to Harmer expressing his and Desmond Bristow's surprise that Vaudreuil and not Verneuil had been the 'selected confidant'. As he understood it:

> We had always agreed (a) that when the French were told about VICTOIRE they should be told not in an unofficial manner, but formally with a dossier of her case, and (b) that you should tell one selected French officer about the facts of BRUTUS qua Special Agent. Course (a) has been pursued by us, and the only thing we wanted you to do you have done, namely tell Vaudreuil that BRUTUS is a Special Agent and ask him for his assistance in preserving its security.[4]

Marriott had written to Harmer in early January to say that 'we' did not agree with all of his premises or conclusions. Presumably, he meant the Twenty Committee, or the deception planners at the London Controlling Section (LCS) and Colonel Noel Wild. The LCS had been established in 1941 to coordinate all military deception plans, with Lieutenant Colonel John Bevan as its controller. Wild was head of Ops B at LCS and had been part of Operation *Bodyguard*. There was still the need to consult with LCS as well as Wild. Marriott requested that Harmer 'apprise the appropriate French officer of the facts of the BRUTUS case' and arrange that KIKI (Robert Kiffer) should not be prosecuted for the time being. KIKI was regarded as the greatest danger to the BRUTUS case, being the first man in the WALENTY organisation to be betrayed, and there was some doubt as to whether he had been working for the Germans all the time. He was currently in the custody of the French Police Judiciare.

Harmer replied to John Marriott on 28 February 1945 to say that the release of 'the people in France who had dangerous information' had brought them full circle with VICTOIRE and what to do with her. He added:

> I find it difficult to see quite what the French will be able to do with her now that they have released the other members of the organisation who collaborated with the Germans. The case of KIKI is one in point, since he was the first of them to go over to the Germans and give away the rest of the organisation. The fact that he subsequently did good work for the Allies is the identical argument which VICTOIRE will use when it comes to discussing the part she played in getting LUCAS out of the country.[5]

The issue now beginning to emerge was how VICTOIRE's case would be handled once she had been handed over to the French. Luke's report of 17 March 1945,[6] addressed to Masterman and Astor, cautioned about the 'dangers in handing her over which ought to be realised'. At their meeting on the 14th Hale had said that he was almost certain the trial of VICTOIRE would be held in camera but, as Luke pointed out, 'this in itself is not a complete safeguard against the proceedings becoming known to the public, as French ideas of "in camera" do not coincide with our own.' He further warned that since she might be tried at the same time as KIKI, information might emerge that BRUTUS had come over to Britain 'with a political mission from the Germans', something that KIKI had already told the French. It was also possible that 'he [KIKI] may have hinted – if he knew it – that BRUTUS came over with an espionage mission'. Someone, either Masterman or Astor, had pencilled 'He did', although it is unclear whether it meant that KIKI had hinted or that he knew about the espionage mission. Furthermore, 'VICTOIRE is as stupid in some ways as she is clever in others, and although she would be ill-advised to do so, she may insist on calling BRUTUS as a witness.' This would mean that under oath he would be forced to reveal his various activities before he escaped from the Germans and afterwards. In turn this could compromise the safety of his family and the past deception plans of British Intelligence (such as the role BRUTUS had played in Operation *Fortitude*).

Luke considered it:

> Most unwise to allow BRUTUS to give evidence, but I see no objection to his making a sworn statement over here of the circumstances surrounding his association with VICTOIRE, both before and after the Germans broke up the INTERALLIEE organisation.

Something else that might complicate matters was if VICTOIRE were to tell a different story to the one LUCAS had given the Germans when they captured him. This would then endanger him, as he was still a prisoner of the Germans at that point.

Other steps that Luke and Hale wanted to take seemed thwarted. Hale had wanted to talk to Vaudreuil about it, but Luke cautioned against it. Luke had wanted to talk to Harmer about it while he was on leave from France, but Dick White did not want to extend Harmer's leave. He therefore thought that Hale should have an initial chat with Vaudreuil and sought Masterman and Astor's agreement. A note was added later to the effect that Luke had met with Harmer while he was on leave, with Harmer agreeing that:

> Whilst there are certain risks in handing VICTOIRE over at this stage, nevertheless it is desirable that we should do so. He thought that the French should agree either to postpone the trial until after the war or else to arrange it to take place in secret. He said that KIKI had disclosed to the French that BRUTUS had come over to this country with the connivance of the Germans on an espionage mission and that it would be unwise for us to allow BRUTUS to be called as a witness at VICTOIRE's trial.[7]

Herbert Hart expressed his view that there was very little danger of the Germans discovering anything about the BRUTUS case, 'though no doubt VICTOIRE will tell her whole tale to the French authorities'. He also thought that the matter needed to be discussed with SOE and SIS, as well as informing the Home Office. In a note by Guy Liddell dated 1 May 1945 he expressed the view that:

Owing to the interplay between BRUTUS and GARBO before Overlord it was important to avoid blowing BRUTUS for as long as possible or at any rate until the cessation of hostilities and the capture or destruction of Abwehr and S.D. records.

GARBO was Juan Pujol García (1912–88), a Catalan who, together with BRUTUS, had played a pivotal role in the D-Day deception plans.[8]

A letter from 105 SCI Unit to Section VB at SIS on 13 April 1945 stated that Captain Kressmann had been asking for the name and address of Mathilde Carré's lawyer, and that her mother, Madame Belard, knew that she was in the UK because of a message broadcast on the BBC saying 'Pierre MARCHAND *embrasse la famille*' ('Pierre Marchand greets the family'). Exactly who had arranged this message is not given in the letter, but it had obviously been pre-arranged. 'Pierre' may actually refer to Pierre de Vomécourt (LUCAS). Townshend at SIS sent a reply on the 17 April giving the name of Mathilde's lawyer as Michel Brault, 'a lawyer of Polish extraction and member of the Franco-American Chamber of Commerce and Industry, who used to be permanently domiciled in Paris', and his address as 22 rue Raynouard, Paris.[9]

Major M. Ryde of B1a wrote to Luke on 28 May 1945 saying that the French were 'very anxious to take action in the Judicial Courts against the principal characters surrounding the VICTOIRE and BRUTUS cases ... which would involve the cases being heard in open court'. Trevor Wilson in the MI5 War Room expressed doubt as to whether it would be entirely possible to protect their interests with the cases being heard in open court. À propos of this, Luke wrote to Bernard Townshend at SIS saying that the case should be held in camera and he would discuss it with Colonel H.G. Trevor Wilson of MI6's Section V, described by Ben Macintyre as a 'jovial eccentric', and Captain Kressman (assistant to Vaudreuil) when he was in Paris at the weekend. After discussions with Guy Liddell, it was decided that Major Luke would accompany VICTOIRE on the flight to Paris, which was scheduled for Friday 1 June. Luke explained in his note that:

Colonel Robertson was not prepared to regard VICTOIRE as a War Room body since she had not been captured in the field, but Major Johnston [*sic*] has arranged matters through the War Office. VICTOIRE will go over as a prisoner of the War Office, although this fact will not be made known to her, or for that matter anyone else.

I have informed Capitaine Ponsard that she will be arriving at Le Bourget on Friday some time between one and three, and he will arrange my accommodation.

VICTOIRE's transport to the aerodrome is being arranged by Inspector (?) Garrett of Special Branch (Ext.325). [Detective Inspector Leslie Garrett, although the document from Special Branch gives his rank as Sergeant]

If there should be any slip-up in the reception arrangements for VICTOIRE I am to telephone Commandant HUGON at Trocadero 3279 in Paris; his address is 2 Boulevard Suhet [*sic* – should be Suchet].[10]

Major Mark Johnstone was with the War Room (WR-A) and had taken over from Geoffrey Wethered as liaison officer with SOE's Bayswater Special Security Section in 1945. Between July 1940 and February 1943 Capitaine Hugon (Hurel) was listed as being in TR 114 (Travaux Ruraux) in Lyons in a reorganisation of French counter-espionage, responsible for eastern France, Alsace, Switzerland and Germany.[11]

On 30 May a Deportation Order was sent from the Home Office Aliens Department to the Metropolitan Police Commissioner, Air Vice Marshal Sir Philip Game, to be served on 'Mathilde Lucie Carre @ La Chatte @ de Roche @ Victoire @ Marguerite de Roche'. On 4 June Luke filed his report, which explained that the handover of VICTOIRE to the French authorities on 1 June had not gone according to plan. He had accompanied her from Croydon airport to Le Bourget, where he found no one there to meet them. Under the impression that they were to pick her up from the airport, he contacted 'French Security Control', but Commandant Hugon, who he had phoned, knew nothing about VICTOIRE or her case. He concluded, 'Capitaine Ponsard's arrangements seem to have fallen down here.' Afterwards he had contacted Trevor Wilson and spoke to Peter (later Sir Peter) Hope, who said he would take care of things. Hope had been attached to MI6 in 1939 and had been involved with the formation of SOE. In 1941 he transferred to MI5 and was attached to Supreme Headquarters Allied Expeditionary Force (SHAEF) in 1944 to track down war criminals. While this was going on, one of the French security officers said that the Département de l'Intérieur was sending a car to take them both into Paris.

The car arrived three-quarters of an hour later with an inspector who also knew nothing about the case but had been given a 'heads-up' about her arrival. He reassured Luke that she would not be allowed to go free. Luke described the journey into Paris as 'hair-raising', although he offered no details as to why, but reported that one piece of VICTOIRE's luggage had gone missing. On arriving at 11, rue Cambereres, in the 8th arrondissment [*sic* – actually, rue Cambacérès, where the Inspection Generale Police Nationale is now located], near the Madeleine, Luke spoke with Monsieur Jean Bernhardt, commissaire divisionnaire at the Direction Surveillance du Territoire [*sic* – DST]. Hope then came over to pick him up. Throughout the entire trip to Paris VICTOIRE had not uttered a single word; now the only word that emerged from her lips was '*Salaud*' ('Bastard'). Luke explained:

> I went round to Warden's office (S.O.E.) and telephoned Capitaine Kressman who seemed to be somewhat perturbed that the woman had been met by the Departement d'Intérieur [*sic*]. It seems that there is some kind of a quarrel going on between the various Police and Intelligence departments in Paris, and they are very jealous of each other. I told him where he could find VICTOIRE, and also gave him the name of Mr. BERNHARDT.
>
> I had a long talk with Warden and Hope about the VICTOIRE case and its connections with BRUTUS. I told them that I considered it was essential that the trial of VICTOIRE should be held in camera, and they are going to write a joint letter to Colonel Chrétien on this subject.[12]

Major Richard Henry Atkinson 'Dick' Warden had been head of SOE's BSS since 1941 and was described by former SOE security officer Peter Lee as a 'wonderful character'; following the liberation of Paris he had been sent there to become their security officer.

On Saturday 2 June Luke and Hope lunched with Kressman and Vaudreuil and composed a letter 'which I think will cover all B.1.a's requirements'. Luke warned that:

> It is not by any means certain that the trial will be held in camera, but it will be made clear to Colonel Chretien that certain documents may have to be withheld if there is to be a public trial, and that BRUTUS will not be allowed to appear as a witness. Kressman and Vaudreuil are toying with the idea of informing the Prosecutor that he [BRUTUS] is dead, and whilst the method of procedure is not my concern I told them that I thought this would be a great mistake.
>
> VICTOIRE has arrived at an opportune moment because Kressman's department are keen to press the charges against KIKI and BARDET both of whom are at present at large. KIKI is a Lt Colonel in the French Army

and was recommended for the Croix de Guerre, but the recommendation was withdrawn when he was denounced as a collaborator. It is considered desirable that he should be prosecuted as soon as possible so as to clarify his position in the French Army.

On Saturday I told Kressman that in Harmer's opinion VIOLETTE should not be prosecuted, and I understand that there is now no question of this. Kressman wanted to know whether there were any questions which we wanted to ask ONCLE MARCO, and I said I would look into this on my return. I must ask Harmer.[13]

Colonel Jean Chrétien was the head of French counter-intelligence, Direction des Services de Documentation (DSDOC or DSDoc), who had previously supervised Services des Renseignements War (SR Guerre) activity in French North Africa.

Luke wrote to Bernard Townshend at SIS on 5 June to inform him of his meeting with Warden, Kressman and Vaudreuil about the prosecution of VICTOIRE and the letter being sent to Colonel Chrétien. After speaking with Harmer there were a couple of questions that he wanted answered and suggested that Trevor Wilson get Kressman to put them to ONCLE MARCO:

1. Was VICTOIRE entirely responsible for his arrest?
2. Had she any opportunity of warning him?

He also wondered whether it would help if they could provide a deposition from BRUTUS. Given her letter to Hinchley-Cooke, where she complained about her health, he thought it would be useful for Wilson to inform Kressman and the DST 'of the true facts, so that the[y] may be ready to meet her complaints'.

Some further evidence against VICTOIRE emerged that MI5 thought might help to corroborate other information they had on her. It may be recalled that on 27 November 1941 VICTOIRE had gone to see YOLÉ at his office, wearing a sling (see Chapter 11). The reason for the sling was later revealed by Luke, writing to Captain Vaudreuil, Major Richard A. 'Tom' Wells at SOE, and Major Desmond Bristow at SIS between 16 and 19 April 1945. In his letter to Bristow on 18 April Luke wrote:

I have had a letter from Wells of S.O.E. in which he gives some information about a conversation which Bourne-Patterson, of S.O.E.'s French Section, had with one Cadett, who used to be with their French Section and is now in Paris working for the B.B.C.[14]

This referred to a conversation Cadett had had with 'an old gentleman called Rene LEGRAND', who had mentioned 'Joel Letaq' [*sic*]. René Legrand was an old friend of his who had been a member of the Resistance and lived at 21, rue de Longchamps, Paris in the 16th arrondissment. Legrand said he had met VICTOIRE while he was working for the Resistance, when she came to see him one day and gave all the right passwords. She told him that it was very important that he should telephone a certain man whose number she gave him, insisting that he write it down. When he told her he could remember it without doing so, she became 'extremely insistent' so he eventually wrote it down very lightly on a map on the wall. When she left, he rubbed it out.

The next thing he knew, the Gestapo arrived and interrogated him about who he knew and the man whose number VICTOIRE had given him. Strangely enough, another Gestapo man went over to the map to look for the number but couldn't find it. Nor could the Gestapo find anything incriminating against him. Legrand told the SOE informant that as a result of VICTOIRE's activities, fifty members of the network were arrested and forty of them shot. Luke suggested to Vaudreuil that it might be useful to interview Legrand and get a statement that could be used in the case against VICTOIRE.

Lieutenant Colonel Robert Bourne-Patterson also confirmed the story in a letter to Buckmaster written on 15 February 1945. He told of a meeting he had had with Tom Cadett of SOE the previous evening. Thomas Tucker-Edwardes Cadett (1898–1982) had joined SOE's F Section in 1940, having covered the German invasion of France for *The Times* as chief Paris correspondent. Cadett later worked for BBC Radio as their correspondent in Paris. He worked for SOE until 1942, during which time he had recruited Georges Bégué. Marcel Ruby's book *F Section SOE* states that Cadett was running the section in 1941 (until 1942) when Bégué and LUCAS were dropped into France.[15] Cadett was also present at the official surrender by General Jodl at a schoolhouse in Reims on 7 May, the advanced HQ of General Eisenhower, as well as reporting from Hitler's bunker in Berlin on 9 May 1945. Cadett had been to see an 'old gentleman of some 60 years of age' who was a friend of his. During their conversation he suddenly mentioned 'Joel Letaq' [*sic*], who had been involved with the OVERCLOUD network (this was Jöel André Letac (1918–2005), mentioned earlier). Cadett's 'old gentleman', mentioned in a report by 'Tom' Wells of SOE, was René Legrand @ YOLÉ.

Legrand, who worked for the Compagnie Générale des Colonies, 282, Boulevard St Germain, Paris, in the 7th arrondissement, had met Cadett at a cocktail party in Paris in November 1944 and they had seen each other four or five times after that. He was the uncle of a girl 'married to one BERGE [Captain Georges Roger Pierre Bergé (1909–97)], who was recruited by Cadett in 1941 for Operation SAVANNAH' – the first attempt by SOE to insert Free French paratroops into German-occupied France between 15 March and 5 April 1941. As Luke noted to Bristow:

> Rene LEGRAND is of course well known to us, and appears in Harmer's famous summary of the VICTOIRE case. On her own confession, on November 23rd 1941, VICTOIRE was questioned by the Germans about three people (YOLÉ, MIKLOS and Robert POULAIN). On November 24th she rang up these three to make appointments to carry into effect a provocation which had been agreed upon with the Germans.[16]

Luke revealed to Bristow that when VICTOIRE had gone to meet with YOLÉ, MIKLOS and Robert Poulain, 'On each occasion she was allowed to make the visits alone with her arm in a sling, which was the excuse for asking them to write down any information or messages they wanted to send to London.' In his biography of Mathilde Carré, Lauran Paine cites Renée Borni (VIOLETTE) as saying that *Interallié* had been in touch with a Frenchman known only as 'Yolo', who is obviously taken to be YOLÉ. Borni claimed that he was a double agent working for a special section based at the Hôtel Majestic upon whom the Germans relied heavily:

> He had never been caught, and Renée implied to Bleicher, for obvious reasons, that Mathilde, who knew this man well, had been protecting him.
> Bleicher confronted Mathilde at once. She admitted knowing Yolo, but scoffed at the allegation that she had been protecting him, and in fact offered to take Bleicher to the double agent's business address.[17]

The Hôtel Majestic on the Avenue Kléber is now the Peninsula Paris. During the war it was the headquarters of the Militärbefelshaber Frankreich (German military high command in France). The rest of the description in Paine's book follows the same story, except for saying in this case that Mathilde had a bandaged hand, and that 'Yolo' had written down the information, which Mathilde then gave to Bleicher. Mathilde is quoted as commenting, 'Well, Yolo had given them proofs of an excellent collaboration. He had played with both sides and that was too much. Now he was finished.' WALENTY denied that VIOLETTE had betrayed YOLÉ, MIKLOS and Robert POULAIN to the Germans:

YOLÉ supplied information about French shipping. It is ridiculous to say that VIOLETTE spoke about YOLÉ. The (her) report betrayed him, his pseudonym and the subject matter. VIOLETTE knew no personal details about YOLÉ. LA CHATTE continually stresses that she was blackmailed. LA CHATTE gives YOLÉ's address. It was easy for her to invent a story which rendered contact with him impossible – for instance, to give a fictitious date for meeting him in a café. As a matter of fact, we had arranged to use this explanation in case of a compromise.[18]

VICTOIRE describes in her memoirs 'Robert P', who is obviously Robert Poulain, and mentions his association with 'Pontiatewsky and Lubiensky'. Pontiatewsky was Prince Michel Casimir Pontiatowski (1922–2002), who later became one of the chief architects of the election of Valéry Giscard d'Estaing to President of France. He was described as an anti-Gaullist. At 21 he had joined the Free French and parachuted into occupied France. Lubiensky was Count Michael Lubienski, *chef de cabinet* (chief aide) to the Polish foreign minister Józef Beck. He became involved in a 'honey trap' with Betty Pack (1910–63), code-named CYNTHIA, described by *Time* magazine in her obituary on 20 December 1963 as the 'Mata Hari of Minnesota … who [used] the boudoir as Ian Fleming's hero uses a Beretta'.[19]

A document in VICTOIRE's file about Legrand seems to support Borni's allegation, as it contains information on Lafont (Henri Chamberlin), quoting from an interrogation report of Pierre Bonny (1895–1944) dated 16 April 1945.[20] Bonny had been a French police inspector who was a member of the French Gestapo, or Carlingue. The Carlingue, based at 93, rue Lauriston in the 16th arrondissement, worked with the Gestapo, SD and GFP between 1941 and 1944. The report alleges that 'Legrand @ Rene LORIS was paid 80,000 francs a month by the Germans and was controller of a gang connected with the paratrooping and parachuting Allied agents.' He worked at 84, Avenue Foch under SS-Hauptscharführer (Master Sergeant) Josef Placke, who was responsible for capturing agents who had parachuted into France. Placke was a Belgian born in Osnabrück-haste in 1897, described in Charles Wendel's file as:

Hauptscharfeuhrer
German; 33-36; fairly robust build; height 1m 75-1m 77; fair hair, going grey, brushed back; grey eyes; long face, pallid complexion; nose reddish blue colour from drinking, and slightly shriveled; sleepy appearance, yet very

active; looks like a detective. Civilian clothes sober and scruplulously tidy. Peculiarities: reeling walk; always agrees with one and then did what he liked. Languages: German and French (had lived in France for 10 years).

Seen: S.D., 84 Avenue Foch, Paris

Note: In charge of a group of some 30 French agents, having as his sector particularly the North and St. Quentin. Almost all these agents accompanied him to Nancy where they had requisitioned the brothels. At the end of July or beginning of August 1944 he was in Berlin and was decorated by HIMMLER for the work done by his French agents. Returned to Paris on the 16th or 17th August, and was just in time to leave for Nancy. With his men he arranged the arrest of many of the 'Normandie' organisation, also English and American airmen.[21]

Charles Wendel was an Austrian/Polish/German born at Merlebach, Lorraine, on 14 October 1913. His mixed nationality was because he was Austrian by birth, Polish after the First World War, and German in 1940 after the Anschluss, the German annexation of Austria, in 1938. His file states that from 1 October 1943 onwards he was working as an interpreter at the SD headquarters at 84, Avenue Foch, Paris. A note on him by Guy Liddell dated 10 January 1945 quotes him as saying that he had a reputation as a 'pitiless torturer'.

Chamberlin (1902–44), described by David Schoenbrun as a gangster, was the head of the French Gestapo who was shot by firing squad on Boxing Day 1944 along with Bonny. They had both been recruited by the Gestapo to root out resistants. Together they had recruited 'the most savage killers, torturers, and sadists in the French underworld'.[22] Another interrogation report on Charles Wendel[23] tells that 'Le Grand René' worked closely with 'Henri', an SD agent working under Placke. This 'Henri' must be Chamberlin. Wendel described 'Le Grand René' as a German agent and one of Robert Mansard's (or Mansac) chiefs, another SD agent working for Placke:

'Le Grand RENÉ' – Agent. Chief of PLACKE's Group.

French, aged 32–36, tall and strong, heavyweight boxer type, height 1m. 82–85, weight 90 kg., Brown hair. Sometimes wears dark glasses as a disguise. Sunburnt complexion, clean shaven, dresses very smartly, speaks French and a little German.

Seen: several times a month at 84, Avenue Foch, Paris (SD) up to August 1944. Last seen at Nancy on 30.8.44.

His mistress is a small woman about 1 m.47 in height, dyed hair. Shot herself in the leg when playing with a revolver.

Le Grand RENE penetrated escape organisations. He and PLACKE also seized all the material of a French resistance network destined for Algiers and London a few hours before it was to be despatched. Parachute landing points in the neighbourhood of St. Quentin and in the north of France were arranged by him and his men in collaboration with SCHROEDER's [sic] group.[24]

The report on Legrand concludes:

'Le Grand René' is presumed to be identical with RENÉ @ LE GRAND RENÉ, surname possibly OHL. In August 1943 he was in charge of a phoney escape organisation working in the Chateauroux area. The name of the organisation was 'L'ALLIANCE'.[25]

A 'Summary of Traces' in Wendel's file indicates no such network, that 'LE GRAND RENÉ' was difficult to identify, and there was 'N.L.T. [no living trace] under RENÉ'. However, the network *is* listed in Wendel's file under 'Resistance or Allied Intelligence Organisations Discovered by SD Paris' in an 'Interim Report on the Case of Charles Wendel' prepared by Camp 020, and in an MI5 interrogation report of Wendel dated 9 November 1944.[26] Mansard was described as:

French; about 23-25 years old; small build; height 1m 58-62; 56-58 kgs; black hair; sometimes wears glasses; bronzed complexion; full set of teeth; cleanshaven. Has a mania for gloves. Rubs his hands when speaking – very nervous. Gigolo type. Dressed rather too smartly. Shrill voice.

Seen at: S.D., 84, Avenue Foch, Paris 1943-44. Last time Nancy end August, with rest of PLACKE's group at 9, Place St. Eve.

His chief in the S.D. was 'Le Grand Rene'. His car as well as himself was [sic] always ready before 84, Avenue Foch, in case it was urgently wanted. Married, and wife with him at Nancy. She is average build, with freckles.[27]

The *Alliance* network was described as intended to unite all former senior French Army officers who, when ordered to do so, would rise against the Germans and fight. 'They were known as the soldiers of DE GAULLE-GIRAUD of tomorrow.' After the leader of *Alliance*, Colonel Léon Faye (1889–1945), was arrested on 16 September, Marie-Madeleine Fourcade (1909–89), code-named HÉRISSON ('Hedgehog'), whom Faye had met in Vichy in January 1941, took over from him until the network was rolled up in October/November 1943. When she died in 1989 she had the distinction of being the first woman to be buried at Les Invalides in Paris.

As noted above, the 'LE GRAND RENÉ' Wendel described was someone who was aged 32–36, not the 60-year-old known to Cadett, so he cannot have been the same person.

Schroeder was SS-Sturmscharführer (Regimental Sergeant Major) Richard Schroetder, whose office was at 84, Avenue Foch, the headquarters of Abt IV (Gestapo):

SCHROETDER, Richard   Sturmscharfeuhrer

German; 42-44; heavy build, (former wrestler); height 1m 70-72; weight 80-85 kg; grey hair, parted on the left, well cared-for, cut short; grey eyes – piercing, evil look. Wears glasses only when working, and then not always; occasionally wears glasses in town; large oval head, dull complexion, two or three teeth missing (often has trouble with his teeth), close-shaven; large, wrestler's hand; calm disposition; Prussian type; in civilian clothes wears a thick dark blue coat, almost black, with a belt, and a large felt hat. Takes at least size 44/45 in shoes (flat feet). Shrill voice, sometimes normal. Like all Prussians, counts on his fingers. Very well educated.

Seen: S.D., 84 Avenue Foch, Paris

Note:

Knows almost all Europe. Has worked in Riga, Salonica, Brussels, and Paris (84, Ave. Foch), S.D. Almost all the dossiers passed through his hands before the chief [Kieffer] saw them. Ardent worker for Germany. When he answered the telephone, gave his No. IV E 12, and never his name. Has the dossiers of all agents, with photo or No. When the 'Alliance', 'Normandie', 'Ajax' 'Grossfuerst', etc, organisations were hit so hard, it was the result of the labours of SCHROETDER and his agents. SCHROETDER knows the majority of agents working for the Germans, both S.D. and Abwehr, and they know him.[28]

Other names mentioned by Wendel appear interchangeably as BOB, an agent who he said had once worked for a British intelligence organisation but had been 'turned around', and Bob ROBERTS, also known as BOBBY, who he claims was an English ex-captain who had played a key role in the interrogation of English agents. He alleged that BOBBY had blown all the W/T operators known to him. In fact, Bleicher's file includes BOB in a list of the Resistance workers turned around:

KLEBER

BARDET @ ROGER

MARSAC @ END

VOLTERS

MICHELINE (Lilly CARRE) @ VICTOIRE @ LA CHATTE

Marcel ETASSE @ MARCEL

Renee BORNI @ VIOLETTE

Pierre SERRE

Claude JOUFFRET @ CLAUDE

Robert KIEFFER @ PAUL @ KIKI @ RAOUL

Capt. TCHERNIAWSKI @ ARMAND [sic]

Mlle. LAVIALLE [sic]

MARCEL (W/T operator)

PARKER @ Jacques DUFRESNES @ JACQUES

Louise MAINGOT @ LOUISE

BOB[29]

Both BOB and BOBBY would seem to tie with the identity of Captain John A.R. Starr, the brother of George Reginald Starr (1904–80), who was also an SOE agent.

—∞—

A poster artist living in Paris before the war, John Ashford Renshaw Starr (1908–96) served in Rouen in 1940 with the KOSB and then joined the Field Security Police in Nantes.[30] When the Germans invaded, he managed to escape from St Nazaire to England, arriving in Winchester, where he re-joined his unit. He later joined F Section SOE, trained at Wanborough Manor, and carried out several missions, the last being in the spring of 1943 when he parachuted into Lons-le-Saunier in the Jura region. He had been the leader of the *Acrobat* network around Montbéliard before being arrested and imprisoned in Dijon in July 1943, then transferred to Fresnes. While in captivity at the Avenue Foch he had begun a portrait of SS-Sturmbannführer (Major) Hans Josef Kieffer, head of *Abt.* IV E of the SD in Paris. Wendel's file describes BOB as:

English; aged 32-36; powerful, athletic build; height 1m 65; hair reddish fair, parted in middle and smoothed back; blue eyes with direct piercing gaze; dull complexion, normal nose, teeth slightly apart in front, small moustache; Well cared-for hands. Elegantly dressed in dark grey with air-force blue pull-over and bow tie. Clear, gay voice. Smokes a pipe a great deal and often speaks with pipe in mouth; speaks French and German, both with strong English accent.

Seen: 84 Avenue Foch, Paris.

W/T specialist. Draughtsman: also could draw a portrait from a passport photograph.[31]

One of Starr's (@BOB's) two radio operators who was captured was SOE agent Diana Hope Rowden (1915–44), code-named PAULETTE, who would later die at Natzweiler-Struthof on 6 July 1944;[32] the other was Lieutenant John Cuthbert Young (1907–44). When she was taken to the Avenue Foch, Rowden was confronted with Starr. As Peter Jacobs' book recalls, 'Whether Starr had been "turned" by the Gestapo is unclear but he survived the war when others did not.'[33]

MI5 reports state that Faye, BOB/BOBBY and 'an Alsatian woman' attempted to escape over the rooftops of 82, 84, and 86, Avenue Foch during an air raid but were apprehended two hours later.[34] This description matches the escape attempt made by Léon Faye (1899–1945), Starr (BOB) and Noor Inayat Khan (MADELEINE) on 25 November.[35] After being captured, Faye and Noor were first sent to Berlin.[36] Noor was later executed at Dachau concentration camp on 12 September 1944; Faye died in Sonnenburg penitentiary in West Prussia on the night of 30/31 January 1945. Starr was imprisoned in Sachsenhausen concentration camp in August 1944 but avoided execution because of a typhus outbreak during which he managed to escape and link up with some French and Belgian prisoners who had been released to the Red Cross. Young died in Mauthausen on 6 September 1944. After the war Jean Overton Fuller alleged that Starr had collaborated with the Germans and detailed the case in *The Starr Affair* in 1954.[37] An investigation by MI5 into his conduct concluded that there were no grounds for criminal prosecution. Interestingly, documents in Wendel's heavily weeded MI5 file relating to 'Bob Staar' [sic] dating from January 1945 were destroyed in 1961. This would seem to imply that perhaps there was more evidence on J.A.R. Starr, who was most likely the same person as 'Bob Staar', than MI5 wished to be made public.

CHAPTER 24

Strong Evidence from Many Sources

With the war coming to an end it was possible to bring over to England for interrogation some of the key persons suspected of betraying *Interallié*, as well as Bleicher once he had been arrested. It was hoped that doing so would shed more light on exactly who was responsible for betraying who in the *Interallié* network. Was VICTOIRE the only culprit, or were there others who were also guilty or culpable? Information gleaned from the interrogation of KIKI and those of VIOLETTE and Bleicher will be the subject of this chapter. The following question in an internal memorandum on Bleicher from Squadron Leader Beddard to Colonel Stephens at Camp 020 dated 9 July 1945 helped to clarify the role of VIOLETTE (Renée Borni):

Q.9. What exactly was VIOLETTE's part (Renée BORNI) after her arrest? What services did she render? What did she reveal which could have led to the arrest of agents of the group? Did the Germans in fact pay VIOLETTE 3,000 francs a month and why exactly? Was she working for them or was it merely to keep the promise made to ARMAND on his acceptance of a mission for the Germans?

A.9. Renée BORNI @ VIOLETTE directly after her arrest revealed to BLEICHER all she knew about the organisation, and denounced MICHELINE [VICTOIRE] of whom she was very jealous.

VIOLETTE took BLEICHER to the office about three minutes' walk from the Villa Léandre, where MICHELINE worked, and gave all the details necessary to effect her arrest. BLEICHER states that since MICHELINE was prepared to give away the entire organisation he had no further need of other assistance. However, VIOLETTE, who had always coded and decoded messages for ARMAND declared that she was prepared to do the same work for the Germans and she was consequently installed at the Katzensteg

['La Chattière' – the Cattery] at St.Germain where BLEICHER was also working and continued deciphering messages from November 1941 to March 1942.

To cover minor expenses (she was free to go by herself to St.Germain, or in company with the N.C.O. PROPST) she was paid Frs. 3,000 a month. By April PROPST had himself learned how to encode messages and BLEICHER was anxious to get rid of VIOLETTE, who was becoming more trouble than she was worth.

Major KAIZER [sic] and others spent most of their time making love to her and the situation was getting out of hand. Major KAIZER had proposed that VIOLETTE should work for him in some not very clearly defined capacity, and BLEICHER at this point stepped in and told her that in recompense for her past service she might return to her parents at Luneville, and this arrangement was finally agreed upon. This had nothing to do with the promises made to ARMAND and which, in fact, occurred much later.

BLEICHER states, however, that after his release from Fresnes, and before leaving for the Zone Libre, ARMAND went to Luneville to see VIOLETTE.[1]

A memo dated 18 February 1946 from B1a to Major Peter Hope, a security officer attached to the SIS station in Paris as a temporary first secretary, outlined the main points of the case against Borni, indicating that the French were considering charges against her:

(i)   That she was equally culpable with Mme. Mathilde CARRE in collaborating with the enemy and giving information which led to the arrest of a number of the persons working in a resistance organisation which had as its leader Armand WALENTY, (Wing Commander Ramon [sic] CZERNIAWSKI).

(ii)   That Mme. Renee BORNI was solely and directly responsible for the arrest of forty or fifty persons, including Mme. CARRE herself.

(iii)   That Mme. Renee BORNI disclosed to the Germans the code which had been used by WALENTY's organisation and thus enabled them to continue transmitting messages to the British Intelligence authorities, and that she herself acted as cypher clerk.[2]

The report further stated that British Intelligence had had ample opportunity to interrogate other members of the WALENTY organisation. In comparing Borni's case with that of Mathilde Carré, they had reached the conclusion that:

Although Mme. BORNI did undoubtedly collaborate to some extent under duress, the service which she rendered to the British Authorities prior to her arrest and the limits which she herself was able to place on the extent of her collaboration would justify the French Authorities in taking a merciful view of her actions immediately following her arrest at German hands.[3]

It went on to say:

Whilst there is no direct evidence to prove that Mme. BORNI supplied the Germans with the name and address of Mme. CARRÉ, and she herself under interrogation denied having done so, [Bleicher's evidence from his interrogations] may be considered to provide fairly strong evidence as to her guilt in this respect.

However:

There is strong evidence from many sources that Mme. BORNI betrayed no other member of the organisation and it is a fact that agents known only to her: M.DEFLY [HECTOR] for instance, head of the Sector H, and M.MARTIN, head of Sector G, both wanted by the Germans but both unknown to Mme. CARRE, escaped arrest. Mme CARRE, on the other hand collaborated wholeheartedly with BLEICHER from the moment of her arrest, to the extent of becoming his mistress and acting as a decoy for the capture of the remainder of the Organisation.[4]

Bleicher was reported to have said that VICTOIRE (Mathilde Carré) was 'insatiable in her treachery, prepared to denounce her nearest and dearest', adding that 'in all his experience he had never seen anyone who betrayed her friends with such cynicism and zest'.

As far as VICTOIRE's accusations were concerned – that Renée Borni had betrayed a number of agents, such as Legrand, Brault, Poulain, Lach and 'several other Poles' – Borni had denied them. WALENTY had also backed her up by saying that she had not known any of the personal information needed to be able to do so. The report said:

It is perfectly clear from the interrogation of BLEICHER and others, as well as from details of Mme. CARRE's memoirs, that Mme. CARRE was herself directly responsible not only for the arrest of these agents but also for the calculated betrayal of DUVERNOY, MARSCHAL, AUBERTIN, DeLYPSKY, FRANCE and others, as well as the leaders of related French Organisations, Mme DAMPIERRE and KRAUS and, by her own confession, for the betrayal of Henri ROUSEL. According to WALENTY's evidence she must also have been responsible for the arrest of the Poles JANOWSKI and his daughter Madeleine [also written as Magdalena], Paulette PORCHER and Mme. BRATOWSKA, as well as for the betrayal of BERTRAND and the agents known as 'COCO' and 'BOB' and the couple Le QUELLEC.[5]

The fact that Mathilde Carré had worked as WALENTY's deputy, whereas Renée Borni had been the cipher clerk, meant that Carré had been privy to much more personal information than anyone else in the organisation. Carré had claimed that any one of the above-named persons had been betrayed by Renée Borni, but this was unsubstantiated:

> Either by the evidence in the hands of the British Authorities, or by BLEICHER who records that it was 'thanks to Mme CARRE's hard work' that the Germans were able to liquidate almost the whole of the WALENTY Organisation, the total number of arrests being almost ninety in all.

It was also stated that when Borni and WALENTY had been arrested on 18 November 1941, the Germans had retrieved the organisation's new code, telegrams in code and *en clair*. Therefore, there would have been no need for Borni to betray this to them. By working for the Germans as a cipher clerk she had had the opportunity to make mistakes while sending messages, alerting the British to the fact that she was working under the Germans' control. It is questionable, however, whether these mistakes were picked up by the British, as SOE in particular was notorious for ignoring such things. Mathilde Carré had also made numerous mistakes, according to Borni, when she visited WALENTY in Fresnes. The report concluded:

> The British Intelligence Authorities do not regard her [Borni's] action in the circumstances as being culpable collaboration with the enemy, and they are satisfied that even under duress Mme. BORNI gave nothing away to the enemy which they would not have discovered otherwise.
>
> In short, it is felt that if Mme. BORNI disclosed the name and address of Mme. CARRE to the Germans she did the British Intelligence Authorities and the French nation a disservice, the gravity of which she cannot possibly

have realised at the time of the offence. It was, however, a case of consequential damage since the real trouble started only when Mme. CARRE allowed herself to be turned immediately into a double agent by the Germans.[6]

It was also felt that 'her subsequent actions under duress might now properly be condoned', saying there was no comparison between the 'grudging and qualified collaboration' of Borni and the 'whole-hearted craven and despicable collaboration' of Carré.

A November 1944 report on Borni by Harmer, who was then OC 104 SCI Unit, sent to Major Berding, OSS SCI 12 Army Group, sets out to establish whether she was guilty of the accusations levelled against her, or whether she should be exonerated on the grounds she claimed, which he said were:

a) That VIOLETTE did not voluntarily give away any agents.

b) That she worked for the Germans merely in connection with cyphering under duress.

c) That she may have given away the sypher [sic] and enabled the Germans to use it (this however, must be a matter of complete indifference because they found already encoded messages and could have worked it out for themselves).[7]

Harmer stated, 'I do not think that VIOLETTE's conduct is very culpable.' However, he added that during her interrogations she had provided very inaccurate information in terms of dates, which are 'hopelessly wrong'. He takes her to task over her claim that she had been in prison for three months, yet the house in which she lived was 'given up by the Germans in the early part of 1941'. Her other claim that she had enciphered messages sent within six weeks of the arrests were 'so patently capable of being checked that I cannot believe that VIOLETTE is deliberately lying and conclude therefore that it proves her to be an unreliable and inaccurate witness on questions of fact'.[8] The messages, he said, all had a basis of truth but were in some cases misinterpreted or muddled. He came to the following conclusions:

a) In the INTER ALLIEE [sic] organisation VIOLETTE was purely and simply a cypher clerk and her knowledge of the organisation and functioning of the service is very small.

b)   That the proximate cause of the arrest of VALENTIN [WALENTY] was the arrest of CHRISTIAN and VIOLETTE confirms that he had not been present at the party held a few days before to celebrate the anniversary of the setting up of the organisation. This point had previously been in some doubt.

c)   The statements made by LA CHATTE that VIOLETTE had identified her and given away the names of various agents including YOLE, MIKLOS and Robert POULAIN are untrue. VIOLETTE states that she had not known any of the last three agents.

d)   VIOLETTE was removed from prison to the house in the rue de Piteure about 31 Dec 41.

e)   She was never fully trusted by the Germans, this is borne out not only by her own statements that BLEICHER said that he did not trust her but also by the fact that various messages sent and received were not shown to her, this means that she was not sufficiently incorporated in the German service to be employed as their cypher clerk.

f)   The date of VIOLETTE's visit to VALENTIN's prison is obscure and further enquiries must be made about it.

g)   MARCEL, the wireless operator who the Germans employed when they were controlling the set, is at large in France at the present time.[9]

There were other recommendations too: such as her contact with the Germans after they had released her to go and live in Lunéville in March 1941, and the fact that she had been paid by the Germans, which he said was obscure. She had claimed that when she was arrested the Germans had confiscated 40,000 francs from her, which she tried to reclaim when she was released. Instead, they had offered her 2,000 francs a month in 1943 and 3,000 in 1944. This she denied 'for obvious reasons that this represented a payment by the Germans to her for services rendered', claiming that it was a partial payment for the money they had taken from her.

Harmer noted that VIOLETTE had admitted to receiving a visit from Eckert while she was in Lunéville in October 1941 [sic]; he had come to enquire whether she had any news about VALENTIN (WALENTY) and informed her that he had escaped. This initially appears to refer to the time when WALENTY was in England in October 1941, and not in 1942 after she had been released, but when Eckert asked how she had been living, she again made a claim for the Germans to repay her money. This means that it must have been in 1942. Clearly, Eckert had not been privy to the escape plan hatched by WALENTY and the Germans.

Keyser also visited her towards the end of 1943 to ask for any news she might have had of WALENTY (always referred to as VALENTIN in the file). In February 1944 GABY visited her, the details of which were set out in a CIC report by Otto Wirth dated 7 October 1944, referred to in the next chapter.[10] Just before Lunéville was liberated, and she was in hiding, the Germans came looking for her, arriving at the house of a Madame Durant at 31, rue Erckmann, although Harmer notes that the purpose of their enquiries was unclear. As there was no further useful information that MI5 obtained about WALENTY's visit to VIOLETTE in August 1942, Harmer noted:

> Indeed it seems too obvious that the result of her experiences with the Germans, the statements by VALENTIN made to her when he saw her, and the subsequent statements made about her by the Germans, has confused her so much that she is hopelessly muddled in her mind about the true position. Her faith in VALENTIN remains unflinching and she is certain that he would never assist the Germans in any way. I[t] is, however, on this aspect of the case that further investigation is necessary.[11]

This 'further investigation' involved letters she told Harmer she had at her home, letters that the Germans had written to her that she was prepared to make available to him. Once Harmer had seen the letters, and obtained an account of WALENTY's side of the story, 'it will be possible to come to a more definite conclusion on this side of the case,' he wrote.

Later in the report Harmer commented that VIOLETTE's account of why she was arrested in Lunéville 'was so illogical and confused that I gave up trying to understand it', adding, 'It seemed that an investigation with the F.F.I. as to why she was on their suspect list would be much profitable as a basis on which to question her further.' Harmer informed Captain Brown, OSS SCI Unit Detachment, 12 Army Group, that he did not consider her a security problem 'merely on her conduct in connection with her collaboration in the INTER ALLIEE affair'. He recommended that:

a) She should be returned to NANCY forthwith where she had proposed that she should live at the house of Dr. William JACKSON, a friend with whom her fiancé is staying. She should be required to undertake not to return to LUNÉVILLE or to move from NANCY without permission.

b) That she should be officially escorted to LUNÉVILLE to collect the letters she received from the Germans and any other documents she may have of interest.

c)   That enquiries should be made from the F.F.I. as to why she was arrested and whether there has been evidence of her working for the Germans in LUNÉVILLE.

d)   That Mme DURANT, 31 Rue Erckmann, LUNÉVILLE, be questioned as to enquiries made by German officers about VIOLETTE and her whereabouts just before the liberation of the town.

e)   That I should have the opportunity of conducting a further interrogation in just about a fortnight's time when material on record in London will also be available.[12]

Further information on VIOLETTE and her arrest can be found in the next chapter.

Harmer thought that the most likely source of the break-up of *Interallié* was a 'male agent who collaborated with the Germans and was released by them. He was MARCEL, the wireless operator and was seen in Paris by VIOLETTE in 1944.' He listed MARCEL's description, and his real name as François Tabet. Whether the letters to which Harmer referred ever came to light is unknown as they are not found in any of the MI5 files consulted.

KIKI had been arrested and was in the hands of the Police Judiciaire. His arrest came as a result of his crossing with Boudet through the German lines near Livarot, close to where the British forces were located, on 18 August 1944, according to a report by Captain O.H. Salmon of the RVPS, dated 29 August 1944. There they contacted an intelligence officer with the Canadian 7th Armoured Division. Afterwards they had returned to Le Mesnil-Germain, a village in the Calvados département of Normandy, to instruct Le Vivier (probably Jack Vivier), chief of the sub-group, to prevent the Germans from blowing the bridge across the stream. When they returned to the Canadian lines Kieffer was taken to Army Headquarters at Hombly. A week later Buckmaster came to see him.

It is unclear to which Boudet Salmon is referring. In a look-up list in Kieffer's MI5 file, Boudet was listed as '*chef de groupe*' in Courson in the Calvados département, although it is appended by the initials 'NLT' – 'no living trace'.[13] Another document in the same file refers to him as being head of Group VI in Courson. This may have been Albert Boudet, a florist at Ducey, Lower Normandy, who from July 1943 was a member of the FTPF (Francs-

Tireurs et Partisans Français) in Redon, Brittany under Louis Petri. The
FTPF was a Resistance group formed by the French Communist Party. There
is also a Louis Boudet listed as being a member of the FTPF.[14] A Madame
Boudet is also mentioned in Salmon's report as having been arrested with
Madame Hautechaud (*née* Andrée Eynard) sometime in June 1944, most likely
after D-Day, as there are mentions of a timeframe 'some while afterwards',
in reference to an earlier mention of 'some while before the Allied invasion
of Normandy'. In Salmon's report there are mentions of various towns in
Normandy, which would fit in with Albert Boudet. Other contenders for
Boudet – Victor Boudet (b.29 January 1896 in Paris) who was liberated from
Dachau on 20 October 1944 (his number at Natzweiler is given as 24089);[15]
Pierre Boudet as a member of the *Éleuthère* network in Bordeaux, as well as
Marcel Boudet, code-named 'Marc', who was deputy head of the *Éleuthère*
network in the Marne from September 1943 until 31 December 1944[16] – must
be eliminated as they do not fit the profile in Salmon's report. The *Éleuthère*
network was part of the Liberation-Nord movement founded in 1942 by
writer Hubert de Lagarde. There was also a Henri Beaudet, who worked in the
same network as Dr Hautechaud (see below),[17] but since Boudet is mentioned
several times, it must the right name.

At this point there is what appears to be a major discrepancy in the
documents found in Kieffer's (KIKI) MI5 file. On the one hand, he was
taken from Arromanches to Newhaven by LCI-379 (Landing Craft Infantry)
on 26 August 1944, from where he was escorted by Sergeant Murray of the
Field Security Police to 32 Weymouth Street, London W1, a hostel used
by F Section SOE agents waiting to go on missions to France.[18] This is
supported by:

(i)   A letter from Captain T.F. Miller of SOE to Colonel [H.J.] Baxter of
      MI5 (London Reception Centre, B1d) which stated that 'the above
      named Frenchman arrived this morning at Newhaven from Normandy
      [26 August 1944], escorted by Sgt. Murray of 65 S.F. Section [*sic*][19]
      ... He has accordingly been R.L.L. [Refused Leave to Land] and is
      being held in one of our safe houses pending interrogation.'[20] That safe
      house was probably 32 Weymouth Street, in Marylebone, listed as a
      hostel for France-bound SOE agents,[21] referred to by Roy MacLaren as
      the 'mad house'.[22]
(ii) The Travel Document and Way Bill for Kieffer's trip to England.[23]
(iii) The MI5 internal memorandum from Miss O'Callaghan to Captain

Milton arranging for KIKI to be interrogated at 10.00 a.m. on Monday 28 August 1944;[24] the RVPS report states that he arrived there on 28 August 1944.

(iv) WS Form 4 (b): 'Form for Particulars of Aliens Sent to London for Further Interrogation';[25] and

(v) Salmon's report, which concludes:

> KIEFFER personally made a favourable impression. He seems to be intelligent, sincere, and competent. I do not consider that the 'Jean' and 'Michel' episode [Kieffer's so-called first but unidentified Resistance contacts] gives us anything to go on, nor do I consider that the doubts concerning Roger BARDET need by [sic] held against KIEFFER since the LOUBA [Jacques Henri Frager] set up appears to have been in a permanent state of intrigue and private dispute. I therefore recommend the release of KIEFFER, so long as no adverse information is forthcoming.[26]

On the other hand, he still appeared to be being held in France, as witness the various meetings held between MI5 and SOE early the following year. However, there *were* plans to return him to France. Miller's letter saying, 'It is desired to send him back to the Field at the earliest moment' and the suggestion that Baxter see KIKI through the 'side door' imply that he was indeed returned, at least to the French authorities, if not to 'the Field' shortly thereafter, although no document exists in his file to confirm this, nor the date when he was returned. It may also be significant that he was shipped over in a landing craft rather than a military aircraft, although at the time this may have been the only transport available. Another document, dated 27 August 1944, is an SOE form for returning him to the field 'shortly as a double agent'.[27] The form, which appears to be simply a Registry form, contains many initials and abbreviations, and gives no indication concerning KIKI's repatriation. However, a Note to File from the LRC signed by Miss O'Callaghan, dated 5 September 1944 with the heading KIEFFER @ MICHEL suggests that perhaps he was returned to France on that date: 'This man was landed under the name of MICHEL on 5.9.44.'[28] Confirmation can be found in a letter to Major Mark Johnstone, who had replaced Major Geoffrey Wethered as MI5 liaison with SOE, from Major John Delaforce of SOE dated 10 November 1944 in which Delaforce states:

Investigations in the Field have revealed that the above French Section ~~accredited~~ agent [Robert Kiffer] has been found on his own confession to have been working for the enemy for some time.

It will be recalled that this agent, who figured in the VICTOIRE case, came to this country after D–Day and returned to France on 27th September, 1944. At present he is in the hands of the French in Paris, and a full report is expected later, when you will receive a copy.[29]

Scrawled underneath is a pencilled note, 'B1B Mr. Wilson [D.I. Wilson].' Exactly what MI5 or SOE proposed to do with him as a double agent is not revealed, nor why – if they were anxious for there not to be a public trial in France – they did not keep him in England, thus avoiding the problems they anticipated.

Ian Wilson sent a report to Major Warden at SOE on 16 November 1944[30] containing information about Kieffer given by WALENTY and VICTOIRE. In it he cited WALENTY as claiming that Kieffer's arrest was the direct cause of the break-up of *Interallié*. Had he been less talkative the organisation might have been saved. 'It seems clear that through information obtained from first KIKI and then CHRISTIAN, the Germans were able to arrest WALENTY and the other principal members of his organisation on 18.11.41 and subsequent days.' CHRISTIAN, while not made to talk, apparently had 'essential addresses or telephone numbers' which the Germans found in his possession. One of these was undoubtedly WALENTY's, which led to his arrest. After that, KIKI was 'cooperating whole-heartedly with the Germans … [and] expressed himself satisfied with his new life,' according to VICTOIRE, 'although on other occasions he appears to have had attacks of conscience'. Since he was at liberty, Wilson presumed that this was 'because he had originally been responsible for the break-up of the organisation', Wilson also said that ADAM had doubted that KIKI would have worked for the Germans:

> but there is strong supporting evidence for VICTOIRE's statement that he did work for the Germans because, in the wireless traffic sent under the German control when they were operating the WALENTY transmitter, they offered on 14.12.41 to send KIKI (referred to as DESIRE) to the Free Zone to await a parachutist bringing money. This clearly suggests that by that time, they were prepared to use KIKI and had complete confidence in him. According to VICTOIRE, some time early in 1942 KIKI was sent off to Normandy where, at the time she left for England, he was engaged in acting as informant and *agent provocateur* for the Germans.[31]

As noted earlier, KIKI had been introduced into the organisation through VICTOIRE, although this seems to have slipped WALENTY's memory. If there was any resentment of WALENTY on KIKI's part it may have been because WALENTY had dissuaded him from going to England to join the RAF, instead sending him to Marseilles, and then to Spain. He never made it as far as Spain as he was arrested in Vichy, imprisoned and tortured before being deported to France.

WALENTY's arrest may have been a set-up by KIKI, who had conveyed a message via MICHEL (KIEFFER) that he wished him to get in touch personally. WALENTY thought that their meeting would be so that KIKI could tell him about the new sea mail route. He was unable to keep the appointment so he sent CHRISTIAN instead. The information he received from KIKI was 'so indefinite as to be of no use at all', so he sent CHRISTIAN back. When he did not return for the celebration WALENTY had planned for the organisation's first anniversary, WALENTY assumed he had been arrested. Wilson's report notes:

> There is satisfactory evidence that KIKI could not have been working for the Germans prior to mid-November 1941. For example, he knew in advance that the English agent ADAM was picked up by aeroplane on 2.11.41 and the Germans would not have permitted ADAM's departure in the fully justified supposition that ADAM would be carrying important mails. Furthermore, the exchange of mails at the Paris postbox on 14.11.41 was not interfered with, although KIKI may have been arrested before that date as there was no report from him. WALENTY points out that the German agent in mufti who arrested him introduced himself with the words, 'I am the fisherman from Cherbourg', and it seems fairly clear that this man, to whom VICTOIRE gives the name BLEICHER, had started his investigations in Cherbourg and got on to the main organisation through KIKI.[32]

Another clue was that the Germans already knew the name of the aerodrome, which was known only to KIKI and WALENTY. WALENTY said that KIKI deserved credit for the good work he had done prior to his arrest, saying that he could have also betrayed the Polish organisation in Marseilles, but he didn't. KIKI did not behave well in times of crisis, which explained why he had betrayed the network so readily. When he worked for the Germans he had also taken a stand, saying he would not work against Frenchmen, but only Communists and Jews, presumably *French* Communists and *French* Jews. This is not untypical behaviour for the time; in some circles the Communists were regarded with suspicion, particularly by the Gaullists, and there had been a long-standing ambivalence towards the Jews in France, a large percentage of whom (about two-thirds) lived in or around Paris.

There was an exchange of correspondence between Paris and London about the KIKI case. On 24 November 1944 Harmer cabled Ian Wilson from Paris:

TOP SECRET
A. Your letter of 14 November arrived 22nd morning.
B. Would like to see KIKI and put a few questions.
C. Which French service holds him and do SCI know about it?
D. Please ask Astor to expedite BRUTUS letter to VIOLETTE as I want to see her within next week.
E. Will not mention case to French for time being.[33]

Noble of B1b replied on 25 November, 'it might be as well to state that it comes from Wilson':

TOP SECRET
A. Reference your ALP/TG 87 OF 24.11.44.
B. Your para. B. We have no interest in your seeing KIKI at least until we have full report promised by S.O.E.
C. We regard further elucidation of VICTOIRE as exclusively French interest and not urgent.
D. Your para. C. We do not know but Warden now in Paris could answer.
E. Your para. D. Will be done but may be delayed as BRUTUS not at the present available.
F. Your para. E. If you mean VICTOIRE there is no hurry but French should be warned about BRUTUS now.[34]

John Marriott wrote to Harmer on 7 December with regard to VIOLETTE, warning him about his interest in the case, saying, 'I have an uneasy feeling that you may be getting yourself personally rather more involved in it and its ramifications than we have any right to expect you to do, and indeed than is really necessary.' He continued:

I am told by Ian Wilson that it has been learnt off the record from the French that KIKI, of whose interrogation no report has officially been received from the French, has stated in terms that BRUTUS, after his arrest, did agree to work for the Germans.

I do not myself think that we need worry ourselves unduly about this, but it is of course a piece of information which we ought to have had, and in view of the uncertainty of the whole position I am wondering what, if anything, you have told any Frenchman about BRUTUS, and what you are proposing to tell the French, and to whom in particular, about KIKI, VICTOIRE, VIOLETTE and BRUTUS ...

As far as VIOLETTE is concerned, I am not clear whether you have seen her again since you were last in London, but I want to make it clear that from our point of view there is nothing in the BRUTUS case which makes it necessary for you to continue interest yourself in her.[35]

Harmer's so-called personal interest in VICTOIRE may stem from his earlier relationship with her which, while platonic, seems to suggest a certain admiration bordering on infatuation with her. The information about WALENTY agreeing to work for the Germans was also confirmed in a note written by Ian Wilson (as background to Marriott's letter of 7 December), who had received confirmation from Townsend in the War Room, adding, 'from information obtained from S.O.E. it seemed clear that after the break-up of the Interalliee Organisation KIFFER had managed to get taken on as an S.O.E. agent and had even passed through this country without being identified'. As noted earlier, he was landed under the name of MICHEL as a Category C prisoner, clearly a blunder by British Intelligence in not identifying him. The Counter-Espionage Section of SIS, Section V, also noted that KIKI had penetrated the Polish organisation and 'had been in the U.K. since D Day', according to a document sent to MI5, dated 7 December 1944. The SIS communication expressed the view that 'Z.B. [SIS symbol for MI5] take the view that it is a matter for the 27 landers [France] to unravel Kiffer's [sic] treachery and that it is no longer of operational interest to us.'

On 27 December 1944 Harmer reported to John Marriott that he had seen Trevor Wilson's officer and 'Dick' Warden's officer Mathe in Paris about the KIKI case. He said he had seen notes taken at his interrogation that were 'most alarming', since Bleicher had told KIKI everything about BRUTUS. There was speculation about what exactly would happen to KIKI: 'I think [Captain] James Hales (or Halles) takes the view that he will be shot and Warden's officer the view that he will get off with a very light sentence, but in any event he is going to be put on trial.'

On 15 January Colonel Noel Wild, based at Ops 'B' Sub-Section, G-3 Division at SHAEF, wrote to Tar a Top Secret note regarding the cases of Kiffer and Roger Bardet, pointing out:

> In the case of BARDET and KIFFER, the danger lies in their mistresses having contact with some German source unknown to us and thereby the fact of their arrest becoming known to the Germans. The story we have concocted is not particularly clever, but it is simple and we feel confident it will meet the case. One thing about which we can all rest assured is that any danger of public trial and publicity in general concerning their arrest, other than through a leak by their mistresses, has been eliminated.[36]

The mistresses to which Wild referred were Madame Cornet for Bardet, and Paulette Besliard for Kiffer, according to notes from a meeting on 14 January 1945 between Colonel Wild, Major Grant, Capitaine Vaudreuil, Capitaine Kressman, Major Trevor Wilson and Captain Hales at 20, rue Pétrarque, Paris. Bardet and Kiffer were being held at 11, rue Cambarcérès, the headquarters of the Contrôle de la Surveillance du Territoire (CST, established in 1937 and predecessor to the DST, now the location of the Inspection General Police National) awaiting interrogation by Kressman on 16 January.

Kressman devised a cunning subterfuge, part of which would be to create the impression, as far as the mistresses were concerned, that he would be defending them because 'he thinks the men have done a wonderful job with the F.F.I.' and therefore they would not be prosecuted. He also planned to tell them that Bardet and Kiffer would be sent to North Africa to prevent a revival of the trial 'and the possibility of revenge against them until their Chief, Henri FRAGER, is able to return from Germany and clear them'. The deviousness of the plan did not end there. En route to North Africa the plane in which they were flying would disappear. The women would be given an address in North Africa to which they could write via Kressman. However, their letters would be intercepted and stopped and:

> It is expected that, in due course, they will make some enquiries as to why they have had no reply to their letters. KRESSMAN will show surprise and volunteer to investigate and, in due course, he will inform them that apparently they had an accident en route to Africa and nothing has been heard of the aeroplane since. If advisable, suitable replies will be concocted at 020, in order to satisfy the women.

Factually, BARDET and KIFFER will be transported from their present place of custody to Camp 020 in the near future.[37]

However, Colonel Wild called a meeting on 23 January 1945 that was attended by Colonel Bevan, Tar Robertson, Masterman, Marriott, 'Buster' Milmo, D.I. Wilson (of MI5's War Room), Herbert Hart, Major Wells of SOE, Capitaine Vaudreuil and Hugh Astor to discuss the four agents of the WALENTY organisation currently being held in France. Wild explained that the four agents were 'all aware of the fact that BRUTUS's escape from German imprisonment had been facilitated and that he was in fact a German spy'. Astor reported:

> Colonel Wild appeared to have little idea as to the charges levelled against these four persons or the extent of their allegations against BRUTUS. He merely insisted that they were in a position to compromise BRUTUS, and that a certain Roger BARDET was a particular danger in this respect. He had clearly not examined the cases of any of these agents with a view to discovering whether the dangers could be neutralized, but had been influenced both by the French and by Major Harmer, whom he met in Paris, into believing that the danger was serious.[38]

Wild went on to explain that following the decision taken at a meeting on 12 January, he had approached General Eisenhower 'and had succeeded in obtaining the concurrence of all parties in France to the four agents being sent to the U.K.'. This, he said, was to prevent a public trial in France. He admitted that perhaps this action had been a hasty one and that the four agents should remain in France, 'and to let the French legal procedure run its course and BRUTUS face the music':

> At this point all of Colonel Wild's observations were rendered irrelevant by the late arrival of Captain Vaudreuil, who brought hot intelligence direct from Paris. To the surprise of one and all, he announced that KIKI and BARDET had been subjected to intense interrogation by Kressman, and as a result of which their innocence of collaborating with the enemy had been established ...
> This new information came as a complete surprise and caused such stupefaction that the original purpose of the meeting was forgotten.[39]

Vaudreuil told the meeting that his officers were satisfied that Bardet and Kiffer (KIKI) were 'wholly innocent men' and that they ought to be released. It had been another party, whose name Vaudreuil did not reveal, who had been responsible for the break-up of the network. Goubeau, he said, was under unlawful arrest. He suggested that Bardet and Kiffer be brought over as free men and subjected to further interrogation, which no one at the meeting agreed with. The participants then set about deciding how they should proceed with them. Wells and B1b remained unconvinced of their innocence as professed by Vaudreuil. When it was pointed out to Vaudreuil that if these two agents were allowed to come to England as free men it would be impossible to interrogate them properly, Vaudreuil backed down. Hugh Astor concluded:

> Thus if B.1.B. and S.O.E. are satisfied by the reports brought by Kressman then the two agents will be released in France. If, however, they are not satisfied, the agents will be brought to this country as Category A for further interrogation.[40]

It was also arranged that Kressman would bring over copies of the interrogations.

Interestingly, in February 1945 Hugh Astor wrote up an account of meetings attended variously by Guy Liddell, Herbert Hart, John Marriott, Major John Masterman, Capitaine Kressman, Major Frank Soskice, John Senter of SOE and himself, the main purpose of which was:

> … to decide whether or not the British authorities had any interest in bringing BARDET, KIKI and GOUBEAU to this country, and it was finally decided that on the evidence at present available we [MI5] have no interest in bringing these men to England. It was agreed that they should be dealt with in the normal way. They are at present under illegal detention and they will probably have to be handed over to the Police Judiciaire and put on trial. It would be dangerous, especially in the case of BARDET and KIKI, for these men to be released at the present time, as they are popularly supposed to be guilty of collaboration and would no doubt fall victim to mob law.[41]

Major Frank Soskice (1902–79), later Sir Frank, then Lord Stow Hill, had replaced Cyril Miller as SOE's Interrogation and Case Officer at Bayswater in May 1944.[42] He became Solicitor-General in Atlee's post-war government and was Home Secretary, then Lord Privy Seal, in Harold Wilson's government (1965–66). A handwritten note by Astor appended at the bottom reads, 'For this reason it might be possible to persuade them to accept a form of voluntary detention.' Astor's comment is interesting as he had attended the meeting on 23 January when everyone had rejected Vaudreuil's suggestion of bringing over Bardet and Kieffer as free men; he now seems to have had a change of heart.

An extract from a report dated 9 April 1945, 'Captured Personnel and Material Branch, Military Intelligence Division, U.S. War Department', gives the following information about Bardet and Kiffer as agents of Sonderführer Verbeck (Bleicher):

ROGER	E-8010, a former French flying officer (Lieutenant), arrested at the beginning of 1943 for belonging to a resistance group, set free by Verbeck and used in the 'Fall Resistance', was around for a very short time as adjutant and the like (cf. the Resistance Case.)
KIKI	E-71010, a former flying sergeant and friend of E-8010 when this man brought into the organisation, worked near Lisieux and Caen to locate resistance groups.[43]

Further information on Roger Bardet had been provided in a B1d/LRC document on Kieffer's contacts, dated 15 January 1945:

Roger BARDET	CHAILLON @ ROGER @ CORNU @ DURAUX @ Roger BARDET, one of LOUBA's local recruits in the field in about March 1943. In about May 1943 he was arrested by the Germans and managed to escape. His escape story seemed very suspicious. In April 1944 Major Boddington stated that he was not sure of ROGER's integrity but that he had no actual proof of his being in communication[n] with the Germans.[44]

It also offered information on Mlle Buffet, who it said was identified with Mme Buffet @ DENISE, who had been a member of *Interallié* and had betrayed Kieffer in November 1941. Another contact of Kieffer's was Henri Dericourt (GILBERT). The story and controversy surrounding his alleged betrayal of many SOE agents has been the subject of a number of books and would require another book to go into here.

Much of the report from the RVPS, otherwise known as the London Reception Centre (LRC), dated 28 August 1944 outlines a brief biography of

Kieffer and his later career but does not discuss the betrayal of *Interallié* or even his recruitment to, or association with, it. According to the first interrogation report on Kieffer (referred to as KIFFER in the report) dated 19 December 1944 and prepared by SCI 105 in Paris following his arrest, he was in close touch with Bleicher (referred to as Jean VERBECK). It lists his contacts as Suzanne Laurent (Bleicher's girlfriend), the Abbé Alesch, ALEX, and Roger Bardet, who had worked for Henri Jacques Paul Frager (1897–1944). He attributes the arrest of several British officers to GILBERT (Dericourt), who had betrayed the *Amiate* group. Buckmaster had apparently been told about this by Frager when he was in England in 1943. Frager would later die in Buchenwald on 5 October 1944.

What is clear from Bleicher's file is that VICTOIRE, referred to in it as MICHELINE, had helped him select a number of agents, of whom KIEFFER was one, and was subsequently set free. The file states that KIEFFER and JOUFFRET were the only two who worked for Bleicher until June 1944.[45] A note in Bardet's file on himself, Robert Goubeau and Claude Jouffret prepared by Edward Blanchard Stamp on 21 January 1945 states:

> We know nothing about them beyond the fact that they are said by Colonel Wilde [*sic*] and Major Trevor Wilson to be in the same position as Robert KIEFFER. That is to say that they must know that BRUTUS [WALENTY] is a German agent and must be German agents themselves and if prosecuted by the French in France would prejudice the security of the BRUTUS case.[46]

Stamp explained that both Wild and Trevor Wilson wanted to keep the three incommunicado until the war in Europe was over. Consequently, they would be sent to Camp 020 as Category 'A' prisoners and kept there for a period not exceeding eight weeks, following which they might be detained permanently at Camp 020.

After his capture by the Germans, it appears that Kieffer became involved in sabotage work for III F in the Caen area between January and March 1942, which had led to the founding of his fictitious resistance group, known to the Abwehr as LYSIANA, containing 150 notional agents operating in Lisieux, Fervacques and the surrounding district. This had been constructed with the help of Dr Paul Hautechaud (1896–1944), a well-known doctor in Lisieux who had founded a group in 1941 consisting of Henri Beaudet, Suzanne Septavaux and Emmanuel des Georges. In 1942 it became established in Lisieux under Roland Bloch (HUGO). The network had come to light from a newspaper cutting of the sabotage of the Paris–Cherbourg express found in the possession of LUCAS's courier when he was arrested at the demarcation line. The later work of KIEFFER in the Marseilles area and Normandy from 1942 onwards is not relevant to this book, only his alleged role in the break-up of *Interallié*. He did, however, use his contacts with the TUDOR organisation, made during his time with *Interallié*, to effect these subsequent activities. A report from Kieffer's later trial in a book on Anders Larsson of the SAS stated, 'By November 1943 Kieffer [*sic*] and three companions had decapitated the Norman Resistance organisation. They left behind tears and mourning.'[47]

Paul François Roger Hautechaud was born in Bordeaux on 4 March 1896; he married Andrée Eynard in Saint Sulpice, Paris in 1919 and qualified as a doctor of medicine in 1922. During Operation *Aquatint*[48] one of the agents, Graham Hayes, became ill with food poisoning and was cared for by him and Suzanne Septavaux. Hayes was betrayed by Robert Kieffer and later shot without trial under Hitler's Commando Order in Fresnes on 13 July 1943.[49] Hautechaud was denounced to the Gestapo on 18 September 1943, tortured by the SD–Sipo at their headquarters in the rue des Jacobins in Caen and imprisoned first in Caen, then in Royallieu near Compiègne, before being transferred to Buchenwald, where he died on 11 March 1944 (prisoner number 44862). His wife, Andrée, was deported and never heard of again.

On 11 February 1945 Harmer prepared a questionnaire to be given to Captain W.J.E. Mathe for KIKI's interrogation. Unfortunately, further interrogation reports of KIKI which may have provided answers to these questions are not to be found in Kieffer's MI5 file. Some are found in a questionnaire which *is* in Kieffer's file, handed to the War Room by Capitaine Vaudreuil on 29 June 1945, but the answers, supplied by Bleicher,[50] help to shed some light on the questions posed in Harmer's questionnaire. The first one regarding who had denounced Robert Kieffer has already been dealt with in Chapter 7. Answers to the second question were discussed in Chapter 11; answers to the third can be found in various chapters throughout the book.

It has not been confirmed whether François Tabet was also a Vaudeville artist. He may have been confused with Georges Tabet (1905–84), who appeared with Jacques Pills as a music hall duo in the 1930s; Georges Tabet also later wrote screenplays for a number of films. There appears to be no record of Georges Tabet being involved with the French Resistance. Harmer's SCI report refers to Tabet as being the son of Maître Tabet, probably of the Paris Bar.

REMARKS	QUESTION
1. The explanation given of the break up of INTERALLIEE has been that a certain Denise BUFFET betrayed KIFFER who was arrested by BLEICHER and forced to write a letter to VALENTIN asking for an interview and fixing a rendez-vous: that VALENTIN failed to turn up but sent CHRISTIAN instead who was arrested.	1. (a) Information on Denise BUFFET. (b) Did KIFFER write letter asking for rendez-vous? (c) Did CHRISTIAN turn up at the rendez-vous?
2. LUCAS returned to France from England at beginning of April 1942 and was arrested towards the end of April in Paris.	2. (a) Circumstances of arrest of LUCAS. (b) Who was responsible? (c) Was he arrested by BLEICHER or another Service? (d) What did LUCAS tell Germans about LA CHATTE's activities in England?
3. The following ex agents of INTERALLIEE are stated to have collaborated with the Germans after the break up: (a) Robert GORRIOT or GORBINET @ BOB @ EDGAR, age 24; 1m82; clean shaven; blue eyes; fair hair. Cadet pilot during the 1939-1940 war. (b) Claude JOUFFRET @ MICHEL @ CLAUDE. Age 27; 1m80; cleanshaven; blue eyes; fair hair. Officier aviateur who lived in Neuilly. (c) Francois TABET @ MARCEL. Age 36; 1m75; cleanshaven; fair complexion; dark brown hair; brown eyes. Said to be son of Maitre TABET. Seen in Paris in March 1944. Lived in spring 1942 in hotel in Rue du Mont d'Or.	3. (a) Further particulars about and subsequent movements of GORRIOT, JOUFFRET and TABET. (b) Is TABET identical with Vaudeville artist?

CHAPTER 25

The Final Reckoning

In Otto Wirth's CIC report of 7 October 1944 he states that VIOLETTE had been released from La Santé on 14 April 1942 and allowed to return to Lunéville, but was kept under surveillance by the Kreiskommandantur 594 (local military command no. 594) and had to report to them once a day for three months. She was required to work as an interpreter for Monsieur Jules Émile Français (1866–1957), the mayor of Lunéville (1943–5), and his secretary Madame Schmidt when issuing *laissez-passer*. However, this was short-lived as she was suspected of being non-Aryan.[1] Where she is mentioned in any of the files there is nothing that can confirm or deny this, and may have just been an act of spite on the part of the Germans or her employer.

Wirth's report also claims that during the winter of 1943/44 VIOLETTE had met a decorator named Émile Arnold, with whom she had also been arrested, and then became engaged to him. It is not clear, however, to which arrest he is referring. At the beginning of February 1944 she wrote to WALENTY using what she believed was his new code name (GABY), addressed it to 45, rue des Écoles saying that she wanted to break with him and to make an appointment to meet him at the Café de la Paix in Paris. In response she received a note saying, *'Je vous attends le Café de la Paix heure prevue'* ('I'll wait for you at the Café de la Paix at the pre-arranged time'). When she arrived he wasn't there so she left a note for GABY. Given that WALENTY was not in the country at the time this is hardly surprising. Whoever sent the note obviously wasn't WALENTY, but probably the Abwehr or GABY on their behalf. There is no information on his true identity, but when he visited her in Lunéville at the end of February she thought his accent might be Algerian. He had come to try to persuade her to return to Paris and continue their work with WALENTY, but she refused, saying that she did not want to leave her fiancé.

She claimed that she and her fiancé had been responsible for rescuing nine English and Canadian aviators who had parachuted into the area surrounding Lunéville. At least one of these may have been Warrant Officer P.R. 'Barney'

Greatrex, the bomb aimer and only survivor of Lancaster QR-O, serial number LL775 of 61 Squadron RAF, shot down on the night of 25/26 February 1944. Other Commonwealth airmen included Australian Flight Lieutenant Allan Frank McSweyn, 115 Squadron RAF, and Captain R.B. Palm, SAAF, both of whom were repatriated via the *Marie-Claire* line run by Ghita Mary Lindell (1895–1986) @ Comtesse de Moncy @ Comtesse de Milleville, described by Airey Neave as 'one of the most colourful agents in the history of Room 900'.[2] Whether VIOLETTE and her fiancé had anything to do with them or their subsequent escape is a matter of speculation.

Hugh Astor reported on 9 January 1945 that VIOLETTE had been arrested in Lunéville by the FFI on 29 September 1944 and subsequently interrogated by the American Third Army. Wirth recommended in his memo dated 7 October 1944 that she be referred to the Twelfth Army for 'further interrogation, verification of her story through sources in the U.K. [and] final disposition'. In his report Astor said:

> She is aware of the fact that BRUTUS is working for the Germans and is therefore able to compromise him. VIOLETTE herself does not present a security danger, and she has therefore been released and allowed to return in liberty to Lunéville. In view of the proximity of Lunéville to the German frontier and of the fact that her case must be fairly widely discussed in the neighbourhood, it is possible that the Germans may learn of her arrest by the F.F.I. and may assume that she has denounced BRUTUS.[3]

Incoming cables from SPEARHEAD to CRUSADE (SAINT) and BLISS (AGNOSTIC) on 11 October, and 15 October from SIS Section VB5 (also shown as VBZ) stated that VIOLETTE had been interrogated by the Third Army.[4] At the top of the SIS cable, the recipient, which appears to be Masterman's initials, has scribbled, 'B1A. Wd. you get into touch with Tim Cohen about this, as there is a possible ISOS trace of this character in connection with one of yours?' Cohen was with SIS at Ryder Street, London. The SIS cable also wondered whether she should be brought to Camp 020 for interrogation. Captain S.H. Noakes, a lawyer with B1b, replied to the SIS cable, stating that MI5 did not require VIOLETTE to be sent to Camp 020 and suggested that Harmer interrogate her in the field as he was the most conversant with the case. This decision had been taken in consultation with Tar Robertson.

Astor also raised the matter in a meeting with Tar on 18 October at which he pointed out that VIOLETTE's interrogation 'would be of primary interest to Tom [redacted – most likely Tom Greene] of S.I.S. and Colonel Gano of the Polish Deuxième Bureau, both of whom are at present in Paris'.[5] On receiving Tar's agreement, Astor communicated with Charles [redacted] in 'Biffy' Dunderdale's office. Others, unnamed, were also 'put in the picture'. A note written by Astor on 18 October observed:

> The arrest of VIOLETTE seriously complicates the case of BRUTUS, as on several occasions BRUTUS has asked the Germans to pass on messages of goodwill to VIOLETTE, as the result of which VIOLETTE was able to deduce that BRUTUS was communicating with the Germans.[6]

He cited a message sent on 21 October 1943 and BRUTUS's reply on the 26th as examples and said that they needed to find out as soon as possible the exact circumstances of VIOLETTE's arrest and how much she had collaborated with the Germans in recent months. He further suggested a plan of action:

> BRUTUS should report in a frenzy of anxiety that S.I.S. have told him of the capture of VIOLETTE and asked him to assist in that part of the interrogation which concerns the break-up of the WALENTY organisation. BRUTUS will remind the Germans of their message telling him that VIOLETTE knows that he is working for the Germans, and will ask to what extent she had been taken in the Germans' confidence and whether she is still likely to collaborate with them. He will point out that the charge against VIOLETTE at the present time concerns her collaboration with the Germans in 1942, and he can point out that his own position is so strong that he can easily justify this action in the eyes of the British. When he meets VIOLETTE, however, he will put his cards on the table and recruit her as a sub-agent. Before attempting to recruit her, however, BRUTUS will have to receive an assurance from the Germans that she is likely to fall in with this suggestion.
>
> The above is, of course, only a brief outline and would require considerable collaboration. If VIOLETTE is recruited she can either work as a sub-agent through BRUTUS, sending chicken-food from France, or possibly she can run entirely independant [sic] of BRUTUS and direct to the Germans. If the latter course is adopted it should be possible to devise a means whereby even if VIOLETTE subsequently becomes blown it would not react against BRUTUS.[7]

Tar appended a note to Astor saying, 'This plan is good, but before deciding definitely we should wait for the first int. report from C.H.H. [Harmer].'

An undated telegram to Major Dykes at 106 SCI Unit, SHAEF, based at
Versailles, marked 'Top Secret. Immediate', asking him to inform Harmer of its
contents, includes the following:

6.   Reference VIOLETTE. We remind you that in October 1943 BRUTUS
     received a message stating that she seemed, owing to their dealings with
     her, to have deduced that BRUTUS was working for the Germans.
     BRUTUS replied protesting at VIOLETTE having been allowed to
     make this deduction, but there was no reaction, and it is therefore not
     clear whether the Germans really blew BRUTUS to her or not.[8]

The message referred to, dated 21 October 1943, was: 'VIOLETTE is very
well. Because of our dealings with her she seems to have deduced that you are
fighting on our side. Her friends are also well.'

BRUTUS replied on 26 October 1943. He had already sent a postcard to António in
English – *not* French – on 10 October from 61 Richmond Park Road, SW14. The
postmark on the envelope is stamped 10.10.43; a subsequent postmark stamped in
Lisbon was 27.10.43 when it was 'Returned to Sender'. The postcard read as follows:

Dear Antonio – for a long time I haven't had any news from you. I suppose
both you and your family are well. Although I am working very hard I am
quite well and my business is going better. I hope to hear from you soon.
    Yours sincerely,
    Henry[10]

The letter was mailed to António da Silva, 62 Rua Marquês Sá da Bandeira,
Lisbon, which is an apartment building right opposite the Jardim da Fundação
Calouste Gulbenkian and the Museu Calouste Gulbenkian. At the bottom of
the letter, which has obviously been opened, was written, 'Não mora nesta casa.
Ha 4 anos. 17.X.1943' ('Hasn't lived at this address for four years'). Clearly, the
information WALENTY had was out-of-date.
    Hugh Astor wrote to Roland Bird in B3a, Liaison with Censorship, on
1 March 1944 reminding him that BRUTUS's original postcard had been
returned, and sending him the original. He also told Bird that BRUTUS had
again written to the same address on 10 November, adding, 'but as it did not
bear the address of the writer, I don't suppose that the Portuguese Post Office
authorities will bother to return it'.[11] Bird replied:

It is difficult to offer any views on the form in this case, but presumably the Germans were relying on the postman on this particular walk to hand over to them any correspondence to Antonio da Silva, well knowing that he had left the address four years ago. I believe a similar arrangement was made in at least one case for a GARBO address. If this should be the same arrangement, I presume that it has fallen down owing to the postman with whom it was made being removed from this particular walk. From the efforts that the Lisbon Postoffice [sic] has made to deliver the letter, the Germans would not appear to have any long-stop arrangement in operation at the Lisbon G.P.O.

Astor wrote at the bottom, 'Not necessarily. The present resident c? receive [sic] mail in the name of a man who had lived there 4 yrs previously.'[12]

MI5 was also worried about what KIKI might disclose, since he was the first one arrested and turned out to be a 'bad hat'. When he returned to France he was arrested by the French. KIKI knew that the Germans had facilitated BRUTUS's escape but they did not know whether he was aware of BRUTUS's espionage mission and that he was still in contact with the Germans. 'This information must by now be known to a fairly large number of Frenchmen who are not intelligence officers.' Astor cautioned that 'the security of the BRUTUS case on the Continent is at present in a bad way' and offered two courses of action depending on whether they (a) decided to close the case, or (b) continued to run it. To the first option (a) he suggested that BRUTUS would have to come clean with the Germans about KIKI's disclosures and explain that this had led to another investigation of his escape. He would promise to tell the Germans that he had told the British that the allegations against him were true, that he had come to Britain with a political mission to foment trouble in Polish circles. He would confess that his arrest had caused him to see the error of his ways and plead for mercy. He had also been under great stress during his arrest by the Germans. Astor saw this as a way of mitigating any further allegations against him. If the second option (b) were adopted, then the necessary arrangements for KIKI's trial should be made but it should be conducted with the miminum of fuss and publicity. He concluded by saying that everyone (Buckmaster, Marriott and himself at their 5 January meeting) agreed that:

In the event of BRUTUS becoming blown, the whole of FORTITUDE would *probably* [added] also be compromised and the Germans would become aware of our deception technique. The strategic deception and the 'Y' Service etc. would therefore be compromised.[13]

Masterman commented in the margin, 'I did not agree this. JCM.' In weighing the advantages of both options, Astor observed that the first, '(a) provides complete protection for our strategic deception technique, but would probably result in the loss of a valuable agent', while '(b) would permit the continued running of BRUTUS as a high-grade agent for a period of time, but there would be a risk that he might be at any moment become compromised.'[14] Again, Masterman commented, 'Only if the Germans swallow it all!'

In mid-December 1945 BRUTUS received a letter from Monsieur G. Margain, the advocate acting for VIOLETTE, which was passed on to MI5. Billy Luke wrote, 'BRUTUS is most anxious that VIOLETTE should not be convicted and wishes to do everything he can, short of appearing in court, on her behalf to establish her innocence.' While VICTOIRE and Bleicher had both said that VIOLETTE had betrayed VICTOIRE's address to the Germans, BRUTUS strongly believed that it had been revealed by someone else and wished to answer the questions put by Monsieur Margain. MI5 agreed that he should be allowed to do so, with copies being sent to Peter Hope in Paris and Colonel Verneuil. Now a wing commander living at 1 Princes Row, SW1, BRUTUS replied to Margain's questions on 13 December:

1. That she wasn't the only one who knew VICTOIRE's address; there were a number of people belonging to the organisation who knew it.
2. He couldn't recall whether there had been a telephone conversation the evening before the arrest, but he did remember being displeased that during the conversation at that meeting CHRISTIAN had given away his telephone number. CHRISTIAN had telephoned the city the day before and he told him that he thought it very indiscreet of him.
3. CHRISTIAN had told him a few times before the arrest that he knew a young German woman soldier working for the Service de Transmission, either telephone or radio, he wasn't sure. It was CHRISTIAN's aim to obtain from her in the future any information that she would unwittingly give him. However, BRUTUS didn't think that she was actually his mistress.
4. When he met with Madame Borni while he was in Fresnes they very quickly discussed how they could limit the number of arrests and in each case not give details of the others.

5. VIOLETTE did not make the distinction between herself and that of the
    network. A typical example, he said, was that she had proposed transporting
    their operations hub to that of her own house close to Paris.
        He said he was unable to answer the questions:
6. Did you know that her work at Saint Germain was deliberately sabotaged?
7. Didn't she help you to escape in August 1943?

He concluded by saying that in his personal opinion Madame Borni had tried
to limit the amount of danger that threatened the other agents and the other
networks. As a codist she knew a lot of information both about their network
and that of neighbouring ones. If she hadn't kept these secrets it would have
led to the inevitable liquidation of the French Underground. He hoped these
opinions would help in Renée Borni's defence, but further enquiries should be
directed through military channels.

The trials of Robert Kieffer and Roger Bardet were held in December 1949
along with Claude Jouffret (MICHEL), Robert Goubeau (BOB), and Suzanne
Laurent. Mathilde had been asked to appear as a witness on 12 December
but when questioned she declined to answer, saying, 'I don't know, I've
forgotten.' Kieffer (KIKI) and Bardet (ROGER) were both condemned to
death. Kieffer was given amnesty in 1953 and died in Senlis on 22 September
1974. Bardet's sentence was commuted to twenty years; he was released in
1955.[15] In 1953 Goubeau was tried and received a sentence of five years'
hard labour.

    During the years that she was in prison in France Mathilde Carré kept a
diary that features in two chapters of her memoirs in which she recorded her
thoughts – 'The Slow Hours in Prison' (1945–8) and 'The Diary of a Woman
condemned to Death' (1948–52). They also appear in French in *My Conversion*.
In the entry on 6 July 1947 she mentions a black-and-white angora cat, Whisky,
which she had somehow acquired and fed with scraps from the 'wardresses'
mess'. On All Saints' Day (1 November 1947), she found herself thinking
about her late husband, Maurice, and wondering where he was buried. He had
declared that if he were to be killed in battle he should be buried along with his
comrades. 'So was he buried at Monte Cassino?' she wondered.

    Later, on 14 November, she wrote, 'They took Whisky from me and I wept.
No little purr to greet me, no little paw to tug at my sleeve or caress my cheek.

I wept for Whisky.' This may be the first time that she had openly revealed any emotion or any empathy for any living thing. She cried because 'since 1939 everything goes, everything leaves me. My life is a series of great and small amputations. I wept for everything which has been taken away from me.'[16]

On 13 May 1949 she was transferred to the women's penitentiary of Maison Centrale de Rennes (Brittany). There she received a visit from a Monsieur B, the chief commissioner at Bordeaux, and a police inspector. They told her that she was not the one who was guilty, but ARMAND; he had joined the Abwehr while she was in England in 1942. As she claims in her memoirs:

> I had always refused to let Bleicher enroll me in the Abwehr. Armand had done so and he was at liberty. At first I refused to believe this story. But the two inspectors showed me photographs, articles and the results of their enquiries. The case was opened before a military tribunal in Bordeaux but immediately squashed.[17]

Mathilde Carré's trial, together with that of Renée Borni, took place in Paris on 3 January 1949 at one' oclock in the afternoon, both charged with 'Intelligence with the Enemy'. The actual indictment against Mathilde as recorded in her autobiography read:

> Having at Paris in 1941 and 1942 and at all events in France between the 16th June, 1940, and the date of the Liberation, with intent to aid the undertakings of the enemy, being a Frenchwoman [sic] passed on intelligence to a foreign power or its agents, with a view to assisting the undertakings of this power against France, a crime envisaged and punished by articles 75 paragraph 5 of the Penal Code[18] (modified by the decree of 29th July, 1939) and paragraphs 1 and 2 of the decree of the 28th November, 1944.[19]

Borni was seriously ill and had to be carried into the courtroom on a stretcher. As Lauran Paine, Carré's biographer noted, 'Renée ... was not going to survive for long.' Mathilde's lawyer was Maître Albert Naud (1904–77), described by Paine as a 'shrewd, capable French barrister'. Arrested in 1941 for his activities with the Resistance and imprisoned in La Santé for two months, Naud was perhaps the ideal person to defend her. Made famous in 1931 for having defended Henri Charrière, popularly known as 'Papillon', perhaps more significantly, he refused in 1945 to defend Pierre Laval (1883–1945), leader of the Milice from 1943 to 1945, which led to Laval's execution on 15 October 1945.

One of the problems Naud faced was who to call as witnesses for the defence as it was felt that some of them could actually do more harm than good. Roman Garby-Czerniawski (WALENTY) declined to take the stand or send any deposition. Nor could the deposition that Bleicher had given the French authorities when they had imprisoned him after his capture be entered into the trial. In fact, he had not wanted to come to Paris at all. Another dead end proved to be René Aubertin, an old friend of Mathilde's with whom she had shared a close relationship at one time, although perhaps not as lovers. However, he had been called as a witness for the prosecution by Maître Becognée, the public prosecutor. Becognée had also decided to call Pierre de Vomécourt (referred to erroneously as Paul in Paine's biography of Carré), Maître Michel Brault (MIKLOS), Wladimir Lipsky, Henri Tabet [sic], Renée Borni and Mireille Lejeune as witnesses. The latter was the wife of Charles Lejeune (1902–45), known as BOBY-ROLAND, who had worked as a concierge in the rue Lamarck. As a result of Carré's treachery Mireille had spent seven months in Fresnes,[20] while her husband had been deported to Mauthausen on 29 March 1943 under Hitler's 'Night and Fog' decree and died of typhus in Hörsching, Austria, on 24 May 1945.[21] He should not be confused with Captain Sidney Charles Jones of SOE, one of whose code names was Sylvain Charles Lejeune, who was betrayed by Roger Bardet and died in Mauthausen on 6 September 1944.[22]

Ever the optimist, Mathilde had suggested to Maître Naud that Colonel Maurice Buckmaster and Major Benjamin Cowburn (BENOIT) of SOE, Major Tom Greene of SIS and Inspector Gale of Scotland Yard be called as witnesses in her defence. However, as her other biographer, Gordon Young, explained, 'Nothing ever came from the British side.' Indeed, Pastor Louis Arbousset, regional prison almoner at St Germain-en-Laye, wrote to Tom Greene at the British embassy in Paris on 25 March 1948 to solicit British support in Mathilde's defence. Someone in MI6's R5 B1 (MI6 post-war counter-espionage section under Kim Philby) wrote to H.K. Morton Evans at MI5, saying, 'We are no longer interested in her fate and I suggest, if you approve, that no reply be made to this approach made on her behalf.'[23] Lieutenant Colonel Kenneth Morton Evans had been appointed deputy controller, Radio Security Service (RSS or MI8c), in 1942.

During the preliminary hearing before the magistrate Mathilde had defended her actions by saying:

In order to make the deception possible … there had to be victims. I was acting as a sort of 'Battalion leader of the Resistance' and so I had to sometimes sacrifice men just as a general on a battlefield may send a group of soldiers to their death in order to save a regiment. That is just the fortunes of war. And besides … I only denounced the more stupid ones, you know.[24]

Throughout the trial, heard before Judge Drappier, president of the Court of Justice, Mathilde had remained, in the words of Paine, 'ambivalent' and 'defiant and hostile'. A female journalist covering the trial commented that she was cynical, insolent and showing 'a clear and obvious hardness'. In spite of this she was modestly dressed, 'suggesting a demure, correctly repentant individual', yet she presented herself as hard-faced and ruthless, 'and also by chewing gum, sneering, indicating disgust, contempt and scorn'. As Paine recorded:

She remained defiant to the last. She did nothing by her manner to arouse sympathy or compassion among the spectators … [she] fastened her green stare upon a witness with obvious baleful malevolence. By expression alone, she impressed people in the courtroom with her capacity for ruthlessness, with her unshakeable conviction that she alone mattered.[25]

Clearly, she was not trying to win any favours from the court by her attitude. She claimed that she had been judged on her behaviour, her replies and her involuntary smiles, justifying this by being shortsighted and a refusal to wear her glasses in court, in order to isolate herself:

I could not see clearly, I could see only shapes. But I could not observe the glances and the changes on their features. I retired into a fog in which I hid my head like some foolish ostrich. When you meet a look of hatred it hurts you: it can make you lose your head and encourage you to return hatred for hatred. I preferred to see nothing.[26]

Madame Belard, her mother, was also called as a witness, declaring that they were an honourable French family – 'How could you imagine that a member of a family such as ours could betray their country?' Still denying her guilt, Mathilde declared: 'In spite of my shortcomings and my mistakes I have always been loyal and goodhearted. Why had they systematically destroyed my true personality by transforming my mistakes into high treason and my shortcomings into vices?'[27]

None of the witnesses for the prosecution had a good word to say about her except for Colonel Achat of the Deuxième Bureau, who declared her to be 'an admirable woman', and not a double agent who had betrayed them; and Commander Simonneau, also of the Deuxième Bureau, who spoke of her 'immense desire' to serve her country. Michel Brault claimed, 'I think that woman had dreams of becoming a second Mata Hari – either a French one or a German one, it didn't really matter to her.' An embittered René Aubertin spoke of the hardships he had endured in Mauthausen and how she had placed her own life above that of those she had betrayed. A name card for Aubertin created by the Gestapo gives his details as being born on 7 June 1922; he was sent to Dachau on 9 June 1945 and released on 16 June 1945. His address when arrested was 30, rue Victor Hugo, Lyons.

When Pierre de Vomécourt (LUCAS) was finally called to the stand Maître Naud asked him: 'Would you say that, at the moment when she confessed to you her liaison with the Germans, Mathilde Carré manifested signs of a sincere desire to make amends?' De Vomécourt paused, then replied, 'Yes, on the whole I would.' In her defence, he professed that she had never done anything to harm him personally and had, in fact, worked loyally with him and his network. As evidence of her self-incrimination Maître Becognée read from her memoirs and quoted from her retort to Borchers when, after being asked what her last request would be if she were to be shot, she had replied: 'To have a good dinner, spend the night in bed with a friend – and then hear the Requiem of Mozart.' 'What kind of woman could write a thing like this?' he asked.

When all the testimonies had been heard it was time for Becognée and Naud to sum up. 'This woman betrayed France because she was without any moral feelings, because she was a woman without scruples,' Becognée said. Turning to the jury, he concluded, 'She betrayed her cause in a manner which I can find no words to pardon ... It is with a heavy heart that I now ask you to punish this woman with the supreme penalty for traitors – with the penalty of death.' Naud tried to mitigate the accusation that she had committed espionage, saying that she had been an amateur while others had been professionals, and 'she showed the human weakness of an amateur in the tough game of espionage'. He admitted that she was guilty, but pleaded for clemency 'for this woman who believed herself to be stronger than she was and then found herself faced with this dilemma: to die or to live'. He reminded the jury that she had been first a heroine in the early days of the Resistance and asked them: 'Are you going to kill one of those who spread patriotic faith in the early days?' and to make a distinction between those who had willingly offered their services to the

Gestapo and she who 'during years of heroism experienced only two months of weakness'. Clearly, he was clutching at straws.

When it came time for the judge to sum up, he posed two questions to the jury:

> 1st Question. Belard, Mathilde, widow Carré, here present and accused, is she guilty of having in Paris between 1941 and 1942, or in any case between June 16, 1940 and the Libération, being a French citizen in time of war, maintained intelligence with a foreign power or with its agents with a view to aiding this foreign power against France?
>
> 2nd Question. Was the action specified above in Question Number 1 committed with the deliberate intention of favouring the enterprises of all kinds of Germany, a power which was the enemy of France, or at any one of the Allied nations at war against the Axis powers?[28]

It should be noted that, according to Mathilde, the jury were all former members of the French Resistance movement, so it is hard to imagine how she could have had a fair trial. The judge also posed similar questions about Renée Borni, but she was not expected to receive a death sentence; indeed, the jury found that there were 'extenuating circumstances' in her case, and recommended mercy. It did not go unnoted that throughout the summing up and allegations made against her, Mathilde had remained totally impassive and devoid of any emotion. One observer drily commented, 'She might have been listening to a sentence being passed on somebody quite different.'

Mathilde Carré was sentenced to death on 7 January and confined to the condemned cell at Fresnes. There she wrote to Naud a letter in which she attempted to absolve herself of her perceived indifference to the whole trial, saying:

> You should not give any credence to the evidence given by certain of the witnesses on the subject of my so-called depravity … I have not been guilty of everything of which I have been accused. To be sure I have not always shown myself very amiable with regard to yourself, just precisely because I feel a great sympathy for you. I should not like to remain in your memory either as a monster or as a woman deprived of all feeling. If only you knew what this has cost me to put on this mask so as the better to hide my real nature! For years I have not had anybody to whom I could show myself as I really am. I have sunk into despair, believing myself incapable of supporting such a situation.[29]

She closed by imploring him to 'do everything you can to try and get me out of this awful cell and this prison of Fresnes'.[30]

In May 1950 her death sentence was commuted to life imprisonment, in spite of protests from former members of the Resistance. This was largely as a result of a plea Naud wrote to Vincent Auriol, first president of the French Fourth Republic (1947–54), in which he emphasised the work she had done on behalf of the Allies prior to her arrest, and the fact that it would only have been a matter of time before Bleicher rounded up the members of the network, with or without her help. His plea can be summarised in the following four points:

1   Mathilde Carré was an authentic, effective and enthusiastic member of the Resistance from September 1940 to November 1941.
2   The defence admits her error of two months during the time of her arrest.
3   Mathilde Carré revealed herself by confiding to an Allied agent [LUCAS] the unfortunate undertaking she had been carrying on, either voluntarily or otherwise.
4   She risked her life both by making this confidence and by organizing her departure for London in January and February 1942. If she had been discovered by Bleicher she would have been pitilessly executed.[31]

—⁂—

A Foreign Office file in the National Archives at Kew contains several letters from Captain George Pitt-Rivers to Lord Selborne regarding the sentence passed on Carré.[32] That correspondence can also be found in Pitt-Rivers' MI5 file. George Henry Lane-Fox Pitt-Rivers (1890–1966), formerly of the Royal Dragoon Guards and cousin of Clementine Churchill, was an anthropologist and eugenics expert who was interned under DR.18B as a member of The Link and the Fascist January Club, a known Mosley-ite and Nazi supporter. As a result, he spent 1940–42 in the Tower of London.[33] Twice divorced (he was first married to the Honourable Rachel Forster, then Rosalind Venetia Henley), after the war he met Stella Lonsdale, who became his mistress and later inherited from him.

In February 1949 Pitt-Rivers had approached Lord Selborne regarding Mathilde's death sentence. He urged the 'War Office to stop what he represented as a miscarriage of justice', according to H.N. Brain, under-secretary at the Foreign Office, writing on 2 February 1949. Henry Norman Brain was the Foreign Office representative in Vietnam (1945–46) who was present as the origins of the Vietnam War unfolded, and UK ambassador to Cambodia. He was the last head of the Services Liaison Department (SLD) and first head of the Permanent Under-Secretary's Department (PUSD) in 1948–50.[34]

A letter to MI5 from Colonel Rupert Harding-Newman, the Deputy Director Military Intelligence, Operations & Security (DDMI O&S) stated:

> I attach a copy of the Private and Personal letter from Mr. George Pitt-Rivers to Lord Selborne for your retention.
>
> Mr. Pitt-Rivers has been informed that we cannot assist him in this matter.
>
> As there is little doubt that he will pursue the matter further, I would appreciate confirmation that there is no information or evidence which your department can make available which would in any way assist Mr. Pitt-Rivers in his efforts to prevent or delay the sentence of the French court on Mathilde Carré.
>
> On the other hand, any evidence which could be used to dissuade Mr. Pitt-Rivers from pursuing the matter would be of equal value.[35]

Bernard Hill of SLB replied to Harding-Newman that 'the Security Service confirm that there is no information which they can make available from their records to Mr. PITT-RIVERS,' adding that he should pursue it through the Foreign Office. Hill wrote a note on 1 February 1949 saying that he had met with Harding-Newman, who had told him he had been forced to meet with Pitt-Rivers and showed him the letter he had written. As Hill put it, 'the letter was a document severely criticising S.O.E. officers and also M.I.5'. Pitt-Rivers had threatened to go public with the story if the Directorate of Military Intelligence (DMI) did not intervene. As Hill pointed out to Harding-Newman, 'neither the M.I. Directorate nor M.I.5 could intervene directly with the administration of justice in a foreign country, to wit, France.' He suggested that Pitt-Rivers should be advised to contact the Foreign Office, and that Harding-Newman contact Sir William Hayter, the assistant under-secretary of state at the Foreign Office and chairman of the Joint Intelligence Committee (JIC), to warn him.

A note dated 3 February 1949 by A.R. Walmsley of the Foreign Office Western Department stated: 'Mlle Carré betrayed 30 or 40 members of the French Resistance to the Germans, and most of them were tortured and killed. She did act for a time on our behalf, according to press accounts, but we quickly found her out.'[36]

The letter to which Harding-Newman was referring was written by Pitt-Rivers to Lord Selborne on 22 January 1949. Pitt-Rivers' letter, which amounts to something of a diatribe or rant, purporting to 'clear the air', as he put it, is worth repeating in full, if only to reveal what he appears to have known about the case, and his prejudices:

No.1. 'What we (any Englishmen) can do in the matter'

It was announced yesterday in the Paris press that the appeal of Mathilde Carré against sentence of death for treason had failed. That was anticipated. There remains, of course, an appeal for clemency and reprieve to the President. Such action can be taken by an Allied Government or by the subjects of an Allied Government.

The British Government handed her over to the French at their request after the War. We have an obvious interest and responsibility. She was first used, then apprehended and imprisoned by the British Secret Service between July 1942 and the summer of 1945.

She worked, as of course you are aware, for the Reseau de Resistance otherwise known as 'Interalliee' or 'Valenty' as our Intelligence Service called it, under the Pole, Czerniawsky, who was arrested by the Germans at the same time, and shot. You being the Ministerial Authority which brought her to England with de Vomecourt, and the authority for our secret service operating in France could hardly claim Ministerial impartiality to her appeal? May I therefore call your attention to the Sunday Despatch January 9th. 'Her life is literally in the hands of a small number of British Intelligence officers.'

I note that you 'haven't the least idea whether she is guilty or not.' But you also say that you understand all witnesses on both sides have been French citizens. This surprises me.

One of the chief witnesses for the prosecution appears to have been this Pierre de Vomécourt, a spy in British service dropped by parachute into France to sabotage and maintain contact with Reseau Interalliee. This creature … according to the report of his evidence in 'Le Monde' of January 8th contacts 'La Chatte' 'soem [sic] months' before he discovers that she is in German hands. He then, presumably posing as a Vichy agent, claims to have bluffed the German Counter-espionage agent, Hugo Bleicher, to let him take her over to England and pose as 'escapee' from German Hands. Yet he testifies 'qu'à ce moment Mathilde Carré avait sincérement le désire de ce racheter.' ['From that moment Mathilde Carré sincerely wanted to redeem herself.'] From that moment, as of course your department knew perfectly well, she was never out of sight or control of your agents, and could only have been used to send fake messages to the Germans.

There seems to have been some doubts about the nationality of and loyalties of de Vomecourt since he becomes a naturalised Frenchman in 1940, and a spy in British service when parachuted into France in May 1941 when he contacts Mathilde Carré, avowedly as a British agent. She is acting as a cryptographer in the Anglo-French underground and on 18th November 1941 is captured by the Germans with her associates and the incriminating list of names. She becomes 'maitresse' [mistress] and decoy to Bleicher, whereupon de Vomecourt saves her from the Germans by arranging for her to be picked up, together with English Major Cowburn of 'the War Office', off the French coast by an English motor boat, after bluffing according also to de Vomecourt's account, the German Counter-Espionage officer, Bleicher by claiming that he is a <u>German</u> (Alsatian or Vichy) agent. He now assures the Court that Mathilde Carré at this time 'sincerely' wished to re-enter the British Service. His evidence then proceeding shows that she accomplished the remarkable feat of bluffing the British War Office for four months during which time she transmitted coded messages from London to Bleicher – presumably from the love nests of Detective-Inspector 'G' [Gale] Central Office (Political) Branch of Scotland Yard, sharing it with Pierre at Porchester Gate; and afterwards M.I. officer 'L' at Brook Street [this was probably Llewellyn, who was not an intelligence officer]. This went of [sic] for months before an exceptionally bright Intelligence Officer becomes suspicious and begins to make enquiries about her: '*Au bout de quatre mois au Londres un officier de l'Intelligence Service, curieux, enquêta sur cette femme et s'aperçu bientôt qu'elle était plus que suspecte. On l'arrêta à Londres le 1 juillet 1942. Jusqu'au 1945 elle resta au secret à la prison de femme de Holloway.*' (L'Intransigeant – January 5th 1949) [Translation: After four months in London an intelligence officer, who was curious and worried about this woman soon saw that she was more suspicious. She was arrested in London on 1 July 1942. Since 1945 she has remained in secret at Holloway women's prison.]

However she continues to trust de Vomecourt's <u>bona fides</u>, who acts under instructions as one of her controls in the Porchester flat. She seals her confidence in this 'reliable' British-French agent by the usual exchange of feminine favours, and was still wearing a gold signet ring he gave her when she finally lodged in the safe-keeping of Aylesbury gaol. She does not appear to have been disillusioned until she leanrt [sic] a little English and the 'peculiar idiom' of English Intelligence. You know, of course, better than I, how reliable an agent was Pierre, but it seems reasonable clear [sic] that he now earns his 'Resistance Medal', instead of bullets, by 'shopping' the girl?

I am far from wanting offend, but to someone like myself, untutored in the ways of our Secret Sercie [sic], it would seem that Anglo-French Military Intelligence shows a greater tactical proficiency in the Camp of Venus than in the Camp of Mars.

No.2. 'Intelligence avec l'ennemi' [Intelligence with the enemy]

I have no personal axe to grind but I well realise unlike yourself I am not constrained by the Official Secrets Act. The names of the 'small number of former British Intelligence officers' are perhaps unfortunately easily identifiable. Secret Service agents who write highly imaginative and romantic accounts of 'The beautiful spies I have met, and Nazi spies I have foiled', etc. find credulous readers only in England.

'La Chatte', it appears, made a point understood better in France than England about the technique of securing glamorous female agents. After serving the Anglo-French-Polish cause as 'amie' [friend] in the French idiom 'contre-Vichy' [against Vichy] with the Pole who enjoyed her _petite amitiee_ [little friendship] with her friend Renne Borni _dites_ 'Violette' [called 'Violette'], now convicted but released in a dying state, is captured by the Germans counter-espionage agent, Bleicher, produced as evidence against her by the prosecution, after the usual examination and conditioning accorded to German prisoners-of-war. She 'Naturally' has <u>intelligence</u> with her captor. The English call it 'social contact'. She is taken to a luxurious apartment in Maison Laffitte:

> A ce moment-là, il me dit: [At that moment he told me]
>
> 'Vous êtes ma prisonnière' [You are my prisoner]
>
> Le President – [The President [of the court]]
>
> Et vous êtes devenue sa maîtress? [And you became his mistress?]
>
> Mettez-vous a ma place! monsieur le president. [Put yourself in my place, Mr President.]

I make the point that Carre's death sentence, it seems clear, is almost entirely attributable to her avowed anti-communist sentiments and the fact that she was <u>not</u> shot when captured by the Germans but proved accommodating in other ways. Faction loyalties in France, then as now, were confusing. Petainists and anti-Petainists; factions against Admiral Darlan who was anti-British and pro-American; for and against Laval; pro-Russian communists and anti-American and British; pro and against de

Gaulle, etc. Even in the Deuxième Bureau during the occupation, all these warring factions and conflicting sympathies were represented.

No.3. British Intelligence

When Carré came to England she had 'Intelligence' with 'a small number of English secret service agents', for which purpose she is installed en luxe [in luxury] first in a flat at Porchester Gate with her Pierre and a Scotland Yard officer of C.O.B.R.A. (Detective Inspector G.) placed with her ostensibly as an Interpreter, and wined, dined, gowned and petted, by the 'small number of officers' of M.I. The list includes Colonel Buckmaster, Richard Lloyd (Llewellyn) of 'How Green is my Valley', gazetted to Welsh Guards, in whose flat in Brook Street Mathilde Carré was subsequently installed before War Dept. decided to arrest her and remove her, first to Aylesbury Prison (July 1st 1942) and then to Holloway. She also wined and dined and 'had intelligence' with Captain Jimmy Langley, Peter Ustinov, C. Mackintosh and others.

No.4. Evidence

The question of guilt in a 'War Crimes' trial as in all political, treason or heresy trials, has, in any case, nothing to do with the jurisprudence of civil or criminal trials – especially in the case of a woman whose political affiliations or sympathies, in French described as 'having intelligence with or having collaboration with the enemy' are in question according to the supposed nationality of the secret service agent who jumps into bed with her. In this case they were successively Polish, French, German and British, and the woman did not speak a word of English or German. She is brought to trial after three years British imprisonment on no charge at all, and nearly four years French imprisonment. She cannot call on the British for whom she worked because official secrets Act preclude them from giving evidence, or of confessing the truth if they do. In any case rules of evidence do not apply in 'War Crimes' courts. As at Nurenburg [sic], War Crimes Tribunals, according to Article 19 of the Charter, 'shall not be bound by technical rules of evidence. – They shall adopt expeditious and non-technical procedure.' Non-technical certainly, but do you call that expeditious? As in 'Alice Through the Looking Glass', first comes the imprisonment, then the trial and, of course, the crime comes last of all! Then the prosecution rely on the evidence of German prisoner-of-war Bleicher, imprisoned, examined and 'conditioned' by the French for several years after the event. And we know what that is worth – vide American lawyer Everitt's evidence on the worth of German prisoner-of-wars' evidence and confessions at mock trials – solitary confinement – near starvation rations – tortures and permanently injured testicles etc.

One may have one's doubts about when American journals and inquisitive citizens question why Allied Intelligence officers found it necessary to 'examine' repeatedly, at midnight cocktail parties, only the younger and prettier wives of Nurenburg [sic] 'war-criminals'– with special reference to young Frau Baldur von Schirach.

All this may not implicate the British Secret Service, it is at least unfortunate that we tolerate the publication of such fictional drivel, inversions and lies as e.g. 'Secrets of the British Secret Service' by E.H. Cookridge (Sampson Low, Marston & Co. 1948), who relies, in his bland advertisement, 'Upon careful investigations and <u>official documents</u>' – documents unspecified. Another volume is called for: '<u>Not Such Secret Secrets of the British Secret Service</u>'.

5. 'We have no status to intervene'

Since the woman's Appeal has been rejected by the French Court, the question of jurisdiction is no longer of practical importance. We can only move to secure reprieve by appeal to the President. It seems obvious that we have more 'status' with a friendly allied Government than for instance in the case of Roman Catholics in Gibraltar moving to secure Colonial Office intervention to secure release of Cardinal Mindszenty of Hungary under trial by an 'ex-friendly' ally, or even without protégé Chiang-Kai-Shek, who received our 'All-aid-to-China' benediction.

Affiliation with Anglo-French section of F.F.I. during the war is now regarded as dangerously near 'collaboration' with an enemy? Anyway the French distinction between 'collaboration' and 'resistance' is a matter of ever-changing political grouping and in the case of a woman – well, there is only one way a Frenchman usually shows her intimate political sympathies, and we relied on that without the German formality of: 'Vous etes ma prisonniere.' Unfortunately for her, the woman has no very wealthy relatives. It would be easy to furnish a list of wealthy men imprisoned for 'collaboration' who escaped the shooting squad by paying 'une amende' [a fine] for a bit extra getting the <u>Medaille de la Résistance</u>. The tariff for acquittal was in some cases 5,000,000 frs. and for an extra half million francs, the Resistance Medal was thrown in as well.

6. Moral Responsibility

I lay stress on the fact that we have the moral responsibility. She worked in France for and with the Anglo-French-Polish sabotage section (linked with Economic Warfare) until captured by the Germans with the incriminating list. She could speak no word of German or English— until imprisoned by us. She escaped from Occupied France of her own accord, with our connivance, and it suited the Germans whom she bluffed successfully, to let her go. They were always far less ready to shoot women than the French or we were. Notwithstanding our Nurse Cavell memorial pretensions. We used her – perhaps not entirely in the way Violet Douglas-Pennant would have approved of – and then kept her three years in a prison without preferring any charge against her, and without allowing her any contact except our MI.

In the English gaols, she was placed with a young English woman who interpreted for her – for the time being I shall call her Mrs. X – who taught her English and supplemented her prison rations by sharing with her small comforts from outside. She was encouraged or invited to earn British approval by reporting back on Mrs. X who was accused of withholding information likely to be useful to the 'war effort'.

After three years in Aylesbury and Holloway prisons, under especially privileged conditions Mrs. X was released, but without any compensation and in broken health.

I am only mentioning or introducing Mrs. X at this stage, because, as my informant, she has asked me to launch an appeal in the right quarters.

My qualifications, such as they are, include an intensive study of 'economic and psychological warfare' and its personnel.

With regard to Mrs. X, I may add a few words to the effect that the conditions of her intimate and isolated association with Mathilde Carré for three years has furnished her with a very complete record.

I feel inclined to observe that it occurred to me during the war that anyone interested in the expenditure of public money on our secret service had only to visit the Lansdowne Club and the Berkeley Restaurant, conveniently situated to the MI5 headquarters in St. James's Street, where their duty so frequently took them.

Perhaps you will forgive the hyperbole of my picture of the Cavell statue blushing for shame, unless something is done.[37]

To clarify some of the persons to whom Pitt-Rivers referred in his letter, not previously mentioned elsewhere in this book:

- **Henriette 'Henny' von Schirach *née* Hoffman** (1913–92) was the wife of Baldur von Schirach (1907–74), *Reichsjugendführer* (Reich Youth Leader) and *Gauleiter* of Vienna. Von Schirach was convicted at the Nuremburg Trials and spent twenty years in Spandau Prison. In 1982 she published a book of anecdotes about Hitler entitled *Frauen um Hitler: Nach Materielen* (*Women Around Hitler: After Materials*) in which she described him as a 'cozy Austrian' who 'wanted to make himself and others a little bit happy'.
- **Lieutenant (later Lieutenant Colonel) James Maydon 'Jimmy' Langley** (1916–83) MC, OBE, was a Coldstream Guards officer wounded at Dunkirk (he lost an arm) who escaped back to Britain and worked alongside Airey Neave at MI9, the escape and evasion organisation of British Intelligence.
- **The Hon. Violet Douglas-Pennant** (1869–1945), sixth daughter of Lord Penrhyn, was the second commandant of the Women's Royal Air Force (WRAF) until she was dismissed in August 1918; she was also a philanthropist.
- **Edith Louisa Cavell** (1865–1915) was the British nurse shot by the Germans for espionage during the First World War on 12 October 1915.
- **Cardinal Jósef Mindszenty** (1892–1975) was the Prince Archbishop of Esztergom, Hungary, imprisoned by the Arrow Cross Party, the pro-Nazi party in Hungary, during the Second World War. In 1949 he appeared at a show trial which provoked worldwide condemnation and a UN Resolution. In 1956, after eight years' imprisonment, he was released during the Hungarian Revolution. Having been granted political asylum, he lived at the US embassy until 1975, when he went to Vienna to live in exile until his death.
- **Generalissimo Chiang Kai-shek** (1887–1975) was the leader of the Kuomintang, the Chinese Nationalist party during the Second World War, and who opposed Mao Tse-tung (Mao Zedong) during the Chinese Civil War. In 1949 Chiang fled to Formosa, now known as Taiwan, where he became president of the Republic of China, until his death in 1975.
- **'Mrs. X'**, Pitt-Rivers' informant may have been **Mary Stanford**, referred to earlier, who had written to various Members of Parliament about Mathilde Carré. More likely, it could have been **Stella Lonsdale**, who became his mistress after the war, who had been in prison with Mathilde.

- **E.H. Cookridge** (1908–79), whose real name was **Edward Spiro**, would write a number of books relating to British Intelligence, including *Inside S.O.E.*, *The Third Man* (about Kim Philby) and *George Blake: Double Agent*.
- The 'exceptionally bright Intelligence Officer' was probably Christopher Harmer.
- It was **Jona 'Klop' von Ustinov** who Mathilde met and stayed with, *not* his son Peter.
- The Everitt referred to was **Colonel Willis M. Everett, Jr.**, a lawyer from Atlanta who directed the defence team at the trial of the so-called 'Malmedy Massacre' of over 300 American prisoners of war by the Waffen-SS on 17 December 1944 during the Battle of the Bulge.[38]

What is interesting about Pitt-Rivers' rant is how many details of Mathilde Carré's case he seemed to know. This could not all have come from the French trial or from his female informant, whoever she may have been. So did he also have contacts in MI5 or SOE? More likely, at least some of the information came from Stella Lonsdale.

A Minute to Mr Halford from John E.D. Street on 11 February 1949 stated:

> Your friends disclaim[ed] any intention of intervening with the French on her behalf, advising any department of H.M.G. to do so'. This was agreed to by MI5. Given some work to keep her busy while Vomécourt returned to France to warn rest of his reseau. There was no further point in keeping Carre at large and she was interned for the rest of the war in company with other fascist friends of Captain Pitt-Rivers.
>
> After the liberation she was deported to France where she was re-arrested and eventually tried. Complete details of her case were handed to French authorities and it was agreed that subsequent action was exclusively a French matter.[39]

After Mathilde's release on 7 September 1954 at eight o'clock in the evening, she returned to her parents' flat in the Avenue des Gobelins: 'Great tears of joy ran down my cheeks. Ave Maria!' Shortly thereafter, in March 1955, a meeting of the National Federation of Former Members of the Resistance in the Loir-et-Cher region in Orléans passed a resolution which it stated that the meeting:

Protests energetically at the final measure of grace accorded to Mathilde Carré, which is an offence against the memory of the victims of this woman, and asks the Minister of Justice to order a new examination of her case, and to communicate the result of this new examination to our Federation.[40]

Whether or not the Federation received any response from the Minister of Justice is not recorded, but protests such as this were to no avail and Mathilde remained a free woman.

Months after Mathilde's release, Gordon Young, who would become one of her biographers, heard about her case by chance through Henry Wales, the foreign news correspondent of the *Chicago Tribune* in Paris. Intrigued by what Wales had told him, he decided to try to interview her. At first he was rebuffed by her mother when he visited the flat, but two days later he was invited back to meet with Mathilde. What, he wondered, was he going to find when he got there? As he mused en route to the flat:

Here was a woman, now just over forty-five, who had given herself freely to many men and whom many had found irresistible. She had been accused of the most base duplicity, and yet she had, by all accounts, aroused admiration amounting almost to devotion from nearly all those men and women who she had recruited to serve her. She had shown, really, not two but a score of different faces affectionate and heartless, idealistic and cynical, generous and selfish, petty-minded and supremely intelligent, traitorous and loyal, cowardly and brave.[41]

When after a few minutes Mathilde entered the 'typical little middle-class Parisian salon', he observed that 'I certainly found none of the things I had expected':

She was small, smaller even than I had expected, and her eyes and expression were totally hidden behind an enormous pair of thick dark glasses [she was half-blind at this point]. Her skin was pale and in her abundant locks of thick dark hair there were many strands now of white. She wore a plain pink blouse, very clean and neat, with a bright yellow woollen cardigan over it, and a slim black skirt. There was no varnish on her finger-nails and only a trace of make-up on her lips. Here was no *femme fatale*, nothing that fitted the conventional novelist's picture of an international spy. This quiet, modestly dressed woman looked like perhaps, a good-class hospital nurse in civilian clothes [it must be remembered she had once been a nurse], or a governess on her day off. If this was The Cat, it was truly a Cat without claws.[42]

Young explained to her that he was seeking the truth about the events in which she had been involved, including the betrayal of the *Interallié* network and the business with the *Scharnhorst* and *Gneisenau* (see Chapter 11). As ever, Mathilde remained defensive. To the first issue she responded, 'What could I do about that?', saying that either she went along with Bleicher's scheme or she would have been shot. To the second she replied, 'What could I say about that?', claiming that she had had no idea what messages Bleicher or Borchers would send from her transmitter. From his account it seems that Young got no closer to the truth about any of it. All her answers were very circumspect or evasive; the truth would have to wait until her official files were made public in 2002. Even now, many documents appear to be missing from them; the same applies to the files of others implicated in the case.

Young reflected on his encounter with Mathilde, how he was 'struck by the totally unexpected character which she presented to me that morning', an experience which made him wonder:

> She seemed so quiet, so modest, so meek, so dignified and so completely harmless that it was hardly possible to believe that this could conceivably have been the woman whose passionate drama I had been investigating. Was this how she really was? Or had the long years of imprisonment, ill-health and fading eyesight so greatly transformed her? Or …was it simply that Mathilde Carré was that morning, as she had done so often in her life before, simply adapting herself with consummate skill to a situation? Was she, in fact, just filling the role most calculated to disarm the inquisitive and persistent foreign newspaper man? Had The Cat adapted herself to impress me, with the same instinctive 'feel' for other people's personalities as she had employed in her encounters with all the varied types whose loyalty she had so completely won for the Resistance network − as she had obviously employed, too, in her perilous relationships with the Germans?[43]

All that being said, he recorded that she left him impressed, 'whether it was through skill or sincerity'.

Once again, Mathilde Carré had succeeded in being manipulative, preying on his emotions and preconceived ideas, luring him into a false sense that she was being honest with him, but in reality pulling the wool over his eyes to obscure the truth. Honesty was not something that came to her naturally; she really didn't know the meaning of the word. She had asked him when writing about her 'to please ask the world to forget The Cat'. Yet, had she really wanted that, she could have easily refused to meet with Young at all. It was not that she was ashamed of what she'd done and wanted to forget about it herself; far from it, she was still unrepentant. Nor was it as Alexander Pope had written, 'To err is Human; to Forgive, Divine'.[44] It was, as Young summed it up, 'due to a national characteristic that is particularly French; for that country which gave birth to the phrase "*Tout comprendre c'est tout pardonner*" ['To understand everything is to forgive everything.'] has always shown a great ability to understand and make allowances for human weaknesses and even human sins.'[45] A cynic might interpret that expression as a typical example of the Gallic duplicity expressed after the war: that it was acceptable to commit these and other acts when it suited them, but it was only for the French (or perhaps God) to judge whether they were indeed ultimately wrong. Ironically, Mireille Lejeune would tell Young:

> Micheline was a very great friend of mine and I would not like even now to speak of her in hatred. She was a mixture in her character. She could be so warm-hearted and generous: if somebody needed something she would give it to them at once.[46]

Yet to a great extent, the world did forget The Cat. Shortly after Young had interviewed Mathilde, she disappeared to the country and lived under an assumed name. Her memoirs suggest that this was in August 1955: 'I left Paris for this little forgotten haven ... it was only on arriving here, 500 miles from Paris, that I felt entirely free.'[47] If that distance is correct, it could be almost anywhere in France. However, a caption to a photograph in her memoirs states that on 18 November 1958 she made a pilgrimage to Montmartre and retraced her steps, stopping at the corner of the rue des Saules and the rue l'Abreuvoir opposite La Maison Rose restaurant, exactly where Bleicher had arrested her in 1941, a restaurant made famous by Maurice Utrillo, who painted several pictures of it.

While in prison in France before her trial it appears that Mathilde underwent some sort of religious conversion that she wrote about in her memoirs, and to which she devoted an entire chapter. While in Holloway the priest, whom she refers to as Father W, had tried unsuccessfully to convert her to Roman

Catholicism, as according to French lawyer Yves-Frédéric Jaffré (1921–2010) she was originally Protestant.[48] This priest, according to her book *My Conversion*, was Father Woodward; he had, however, been successful in teaching her the Lord's Prayer and the Ave Maria. At that point she was still unrepentant. As the entry for 26 April 1953 recalls:

> Condemned to death, when the priest and the pastor tried to baptize me I refused with great energy. I would have no bargaining with God. Salvation of my soul in exchange for font water? No! It was an undignified and cowardly bargain. But in secret I had said to God that if one day things turned out well and I was freed then I would be baptized of my own accord.[49]

Later, in May, she talked about not understanding the Mass, but it appears that shortly thereafter she had become fully absorbed with Roman Catholicism. On 2 June she declared that she wanted to be baptised before her birthday (29 June), but in secret so as to avoid any publicity from the press. This took place on 27 June at 8.30 in the morning in a convent chapel, with nuns and a friar participating; her godmother, Marthe, was a former prostitute. She would take her first Communion the following day and attend her first Mass on Sunday 5 July. In the remainder of her entry for that day she quotes Jean-Baptiste Henri-Dominique Lacordaire (1802–61), the French ecclesiastic, preacher and journalist who re-established the Dominican order in post-Revolutionary France in 1837. On 3 October she wrote that, having read Romano Guardini, she had realised her sin, declaring 'What an ignoble creature I am.'[50]

Romano Guardini (1885-1968) was an Italian-German Roman Catholic priest, author, academic and intellectual who had a major influence on the Liturgical Movement in Germany, and who was able to interpet the major philosophers into layman's language.

One source has claimed that she died in Paris on 30 May 1970, but it now seems that she died there in the 6th arrondissement on 30 May 2007, aged 98 and 11 months; the reference by Michel Jack Masson even includes a death registration number.[51] Apart from her memoires, two other books were published under the name Lily Carré: in 1975, *Ma Conversion* (*My Conversion*), with a Preface by Jesuit priest Père Roger Braun (1910–81); and in 1980, *Ainsi vécut Marie, jeune-fille de Nazareth, mère du Christ* (*Thus Lived Mary, Young Girl of Nazareth, Mother of Christ*).[52] Had she found redemption in her religion? Was she comparing herself to Mary in some sacrilegious way? Or was she just trying to assuage her conscience?

Who Were the Guilty Parties?

In summary, we must consider who was guilty of what and to what degree; whether the punishments they received were justified; and what motivated them to do so. But to try to unravel exactly who is like trying to determine which, if any, of the disparate Resistance movements in France were more or less successful, or which actually liberated Paris. Each of them, as well as the Allies, laid claim to equal importance in that respect, a topic discussed at some length in Ronald Rosbottom's study, *When Paris Went Dark*, about how Parisians dealt with the German occupation of their city.[1] As we have seen, Mathilde Carré was not the only one guilty, but exactly what motivated her and the other guilty parties still remains open to conjecture.

In Michael Smith's recent book *The Anatomy of a Traitor*[2] he cites the FBI as defining the factors influencing a person's decision to commit espionage or treason by the acronym MICE: Money, Ideology, Coercion (or Compromise) and Ego (or Excitement). However, Smith feels that this is too simplistic an explanation, and divides his book into chapters entitled 'Sexual Relationships', 'Money', 'Patriotism', 'Adventurers, Phantasists and Psychopaths', 'Revenge' and 'The Right Thing to Do' and cites examples of each of these traits in respective chapters. But, as he says, 'Agent motivation – why spies spy – is a complex subject … what seems at first sight to be the reason for betrayal is often not the sole one, or even the defining one.' He quotes a former CIA officer as saying, 'An agent's motivation can be changed, either by circumstances or through the efforts of an interested and patient case officer,' and a former SIS officer as saying, 'Motives are often mixed or become mixed even if they aren't to start with.'[3]

While none of the characters mentioned in this book are featured in Smith's examples, many of the traits he mentions were exhibited, individually or in combination, by the main protagonists here. Money, it has been suggested, is a more recent (i.e. post-Second World War/Cold War/post-Cold War) phenomenon. Perhaps this is because with modern-day consumerism it is so much easier to 'keep up with the Joneses' and get into debt. Smith uses the analogy of Samson and Delilah and how the Philistines had offered 1,100 pieces of silver to Delilah to betray him. One could also perhaps use the other Biblical example of Judas betraying Jesus for thirty pieces of silver. Money was not necessarily a motivating factor in our main protagonists' cases, but Mathilde Carré had been offered a financial inducement in return for her cooperation and did briefly enjoy the high life lavished upon her by the Germans. Certainly what she and WALENTY had in common was that they became emotionally and sexually involved with various members of their network. WALENTY in particular, had many girlfriends, which was bound to cause friction, lead to petty jealousies and ultimately betrayal. So much so in his case, that British Intelligence warned him to choose one and leave the rest alone.

Let us now try to establish what motivated the guilty parties to betray each other and the *Interallié* network.

Mathilde Carré (VICTOIRE)

What caused this vivacious woman from a decent bourgeois French background, who had so fervently wanted to strike back against the Nazis, to betray her country? By becoming involved in the *Interallié* network instead of living in comparative safety in the Middle East with her husband, Mathilde had expressed the same degree of patriotism as many of her fellow French men and women at the time who wanted to 'do their bit'. Apart from that, she seems to have run the gamut of Smith's criteria. There is no doubt whatsoever that she was guilty as charged. That she had no compunction in betraying her comrades and defecting so easily to the other side, without a by-your-leave, is unquestioned, and has been commented on by all with whom she came into contact. She also showed complete indifference and no remorse both at her trial and later when interviewed by Gordon Young, and was completely unrepentant. Her own opinion of things in her memoirs was:

> I have never considered myself guilty of any of the treacheries of which I have been accused … there are only two unforgiveable actions for which I can reproach myself. One was to have left my husband – the other we shall see later.[4]

Most accounts rightly accuse her of betraying the *Interallié* network, but the number of members she allegedly betrayed frequently becomes inflated to an estimated 100 people, tending to turn her story into tabloid sensationalism.

The exact number she actually betrayed, and of which she was eventually accused, was probably about two-thirds of that (around sixty or so), not an insignificant number, but this in turn created a 'domino effect' by others in the network who followed suit, whether willingly or otherwise, which probably gives rise to the figure frequently cited. Contrary to popular belief, apart from the two who died as a result of the betrayals (Lucien de Rocquigny, who was beaten to death at Mauthhausen where he died on 19 April 1943, and Madame Hugentobler, who had hanged herself in her cell), none of the other members of the network died at the hands of the Germans; they all spent the rest of the war in prison or in concentration camps and survived. That is not to say, of course, that they did not suffer during that incarceration, or afterwards from post-traumatic stress disorder.

Sexual Relationship

Sex undoubtedly played 'an important role in this woman of waning sexual powers', as Klop Ustinov observed in his report, 'and that she therefore never misses an opportunity depicting herself as being desired'. Men seemed to be attracted to her, or at least that is what she fantasised. The breakdown of her marriage, her husband's inability to satisfy her carnal needs, and his initial antipathy to want to fight, likely contributed to her insecurity. She may or may not have been involved in a brief sexual relationship with Garby-Czerniawski (they both always denied it), but when he later switched his attentions to Renée Borni (VIOLETTE), that was enough to inflame her jealousy, in spite of her protestations to the contrary. The fact that he directed his attention towards Renée Borni, whom she despised or even hated, suggests that Mathilde's motivation to betray the network had to have been primarily sexual.

Did Bleicher also find her desirable? We may never know as he never mentions it anywhere. She played down her relationship with him and insisted that she only spent one night with him, and that by mistake. His 'slapping me on the thigh, which only made him appear more repulsive in my eyes. I could not hide my disgust,' gives the impression that while she had been prepared to sleep with him on her first night as a German spy, she did it purely to lure him into thinking she was now on his side.

In spite of his initial misgivings about her trustworthiness, LUCAS also slept with her, as did Richard Llewellyn. Neither really expressed any opinion of how much they were enamoured of her, if indeed they were. Most likely, it was just part of a wartime 'fling'.

Christopher Harmer also appeared somewhat smitten with her, in spite of her telling him that she 'had every fault and was an impossible woman'. In a strange sort of way, he may have been attracted to her, even though he didn't trust her, as a sort of *femme fatale*. He would later in 1943 marry his secretary, Peggy.

Ego

Mathilde Carré had an inate inferiority complex developed during her early childhood, and an ego that always needed stroking. Dealing with her was like handling a gun with a hair trigger or trying to defuse a bomb: at any moment anything could have set her off.

While Garby-Czerniawski was away in England Mathilde was still nominally in charge, not Renée. She had always wanted to be the centre of attention, but she now believed that she was not. Yet when Garby-Czerniawski began to favour Renée Borni he had not assigned her extra duties, taking them away from Mathilde, and Renée Borni was not usurping what power he had already given Mathilde. But in her twisted mind it was as if her influence in the *Interallié* network was beginning to wane, and so she sought revenge because she so despised Renée Borni. This led to a downward spiral of betrayals, some made by her, some made by others as a result of her treachery.

Manipulation

Mathilde Carré's time spent in London, as well as in Aylesbury and Holloway prisons, are examples of how manipulative she could be. The various British Intelligence agencies who became involved in her case showed an inordinate amount of patience in dealing with her many gripes, and they felt somehow compelled to bend over backwards to accommodate her. Handling her case was always as if they were tip-toeing on egg shells. She led a charmed life and was, to use a term once coined by an intelligence contact of mine, 'high maintenance'. She was extremely manipulative and managed to twist men around her little finger in order to get what she wanted, and to which she believed she was entitled. Inspector Gale was forbidden to have anything more to do with her, and the foolish Lord Selborne managed to avoid making a complete ass of himself and creating a potential disaster by almost falling for her charms, but only after being warned off by MI5. But how was it that LUCAS could apparently fall in love with her when she had just confessed to him of betraying her comrades to the Germans, and whom he had considered killing? Was it infatuation, or was he just using her to ensure that she could be 'turned' as a double agent?

Phantasist

That she was a phantasist is exemplified in her imagining herself as the 'Mata Hari of the Second World War', or a second 'Jeanne d'Arc' although of course, it didn't end well for either of them – Joan of Arc was burnt at the stake in 1431 and Mata Hari was executed by firing squad in 1917 – so not exactly good role models!

Like most defectors, she retained some information for her interrogators to prise out of her rather than spilling all the beans at once – what is sometimes referred to as a 'meal ticket'. To do otherwise would have devalued her importance. The longer she could hold on to some titbits of information, the longer she could retain some credibility. Once it had all been told there would have been no further use for her, and she would have been discarded like flotsam on the shores of washed-up spies. She claimed that she had always been loyal, as noted in the previous chapter, but there was a distinct absence of any deep-rooted loyalty, referred to by MI5 in Chapter 1.

Revenge

Mathilde sought revenge against Renée Borni because Garby-Czerniawski had directed his attention (and favours) towards her. But why did she not find some other way of getting back at Renée without her actions leading to the total destruction of the network? Was this hatred of Renée directed at him as well? Nothing that has come to light so far indicates that this was the case; all the venom is directed at Renée. In none of MI5's interrogations of Mathilde does she speak disparagingly about him. The fact that *Interallié* was *his* network, which he had painstakingly built up from scratch, indicates that perhaps it was her way of punishing him as well. Once, when she threatened to leave, he warned her that she was not indispensable, which would have only rubbed salt into an already open wound and antagonised her. It has to be understood that Mathilde Carré was by no means a rational woman. As Christopher Harmer said, she was 'completely out for her own advancement and accordingly unworthy of any real long-term trust'. She suffered from delusions of grandeur and a sense of self-importance. She was also resentful of not receiving any formal recognition from the British (i.e. a medal). This made it easier for her to betray her colleagues with an easy conscience.

Money

Mathilde had claimed that her betrayal was simply for the 6,000 francs a month Bleicher had offered her to cooperate, in return for her life.[5]

Psychopathic Tendencies

MI5 described Mathilde Carré as having a 'complete lack of ordinary human understanding and sympathy'. Her lack of empathy and cold-heartedness, shallow emotions, irresponsibility and selfishness lead one to now ask if she was, in fact, a psychopath or a sociopath.

The traits referred to in the 'Psychopathic Personality Inventory' of Lilienfeld and Andrews[6] suggest possibly the former, although they consider a sociopath to be less dangerous, with a personality shaped by her environment. More likely is that she suffered from 'Narcissistic Personality Disorder', traits of which had started to develop during her early adulthood. In her autobiography she speaks of 'this girl who was irresistibly drawn towards evil', for which she gives as an excuse that her mother was 'always pulling me to pieces' by telling her, 'Be quiet, you don't know how to speak properly'; 'How ugly you are'; 'You're completely lacking in elegance'; and 'You have no taste.'[7] This, she said, gave her a 'violent inferiority complex'. By her own admission, she was neurotic, a 'complete egoist', and showed no interest in her close friend Sophie (possibly not her real name) while she was a student. WALENTY said she was highly strung. As a young woman, the stance she opted to take was that:

> I pretended to be older than I really was and to my misfortune I adopted the fashion of the moment – the 'tough woman'. A cigarette between my lips, a cynical laugh and ruthlessly stifling all sentiment and emotion … I denied everything in the nature of sweetness, sensibility and love – 'all that old-fashioned rubbish' as the young people of the period used to say.[8]

In his introduction to her book her lawyer, Albert Naud, best sums her up when she appeared at her trial:

> A picture was formed of her … the Cat did not conjure up a picture of a sweet, feminine woman with soft, voluptuous gestures and half-closed eyes, full of tenderness and ardour. Look at the photograph of Mathilde Carré taken during this theatrical trial, the one in which her forehead is supported by her two hands pointing downwards, making them look like a pair of ears. Look at her cold eyes which seem to pierce beyond this world and you will have the conventional Cat as she was represented by the Press and whom the public would have been disappointed not to find in the dock of infamy, conforming to its pre-conceived image.[9]

Renée Borni (VIOLETTE)

If what WALENTY wrote in his critique of VICTOIRE's manuscript is to be believed in its entirety, Renée Borni was also guilty, perhaps equally so, although this was never proven in a court of law. Consequently, her punishment was commensurate with her offence and mitigated by her ill health at the time of the trial. MI5 also appears to have practically absolved her of all wrong-doing on account of her having to work under duress, which they referred to as 'grudging and qualified collaboration', unlike the 'whole-hearted craven and despicable collaboration' of Mathilde Carré. By all accounts, Renée Borni was much liked by most members of the network, perhaps because she was young and pretty, unlike the abrasive Mathilde, who was neither, and had an inflated sense of her own importance. Both Renée Borni and Mathilde Carré had allowed their petty jealousies to come between them and their work, which led to *Interallié*'s destruction and affected the lives of those with whom they came into contact.

Borni received a two-and-a-half year prison sentence, '*indignité nationale*' ('national indignity') and the equivalent of a £50 fine. '*Indignité nationale*' was a legally defined offence created following the Liberation of France and adopted by the Assemblée Nationale on 26 August 1944. It involved any act of aid to the Axis powers after 16 June 1940 (the Occupation) or:

- participation in the Vichy Cabinet;
- executive posts in the Vichy propaganda or the Commissariat for Jewish Affairs;
- active participation in pro-collaboration demonstrations; or
- mere membership in pro-collaboration organisations.

It also served to fill a legal void that was not covered by the existing laws of treason, murder, etc. during the Occupation or the Vichy regime and did not take into consideration participation in the Milice or the Waffen-SS. The punishment was confiscation of property, loss of election rights, banning from public service or trade unions, mass media or semi-public companies, and could last from five years to life. It ceased to be a punishment at the beginning of 1951. It is not known how long Borni's 'state of indignity' lasted, but given Borni's comparatively light sentence, it can be assumed it was for the minimum five years. She was never required to serve much of her sentence as, at the time of her trial she had been 'grievously ill' and was discharged from the clinic in which she was receiving treatment and disappeared into obscurity 'in an unnamed part of the French countryside'. As of 1961 she was 'now married and living in France', according to Garby-Czerniawski at the end of his memoirs. The date of her death and the name of her husband are unknown.

The Others

And what of the others? Did Mathilde Carré 'cast the first stone', as the question was posed earlier, or was it someone else? It seems as if it might have actually been Émile Lemeur, the half-drunk docker in Cherbourg who first betrayed Kieffer (KIKI), which then alerted the Germans to the existence of the network when these two began to talk. His motivation, and that of Denise Buffet (referred to by Marcel Ruby as Madame Bonnet), are unclear, but it may have been money.

It is hard to pinpoint exactly what motivated them to betray their fellow members of *Interallié*. For some it was probably revenge; for others it was simply fear or coercion. Exactly how many in total were guilty is also hard to nail down, but the principal ones were:

- Robert/Jean Lucien Kieffer (KIKI)
- Roger Bardet (ROGER)
- Claude Jouffret (MICHEL)
- Robert Goubeau (BOB)
- Suzanne Laurent, Bleicher's girlfriend

They were all found guilty of betraying members of the network and received sentences that served to teach that no crime goes unpunished, yet Kieffer and Bardet, along with Carré, were spared the firing squad.

Denise Buffet was also considered guilty, but because she had spent time in a German concentration camp she had suffered enough and was not brought to trial. Perhaps it was a testament to how the French were prepared, to some extent, to forgive and forget, as mentioned above, even though the crimes had cost many lives and ruined others.

Some members of the network easily capitulated under interrogation. There may have been the threat of, or actual, torture; while others were obviously quite willing to betray each other without batting an eyelid, even before any threats were uttered. Their motive was not money, but to save their own skin, or as revenge against Mathilde Carré, whom they resented or hated. Some lacked the 'moral fibre' or inner strength to resist interrogation, such as **Duvernoy**, who 'wept like a woman'. But being mostly amateurs, unlike the SOE-trained officers, it is likely that none of those involved would have received any formal training in resistance to torture – the maxim being to try to stay silent for forty-eight hours to allow agents to go into hiding or networks to disperse. In reality, most people will crumble under duress, even without being tortured. Under torture people will confess to anything to avoid physical and mental pain. Information extracted under these conditions may or may not be admissible in a court of law, certainly not in today's context. If this is the case, are those people then guilty of treachery and therefore considered traitors? Or should they be forgiven for capitulating so easily? That is a discussion best addressed by lawyers, and outside this author's experience.[10] But, just like Mathilde Carré's, their actions caused harm to others, and sent many to concentration camps. Their duplicity, and that of others not covered here, would not be forgotten and would remain a source of deep resentment in France for decades to come. So much so that it has only been comparatively recently that French authorities have released files dating back to the war now that the guilty parties are mostly dead. The late Richard Deacon (Donald McCormick) has suggested that the mysterious deaths of British citizens driving or camping in the south of France may in some cases have been connected to wartime revenge killings.[11] Undoubtedly, the mysterious deaths of French citizens who were collaborators may also be explained in this way, but there is no evidence that has so far come to light to suggest that this was the case with those involved in the *Interallié* affair.

Alfred Ignatz Maria Kraus

Kraus had a dubious and shady past. He claimed that he had been coerced, reluctantly at first, into working for German Intelligence, but later willingly offered to help them. As a member of the Abwehr he played an active role in the arrests of several members of *Interallié*, but it is debatable just how influential he was in that respect. Certainly he was able to supply his German masters with important information 'borrowed' from Michel Courtois (EVE); with or without Kraus, members of *Interallié* would have been arrested sooner or later by the treachery of others. He also managed to move into Parisian society by way of his marriage of convenience to **Jacqueline de Broglie** as a noble act to save her from arrest. If she was complicit in helping him in his work, in spite of claiming that she never shared with him any of the information given to her by Courtois, it has never been proven. Kraus's deviousness extended into persuading a renowned – and later discredited – hero of the SAS (Captain Lee) to take him to England to join the elite Parachute Regiment, but rightly fell under the suspicion of MI5 as not to be trusted, and was interned. In many ways, like Mathilde Carré, he led a charmed life, always managing to scrape through relatively unscathed. His later life in Canada and elsewhere is unrecorded.

Hugo Bleicher

Hugo Bleicher was not a traitor; he was just a devious German intelligence officer who succeeded in doing his job by using Mathilde Carré to break up *Interallié*. He did not commit any 'war crimes' *per se*, nor cause any lives to be lost directly by his actions – only the actions of those who worked for him did that. Having been extensively interrogated by British Intelligence at the end of the war and providing them with his side of the *Interallié* and LUCAS affairs, as well as a breakdown of the German intelligence services in Paris, he retreated to Tettnang, his hometown, where he opened a tobacconist's shop. His account of events, such as it is, was published in *Colonel Henri's Story* in 1954. Even so, the account was not without controversy (see below). As noted earlier, he doesn't mention Mathilde Carré by name and only alludes to her; there is no mention of an 'affair', not even to justify using her to his own ends. How competent he really was as an intelligence officer remains to be seen. Certainly he was instrumental in the break-up of other networks in France, which are beyond the scope of this book. Many of his achievements were the result of others' handiwork and not entirely of his own doing. A photograph online shows him and Roman Garby-Czerniawski in Paris in 1972, meeting in front of the Eiffel Tower. However, neither his book nor Garby-Czerniawski's make any mention of that meeting, nor how or if they got along. According to Roman's son, Gerry Czerniawski, the meeting with Bleicher in Paris was good-natured and the two shared a mutual respect as two professionals. It may have been a French TV programme that brought them together. Bleicher died in August 1982.

Roman Garby-Czerniawski

It must be said that Roman Garby-Czerniawski was *not* a traitor either and has been exonerated for any misdemeanours he might have committed in the eyes of the Poles and the British. To many he was a war hero, and was decorated by both Poland and Britain, but nor had he been squeaky clean. When he returned to England with his plan to set up a Polish Fifth Column it raised a number of concerns among British and Polish Intelligence officials, causing them to suspect that he too was a double agent 'turned' by the Germans.

However, this was later disproved. What he succeeded in doing was to convince the Germans to release him and allow him to go back to England, in order to continue working against them. This shows a particular kind of ingenuity and deviousness. But there were also alleged lapses in operational security, and his many girlfriends only served to make Carré's and others' task easier when it came to betraying the *Interallié* network. As his son Gerry told me, his father was always a 'ladies' man' and his mother's friends all went 'gooey-eyed' over him.

As noted earlier, as BRUTUS he went on to play a key role in the D-Day deception plans, for which he was awarded the OBE. The spurious allegations that he may have been a German agent do not stand up to scrutiny as they would surely have been investigated as far as possible before ever allowing him to become part of the cadre of D-Day planners. Those making the allegations were themselves guilty of collaborating with the Germans and so were inclined to sow seeds of doubt in MI5's collective mind and besmirch his character. Most of the allegations were made retrospectively, after the Allied invasion of France, and by people after they had been captured and taken into custody by either the French or the British. No evidence has come to light to suggest that BRUTUS ever compromised the D-Day deception plans by leaking information to the Germans, nor that they became aware of the deception technique. The transmitter he used at that time was closely monitored so that, were he to have made any 'mistakes' to warn the Germans that the information he was sending them was false, they would have been easily detected.

After the war he married Monique Deschamps, referred to by his son Gerry as 'Bambi', but later married Thelma, Gerry's mother. At some point, Monique was involved in an explosion that disfigured her face. Gerry thought that this may have been a contributing factor to their splitting up, although the two women remained friends. Later still, Roman married Lola Modzelewska, a Polish actress. He became Director of Resettlement for the Polish Air Force – the Polish Resettlement Corps (Royal Air Force). The Polish government-in-exile also appointed him Minister of Information, which, according to intelligence historian Nigel West, he held until his death.[12] He got to know the comedian Michael Bentine (1922–96), one of the founding members of the Goons, who had been an RAF intelligence officer attached to 300 'Land of Masovia' Polish Bomber Squadron and 626 Bomber Squadron at one time. Another person with whom he came into contact was Monsignor Bruce Kent (b.1929), the former Catholic priest who became active in the Campaign for Nuclear Disarmament. As a printer in Fulham, Roman printed *Felix*, the newspaper of Imperial College

Union, amongst others. According to Nigel West, at one time he lived just doors away from him. He died in London on 26 April 1985, aged 75, and is buried in Newark-on-Trent cemetary for RAF burials (P-2554).

Pierre de Vomécourt (LUCAS)

LUCAS also came under suspicion of being a German agent. He claimed that if he had betrayed any names to the Germans, it was only those who had already been betrayed to them by others – 'I gave the names only of those whom The Cat had already betrayed.'[13] As Colonel Gano of the Polish Intelligence Service observed, he had made the major mistake on his first meeting with VICTOIRE of giving away too much information even though he knew nothing about her at that point. And, like almost everyone else who came under her spell, de Vomécourt chose to sleep with Mathilde instead of killing her because of her betrayals. He too had become infatuated with her, yet, as Guy Liddell observed, 'although VICTOIRE was very much in love with him, he was not nearly so enamoured with her'. Even at her trial he continued to defend her, professing that she had never done anything to harm him personally, which was true, but still does not absolve her of her crimes. At that time de Vomécourt was already married: he had married Micheline Sailly (1907–2010) on 21 December 1927; he later remarried on 13 April 1951 to Thérèse-Geneviève-Augustine Leblond (1906–86). It appears that Micheline Sailly died on 25 April 2010 in Villedieu-sur-Indre at the remarkable age of 103; de Vomécourt died on 7 March 1986.[14]

The Future of *Interallié*

Would the *Interallié* network have gone on being successful for some time longer without Mathilde's treachery and that of the others? There is a certain inevitability that, like many of the networks in France, *Interallié* would have eventually collapsed due to betrayals or the Germans becoming more aware of its activities. Apart from the obvious treachery, its break-up was due in part to the risks the members ran, the lack of good operational security and the dubious reliability of some members, some of whom were associated with VICTOIRE and unlikely to have been properly vetted when they were recruited. Like some other networks, it got too big and too difficult to handle – too many people knew too much, either in terms of operational details, or the names of those involved. There were few or no 'cutouts' to avoid this from happening. As WALENTY said in his memoirs, when discussing with VICTOIRE the friction between her and Fernand Gane (MONO/KENT), 'it just proves what I have felt for a long time; we are centralizing too much now, and the organization is growing too big to be safe!' Prescient words indeed. He also admitted:

> There is no doubt that even without her assistance the Organisation would have been entirely liquidated ... Her guilt, therefore, consists chiefly in having facilitated to the Germans the quick arrest of other and numerous agents, who might have escaped in view of the notoriety, which the affair immediately won.[15]

Other networks throughout France were also periodically betrayed, some of which involved Bleicher's handiwork, others allegedly by Henri Déricourt. These break-ups were caused in part by internecine squabbling among the many factions working under the umbrella of the French Resistance. They were often politically and diametrically opposed to one another, all working to their own agendas, but supposedly all for the good of France. Many more mistakes were made in terms of recruitment and operational security. Nevertheless, what happened to these agents and networks should have served to instil more caution into British Intelligence, in particular SOE. How effective SOE's operations were has to some extent already been evaluated by M.R.D. Foot and others.[16] How useful *Interallié*'s intelligence was to British Intelligence needs to be properly studied and evaluated once more documents become publicly available, if indeed after the passage of time they still exist. The *Interallié* affair serves as an example of human failings and the damage that they can cause when these interfere and are left to run their course.

In this author's mind, from the evidence presented throughout these chapters, those who were punished got their just desserts. Of course, not all of those involved were accused of, or found guilty of, treachery, but they were guilty on occasion of other character flaws that under duress manifested themselves and caused considerable damage in some cases, contributing to the collapse of the *Interallié* network.

Should the French have executed Mathilde Carré instead of commuting her sentence? Others had been executed for similar or even lesser crimes, so perhaps the French would have been justified in carrying out the original sentence. It is perhaps fitting for Mathilde Carré, someone who craved to be the centre of attention at all times, no matter what the cost, that her sentence should be that she died in obscurity, largely unknown to the French public, her career only mentioned briefly in wartime intelligence books since then. Only now, seven decades later, can the effects of her treachery on the networks in which she played a key role in betraying be better known. The cat initially got the cream, but then it went sour.

APPENDIX 1

Members and Contact of the WALENTY Organisation Carded in VICTOIRE

From KV2/926.

ADAM *see under* MITCHELL Lt Roger
ALBERT*see under* COTTIN Roger
ALBERT I *see under* see under LEJEUNE Jean
ALBERT II
ALICE
ANGELLO *see under* MAILLET Charles
APOLLON *see under* METEOS Marcelino
ARTOS
AUBERTIN *see under* cover name RENÉ
AUTIER Philippe
ACHAT Capt. André
BAILLY Auguste
BAILLY Jean or Oscar
BENOIT *see under* COWBURN Benjamin Hodkinson
BERNARD
BERNARDSKI *cover name* TADY, CAROLA
BERTHE
BERTRAND
BLAVETTE Mme
BOB
BOB-EDGAR } *see under* GORRIOT Robert
BOBY-ROLAND *see under* LEJEUNE Charles

BORNI Renée *see under* PETITJEAN
BRADOWSKA Mme *cover name* METCHKA
BRAULT Michel *cover name* MIKLOS, NIKLAUSS, JEROME
BUFFET Mme *cover name* DENISE
BURLOT Théophile *cover name* CHARLES
CARBONNIER Jean *cover name* DANIEL
CAROLA *see under* BERNARDSKI
CESAR
CHARLES *see under* BURLOT Théophile
CHON *see under* JANOWSKI Madeleine
CHRISTIAN *see under* KROTKI
CLAUDE
CLAUDE *see under* JOUFFRET Claude
COCO
COTTIN Roger *cover name* ROGER, ALBERT
COURTOIS Michel *cover name* EVE
COWBURN Benjamin Hodkinson *cover name* BENOIT
CZYZ Lt Stefan *cover name* STEPHEN
DANIEL *see under* CARBONNIER Jean
DAMPIERRE Comte Armand
DAMPIERRE Comtesse Colette
DANIEL Capt
DEFLIE *cover name* HECTOR
DENISE *see under* BUFFET Mme
DESCHAMPS-CZERNIAWSKA *cover name* MOUSTIQUE
MONO
DUPRÉ *cover name* EUGENE
DUVERNOY *see under* WIRTZ
EDGAR *see under* GORRIOT Robert
ÉMILE
ENGELMANN Paul *cover name* APOLLON
ERNESTINE *see under* JEANNINE
EUGENE *see under* DUPRÉ
EVE *see under* COURTOIS Michel
FERGA *see under* GANE Fernand
FERNAND

FRANCK

FROMENT Pierre de

GANE Fernand @ GAUTHIER *cover name* MONO, KENT, PIANISTE, JACQUOT
Lt @ GRENIER @ GARNIER

GEORGES I

GEORGES II

GORCE Henri *cover name* LOUIS

GORRIOT Robert *cover name* BOB-EDGAR, BOB, EDGAR

GUY *see under* VEDERO Guy

D'HARCOURT Richard *cover name* RICHARD Georges or Pierre or Pierre

IRINEE I *see under* VEDERO Guy

IRINEE II

ISIDORE

JACQUES *see under* JAGIELOWICZ

JACKIE *see under* LABOUROT Jacques

JAGIELOWICZ *see under* JAG, JACQUES

JAG *see under* JACQUES

JANKOWSKI

JANOWSKI Madeleine *cover name* CHON

JEAN *see under* LURTON Georges

JEANNINE *cover name* ERNESTINE

JEROME *see under* BRAULT Michel

JOUFFRET Claude *cover name* MICHEL, CLAUDE

KRAUSS Freddie

KAWOVIC @ MARSCHALL *cover name* ONCLE MARCO

KENT *see under* GANE Fernand

KIFFER Robert *cover name* KIKI, DESIRE, POVIC

KLEBER Marcel

KLEIND *see under* KROTKI Lt

KROTKI Lt @ ORSIVAL @ *cover name* CHRISTIAN KLEIND

LABOUROT Jacques *cover name* JACKIE

LACH *cover name* RAPIDE

LAPORTE Lt André *cover name* MARIUS

LECQUELLEC Mme Maud *cover name* ORION

LEGRAND *see under* ROBERT Lt

LEGRAND René *cover name* YOLÉ

LEGRAND Jacques *cover name* W.O.L./T.A.R.
LEJEUNE Mme *cover name* MIREILLE
LEJEUNE Charles *cover name* BOBY-ROLAND, ROLAND
LEJEUNE Jean *cover name* ALBERT I
LIPSKI de *cover name* OBSERVATEUR
LURTON Georges *cover name* JEAN
LYPSKY de *see under* LIPSKI de
MAILLET Charles *cover name* ANGELLO
MARCEL *see under* TABET Francis
MARCO Oncle *see under* KAWOVIC
MARIUS *see under* LAPORTE Lt André
MARSCHALL *see under* KAWOVIC
MASLOWSKI @ MASSENET
MATEOS Marcelino *cover name* ANTONIO
MAURICE *see under* WLODARCZYK Janusz
MAX
METCHKA *see under* BRADKOWSKA Mme
MICHEL *see under* JOUFFRET Claude
MIKLOS *see under* BRAULT Michel
MIREILLE *see under* LEJEUNE Mme
MITCHELL Lt Roger *cover name* ADAM
MOUSTIQUE *see under* DESCHAMPS-CZERNIAWSKI Mono [*sic*]
NOEL
NOEUD Richard *cover name* RICHARD
OBSERVATEUR *see under* DE LIPSKI
ORSIVAL @ KLEIND *cover name* CHRISTIAN
POULAIN Robert
PAOLI *see under* ROBERT Lt
PAUL *see under* ROCQUIGNY Lucien
PETIT *see under* ROBERT Lt
PETITJEAN Renée née BORNI *see under* VIOLETTE
PHILIPPE
PIANISTE *see under* GANE Fernand
PORCHER Paulette
RAOUL
RAPIDE *see under* LACH

RAYMOND
RENÉ *see under* AUBERTIN René
RICHARD *see under* NOEUD Richard
RICHARD Georges *see under* D'HARCOURT Richard
RICHARD Pierre *see under* D'HARCOURT Richard
ROBERT Lt @ PETIT @ LEGRAND *cover name* PAOLI
ROCQUIGNY Lucien *cover name* PAUL
ROGER *see under* COTTIN Roger
ROLAND *see under* LEJEUNE Charles
STEPHEN *see under* CZYZ Lt Stefan
TABET Francis *cover name* MARCEL
TADY *see under* BERNARDSKI
VEDERO Guy *cover name* GUY, IRINEE I
VIOLETTE *see under* PETITJEAN Renée
VOLTA
WIRTZ *cover name* DUVERNOY
WLODARCZYK Janusz *cover name* MAURICE
WALTERS Gu *cover name* LEON
YOLÉ *see under* LEGRAND
YVES

Particulars of Members and Associates of WALENTY Organisation

Note: Information is taken from KV2/931 and may contain some mistakes, which have been corrected in the text.

WALENTY	Captain CZERNIAWSKI. Age 33, short, thin and strong, brown wavy hair, green bloodshot eyes, bad teeth. Pilot in Polish air Force. Passed Staff College in Warsaw and during war on General Staff. Stationed at Lunéville on capitulation of France and escaped to unoccupied zone after being taken prisoner.
A	
[ADAM]	Lieut. Roger MITCHELL, F.F.F. @ MICHEL. Half American, half French, mother living in Paris. S.I.S. agent. Visited WALENTY organisation in Paris in August 1941 and remained in touch until his return to England in November. Subsequently returned to unoccupied France in early part of 1942 to make investigations.
ALBERT	Formerly agent of Sector A, friend of JACKIE. Name and address unknown. Left organisation before arrests took place and therefore still at liberty.
ALICE	One of VICTOIRE's landladies in the rue Cortot.
ANGELLO	Sub-agent of MOUSTIQUE for Sector A. Name and address unknown.

ANTONIO	Spanish sub-agent of MOUSTIQUE for Sector A, employed for arranging escapes into Spain. Name and address unknown.
ARTOS	Painter living at 217 Faubourg St. Honoré. Apartment used for one of alternative wireless stations.
B	
BAILLY, Auguste	Godfather of VICTOIRE. Novelist living in rue Faraday, Paris. Casual contact of VICTOIRE.
BAILLY, Oscar @ Jean	Son of above living in rue Paul Adam. Casual contact of VICTOIRE.
BERNARD	Sub-agent of Sector B. Air N.C.O. Introduced by IRINEE II. Name and address unknown.
BERTHE	Fisherman recruited by BERNARD as sub-agent for Sector B. Name and address unknown.
BERTRAND	Agent of Sector B. Air N.C.O. aged 20. Friend of BOB-EDGAR and COCO. Name and address unknown.
BOB-EDGAR	See EDGAR.
BOBY-ROLAND	See ROLAND.
C	
CÉSAR	Fisherman of Roscoff with nine children. Employed in sea liaison between Brittany and England. Name and address unknown.
CLAUDE	Sub-agent of CHARLES for Sector C. ? Guy CHAUMET, son of ex-Minister, CHAUMET.
CHARLES	Theophil BURLOT, aged 33, small, curly hair. Sub-agent for Sector C. Responsible for betraying OVERCLOUD organisation to Germans.
LA CHATTE	VICTOIRE
CHON	Eldest daughter of JANKOWSKI, Pole living at 64, Avenue de la Grande Armée. Employed in identification of vehicles at fee of 300 francs per month. Girlfriend of WALENTY.

CHRISTIAN	ORSIVAL @ KLEIND. Pole living in Paris. Friend of WALENTY. Employed for liaison and general work. Spoke Italian.
COCO	Young French pilot aged 20. Chief of Sector C. Name and address unknown.
D	
DAMPIERRE	Comte and Comtesse de D. Contacts of VICTOIRE and EVE.
DANIEL	Jean CARBONIER. Aged 50. Commercial traveller. Spoke many languages. Formerly Chief of Sector D, but arrested in spring of 1941. Now probably shot.
DANIELLE	Capt. Contact of VICTOIRE with Deuxième Bureau.
DEFLIE, M.	Friend of MONO who worked occasionally in Sectors G and H.
DENISE	Mme. BUFFET, sub-agent of Sector D, who betrayed KIKI.
DÉSIRE	See KIKI.
D'HARCOURT, Richard	Agent of Deuxième Bureau in Occupied France and contact of VICTOIRE's. Tall, short-sighted. Very intelligent and courageous.
DUVERNOY	WIRTZ. French-Russian, born in Cairo. One of VICTOIRE's links with the Deuxième Bureau. Had formerly been engaged in espionage in Italy for France.
E	
EDGAR	GORRIOT or GOBINOT. Pilot aged 20. Head of Sector E.
ÉMILE	Belgian, living in Courbevois or Asnières. Sub-agent of Sector E. Name and address unknown.
ERNESTINE	See JEANNINE.
EUGÈNE	DUPRÉ. Reputed to be half-brother of ÉMILE. Name and address unknown.

[EVE]	British S.I.S. agent sent to France in 1941 under name Michel COURTOIS. Contact of WALENTY, VICTOIRE, DAMPIERRE and KRAUSS. Arrested beginning of July, 1941.
F	
FERNAND	Young French Air Force N.C.O. living at Boulogne. Friend of IRINEE II. Sub-agent of Sector F.
FRANCK	Jew who helped to change money on black market and subsequently became chief of Sector F.
FROMENT, Pierre de	French lieutenant aged 32. Friend of VICTOIRE. Lived near demarcation line and helped organisation in early stages but never took active part later on.
G	
GEORGES I	Pole, name unknown. Sent up to Paris from Marseilles in early stages of organisation to deal with W/T side, but was injured in a train accident early in 1941 and left.
GEORGES II	French Air Force N.C.O. Name and address unknown. Was in charge of Sector G for some time.
GUY	Guy VEDERO. French Air Force N.C.O. Originally in charge of Sector I under code name of IRINEE, but subsequently took over Sector G under his Christian name, GUY. In autumn of 1941, by pretending that the Gestapo were after him, managed to get 10,000 francs out of VICTOIRE and re-joined his old squadron at Pau. Never arrested by Germans.
H	
HENRIETTE	French girl engaged by VICTOIRE shortly before break-up to act as her secretary. Name unknown.
I	
IRINEE I	See GUY.

IRINEE II	Chief of Sector I. Name and address unknown.
ISIDORE	Young French Air Force N.C.O. Friend of IRINEE II and sub-agent of Sector I.

J

JACKIE	Jacques LABOUROT, son of music dealer of Montmartre. Young French Air Force N.C.O. Sent by Deuxième Bureau as contact.
JAG (JACQUES)	Pole, name unknown. N.C.O. Friend of WALENTY. Used for general liaison work and microphotography. Escaped after being warned by MAURICE.
JANKOWSKI	Pole living at 64, Avenue de la Grande Armée. Friend of WALENTY. Took no active part in organisation. See also CHON.
JEAN	Georges or Gaston LURTON, aged 40–45. Kept radio shop near Tours. Chief of sector J.
JEANNINE (ERNESTINE)	Waitress in restaurant at Loches. Name and address unknown. Became girlfriend of JEAN and worked in Sector J with him.

K

KENT	Sub-agent of Sector K. Name and address unknown.
KIKI	Robert KIFFER. Head agent of Sector D.
KLEBER, Marcel	Chief agent of Sector K.

L

LOUIS	Henri GORCE. Frenchman aged 35-40. Friend of MONO and MOUSTIQUE and agent of Sector L.

M

MARCEL	Francis TABET. Friend of VICTOIRE and used by Germans to operate W/T set after break-up.

MARCO, ONCLE	Distinguished French scientist of Russian extraction named KAWOVIC @ Marco MARSCHALL. President of Association of French Chemists. Contact of VICTOIRE for liaison with PATRIE network.
MARIUS	Lieut. Aviateur André LAPORTE. Young, fair. Agent provided for VICTOIRE by Deuxième Bureau who worked for INTERALLIÉE for a time in obtaining information about aerodromes in Paris region.
MASLOWSKI @ MASSENET	Pole. W/T operator sent from Marseilles to Paris in early summer, 1941 to organise W/T side. Later left occupied zone and has since reached England.
MAURICE	Janusz WLODARCZYK. Pole. Wireless operator. Escaped and later reached England.
MAX	Radio operator, friend of MONO and MAURICE. Name and address unknown.
METCHKA	Mme. BRATKOWSKA. Wife of Polish captain in London. No particular function in organisation but friend of WALENTY.
MICHEL	Claude JOUFFRET. Friend of VICTOIRE, who gave her general help. Arrested and later let out of prison at her request to become her liaison with LUCAS under the name CLAUDE.
MIKLOS	Maître Michel BRAULT. Lawyer of Polish extraction, working for various underground movements and VICTOIRE's liaison with the L.N. organisation.
MIREILLE	Mme. LEJEUNE. Wife of ROLAND-BOBY and concierge at 6, Avenue Lamarck, one of the original post boxes.
MONO	Fernand GANE or GANNE (@ GAUTIER, GRENIER, GARNIER). Frenchman aged 35–40, recruited to organise W/T side, but later relegated to chief agent of Sector A.
MOUSTIQUE	Simone DESCHAMPS [sic]. French. Mistress of MONO and afterwards agent in Sector A.

O	
OBSERVATEUR	DE LIPSKY. Pole living in Paris. Responsible for information about small French industry.
ORION	Mme. Madeleine DE QUELLEC. French girlfriend of WALENTY. Took no active part in organisation as such.
P	
PAOLI	Lieut. ROBERT @ PETIT @ LEGRAND. French officer aged 26, living at 26, rue Légion d'Honneur. Contact of VICTOIRE with Deuxième Bureau.
PAUL	Lucien ROCQUIGNY. ExPolish journalist living in Boulevard St. Michel, who had travelled extensively in Germany. Responsible for review of Press and Propaganda.
PORCHER, Paulette	Girlfriend of WALENTY.
R	
RAPIDE	LACH. Pole, ex-railway employee. Acted as courier in early stages of organisation and to a certain extent later on.
RAOUL	French police officer. Sub-agent of ROLAND for Paris Sector. Name and address unknown.
RAYMOND	French police officer. Sub-agent of ROLAND for Paris Sector. Name and address unknown.
RENÉ	René AUBERTIN. French officer, lover of VICTOIRE. In charge of industry in Paris Sector, and also gave VICTOIRE a great deal of help in preparing reports and in other ways.
RICHARD (NOEUD)	
[HUGENTOBLER]	Frenchman with German-sounding name who spoke German well and occupied himself with obtaining information from Germans in Paris region. His wife was concierge at 1, Avenue Lamarck, which was used as a post box.

ROLAND-BOBY	Charles LEJEUNE. French police officer. Chief agent for Sector R (Paris region). Husband of MIREILLE.
S	
STEPHEN	Pole. Name, address and function unknown. Arrived shortly before break-up from Marseilles.
T	
TADY (CAROLA)	BERNARDSKI. Czech. Friend of METCHKA. Contact of organisation for general information. Probably worked to a certain degree also for the Germans.
TILLOT, Dr.	French doctor. Friend of JACKIE and BOB. Did no work for organisation but was prepared to supply poison.
V	
VIOLETTE	Renée PETIJEAN (*née* BORNI). Mistress of WALENTY.
VOLTA	Head of photographic laboratory. Name and address unknown.
Y	
YOLÉ	René LEGRAND. Frenchman. Gave information on sea transport, especially between French North Africa and Unoccupied France. Also giving information to Germans.
YVES	(Le Petit Turc). Frenchman (half Turkish). Engineer giving information about transport generally. Name and address unknown.

Chronology of the Betrayal and Arrests of Interallié

Synthesised from KV2/926 and KV2/931.

3 November 1941: KIKI denounced by Mme BUFFET.

10 November 1941: KIKI arrested on Cherbourg Station.

11 November 1941: ARMAND returned from England.

15? November 1941: KIKI forced to write letter fixing rendezvous at Paris.

? November 1941: KIKI forced to make second rendezvous, as first not kept (second rendezvous with CHRISTIAN at Café de Monte Carlo).

17? November 1941: CHRISTIAN arrested.

18 November 1941: *0530*: ARMAND and VIOLETTE arrested at Villa Léandre; MAURICE and GEORGES [*sic*] escaped; MONO, MAX and JAG warned; *1015*: VICTOIRE went to café in rue Lamarck; *1030*: CLAUDE failed to keep rendezvous at café, corner of rue Lamarck; *1045*: VICTOIRE called at 8, rue Lamarck and received news of arrest; VICTOIRE arrested on way to rue Cortot to destroy papers; *1300*: VICTOIRE taken to Villa Léandre then Hôtel Edward VII and searched; *1600*: VICTOIRE taken to La Santé.

19 November 1941: *0800*: VICTOIRE questioned by captain in Deuxième Bureau with two female interpreters; VICTOIRE returned to Hôtel Edward VII and interrogated by Captain Eric BORCHERS (Gestapo chief at Cherbourg), Hugo BLEICHER and 3 or 4 others; *1100*: Rendezvous with DUVERNOY (WIRTZ) in Champs-Élysées. VICTOIRE assisted in WIRTZ's arrest; *1200*: VICTOIRE telephoned her mother, and at her request, ONCLE MARCO to reassure him and remind him of evening rendezvous; VICTOIRE went with BLEICHER to arrest MIREILLE; VICTOIRE went with BLEICHER to arrest ROLAND-BOBY; *1830*: Rendezvous with ONCLE MARCO (MARCHAL) and RENÉ at

Café Graff. Both arrested; VICTOIRE went with BLEICHER to arrest Richard NOEUD; VICTOIRE met ANDRÉ with BLEICHER and introduced him as a personal friend and he was not arrested; VICTOIRE moved to Harry BAUR's house where later Leutnant KAISER and VON EHFELD arrived.

20 November 1941: Meeting at Hôtel Edward VII. Present KAISER, BLEICHER, VON EHFELD; VICTOIRE went with BLEICHER to arrest RAPIDE-LACH; ARTOS and second radio station taken without VICTOIRE's assistance; radio set moved to La Chattière, St Germain; arrest of MAX who sold MARCEL.

21 November 1941: VICTOIRE confronted with MAX but failed to recognise him; *1600*: Conference during which VICTOIRE told that they had decided to continue L'AFFAIRE INTERALLIÉE [*sic*], and that MARCEL should be the radio operator and that she should choose a new name (i.e. VICTOIRE); VICTOIRE questioned about Dr COLLINS and Jean BAILLY, given away by VIOLETTE, whose veracity put in issue successfully by VICTOIRE; first false message sent by Germans.

22 November 1941: *1100*: VICTOIRE accompanied BLEICHER to address of PAUL (letter from PAUL found in her bag), who was not there; VICTOIRE accompanied BLEICHER to Town Hall of 18th arrondissement to arrest colleagues of ROLAND-BOBY, who had all escaped except one; VICTOIRE returned with BLEICHER to PAUL's lodging, where they arrested him; VICTOIRE accompanied BLEICHER to arrest OBSERVATEUR; VICTOIRE accompanied BLEICHER to the rue de la Michodière, where letter from FRANCK was found, saying he was coming back at 1700; *1800*: VICTOIRE returned with BLEICHER to the rue de la Michodière and arrested FRANCK, who gave away FERNAND.

23 November 1941: STEPHEN arrested on his return to Villa Léandre; VICTOIRE cross-examined about YOLÉ, whom VIOLETTE had said she knew all about: she revealed his identity; also questioned about MIKLOS and Robert POULAIN; scheme designed to trap them.

24 November 1941: VICTOIRE went to La Palette for reunion of agents; only COCO arrived, late and disguised; COCO arrested; VICTOIRE rang up YOLÉ, MIKLOS and Robert POULAIN.

25 November 1941: Arrest of MARCEL outside his Hôtel and his agreement to work for the Germans; second meeting between VICTOIRE and VIOLETTE when latter announced her engagement.

26 November 1941: VICTOIRE accompanied BLEICHER to Fresnes and La Santé; *1415*:VICTOIRE and BLEICHER met at La Madeleine Restaurant, where she was confronted with KLEBER, who denied knowing her, but whom she recognised; *1800*:VICTOIRE accompanied BLEICHER to Café Ruc to meet YVES, who was arrested going out.

27 November 1941: *1100*:VICTOIRE went alone to YOLÉ's office and by pretending to have a bad hand got him to write incriminating news; *1500*:VICTOIRE visited MIKLOS alone and got him to write a short message to London; YOLÉ arrested.

28 November 1941: VICTOIRE rang up and subsequently lunched with Robert POULAIN, but failed to get any incriminating evidence; VICTOIRE had dinner with VIOLETTE and later stipulated that she should not see her again; sent to another villa.

29 November 1941: First message signed 'VICTOIRE' received.

November/December 1941: VICTOIRE went with BLEICHER to La Santé to fetch KLEBER's mistress, who took them to address of MONO and MOUSTIQUE and to IRINÉE's address near Rambouillet; KLEBER's mistress escaped at Café des Sports, Porte Maillot; VICTOIRE returned with BLEICHER to arrest IRINÉE, who gave address of ISIDORE; VICTOIRE went with BLEICHER to arrest ISIDORE, who told them that the free agents were meeting on 6 December at Café Louis XIII, then arrested; after dinner one night VICTOIRE accompanied BLEICHER to arrest ÉMILE in his villa at Courbevoie or Asnières; EUGÈNE also arrested.

6 December 1941: VICTOIRE attended at Café Louis XIII; BERTRAND and BOB arrived and were arrested; the latter told VICTOIRE before being arrested that CHARLES was staying with CHAUMET; he also had on him the plan of the OVERCLOUD organisation; BERTRAND gave away BERTHE and BERNARD; VICTOIRE accompanied BLEICHER to the house of the family CHAUMET, where after a long wait GUY returned; after having recounted to VICTOIRE that CHARLES was coming round next morning, GUY was arrested.

7 December 1941: CHARLES arrested on his arrival at house of CHAUMET family, by PROPST and TRITCHE; CHARLES gave away CÉSAR and offered to work for Germans; VICTOIRE learned that M. and Mme LEQUELLEC, given away by the indiscretions of ÉMILE, had been fetched from Rouen.

14? December 1941: VICTOIRE and BLEICHER visited La Palette and JEANNINE was caught.

15? December 1941: VICTOIRE arranged tea party between Austrian called KRAUSS and the Comte and Comptesse DAMPIERRE, as a result of which they were all three arrested.

22 December 1941: BLEICHER and VICTOIRE arrested JANKOWSKI and Paulette PORCHER; *1800*: VICTOIRE visited METCHKA and induced her to write compromising letter.

23 December 1941: TADY arrested and released; VICTOIRE, on instructions from BLEICHER, visited MIKLOS and gave him phoney message from London; BLEICHER with VICTOIRE went off one morning to arrest family of Capitaine PHILIPPE, but they had gone away for Christmas.

25 December 1941: First meeting between VICTOIRE and LUCAS.

27 December 1941: Second meeting between VICTOIRE and LUCAS, after which latter left for Chartres.

30? December 1941: LUCAS returned from Chartres.

31 December 1941: First message signed 'LUCAS' sent.

5 January 1942: VICTOIRE confessed to COLLINS.

18 January 1942: BLEICHER decided to arrest MIKLOS.

19 January 1942: MIKLOS arrested.

20 January 1942: VICTOIRE confessed to LUCAS.

? February 1942: Break-up of FELIX and OVERCLOUD organisations.

3 February 1942: VICTOIRE becomes LUCAS's mistress.

12/13 February 1942: Unsuccessful operation at Moulin-de-la-Rive. Officer and 2 W/T operators taken prisoner.

[26/27 February 1942: VICTOIRE and LUCAS departed France for the UK.]

24 April 1942: Arrest of ROGER.

27 April? 1942: Arrest of LUCAS.

1 July 1942: VICTOIRE interned.

The Case Against VICTOIRE: The Allegations of her Betrayals

From KV2/931.

The case against her is:

1.   That on November 19th, 1941, she consented to work for the Germans without resistance. VICTOIRE states that the matter was put to her in such a way that she could not refuse. On the other hand, the methods employed by the Germans, as admitted by her, are only consistent with a fairly good certainty on their part that she would be prepared to work for them. Such incidents as offering the cigarettes to TRITCHE, having her mattress changed in her cell, and the food given her are wholly inconsistent with any really hostile methods of persuasion.

2.   That on November 19th, 1941, she was responsible for the arrest of:

    (a)   DUVERNOY (WIRTZ). VICTOIRE's justification is that the rendezvous with him was entered in her diary and that she had no option. The rendezvous was, however, at a café and the Germans would not have been able to identify him without her assistance.

    (b)   ONCLE MARCO and RENÉ. In these cases she justified her action on the ground that VIOLETTE was ultimately responsible for their names being disclosed, which appears to be improbable. In any case the same considerations as in 2(a) apply.

3.   That on November 19th, 1941, she identified for the purpose of arrest by the Gestapo, the following agents of the WALENTY Organisation:

(a)   Roland BOBY
(b)   Richard NOEUD
(c)   MIREILLE

All these appear to have been identifiable by the Germans without VICTOIRE's assistance and, therefore, it cannot be said that she was directly responsible for their arrests. It does, however, demonstrate that t[h]e Germans, on the first day of her collaboration, had suffi[cien]t confidence in her to use her where her assistance was not vital.

4.   That on November 20th she was responsible for the arrest of RAPIDE-LACH and his wife. Her explanation of this is that the Germans had found his address in a letter from TUDOR to WALENTY. If so, it would have been unnecessary for VICTOIRE to accompany the German Officer making the arrest, unless she is charged merely with identifying these persons for the purpose of their arrest.

5.   That on November 21st she consented to collaborate with the Germans in running the wireless transmitter to deceive the British. Once again her account presents the picture of an ultimatum by the Germans to VICTOIRE which she had no option but to accept. On the other hand, the first message appears to have been written by her and her choosing her new name (VICTOIRE) is hardly consistent with an unwilling collaboration.

6.   That on November 22nd she was responsible for the arrest of PAUL and, through him, of OBSERVATEUR. She says that a letter from PAUL was found in her handbag and this may be true, in which case her responsibility is that she identified him. If a letter really was found it is peculiar that they did not, as they could, arrest PAUL immediately, i.e. on November 19th.

7.   That on November 22nd she identified FRANCK at the Rue de la Michodière, who gave away FERNAND. FRANCK might have been arrested without her assistance, so that she may not be responsible for this arrest.

8.   That on November 24th VICTOIRE kept the rendezvous at the La Palette Restaurant and acted as a decoy to catch COCO, who was arrested and subsequently shot. [*He could not have been shot for the reasons previously stated.*]

9.   That VICTOIRE, according to her own story, had two opportunities on November 26th of escaping or at any rate of taking steps to warn other members of the organisation still free. These two opportunities were:

   (a)   on being left at her parents' house for lunch and being allowed to proceed from there alone to her next rendezvous, and
   (b)   later when she went off alone into a café near La Santé.

10.   That on November 26th VICTOIRE went to La Palette Restaurant, where she acted as a decoy for the identification and arrest of YVES. A letter had been found at the café from YVES making the appointment, so that the Germans might have arrested him without VICTOIRE's collaboration.

11.   That on November 27th VICTOIRE acted without supervision as an agent provocateur to incriminate YOLÉ, MIKLOS and Robert POULAIN. On each occasion she was allowed to make the visit alone, with her arm in a sling which was the excuse for asking them to write down any information or messages they wanted to send to London. She succeeded in getting evidence in the cases of YOLÉ and MIKLOS, the former of whom was arrested. In consequence, MIKLOS was also nearly arrested but managed to escape.

12.   That on some date prior to December 6th VICTOIRE wrote a note to IRINEE which was left at his address (which had been given away by KLEBER's mistress) and later when KLEBER's mistress escaped, returned to the address and assisted in the arrest of IRINEE.

13.   That on the same date as in paragraph 12 VICTOIRE was present when ISIDORE (who had been given away by IRINEE) was arrested and acted as a decoy, with the result that ISIDORE told her voluntarily and thinking that she was free, that an important meeting of free agents was to take place on December 6th at the Café Louis XIII.

14.   That on some date prior to December 6th VICTOIRE assisted BLEICHER in the arrest of ÉMILE and EUGENE, the former of whom VICTOIRE states had been given away by YVES, who is referred to in 10.

15.   That on some date prior to the arrest of ÉMILE referred to in 14, VICTOIRE had another opportunity of escaping or warning the remaining agents. She admits in her book to having been allowed to visit her parents alone.

16. That on December 6th VICTOIRE went to the meeting at the Café
     Louis XIII, referred to in 13, where she acted as a decoy for the arrest
     of BERTRAND and BOB who, before being arrested and thinking
     VICTOIRE was free, told her the whereabouts of CHARLES; and that
     through the arrest of these two the Germans later arrested BERTHE
     and BERNARD and pe[ne]trated and broke up the OVERCLOUD
     Organistaion.

17. That on the night of December 6th/7th VICTOIRE acted as a decoy
     for the arrests of the CHAUMET family; and that the latter CESAR was
     arrested and subsequently shot.

18. That on December 7th, VICTOIRE on her own admission, was allowed
     to go alone to her tailors and thereby neglected a further opportunity
     to escape.

19. That on some date around December 14th VICTOIRE acted as decoy for
     the arrest of JEANNINE. According to her own story, VICTOIRE tried
     to give her warning by pretending not to know who she was.

20. That on some date in December VICTOIRE, having acted as an agent
     provocateur under the orders of the Germans was responsible for the
     arrest of an Austrian Engineer named KRAUSS [sic] and the Count and
     Countess DAMPIERRE, by presenting the former with a forged message
     to him alleged to be from the British agent EVE.

21. That on some date around December 18th VICTOIRE admits to having
     had BORCHERS in her power and a good opportunity to escape, of
     which she did not take advantage.

22. That at some time around December 22nd VICTOIRE was responsible,
     by acting as an agent provocateur, for the arrest of TADY.

23. That VICTOIRE, from about December 20th onwards, knew that the
     Germans were trying to arrest the family of Capitaine PHILLIPE and
     neglected every opportunity to try to warn them.

24. That on December 26th VICTOIRE met and voluntarily betrayed
     LUCAS. Her account of the meeting is considered to be false so far as
     she maintains that her meeting with LUCAS and the reasons for it were
     known to the Germans before it took place.

25. That on January 6th, 1942, VICTOIRE admits to having had BLEICHER
     entirely in her power in company with LUCAS and other loyal agents, but
     failed to do anything.

26. That on and after January 6th VICTOIRE admits to having had complete liberty, yet failed to take any steps to warn LUCAS or outwit the Germans until January 20th when, after the attempt to arrest MIKLOS, LUCAS taxed her with working for the Germans.

27. That VICTOIRE, through her wholehearted collaboration with the Germans and her failure to take opportunities presented to her of escaping from their clutches, was responsible for, or alternatively could have prevented, the arrests and break up (besides those of the WALENTY groups and persons associated with these) of:

   (a)   The OVERCLOUD Organisation.
   (b)   The Capitaine PHILLIPE Organisation.
   (c)   The LUCAS Organisation.
   (d)   The W/T operators sent over on the operation of February 13th.

28. That VICTOIRE was responsible, through her betrayal of LUCAS, for giving the Germans evidence compromising the activities of the U.S. Military Attaché at Vichy.

APPENDIX 5

Members of the Interallié Organisation who Escaped to England

From KV2/932.

Taken from a CX report by B.H. Townshend of MI6, Section VB5, 20 November 1944, sent to D.I. Wilson, MI5

1. Mme CARRÉ @ VICTOIRE @ LA CHATTE
   Arrived U.K. by sea operation 27.2.42
2. WLODARCZK, Janusz @ MAURICE
   Polish W/T operator. Arrived U.K. March 1942
3. MASLOWSKI @ MASSENET
   Polish W/T operator. Arrived U.K. March 1942
4. GANE, Fernand @ MONO, KENT, GAUTIER, GRENIER, GARNIER, FERGA, RENÉ
   French, helped with W/T. Arrived U.K. 5.10.42.
5. GORCE, Henri @ LOUIS
   French. Arrived U.K. 5.10.42.
6. Captain CZERNIAWSKI @ WALENTY
   Polish. Arrrived U.K. 10.10.42.
7. DESCHAMPS, Mono Simone @ MOUSTIQUE
   Arrived U.K. 12.10.42.

Associates
   MITCHELL, Roger @ ADAM, BRICK
   Arrived U.K. 1.3.42.

APPENDIX 6

Regulations for Special Internees at Aylesbury

From KV2/538.

1. Subject to the exceptions mentioned in paragraphs 2–5 inclusive Internees will not be permitted to associate or have any contact with any other persons except fellow internees who are interned in the same part of the prison and arrangements should be made whereby it will be impossible for them to communicate with other prisoners and the outside world.

2. <u>Letters.</u>
    (A) All letters, both in-coming and out-going, will be subject to 100% censorship by M.I.5, and in order that delay should be reduced to a minimum, internees should be instructed
        (i) that out-going letters should bear the date on which they are handed to the Prison Authorities,
        (ii) that out-going letters should be handed to the Prison Authorities before [*illegible*]/p.m. daily.
    (B) It is desirable that when possible out-going mail should be posted to Box 500, Parliament Street Box Office, London, S.W.1, so that it arrives the following day and can be examined and released with a minimum of delay. Out-going inland mail will be posted to a letter box but overseas mail will be passed by M.I.5 direct to Postal Censorship with a note to the effect that it has been seen by M.I.5. The number of out-going letters will not be restricted beyond the limits usually imposed in 18B cases.
    (C) Incoming mail will be sent by the Prison Authorities to Box 500 and after examination by M.I.5 it will be returned to the Governor with a note to the effect that M.I.5 have no objection to it going forward.

3.   Telegrams.

Telegrams, both in–coming and out-going, unless they are prima facie objectionable, be allowed to go forward but copies should be sent to M.I.5. In doubtful cases the Governor should consult M.I.5.

4.   Telephone Calls.

Telephone calls wil not be permitted without reference to M.I.5 except in cases of serious illness, and then only when the Governor sees fit and under such restrictions as she considers it proper to impose.

5.   Visits.

(A) Permits to visit will only be issued with the written approval of M.I.5 who will bear in mind that it is not desirable that any restrictions imposed should compare unfavourably with those in force at the previous place of detention.

(B) All visits will be supervised and conversation will be in English only unless the Internee has reasonable grounds for requesting that a particular interview should be given in any other language at the time the permit to visit is applied for.

(C) It will be the duty of the Officer who supervises the visit to stop any objectionable conversation and in particular any conversation which may convey to the visitor anything to do with **ANY** Internee's association with, or activities on behalf of, any British or Allied organisation either in this country or abroad. Internees should be warned in this sense before receiving each visitor.

6.   Should any of these Internees desire to be visited by a priest permission for such visit should be given by the Governor, but the priest should be told that if an Internee makes any statement outside the seal of the confessional it is his duty to report the full facts to the Governor. If a suitable priest is not available M.I.5 should be consulted.

7.   The examination of mail by M.I.5 will be complementary to and not in substitution for, the normal prison censorship which should continue to operate as usual. Parcels will be examined by the Prison Authorities only but any written communications which they contain should be submitted to M.I.5.

8.   The contents of paragraphs 2(A) (i) & (ii) and 5(B) & (C) supra are the only parts of the regulations which should be disclosed to Internees.

9.   Neither the fact that it is M.I.5 which is interested in the correspondence of these Internees nor the proper names of any M.I.5 officers should be communicated to them.

M.I.5/B.1.A

6.7.42

Major Ische's Personnel in 1942

From *German Intelligence Service. Personnel of the Abwehr Stations in France*, CIA document declassified in 2001 and 2007, p. 36.

Alst Paris. III F
Major Ische @ MALLY @ FREDDIE (Aug 42)
Hptm. Borcher(s), Erich (Feb 42)
Oblt. Kaiser @ DE JUIF (Jan 42)
Cmdt. Ehfeld, von @ EIFFEL, von (Dec 41)
Fdw. Bleicher, Hugo @ CASTEL, Jean @ JEAN, Monsieur (Dec 42)
NCO Propst, Karl Gustave (Nov 41)
NCO Todt (Aug 42)
? NCO Tritche (Feb 42)
    Kleiber (Chauffeur to BLEICHER)
? Major Braune (Feb 43)
? Major Boehl (1942)
Major Scherz (Nov 42)
Hptm. Schmitz (Nov 42)
Lt. Neumann (Dec 42) (D/F expert)

From Hugo Bleicher (KV2/166).

1. Alst Paris (III F)
    (a) At Headquarters
         Obstlt. Reile   Head of III F
         Maj. Schaefer   Adjutant to REILE
         Hptm. Leyrer   Clerical work
         Hptm. Moeller   Clerical work, later with FAK 306 in Holland
         Gefr. Graf   Chauffeur

(b) <u>External Services</u> (Working with agents)
Major Eschig @ SALZBERG (Also under Ast. St. Germain)
Hptm. Wiegand @ WALTER (Also under FAT 350 – Zwolle)
Hptm. Kramer @ FRED
Hptm. Radeke (Liaison with HENRI group of agents)
Hptm. Schmitz at Hôtel Cayre
U/Off. Schwann at Hôtel Cayre
Gefr. Kuchenberger @ KUKI
Sdf. LINK (Also under FAK 306 Rorup)
? Hachmann
Sdf. Graf Kreuze @ PIERRE
Sdf. Scheide @ BERGER

(c) <u>Funkabwehr</u>
Inspector Strassenschulte @ PHILIPPE

2. <u>Ast. St. Germain</u>

Obstlt. Stephan	Chief of Ast St. Germain
Obstlt. Weber	Chief of Abwehr I, St. Germain
Major Eschig @ SALZBERG	III F
Hptm. Kaiser	III F (External work)
O/Lt. Simon	III F
U/Off. Propst	III F
U/Off. Tritsche, Charles	III F
Sdf. Eckert @ EVANS	III F (also under Rouen)
Weber	III F (civilian clerk)

APPENDIX 8

Proposed Messages Relating to the Return of LUCAS and VICTOIRE to France

From TNA KV2/927 (see Chapter 16).

To be sent 21st or 23rd April:
Reference your telegram 1125, understand your anxiety. You need not worry, preparations are going ahead for my return. All here appreciate the way you have kept things going during the last weeks and I am arranging for you to visit England after my return. Above all else be careful since around us the British are building their most important organisation. Do not send me any messages. Keep everything but urgent details until my return when a full report will be prepared and many channels of communication assured.

To be sent on 25th April:
Details regarding return will be definitely settled this weekend and you will receive instructions on Tuesday. Everything going all right. LUCAS has returned from special training. Reference your telegram 1130, several new W/T sets will be brought back by ~~him~~ me and also radio specialists.

To be sent on 28th April:
Details of return as follows. LUCAS will be dropped on the night of Saturday or Sunday the 2nd or 3rd in unoccupied zone. He will stay there for sufficient time to prepare a full report on new situation there as a result of change of Government. ROGER should go to Vichy again on May 1st to collect further money out of which he wil pay you 100,000 to cover the period until my return. On completion of enquiries LUCAS will move into unoccupied zone. There he must meet COCO and investigate landing place on coast for my

return by sea. On account of numbers of new agents arrived in France as part of this organisation, a sea landing is necessary. LUCAS, through COCO, will communicate the landing place chosen for my return. Details for the meeting between LUCAS and COCO later.

To be sent on May 5th:
LUCAS landed safely near X on night of ….. No further details yet. Will let you know as soon as possible.

To be sent on 9th May:
Have heard from LUCAS. Everything O.K. The position at Vichy requires fuller investigation than anticipated. He will move into occupied zone at the end of next week. ROGER should go to meet him on May 15th. Meet at …..between….. and ….. My return definitely fixed for week ending 23rd May.

To be sent on 12th May:
COCO should be in the ….. Café at ….. each day from Tuesday 19th May at 1200, 1700 & 1900. LUCAS, who has COCO's description, will approach him. Password …..

To be sent on 21st May:
Has COCO met LUCAS. Nothing from LUCAS since he left the unoccupied zone. Has ROGER returned to Paris.

NOTES

Introduction

1   Curry, John, *The Security Service 1908–1945. The Official History* (London: Public Record Office, 1999).
2   Stephens, Robin, *Camp 020. MI5 and the Nazi Spies*, ed. Oliver Hoare, (London: Public Record Office, 2000).
3   Masterman, J.C, *The Double-Cross System* (London: Vintage Books, 2013), paperback edition.
4   TNA KV2/933.
5   Garby-Czerniawski, Roman, *The Big Network* (London: George Ronald, 1961), pp. 11–12.
6   http://www.filmportal.de/film/doppelspiel-in-paris_2a7f7d847b1f443d8 3889de9f057a4ce

Chapter 1. 'An Exceedingly Dangerous Woman'

1   TNA KV2/931.
2   Carré, Mathilde-Lily, *I Was The Cat* (London: Souvenir Press, 1960), p. 16.
3   *Ibid.*, p.17.
4   Young, Gordon, *The Cat with Two Faces* (New York: Coward-McCann Inc, 1957), p. 15.
5   TNA KV2/931.
6   Carré, *op. cit.*, p. 38.
7   Paine, Lauran, *Mathilde Carré: Double Agent* (London: Robert Hale, 1976), p.26; Carré, *op. cit.*, p. 34.
8   TNA KV2/931.
9   One of her files (TNA KV2/931) says 'in about 1935', yet an account of her life gives it as 18 May 1933.
10 Carré, *op. cit.*, pp. 40–1.
11 TNA KV2/933.

12   According to a blog by Nik Morton (aka Ross Morton): http://nik-writealot.blogspot.ca/2015/01/i-was-cat.html and TNA KV2/931.

13   Young, *op. cit.*, p. 18, and Carré, *op. cit.*, p. 56.

14   TNA KV2/931.

15   Walker, Robyn, *The Women who Spied for Britain. Female Secret Agents of the Second World War* (Stroud: Amberley Publishing, 2014), paperback edition, Chapter 7, p. 163.

16   http://www.lejsl.com/edition-du-creusot/2012/06/16/une-etrange-creusotine-meconnue-mathilde-carre

17   TNA KV2/931.

18   Young, *op. cit.*, p. 15.

19   Nash, Jay Robert, *Spies: A Narrative Encyclopedia of Dirty Tricks and Double Dealing from Biblical Times to Today* (New York: M. Evans and Company, 1997), pp. 138–9.

20   Young, *op. cit.*, p. 17.

21   Nash, *op. cit.*, p. 138.

22   Walker, *op. cit.*, p. 163.

23   Paine, *Mathilde Carré*, jacket; Paine, Lauran, *German Military Intelligence in World War II. The Abwehr* (New York: Military Heritage Press, 1984), p. 16.

24   TNA KV2/931.

25   TNA KV2/927.

26   Andrew, Christopher, *Defence of the Realm* (Toronto: Viking Canada, 2009), pp. 242–3; Day, Peter, *Klop. Britain's Most Ingenious Secret Agent* (London: Biteback, 2014), p. 299.

27   For more information on Barton/Ashley see: O'Connor, Bernard, *Agent Fifi and the Wartime Honeytrap Spies* (Stroud: Amberley, 2016), paperback edition, p. 155; Loftis, Larry, *Into the Lion's Mouth. The True Story of Dusko Popov: World War II Spy, Patriot and the Real-Life Inspiration for James Bond* (New York: Berkley Caliber/Penguin Books, 2016), pp. 78, 262; Day, op. cit, pp. 119, 146–7; West, Nigel, *Historical Dictionary of British Intelligence* (Lanham, MD: Rowman & Littlefield, 2014), 2nd edition, p. 42; Macintyre, Ben, *Double Cross* (London: Bloomsbury, 2012), pp. 71–2, 81, 122, 126, 127, 142, 196, 234, 328, 342; Andrew, op. cit., pp. 242–3; Elliott, Geoffrey, *Gentleman Spymaster* (London: Methuen, 2011), pp. 263–4.

28   Macintyre, *Double Cross*, p. 71. Lennox was in charge of Room 055 at the War Office, responsible for liaison between MI5 and the military. He had been a successful playwright before the war.

29   Young, *op. cit.*, p. 20.

30   Carré, *op. cit.*, p. 61.

31   *Ibid.*, p. 66.

32   Listed in *Guerre de 1939–1945. Archives du Comité d'histoire de la Deuxième Guerre mondiale et fonds d'origine privée*, as code-named PRALINE: https://www.siv.archives-nationales.culture.gouv.fr/siv/rechercheconsultation/consultation/ir/pdfIR.action?irId=FRAN_IR_054523

33   The restaurant on the Place Wilson closed its doors in 2009.

34   Langenfeld had commanded Office No. 6 in Łódź of the Polish General Staff Deuxième Bureau just prior to the German invasion of Poland in 1939.

35   Garby-Czerniawski, *op. cit.*, p. 43.

36   TNA KV2/936.

37   Young, *op. cit.*, p. 23.

38   Carré, *op. cit.*, p. 69.

39   TNA KV2/72.

40   TNA KV2/928.

Chapter 2. 'A Man of Great Daring and Initiative'

1   http://www.polishairforce.pl/czerniawski.html

2   Garby-Czerniawski, *op. cit.*, p. 36.

3   TNA HS9/1224/6; Masson, Madeleine, *Christine. SOE Agent and Churchill's Favourite Spy* (London: Virago, 2005), paperback edition, pp. xxi, 64, 71, 283, 288; Mulley, Clare, *The Spy who Loved* (London: Pan Books, 2013), paperback edition, pp. 34–5, 40, 50, 50n., 52, 70.

4   TNA HS9/66/4.

5   TNA KV2/72.

6   TNA KV2/933.

7   TNA KV2/933.

8   Dear, Ian, *Spy and Counterspy: Secret Agents and Double Agents from the Second World War and the Cold War* (Stroud: Spellmount/History Press, 2013), paperback edition, p. 150; Richelson, Jeffrey T., *A Century of Spies. Intelligence in the Twentieth Century* (Oxford and New York: Oxford University Press, 1995), p. 129; Lyman, Robert, *Operation Suicide* (London: Quercus, 2012), p. 62; West, Nigel, *MI6. British Secret Intelligence Service Operations 1909–45* (London: Weidenfeld & Nicolson, 1983),

p. 141. See also: http://www.wikiwand.com/de/Mieczys%C5%82aw_ Zygfryd_S%C5%82owikowski Col. Wicenty Zarembski (1897-1966)

9 Official citation: Bogomila Zongollowicz, 'Kleeberg Juliusz Edward (1890–1970)', *Australian Dictionary of National Biography*, National Centre of Biography, Australian National University. http://adb.anu.edu.au/ biography/kleeberg-juliusz-edward-10756/text19069, published first in hardcopy 2000.

10 Bleicher, Hugo, *Colonel Henri's Story* (London: William Kimber, 1954), pp. 117–21.

11 *Ibid.*, pp. 119–20.

12 Bennett, Gill, 'The Zinoviev Letter of 1924', *History Notes*, no. 14 (February 1999), p. 42.

13 Carré, *op. cit.*, p. 73.

14 Lerecouvreux, Maurice, *Résurrection de l'Armée française, de Weygand à Giraud* (Paris: Nouvelles Éditions Latine, 1955), p. 379.

15 TNA KV2/933.

16 Ruffin, Raymond, *Résistance P.T.T.* (Paris: Presses de la Cité, 1983), mentioned in Cornick, Martyn, *The French Secret Services* (London: Routledge, 1993), p. 67.

17 http://www.aassdn.org/POSTES.pdf and https://rha.revues.org/1843

18 http://www.cf2r.org/fr/notes-historiques/un-homme-est-passe-pierre-marion-et-la-dgse.php

19 D'Harcourt, Pierre, *The Real Enemy* (London: Longmans, 1967).

20 TNA KV2/934.

21 Ruby, Marcel, *F Section SOE* (London: Leo Cooper/Heinemann, 1988), p. 165.

22 Garby-Czerniawski, *op. cit.*, p. 50.

23 TNA KV2/928.

24 TNA KV2/928.

25 TNA KV2/928.

Chapter 3. *Interallié* is Born

1 Nigel Perrin's blog, 'Set Europe Ablaze': http://blog.nigelperrin. com/2013/03/brutus-and-naked-heroine.html#.WSzY5uvyuiM

2 TNA KV2/933.

3   Polish Genealogical Society of Connecticut and the Northeast,
     'Focus on D-Day. The D-Day Spies: Part III, Roman Czerniawski'
     (quoting Ben Macintyre): https://www.facebook.com/permalink.
     php?id=175145372572821&story_fbid=396511003769589

4   Izbicki, John, *The Naked Heroine* (London: Umbria Press, 2014), p. 30.

5   Mikaberidze, Alexander (ed.), *Atrocities, Massacres and War Crimes.
     An Encyclopedia* (Santa Barbara, CA: ABC-CLIO, 2013), vol. 1, *A–L*,
     pp. 501–2.

6   Izbicki, *op. cit.*, p. 30.

7   TNA KV2/928.

8   Brault was Michel Henri Robert Brault @ Jerome Levy @ Colonel
     Jerome @ Marcel Robert Barrault @ MIKLOS @ Maizeray, born 1893.
     See TNA HS9/203/5.

9   There are two Labourots listed in *Service historique de la Défense / Centre
     historique des archives, Vincennes*: Marcel Jean, born in Arc-en-Senans in the
     Doubs département, 25 June 1920, and Roger, born in Bouafles in the
     Eure, 27 December 1901, both confirmed as being members of the FFI,
     but no Jacques. http://www.servicehistorique.sga.defense.gouv.fr/sites/
     default/files/SHDGR_16P_L.pdf

10   TNA KV2/931.

11   http://monument-mauthausen.org/spip.php?page=print-fiche&id_
     article=10512&lang=fr

12   https://www.academia.edu/30261887/Liste_des_r%C3%A9seaux_
     et_mouvements_de_la_R%C3%A9sistance_int%C3%A9rieure_
     fran%C3%A7aise

13   CIC Interrogation Center, 3rd United States Army, APO 403, 7 October
     1944, in: TNA KV2/932.

14   TNA KV2/932.

15   Garby-Czerniawski, *op. cit.*, pp. 116–17.

16   TNA KV2/931.

17   For more information on escapes such as this see: Stourton, Edward, *Cruel
     Crossing. Escaping Hitler Across the Pyrenees* (London: Transworld, 2014),
     paperback edition.

18   Jean Carbonnier was later part of the Shelburne escape line in Brittany.

19   Oliver, David, *Airborne Espionage. International Special Duty Operations
     in the Second World War* (Stroud: The History Press, 2013), eBook,
     no pagination.

20   Garby-Czerniawski, *op. cit.*, p. 109.

21   *Ibid.*, p. 106.

22   Noguères, Henri, *Histoire de la Résistance en France* (Paris: Robert Laffont, 1972), vol. 1, p. 428; cited in Verity, *op. cit.*, n.9, p.224.

23   'The History of World War II Infiltrations into France', p.15: http://www. plan-sussex-1944.net/anglais/infiltrations_into_france.pdf It also cites the reference as Faure, Claude, *Aux services de la République : du BCRA à DGSE* (Paris: Librairie Arthème Fayard, 2004).

24   https://beforetempsford.org.uk/tag/sis/page/4/

25   Verity, Hugh, *We Landed by Moonlight. The Secret RAF Landings in France 1940–1944* (Manchester: Crécy Publishing, 1998), 2nd revised edition , p. 191; 'Before Tempsford. Royal Air Force Operations for SIS and SOE 1940–1942. Operation BRICK', http://beforetempsford.org.uk/2-october-1941/

26   Verity, op. cit., p. 191; https://beforetempsford.org.uk/tag/dufort/ pp. 6–7; Tebbutt, Roy, Carpetbagger Aviation Museum, Harrington, p. 13; Clark, Freddie, *Agents by Moonlight. The Secret History of RAF Tempsford During World War II* (Stroud: Tempus Publishing, 1999), p. 42; https://aviation-safety.net/wikibase/ wiki.php?id=89762

27   http://www.anciens-aerodromes.com/illustrationsterrains/lieux%20 atterrissages%20clandestins%20departement%20Indre%20et%20Cher. htm; https://beforetempsford.org.uk/tag/dufort/

28   TNA KV2/753.

29   TNA KV2/932.

Chapter 4. 'A Squalid Tale'

1   TNA KV2/929.

2   Verity, *op. cit.*, p. 191.

3   Giskes, H.J., *London Calling North Pole* (London: William Kimber, 1953), p. 40.

4   TNA KV2/1728.

5   Booth, Nicholas, *Zigzag. The Incredible Wartime Exploits of Double Agent Eddie Chapman* (New York: Arcade Publishing, 2007), trade paperback, pp. 262; 283.

6   Macintyre, Ben, *Agent Zigzag. The True Wartime Story of Eddie Chapman. Lover, Betrayer, Hero, Spy* (London: Bloomsbury, 2007), p. 261.

7   Wilson, Christopher, 'She lived on grouse, cocaine and other women's husbands. As her gems are sold at Sothebys, the jaw-dropping story of … the most wicked woman in High Society', *Daily Mail*, 29 March 2014.

8   Roger Richard Charles Henri Étienne de Dampierre (1892–1975), married 9 May 1931, Paris (75016), first marriage to Enid Rylda Aileen Lindsay-Toone (1903–34), who had a son, Armand Roger Étienne de Dampierre (1932–53). Second marriage 8 October 1937, Paris (75016), to Raymonde Dreyfus (1907–67), who had a daughter, Christianne Germaine Marie Georges de Dampierre.

9   TNA KV2/929. A note at the top says, 'Original in R.P.S. 10,221 – Vicomte de DAMPIERRE'.

10   TNA KV2/929.

11   West, *MI6*, p. 146; Jacques Collardey, in: de Ruffay, Françoise, *Histoire Orale. Armée de l'Air* (Paris, Vincennes: Archives de la Défense, 2015), vol.VII, AI 8 Z 768 à AI 8 Z 968 DE 2007 TO 3 à DE 2007 TO 4, pp. 131, 132, 133. http://www.servicehistorique.sga.defense.gouv.fr/sites/default/files/SHDAI_INV_HISTORALE_TOME7.pdf. Also: vol. 3, 1995, Entretiens 271 à 410, pp.14, 217–18, http://www.servicehistorique.sga.defense.gouv.fr/sites/default/files/SHDAI_INV_HISTORALE_TOME3.pdf, mentions he was a colonel, and his imprisonment at Gusen. Mentioned in Demeude, Hugues, 'La Chatte dans les griffes de l'aigle Nazi', *Historia Numéro Spéciale, Les Archives Secrète de la Second Guerre Mondiale*, (January–February 2017), pp. 50–1. Collardey was sent to Mauthausen concentration camp on 27 March 1943, from where he was liberated on 5 May 1945.

12   TNA KV2/1313.

13   TNA KV2/1728.

14   TNA KV2/961.

15   TNA KV2/961.

16   TNA KV2/961.

17   TNA KV2/932.

18   TNA KV2/72.

19   Oberstleutnant Oskar Reile, Leiter III F, listed in: *German Intelligence Service Personnel of the Abwehr Stations in France 1945?* Declassified in 2001 and 2007: http://numbers-stations.com/cia/German%20Intelligence%20Service%20(wwii),%20%20Vol.%201/GERMAN%20INTELLIGENCE%20SERVICE%20(WWII),%20%20VOL.%201_0004.pdf. Also listed in Bleicher's file: TNA KV2/164 as colonel, and head (Leiter) of III F, based at the Hôtel Letitia.

20   Graf (Count) Alex Kreutz, *Ast.* Paris, III F (December 1943), listed
      in: *German Intelligence Service Personnel of the Abwehr Stations in France
      1945?* Declassified in 2001 and 2007. http://numbers-stations.com/
      cia/German%20Intelligence%20Service%20(wwii),%20%20Vol.%201/
      GERMAN%20INTELLIGENCE%20SERVICE%20(WWII),%20%20
      VOL.%201_0004.pdf. Also listed in Bleicher's file: TNA KV2/164 as
      Sonderführer Kreuz @ PIERRE 'working outside with agents'.
21   TNA KV2/166.
22   He is listed in 'La Mémoire de la Déportation': http://www.bddm.org/
      liv/details.php?id=I.136. and: http://buchenwaldcamp.blogspot.ca/
23   TNA KV2/2853, MI5 file of Comte Alexandre Casteja, extracted from
      a report in the Kraus file which was in turn taken from an SCI report
      (OSS Special Counter-Intelligence), c.23 March 1945. However, the
      Kraus file is almost totally illegible due to being a poor-quality copy of a
      photostat copy.
24   TNA KV2/2853.
25   Verity, *op. cit.*, p. 202; see: http://www.plan-sussex-1944.net/anglais/pdf/
      infiltrations_into_france.pdf
26   King, Stella, *'Jacqueline'. Pioneer Heroine of the Resistance* (London: Arms &
      Armour Press, 1989).

Chapter 5. An American in France

1   Her file is GR28 P4 202-63, operating in 1944, listed in *Dossiers
     individuels des agents de la France combattante*, Service historique de la
     Défense, Département des archives définitives, Division defense, GR28
     P4 1-233, 2015: http://www.servicehistorique.sga.defense.gouv.fr/sites/
     default/files/SHDGR_28P4.pdf
2   Lownie, Andrew, *Stalin's Englishman* (London: Hodder & Stoughton,
     2015), p. 105.
3   TNA KV2/1729.
4   TNA HS9/1250/3, closed until 2025.
5   TNA HS9/1250/1; closed extract (1 page) from HS9/1250/9. The
     National Archives' entry also states that she is referred to in the Appendix
     and Index of the 2004 revised edition of Foot's book, *SOE in France*, and
     is identical to the author of *Full Moon to France*.

6   http://www.specialforcesroh.com/showthread.php?31705-Devereux-Rochester-Elizabeth-(Miss);Thomas, Gordon and Greg Lewis, *Shadow Warriors of World War II. The Daring Women of OSS and SOE* (Chicago: Chicago Review Press, 2017), no pagination in online version accessed; Escott, Beryl, *The Heroines of SOE F Section* (Stroud: The History Press, 2010), pp. 130–4.

7   http://wartimespyladies.blogspot.ca/2013/11/elizabeth-devereaux-rochester-1917.html

8   Petersen, Neal H. (ed.), *From Hitler's Doorstep. The Wartime Intelligence Reports of Allen Dulles 1942–45* (University Park, PA: Pennsylvania State University Press, 1996), p. 566.

9   Verity, *op. cit.*, p. 202.

10   Rochester, Devereux, *Full Moon to France* (London: Robert Hale, 1978), p. 198.

11   Bourne-Patterson, Major Robert, *SOE in France 1941–1945* (Barnsley: Frontline Books/Pen & Sword, 2016), pp. 241–2. See also: Maclaren, Roy, *Canadians Behind Enemy Lines* (Vancouver: UBC Press, 2004), pp. 110–13.

12   Jacobs, Peter, *Setting France Ablaze. The SOE in France During WWII* (Barnsley: Pen & Sword, 2015), p. 138.

13   https://www.resistance-ain-jura.com/42-non-categorise/407-atterrissages-s-o-e-aide-des-allies-ain.html

14   Verity, *op. cit.*, p. 201.

15   Binney, Marcus, *The Women who Lived for Danger. The Women Agents of SOE in the Second World War* (London: Hodder & Stoughton, 2002), pp. 319–20.

16   TNA KV2/1729.

Chapter 6. 'The Kraus Affair'

1   TNA KV2/1727.

2   TNA KV2/1727.

3   TNA KV2/1727.

4   TNA HS9/1647; https://alchetron.com/Raymond-Couraud-808655-W

5   Mortimer, Gavin, *Stirling's Men* (London: Weidenfeld & Nicolson, 2004), pp. 249, 251; Asher, Michael, *The Regiment* (London: Viking Penguin, 2007), p. 271. Strangely, he does not mention Lee in his earlier book *Get Rommel*, a book about the plot to kill Rommel.

6   TNA WO373/6/304.
7   TNA KV2/2853.
8   TNA KV2/2853.
9   TNA KV2/1729.
10 http://www.gentet.fr/Couraud/Raymond/Raymond.htm
11 Marnham, Patrick, *Wild Mary. A Life of Mary Wesley* (London: Vintage Books, 2007), p. 105.
12 Chisholm, Anne, 'The Dangerous Edge of Things' (review of *Wild Mary. A Life of Mary Wesley*), *Spectator*, 7 June 2006; Angela Lambert's obituary in the *Independent*, 31 December 2002 says it was a section of the War Office (a frequent euphemism for MI5); an article from the Open University says it was a codebreaking section of MI6 as Mary Siepmann (her second husband's name was Eric Siepmann): http://www.open.edu/openlearn/history-the-arts/history/history-science-technology-and-medicine/history-technology/the-bletchley-park-connection
13 McLeod, Marion, 'In Beds with Mary', *The Listener*, 12 August 2006.
14 Marnham, *op. cit.*, pp. 106–8.
15 Beevor, Anthony and Artemis Cooper, *Paris After the Liberation 1944–1949* (London: Penguin, 2004), no pagnation in online version consulted.
16 TNA KV2/1727.
17 TNA KV2/1727.
18 TNA KV2/1727.
19 TNA KV2/1727.
20 TNA KV2/1727.
21 'Inga Haag: Conspirator in, and Last Link to, the 1944 Plot to Kill Hitler', *Sunday Times*, 20 December 2009: https://www.pressreader.com/south-africa/sunday-times/20091220/282260956571536; 'Inga Haag: Co-conspirator in the plot to assassinate Hitler', *Independent*, 11 January 2010: http://www.independent.co.uk/news/obituaries/inga-haag-co-conspirator-in-the-plot-to-assassinate-adolf-hitler-1863930.html; Obituary, *Scotsman*, 30 December 2009: https://www.scotsman.com/news/obituaries/inga-haag-1-784167; Fryer, Jonathan, 'Obituary', *Guardian*, 13 January 2010: https://www.theguardian.com/theguardian/2010/jan/13/inga-haag-obituary; Bassett, Richard, *Hitler's Spy Chief* (London: Cassell, 2005), p. 98, paperback edition; Mueller, Michael, *Canaris. The Life and Death of Hitler's Spymaster* (London: Chatham Publishing, 2007), pp. 175; 218; 'Why my Friends Felt they Had to Kill Hitler', *Guardian*, 11 July 2004: https://www.theguardian.com/uk/2004/jul/11/germany.secondworldwar

22 TNA KV2/961.
23 TNA KV2/2853.
24 TNA KV2/1728.
25 TNA KV2/1728.
26 *Hansard*, House of Commons, vol. 410, no. 68, 26 April 1945, Oral Answers, German National (Internment); TNA KV2/1729. Not available online from *Hansard* or Millbank Systems.
27 Farago, Ladislas, *The Game of Foxes* (New York: David McKay & Co., 1971), pp. 633–6.
28 TNA KV2/1729.
29 TNA KV2/1729.

Chapter 7. The *Interallié* Network

1   TNA KV2/72.
2   West, *MI6*, p. 143.
3   http://beaucoudray.free.fr/1940.htm
4   TNA KV2/926.
5   TNA KV2/164, the file of Hugo Bleicher. The same report appears in KV2/753, the file on Jean Lucien Kieffer.
6   Lefebvre-Fileau, Jean-Paul and Gilles Perrault, *Ces Français qui on collaboré avec le IIIe Reiche* (Monaco: Éditions du Rocher, 2017), no pagination in online edition.
7   In 1942 he is listed on the staff of Major Ische in III F. See declassified CIA document, *German Intelligence Service Personnel of the Abwehr Stations in France 1945?* Declassified in 2001 and 2007: http://numbers-stations.com/cia/German%20Intelligence%20Service%20(wwii),%20%20Vol.%201/GERMAN%20INTELLIGENCE%20SERVICE%20(WWII),%20%20VOL.%201_0004.pdf
8   Lefebvre-Filleau & Perrault, *op. cit.*, no pagination in online version.
9   TNA KV2/931.
10 Garby-Czerniawski, *op. cit.*, pp. 237; 241.
11 TNA KV2/926.
12 Verity, *op. cit.*, p. 191; the pilot was Nesbitt-Dufort; West gives the date as 11 October and the pilot as Flight Lieutenant Phillipson: West, *op. cit.*, p.142; Wake-Walker, Edward, *House for Spies* (London: Robert Hale, 2011), p. 160 simply says October 1941 and the pilot as Nesbitt-Dufort. This is

confirmed in Robertson, K.G. (ed.), *War, Resistance and Intelligence. Essays in Honour of M.R.D. Foot* (Barnsley: Leo Cooper, 1999), p. 171.

13 Verity, *op. cit.*, pp. 40–3.
14 *Ibid.*, p. 41.
15 Garby-Czerniawski, *op. cit.*, p. 197.
16 *Ibid.*, p. 203.
17 *Ibid.*, p. 221.
18 *Ibid.*, pp. 119–20.
19 West, Nigel, *Historical Dictionary of Sexpionage* (Lanham, MD: Scarecrow Press, 2009), p. 46.
20 Verity, *op. cit.*, p. 191.

Chapter 8. Betrayal

1 TNA KV2/928.
2 http://www.bandcstaffregister.com/page156.html and TNA KV2/928. This may have been the Gordon Road workhouse, renamed the Camberwell Reception Centre: http://www.workhouses.org.uk/Camberwell/
3 Taken from TNA KV2/931.
4 TNA KV2/1727.
5 In 1942 he is listed as an NCO on the staff of Major Ische in III F. See declassified CIA document, *German Intelligence Service Personnel of the Abwehr Stations in France 1945?* Declassified in 2001 and 2007. http://numbers-stations.com/cia/German%20Intelligence%20Service%20(wwii),%20%20Vol.%201/GERMAN%20INTELLIGENCE%20SERVICE%20(WWII),%20%20VOL.%201_0004.pdf. He is also listed as Unteroffizier Charles Triesche in III F of *Ast.* St Germain in Bleicher's file, TNA KV2/166.
6 TNA KV2/72.
7 TNA KV2/926.
8 TNA KV2/926.
9 TNA KV2/930.
10 TNA KV2/926.
11 TNA KV2/931.
12 TNA KV2/936.

13 Carré, *op. cit.*, p. 108.
14 TNA KV2/931.
15 http://www.zrobtosam.com/PulsPol/Puls3/index.php?sekcja=1&arty_id=13193
16 Carré, p. 113.
17 Paine, *Mathilde Carré*, p. 80, and Young, *op. cit.*, pp. 80–1.
18 TNA KV2/931.
19 TNA KV2/931.
20 Carré, *op. cit.*, p. 115.

Chapter 9. MAURICE's Escape

1 TNA KV2/928.
2 TNA KV2/928.
3 See Chapter 1, note 34 re: Langenfeld.
4 West, Nigel and Oleg Tsarev, *Triplex. Secrets from the Cambridge Spies* (New Haven and London: Yale University Press, 2009), p. 315.
5 TNA KV2/928.

Chapter 10. Colonel Henri's Story

1 Bleicher, *op. cit.*
2 The *London Gazette* for 21 November 1939, p. 7807 lists him as an acting pilot officer (90510) with 906 (County of Middlesex) Squadron; promoted to flight lieutenant, 10 June 1941 (*London Gazette*, p. 3327). He is listed in the *Air Force List* for May 1941 (p. 1326).
3 TNA KV2/164.
4 TNA KV2/164.
5 Melvin, Major General Mungo, *Manstein. Hitler's Greatest General* (New York: St Martin's Press, 2011), no pagination in online version.
6 Tickell, Jerrard, *Odette. The Story of a British Agent* (London: Chapman & Hall, 1950), 5th impression, p. 216.
7 *Ibid.*, p. 216.
8 Sweet, Matthew, *The West End Front. The Wartime Secrets of London's Grand Hotels* (London: Faber & Faber, 2012), paperback edition, p. 163.

9   The *Army List* of 1942, p. 21B lists him as a staff captain (temporary captain, appointed 6 December 1941) on the Quarter-Master-General's staff, Royal Army Service Corps.

10 The National Archives at Kew has a file on Edward Jerrard Tickell, accused with George de la Vatine aka Georges Frédérick Montague de Fossard, Comte de la Vatine, of the murder of Helen Mary Pickwoad by criminal abortion at the Mount Royal Hotel, Oxford Street, London on 20 May 1941. TNA MEPO/2219 and MEPO/2219/1 (closed extracts until 2027). Sweet gives an account of Tickell's involvement in this business in his book.

11 Tickell, *op. cit.*, p. 220.

12 Bleicher, *op. cit.*, pp. 23–4.

13 There is now a café bar, Le Pélican at 107, Avenue Capitaine Georges Guynemer which is unlikely to be the same one; nor is Le Pelican at 10, Avenue de France, Maubeuge.

14 Bleicher, *op. cit.*, p. 29.

15 *Ibid.*, between pp. 96 and 97.

16 NARA M1944. Records of the American Commission for the Protection and Salvage of Artistic and Historic Monuments in war Areas, 1943-46; NARA catalogue number 1518806: *OSS – Works of Art, etc. Stolen in France, undated and dated.* Roll 22, Target 10.

17 Suzanne Laurent. Mentioned in Internal Report by Squadron Leader Beddard, 'Bleicher. FAK 306 and R.Netz', dated 7.8.45. Also in Bleicher's MI5 file, TNA KV2/166.

18 TNA KV2/164: 'Extract of an Interrogation Report No.S 1504', dated 29.5.45. Headquarters 12th Army Group, SCI Detachment, APO 655. Interrogation report on SCI Penetration Agent BABY after returning from a mission.

19 TNA KV2/1491.

20 http://www.peacearchnews.com/obituaries/lorne-davidson/

21 In 2008 the DST merged with the RG (Renseignments Généraux) to form the DCRI (Direction Centrale du Renseignement Intérieur); in 2012 this became the DGSI (Direction Générale de la Sécurité Intérieure). It is now located at 84, Rue des Villiers, Levallois-Perret, France.

22 Bleicher, *op. cit.*, pp. 192–4.

23 TNA KV2/166.

24 TNA KV2/166.

25 TNA KV2/166.

Chapter 11. Turning the Tables

1   Carré, *op. cit.*, p. 117.
2   Listed in declassified CIA document, *German Intelligence Service Personnel of the Abwehr Stations in France 1945?* Declassified in 2001 and 2007. http://numbers-stations.com/cia/German%20Intelligence%20Service%20(wwii),%20%20Vol.%201/GERMAN%20INTELLIGENCE%20SERVICE%20(WWII),%20%20VOL.%201_0004.pdf
3   TNA KV2/931.
4   TNA KV2/931.
5   TNA KV2/931.
6   TNA KV2/931.
7   TNA KV2/931.
8   http://www.zrobtosam.com/PulsPol/Puls3/index.php?sekcja=1&arty_id=13193
9   This may have actually been Raymond Poulain (b.1922).
10 TNA KV2/931.
11 TNA KV2/931.
12 Carré, *op. cit.*, p. 126.
13 TNA KV2/931.
14 Mentioned by Lucas, E.V. in *A Wanderer in Paris* (London: Methuen, 1923), p. 149.
15 Richards, (Sir) Brooks, *Secret Flotillas. Volume 1: Clandestine Sea Operations to Brittany 1940–44* (Abingdon: Routledge, 2011), 2nd edition. See also TNA HS6/41612.
16 See TNA HS9/302/6.
17 TNA KV2/926.
18 TNA KV2/931.
19 All these messages can be found in Mathilde Carré's file, TNA KV2/931.
20 Wilkinson, Peter and Joan Bright Astley, *Gubbins and SOE* (Barnsley: Pen & Sword, 2010), p. 118.
21 Ricks, Thomas E., 'Who Whacked Admiral Darlan? My Guess is that Winston Churchill Ordered it', *Foreign Policy*, 16 December 2014, no pagination in online version accessed; http://barnesreview.org/who-ordered-the-death-of-french-admiral-darlan/; Montmorency, Alec de, *The Enigma of Admiral Darlan* (New York: E.P. Dutton, 1943), reprinted by Kessinger Publishing, 2007.
22 TNA KV2/933.

23   TNA KV2/926.

24   TNA KV2/926.

25   TNA KV2/926.

26   TNA KV2/926, and West, *MI6*, p. 146; Garby-Czerniawski, *op. cit.*, pp. 208–9.

27   *German Documents among War Crimes Records*, p. 28: https://www.fold3.com/image/233805039

Chapter 12. Penetration of the LUCAS Network

1   Foot, M.R.D, *SOE in France* (London: HMSO, 1966), p. 175.

2   West, Nigel, *Secret War* (London: Hodder & Stoughton, 1992), pp. 33–4.

3   Ibid., p. 127; Ruby, *op. cit.*, p. 59.

4   Mackenzie, William, *The Secret History of SOE. The Special Operations Executive 1940–1945* (London: St Ermin's Press, 2000), p. 249.

5   Clark, *op. cit.*, p. 12.

6   Max Shoop had filed an application on 29 November 1920 to practise law in the Philippines: http://www.lawphil.net/judjuris/juri1920/nov1920/maxshoop_1920.html

7   Waller, Douglas, *Disciples. The World War II Missions of the CIA Directors who Fought for Wild Bill Donovan* (New York: Simon & Schuster, 2015), p. 72.

8   TNA HS9/203/5.

9   http://lesamitiesdelaresistance.fr/lien16-auvergne.php

10   TNA KV2/931.

11   Boussel, Louis-Henri, 'Le Réseau *Rail*. Ma determination dans l'Honneur et le Devoir', *Le Lien*, no date, p. 45: http://lesamitiesdelaresistance.fr/lien19-boussel.pdf

12   Knowlson, James, *Damned to Fame: The Life of Samuel Beckett* (New York: Simon & Schuster, 1996), p. 281.

13   TNA KV2/931.

14   Carré, *op. cit.*, p. 131.

15   TNA KV2/931.

16   TNA KV2/931.

17   TNA KV2/926.

18   TNA KV2/933.

19   http://www.francaislibres.net/liste/fiche.php?index=111646

20   http://memoires52.blogspot.ca/2010/04/

21 TNA KV2/1313.
22 TNA KV2/166.
23 TNA KV2/165.
24 TNA KV2/931.
25 Cowburn, Benjamin, *No Cloak No Dagger* (London: Frontline Books, 2009), p. 72.
26 Carré, *op. cit.*, pp. 137–8.
27 TNA KV2/933.
28 Richards, *op. cit.*, p. 314. Richards gives Black's rank as lieutenant.

Chapter 13. Gloria in Excelsis

1   Knowlson, *op. cit.*, p. 279.
2   TNA KV2/1312.
3   TNA KV2/1312.
4   TNA KV2/164. Lieutenant François (or Francis) Marcel Basin, born 6 August 1903, was arrested by the French in Cannes on 20 September 1941 on the morning after his arrival via Gibraltar on the 19th. Lieutenant Ted Cyril Coppin, born 20 May 1915, was a member of SOE and was executed by the Germans on 27 September 1943 (location unknown). He was awarded the Croix de Guerre with Silver Star by the French and a posthumous MBE in 1947.
5   TNA HS9/350/9; WO373/185/1084.
6   TNA HS9/55/7.
7   TNA KV2/1312.
8   TNA KV2/1312.
9   TNA KV2/937.
10 TNA HS6/408.
11 TNA KV6/32.
12 TNA KV2/938.
13 TNA KV2/938.
14 TNA KV2/937.
15 TNA KV2/926.
16 TNA KV2/937.
17 TNA KV2/927.
18 TNA KV2/930.
19 TNA KV2/930.

20 TNA KV2/930.
21 Knowlson, *op. cit.*, p. 283; see also note 51, p.679 of *Damned to Fame*.
22 TNA KV2/1312.
23 Knowlson, James, 'Samuel Beckett's Biographer Reveals Secrets of the Writer's Time as a French Resistance Spy', *Independent*, 23 July 2014: http://www.independent.co.uk/arts-entertainment/books/features/samuel-becketts-biographer-reveals-secrets-of-the-writers-time-as-a-french-resistance-spy-9638893.html
24 Knowlson, *Damned to Fame*, p. 279; note 31, p.679.
25 TNA KV2/1313.
26 Godlewski, Susan Glover, 'Warm Ashes. The Life and Career of Mary Reynolds': http://www.artic.edu/reynolds/essays/godlewski.PDF
27 Delano, Page Dougherty, 'Kay Boyle and Mary Reynolds: Friendship Intensified by War': https://erea.revues.org/3132
28 TNA KV2/1312.

Chapter 14. LUCAS's Story

1 TNA KV2/926.
2 TNA KV2/931.
3 TNA KV2/933.
4 TNA KV2/926.
5 See: West and Tsarev, *op. cit.*, pp. 132–3: according to 'SIS Internal Country Codes Used Up to the Second Half of 1946', p. 133, 48000 = USA; Jeffrey, Keith, *The Secret History of MI6, 1909–1949* (New York: Penguin Press, 2010), p. 453, 'European theatre reports obtained from 48-land [USA] sources'.
6 TNA KV2/926.
7 TNA KV2/926.
8 Smith, Richard Harris, *OSS. The Secret History of America's First Central Intelligence Agency* (Guilford, CT: Lyons Press, 2005), paperback edition, p. 34. Schow would later serve as assistant director of the CIA, 1949–51 (listed as assistant director for Special Operations (ADSO) see: https://www.cia.gov/library/readingroom/docs/1950-12-26a.pdf and https://www.cia.gov/library/readingroom/docs/1950-05-01.pdf), and chief of Army Intelligence, 1956–8.

9   TNA KV2/926.
10 TNA KV2/926.
11 TNA KV2/926.
12 Davies, Philip H.J., *MI6 and the Machinery of Spying* (London and Portland, OR: Frank Cass, 2004), paperback edition, pp. 111–12; see also: West, Nigel and Oleg Tsarev, *The Crown Jewels* (London: HarperCollins, 1999), paperback edition, p. 304.
13 TNA KV2/937.
14 TNA KV2/938.

Chapter 15. BENOIT's Story

1   Cowburn, *op. cit.*, pp. 69–70.
2   *Ibid.*, p. 83.
3   *Ibid.*, p. 85.
4   TNA HS9/3/10.
5   Bailey, Roderick, *Forgotten Voices of the Secret War* (London: Ebury Press, 2009), paperback edition, pp. 103–4.

Chapter 16. An Important Affair

1   TNA KV2/933.
2   TNA KV2/926.
3   Foot, M.R.D., *Memories of an S.O.E. Historian* (Barnsley: Pen & Sword, 2009), p. 179.
4   TNA KV2/926.
5   TNA KV2/926.
6   Jeffrey, *op. cit.*, pp. 379, 507; TNA WO339/84288.
7   TNA KV2/926.
8   TNA KV2/926.
9   TNA KV2/926.
10 Murphy, Christopher J., *Security and Special Operations. SOE and MI5 during the Second World War* (Basingstoke: Palgrave Macmillan, 2006), p. 158.
11 Mackenzie, *op. cit.*, p. 270, n.; West, *SOE*, pp. 261, 263.
12 TNA KV2/926.

13 A Dr Yolande Friedl is listed as living in East Grinstead, Sussex in 1948: http://archive.ioe.ac.uk/DServe/dserve.exe?dsqIni=Dserve.ini&dsqApp=Archive&dsqDb=Catalog&dsqCmd=Show.tcl&dsqSearch=(RefNo==%27GER/8/4/17%27)
14 TNA KV2/926.
15 TNA KV2/926.
16 TNA KV2/926.
17 TNA KV2/926.
18 TNA KV2/926.
19 TNA KV2/926.
20 TNA KV2/926.
21 It is interesting to note that there is an SOE file on a Cecile Eugenie Picard @ Josette Crusset @ Jacqueline Pradier @ Annie Cordier, born 5 April 1915, although no connection between the two women has been made. TNA HS9/1185/4.
22 TNA KV2/926.
23 TNA KV2/926.
24 TNA KV2/927.
25 TNA KV2/926.
26 TNA KV2/926.
27 TNA KV2/926.
28 TNA KV2/926.
29 TNA KV2/926.
30 TNA KV2/927.
31 Sisman, Adam, *John le Carré. The Biography* (London: Bloomsbury, 2015), p. 187.
32 TNA KV2/926.
33 Colonel, later General, Stanisław Gano (1895–1968), was the leader of Polish Military Intelligence during the Second World War. http://www.msz.gov.pl/en/news/heroic_leader_of_polish_military_intelligence_in_the_west_commemorated_in_morocco?printMode=true
34 TNA KV2/926.
35 TNA KV2/926.
36 TNA KV2/926.
37 TNA KV2/926.
38 TNA KV2/926.
39 TNA KV2/926.
40 TNA KV2/926.

41 A Harold John Bourn, a solicitor with the firm of Herrington, Willings & Penry Davey, of 23 Cambridge Road, Hastings, Sussex, is mentioned as the personal representative in connection with the late Mrs Florence Billiter Bourn, of 2 White Rock Road, Hastings in the *London Gazette*, 7 June 1963, p. 4986.
42 TNA KV2/931.
43 TNA KV2/931.
44 Clark, *op. cit.*, pp. 55–6. Davies was killed on 30 July 1942 when his Whitley V bomber Z9230 NF-N was shot down by a Messerschmitt Me 110 west-north-west of Rijssen on SOE Operation *Lettuce* 5; he is buried in Holten General Cemetary in the Netherlands. See: Bowman, Martin W., *Nachtjagd. Defenders of the Reich 1940–1943* (Barnsley: Pen & Sword Aviation, 2015), p. 92.
45 TNA KV2/933.
46 West, Nigel (ed), *The Guy Liddell Diaries. Vol. I, 1939–1942* (Abingdon: Routledge, 2005), p. 240.
47 TNA KV2/932.
48 TNA KV2/931.
49 TNA KV2/927, serial 113b.
50 Weisberg, Richard H., *Vichy Law and Holocaust France* (London and New York: Routledge, 1996), p. 215.
51 TNA KV2/931.
52 TNA KV2/931.
53 TNA KV2/931.
54 TNA KV2/927.

Chapter 17. 'A Nasty Taste in One's Mouth'

1 TNA KV2/927.
2 TNA KV2/927.
3 Carré, *op. cit.*, p. 155.
4 In Greek mythology, it was a poisoned shirt, tainted with the blood of the centaur Nessus, given to Heracles by his wife Deianeira, which killed him. Metaphorically it represents 'a source of misfortune from which there is no escape; a fatal present; anything that wounds the susceptibilities' or a 'destructive or expiatory force or influence': Brewer, E. Cobham, *Dictionary of Phrase and Fable* (1898), cited in: https://en.wikipedia.org/wiki/Shirt_of_Nessus. She might also be described as a poisoned chalice.

5 TNA KV2/927.
6 TNA KV2/928.

Chapter 18. WALENTY and the 'Great Game'

1 Hennessey, Thomas & Claire Thomas, *Spooks. The Unofficial History of MI5 from Agent Zigzag to the D-Day Deception, 1939–45* (Stroud: Amberley, 2010), paperback edition, Ch. 8, 'Enter BRUTUS', pp. 248–77.
2 TNA KV2/72.
3 Hinsley, F. H. and C.A.G. Simkins, *British Intelligence in the Second World War. Vol. 4: Security and Intelligence* (London: HMSO, 1990), pp. 98–102; 118–19; and West, Nigel, *Historical Dictionary of World War II Intelligence* (Lanham, MD: Scarecrow Press, 2008), p. 261.
4 Beavers may have been the captain from the Field Security Police of the Intelligence Corps assigned to keep an eye on WALENTY. A declassified CIA file on Obersturmbannführer Hans-Walter Zech-Nenntwich @ Dr NANSEN mentions a Captain Beavers who was with 7 CCU (FSS) (Canadian Concentration Unit; Field Security Section). Since Zech-Nenntwich worked for MI5 and was also later involved with the Political Warfare Executive (PWE) propaganda unit at Milton Bryan, Bedfordshire, it may be that Beavers was working for PWE at the time, and Harmer's report was circulated for propaganda purposes. https://www.cia.gov/library/readingroom/docs/ZECH-NENNTWICH,%20HANS_0001.pdf. Christopher Andrew also mentions 'Beavers' in B1b who analysed ISOS decrypts, Abwehr communications with the double agents and other intelligence relevant to the Double-Cross System. Andrew, *op. cit.*, p. 249; n. 54, and Curry, *op. cit.*, pp. 232–3.
5 TNA KV2/72.
6 TNA KV2/2127.
7 Neave, Airey, *Saturday at MI9* (London: Hodder & Stoughton, 1969), p. 129.
8 TNA KV2/72, with the file number PF 600,226. Unfortunately, that file is not available from the National Archives. He is also mentioned as @ Pierre Puissegur, as being dropped near Saint-Prancher, 10 kilometres north-east of Chatenois in the Vosges region on 30 August 1944, together with Pierre Diamant @ Pierre Cambon @ Pierre Conlon as part of Plan Sussex. http://www.plan-sussex-1944.net/anglais/infiltrations_into_france.pdf.

9   http://www.plan-sussex-1944.net/anglais/infiltrations_into_france.pdf
    and: TNA HS7/246 SOE RF RF Section War Diaries; TNA HS7/248
    SOE RF Index & App 1-5 C Faure du BCRA à DGSE. Verity, *op. cit.*,
    App. B, p. 193: Operation PIKE/CARP/RUFF, agent, Lt. Harrow. Verity
    gives the landing zone as 25 kilometres south of Bourges, 800 kilometres
    north of Chavannes; Clark, *op. cit.*, p. 113.

    The pilot was Flight Lieutenant James Atterby 'Mac' McCairns, DFC★★,
    MM, although Verity gives his rank as pilot officer, as does Freddie
    Clark (and at that time with only the Military Medal awarded when
    he was a sergeant pilot with 616 Squadron). He was also the pilot who
    would carry Diana Rowden (1915–44) @ Paulette and Captain Charles
    Milne Skepper (1905–44) @ Henri Charles Truchot @ Bernard on
    16 June 1943.

10 Foot, *SOE in France*, pp. 138, 379; and: http://www.plan-sussex-1944.net/
    anglais/infiltrations_into_france.pdf.

    On 28 January 1944 there is also a SOE agent F.J. Poirier @ NESTOR
    @ DIGGER dropped from an RAF Halifax bomber on a farm, La
    Luzette, 2.5 kilometres north-west of Labastide du Haut Mont in the
    Lot/Cantal region. He also carried out another drop on 11 August 1944
    in the Dordogne.

11 See: Mejer, Elijah, *The Most Secret List of SOE Agents*: Jean Nestor
    Eugène ST. AUBIN, b. 24 April 1912 (TNA HS9/62/1); Nestor Armand
    BODSON, b. 13 April 1921 (TNA HS9/171/7); José DECHVILLE @
    Jean Nestor Eugène DELWICH, 8 December 1910–30 August 1944
    (TNA HS9/411/3).

12 Young, *op. cit.*, p. 209.

13 TNA HS9/611/4.

14 The report was 'intended to be a continuation of the report on the
    BRUTUS case', dated 30.11.42, filed at 29Z of Volume II of PF.65363
    and the conclusions filed at 29Y of that file; however, only Volume I –
    'Selected Historical Papers from the ARMAND WALENTY (BRUTUS)
    Case' (KV2/72), and 'Main File' (KV2/73) are currently available from the
    National Archives at Kew.

15 http://www.zrobtosam.com/PulsPol/Puls3/index.php?sekcja=47&arty_
    id=13193

16 TNA KV2/72.

17 TNA KV2/72.

18 TNA KV2/72.

19   TNA KV2/72.
20   TNA KV2/164.
21   TNA HS9/1617/5; Foot, *op. cit.*, p.193.

Chapter 19. Pointing Fingers

1   TNA KV2/72: 'Reasons and Causes of the Liquidation of the "INT" I.O. – according to my suppositions'.
2   The name Tadeusz Biernacki is mentioned by WALENTY in KV2/72, but this cannot be the same man born in 1923, as he had been arrested by the Gestapo in 1940 and sent to Dachau in 1943. This may be referring to General Stefan Dąb-Biernacki (1890–1959), rejected by General Sikorski and exiled on the Isle of Bute after the fall of France, who plotted against Sikorski's government. He was court-martialled in 1941 by the Poles and reduced to the rank of private; imprisoned by the British for four years, but released in 1943 on the grounds of ill health; he went to live in Ireland.
3   Langbein, Hermann, *People in Auschwitz* (Chapel Hill and London: University of North Carolina Press, 2004), p. 179.
4   TNA KV2/929.
5   See: TNA KV2/373.
6   There was a P&O liner named SS *Narkunda* but no Royal Navy trawler of that name; the liner seems more likely.
7   TNA KV2/373.
8   TNA KV2/373.
9   TNA KV2/373.
10 *Sipo and SD Kommandos in France. Personnel and Chief Groups of Agents.* Central Intelligence Agency (CIA), declassified 2001 and 2007: https://ia601301.us.archive.org/11/items/GERMANINTELLIGENCESERVICEWWIIVOL1-0001/GERMAN%20INTELLIGENCE%20SERVICE%20(WWII),%20%20VOL.%201_0001.pdf
11 TNA KV2/932.
12 TNA KV2/932.
13 TNA KV2/72.
14 TNA KV2/926.
15 TNA KV2/926.
16 Garby-Czerniawski, *op. cit.*, p. 247.
17 TNA KV2/929.

18   TNA KV2/72.

19   TNA KV2/72.

20   TNA KV2/72.

21   TNA KV2/72.

22   TNA KV2/72.

23   TNA KV2/72.

24   TNA KV2/72.

25   TNA KV2/926.

26   Congreve, William, *The Mourning Bride* (1697), Act III, Scene 2.

27   TNA KV2/72.

28   Verity, Hugh, 'Some RAF Pick-ups for for French Intelligence',
     in: Robertson, *op. cit.*, p. 171. Verity stated that Mathilde Carré had
     denounced Paul Shiffmacher.

29   www.montigny-asme.fr

30   http://www.mortonandeden.com/pdfcats/53web.pdf : Morton & Eden,
     Catalogue for 1 December 2011, Lot 1477. Notes by Nicolas Livingstone.

31   Verity, *op. cit.*, p. 39.

Chapter 20. Winding Up a Troublesome Affair

1   TNA KV2/927.

2   TNA KV2/928.

3   West, Nigel, *MI5. British Security Service Operations 1909–1945* (London:
    Bodley Head, 1981), p. 123; TNA HS9/582/6.

4   http://www.cwgc.org/find-war-dead/casualty/3069800/GILLSON,%20
    GODFREY%20ANTHONY. See also: http://www.specialforcesroh.
    com/showthread.php?23570-Gillson-Godfrey-Anthony

5   Murphy, *op. cit.*, p. 55.

6   West, *MI5*, pp. 27, 123. One source gives the date of his death as
    3 March 1944 in Burma: https://www.wikitree.com/wiki/Gillson-16;
    the Commonwealth War Graves Commission also confirms this date.
    He is buried in Rangoon, Burma (Yangon, Myanmar): http://www.cwgc.
    org/search/casualty_details.aspx?casualty=3069800; his file at TNA is
    HS9/582/6. Also listed in: http://www.academia.edu/2299311/THE_
    MOST_SECRET_LIST_OF_SOE_AGENTS_G. His wife, Priscilla, was
    born in New York City. The couple divorced and in 1947 she remarried
    to Count Guy de la Fregonnière; she died on 22 February 1979.

7   West, *MI5*, p. 45.

8   David Lloyd, in: Gourvish, Terry, *Dolphin Square. The History of a Unique Building* (London: Bloomsbury, 2014), p. 99; n. 116.

9   Murphy, *op. cit.*, pp. 51–6, 61, 69.

10 Sisman, *op. cit.*, pp. 207–8.

11 As a detective chief inspector, Gale would later be responsible for arresting British spy George Blake on 4 April 1961: Allason, Rupert, *The Branch* (London: Secker & Warburg, 1983), p. 140; Hermiston, Roger, *The Greatest Traitor* (London: Aurum Press, 2014), pp. 229, 230, 232. Hermiston refers to Gale as detective superintendent.

12 Bonhams states she was British; artuk.org states German. See also: Vincent, Jutta, 'Muteness as Utterance of a Forced Reality – Jack Bilbo's Modern Art Gallery (1941–1948)' in: Behr, Shulamith and Marian Malet (eds), *Arts in Exile in Britain 1933–1945. Politics and Cultural Identity* (Amsterdam and New York: Editions Rodopi B.V., 2004). *The Yearbook of the Research Centre for German and Austrian Exile Studies*, Vol. 6, p. 331, n. 78; note 79 of the same source states that 'as far as is known, Mayerson was not involved in any political movement'. See also: modernbritishpictures.co.uk; http://theamericanreader.com/20-march-1951-truman-capote-to-robert-linscott/

13 TNA KV2/928.

14 TNA KV2/928.

15 TNA KV2/928.

16 Carré, *op. cit.*, p. 153.

17 TNA KV2/928.

18 TNA KV2/928.

19 Thomas and Lewis, *op. cit.*, p. 52.

20 TNA KV2/927.

21 TNA KV2/927.

22 TNA KV2/927.

23 TNA KV2/928.

24 Gray, Chris, 'How a Triple Agent Called "The Cat" Got the Cream of Britain's Spy Network', in *Independent*, 28 November 2002.

25 TNA KV2/928.

26 TNA KV2/931.

27 TNA KV2/928.

28 TNA KV2/928.

29 TNA KV2/931.

30 TNA KV2/931.

31 TNA KV2/931.

32 TNA KV2/928.

33 TNA KV2/928.

34 See: Simpson, A.W. Brian, *In the Highest Degree Odious. Detention without Trial in Wartime Britain* (Oxford: Oxford University Press, 1984), p. 258.

35 TNA KV2/928.

36 Molly Mellanby, CBE was born on 13 September 1898. In 1939 she was governor and living in the Governor's House along with Elsie Woodley, a domestic. She later became director of women's establishments on the Prison Commission for England and Wales and was awarded the CBE (Civil Division) in the 1957 New Year's Honours List. According to Smith, Ann D., *Women in Prison. A Study of Penal Methods* (London: Stevens & Sons, 1962), Ch. 16, pp. 256–72, 'Borstal Training', she took over as governor in 1934 and was succeeded by the Hon. Victoria Bruce c.1943.

37 See: TNA KV2/832 and KV2/833; Clough, Bryan, *State Secrets. The Kent-Wolkoff Affair* (Hove: Hideaway Publications, 2005), pp. 183–4; Quinlan, Kevin, *The Secret War between the Wars. MI5 in the 1920s and 1930s* (Woodbridge: Boydell Press, 2014), p. 119; Willetts, Paul, *Rendezvous at the Russian Tea Rooms* (London: Constable, 2016), paperback edition, pp. xvi, 153, 180, 202–3, 216, 229, 231, 252.

38 TNA KV2/928.

39 TNA KV2/928.

40 TNA KV2/539.

41 TNA KV2/538.

42 TNA KV2/928.

43 TNA KV2/930.

44 TNA KV2/929.

Chapter 21. Accounts Payable: The Cost of Doing Business

1   Author of numerous books about the anatomy of the eye. He had prescribed lenses as –15 in each eye, with –1 cylinder in the right eye.

2   TNA KV2/935.

3   Bourne-Patterson, *op. cit.*

4   TNA KV2/935.
5   Davies, *op. cit.*, p. 113.
6   TNA KV2/935.
7   TNA KV2/935.
8   TNA KV2/935.
9   TNA KV2/935.
10 The Hon. Victoria A.K. Bruce was born on 2 November 1894.
    According to the 1939 register, she was deputy governor of Aylesbury
    Borstal Institution and lived in the Gate House. Other occupants of
    the house were Florence A. Marsh, Borstal officer, Joan Martyn, Borstal
    housemistress, and Ada Woodland, in charge of housekeeping.

Chapter 22. What Are we Going to Do about Mathilde?

1   TNA KV2/539.
2   TNA KV2/930.
3   Cited in: Bailey, Roderick, *Target: Italy. The Secret War Against Mussolini, 1940–1943* (London: Faber & Faber, 2014), pp. 91–3; see also: Fedorowich, Kent, 'The Mazzini Society and Political Warfare', in: Wylie, Neville (ed.), *The Politics and Strategy of Political Warfare, 1940–1946* (London and New York: Routledge, 2007), pp. 163–4; and TNA KV2/3172 and FO371/34202.
4   *Ibid.*, p. 93.
5   The full article can be read in the *Chicago Sunday Tribune* for 12 September 1943 at: http://archives.chicagotribune.com/1943/09/12/page/2/article/display-ad-1-no-title
6   See: Neave, Airey, *Little Cyclone* (London: Coronet/Hodder & Stoughton, 1985), 4th impression, paperback edition; Stourton, Edward, *Cruel Crossing. Escaping Hitler across the Pyrenees* (London: Transworld/Random House, 2014), paperback edition; Foot, M.R.D., *Six Faces of Courage* (Barnsley: Leo Cooper, 2003); Clutton-Brock, Oliver, *RAF Evaders* (London: Bounty Books, 2009).
7   Internees at liberty in UK in 1939–42: TNA HO396/46/99 and HO396/46/100 respectively.
8   TNA KV2/930.
9   Rees, Goronwy, *A Chapter of Accidents* (London: Chatto & Windus, 1972).

10 TNA KV2/930.

11 TNA KV2/930.

12 TNA KV2/930.

13 TNA KV2/902, KV2/903, KV2/904.

14 Cooper, Alan W., *The Dambuster Raid. A Reappraisal 70 Years On* (Barnsley: Pen & Sword Aviation, 2013), p. 149.

15 TNA KV2/930.

16 See TNA KV2/1094-97; West, Nigel, *Historical Dictionary of World War 1 Intelligence* (Lanham, MD: Rowman & Littlefield, 2014), p. 40.

17 TNA KV2/930.

18 The Latin expression *a fortiori* is defined by (i) the *Oxford English Dictionary* as something which is 'Used to express a conclusion for which there is stronger evidence than for a previously accepted one'; (ii) 'This phrase is used in logic to denote an argument to the effect that because one ascertained fact exists, therefore another which is included in it or analogous to it and is less improbable, unusual, or surprising must also exist'; and (iii) 'conclusively, with even stronger reason'. See: *West's Encyclopedia of American Law, Edition 2*. S.v: http://legal-dictionary.thefreedictionary.com/a+fortiori; Buchanan-Bown, John, et al. (eds), *Le Mot Juste. A Dictionary of Classical and Foreign Words and Phrases* (New York: Vintage Books, 1981), paperback edition, p. 14.

19 TNA KV2/930.

20 TNA KV2/930.

21 TNA KV2/930. Kinnaird House, 1 Pall Mall East, St James's was the headquarters of the Security Executive during the Second World War.

22 TNA KV2/930.

23 TNA KV2/930.

24 TNA KV2/930.

25 TNA KV2/930 (322k and 325k respectively).

26 TNA KV2/930.

27 TNA KV2/931.

28 TNA KV2/931.

29 TNA KV2/931.

30 TNA KV2/931.

31 TNA KV2/934.

32 TNA HS9/576/3.

33 TNA KV2/931.

34 TNA KV2/926.

35 TNA KV2/931.

36 TNA KV2/931.

37 TNA KV2/931.

38 The president at that time was Max Huber (1874–1960), who had served in that capacity from 1928 to 1944, when he was succeeded by Carl Jacob Burckhardt (1891–1974).

39 TNA KV2/931.

40 TNA KV2/932.

41 TNA KV2/932.

42 Ruby, *op. cit.*, p. 169.

43 Bourne-Patterson, *op. cit.*, p. 5.

44 TNA KV2/930.

45 Bailey, *op. cit.*, pp. 110, 111, 195, 298.

46 TNA KV2/932.

47 TNA KV2/932.

48 TNA KV2/932.

49 O'Connor, Bernard, *Agents Françaises* (Kobo eBook, 2016), no pagination; Sergeuiew, Lily and Mary Kathryn Barbier (ed.), *I Worked Alone: Diary of a Double Agent in World War II Europe* (Jefferson, NC: McFarland & Co., 2014), p. 297; Faure, Claude, *Aux Services de la République: BCRA à la DGSE* (Librairie Arthème Fayard, 2004), Kindle edition, no pagination.

50 TNA KV2/932.

Chapter 23. Disposing of the Body

1 TNA KV2/932.

2 For information on Mitzi Smythe, an active Fascist in the 1930s, see: KV2/1341-1342; for Helene Louise ten Cate Brouwer @Gerda Hoffman @ Debruyn @ Anneke Vantuyll, an SD agent, see: KV2/219; WO204/11652 and https://www.cia.gov/library/readingroom/docs/RAUFF,%20WALTER_0008.pdf; for Jessie Jordan @ Wallace see: KV2/193–194; KV2/3532–3534.

3 TNA KV2/932.

4 TNA KV2/932.

5 TNA KV2/932.

6   TNA KV2/932.
7   TNA KV2/932.
8   For more information on GARBO see: Pujol, Juan with Nigel West, *Garbo* (London: Weidenfeld & Nicolson, 1985); Harris, Tomás, *Garbo. The Spy who Saved D-Day* (London: Public Record Office, 2000); Talty, Stephen, *Agent Garbo* (Boston and New York: Marriner Books/Houghton Mifflin Harcourt, 2013), paperback edition.
9   TNA KV2/932.
10 TNA KV2/932.
11 http://www.aassdn.org/TR.pdf. Interestingly, there was also a Jean Hugon (1909–45) who was arrested on 14 April 1944 by the Milice in Vichy and deported to Neuengamme concentration camp on 5 May, where he died on 1 February 1945.
12 TNA KV2/932.
13 TNA KV2/932.
14 TNA KV2/932.
15 Ruby, *op. cit.*, p. 113.
16 TNA KV2/932.
17 Paine, *Mathilde Carré*, pp. 110–11.
18 TNA KV2/932.
19 Blum, Howard, *The Last Goodnight* (New York: HarperCollins, 2016); 'Espionage: A Blond Bond', *Time*, vol. 82, no. 25 (20 December 1963): http://content.time.com/time/magazine/article/0,9171,938947,00.html
20 Under the title 'P.F.600, 286, LAFONT'. He should not be confused with Marius Lafont (b.1901), HS9/875/6 or Luc Jean Le Fustic @ LAFONT (b.16 July 1917), HS9/908/5.
21 TNA KV2/312.
22 Schoenbrun, David, *Soldiers of the Night. The Story of the French Resistance* (New York: E.P. Dutton, 1980), p. 350.
23 TNA KV2/312.
24 TNA KV2/312.
25 TNA KV2/312.
26 TNA KV2/312.
27 TNA KV2/312.
28 TNA KV2/312.
29 TNA KV2/166.

30   TNA HS9/1406/8; FO950/1292. The *Supplement to the London Gazette* entry for 28 April 1942 (p. 1856) lists L/Cpl John Ashford Renshaw Starr (230430) from the I.C. (Intelligence Corps) to the General List as of 6 March 1942.

31   TNA KV2/312.

32   For more information see: McDonald-Rothwell, Gabrielle, *Her Finest Hour* (Stroud: Amberley, 2017).

33   Jacobs, Peter, *Setting France Ablaze. The SOE in France During WWII* (Barnsley: Pen & Sword, 2015), p. 106.

34   TNA KV2/312.

35   Fuller, Jean Overton, *Noor-un-nisa Inayat Khan* (London and The Hague: East–West Publications, 1988), revised paperback edition, pp. 228–38; Starr's testimony of the escape is detailed on pp. 222–38; Basu, Shrabani, *Spy Princess. The Life of Noor Inayat Khan* (Stroud: Sutton Publishing, 2006), pp. 162, 163–6, 167.

36   http://maitron-fusilles-40-44.univ-paris1.fr/spip.php?article178801

37   Fuller, Jean Overton, *The Starr Affair* (London: Victor Gollancz, 1954); TNA HS9/1406/8.

Chapter 24. Strong Evidence from Many Sources

1   TNA KV2/933; also found in KV2/753.

2   TNA KV2/933.

3   TNA KV2/933.

4   TNA KV2/933.

5   TNA KV2/933.

6   TNA KV2/933.

7   TNA KV2/932.

8   TNA KV2/932.

9   TNA KV2/932.

10 TNA KV2/932.

11 TNA KV2/932.

12 TNA KV2/932.

13 TNA KV2/753.

14 http://www.archives18.fr/arkotheque/client/ad_cher/_depot_arko/articles/993/repertoire-140-j_doc.pdf

15   http://www.bddm.org/liv/details.php?id=I.274.

16   http://museedelaresistanceenligne.org/mediasmusee/Listing_libenord.pdf

17   For more information on Beaudet see: *Inventaire Archives Imprimées et Manuscrites. Fond France Résistance*: http://s3.amazonaws.com/zanran_storage/www.memorial-caen.fr/ContentPages/47398126.pdf

18   Stafford, David, *10 Days to D-Day* (London: Abacus, 2004), paperback edition, p. 57 (p. 61 in hardcover); Osborne, Mike, *Defending London. The Military Landscape from Prehistory to the Present* (Stroud: The History Press, 2012), Appx 8 (no pagination in online edition); Maclaren, *op. cit.*, p. 95.

19   65 Field Security Section (65 FSS) based at Aylesbury was assigned to SOE duties, 1941–44; Holland 1944. See: Clayton, Anthony, *Forearmed. A History of the Intelligence Corps* (London: Brassey's, 1996), p. 266.

20   TNA KV2/753, serial 3A.

21   Osborne, *op. cit.*

22   Maclaren, *op. cit.*, p. 96.

23   TNA KV2/753, serial 4B.

24   TNA KV2/753, serial 4A.

25   TNA KV2/753, serial 6A.

26   TNA KV2/753, serial 5A.

27   TNA KV2/753, serial 4C.

28   TNA KV2/753, serial 7A.

29   TNA KV2/753, serial 8A.

30   TNA KV2/753.

31   TNA KV2/753.

32   TNA KV2/753.

33   TNA KV2/753.

34   TNA KV2/753.

35   TNA KV2/753.

36   TNA KV2/753.

37   TNA KV2/753.

38   TNA KV2/1175.

39   TNA KV2/1175.

40   TNA KV2/753.

41   TNA KV2/753.

42   Murphy, *op. cit.*, p. 201; Mackenzie, *op. cit.*, p. xviii states that he was head of security at Bayswater.

43   TNA KV2/753.

44   TNA KV2/753.
45   TNA KV2/166.
46   TNA KV2/1175.
47   TNA KV2/166; Langley, Mike, *Anders Larsson VC, MC of the SAS* (Barnsley: Pen & Sword, 2016), p. 104.
48   https://combinedops.com/Op_Aquatint.htm
49   Lett, Brian, *The Small Scale Raiding Force* (Barnsley: Pen & Sword, 2013), Ch. 14, 'Graham Hayes', no pagination in online version; Lewis, Damien, *The Ministry of Ungentlemanly Warfare* (NY& London: Quercus, 2015), p. 222.
50   TNA KV2/753.

Chapter 25. The Final Reckoning

1   https://fr.wikipedia.org/wiki/Canton_de_Lun%C3%A9ville-Sud. This is contradicted by http://www.francegenweb.org/mairesgenweb/resultcommune.php?id=412 (12.5.39-17.6.1939) and Albert Mayer (17.6.39-10.6.44; 19.10.45-14.3.47).
2   Neave, *op. cit.*, p.183.
3   TNA KV2/72.
4   SPEARHEAD was the code name for the OSS; it was also the name of the American 3rd Armored Division; SAINT was the OSS code name for its chiefs of station in Washington, London and Paris. CRUSADE was an OSS field unit in France and AGNOSTIC was the OSS in London. Nigel West, personal communication.
5   TNA KV2/932.
6   TNA KV2/72.
7   TNA KV2/72.
8   TNA KV2/72.
9   TNA KV2/72.
10   TNA KV2/72.
11   TNA KV2/72.
12   TNA KV2/72.
13   TNA KV2/72.
14   TNA KV2/72.
15   Prados, John, *Lost Crusader. The Secret Wars of CIA Director William Colby* (New York: Oxford University Press, 2003), p. 16.

16   Carré, *op. cit.*, p. 179.

17   *Ibid.*, p. 200.

18   'Any French citizen who in time of war, corresponds with a foreign power or with its agents, with a view toward favoring this power's undertakings with France.' Cited in: Céline, Louis-Ferdinand, *Fable for Another Time* (Lincoln, NB: University of Nebraska Press, 2003), p. 223; and 'any French person who in time of war, was found guilty of collusion with a foreign power or its representatives with a view to promoting the foreign projects of this foreign power against France should be executed.' Cited in: Drake, David, *Intellectuals and Politics in Post-War France* (Basingstoke and New York: Palgrave Macmillan, 2002), pp. 17–18.

19   Carré, *op. cit.*, p. 9.

20   O'Connor, *Agents Françaises.*

21   Young, *op, cit.*, p. 73; see: http://www.monument-mauthausen.org/25525.html?lang=fr

22   Grehan, John and Martin Mace, *Unearthing Churchill's Secret Army* (Barnsley: Pen & Sword, 2012), pp. 88–9.

23   TNA KV2/933.

24   Young, *op. cit.*, p. 179.

25   Paine, *Mathilde Carré*, p. 176.

26   *Ibid.*, p. 201.

27   *Ibid.*, p. 201

28   Young, *op. cit.*, p. 194.

29   *Ibid.*, pp. 196–7.

30   *Ibid.*, p. 184.

31   *Ibid.*, p. 200.

32   TNA FO371.

33   See: TNA KV2/831; TS 27/514 (Treasury Solicitor and HM Procurator-General, Application for Writs of Habeus Corpus under DR.18B); HO 283/58/1 (closed extracts, 3 pp); HO 45/25725; HO 283/58; Hart, Bradley W., *George Pitt-Rivers and the Nazis* (London: Bloomsbury Academic, 2015).

34   Aldrich, Richard J., *Espionage, Security and Intelligence in Britain 1945–1970* (Manchester: Manchester University Press, 1998), p. 116; Rust, William J., *Eisenhower and Cambodia, Diplomacy, Covert Action and the Origins of the Second Indochina War* (Lexington: University Press of Kentucky, 2016), no pagination in online version; Smith, T.O., *Britain and the Origins of the Vietnam War* (Basingstoke: Palgrave Macmillan, 2007), p. 44; and http://www.gulabin.com/britishdiplomats/pdf/BRIT%20DIPS%201900-2011.pdf

35 TNA KV2/831.

36 TNA FO371.

37 Found in TNA FO371 and KV2/831. *L'Intransigeant*, mentioned under point No. 1, was a left-wing French newspaper founded in 1880, which became right-wing in the 1920s; it ceased publication in 1940, only to re-emerge in 1947 as *L'Intransigeant-Journal de Paris*.

38 See: https://www.loc.gov/rr/frd/Military_Law/pdf/Malmedy_report. pdf and Weingartner, James J., *A Peculiar Crusade. Willis M. Everett and the Malmedy Massacre* (New York: New York University Press, 2000); Weingartner, James J., *Crossroads of Death. The Story of the Malmédy Massacre and Trial* (Berkeley & Los Angeles: University of California Press, 1979).

39 TNA FO371.

40 Young, *op. cit.*, p. 213.

41 *Ibid.*, p. 203.

42 *Ibid.*, pp. 203–4.

43 *Ibid.*, pp. 206–7.

44 Pope, Alexander, *An Essay on Criticism* (1711), Part II.

45 Young, *op. cit.*, p. 216.

46 *Ibid.*, p. 214.

47 Carré, *op. cit.*, p. 219.

48 Jaffré, Yves-Frédéric, *Les tribunaux d'exception 1940–1962* (Paris: Nouvelles Éditions Latines, 1962), p. 200.

49 Carré, *op. cit.*, p. 210.

50 *Ibid.*, p. 216.

51 (1) https://www.revolvy.com/topic/Mathilde%20Carr%C3%A9&uid=1575; (2) https://en.wikipedia.org/wiki/Mathilde_Carr%C3%A9; (3) http://www.auffargis.com/W/2017/02/XX-4-d%C3%A9cembre-1941.pdf. This last reference includes a death registration number.

52 Published by Beauchene, Paris, and Droguet et Ardant respectively.

Epilogue. Who Were the Guilty Parties?

1   Rosbottom, Ronald C., *When Paris Went Dark* (New York: Little, Brown & Company, 2015), paperback edition.

2   Smith, Michael, *The Anatomy of a Traitor* (London: Aurum Press, 2017), p. 14.

3   *Ibid.*, pp. 13–14.

4   Carré, *op. cit.*, p. 73.

5   Carré, *op.cit.*, p.115, and see quote, p.119.

6   Lilienfeld, S.O. & B.P. Andrews, 'Development and Preliminary Validation of a Self-report Measure of Psychopathic Personality Traits in Noncriminal Populations', *Journal of Personality Assessment*, vol. 66 (1996), pp. 488–524.

7   Carré, *op. cit.*, p. 29.

8   *Ibid.*, p. 33.

9   *Ibid.*, p. 10.

10 Thienel, Tobias, 'The Admissibility of Evidence Obtained by Torture Under International Law', *European Journal of International Law*, vol. 17, no. 2 (2006), pp. 349–67.

11 Deacon, Richard, *Escape!* (London: BBC, 1980), Ch. 5 'The Cartland Murder', pp. 151 et seq.

12 West, *Historical Dictionary of British Intelligence*, p. 204.

13 Vine, George, 'Spy Fights for his Honour in Case of The Cat', *News Chronicle*, 22 April 1959, cited in TNA KV2/166 (Bleicher) and PF64216 (Carré), vol. 9, currently not available from the National Archives.

14 http://gw.geneanet.org/touvet?lang=en&pz=cedric&nz=touvet&ocz=0&p=pierre&n=de+crevoisier+de+vomecourt; https://www.avis-de-deces.net/f_micheline-sailly-villedieu-sur-indre-36320-indre_282957_2010.html

15 TNA KV2/72.

16 See: Foot, M.R.D., 'Was S.O.E. Any Good?', *Journal of Contemporary History*, vol. 16, no. 1 (January 1981), pp. 167–81; Seaman, Mark (ed.), *Special Operations Executive. A New Instrument of War* (London and New York: Routledge, 2006).

Select Bibliography

Primary Sources

The National Archives, Kew (TNA):

KV2/164–166, 2127 (Bleicher)
KV2/72–73 (BRUTUS)
FO371/79181
KV2/926–936 (Carré)
KV2/2856 (De Casteja)
KV2/539 (Eriksson)
KV2/961 (Giskes)
KV2/753 (Kieffer)
KV2/1727–1729 (Kraus)
KV2/903–904 (Nicholson)
KV2/1312–1313 (Picabia)
KV2/937–938 (Pierrat)
KV2/831; FO371 (Pitt-Rivers)
KV2/1491 (Schuchmann)
KV2/832–833 (Stanford)
KV2/373 (Szumlicz)
KV2/312 (Wendel)

Secondary Sources

Adams, Jefferson, *Historical Dictionary of German Intelligence* (Lanham, MD: Scarecrow Press, 2009).

Andrew, Christopher, *Defence of the Realm* (Toronto: Viking Canada, 2009).

Bailey, Roderick, *Forgotten Voices of the Secret War* (London: Ebury Press, 2009), paperback edition.

Binney, Marcus, *The Women who Lived for Danger. The Women Agents of SOE in the Second World War* (London: Hodder & Stoughton, 2002).

Bleicher, Hugo, *Colonel Henri's Story* (London: William Kimber, 1954).

Booth, Nicholas, *Zigzag. The Incredible Wartime Exploits of Double Agent Eddie Chapman* (New York: Arcade Publishing, 2007); trade paperback.

Bourne-Patterson, Major Robert, *SOE in France 1941–1945* (Barnsley: Frontline Books/Pen & Sword, 2016).

Boyd, Douglas, *Voices from the Dark Years. The Truth about Occupied France 1940–1945* (Stroud: The History Press, 2007).

Boyer, Régis and Jean-Marc Binot, *Nom de code: BRUTUS: Histoire d'un réseau de la France* (Paris: Librairie Arthème Fayard, 2007).

Carré, Mathilde-Lily, *I Was the Cat* (London: Souvenir Press, 1960); originally published in French as *J'ai été la Chatte* (Paris: Éditions Morgan, 1959).

Cave Brown, Anthony, *Bodyguard of Lies* (Toronto: Fitzhenry & Whiteside, 1975).

Clark, Freddie, *Agents by Moonlight. The Secret History of RAF Tempsford during World War II* (Stroud: Tempus Publishing, 1999).

Clough, Bryan, *State Secrets. The Kent-Wolkoff Affair* (Hove: Hideaway Publications, 2005).

Cookridge, E.H., *Inside SOE* (London: Arthur Barker, 1966).

Cowburn, Benjamin, *No Cloak No Dagger* (London: Frontline Books, 2009).

Crowdy, Terry, *Deceiving Hitler. Double Cross and Deception in World War II* (Oxford: Osprey, 2008).

Curry, John, *The Security Service 1908–1945. The Official History* (London: Public Record Office, 1999).

Davies, Philip H.J., *MI6 and the Machinery of Spying* (London and Portland, OR: Frank Cass, 2004), paperback edition.

Day, Peter, *Klop. Britain's Most Ingenious Secret Agent* (London: Biteback, 2014).

Farago, Ladislas, *The Game of the Foxes* (New York: David McKay & Co., 1971), first US edition.

Foot, M.R.D., *Memories of an S.O.E. Historian* (Barnsley: Pen & Sword, 2009).

Foot, M.R.D, *SOE 1940–46* (London: BBC, 1984).

Foot, M.R.D, *SOE in France* (London: HMSO, 1966).

Foot, M.R.D, *Resistance. European Resistance to Nazism 1940–45* (London: Eyre Methuen, 1976).

Garby-Czerniawski, Roman, *The Big Network* (London: George Ronald, 1961).

Haufler, Hervé, *The Spies who Never Were* (New York: New American Library, 2006), paperback edition.

Hayward, James, *Hitler's Spy. The True Story of Arthur Owens, Double Agent Snow* (London: Simon & Schuster, 2012), paperback edition.

Helms, Sarah, *A Life in Secrets* (London: Little, Brown, 2005).

Hennessey, Thomas and Claire Thomas, *Spooks. The Unofficial History of MI5 from Agent Zigzag to the D-Day Deception, 1939–45* (Stroud: Amberley, 2010), paperback edition.

Hesketh, Roger, *Fortitude. The D-Day Deception Campaign* (London: St Ermin's Press, 1999).

Hinsley, F.H. and C.A.G. Simkins, *British Intelligence in the Second World War. Vol. 4: Security and Counter-Intelligence* (London: HMSO, 1990).

Holt, Thaddeus, *The Deceivers. Allied Military Deception in the Second World War* (London: Weidenfeld & Nicolson, 2004).

Irwin, Will, *Jedburghs. The Secret History of the Allied Special Forces, France 1944* (New York: Public Affairs, 2005).

Izbicki, John, *The Naked Heroine* (London: Umbria Press, 2014).

Jacobs, Peter, *Setting France Ablaze. The SOE in France During WWII* (Barnsley: Pen & Sword, 2015).

Jeffrey, Keith, *The Secret History of MI6, 1909–1949* (New York: Penguin Press, 2010).

Kahn, David, *Hitler's Spies. German Military Intelligence in World War II* (London: Hodder & Stoughton, 1978).

Knowlson, James, *Damned to Fame. The Life of Samuel Beckett* (New York: Simon & Schuster, 1996).

Lefebvre-Fileau, Jean-Paul and Gilles Perrault, *Ces Français qui on collaboré avec le IIIe Reiche* (Monaco: Éditions du Rocher, 2017).

Lerecouvreux, Maurice, *Résurrection de l'Armée française, de Weygand à Giraud* (Paris: Nouvelles Éditions Latine, 1955).

Levine, Joshua, *Operation Fortitude. The Greatest Hoax of the Second World War* (London: Collins, 2012), paperback edition.

Lloyd, Christopher, *Collaboration and Resistance in Occupied France. Representing Treason and Sacrifice* (Basingstoke: Palgrave Macmillan, 2003).

Macintyre, Ben, *Agent Zigzag. The True Wartime Story of Eddie Chapman, Lover, Betrayer, Hero, Spy* (London: Bloomsbury, 2007).

Macintyre, Ben, *Double Cross* (London: Bloomsbury, 2012).

Mackenzie, William, *The Secret History of SOE. The Special Operations Executive 1940–1945* (London: St. Ermin's Press, 2000).

Maclaren, Roy, *Canadians behind Enemy Lines* (Vancouver: UBC Press, 2004), paperback edition.

Marnham, Patrick, *Wild Mary. A Life of Mary Wesley* (London: Vintage Books, 2007).

Masterman, J.C, *The Double-Cross System* (London: Vintage Books, 2013), paperback edition.

Miles, Rosalind and Robin Cross, *Warrior Women. 3000 Years of Courage and Heroism* (London: Quercus, 2011).

Moon, Tom, *Loyal and Lethal Ladies of Espionage* (San José: iUniverse.com, Inc., 2000).

Murphy, Christopher J., *Security and Special Operations. SOE and MI5 during the Second World War* (Basingstoke: Palgrave Macmillan, 2006).

Nash, Jay Robert, *Spies: A Narrative Encyclopedia of Dirty Tricks and Double Dealing from Biblical Times to Today* (New York: M. Evans and Company, 1997).

Neave, Airey, *Saturday at MI9* (London: Hodder & Stoughton, 1969), 1st UK edition.

Neave, Airey, *Little Cyclone* (London: Coronet Books/Hodder & Stoughton, 1985) paperback edition, 4th impression.

O'Connor, Bernard, *Agents Françaises* (Kobo eBook, 2016).

Osborne, Mike, *Defending London. The Military Landscape from Prehistory to the Present* (Stroud: The History Press, 2012).

Paine, Lauran, *Mathilde Carré: Double Agent* (London: Robert Hale, 1976).

Richards, (Sir) Brooks, *Secret Flotillas, Volume 1: Clandestine Sea Operations to Brittany 1940–44* (Barnsley: Pen & Sword, 2013), trade paper.

Richelson, Jeffrey T., *A Century of Spies. Intelligence in the Twentieth Century* (Oxford; New York: Oxford University Press, 1995).

Robertson, K.G. (ed.), *War, Resistance and Intelligence. Essays in Honour of M.R.D. Foot* (Barnsley: Leo Cooper, 1999).

Ruby, Marcel, *F Section SOE* (London: Leo Cooper/Heinemann, 1988).

Simpson, A.W. Brian, *In the Highest Degree Odious. Detention without Trial in Wartime Britain* (Oxford: Oxford University Press, 1984), trade paperback.

Sisman, Adam, *John le Carré. The Biography* (London: Bloomsbury, 2015).

Stephens, Robin, *Camp 020. MI5 and the Nazi Spies*, ed. Oliver Hoare, (London: Public Record Office, 2000).

Suttill, Francis J., *Shadows in the Fog* (Stroud: The History Press, 2014).

Sweet, Matthew, *The West End Front. The Wartime Secrets of London's Grand Hotels* (London: Faber & Faber, 2012), paperback edition.

Thomas, Gordon and Greg Lewis, *Shadow Warriors of World War II. The Daring Women of OSS and SOE* (Chicago: Chicago Review Press, 2017).

Tickell, Jerrard, *Odette. The Story of a British Agent* (London: Chapman & Hall, 1950), 5th impression.

Verity, Hugh, *We Landed by Moonlight. The Secret RAF Landings in France 1940–1944* (Manchester: Crécy Publishing, 1998), 2nd revised edition.

Vomécourt, Philippe de, *An Army of Resisters: The Story of the SOE Resistance Movement in France, by One of the Three Brothers who Organized and Ran it* (London: Doubleday, 1961).

Wake-Walker, Edward, *House for Spies* (London: Robert Hale, 2011).

Walker, Robyn, *The Women who Spied for Britain. Female Secret Agents of the Second World War* (Stroud: Amberley Publishing, 2014).

West, Nigel, *MI5. British Security Service Operations 1909–1945* (London: Bodley Head, 1981).

West, Nigel, *MI6. British Secret Intelligence Service Operations 1909–45* (London: Weidenfeld & Nicolson, 1983).

West, Nigel, *The Friends. Britain's Post-War Secret Intelligence Operations* (London: Weidenfeld & Nicolson, 2008).

West, Nigel, *Historical Dictionary of British Intelligence* (Lanham, MD: Scarecrow Press, 2005), 1st edition.

West, Nigel, *Historical Dictionary of Sexpionage* (Lanham, MD: Scarecrow Press, 2009).

West, Nigel, *Secret War* (London: Hodder & Stoughton, 1992).

West, Nigel (ed.), *The Guy Liddell Diaries. Vol. I: 1939–1942* (Abingdon: Routledge, 2005).

West, Nigel (ed.), *The Guy Liddell Diaries. Vol. II: 1942–1945* (Abingdon: Routledge, 2005).

West, Nigel and Madoc Roberts, *SNOW. The Double Life of a World War II Spy* (London: Biteback, 2011).

West, Nigel and Oleg Tsarev, *Triplex. Secrets from the Cambridge Spies* (New Haven and London: Yale University Press, 2009).

Willetts, Paul, *Rendezvous at the Russian Tea Rooms* (London: Constable, 2016), paperback edition.

Yarnold, Patrick, *Wanborough Manor. School for Secret Agents* (Guildford: Hopfield Publications, 2009).

Young, Gordon, *The Cat with Two Faces* (New York: Coward-McCann Inc, 1957).

INDEX

Abbott, G.W. 172, 186, 195-6, 319

Abwehr 19–21, 30, 50, 58, 62–4, 74, 85–6, 92–3, 95, 99, 112, 114, 129, 134, 136, 138–9, 156, 161, 163, 171–2, 246, 257–9, 327, 336, 357, 360, 367, 394

Achat, André 39, 40–2, 49, 370

Agent U.35, *see* Ustinov, Jona von 'Klop'

Alesch, Abbé 184, 357

Aliona, Mustapha Ben 28

Alliance 335–6

Amiate 357

Aouta (MOUSTIQUE) 107, 126

Apollinaire, Guillaume 173

ARMAND, *see* Garby-Czerniawski, Roman

Ashley, Gisela, *see* Barton, Susan

Astor, Hugh 39, 182-3, 253, 321–3, 325–6, 351, 354–6, 361–5

Atkins, Vera 198, 298-9

Aubertin, René 33, 46, 50, 55, 168, 342, 368, 370

Auerstaedt, Jacques Davout d' 163–4

Auschwitz *see* concentration camps

Author/Digger 250

Autier, Philippe 39, 72, 162, 177

Aveling, A.V. 289

Aylesbury Prison 284, 290–5, 297–8, 300, 302, 303, 305–7, 310–12, 317, 375, 377, 379, 389

Bailly, Auguste 143

Bailly, Jean 143, 188

Bardet, Roger 58, 137, 213, 320, 329, 337, 348, 353–7, 366, 368, 393

Barry, Lt Col P.R. 94, 97

Barton, Susan 30–2, 62, 213, 224, 277–82, 290

Baxter, E.A.S. 290

Baxter, Col H.J. 60, 92, 347–8

Bayswater Special Security Section (BSS) 321, 328, 355

Beaudet, Henri 347, 357

Beckett, Samuel 163, 173, 175, 182–4

Becognée, Maître 368, 370

Beddard, S/Ldr T.E. 100, 129, 169, 339

Bégué, Maj. Georges 161, 194, 331

Belard, Arsène, father of Mathilde Carré 25

Belard, Jeanne (*née* Gross), mother of Mathilde Carré 25, 141, 327, 369, 371

Benois, Nadia 225

BENOIT, *see* Cowburn, Ben

Bentine, Michael 396

Berenberg-Gossler, Sfr Heinrich Cornelius 64

Bereznicki, Tadeusz 257–8

Bergé, Capt. Georges Roger Pierre 332

Bergen-Belsen *see* concentration camps

Bergeret, Gen. Jean Marie Joseph 39

Berthold, Obgfr. 67

Besliard, Paulette 353

Best, Sigismund Payne 32

Besthorn, Kurt 32

Bevan, Lt Col John 325, 354

Biernacki, Tadeusz 256–7, 265

Bingham, John 273–4

Birtwistle, Lt Edmund Frederick Astley 88

Black, Lt Cmdr Ivan 172, 196

Bleicher, Gerhard, son 133

Bleicher, Hugo 20–2, 40–1, 61, 69,
        72–5, 94, 100–3, 112–9, 127, 129–
        42, 144–53, 160–1,163, 166–71,
        175, 181, 187, 194–5, 212, 222,
        226–7, 229–32, 235, 239, 248,
        250, 254–5, 266, 316, 319–20,
        332, 336, 339–42, 344, 350, 352,
        356–9, 365, 367–8, 372, 374–7,
        383–4, 388, 390, 393, 395, 398

Bleicher, Luzie (Lucie) (née Mueller),
        wife 133

Bloch, Roland 177, 357

Bodington, Maj. Nicholas Redner 129,
        180, 197–8, 201-3, 205, 207–11,
        217–8

Bonny, Pierre 333-4

Bono, Hélène de 89

Borchers, Hptm. Erich 56, 101, 112,
        116, 129, 138–40, 142–3, 145,
        150–1, 153, 157, 239, 242–5, 268,
        370, 383, 416, 423

Borea, Maximilienne (Baby) 77–8, 82–4,
        136

Borni, Ernest, husband of Renée 54

Borni, Renée (née Petitjean) 22, 53–6, 61,
        94, 102–4, 106–8, 110, 112, 116,
        118, 120, 122–7, 139, 142–6, 148,
        152, 155, 158, 164, 167, 175, 184,
        214, 227–8, 234, 239–40, 245–7,

253, 256, 263–9, 330, 332–3, 337,
        339–40, 343–6, 351–2, 360–3,
        365–6, 371, 376, 388–90, 392

Bourn, Rosina 'Peggy' 210, 217–8

Bourne-Paterson, Maj. Robert 80–1,
        298–9, 319, 330–1

Boussel, Louis-Henri 163–4, 174, 184

Boyle, A/Cdre Archie 303, 305–6

Bradkowska, Mme 150, 153, 227

Brain, H.N. 372

Brault, Maître Michel 22, 49, 72, 144,
        162-3, 174, 177–8, 185, 188, 239,
        265, 327, 341, 368, 370

Brett-Perring, Marie Anne Teresa de
        Styczinska 308–9

Bristow, Desmond 324, 330, 332

Broglie, Princess Jacqueline Marguerite
        de 42, 62, 64, 65-6, 69–72, 76,
        92–3, 95, 98, 394

Brook, Robin 202

Brooke-Booth, Capt. Septimus 317,
        323–4

Bruce, Hon. Victoria A.K. 301

Brun, Auguste (VOLTA) 104

BRUTUS see Garby-Czerniawski,
        Roman 20, 22, 39, 46–7, 100,
        107, 171, 237, 249, 251–4, 300–1,
        320–1, 323, 325–7, 329–30,
        351–2, 354, 357, 361–5, 396

Buchenwald see concentration camps

Buckmaster, Col Maurice 82–3, 129,
        158, 174, 191, 197–8, 201, 206,
        282–3, 291, 299, 320, 331, 346,
        357, 364, 368, 377

Buffet, Denise (née Marie-Thérèse Fillon)
        47, 58, 100–1, 127, 139, 173, 227,
        266, 356, 359, 393

Buffet, Gabrièlle 173

Burdeyron, Lt Noël Fernand Raoul 319

Burgess, Guy 78, 295

Burke, P.M. 307

Burlot, Théophile 47, 61, 149, 404, 409

Burt, Supt Leonard 88

Cadett, Thomas 198, 330–2, 336

Capote, Truman 276

Carbonnier, Jean 59

Carré, Mathilde-Lucie (Lily) 19–21, 25, 28, 35–6, 38–9, 41, 44–58, 60–2, 65–6, 71–5, 85–6, 90–1, 94, 99–118, 126–7, 129, 130, 134, 139–207, 211–9, 221–37, 239–240, 245, 247, 250–1 254–5, 258–62, 265, 268–9, 271–318, 320–33, 337, 339, 340–3, 349–52, 357, 365, 366–68, 370–7, 379, 380–3, 385–7, 389–96, 398

Carré, Maurice Henri Claude, husband 27, 41

Carte network 49, 175

Cartwright circuit 63, 66

Casteja, Alec de 76

Casteja, Emeline de (*née* de Broglie) 76, 79, 81–4, 86, 88, 90–1, 94–5

Cavell, Edith Louisa 379, 380

CELERY *see* Dicketts, Walter

Chagall, Marc 89

Chamberlin, Henri *see* Lafont, Henri

Chapelle, Fernand Bonnier de la 64

Chapman, Eddie (ZIGZAG) 291, 289, 292–3, 302, 324

Château-Thierry, Duchesse de 289, 292–3, 302, 324

Chaumet, Guy 47, 151

Chiang, Kai-shek 378, 380

Churchill, Odette (*née* Hallowes) 131

Churchill, Winston 21, 96, 98, 280

Clark, Norman Maynard 95

Clayton, Mr 290

Clemenceau, Georges 145

Clemenceau, Michel 260

Colditz Castle (Oflag IVc) 196, 208, 319

Cole, J.A. 293

Collardey, Jacques (COCO) 66

Colledge, Magdalena Cecilia 308

'Colonel Passy' *see* Dewavrin, André

'Colonel Rémy' *see* Renault-Roulier, Lt Col Gilbert

concentration camps:

    Auschwitz 49, 183, 244, 257

    Bergen-Belsen 77, 151

    Buchenwald 40, 42, 49, 70, 76, 269, 319, 357-8

    Dachau 108, 150, 338, 347, 370

    Dora 76, 150

    Drancy 75, 184

    Gross-Rosen 150

    Mauthausen 48, 50, 52, 101, 141, 163, 168, 187, 251, 305, 338, 368, 370

    Natzweiler-Struthof 150, 338, 347

    Neue-Bremme 42

    Neuengamme 150, 173

    Orianenberg 160

    Ravensbrück 48–9, 52, 77, 101, 175, 305

    Sarrebrück 27, 101, 183

Constant, Miss 298

Cookridge, E.H. 378, 381

Cooper, Duff 90, 96, 319

Copernicus network 47

Coppin, T.C. 175

Cornet, Mme 353

Cottin, Roger 52, 168, 170, 178, 181, 206, 208, 210, 218, 319

Coulomb, Lt Michel 56, 62–4, 66–75, 93, 146, 214, 394

Couraud, Raymond, *see* Lee, Capt. Jack William Raymond

Courtois, Michel *see* Coulomb, Lt Michel

Cowburn, Ben (BENOIT) 21, 170, 172, 189, 191–2, 194–6, 198, 368, 370, 377

Cowgill, Maj. Felix 269, 275

Creswell, Michael Justin 249

CST 353

Cullis, M.F. 97

Czaykowski, Zbigniew 37

Czerniawski, Gerry, son of Roman 395

Czyż, Lt Stefan 38, 144

Dachau *see* concentration camps

Dampierre, Comte Armand de 57

Dampierre, Comtesse Colette 'Coco' de (*née* Cahen d'Anvers) 56–7, 62, 65–6, 69, 71–5, 83, 164–5, 184, 188, 268, 342

Dansey, Col Claude 191–2, 199, 200, 296

Darlan, Adm.Jean Louis Xavier François 76, 155, 376

Darling, George 79

Dashwood, Edmee Elizabeth Monica *see* Delafield, E.M.

Davenport, Miriam 89

Davies, S/Ldr William Twiston 220

Davis, J.M. 88

Davis, Katherine 89

Davout, Capt. *see* Auerstaedt, Jacques Davout d'

Day, 2/Lt J.P. de C (John) 258

De Cellis 198

De Couëdic, Capt. 324

Delafield, E.M. 203

Déricourt, Henri 201, 356–7, 398

Deschamps, Monique 47, 53, 104, 253, 396

Deuxième Bureau:
    France 40–3, 50–2, 58, 62, 112, 115, 145, 149, 164, 262, 316, 370, 377
    Poland 38, 40, 105, 127, 173, 192, 238, 251, 258, 362

Devereaux-Rochester, Elisabeth 76, 78–9, 804, 90

Dewavrin, André 53

Dicketts, Walter 246

Dirksen, Herbert von 86

Dora *see* concentration camps

Douglas-Pennant, Hon. Violet 379–80

Drancy *see* concentration camps

Drappier, Judge 369

Drew, Mr 97

DSDOC 330

DST 137, 329–30, 353

Duch, Brig. Gen. Bolesław Bronisław 38

Duchamp, Marcel 173, 183

Dunderdale, Cmdr Wilfred 'Biffy' 66, 105, 120, 191–2, 200–2, 206, 208, 211, 214–5, 238, 252, 283, 285–6, 362

Duvernoy (Wirtz) 42, 114, 316, 342, 394

Eady, Charles 'Carol' Swinfen, Lord Swinfen 89

Eckert, Sfr Joseph von 172, 186, 195, 198, 239, 244–5, 344

Ehfeld, Cmdt Von 141

Ehrenburg, Lt 127

Eriksson, My 289, 292–3, 300, 302–3, 305

Eschig, Maj. 74, 101

Farago, Ladislas 95–6, 98

Farran, Maj. Roy 87

Faye, Col Léon 335, 338

Fellowes, Hon.Daisy (*née* Marguerite Séverine Philippine Decazes de Glücksbierg) 62, 65, 90, 94, 96, 169

FFI 82, 251, 361

Fitz-George, Cmdr George William Frederick 68

Foley, Maj. Frank 127, 238, 283, 285, 291, 294, 299, 302, 304

Foot, M.R.D. 198, 208, 218, 250, 282, 398

Fourcade, Marie-Madeleine 335

Fresnes Prison 40, 47–8, 50, 70, 75, 77, 81, 90, 116, 137, 146–7, 163, 183, 196, 206, 208, 213, 239, 245, 269, 305, 319–20, 337, 340, 342, 358, 365, 371–2

Friederich, Max 132

Friedl, Dr Yolande 203

Froment, Pierre de 49

Fry, Varian 89

Gaby, Mme 115, 247, 345, 360

Gale, Sgt/Insp. Louis V. 275, 281, 296, 314–5, 368, 375, 389

Game, A/M. Sir Philip 328

Gane, Fernand 47, 53, 106–7, 148, 397

Gano, Col Stanisław 105, 164, 215, 238, 251–2, 362

Garby-Czerniawski, Roman 20–2, 33–7, 48–50, 52–54, 55–7, 59–61, 65, 72–3, 75, 85–6, 94, 99–113, 117, 119–20, 122, 124–7, 130, 140, 142–3, 146, 150–1, 153–5, 158–60, 162–4, 167, 171, 173–4, 186, 188, 190, 206–7, 213, 219, 221–2,

226–9, 232–5, 236–45, 247–56, 259–62, 265–68, 285–89, 291, 294–5, 300–1, 316, 320–1, 323, 325–7, 329–30, 332, 337, 340–2, 344–51, 349–52, 354, 357, 360–5, 367–8, 387–92, 393, 395–6, 398

Garby-Czerniawski, Stefan, father of Roman 37

Garby-Czerniawski Zusanna, or Susanna (*née* Dziunikowska), mother of Roman 37

García, Juan Pujol (GARBO) 22, 327

Garrow, Lt Ian Grant 33

Gartner, Friedl 31

Garton, C.H.S. 68–9

Geheime Feldpolizei 100, 133, 258

GELATINE *see* Gartner, Friedl

Georges, Emmanuel des 357

Gestapo 20, 39, 50, 52, 57, 59–60, 64, 70, 76–7, 79, 81, 83, 92-3, 100–2, 109–11, 118–20, 122–4, 126, 137, 140, 145, 148, 150, 164, 166–7, 170–1, 174–5, 178, 181–2, 188, 194, 199–200, 203–4, 206, 208, 226, 257–8, 269, 305, 309, 314–5, 331, 333–4, 336, 338, 358, 370–1

Gielgud, Lewis 198

Gillson, Maj. Godfrey Anthony (Tony) 271, 273–4

Gimpel, René 173

Giscard d'Estaing, Valéry 333

Giskes, Maj. Hermann 62–4, 66–7, 69, 70–2, 93, 98

Gladstone, Capt. James Gustavus 90

Gladstone, Mrs Rosamond Daisy 90

Goering, Reischmarshall Hermann 155

Gold, Mary Jane 88

Gorbinot, Robert 47

Gorce, Henri 47, 53

Gorriot, Robert 47, 57, 139, 249, 268, 359

Grant, Maj. 353

Granville, Lord Edgar 95-6

Grassal, Jacques Marie Christophe 251

Greene, Tom 127, 192, 198, 200–7,
    209, 211, 214, 216, 260, 274, 278,
    280–1, 283, 291, 293–4, 299, 311,
    316, 320–1, 362, 368

Gregory, Ann 65

Grist, Evelyn 213–4

Grogan, Alan 293

Gross-Rosen *see* concentration camps

Guardini, Romano 385

Gubbins, Maj. Gen. Colin McVean 48,
    202, 206, 210–11, 214, 282, 309

Guérisse, Albert 33

Haag, Ingeborg Helen (*née* Abshagen) 64,
    92–3

Hale, J.L.S. 294, 299, 300, 304, 307, 309,
    310, 312, 325–6

Hales, Capt. 352–3

Hall, Virginia 319

Hambro, Sir Charles 312

Harcourt, Pierre d' 42, 50–2, 58, 62, 71,
    93–4

Harding-Newman, Col. Rupert 373–4

Harmer, Christopher 19, 35–6, 44, 52–3,
    55–6, 60–2, 65, 75, 101–4, 107,
    110–18, 120, 127, 141–3, 145,
    147–9, 151, 156, 158, 162, 164,
    166–7, 169, 174, 178–81, 184,
    187–8, 191, 193, 197, 199, 201,
    203–7, 209–14, 216–7, 222–3,
    236, 238, 252–4, 260–1, 268, 273–
    85, 288–91, 293, 296, 299–301,
    303–8, 310, 313, 320, 324–6, 332,

343–6, 351–2, 354, 358, 361–3,
    381, 389–90

Hautechaud, Dr. Paul 347, 357–8

Hentic, Pierre 108

Herbert, Dr E.M. 275–6, 280–1, 290,
    298, 314–5

Heslop, Lt Col Richard 80–1, 319

Hill, Bernard 373

Hinchley-Cooke, Col W.E. 17, 85,
    90–1, 288–90, 302, 312–3, 315–6,
    318–9, 321, 330

Hoare, Sir Samuel 282, 289–90

Hohenburg, Dr Erich 293

Hohenburg, Felicia (*née* Tyndal) 293

Holloway Prison 28, 290, 292–3, 297,
    301–3, 305, 307, 309–10, 312,
    314–16, 318, 321, 323–4, 375,
    377, 379, 384, 389

Home Office, Aliens Department 88,
    289, 290, 299, 300, 317, 324, 328

Hope, Peter 328, 340, 365

Horsfall, St. John 'Jock' 290–1

Hugentobler family 117, 388

Hugon, Capt. (HUREL) 328

Humphreys, L.A.L. (Leslie) 92, 198

Hunter, Harry 209

Ingrao, Dr Andrew R. 303–4

Invernell, Robert 68, 70

Ische, Maj. 131, 141, 151–2, 168–9, 172,
    231–2, 239, 243, 245–7

Jade-Fitzroy 108

Jaffré, Yves-Frédéric 385

Jagielowicz 59

James, Lt David 196

Jankowski, Madeleine (CHON) 37, 55,
    150, 152

Johnson, Capt. D. (GAËL) 80

Johnstone, Maj. Mark 328, 348

Jongh, Andrée 'Dédée' de 249, 305

Jordan, Jessie 293, 324

Jouffret, Claude 46, 61, 108, 137, 139, 149, 168, 181, 222, 249, 337, 357, 359, 366, 393

Kayser, Oblt 141–3, 145, 149, 153

Keswick, Maj. David Johnston 201–2, 204, 208, 211, 220, 281, 282–3, 296

Khan, Noor Inayat (MADELEINE) 338

Kieffer, Sturmbannführer Hans Josef 57, 337

Kieffer, Jean Lucien @ Kieffer, Robert 57–8, 60–1, 100–1, 111, 138–9, 234, 336–7, 346–9, 356–8, 366, 393

Kirsch, Elisabeth 306

Kirsch, Eva 306

Kléber, Marcel 139, 147–8, 153, 265, 268, 37

Kleeberg, Gen. Juliusz Edward 40, 60

Klimecki, Gen. Tadeusz 105, 252

Knight, Maxwell 274, 283

Knowlson, James 173, 175, 182–3

Konarska, Franciszka 144

Kosseki de 221, 247

Kossowski, Jerzy 38

Krafft, Mathilde 289, 292, 302, 318

Krämer, Dr Karl-Heinz (HEKTOR) 246

Kraus, Alfred Ignatz Maria ('Freddie') 42, 62–79, 81–3, 85–98, 111, 169, 268, 319, 342

Kressman, Capt. 327, 329–30, 353–5

Kreuz, Sfr Alex Graf 67, 75

Krótki, Lt Bernard 38, 101, 234, 256, 264, 266

Kukiel, Gen. Marian 48

Labourot, Jacques 42, 50

Lach, Stanislas (RAPIDE) 46, 50, 59, 73, 140–1, 179, 341

'La Chatte', see Carré, Mathilde-Lucie (Lily)

Lacordaire, Jean-Baptiste Henri-Dominique 385

Lafont, Henri 333–4

Lamirault, Claude 60, 108

Langenfeld, Maj. Witold 34, 72, 127, 256

Langley, Lt James 'Jimmy' Maydon 82, 377, 380

Lapeyre-Mensignac, Jean 47

Laporte, Lt André 49–50

La Santé Prison 44, 48, 56, 75, 112–3, 116, 146, 148, 258, 360, 367

Laurencie, Gen. Benoît de Fornel de la 144

Laurent, Marie-Suzanne (née Renouf) 134–5, 250–1, 359, 368, 396

Leblon 174

Le Carré, John 213, 275

Lee, Capt. Jack William Raymond (Ramon) 86–92, 96–8

Lee, Mrs K.G. 88

Legentilhomme, Maj. Gen. Paul Louis Victor Marie 296, 310

Leggatt, Hugh 181

Leggett, Hester 287–8

Legrand, René 47, 144, 174–6, 268, 331–3, 341

Legros, Dr. Raymond 32

Le Hideaux, Mme 76

Lejeune, Charles 46, 50, 368

Lejeune, Mireille 53, 111, 368, 384

Le Quellec, Madeleine (née Hamel) 52, 227, 342

Le Tac, Joël 149, 331

Le Tac, Yves 149

Letaq, *see* Le Tac

Letonturier, Ginette 58, 162

Lévitan, Wolff 75

Lewinski, Fritz Erich George Edouard von *see* Manstein, Gen.Erich von

Lewis, Sarita 210

Liddell, Guy 20, 182, 211, 220, 252, 303–4, 309, 311–3, 326–7, 334, 355, 397

Lindley, Sir Francis O. 289, 316

Lipchitz, Jacques 89

Lipski, Lydia Lova de Korczak ('Cipinka') 48, 51

Lipsky/Lipski, Prince Wladimir de Korczak 46, 48, 144, 368

Lloyd, Capt. Richard Dafydd Vivian Llewellyn 275–9, 283, 289–90, 295, 375, 377, 388

Loesch, Jutta Sybill Viktoria Elisabeth von 131

Lonsdale, Stella 33, 289, 292, 302, 308, 324, 372, 380–1

Luke, Maj. W.E. 'Billy' 100, 117–8, 321, 325–32, 365

Lurton, Gaston 47, 51, 58

MacDermot, Lt Col N. 94

Machugh, Dr 203

McCallum, Patricia 19, 28, 41, 46, 53, 55–6, 107, 156–7, 167, 172, 197, 220

Mackintosh, Charles Ernest Whistler 271, 273–4, 276–8, 283, 377

Majewski, Capt. 258

Manners, Lt Lord John 86–8, 90–1

Manstein, Gen. Erich von 131

Marie-Claire line 361

Marksman 80

Marlag O (Milag und Marlag Nord) 196

Marriott, Henry 198

Marriott, John 30, 182, 198, 201, 216–7, 224, 238, 269, 275, 281–3, 298, 300–1, 307, 309, 313, 320, 323–5, 352–4, 354–5, 364

Marschall, Marco (*née* Kawovic) 46

Marshall, L.C. 298, 301

Martin, Denise, *see* Carré, Mathilde

Martin, Paul 55

Masłowski, Zygmunt 48, 57

Masterman, Maj. J.C. 19–20, 238, 252, 275–6, 279, 283, 290, 299, 319–21, 325–6, 354–5, 361, 365

Mathe, Capt. W.E. 352, 358

Matheson, Dr John Campbell McIntyre 297–8, 315

Mauthausen *see* concentration camps

Mayerson, Anna 275–6, 280

Mazzini Society 303–4

Mellanby, Aliss Molly 292, 295, 297, 300–1, 313

Mercieaux, Capt. Jean 33

MI5 19–21, 25, 27–37, 39, 40–3, 47, 52–4, 57, 60–2, 68, 71, 77–9, 82, 85, 88–92, 94–5, 97–8, 101, 103, 107, 110, 127, 130–2, 138–9, 142, 161–2, 165, 175, 177–8, 180, 182–4, 186, 197, 199, 201–3, 205, 209, 210–14, 218, 221–2, 224–5, 237–9, 250–2, 256–8, 273–5, 280, 282–300, 302–5, 311, 313, 315, 320, 323, 327, 328, 330, 335, 338, 345–49, 352, 354–5, 358, 361, 364–5, 368, 372–3, 379, 381, 389, 390–2, 395–6

MI6 *see also* Secret Intelligence Service

54, 66, 77, 89, 159, 198, 203, 253, 306, 327–8, 368
MI9 79, 82, 249, 380
Mills, Cyril Bertram 199-201, 205, 210, 292–4, 380
Milmo, Helenus 'Buster' 81, 85, 88, 91, 97, 136, 258, 288, 304–5, 310–1, 313, 354
Milton, Capt. 348
Mindszenty, Cardinal Jósef 378, 380
Ministry
    of Economic Warfare 281-2
    of Information 78, 132
Mitchell, Lt Roger (ADAM) 56, 59–60, 104, 214, 225, 234
Mitford, Hon. Diana 78, 308
Moreau, Pierre 249
Morrison, Herbert 95–6, 98, 290, 315–6, 322
Morton Evans, Lt Col Kenneth 368
Mosley, Sir Oswald 308, 372
Mousseigt, Simone Marie Antoinette 315
Moylan, Sir John 309–12, 314
Muet, Mimi 34
Murphy, Christopher 274
Murray, Sgt F. 347
Muselier, V/Adm. Émile Henry 303

Natzweiler-Struth of see concentration camps
Naud, Maître Albert 367
Neave, Maj. Airey 249, 361, 380
Nesbitt-Dufort, S/Ldr John 'Whippy' 60, 104, 108
Neue-Bremme see concentration camps
Neugebauer, Dr 257–8
Neuengamme see concentration camps

Nevile, Brig. 279, 283
Newsam, Sir Frank 97, 289, 302, 312, 323
Nicholson, Mrs Christabel Sybil Caroline 308
Nieuwenhuis, Hendrick 218
Noël, Mlle 249
Noeud, Richard 47, 50–1, 117, 153, 266
Nornable, Lt Gordon (BAYARD) 81
Nunn, Miss 288
Nye, Lt Gen. Sir Archibald 97

O'Callaghan, Miss 347
Ołpiński, Stefan Eugeniusz 257
Operation:
    Amoureuse 77
    Aquatint 358
    Bodyguard 325
    Brick 56, 59–60, 108
    Chariot 157, 196, 219
    Dragoon 68
    Fortitude 22, 237, 326, 364
    Gaff 87
    Jericho 206
    Savannah 332
    Waterworks 172, 195
Orianenberg see concentration camps
Overcloud 149, 172, 331

Pack, Betty (CYNTHIA) 333
Paine, Lauran 27, 30, 42, 140, 332, 367–9
Palson, Betty 88
Park, S/Ldr Hugh E. 323
Pat line 33
Pétain, Maréchal Henri Philippe 144, 155, 376
Petrie, Sir David 217
Peulevé, Henri 250

Philipson, F/Lt 105, 198, 203, 205, 214, 269, 272, 299
Philipson, Simone 269
Physician 79, 269
Picabia, Francis Martinez 173
Picabia, Gabrielle Cecile Martinez (GLORIA) 66, 173, 181–3
Picabia, Jeannine 184
Pickwoad, Margaret 133
Pilcher, 'Toby' 288–90, 294, 310
Pitt-Rivers, Capt. George Henry Lane-Fox 372–4, 380–1
Placke, SS-Hauptscharführer Josef 333–5
Ponsard, Capt. 322, 328
Pontiatowski, Prince Michel Casimir 333
Porchers, Paulette 152
Poulain, Robert 144–5, 147–8, 332–3, 341, 344
Pradier, Jeannine 208–10
Propst 72, 141, 145, 150, 268, 340

Quellec de *see* Le Quellec, Madeleine

Radzimiński, Jósef 38
Ralfe, F.J. 86
Ravensbrück *see* concentration camps
Rebattet, Georges 162
Redding, G.C.B. 172, 186, 195
Redfern, J.P.L. 276, 317
Reile, Oberstl. 74, 100, 134, 254
Renault-Roulier, Lt Col Gilbert 156
RENÉ 33, 46–7, 50–1, 55–7, 108, 116–8, 157, 168, 221–2, 265–7, 331, 334–401
Richard, Mme 311
Riddell, Enid 293
Ritter, Dr Nikolaus 246

Riy, Camille 33
Robertson, A.H. *see* Robson, Capt.
Robertson, Thomas Argyll 'Tar' 31, 160, 166, 185, 191, 199, 206, 209,224, 238, 252, 284, 288, 290, 308, 310, 327, 354, 361
Robson, Capt. 288, 295, 297
Roche, Maj. Hon.Thomas Gabriel 314, 322
Rochester, Devereaux 79, 81–4, 90
Rochester, Deverell Denise 76, 78–80, 82–4
Rocquigny, Lucien 46, 117, 144, 388
Rodriguez, Rachel 88
Roussel, Hélène 175–6, 183
Rowden, Diana Hope (PAULETTE) 338
Roy, Ian 300, 314–5, 317
Rudellat, Yvonne 77
Rumbelow, R.H. 317, 324
Ryde, Maj. M. 327
Rzepka, Lt Jósef 110

Salmon, Capt. O.H. 58, 346–8
Saner, Dr 298
Sarrebrück *see* concentration camps
Schade, Hptm. Theo 63, 68
Schmidt, Wulf (TATE) 246, 360
Schneidau, F/Lt Alfred Philip Frank, *see* Philipson, F/Lt
Schirach, Henriette 'Henny' von 378, 380
Schow, Col Robert A. 191, 200
Schroetder, SS-Sturmscharführer Richard 336
Schuchmann, Kplt Behrend 136
Schultze, Gen. Adm.Otto 172
Schutzstaffel (SS) 32
Schwerbel 256–8

Scott, Capt. *see* Stokes, M.B.

Secret Intelligence Service (SIS) 32, 40, 56, 60, 63, 66, 68, 78, 92, 94–5, 97, 104–5, 108, 120, 127, 132, 171, 176, 181, 184, 189, 191–2, 197–8, 200–3, 205, 207, 211–12, 214, 217, 221, 238, 260, 269, 275, 283, 287, 289, 291, 294, 296, 298, 302, 304–5, 321–3, 326–7, 330, 340, 352, 361, 368, 386

Selborne, Lord (3rd Earl of) 275–6, 280–2, 372–4, 389

Senter, Cmdr John 18, 283, 291, 304–6, 308–9, 312, 315, 319, 320, 355

Septavaux, Suzanne 357–8

Serguiew, Natalie 'Lily' 31–2

Shiffmacher, Paul 269

Shoop, Max 162

Sicherheitsdienst (SD) 32, 57

Sikorski, Gen.Władisław 38, 105, 178, 245

Simonaux, Capt. Léon 41, 166

Sinclair, Maj. Gen. Sir John 97

Sipo und SD 258, 358

Skardon, William 162, 214

Słowikowski, Maj. Mieczysław Zygfryd 40

SMH/GLORIA 22, 173–4, 182–3

Smiro, Jane 32

Smith, H.L. 289

Sol network 47

Soskice, Maj. Frank 355

Southby, Sir Archibald, Bt 307–8

Special Operations Executive (SOE) 19, 21, 38–9, 48–9, 68, 79–83, 91–2, 132, 149, 161, 170–2, 175, 177, 182, 185–6, 191, 194, 197–8, 201–2, 204–5, 207–8, 211, 214, 220, 250–1, 274, 276, 283, 285,

287, 291, 296, 298–300, 302–6, 309–10, 312, 314–15, 317, 319–23, 326, 328–32, 337–8, 342, 347–9, 354–6, 368, 381, 394, 398

Sporborg, Harry 308–9, 312, 314

SR Guerre 12, 330

Stanford, Mary 'Molly' Agnes Geraldine 307–9, 312–3, 380

Starr, George Reginald 337

Starr, John Ashford Renshaw 337–8

Stephens, Lt Col Robin 'Tin-Eye' 20, 91, 95, 100, 254, 339

Stevens, Maj. Richard 32

Stokes, M.B. 109, 127

Stokes, Richard 303

Stone, Mrs Gerald 'Mollie' 293

Stopford, Richman 89–90, 92

Street, John E.D. 381

Stülpnagel, Gen. Carl-Heinrich von 173, 242

Swinfen, Lady (*née* Averil Kathleen Suzanne Humphreys) 88–9, 92

Szumlicz, Tadeusz Wojciech 256–8

Tabat, François (Henri Tabet) 47

TATE *see* Schmidt, Wulf

Thierry-Mieg, Capt. François 322

Thionne de la Chaume, Mme 76–9, 82–3

Thomason, Gilbert 175

Tickell, Edward Jerrard 131–2

Todt 145, 247

Townshend, B.H. 92, 94, 253, 321, 327, 330

TREASURE *see* Serguiew, Natalie 'Lily'

Trevor Wilson, Col H.G. 327–8, 330, 353, 357

Tritche 111, 113, 145, 150

TUDOR 40–1, 48, 50–1, 59–60, 73, 111–2, 119, 123, 140, 227–8, 239, 250, 264, 266, 358
Twenty Committee 20, 237–8, 252, 275, 324

Unternehemen Zerberus (Operation Cerberus) 156
Ustinov, Jona von 'Klop' 32, 203, 205, 222, 224, 303, 315, 377, 381, 388

Vanden Heuvel, Count Frederick 'Fanny' 200
Vaudreuil, Capt. 322, 324, 326–7, 329–31, 353–6, 358
Vedero, Guy 51, 56, 148
Veilleux, Lt Marcel (YVELLO) 81
Verbeck, Sfr see Bleicher, Hugo
Verity, Hugh 59, 63, 77, 81, 104, 269
Vernette, Dr Pierre 32
Viana, Maria Jose 88
VICTOIRE see Carré, Mathilde-Lucie (Lily)
VIOLETTE see Borni, Renée (née Petitjean)
Vomécourt, Jean de 161, 174
Vomécourt, Philippe de 161, 169, 177
Vomécourt, Pierre de (LUCAS) 19, 22, 43, 160–1, 169, 171, 194, 225, 249, 327, 370, 372, 374–5, 381, 397

Wireless Board (W Board) 237–8, 252
Wake, Nancy 33, 309
WALENTY see Garby-Czerniawski, Roman
Walmsley, A.R. 373

Warden, Col 79, 178, 181, 320, 329–30, 349, 351–2
Waters, Lt Ben 196
Wells, Maj. R. Ansell 'Tom' 78, 321, 330–1, 354–5
Wendel, Charles 333–8
Wesley, Mary Aline Mynors (née Farmar) 89–90, 92
West, Nigel 66, 127, 159, 161, 274, 396–7
Wharton, Cmdr E.L. 68
White, Dick 201, 203, 205–6, 211–2, 214, 224, 284, 286, 288, 304, 321, 326
Whyte, Maj. Jock 295
Wiart, Lt Gen. Sir Adrian Carton de 48
Wiegand, Htpm. 134
Wild, Col Noel 325, 353–4, 357
Wilkinson, Ellen 96
Wilson, Miss D. 306, 309
Wilson, Derek Ian 66, 68–9, 78, 87–8, 90, 94, 100, 254, 323–4, 327–8, 330, 349–55, 357
Włodarczyk, Janusz 46–7, 56, 59, 103, 127, 225, 234
Wolff, Dr Eugene 297
Wolkoff, Anna 292, 307–8

Young, Gordon 21, 27, 29, 117, 250, 368, 382–5, 387
Younger, Maj. Kenneth 209, 317

Zarembski, Col Wincenty 38, 40, 60, 123, 250-1
Zembsz, Abraham 66
Ziromski, Jean 44
Żychón, Maj. Jan Henryk 105, 251